A+® Certification Study Guide, Fourth Edition

Nancy Ward
and Syngress Media, Inc.

McGraw-Hill/Osborne

New York   Chicago   San Francisco   Lisbon   London   Madrid   Mexico City
Milan   New Delhi   San Juan   Seoul   Singapore   Sydney   Toronto

McGraw-Hill/Osborne
2600 Tenth Street
Berkeley, California 94710
U.S.A.

For information on translations or book distributors outside the U.S.A., or to arrange
bulk purchase discounts for sales promotions, premiums, or fund-raisers, please contact
McGraw-Hill/Osborne at the above address.

A+® **Certification Study Guide, Fourth Edition**

1234567890 DOC DOC 0198765432

Book P/N 0-07-222-280-8 and CD P/N 0-07-222-281-6
parts of
ISBN 0-07-222-279-4

Publisher	**Acquisitions Editor**	**Copy Editor**
Brandon A. Nordin	Timothy Green	Darlene Bordwell
Vice President and Associate Publisher	**Acquisitions Coordinator**	**Production and Editorial**
Scott Rogers	Jessica Wilson	Black Hole Publishing Services
Editorial Director	**Series Editor**	**Series Design**
Gareth Hancock	D. Lynn White	Roberta Steele
	Technical Editor	**Cover Design**
	Paul Stansel	Greg Scott

This book was published with Corel VENTURA™ Publisher.

About Syngress Media

Syngress Media creates books and software for Information Technology professionals seeking skill enhancement and career advancement. Its products are designed to comply with vendor and industry standard course curricula, and are optimized for certification exam preparation. You can contact Syngress via the Web at www.syngress.com.

Authors

Amy Thomson (A+, MOUS Master) is an A+ Certified Technician and has been involved in several A+ and MCSE certification projects for Syngress Media. Now a Technical Writer in Halifax, Nova Scotia, Amy has previously worked as a computer technician and instructor in private colleges all over Canada.

Amy started her career in the computer industry as a Communicator in the Canadian Armed Forces, where she helped develop the military computer training curriculum for the Atlantic provinces. Amy has an Honors B.Sc. in Psychology and is a Microsoft MOUS Master. She currently resides in Bedford, Nova Scotia with her husband, Jeff, and hedgehog, Hannah.

Nancy Ward has been a member of the HAL-PC (Houston Area League of PC Users) group since 1992 and served on the Board of Directors for two years. Nancy has authored numerous articles and reviews on Hardware and OS topics, and started teaching in 1995 for the PC Upgrade SIG (Special Interest Group) of HAL-PC. Nancy also helped start the A+ Computer Technician Certification SIG, a reformation of HAL-PC that launched with the beginning of CompTIA's A+ certification. During her time as an A+ instructor, Nancy was involved in ensuring her students received hands on experience by starting a community outreach program to provide computers to those who couldn't afford them called PCs for People. Nancy spends her time building computers for herself and friends, and even donated the very first computer she built (an AMD K6 233 Gigabyte system) to a friend who didn't have one.

Series Editor

D. Lynn White (MCPS, MCSE, MCT, MCP+Internet, CTT) is President of Independent Network Consultants, Inc. Lynn has more than 15 years in programming and networking experience. She has been a system manager in the mainframe environment, as well as a software developer for a process control company. She is a technical author, editor, trainer, and consultant in the field of networking and computer-related technologies. Lynn has been presenting mainframe, Microsoft official curriculum and other operating systems and networking courses in and outside the United States for more than 13 years. Lynn is the Series Editor for Syngress for both the Network + and A+ Series. Her latest certification has been to receive her CTT (Certified Technical Trainer) by the Chauncey Group International. Lynn would like to extend thanks to her family and friends for always being there over the years.

Technical Editor

Paul Stansel (CCEA, MCSE, MCP+I, CNA, A+) works as a consultant specializing in remote access and Citrix technologies in Research Triangle Park, North Carolina, where he lives with his wife, Rachel, and their cat. Paul started working with computers when his father got the family a TRS-80 and has never looked back. He enjoys good science-fiction, computer games, and the football season.

What's on the enclosed CD?

- Step-by-step video clips from the author of this book
- Simulation exercises that reinforce certification objectives
- Test Prep tools to help you prepare for the certification exams
- Electronic version of the *A+ Certification Study Guide*
- Your link to comprehensive Online Training Resources from LearnKey

In the Online course from LearnKey, expert Mike Meyers utilizes full-motion video and audio to take you inside the computer for a practical and intimate exposure to PC components. With this interactive experience, you'll develop the skills to build, configure, and troubleshoot PC hardware and be fully prepared to pass the most recent A+ certification exams.

Load the enclosed CD for dynamic Online instruction from LearnKey and McGraw-Hill/Osborne. Your first Session is FREE!

With the Online resources you will learn to:

- Conceptualize and deal with the most common technical problems for a PC
- Build, configure, and troubleshoot PC hardware
- Recognize every major PC component and understand what it does
- Understand system software
- Identify how PC components work together
- Master the skills of an A+ Certified Technician

As you master these objectives, you'll have the skills to become an A+ Certified Technician and be fully prepared to pass the A+ certification exams.

For additional Online training contact LearnKey.

Learn From The Experts™

ACKNOWLEDGMENTS

We would like to thank the following people:

- All the incredibly hard-working folks at Osborne/McGraw-Hill: Brandon Nordin, Scott Rogers, Timothy Green, Gareth Hancock, and Jessica Wilson.

- Bob Glennon of ComputerCrafters, Hingham, MA, www.compucrafters.com, for use of their equipment.

CONTENTS

This book's primary objective is to help you prepare for and pass the required A+ exam so you can begin to reap the career benefits of certification. We believe that the only way to do this is to help you increase your knowledge and build your skills. After completing this book, you should feel confident that you have thoroughly reviewed all of the objectives that CompTIA has established for the exam.

In This Book

This book is organized around the actual structure of the A+ exam administered at Sylvan Prometric and VUE Testing Centers. CompTIA has let us know all the topics we need to cover for the exam. We've followed their list carefully, so you can be assured you're not missing anything.

In Every Chapter

We've created a set of chapter components that call your attention to important items, reinforce important points, and provide helpful exam-taking hints. Take a look at what you'll find in the chapters:

- Each chapter begins with the **Certification Objectives**—what you need to know in order to pass the section on the exam dealing with the chapter topic. The Certification Objective headings identify the objectives within the chapter, so you'll always know an objective when you see it!

- **Exam Watch** notes call attention to information about, and potential pitfalls in, the exam. These helpful hints are written by authors who have taken the exams and received their certification—who better to tell you what to worry about? They know what you're about to go through!

- **Certification Exercises** are interspersed throughout the chapters. These are step-by-step exercises. They help you master skills that are likely to be an area of focus on the exam. Don't just read through the exercises; they are hands-on procedures that you should be comfortable completing. Learning by doing is an effective way to increase your competency with the language and concepts presented.

■ **On the Job** notes describe the issues that come up most often in real-world settings. They provide a valuable perspective on certification- and product-related topics. They point out common mistakes and address questions that have arisen from on the job discussions and experience.

■ **From the Classroom** sidebars describe the issues that come up most often in the training classroom setting. These sidebars give you a valuable perspective into certification- and product-related topics. They point out common mistakes and address questions that have arisen from classroom discussions.

■ **Scenario and Solution** sections lay out potential problems and solutions in a quick-to-read format:

SCENARIO & SOLUTION

What causes GPFs?	GPFs occur when an application tries to perform an activity that would compromise the data or integrity of another application, such as trying to take over its memory space
How do Illegal Operations affect the system?	They are typically limited to a single application. However, they may cause the gradual degradation of the system after the offending program has been closed.
What should I do if an application keeps causing errors, even after I have reinstalled it?	There may be a problem (bug) in the application itself. Check with the manufacturer for known errors and patches.

■ The **Certification Summary** is a succinct review of the chapter and a re-statement of salient points regarding the exam.

✓ ■ The **Two-Minute Drill** at the end of every chapter is a checklist of the main points of the chapter. It can be used for last-minute review.

Q&A ■ The **Self Test** offers questions similar to those found on the certification exam. The answers to these questions, as well as explanations of the answers, can be found in at the end of each chapter. By taking the Self Test after completing each chapter, you'll reinforce what you've learned from that chapter, while becoming familiar with the structure of the exam questions.

■ The **Lab Question** at the end of the Self Test section offers a unique and challenging question format that requires the reader to understand multiple chapter concepts to answer correctly. These questions are more complex and more comprehensive than the other questions, as they test your ability to take all the knowledge you have gained from reading the chapter and apply it to complicated, real-world situations. These questions are aimed to be more difficult than what you will find on the exam. If you can answer these questions, you have proven that you know the subject!

Some Pointers

Once you've finished reading this book, set aside some time to do a thorough review. You might want to return to the book several times and make use of all the methods it offers for reviewing the material:

1. *Re-read all the Two-Minute Drills,* or have someone quiz you. You also can use the drills as a way to do a quick cram before the exam.

2. *Review all the S & S scenarios* for quick problem solving.

3. *Re-take the Self Tests.* Taking the tests right after you've read the chapter is a good idea, because it helps reinforce what you've just learned. However, it's an even better idea to go back later and do all the questions in the book in one sitting. Pretend you're taking the exam. (For this reason, you should mark your answers on a separate piece of paper when you go through the questions the first time.)

4. *Complete the exercises.* Did you do the exercises when you read through each chapter? If not, do them! These exercises are designed to cover exam topics, and there's no better way to get to know this material than by practicing.

6. *Check out the Web site.* Global Knowledge invites you to become an active member of the Access Global Web site. This site is an on-line mall and an information repository that you'll find invaluable. You can access many types of products to assist you in your preparation for the exams, and you'll be able to participate in forums, on-line discussions, and threaded discussions. No other book brings you unlimited access to such a resource. You'll find more information about this site in Appendix B.

A + Certification

This book is designed to help you pass the A+ Certification exam. At the time this book was written, the exam objectives for the exam were posted on the CompTIA Web site, www.comptia.org. We wrote this book to give you a complete and incisive review of all the important topics that are targeted for the exam. The information contained here will provide you with the required foundation of knowledge that will not only allow you to succeed in passing the A+ certification exam, but will also make you a better A+ Certified Technician.

How to Take an A+ Certification Exam

This chapter covers the importance of your A+ certification as well as prepares you for taking the actual examinations. It gives you a few pointers on methods of preparing for the exam, including how to study, register, what to expect, and what to do on exam day.

Importance of A+ Certification

The Computing Technology Industry Association (CompTIA) created the A+ certification to provide technicians with an industry recognized and valued credential. Due to its acceptance as an industry-wide credential, it offers technicians an edge in a highly competitive computer job market. Additionally, it lets others know your achievement level and that you have the ability to do the job right. Prospective employers may use the A+ certification as a condition of employment or as a means of a bonus or job promotion.

Earning A+ certification means that you have the knowledge and the technical skills necessary to be a successful computer service technician. Computer experts in the industry establish the standards of certification. Although the test covers a broad range of computer software and hardware, it is not vendor-specific. In fact, more than 45 organizations contributed and budgeted the resources to develop the A+ examinations.

To become A+ certified you must pass two examinations: the Core Hardware exam and an OS Technologies exam. The Core exam measures essential competencies for a break/fix microcomputer hardware service technician with six months of experience. The exam covers basic knowledge of desktop and portable systems, basic networking concepts, and printers. Also included on the exam is safety and common preventive maintenance procedures.

The newest revision of the A+ certification (January 2001) includes the OS Technologies exam, which covers basic knowledge of Windows 95, Windows 98, and Windows 2000 Operating Systems for installing, upgrading, troubleshooting, and repairing microcomputer systems.

Computerized Testing

As with Microsoft, Novell, Lotus, and various other companies, the most practical way to administer tests on a global level is through Sylvan Prometric or VUE testing centers, who provide proctored testing services for Microsoft, Oracle, Novell, Lotus, and the A+ computer technician certification. In addition to administering the tests, Sylvan Prometric and VUE also score the exam and provide statistical feedback on each section of the exam to the companies and organizations that use their services.

Typically, several hundred questions are developed for a new exam. The questions are reviewed for technical accuracy by subject matter experts and are then presented in the form of a beta test. The beta test consists of many more questions than the actual test and provides for statistical feedback to CompTIA to check the performance of each question.

Based on the performance of the beta examination, questions are discarded based on how good or bad the examinees performed on them. If a question is answered correctly by most of the test-takers, it is discarded as too easy. The same goes for questions that are too difficult. After analyzing the data from the beta test, CompTIA has a good idea of which questions to include in the question pool to be used on the actual exam.

Test Structure

At the time of publication, the A+ exam was being offered as an Adaptive type test. To learn more about CompTIA's computerized adaptive test (CAT), please visit the CompTIA web site at http://www.comptia.org.

This interactive test weights all of the questions based on their level of difficulty. For example, the questions in the form might be divided into levels one through five, with level one questions being the easiest and level five being the hardest. Every time you answer a question correctly you are asked a question of a higher level of difficulty, and vice versa when you answer incorrectly. After answering about 15–20 questions in this manner, the scoring algorithm is able to determine whether or not you would pass or fail the exam if all the questions were answered. The scoring method is pass or fail.

The exam questions for the A+ exams are all equally weighted. This means that they all count the same when the test is scored. An interesting and useful characteristic of the form test is that questions may be marked and returned to later. This helps you manage your time while taking the test so that you don't spend too much time on any one question. Remember, unanswered questions are counted against you. Assuming you have time left when you finish the questions, you can return to the marked questions for further evaluation.

The form test also marks the questions that are incomplete with a letter "I" once you've finished all the questions. You'll see the whole list of questions after you finish the last question. The screen allows you to go back and finish incomplete items, finish unmarked items, and go to particular question numbers that you may want to look at again.

Question Types

The computerized test questions you will see on the examination can be presented in a number of ways. The A+ exams are comprised entirely of one-answer multiple choice questions.

True/False

We are all familiar with True/False type questions, but due to the inherent 50 percent chance of guessing the right answer, you will not see any of these on the A+ exam. Sample questions on CompTIA's Web site and on the beta exam did not include any True/False type questions.

Multiple Choice

A+ exam questions are of the multiple choice variety. Below each question is a list of 4 or 5 possible answers. Use the available radio buttons to select one item from the given choices.

Graphical Questions

Some questions incorporate a graphical element to the question in the form of an exhibit either to aid the examinee in a visual representation of the problem or to present the question itself. These questions are easy to identify because they refer to the exhibit in the question and there is also an "Exhibit" button on the bottom of the question window. An example of a graphical question might be to identify a component on a drawing of a motherboard.

Test questions known as hotspots actually incorporate graphics as part of the answer. These types of questions ask the examinee to click on a location or graphical element to answer the question. As a variation of the above exhibit example, instead of selecting A, B, C or D as your answer, you would simply click on the portion of the motherboard drawing where the component exists.

Free Response Questions

Another type of question that can be presented on the form test requires a *free response* or type-in answer. This is basically a fill-in-the-blank type question where a list of possible choices is not given. You will not see this type of question on the A+ exams.

Study Strategies

There are appropriate ways to study for the different types of questions you will see on an A+ certification exam. The amount of study time needed to pass the exam will vary with the candidate's level of experience as a computer technician. Someone with several years experience might only need a quick review of materials and terms when preparing for the exam.

For others, several hours may be needed to identify weaknesses in knowledge and skill level and working on those areas to bring them up to par. If you know that you are weak in an area, work on it until you feel comfortable talking about it. You don't want to be surprised with a question knowing it was your weak area.

Knowledge-Based Questions

Knowledge-based questions require that you memorize facts. The questions may not cover knowledge material that you use on a daily basis, but they do cover material that CompTIA thinks a computer technician should be able to answer. Here are some keys to memorizing facts:

- **Repetition** The more times you expose your brain to a fact, the more it "sinks in" and increases your ability to remember it.

- **Association** Connecting facts within a logical framework makes them easier to remember.

- **Motor Association** It is easier to remember something if you write it down or perform another physical act, like clicking on the practice test answer.

Performance-Based Questions

Although the majority of the questions on the A+ exam are knowledge-based, some questions are performance-based scenario questions. In other words, the performance-based questions on the exam actually measure the candidate's ability to apply one's knowledge in a given scenario.

The first step in preparing for these scenario type questions is to absorb as many facts relating to the exam content areas as you can. Of course, actual hands-on experience will greatly help you in this area. For example, knowing how to install a video adapter is greatly enhanced by having actually done the procedure at least once. Some of the questions will place you in a scenario and ask for the best solution to the problem at hand. It is in these scenarios that having a good knowledge level and some experience will help you.

The second step is to familiarize yourself with the format of the questions you are likely to see on the exam. The questions in this study guide are a good step in that direction. The more you're familiar with the types of questions that can be asked, the better prepared you will be on the day of the test.

The Exam Makeup

To receive the A+ certification, you must pass both the Core and the OS Technologies exams. For up-to-date information about the number of questions on each exam and the passing scores, check the CompTIA site at www.comptia.org, or call the CompTIA Certification office nearest you.

The Core Hardware Exam

The Core Hardware exam is comprised of six domains (categories). CompTIA lists the percentages as the following:

Installation, configuration, upgrading	30%
Diagnosing and troubleshooting	30%
Preventive maintenance	5%
Motherboard, processors, memory	15%
Printers	10%
Basic networking	10%

The OS Technologies Exam

CompTIA's breakdown of the OS Technologies exam is as follows:

OS Fundamentals	30%
Installation, configuration, and upgrading	15%
Diagnosing and troubleshooting	40%
Networks	15%

Signing Up

After all the hard work preparing for the exam, signing up is a very easy process. Sylvan operators in each country can schedule tests at any authorized Sylvan Prometric Test center. You can register for an exam on-line at www.prometric.com or by calling the Sylvan Prometric Test Center nearest you. There are a few things to keep in mind when you call:

1. If you call Sylvan during a busy period, you might be in for a bit of a wait. Their busiest days tend to be Mondays, so avoid scheduling a test on Monday if at all possible.

2. Make sure that you have your social security number handy. Sylvan needs this number as a unique identifier for their records.

3. Payment can be made by credit card, which is usually the easiest payment method. If your employer is a member of CompTIA you may be able to get a discount, or even obtain a voucher from your employer that will pay for the exam. Check with your employer before you dish out the money.

4. You may take one or both of the exams on the same day. However, if you only take one exam, you only have 90 calendar days to complete the second exam. If more than 90 days elapse between tests, you must retake the first exam.

Taking the Test

The best method of preparing for the exam is to create a study schedule and stick to it. Although teachers have told you time and time again not to cram for tests, there just may be some information that just doesn't quite stick in your memory. It's this type of information that you want to look at right before you take the exam so that it remains fresh in your mind. Most testing centers provide you with a writing utensil and some scratch paper that you can utilize after the exam starts. You can brush up on good study techniques from any quality study book from the library, but some things to keep in mind when preparing and taking the test are:

1. Get a good night's sleep. Don't stay up all night cramming for this one. If you don't know the material by the time you go to sleep, your head won't be clear enough to remember it in the morning.

2. The test center needs two forms of identification, one of which must have your picture on it (i.e. driver's license). Social security cards and credit cards are also acceptable forms of identification.

3. Arrive at the test center a few minutes early. There's no reason to feel rushed right before taking an exam.

4. Don't spend too much time on one question. If you think you're spending too much time on it, just mark it and go back to it later if you have time. Unanswered questions are counted wrong whether you knew the answer to them or not.

5. If you don't know the answer to a question, think about it logically. Look at the answers and eliminate the ones that you know can't possibly be the answer. This may leave with you with only two possible answers. Give it your best guess if you have to, but most of the answers to the questions can be resolved by process of elimination.

6. Books, calculators, laptop computers, or any other reference materials are not allowed inside the testing center. The tests are computer based and do not require pens, pencils, or paper, although as mentioned above, some test centers provide scratch paper to aid you while taking the exam.

After the Test

As soon as you complete the test, your results will show up in the form of a bar graph on the screen. As long as your score is greater than the required score, you pass! Also a hard copy of the report is printed and embossed by the testing center to indicate that it's an official report. Don't lose this copy; it's the only hard copy of the report that is made. The results are sent electronically to CompTIA.

The printed report will also indicate how well you did in each section. You will be able to see the percentage of questions you got right in each section, but you will not be able to tell which questions you got wrong.

After you pass the Core exam and the OS Technologies exam, an A+ certificate will be mailed to you within a few weeks. You'll also receive a lapel pin and a credit card-sized credential that shows your new status: A+ Certified Technician. You're also authorized to use the A+ logo on your business cards as long as you stay within the guidelines specified by CompTIA. If you don't pass the exam, don't fret. Take a look at the areas where you didn't do so well and work on those areas for the next time you register.

Once you pass the exam and earn the title of A+ Certified Technician, your value and status in the IT industry increases. A+ certification carries along an important proof of skills and knowledge level that is valued by customers, employers, and professionals in the computer industry.

The contents of this training material were created for the CompTIA A+ exam covering CompTIA certification exam objectives that were current as of January 2002.

How to Become CompTIA Certified

This training material can help you prepare for and pass a related CompTIA certification exam or exams. In order to achieve CompTIA certification, you must register for and pass a CompTIA certification exam or exams.

In order to become CompTIA certified, you must:

1. Select a certification exam provider. For more information please visit http://www.comptia.org/certification/test_locations.htm.

2. Register for and schedule a time to take the CompTIA certification exam(s) at a convenient location.

3. Read and sign the Candidate Agreement, which will be presented at the time of the exam(s). The text of the Candidate Agreement can be found at http://www.comptia.org/certification.

4. Take and pass the CompTIA certification exam(s).

For more information about CompTIA's certifications, such as their industry acceptance, benefits, or program news, please visit http://www.comptia.org/certification. CompTIA is a non-profit information technology (IT) trade association. CompTIA's certifications are designed by subject matter experts from across the IT industry. Each CompTIA certification is vendor-neutral, covers multiple technologies, and requires demonstration of skills and knowledge widely sought after by the IT industry.

To contact CompTIA with any questions or comments, please call (630) 268-1818; e-mail: questions@comptia.org.

Part 1

A+ Core
Hardware

1

Identifying, Adding, and Removing System Components

This chapter introduces you to basic computer concepts, including how to identify and replace common components. Familiarity with the components, as well as a good working knowledge of their function, will allow you to work comfortably with most types of computers, in spite of different layouts or new component designs.

You will also be introduced to installation procedures for some common devices. The installations discussed in this chapter are limited to those components that require very little other than physical attachment to the computer to function properly. More complex installations are discussed in Chapter 2.

This chapter also discusses the system resources that allow components to operate within the computer without conflicting with one another. Finally, this chapter describes the physical cables and connections used by devices to communicate with one another, as well as various methods of communication.

CERTIFICATION OBJECTIVE 1.01

Safety First: Before You Begin

You must thoroughly understand two areas before opening the cover of a computer: ESD (electrostatic discharge) can kill your computer; and high voltage (inside the power supply and monitor) can kill you. Following are some basics you should know.

Electrostatic discharge, or static electricity, can cause irreparable damage to the devices inside your computer. Although your body can withstand 25,000 volts, damage to computer components can occur with as few as 30 volts. Typical ESD discharges range from 600 to 25,000 volts.

You must equalize the electrical charge between your body and the components inside your computer in order to prevent damage to the system. Touching a grounded portion of your computer's chassis will work to some extent, but for complete safety, use an antistatic wristband with a ground wire attached to the computer frame.

Leave servicing high-voltage peripherals such as monitors and power supplies to technicians trained in that area. Even when left unplugged for an extended period, enough voltage can be stored to cause severe injury, even death. Do not use an antistatic wristband when working with high-voltage devices.

For complete power protection and safety procedures, it is suggested you read Chapter 4 first; read it again after you've read Chapters 1 through 3.

System Modules

This section describes common devices called *field-replaceable modules* as well as their role in the computer system as a whole. This information will form the foundation of your ability to discover and resolve computer problems. If you know the functions of each component, you will more easily be able to determine which component is at fault when something goes wrong.

System Board

Each internal and external component is connected to the *system board*. The system board, also referred to as the *main board*, the *motherboard,* or the *planar board,* is made of fiberglass and is typically brown or green, with a meshwork of copper lines (see Figure 1-1). These "lines" are the electronic circuits through which signals travel from one component to another and are collectively called the *bus*.

The Processor or CPU

Most computer components are designed to perform only one or a limited number of functions, and they only do so when it is specifically requested of them. The device responsible for organizing the actions of these components is the *processor*, also referred to as the *central processing unit,* or *CPU*. As the "brain" of the computer, the processor receives requests from you, the user; determines the tasks needed to fulfill the request; and translates the tasks into signals that the required component(s) can understand. The processor also does math and logic calculations. For more information about this feature, see Chapter 5, "Motherboard, Processors, and Memory."

The processor itself comes in several physical forms. Older processors, such as the Intel 80286, 80386, 80486, and Pentium, have pin grid array (PGA) forms. PGA processors, as shown in Figure 1-2, are square, with several rows of pins on the bottom. These pins are used to attach the processor to the motherboard.

FIGURE 1-1 A system board and its components

Power input connector   Battery socket

Power supply

Microprocessor

Secondary EIDE
channel connector

PCI expansion-card
connectors

ISA expansion-card
connector

3.3-V power input
connector

Diskette drive
interface connector

Primary EIDE
channel connector

Control panel
connector

System Board jumpers

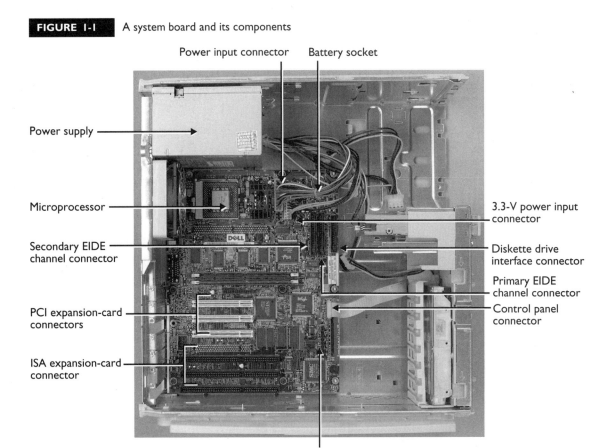

A newer processor form (used in Pentium II, early Pentium III, and early Celeron) is the single-edge contact (SEC) cartridge, which has an upright design and attaches to the motherboard using a slot-1 connector. An SEC processor is shown in Figure 1-3. Processor designs, models, and speeds are discussed in more detail later in the chapter and again in Chapter 5.

FIGURE 1-2

PGA processors
are rectangular,
with pins along
the bottom.

FIGURE 1-3

SEC processors have an upright design and are larger than other processors.

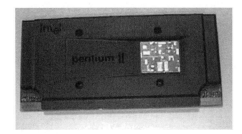

The Power Supply

The *power supply* (shown in Figure 1-4), typically located at the back of the computer's interior, has several very important functions. It is responsible for converting the alternating current (AC) voltage from wall outlets into the direct current (DC) voltage that the computer requires. The power supply accomplishes this task through a series of switching transistors, which gives rise to the term *switching mode* power supply.

Another function of the power supply is to ensure that the computer receives the proper amount of voltage. Typical North American wall outlets generate about 110–120 vAC (volts AC). However, computers require comparatively smaller voltages—±12, ±5, or ±3.3 vDC (volts DC). The computer's power supply removes the excess voltage and dissipates it in the form of heat.

e x a m
ⓦa t c h
Make sure you are familiar with the voltages required by computer components: ±12, ±5, and ±3.3 vDC.

This build-up of heat can cause computer components (including the power supply itself) to fail. Therefore, the power supply has a built-in fan that draws air in from outside the computer case and cools off the components inside.

Memory

Memory is one of the most important but perhaps most misunderstood computer components. Its function is often mistaken for that of hard drive space. Furthermore,

FIGURE 1-4

A typical computer power supply.

computers use several types of memory, each with a different function and different physical form. Typically, when people discuss memory, they are referring to *random access memory,* or *RAM.*

RAM

Recall that when a user makes a request, it is intercepted by the processor, which then organizes the request into component-specific tasks. Many of these tasks must occur in a specific order, with each component reporting its results back to the processor before the next task can be completed. The processor uses RAM to store these results until they can be compiled into the final result(s).

RAM is also used to store instructions about currently running applications. For example, when you start a computer game, a large set of the game's instructions (e.g., how it works, how the screen should look, which sounds must be generated) is loaded into memory. The processor can retrieve these instructions much faster from RAM than it can from the hard drive, where the game normally resides until you start it. Within certain limits, the more information that's stored in memory, the faster the computer will run. In fact, one of the most common computer upgrades is to increase the amount of RAM.

The information in RAM is continually being read, changed, and removed. It is also *volatile,* meaning that it cannot work without a steady power supply. When a computer is turned off, the information in RAM is lost.

Cache

Recently, another type of memory has emerged—*cache memory.* Cache memory carries out a similar function to that of RAM, but it resides directly on the processor itself or physically close to the processor on the motherboard. Cache memory runs faster than typical RAM and is able to "guess" which instructions the processor is likely to need, then retrieve those instructions from RAM or the hard drive in advance.

ROM

Although *read-only memory,* or *ROM,* has an important function, it is rarely changed or upgraded, so it typically warrants less attention by most computer users. Unlike RAM, ROM is read-only, meaning its instructions can be read by the processor, but it cannot be used to store new information.

ROM is *nonvolatile,* so it does not lose its contents when the computer's power is turned off. This makes ROM ideal for storing a device's most basic operation and communication instructions. A number of computer components include ROM chips, which contain device-specific basic instructions. Information on these ROM chips is said to be *hard-wired* or *hard-coded* because it cannot be changed. These types of devices are termed *firmware*, to indicate that they are a mixture of hardware and software.

Test your understanding of the memory types we've discussed so far by answering the next Scenario & Solution questions.

Storage Devices

The function of all storage devices is to hold, or store, information, even when the computer's power is turned off. Unlike information in RAM, files that are kept on a storage device remain there unless they are manually removed or altered by the user or the computer's operating system.

A great variety of storage devices are available, including floppy drives, hard drives, and Zip drives. However, the A+ tests focus only on the "standard" storage devices explained in the following sections.

Floppy Drives

A 3.5-inch *floppy drive* reads data from removable floppy disks and provides a good method for transferring data from one machine to another. *Floppy disks* contain a thin internal plastic disk, capable of holding magnetic charges. The disk is surrounded by a hard plastic protective casing, part of which can be retracted to reveal the storage medium inside (see Figure 1-5). The back of the disk has a coin-sized metal circle that is used by the drive to grasp the disk and spin it. When a floppy disk is inserted in a computer's drive, the drive spins the internal disk and retracts the protective cover. The drive's *read/write head* moves back and forth along the exposed area, reading data from and writing data to the disk.

SCENARIO & SOLUTION

Which type of memory is responsible for...	Solution
Maintaining a device's basic operating instructions?	ROM.
Anticipating processor requests and making the proper data available?	Cache.
Providing temporary storage for application files?	RAM.

FIGURE 1-5

The front
and back sides
of a 3.5-inch
floppy disk.

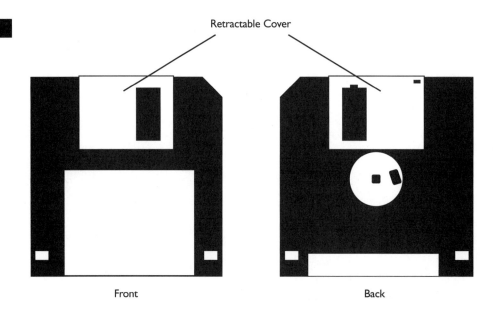

Retractable Cover

Front

Back

Floppy disks themselves are available in several different forms and capacities. The first floppy disks used in PCs were 5.25 inches square and could hold either 360KB or 1.2MB of information. However, these are no longer considered standard computer equipment, so you shouldn't expect to see questions about them on the A+ tests.

The newer 3.5-inch disk can hold 720KB (double density), 1.44MB (high density), or 2.88MB (extra density) of information. The most commonly used such disk is the 1.44MB. Floppy drives are limited in the types of disks they can access. The obvious size difference precludes a 5.25-inch drive from using a 3.5-inch disk, and vice versa. A 720KB drive can read only 720KB disks. However, a 1.44MB drive can access either a 1.44MB or a 720KB disk, and the 2.88MB drive can read all three 3.5-inch disk densities.

Hard Drives

Hard drives store data in a similar fashion to floppy drives, but they typically are not removable and have a different physical structure (see Figure 1-6). A hard drive, also referred to as a *fixed drive*, consists of several hard platters, stacked on top of but not touching one another. The stack of platters is attached through its center to a rotating pole, called a *spindle*. Each side of each platter can hold data and has its own read/write head. The read/write heads all move as a single unit back and forth along the stack.

Hard drives are available in a wide range of capacities and can hold much more data than a floppy disk. Most newer hard drives have a capacity between 2GB and 20GB. The disk must be divided into smaller units, called *clusters*, before it can store

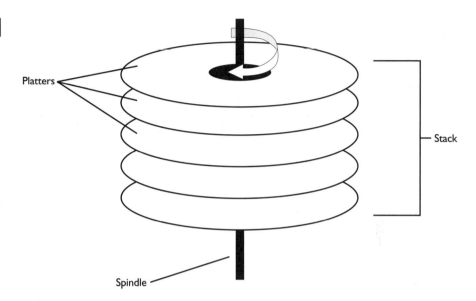

FIGURE 1-6

The internal structure of a hard disk.

data. This division is accomplished through formatting. Depending on the capacity and file system used, each cluster can hold between 512B to 32KB of data. Data storage and file systems are discussed in more detail in Chapters 8 and 9.

CD-ROMs

Compact disk–read-only memory (CD-ROM) offers a balance between the portability of a floppy disk and the capacity of a hard drive. CD-ROMs are composed of a hard medium that contains very small depressed and raised areas, called *pits* and *lands*, respectively. CD-ROM drives read data from the CD using a laser instead of a read/write head.

on the
Job

Because CDs have no protective covering, it's important to handle them with care. Scratches, dust, or other material on the CD surface can prevent data from being read correctly. Because data is located on the bottom side of the CD, always lay the CD label side down.

CD-ROMs can hold roughly 650MB of data and generally cannot be written to, except in the case of CD-Rs (recordable) or CD-RWs (rewritable). Data can be accessed faster from a CD than a floppy disk but much more slowly than from a hard drive.

The Monitor

The function of a *monitor* is to produce visual responses to user requests. Most desktop computers use cathode ray tube (CRT) monitors. CRTs use an electron gun to activate phosphors behind the screen. Each dot on the monitor, called a *pixel,* has the ability to generate red, green, or blue, depending on the signals it receives. This combination of colors results in the total display you see on the monitor.

Monitors are available in a wide array of colors and resolutions. The word *resolution* refers to the size and number of pixels that a monitor can display. Higher resolutions display more pixels and have better visual output. Lower resolutions result in grainy displays.

Color graphics adapter (CGA) monitors are an older type and can display combinations of red, green, and blue at different intensities, resulting in 16 different colors. The maximum resolution of a CGA monitor is 640 x 200 pixels in monochrome mode and 160 x 100 pixels in 16-color mode.

Enhanced graphics adapter (EGA) monitors are capable of generating up to 64 colors, of which 16 can be displayed at any one time. EGA monitors have a maximum resolution of 720 x 350 when displaying text only and 640 x 350 in graphics mode.

Virtual graphics array (VGA) monitors were the first to use analog rather than digital output. Instead of creating displays based on the absence or presence of a color (as in digital CGA and EGA monitors), VGA monitors can display a wide range of colors and intensities. They can produce around 16 million different colors but can display only up to 256 different colors at a time. This color setting is often called *16-bit high color*. VGA monitors have a maximum resolution of 720 x 400 in text mode and 640 x 480 in graphics mode.

Super VGA (SVGA) monitors introduce yet another improvement: They also use analog input and can provide resolutions as high as 1280 x 1024. Some SVGA monitors can provide even higher resolutions. SVGA monitors can display up to 16 million colors at once, referred to as *32-bit true color*. Because the human eye can distinguish only approximately 10 million different colors, it is likely that monitor technology will focus on improving resolution only.

All monitors receive their signals from video cards attached to the motherboard. The monitor technology must match the technology of the video card to which it is attached. That is, an EGA monitor will work only with an EGA video card, and an SVGA monitor must be attached to an SVGA video card. Table 1-1 presents a summary of monitor types and characteristics.

Modems

Modems allow computers to communicate with one another over existing phone or cable lines. Internal modems attach directly to a computer's motherboard and connect to a regular phone jack using the same connector as a phone. External modems also connect to the phone jack but are attached to the computer via an external port. External modems are typically easier to configure and troubleshoot than internal modems and have the benefit of being easily transported to another computer.

TABLE 1-1		Monitor Types and Their Characteristics		
Monitor	**Total Number of Colors**	**Number of Colors That Can Be Simultaneously Displayed**	**Maximum Resolution**	**Input**
CGA	16	16	Monochrome: 640 x 200 Color: 160 x 100	Digital
EGA	64	16	Text mode: 720 x 350 Graphics mode: 640 x 350	Digital
VGA	More than 16 million	256	Text mode: 720 x 400 Graphics mode: 640 x 480	Analog
SVGA	More than 16 million	More than 16 million	1280 x 1024	Analog

Analog Modems

Traditional modems, also called *analog modems*, convert the computer's digital signals into analog signals so they can be sent out over phone lines. This process is called *modulation*. The modem is also responsible for converting incoming analog signals from the phone line into digital signals that the computer can use. This is called *demodulation*. In fact, the word *modem* is an acronym for *mo*dulator/*dem*odulator.

When one computer tries to connect to another via its modem, it must first dial the receiving computer's phone number. This process is known as the *dial-up*. The receiving computer answers, and the two modems engage in a process known as a *handshake*, in which the speed, encryption, and other rules of communication are established. Analog modems take up the phone line, just as a regular phone call would. That is, you cannot use your analog modem and your phone at the same time if they share a line.

Cable Modems

Cable modems use the same cable that televisions use. Because television cables transmit only digital signals, cable modems are not really modems at all; that is, they do not modulate or demodulate signals.

Unlike analog modems, cable modems do not need to perform a dial-up or handshake. To understand this concept, compare your phone to your television. When you phone a friend, you can't simply pick up the phone and speak to him; you must first dial his number and wait for him to answer. The same is true for analog modems. Television channels, however, are always there. You don't need to dial up the cable company through your television to request a channel; all you need to do is switch to that channel, which was there all along. This is the case with cable modems. As long as there is a physical connection between cable modems, they can communicate.

Peripherals

The term *peripheral* is typically used to refer to noncritical external computer components. For example, although monitors are external components, they are critical to the computer's function so are generally not thought of as peripherals. Interestingly, keyboards are considered peripherals, even though the computer will not properly boot without one. With the exception of keyboards, pointing devices, and printers, most peripheral devices are proprietary (in other words, nonstandardized) and are not covered on the A+ exams.

Peripherals can be categorized as either input or output devices. *Input devices* are used for entering data and commands into the computer; these devices include mice, microphones, digital cameras, joysticks, and scanners. *Output devices* are used for seeing or hearing the result of some computer process; they include printers and speakers. Chapter 6 is devoted entirely to printers.

Keyboards

There are several types of keyboards, including 84- and 101-key designs. Newer keyboards might include a variety of additional keys for accessing the Internet, using Microsoft Windows, and other common functions. Some keyboards even include a pointing device, such as a mouse or touch pad.

There are also several keyboard layouts. The keyset on an *ergonomic keyboard* (see Figure 1-7) is split in half and slants outward to provide a more relaxed, natural hand

---

FIGURE 1-7

Ergonomic keyboards have a different structure from regular keyboards.

position. The placement of the keys themselves can also vary. Typical keyboards have a QWERTY layout, the name of which is taken from the first six letters on the second row of the keyboard. The Dvorak keyboard has an entirely different key layout (shown in Figure 1-8) and is designed to allow faster typing speeds.

You don't have to actually *buy* a Dvorak keyboard; you can set the layout of your existing keyboard to either Dvorak or QWERTY using your operating system. If you are using Microsoft Windows, follow the steps in Exercise 1-1 to configure your keyboard to use the Dvorak layout.

FIGURE 1-8

Note the different key positions of the QWERTY and Dvorak keyboards.

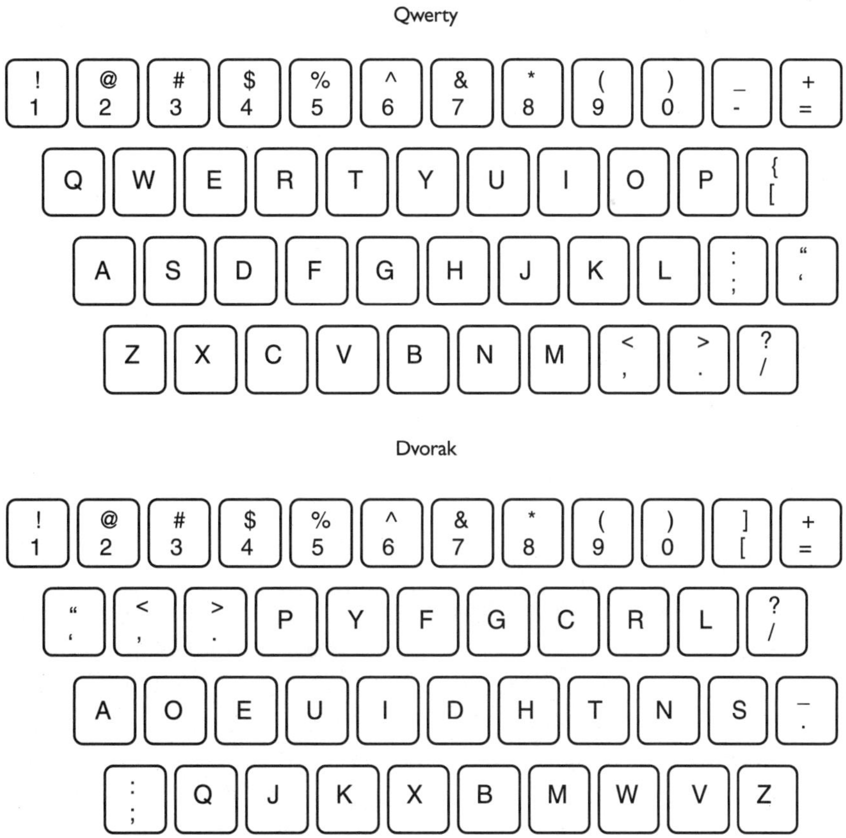

Qwerty

Dvorak

Switching to the Dvorak Keyboard Layout

1. Double-click the My Computer icon.

2. Double-click the Control Panel icon.

3. Double-click the Keyboard icon.

4. Select the Language tab in Windows 9x or the Input Locales tab in Windows NT.

5. Click the Properties button.

6. Select US-Dvorak from the Keyboard Layout drop-down list.

7. Click OK, then click OK again.

8. If you want, you can physically change the keycaps on the keyboard to correspond to their new settings.

FROM THE CLASSROOM

What Happened to the Alphabet?

Ever wonder why the QWERTY keyboard is laid out the way it is—why it's not laid out in alphabetical order? When the keyboard was invented (by Christopher Sholes, in the late 1800s), the keys *were* arranged in alphabetical order. However, due to their primitive nature, early typewriters were prone to jammed keys. To remedy this problem, Sholes created the QWERTY layout. This layout was designed to slow typists down so that they couldn't type fast enough to jam the keys!

Today, computer keyboards are practically impossible to jam, so there is little benefit to using the QWERTY layout. In the 1930s, August Dvorak redesigned the keyboard layout so that the most commonly used characters are in or closest to the home row and are accessed by the strongest fingers. This layout allows for faster typing speeds, less hand strain, fewer typing mistakes, and less overall "finger travel." Although most people cannot exceed about 60 words per minute on

FROM THE CLASSROOM

a QWERTY keyboard, speeds on a Dvorak keyboard can reach about 100–120 words per minute—double the rate. Furthermore, the same passage that requires fingers to travel a total of 12 miles on a QWERTY keyboard requires only about 1 mile of travel on a Dvorak keyboard.

Unfortunately, the Dvorak keyboard has been slow to catch on. Most people learn to type on the QWERTY layout because that is the layout they are most likely to encounter. It is exceptionally difficult to learn and accurately use both layouts, so most people stick to the old QWERTY standby.

—Amy Thomson, A+ Certified Technician, MOUS Master

Firmware

As discussed previously, the term *firmware* is used to refer to hardware components that include hard-wired instructions on ROM chips. These instructions are always available, so they do not have to be reprogrammed every time the computer is started. The firmware in a computer keeps settings such as the time, security passwords, screen colors, and component resources. Without firmware, you would have to do things such as set the time yourself and inform the computer about which types of devices are present each time you turn the computer on.

The concept of firmware can be difficult to understand, but it can be explained using the example of a standard calculator. Any calculations you make on a calculator are "erased" once you turn the calculator off. However, the calculator retains the basic rules for adding, subtracting, multiplying, and the like, even when it is turned off. That is, you don't have to tell the calculator how to add or subtract every time you use it. These basic rules of calculation are hard-wired into the calculator and so, in effect, are the calculator's firmware.

BIOS

One type of computer firmware is the *Basic Input/Output System (BIOS)*. The BIOS is responsible for informing the processor about which devices are present as well as how to communicate with them. Whenever the processor makes a request from a component, the BIOS steps in and translates the request into instructions that the required component can understand.

Older computers contained true read-only BIOSs that could not be altered. This meant that new components could not be added to the computer, because the BIOS would not know how to communicate with them. This seriously limited users' ability to upgrade their computers, so *flash BIOS* was introduced. Now when a new component is installed in the computer, the flash BIOS can be electronically upgraded (or *flashed*) so that it can recognize and communicate with the new device.

CMOS

Another important type of firmware is *complementary metal-oxide semiconductor (CMOS)*. The CMOS chip retains settings such as the time, keyboard settings, and boot sequence. (These settings are described in more detail in Chapter 5.) The CMOS also stores the interrupt request line (IRQ) and input/output (I/O) resources that the BIOS uses when communicating with the computer's devices. The CMOS chip is able to keep these settings in the absence of computer power because it is attached to a small *CMOS battery*, which can last between 2 and 10 years.

exam
ⓦatch

As complicated as it might seem, make sure you that have an iron-clad understanding of the relationship between the computer's BIOS and CMOS as well as the differences in their functions. The BIOS is a set of instructions, and the CMOS is used to store those settings.

You can view and modify the computer's CMOS settings by entering the computer's Setup program during bootup. Watch the screen for instructions such as "Press CTRL+S to access Startup Configuration" or "Press DEL to enter Setup." From the time such a message is displayed, you will have about 3 seconds to enter the appropriate key combination. (This delay itself can be configured in the CMOS settings; configuration of the CMOS settings is discussed in more detail in Chapter 5.)

on the
ⓙob

Interestingly, the term CMOS settings is a bit of a misnomer. When people talk about the computer's CMOS or its settings, they are referring to the items described in the preceding discussion. However, a CMOS is really just a physical type of chip. CMOS chips are used for a variety of things other than retaining CMOS settings. In fact, many processors are actually CMOS chips.

Boot Process

When the computer is started (booted), the BIOS runs a *power -on self-test (POST)*. During the POST, the BIOS checks for the presence and function of each component it has been programmed to manage. It first checks the processor, then RAM, and then system-critical devices such as the floppy drive, hard drive, keyboard, and monitor. It then tests noncritical components such as the CD-ROM drive and sound card.

Next, the BIOS retrieves the resource (IRQ and I/O address) settings from the CMOS and assigns them to the appropriate devices. The BIOS then processes the remaining CMOS settings, such as the time or keyboard status (for example, whether the number lock should be on or off). Finally, the BIOS searches for an operating system and hands it control of the system. The CMOS settings are no longer required at this point, but the BIOS continues to work, translating communications between the processor and other components.

LCD Portable Systems

Portable systems are small, easily transported computers. They generally weigh less than 6 pounds, can fit easily in a large bag or briefcase, and have roughly the same dimensions as a 2- or 3-inch stack of magazines.

As well as the size difference, portables and desktops (also called *PCs* or *personal computers*) differ in their physical layout. Portable computers have an all-in-one layout in which the keyboard, pointing device, and display are integrated with the computer chassis. Typically, portable computers open in the same manner as a briefcase. The top half contains the display, and the bottom half contains the keyboard and the rest of the computer's components.

Finally, although portable computers are functionally similar to desktop computers, they are primarily proprietary and tend to use components other than the ones described thus far. For example, portables use liquid crystal display (LCD) monitors rather than CRT monitors and can use docking stations and PC Cards. Working with portables requires a skill set beyond what is necessary to service desktop PCs. Therefore, many of the chapters in this book are divided into "Desktop" and "Portable" sections.

The term *portable* is often confused with the terms *laptop* and *notebook*. Portable computers are any type of computer than can be easily transported and that contain an all-in-one component layout. A few years ago, most portable computers were called *laptops* because they could fit comfortably on the user's lap. As technology improved, portable computers became smaller and smaller. The newer term, *notebook*, is often used now to refer to portable computers, to reflect their smaller size. Within most of the computer industry and throughout the remainder of this book, the terms *notebook* and *laptop* are used interchangeably.

Another type of portable computer is the *handheld* or *palmtop* computer. Although still considered portables, these computers are physically and technologically different from laptops. A+ exam questions about portable computers will be limited to laptops.

Personal Digital Assistants

Personal Digital Assistants, known as PDAs, are even smaller than laptop computers. Typically, PDAs are small enough to fit in your hand, and they are often referred to as "palmtop" or "handheld" computers. Because they are so small, PDAs do not have the functionality of a laptop or desktop computer. In other words, most PDAs allow you to perform only a small number of functions.

One of the most common uses for a PDA is an organizer. That is, to keep track of appointments, record addresses, and phone numbers, and to keep small notes. Many PDAs also allow you to plug into a fax machine to send faxes, or to plug into a network to send mail or access the Internet. PDAs are too small to include a regular keyboard layout, so the primary input device is a small stylus, which is shaped like a pen. The stylus can be used to press small keys on a keypad, to select items that are displayed on the screen, or to write data on the screen itself. PDAs are entirely proprietary, nonservicable by regular technicians, and different from one another in their technology and functions. Therefore, although you should be aware of their existence, you shouldn't expect to see many questions about PDAs on the A+ exam.

CERTIFICATION OBJECTIVE 1.02

Adding and Removing Field-Replaceable Modules

Most hardware failures are resolved by replacing a "bad," or nonworking, component with a "good," or working, one. This section discusses basic techniques for replacing and installing common computer components. Desktop and portable systems are discussed separately because different skills are required for each.

Whenever you install or replace a computer component, you must turn the computer's power off and ensure that you follow the electrostatic discharge (ESD) procedures discussed in Chapter 4. The exception to this rule comes in the case of a *hot-swappable device*, which is one that can be added or removed while the computer is operating. Proper removal of the computer's cover will vary, depending on the cover style and attaching mechanisms. In all cases, unfasten all the screws or clips, then *gently* slide or lift the cover away from the chassis. Computer covers are designed to move smoothly, so you should never need to use force. All the exercises described in this section assume that your computer's power has been turned off and that the cover has been removed.

Desktop System Components

Many desktop components, such as the processor, power supply and RAM, are installed through simple physical attachment to the computer. That is, physical installation is all that is required to make the component functional. Other devices, such as hard drives and keyboards, require the additional assignment of system resources. This section focuses on the physical installation of common components; resource assignment is discussed in the next section, "IRQs, DMAs, and I/O Addresses." Special hardware configurations are discussed in Chapter 2.

Many of the components discussed here conform to some type of standard. This means that you can replace a component with one that was made by a different manufacturer. The skills discussed here can be used on practically any desktop PC. Whenever you install or replace a PC component, it is recommended that you start the PC to ensure that the component works before you replace the cover.

System Board

Because most components are physically attached to the system board, this can be one of the most time-consuming replacements. If you are replacing one system board with another *of exactly the same brand and version*, you should make notes about the jumper and BIOS settings, in case they need to be changed on the new board. Most likely, however, you will replace a system board with a newer version, and should follow the new board's manual rather than the original setup.

All the expansion cards and cables must be removed from the system board. You might also need to remove hard drive and floppy drive bays to get them out of the way. Next, remove any screws or fasteners attaching the system board to the chassis, and lift the board out.

To place the new (or replacement) board in the computer, line it up properly on the chassis screw holes, and fix it into place. Although the BIOS, CMOS, and CMOS battery are included with the system board, you will need to install the processor, memory, and expansion cards separately. Finally, attach the power and drive connectors.

Storage Devices

Storage devices are a common replacement task because they are one of the most common causes of computer failure. They are also the source of common computer upgrades. Fortunately, since most drives are standardized, they can be recognized by any PC and don't need special configuration.

Hard Drives   Follow the procedure in Exercise 1-2 to remove a hard drive.

EXERCISE 1-2

Removing a Hard Drive

1. Remove the power supply and ribbon cables from the back of the hard drive. Ensure that you grasp the plastic connector, not the wires themselves. If the connector doesn't come out easily, try gently rocking it lengthwise from side to side (never front to back) while you pull it out.

2. Remove the restraining screws that attach the hard drive to the drive bay (these are usually located on the sides of the drive).

3. Slide the drive out of the computer.

To install a hard drive, the procedure is reversed, with a few important notes. The top of the drive is typically smooth and includes a manufacturer's label. The circuit board is on the bottom of the drive. Never install a hard drive upside down.

Some ribbon cables have connectors for two hard drives. If the system has only one hard drive, attach it to the end of the ribbon cable. Special configuration procedures are necessary for installing more than one hard drive. These procedures are discussed in Chapter 2.

Some ribbon connectors can physically fit either way in the drive's socket. The red stripe along the length of the cable represents "pin 1." Make sure that this stripe is aligned with pin 1, as indicated on the hard drive itself.

e x a m
ⓦatch *The primary hard drive is attached to the end connector on the ribbon cable.*

Floppy Drives   Floppy drives are installed and removed in a fashion similar to hard drives. To remove the floppy drive, disconnect the power and ribbon cables, unfasten the retaining screws, then slide the drive out of the bay.

Like a hard drive ribbon, a floppy drive ribbon works only one way. Attach the first floppy drive to the end of the ribbon, and, if necessary, attach the second floppy drive to the middle of the ribbon. Also, ensure that the red stripe on the ribbon cable is lined up with pin 1 on the floppy drive itself.

e x a m
ⓦatch *The red stripe on a drive cable indicates pin 1.*

CD-ROM Drives   The physical removal and installation of a CD-ROM drive is the same as that for hard and floppy drives. However, the CD drive could require the connection of a sound cable to the sound card.

If the computer doesn't recognize or can't communicate with the new drive, you need to load a driver for it. Insert the floppy disk that came with the CD, and run the Setup or Install program. This will load the CD driver and allow the computer to recognize the drive.

Power Supplies

Power supplies come with the chassis of the computer. However, they do fail from time to time and can be replaced using the procedure outlined in Exercise 1-3.

EXERCISE 1-3

Removing a Power Supply

1. Remove the power connector(s) (P1 on an ATX system or P8 and P9 on an AT) from the system board, using the plastic connector, not the wires.

2. Remove the power connectors from all other components, including the hard, floppy, and CD-ROM drives.

3. Remove the screws that hold the power supply to the chassis. Do *not* remove the screws from the power supply case itself!

4. Slide the power supply away from the computer.

Reverse this procedure to install a power supply. It is important to note that the P8 and P9 (AT system) connectors look almost identical. Although each will attach to the system board only one way, it is possible to place them beside each other the wrong way. When attaching them to the system board, make sure the *black* wires of the connectors are together.

The ATX (P1) power supply connector for the ATX system board offers more safety—it is a one-piece 20-pin keyed connector.

exam
Ⓦatch   *The P8 and P9 connectors are attached to the system board with the black wires together.*

Processor/CPU

When you install a CPU, it is important to make sure that it is compatible with the type and speed of the system board. System boards can typically use only one processor model and can usually handle only two or three different speeds of that particular model.

PGA/ZIF   Older processors, such as the Intel 80486 and Pentium, are PGA processors and fit into square sockets on the system board. If the socket is of the low insertion force type, simply remove the processor using a special PGA chip puller, then push the new processor into the socket. However, if the system board has a zero insertion force (ZIF) socket, follow the instructions in Exercise 1-4.

EXERCISE 1-4

Removing a PGA Processor

1. Lift the socket lever. You might have to move it slightly to the side to clear it of a retaining tab.

2. Pull out the processor. Because this is a ZIF socket, there should be no resistance when you remove the CPU.

To install a processor in a ZIF socket, ensure that the lever is raised, line up the pins, and place the processor in the socket, but do not push. Lower the lever to grip the CPU pins.

SEC/Slot I   Processors such as Intel's Pentium II, early Pentium III, and early Celeron, as well as AMD's Athlon are in SEC (single edge cartridge) form. To remove an SEC processor from its slot, locate the retaining clips on each side. Push the clips out, away from the processor. You might first need to slide a locking tab out of place. Pull the CPU out of the slot.

Intel and AMD abandoned Slot 1 and Slot A SEC porcessors in favor of Socket 370 and Socket A, respectively. To learn more about these and their subsequent processors, such as Intel's Pentium 4 and AMD's Athlon XP, go to http://www.intel.com and http://www.amd.com/us-en/.

Memory

The first RAM chips were dual inline packages (DIPs), which attached directly into sockets on the system board. However, their design made them prone to loosening due to the alternating heating and cooling of the system board. Newer memory modules are actually small cards with DIP chips on one or both sides. These cards fit upright into slots on the system board and are held in place by clips that prevent "chip creep" (loosening).

RAM is automatically detected and counted on startup, so its installation is limited to physical placement it in the computer. That is, once RAM is physically installed, no additional configuration is required.

SIMM Memory   Single inline memory module (SIMM) memory is available in 30- and 72-connector configurations. Most 80386, 80486, and Pentium computers include slots for both SIMM types. Follow the steps in Exercise 1-5 to install SIMM.

EXERCISE 1-5

Installing a SIMM

1. Line up the SIMM's connector edge with the appropriate-sized slot on the system board, keeping the SIMM at a 45-degree angle to the slot.

2. Gently rotate the SIMM upright until it clicks into place. Note that SIMMs will fit in a slot only one way. If you have trouble installing the SIMM, reverse its orientation in the slot.

To remove a SIMM, pull outward on the slot's retaining clips. The SIMM should fall to a 45-degree angle. Remove the SIMM.

DIMM Memory The dual inline memory module (DIMM) memory design is newer than the SIMM and is typically used in Pentium, Pentium II, and Pentium III computers. A common misconception is that DIMMs have DIP chips on both sides, and SIMMs have DIP chips on only one side. This is incorrect: DIMMs are so named because they have two rows of connectors, whereas SIMMs have only one row of connectors. DIMM packages, which have 168 connectors, are slightly longer than SIMMs. The technique for installing a DIMM (as shown in Exercise 1-6) is slightly different than for a SIMM.

EXERCISE 1-6

Installing a DIMM

1. Place the DIMM upright in the slot, so that the notches in the DIMM are lined up with the tabs in the slot.

2. Gently press down on the DIMM. The retention clips on the side should rotate into the locked position. You might need to guide them into place with your fingers.

To remove a DIMM, press the retention clips outward, as shown in Figure 1-9. The DIMM should pop out of the slot. Once it is free of the slot, remove it from the computer.

FIGURE 1-9

Removing a DIMM.

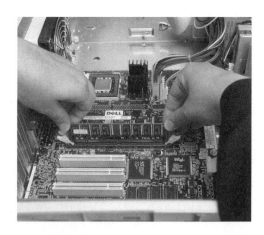

The word single in SIMM and the word dual in DIMM refer to the rows of connectors on each side rather than the number of sides that contain memory chips. For example, each side of each pin (connector) on a DIMM (Dual Inline Memory Module) has a separate function; however, each side of the pin is the same on a SIMM (Single Inline Memory Module). This allows for only one DIMM instead of two SIMMs to make up the 64-bit data path.

Input Devices

Most input devices, such as keyboards and mice, are installed by simply plugging them into the appropriate port on the back of the computer. Keyboards can have either DIN-6 or Mini DIN-5 connectors. Mice typically use either an existing 9-pin serial (COM) port or a Mini DIN-5 port. Note that although it will physically fit, a Mini DIN-5 keyboard will not work in a Mini DIN-5 mouse port, or vice versa.

Another type of mouse, the *bus mouse*, requires a more complicated physical installation. A bus mouse expansion card must be installed on the system board and the mouse then connected to the port at the back.

Portable System Components

Because portable systems are largely proprietary, components cannot be mixed among them. Most portables must be returned to the manufacturer to be repaired or upgraded. This section introduces you to some laptop-specific components and describes installation procedures, where applicable.

on the
ⓙ o b

Portable computers are much more difficult and costly to repair than desktop PCs. To make matters worse, they are also much more likely to need repairs. Because portable are "portable," it's easy to drop them, bang them into things, and so on, all of which can cause damage. Always use a proper carrying case or bag for your portable to avoid the lengthy and costly process of having it repaired.

AC Adapter

The AC adapter's function is to convert AC power to DC power, in the same way that the power supply does in a desktop. The AC adapter is also responsible for recharging the battery. If an external adapter must be replaced, simply unplug it and attach a new one. Because laptops have proprietary designs, check with the manufacturer for instructions on replacing an internal adapter. Furthermore, since AC adapters have varying output voltages, never use an AC adapter with any laptop other than the one for which it was made.

Hard Drive

Laptop hard drives vary in physical size and interface and are typically either 2.5-inch Ultra Direct Memory Access (UDMA) or 2.5-inch Enhanced Integrated Drive Electronics (EIDE). Replace a hard drive only with another of the same type from the same manufacturer. Usually, you can remove a small plastic cover on the bottom of the laptop to access the hard drive. Slide the drive out (see Figure 1-10), then replace it with a new drive and replace the cover.

Keyboard

Most laptops come with small, integrated keyboards. Some laptop keyboards include a pointing device such as a pointing stick or touch pad. Unfortunately, since keyboards are integrated into laptops, they are not easily replaced and the entire computer must usually be sent back to the manufacturer when there is a problem.

Processor Board

The laptop version of a system board is called a *processor board*. It typically contains both the processor and RAM and in most cases can be repaired or upgraded only by the manufacturer.

Video Board

A portable computer's video output is controlled by a *video board*, in much the same way that a PC's video is controlled by a video expansion card. Video boards are

FIGURE 1-10

Removing a hard drive from a portable system.

typically integrated with the system and are difficult to upgrade. In most cases, a faulty video board needs to be replaced by the manufacturer.

DC Controllers

Most portable computers include a *DC controller*, which is designed to monitor and regulate power usage. The function of DC controllers can vary with the manufacturer, but typically, they provide short-circuit protection, give "low battery" warnings, and can be configured to automatically shut down the portable when the power is low.

LCD Panel

To add to their portability, portable computers use thin LCDs. Although their display abilities are typically not as good as those of CRTs, LCDs are much thinner (1 to 2 inches thick) and require much less power. The first LCD panels were called *passive matrix displays*. A passive matrix display is made up of a grid of horizontal and vertical wires. At one end of each wire is a transistor, which receives display signals from the computer. When two transistors (one at the *x* axis and one at the *y* axis) send voltage along their wires, the pixel at the intersection of the two wires is lit.

Active matrix displays are newer and use different technology, called *thin-film transistor (TFT)* technology. Active matrix displays contain transistors at each pixel, resulting in more colors, better resolution, a better ability to display moving objects, and the ability to be viewed at greater angles. However, active matrix displays use more power than passive matrix displays.

LCD displays cannot be repaired. That means a faulty display in a portable will need to be replaced by the manufacturer of the portable.

CERTIFICATION OBJECTIVE 1.03

IRQs, DMAs, and I/O Addresses

You should now be familiar with the physical installation procedures for common computer components. As discussed, physical installation is all that is required to make some components functional. However, some components also require system resources, such as processor time and memory space.

One type of computer resource is called an *input/output (I/O) address*. When the computer is started, the BIOS loads into RAM device-specific information about the existing devices, including their drivers and other rules of communication. Whenever the processor needs to communicate with a device in the computer, it first checks RAM for the entries pertaining to that device. Without an I/O address, components would appear nonexistent to the processor.

Once the processor has finished communicating with or requesting a task from a device, it continues on with other functions, rather than waiting for the device to finish its task. When the device has a result to report to the processor, it places the result in RAM. Next, the device "interrupts" the processor's function to indicate that the task is completed. Devices accomplish this through *interrupt request (IRQ) lines*. When the processor receives an interrupt, it can identify the initiating device by its IRQ and then turns to that device's I/O (RAM) address to retrieve the information.

In some cases, devices require data from other components in order to complete their tasks. In these cases, it is more efficient to allow the two devices to communicate directly with each other than it is for them to communicate via the processor. Devices communicate with one another using *direct memory access (DMA)* channels. DMA channels allow devices to write data directly into memory without first being asked by the processor. Other devices can read this data directly from memory without asking the processor for it.

In some cases, IRQs, DMAs, and I/O addresses are automatically assigned to devices by the BIOS. Plug and Play operating systems, such as Microsoft Windows 95 and 98, can also automatically assign resources. However, in older machines, you might need to allocate resources manually. For this reason, and because they will appear on the A+ exams, you should become very familiar with the concepts presented in this section.

If you are using Microsoft Windows 9x (95 or 98) or 2000, you can view your computer's resource settings in the Device Manager window. Follow the steps in Exercise 1-7 to view your computer's resource allocations.

EXERCISE 1-7

Viewing the Computer's Resource Assignments

1. Right-click the My Computer icon on the desktop.
2. Select Properties from the shortcut menu.

3. Click the Device Manager tab.

4. Select the Computer icon, and click the Properties button.

Hexidecimal Addresses

When you view a device's I/O address setting, you will probably notice that it contains letters and numbers. This is the device's memory address, in other words, the location in memory where the processor must go to find a particular piece of data. This type of numbering is called *hexidecimal*, and it is based on multiples of 16, rather than 10.

The hexidecimal system is mainly used because it is easier to understand than binary. The binary number 0001, for example, is 1 in our decimal system, as well as in the hexidecimal system. 1111 in binary is 16 in our decimal system and F in hexidecimal. The hexidecimal memory address 3D9A is much easier to understand than the equivalent binary representation 11110110011010. See Table 1-2 for related binary, decimal and hexidecimal numbers.

TABLE 1-2	Decimal	Hexidecimal	Binary
Decimal Numbers and their Corresponding Hexidecimal and Binary Numbers	0	0	0000
	1	1	0001
	2	2	0010
	3	3	0011
	4	4	0100
	5	5	0101
	6	6	0110
	7	7	0111
	8	8	1000
	9	9	1001
	10	A	1010

TABLE 1-2	Decimal	Hexidecimal	Binary
Decimal Numbers and their Corresponding Hexidecimal and Binary Numbers (*continued*)	11	B	1011
	12	C	1100
	13	D	1101
	14	E	1110
	15	F	1111

Standard IRQ Settings

When the first PCs were designed, eight IRQs were available. However, as more devices were introduced, more IRQs had to be made available so that devices would not be in competition for them (each device must have a unique IRQ address). Eight more IRQs were added, for a total of 16 (numbered 0–15).

Although some devices can use one of several IRQs, other devices (typically internal components) are hard-wired to use a specific IRQ and cannot be configured otherwise. Although most devices adhere to industry-set standards, some have manufacturer-specific IRQ settings. A device's preferred IRQ setting can usually be found in the manufacturer's documentation that came with the device.

IRQ 0 is set aside for the computer's system timer. The *system timer* is responsible for synchronizing the speed of the computer's activities. Computer systems contain a small quartz that vibrates when exposed to electricity. Each vibration represents a cycle. A computer whose quartz vibrates 100 million times a second runs at a speed of 100 megahertz, abbreviated MHz. Because the system timer is such an important component, it is given the IRQ with the highest priority.

IRQ 1 is assigned to the computer's keyboard. IRQ 1 has the second-highest priority, so keyboard commands take precedence over many other computer functions (as evidenced by the ability to halt some computer operations using special key combinations).

IRQ 2 is typically listed as "cascade" or "redirect to IRQ 9." Recall that the earliest computers had only eight IRQs (0–7) and that IRQs 8–15 were introduced later. The interrupt controller for the new IRQs uses IRQ 2 for itself to access IRQs 8–15. Additionally, some devices at the time were hard-wired to use IRQ 2 only. The "redirect" is used to trick devices into using IRQ 9 instead of IRQ 2.

IRQ 3 is assigned to COM2 and COM4. However, as you already know, devices cannot share an IRQ. Fortunately, most computers include only two COM ports: COM1 and COM2. If COM2 and COM4 both have devices attached, only one can be used at a time. For example, if a modem uses COM2 and a scanner is attached to COM4, you can use one device or the other but not both at the same time. The same principle is true for IRQ 4, which is assigned to COM1 and COM3.

The standard assignment for IRQ 5 is the secondary parallel port (LPT2). However, because most computers include only one LPT port, IRQ 5 is typically available for other devices. IRQ 6 is assigned to the floppy drive, and IRQ 7 is assigned to the primary parallel port (LPT1). Neither of these devices can be reconfigured to use other IRQs.

IRQ 8 is assigned to the computer's real-time clock. This is the clock responsible for keeping the actual time and date. IRQ 9, which was discussed previously, is available for assignment but typically is reserved for devices that are hard-wired to use IRQ 2.

IRQ 10 and IRQ 11 are "available." This means that they are not in use by a critical component and are available to be assigned to peripheral devices, or noncritical components, such as Small Computer Systems Interface, or SCSI (pronounced "scuzzy") controllers or network cards. IRQ 12 is set aside for the PS/2 mouse. If the computer uses a bus or serial mouse instead, IRQ 12 is available for another device.

IRQ 13 is reserved for the math coprocessor, found in Intel 80486DX and newer processors. If the processor is older and doesn't use a math coprocessor, IRQ 13 is available. IRQ 14 is assigned to the primary hard drive controller, and IRQ 15 is reserved for the secondary hard drive controller, if one exists. Table 1-3 presents a summary of standard IRQ assignments.

TABLE 1-3	IRQ	Device
Standard IRQ Assignments	0	System timer
	1	Keyboard
	2	Cascade, redirect to IRQ 9
	3	Serial ports (COM2 and COM4)
	4	Serial ports (COM1 and COM3)
	5	Parallel port (LPT2)
	6	Floppy drive controller
	7	Parallel port (LPT1)
	8	Real-time clock
	9	Redirected from IRQ 2

TABLE 1-3	IRQ	Device
	10	Available
Standard IRQ Assignments *(continued)*	11	Available
	12	PS/2 mouse
	13	Math coprocessor
	14	Hard disk controller
	15	Secondary hard disk controller

exam
Watch

You need to memorize these IRQ assignments for the A+ exam and to properly diagnose and resolve IRQ-related computer problems. There is no apparent order or intuitive structure to these assignments, so it might be helpful to write them out on paper, over and over, recalling more of them from memory each time. After enough exposure to them, you will be able to mentally associate an IRA address with its component, rather than merely calling them up by reciting the whole table of addresses.

All of the above IRQs are *maskable interrupts*, meaning that the processor can ignore them in order to complete a current task. However, in the presence of certain memory errors, the processor must be halted to prevent corruption or loss of data. *Nonmaskable interrupts* are used by memory to indicate a possibly fatal condition, and the processor is stopped mid-task.

Use the following Scenario & Solution questions to reinforce your knowledge about IRQ addresses.

SCENARIO & SOLUTION

Which interrupts are maskable?	0–15.
Which IRQ address has the highest priority?	0.
I'm attaching a device that can use either IRQ 11 or 15. Which should I use?	If the computer uses the secondary hard drive controller, you must use 11 for the new device. If there is no secondary hard drive, you can use either 11 or 15, with no noticeable performance difference.

Modems

Modems require an IRQ and I/O address to function properly but require a good knowledge about resources for proper configuration. If the modem is external, it attaches to one of the computer's serial ports, typically COM2. Because the modem is attached to COM2, it uses the COM2 resources, namely IRQ 3 and I/O 2F8-2FF.

Internal modems present a unique configuration procedure. Even though the internal modem occupies a regular expansion slot inside the computer, it is still assigned the resources of one of the computer's serial ports. This means that the internal modem uses a COM port's resources, even though it is not physically attached to that port. Furthermore, no device can be physically attached to the port with which the internal modem is associated. In most cases, internal modems are configured to use COM3's resources (IRQ 4 and I/O address 3E8-3EF) or COM4's resources (IRQ 3 and I/O address 2E8-2EF).

Floppy Drive

As well as using IRQ 6, floppy drive controllers are also assigned I/O address 3F0–3F7. Floppy drives also require the use of a DMA channel and are typically assigned DMA 2.

Hard Drive

The primary hard drive controller is assigned IRQ 14 and I/O address 1F0–1F8. The secondary hard drive controller uses IRQ 15 and I/O address 170–178. Older hard drive controllers use DMA channel 3. However, newer drives are able to access RAM directly using a protocol called Ultra DMA (UDMA). UDMA is a protocol used only by hard drives and is not functionally associated with a computer's standard DMA channels.

USB Port

The *Universal Serial Bus (USB)* port is a relative newcomer in the computer industry. It is a physical port, located at the back of the computer, which can be used to connect up to 127 external devices to the computer. Low-speed USB transmits data up to 1.5MBps; and high-speed USB supports speeds up to 12MBps.

USB ports can be used only with specially designed USB-compatible components. One benefit of a USB port is that it supports Plug and Play, meaning that devices attached to the port are automatically recognized by the computer and are automatically assigned computer resources, such as IRQs and I/O addresses. The USB port's controller itself typically uses IRQ 9 and I/O address 1020-103F.

In traditional device installation, the computer must be turned off before a component can be installed. When the computer is restarted, it can recognize and use the component. Even devices that can be physically connected while the computer is running (e.g., a printer or scanner) will not be recognized until the computer is restarted. USB ports, however, support *hot swapping*, which means that devices can be attached while the computer is running and can be recognized and used immediately.

Infrared Port

Infrared (wireless) computer devices use infrared light waves, rather than physical connections, to communicate with each other. Most infrared ports support either the Bluetooth or Infrared Data Association's (IrDA's) data transmission standards. Any two wireless devices can communicate with each other, as long as they adhere to the same standards. The Bluetooth infrared standard is not currently supported by Microsoft Windows, so you can expect the A+ exam to focus on the IrDA standard.

IrDA infrared devices support a maximum transmission speed of 4Mbps. Connections can be *point to point*, as in a computer and printer, or *multipoint*, as in computers on a network. One limitation of infrared devices is that they use "line-of-sight" transmission, so the port on the communicating devices must be directly facing one another. Infrared communications are limited to approximately 1 meter.

Microsoft Windows (9x and 2000) supports Plug and Play for IrDA infrared devices. Again, this means that devices are automatically recognized and assigned system resources. Some computers come with an infrared port already installed. However, you can add one by installing an infrared adapter. External adapters are attached to the computer via a serial port, so they use that port's system resources. Like most other expansion cards, internal adapters can be installed in an available expansion slot and assigned an available IRQ and I/O address.

Peripheral Ports, Cabling, and Connectors

Earlier, this chapter discussed procedures for installing various internal components. As a technician, you will also be expected to install and replace external components, such as mice, scanners, and printers. Many external components are installed by simply plugging them into a port at the back of the computer. However, some components can be attached to a computer in more than one way. How then do you decide which way is the best?

This section introduces you to a number of basic peripheral installation concepts, such as cable and connector types, as well as methods of communication. This information will allow you to determine the pros and cons of various connection methods as well as when a peripheral's connection to the computer is the cause of a problem.

Cable Types

Cables are used to physically connect components and are responsible for transmitting signals between them. The majority of computer cables transmit electronic signals and can come in several physical forms. *Straight-pair cables* consist of one or more metal wires surrounded by a plastic insulating sheath. *Twisted-pair cables* consist of two or more metal wires that are twisted around each other along the entire length of the cable. These wires are also surrounded by a plastic sheath. *Coaxial cables* contain a single copper wire surrounded by several layers of insulating plastic. Figure 1-11 illustrates some common cable types.

Another distinction between cable types is the presence or absence of an interference shield. Cables that transmit electronic signals are susceptible to interference from surrounding objects and the atmosphere itself. This interference is technically referred to as *electromagnetic interference (EMI)* and is commonly known as "noise." *Shielded cables* have an extra wire or Mylar covering that can help protect signals from EMI. Cables without this type of protection are called *unshielded.* Both straight-pair and twisted-pair cables are available in shielded and unshielded form. Coaxial cables are shielded. *Fiber-optic cables*, which transmit light signals, are unaffected by EMI, so they do not have noise shields.

FIGURE 1-11

Common
cable types.

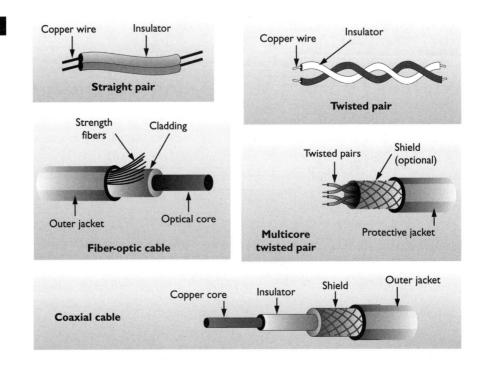

The specific names of peripheral cables are almost as varied as the types of peripherals themselves. Some devices even use nonstandardized cables that cannot be used by other devices. The cable types just discussed are examined in more detail in Chapter 7, "Basic Networking." Other features of cables, such as their use of duplex mode and maximum effective length, are discussed throughout the book as they pertain to different components and hardware configurations.

Cable Orientation

Many computer cables are *bi-directional*, meaning that signals can travel in either direction along the cable. In these cases, the orientation of the cable between devices is not a limiting factor. For example, when you plug a modem into a phone jack, there is no wrong way to orient the cable; either connector can plug into either the modem or the jack. This is also true for network cables. You can try this by following the steps in Exercise 1-8.

Other cables, however, are strictly *unidirectional*, such as the cable that attaches the monitor to the computer. This type of cable transmits signals in one direction only (for example, from the computer to the monitor) and never in the opposite direction. The function of a unidirectional component is entirely dependent on the proper cable orientation. Fortunately, most, if not all, of the unidirectional cables you will use as a technician will have a different type of connector on each end. This makes it physically impossible to connect the wrong end to a device.

The orientation of the cable connector in the device's port is another important factor. In most cases, the wires in a cable must be lined up properly with the pins in a device's port. For example, if you were to attach a modem's cable upside-down in the phone jack, the modem would not work. Again, almost all cables for which port orientation is a factor are designed so that they can be physically connected only one way. Some cables, however, are not limited by port orientation. Coaxial cables, for example, have only one internal wire that is "twisted" into place. In this case, there is no way to attach the cable upside-down.

EXERCISE 1-8

Experimenting with Cable Orientation

1. On the modem itself, locate the port that attaches to the wall outlet (not the port that attaches to a phone).

2. Plug one end of the modem cable into this port, and plug the other end of the cable into the phone jack in the wall.

3. Test the modem to verify that it works.

4. Unplug the cable from both the modem and the wall.

5. Reverse the cable: Plug the end that was originally plugged into the modem into the phone jack, and vice versa.

6. Test the modem. It works!

Pin Connections

There is a great variety of connector and port types among peripheral devices, and different devices use different cable/port combinations. For example, the straight-pair cable for a printer has a different connector than the straight-pair cable for a monitor. It is important to make the distinction between a connector and a port. Typically, the term *connector* refers to the end of a cable, and *port* refers to its place of attachment on a device. Additionally, the distinction between male and female should be made here. A *male* port or connector has pins, and a *female* port or connector has holes.

Some common connector types are described in the following sections. Reference to the names of manufacturer-specific type/port combinations is beyond the scope of this book, and you shouldn't expect to see them on the A+ exams.

DB-9

DB-type connectors can be identified by their trapezoidal shape (see Figure 1-12). In fact, the *D* in *DB* stands for *D-shell*, a reference to the connector's shape. A DB-9 connector has nine connections in two rows (five in one row and four in the other row). Female DB-9 ports on the computer are typically used for parallel communications, which we'll discuss later. Almost all computers include at least one and usually two or more male DB-9 ports at the back. These ports are most commonly used for serial devices such as mice and external modems.

DB-25

DB-25 connectors are D-shell connectors with 25 pins or holes, with 13 in one row and 12 in the other. Most computers include one or two DB-25 connectors for devices such as printers and scanners. Female DB-25 connectors are typically used for parallel communications; the male ports are used for serial communications.

RJ-11

Registered jack (RJ) connectors are rectangular-shaped and have a locking clip on one side (see Figure 1-13). The number designation of an RJ connector refers to its size rather than to the number of wire connections within it. RJ-11 connectors contain only two wires and are used to attach phone cables to modems and to phone jacks in the wall.

RJ-45

RJ-45 connectors are larger than RJ-11 connectors and contain eight, rather than two, wires. RJ-45 connectors are most commonly used to attach twisted-pair cables to network cards.

BNC

The acronym *BNC* is the subject of some debate. Depending on the source you use, you will find that it possibly stands for *broadband network connector, Bayonet Neill-Concelman, Bayonet Neill connector, British Naval Connector, Bayonet Navy Connector, Bayonet Nut Connection...* There seems to be no real consensus as to the origin of its name.

In any case, BNC connectors are used to attach coaxial cables to BNC ports. As you can see in Figure 1-14, the cable connector is round and has a twist-lock mechanism to keep the cable in place. BNC connectors have a protruding pin that corresponds to a hole in the port. BNC connectors are commonly used in computer networks but cannot connect your television to the cable outlet in the wall.

FIGURE 1-13

RJ connectors are rectangular and have a locking tab.

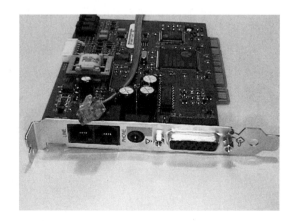

FIGURE 1-14

A BNC
connector
and port.

PS/2 and Mini-DIN

DIN connectors get their name from *Deutsche Industrinorm*, which is the standards
organization for Germany. Most (but not all) DIN connectors are round with a
circle or semicircle of pins (see Figure 1-15). The Mini-DIN connector, or more
accurately, the Mini-DIN-6 connector, gets its name from the fact that it is smaller
than a customary DIN-6 keyboard connector. Mini-DIN connectors are most
commonly used for PS/2 (Personal System/2) mice and keyboards. For this reason,
Mini-DIN connectors are often referred to as PS/2 connectors.

IEEE-1394

IEEE stands for *Institute of Electrical and Electronics Engineers*, a standards organization.
IEEE-1394 is a computer bus standard that supports very high speeds for external
devices. IEEE-1394 (also called FireWire) supports many of the same features as USB
(described earlier).

FIGURE 1-15

Two Mini-DIN-6
connectors, used
for some mice
and keyboards.

IEEE-1394 connectors are slightly smaller than DB-15 monitor connectors and contain two sockets. Each socket is round and contains six wires. The connector is roughly rectangular, with one rounded side to ensure proper orientation in the port (see Figure 1-16).

USB

Because there are two types of USB (slow and fast), there are two types of USB cable. Each of these has a unique connector to ensure that only the proper cable type is attached to a slow or fast USB port. A typical USB connector is shown in Figure 1-17.

Serial vs. Parallel

Another important characteristic of an external peripheral is its method of communication. Serial and parallel communications differ in their speed, transfer modes, and control signals. As discussed previously, a device's use of serial or parallel communication will play a large role in the type of cable and connector that it uses.

Serial Communications

Serial communications are most notably distinguished by the fact that they transfer data one bit at a time (in series). Serial communications implement the Recommended Standard-232 (RS-232) standard, which defines the connection methods for serial devices. For this reason, serial ports are sometimes referred to as *RS-232 ports*.

FIGURE 1-16

An IEEE 1394 connector.

FIGURE 1-17

A USB
connector.

Serial communications can be either *synchronous*, in which data is sent in a continuous stream, or *asynchronous*, in which data is sent in intermittent bursts. In synchronous serial communications, the stream of data never stops. When there is no "real" data to send, the devices send "dummy" bits to remain synchronized with one another. This constant activity keeps the devices ready to receive real data.

Asynchronous data is intermittent, so it is accompanied by start and stop bits that indicate the beginning and end of a data stream. This system helps the receiving device distinguish real data from line noise. Most serial devices, such as serial mice and modems, use asynchronous communications.

Parallel Communications

Parallel communications are defined by the fact that they can transmit more than one data bit at a time. This results in faster data transfers for large packets. Imagine an elevator that can carry only one person at a time. It would take eight trips to get eight people from one floor to another using this elevator. An elevator that could carry eight people at once could do the same thing in only one trip. The same principle is true for parallel communication.

Most data inside the computer is transmitted in parallel—one bit on each of several physical wires. Many external devices—including printers and scanners, which typically receive or send large amounts of data—also use parallel communications. The term #-bit (8-bit, 16-bit, 32-bit) is used commonly in the computer industry to refer to the number of data bits that can be sent at once (in parallel) between two devices.

Parallel devices must be synchronized with each other to properly send or receive data. To achieve synchronization, the devices carry out a *handshake routine*, in which the speed and rules of communication are agreed on before any data is transmitted. Although functionally similar, the parallel communications handshake should not be confused with the modem handshake, which is much more complex.

Now that you are familiar with serial and parallel communications, you should be able to answer the following Scenario & Solution questions.

SCENARIO & SOLUTION

Why do mice use serial communications?	Because they tend to send intermittent, small bursts of data.
Why do printers tend to use parallel communications?	Because parallel communications are faster at transmitting the large data packets typically sent to printers.
How can I tell a serial port from a parallel port at the back of the computer?	Serial ports tend to be male, and parallel ports tend to be female.

CERTIFICATION SUMMARY

Common computer components include the processor, memory, storage devices, and input and output devices. All of these devices have specific functions, and your familiarity with them will help you to quickly determine when a component must be upgraded or replaced. Your knowledge of proper installation procedures will allow you to install or replace devices without causing physical damage or interfering with the proper function of other devices.

In addition to physical installation, many devices require system resources, such as IRQ and I/O addresses, to function properly. Because no two devices can share a resource, you must be very familiar with their standard assignments so that you do not cause, and can resolve, resource conflicts.

Another important factor in device operation and installation is the way that the device is attached to the computer. There are many types of computer cables, including straight-pair, twisted-pair, and coaxial. Cables can be attached to devices using a variety of connectors. Fortunately, most devices come with the proper cable or connector and fit only one way on the device. A good knowledge of connectors will help you quickly distinguish one cable from another and determine which devices can use it.

✓ TWO-MINUTE DRILL

Here are some of the key points from each certification objective in Chapter 1.

System Modules

❑ All components, including external peripherals, are connected to each other via the system board.

❑ The computer's processor uses RAM as a temporary storage space for its processes and uses the system BIOS to communicate with other devices in the system.

❑ Data is stored permanently on storage devices, such as hard, floppy, and CD-ROM disks, each of which offer different capacities and portability.

❑ Portable systems are proprietary (nonstandardized) and use components, such as LCD displays that desktop systems do not.

Adding and Removing Field-Replaceable Modules

❑ Always turn the computer off and follow ESD procedures before installing or removing a computer component.

❑ If you must rock a component to remove or install it, always rock it lengthwise (from end to end), never back and forth (from side to side).

❑ The red stripe on a drive ribbon must be aligned with pin 1 on the port.

❑ When installing the P8 and P9 power connectors, place the two black wires together.

IRQs, DMAs, and I/O Addresses

❑ The processor uses I/O addresses to locate and communicate with devices, and devices use IRQs to get the attention of the processor.

❑ Some devices use DMA channels to directly read from or write to RAM.

❑ No two devices can share an IRQ or I/O address.

Peripheral Ports, Cabling, and Connectors

❑ Common electronic cables include straight-pair, twisted-pair, and coaxial.

❑ Most cables are physically configured to fit only one way in a port or device.

❑ Common connectors include DB-9, DB-25, RJ-11, RJ-45, BNC, and Mini-DIN-6.

❑ Serial devices transmit one bit at a time; parallel devices transmit more than one bit at a time.

SELF TEST

The following questions will help you measure your understanding of the material presented in this chapter. Read all of the choices carefully because there might be more than one correct answer. Choose all correct answers for each question.

System Modules

1. Which of the following connections can be used to attach an 80486 processor to the motherboard?

   A. PGA

   B. Slot-1

   C. ZIF

   D. SEC

2. Which of the following most accurately describes a function of the computer's cache memory?

   A. To store instructions used by currently running applications

   B. To provide temporary storage of data that is required to complete a task

   C. To anticipate the processor's data requests and make that data available for fast retrieval

   D. To store a device's most basic operating instructions

3. You are planning to upgrade your computer's display to one that can use 256-color mode and has a resolution of at least 1024 x 768. Which type(s) of display can fulfill these requirements?

   A. Any type of CRT

   B. Any analog CRT

   C. VGA and SVGA

   D. SVGA

4. Each time you start your computer, it asks you for the proper time. Which component will you most likely need to replace?

   A. The BIOS

   B. The system timer

   C. The CMOS battery

   D. The processor

5. Which statement most accurately describes the relationship between the computer's BIOS and CMOS?

   A. The CMOS uses information stored in the BIOS to set computer configurations, such as the boot sequence, keyboard status, and hard drive settings.

   B. The BIOS's configuration settings are stored on the CMOS chip so that they are not lost when the computer is turned off.

   C. The CMOS uses information stored in the BIOS to communicate with the computer's components.

   D. They perform the same functions, but the BIOS is found only in newer computers.

Adding and Removing Field-Replaceable Modules

6. Which procedures should you follow to properly install a single hard drive in a computer system?

   A. Install the hard drive in the bay closest to the motherboard and align the cable's red stripe with pin 1.

   B. Use the manufacturer's label to identify the top side of the drive, and attach the drive to the ribbon connector closest to the motherboard.

   C. Align the cable's red stripe with pin 1, and attach the hard drive to the end of the cable.

   D. Use the manufacturer's label to identify pin 1, and install the drive in the bay furthest from the motherboard.

7. You have just installed a new power supply, but the computer doesn't seem to be getting any power. Which of the following should you do?

   A. Ensure that the P8 and P9 connectors are attached to the motherboard with the black wires together.

   B. Ensure that the P8 and P9 connectors are attached to each other with the black wires at opposite ends.

   C. Ensure that the red stripe on the cable is aligned with pin 1 on the motherboard.

   D. Ensure that the P8 and P9 connectors are properly attached to the hard drive.

8. You are instructing a computer user in the proper removal of a PGA processor, and you tell her to raise the lever on the side of the socket. What should she expect the processor to do when the lever is raised?

   A. The processor will slowly rise out of the socket, in correspondence with the raising of the lever.

   B. The processor will "pop" upward, out of the socket.

    C. The processor will fall to a 45-degree angle with the motherboard.

    D. Nothing.

9. The *D* in the acronym DIMM refers to:

    A. Direct—the type of communication between the DIMM and the processor

    B. Dual—the number of connector rows on the DIMM

    C. Double—the number of sides on the DIMM that contain memory chips

    D. DIP—the type of memory chips embedded on the DIMM

10. Which of the following statements about a portable's display panel is true?

    A. Most passive matrix displays use TFT technology.

    B. They use CRT technology.

    C. Active matrix displays have better resolution than passive matrix displays.

    D. Older display panels use CRT technology, and newer display panels use LCD technology.

IRQs, DMAs, and I/O Addresses

11. Which of the following most accurately describes the function of I/O addresses?

    A. They are used by the processor to identify and communicate with components.

    B. They are used by components to identify themselves when they communicate with the processor.

    C. They are used by components to interrupt the processor.

    D. They are used by components for direct access to the information in RAM.

12. Which term refers to an IRQ that cannot be ignored by the processor?

    A. Maskable

    B. Nonmaskable

    C. Cascaded

    D. Noncascaded

13. You are planning to install a sound card on a Pentium computer that uses both hard drive controllers and whose only noncritical peripheral is a serial mouse. According to the standard assignments, which IRQ(s) is (are) available to be assigned to the sound card?

    A. IRQs 3 and 4

    B. IRQs 4 and 15

    C. IRQs 7 and 13

    D. IRQs 10 and 12

14. A Pentium computer uses a serial mouse and one hard drive controller. From this information only, what can you tell about this computer?

    A. IRQs 12 and 13 are both in use.

    B. IRQ 13 is in use.

    C. IRQs 12, 13, and 15 are all available.

    D. IRQs 12 and 15 are both in use.

15. An 80386 computer has a printer connected to the parallel (LPT) port, a serial mouse, and an external modem, and it uses standard IRQ settings. A math coprocessor has not been installed in the 80387 slot provided on the system board. The only other noncritical peripheral in the system is a sound card that works only intermittently. Which of the following statements is true?

    A. You should change the IRQ assignment of the sound card to IRQ 5.

    B. There is an IRQ conflict between the math coprocessor and the sound card.

    C. You should unplug the modem.

    D. The sound card problem is unrelated to IRQ assignment.

Peripheral Ports, Cabling and Connectors

16. In telling a customer how to properly attach a cable modem to a wall outlet, which are you most likely to mention?

    A. The larger cable connection goes in the outlet and the smaller connection attaches to the modem.

    B. The cable is attached to the modem with the retention tab at the bottom.

    C. The connector will fit only one way into the wall outlet.

    D. The modem uses a coaxial cable.

17. What differentiates a male connector from a female connector?

    A. Male connectors have pins; female connectors have holes.

    B. A female connector has a shape similar to the universal symbol for "female."

    C. Female connectors are attached to the computer; male connectors are attached to peripheral devices.

    D. Male connectors have an uneven number of wires; female connectors have an even number.

18. Which type of connector can be identified by its rectangular shape, retaining tab, and flat copper connections?

   A. DB

   B. RJ

   C. BNC

   D. Mini-DIN

19. Which of the following ports are *not* used by mice?

   A. DB

   B. Mini-DIN

   C. PS/2

   D. BNC

20. You are planning to buy a printer for your computer. Which of the following factors should you consider when making your choice?

   A. Parallel communications are faster than serial communications.

   B. Serial communications result in fewer errors than parallel communications.

   C. Parallel communications are compatible with more computer types than serial communications.

   D. Serial communications devices are easier to configure than parallel communications devices.

LAB QUESTION

You turned on the computer, opened a word processing program (using the mouse), then created a document (using the keyboard). Next, you saved and printed the document. Using the information in Chapter 1, provide as much detail as you can about the resulting processes that took place in the computer.

SELF-TEST ANSWERS

System Modules

1. ☑ **C.** An 80486 processor can be attached to the motherboard using a ZIF. ZIF stands for *zero insertion force* and is a socket design used for PGA-form processors. A ZIF socket includes a lever that grips and releases the processor so that it can be easily inserted or removed.

   ☒ **A**, PGA, is incorrect because this refers to a type of processor chip design, a pin grid array. In fact, the 80486 processor *is* a PGA chip. PGA chips are attached to ZIF or LIF sockets on the motherboard. **B**, Slot-1, and **D**, SEC, are incorrect because they refer to chip/connection forms for Pentium II and higher processors. Pentium II and Pentium III processors are SEC cartridges and are attached to the motherboard using a connector called Slot-1.

2. ☑ **C.** A function of the computer's cache is to anticipate the processor's data requests and make that data available for fast retrieval. Cache memory can be accessed faster than regular RAM, so the more data that can be stored there, the faster the computer will run overall. The computer's cache includes a cache controller that is able to anticipate the processor's data needs, retrieve them from regular RAM, and store them in the faster cache memory chips.

   ☒ **A**, to store instructions used by currently running applications, and **B**, to provide temporary storage of data that is required to complete a task, are incorrect because these are both functions of RAM memory. **D**, to store a device's most basic operating instructions, is incorrect because this is a function of a device's ROM memory.

3. ☑ **D.** You can use an SVGA display to use 256-color mode with a 1024 x 768 resolution. SVGA monitors can display around 16 million colors at once (32-bit true color) and have a maximum resolution of 1280 x 1024.

   ☒ **A**, any type of CRT, is incorrect because this would include CGA, EGA, and VGA monitors. CGA and EGA monitors can display only 16 colors at once, at resolutions of 160 x 100 and 640 x 350, respectively. VGA monitors have a maximum resolution of 640 x 480. **B**, any analog CRT, and **C**, VGA or SVGA, are both incorrect because they refer to VGA technology (VGA is a type of analog monitor).

4. ☑ **C.** The CMOS battery is most likely not working properly. The computer's CMOS is responsible for retaining computer settings, such as the time, BIOS settings, and boot sequence. The CMOS can retain these settings when the computer is turned off because it is attached to a CMOS battery. When this battery starts to get low, the CMOS is no longer able to keep its settings.

   ☒ **A**, the BIOS, is incorrect because its function is to translate communications between the processor and other computer components. The CMOS battery ensures the BIOS settings are not lost when the power is turned off. The BIOS settings and the time are both retained because of the CMOS battery but otherwise are not related to one another. **B,** the system timer, is incorrect because its function is to synchronize the timing of processes in the computer. It works like a metronome, setting the speed of the computer, and is unrelated to the "real" time. **D,** the processor, is also incorrect. The processor is the brain of the computer, and although it might be responsible for incorporating the time information into other tasks, it does not keep track of the time, even while the computer is turned on.

5. ☑ **B.** The BIOS's configuration settings are stored on the CMOS chips so that they are not lost when the computer is turned off. The CMOS is attached to a small battery, which allows it to retain information when there is no power. When the computer is turned on, the BIOS retrieves its settings from the CMOS.

☒ **A** is incorrect because it states that the CMOS uses information stored in the BIOS to set computer configurations, such as the boot sequence, keyboard status, and hard drive settings. It is the CMOS, not the BIOS, that stores computer configurations. **C** is incorrect because it suggests that the CMOS communicates with computer components, based on the information stored in the BIOS. As explained, this is the opposite of the actual relationship between the BIOS and CMOS. It is the *BIOS* that communicates with components, based on information stored in the *CMOS*. **D** is incorrect because it suggests that the BIOS is a newer version of the CMOS. The functions of the BIOS and CMOS are different, and both are found in all computers, old and new.

Adding and Removing Field-Replaceable Modules

6. ☑ **C.** When installing a hard drive, align the cable's red stripe with pin 1 and attach the hard drive to the end of the cable. The red stripe on any ribbon cable exists solely to identify the pin 1 connection. Use it to ensure that the cable is properly oriented. Because you are installing a single drive, it must be attached to the connector at the end of the ribbon cable.

☒ **A,** install the hard drive in the bay closest to the motherboard and align the cable's red stripe with pin 1, is incorrect. The drive's bay is simply a compartment in the chassis used to hold the hard drive in place. If there is more than one drive bay, the hard drive can be attached to either one. **B,** use the manufacturer's label to identify the top side of the drive, and attach the drive to the ribbon connector closest to the motherboard, is also incorrect. It is good practice to use the label to identify the top of the drive, but the drive itself must be attached to the cable connector that is furthest from, not closest to, the motherboard. **D** is incorrect because is suggests using the label to identify pin 1 and installing the drive in the bay furthest from the motherboard. Although the manufacturer's label on the top of the drive can sometimes be used to indicate pin 1, this is rarely the case. Furthermore, as discussed, the drive's installation in one bay or another is not a factor in the drive's operation.

7. ☑ **A.** When installing a power supply, ensure that the P8 and P9 connectors are attached to the motherboard with the black wires together. Although each (P8 or P9) connector can fit only one way onto the motherboard, it is physically possible to connect them in the wrong ports. That is, the P8 connector will fit in the P9 port, and vice versa. When this is the case, the computer will not work. To ensure that the connectors are in the proper ports, place them beside each other so that the black wires of the P8 connector are beside the black wires of the P9 connector.

   ☒ **B,** ensure that the P8 and P9 connectors are attached to each other with the black wires at opposite ends, and **D,** ensure that the P8 and P9 connectors are properly attached to the hard drive, are both incorrect. The P8 and P9 connectors are attached to the motherboard, not to each other or to the hard drive. **C** is incorrect because it states that you should ensure that the red stripe is aligned with pin 1 on the motherboard. This procedure applies to the installation of hard, floppy, and CD-ROM drives, not power supplies.

8. ☑ **D.** When the user raises the lever on the side of the processor's socket, the processor should do nothing. If the processor's socket has a lever, it must be a ZIF socket. The function of the lever is to grip and release the processor's pins. When the lever is raised, the grip on the pins will be released, but the processor itself should not move.

   ☒ **A** is incorrect because it states that the processor will slowly rise out of the socket, in correspondence with the raising of the lever. As discussed, the lever's position, not the insertion of the processor in the socket, determines the grip on the processor's pins. **B,** the processor will "pop" upward, out of the socket, is incorrect because this refers to the action of a memory DIMM when the retaining tabs are released. **C,** the processor will fall to a 45-degree angle with the motherboard, is incorrect because this refers to the action of a memory SIMM when the retaining tabs are released.

9. ☑ **B.** The *D* in DIMM refers to *dual*–the number of connector rows on the DIMM. That is, a dual inline memory module has two rows of connectors on the bottom.

   ☒ **A** is incorrect because it suggests that the DIMM uses a "direct" communication type to communicate with the processor. The *D* stands for *dual,* and in fact, there is no communication type known as *direct.* **C** is incorrect because it states that the *D* in DIMM refers to *double*–the number of sides on the DIMM that contain memory chips. DIMMs can have memory chips on both sides or on only one side. **D** is incorrect because it suggests that DIMMs are so named because they have DIP chips embedded on them. Although it's true that DIP chips are embedded on the DIMM, the *D* stands for *dual,* not DIP.

10. ☑ **C.** Active displays have better resolution than passive displays. Most portables use LCD displays, which can be either passive or active matrix. Active matrix displays are newer and incorporate a technology that allows them to provide more colors, better resolution, and a smoother display of moving objects.

☒ **A** is incorrect because it states that most passive matrix displays use TFT technology. However, TFT technology is used in active matrix, not passive matrix displays. **B**, they use CRT technology, is incorrect. Although portables can be connected to CRT monitors, the portable's display panel, which is integrated with the portable itself, is an LCD display. **D** is incorrect because it states that older display panels use CRT technology and newer display panels use LCD technology. In fact, most display panels use LCD technology, and none of them uses CRT technology.

IRQs, DMAs, and I/O Addresses

11. ☑ **A.** I/O addresses are used by the processor to identify and communicate with components. When the computer is started, information about each device is placed in a specified range in RAM memory. When the processor needs to communicate with a device, it uses that device's I/O address in RAM to retrieve instructions on how to communicate with it.

☒ **B** and **C** are incorrect because they both suggest that I/O addresses are used by components to either identify themselves during communication or to interrupt the processor. These are, in fact, functions of IRQs, not I/O addresses. **D**, they are used by components for direct access to the information in RAM, is incorrect because this is the function of DMA channels.

12. ☑ **B.** The term *nonmaskable* refers to an IRQ that cannot be ignored by the processor. Most IRQs can be temporarily ignored, but some are used to halt the processor during certain error conditions, to prevent loss or corruption of data. Nonmaskable IRQs are typically used to warn the processor of a parity (data transfer) error. The processor must stop and deal with the error before it can continue with other processes.

☒ **A**, maskable, is incorrect because this term is used to refer to IRQs that can be ignored (masked) by the processor. IRQs 0–15 are all maskable. **C**, cascaded, is incorrect because this term refers to the secondary IRQ controller's use of IRQ 2 to provide access to IRQs 8–15. **D**, noncascaded is incorrect because this is not a valid term.

13. ☑ **D.** IRQs 10 and IRQ 12 are available. One key to answering this question is the fact that the computer's only noncritical peripheral is a serial mouse. Because the computer uses a serial mouse, IRQ 12 (which is typically reserved for a PS/2 mouse) is not in use, so it is available. Furthermore, IRQ 10 is typically available for assignment to noncritical peripherals. Since there are no other noncritical peripherals in the system, IRQ 10 is available for use.

☒ **A**, IRQs 3 and 4, is incorrect because the serial mouse must use the resources of the COM port to which it is attached. If the serial mouse is attached to COM1 or COM3, it will use IRQ 4. If it is attached to COM2 or COM4, it will use IRQ 3. This means that IRQ 3 *and* IRQ 4 cannot both be available. **B**, IRQs 4 and 15, is incorrect because this system uses its secondary hard drive controller. When in use, this controller is assigned IRQ 15. **C**, IRQs 7 and 13, is incorrect because IRQ 7 is assigned to the primary parallel port (LPT1) and IRQ 13 is assigned to the math coprocessor.

14. ☑ **B.** IRQ 13 is in use. This computer is a Pentium, which means it has a math coprocessor. The math coprocessor uses IRQ 13.

☒ **A**, IRQs 12 and 13 are both in use, and **D**, IRQs 12 and 15 are both in use, are incorrect. IRQ 13 is, in fact, in use by the math coprocessor. However, recall that this computer uses a serial mouse. Because there is no PS/2 mouse in this system, IRQ 12 is available. In addition, because the computer uses only one hard drive controller, IRQ 15 is available. (As an aside, although IRQs 12 and 15 might be assigned to peripheral devices, you cannot determine that from the information given in the question.) **C**, IRQs 12, 13, and 15 are all available, is incorrect because IRQ 13 is being used by the math coprocessor.

15. ☑ **D.** The sound card problem is unrelated to IRQ assignment. From the information given, you know that the sound card uses IRQ 13 and that it is not working correctly. You can only deduce that an IRQ conflict is responsible for the problem if you can verify that another device is also trying to use IRQ 13. Your knowledge of IRQ addresses should have led you to the following conclusions.

☒ **B** is incorrect because it states that there is an IRQ conflict between the math coprocessor and the sound card. However, because this is an 80386 computer, you check to see whether a math coprocessor is installed in the 80387 socket provided. Therefore, IRQ 13 is available for assignment to another device. **C**, which states that you should unplug the modem, is incorrect. The modem is external, so it must use a COM port. COM ports use either IRQ 3 or 4, so the modem cannot be in conflict with the sound card for IRQ 13. Unplugging the modem will have no effect on the sound card. **A**, you should change the IRQ assignment of the sound card to IRQ 5, is also incorrect. As demonstrated by **B**, the sound card IRQ address is not in conflict with that of another device. Reassigning the sound card to another IRQ will not solve the problem. Furthermore, this computer uses two LPT ports. This means that IRQ 5, which is assigned to LPT2, is unavailable for the sound card to use.

Peripheral Ports, Cabling and Connectors

16. ☑ **D.** You are most likely to mention that the modem uses a coaxial cable, because all the other statements are incorrect. Cable modems use the same cable that your television does, and they plug into the same type of wall outlet.

☒ **A, B,** and **C** are all incorrect because these are not properties of a coaxial cable. Coaxial cables have the same type of connector on both ends, either of which can be attached to the modem or wall outlet. The connector itself is round and contains only one wire. The connector is twisted into place, so there is no wrong orientation of the connector in the port. Finally, the locking mechanism on a coaxial cable is an outer ring that is twisted into place, not a tab on one side (as in an RJ connector).

17. ☑ **A.** Male connectors have pins; female connectors have holes. As inelegant as this might seem, the basic differences between men and women are used to differentiate male from female connections.

☒ **B, C,** and **D,** which make reference to the connector's shape, location of attachment, and number of wires, are all incorrect. Connector shapes, attachment locales, and number of wires are all unrelated to the characteristic of having either pins or holes.

18. ☑ **B.** The RJ connector can be identified by its rectangular shape, retaining tab, and flat copper connections. RJ connectors are often used in network and analog modem connections.

☒ **A,** DB, is incorrect because this type of connector is trapezoidal and has no copper connectors or retaining tab. **C,** BNC, and **D,** Mini-DIN, are incorrect because they are both round.

19. ☑ **D.** Mice do not use BNC connectors. BNC connectors are used by coaxial cables and are designed for network or modem connections.

☒ **A,** DB, is incorrect because this type of connector is used by serial mice. **B,** Mini-DIN, and **C,** PS/2, are incorrect because PS/2 mice use a Mini-DIN connector, which is often referred to as a PS/2 connector.

20. ☑ **A.** Parallel communications are faster than serial communications. This is because parallel communications support the transfer of multiple bits at a time, whereas serial communications are marked by the transfer of one bit at a time. Most printers are parallel due to the large amounts of data that they are sent by the computer.

☒ **B** is incorrect because it states that serial communications result in fewer errors than parallel communications. Parallel and serial communications differ in their methods of data transfer, not in their reliability or error rates. **C** is incorrect because it states that parallel communications are compatible with more computer types than serial communications. All computers use both serial and parallel communications. **D,** serial communications devices are easier to configure than parallel communications devices, is also incorrect. These communications types refer to *data* transfer methods, not different device types or configurations. In fact, some devices, such as printers and scanners, are available in either parallel or serial versions.

LAB ANSWER

When you turned on the computer, the processor initiated the BIOS. The BIOS retrieved settings about the computer's components from the CMOS, where they were stored when the power was turned off last. The BIOS used these settings to perform a POST, whereby it checked for the presence and function of critical system components. The BIOS then searched the hard drive for an operating system and handed it control of the computer. Throughout this entire operation, the BIOS was responsible for intercepting and translating communications between the processor and the other devices, and the processor used the video adapter's I/O address to send it data about what to display on the monitor.

When you opened the word processor, your mouse used serial communication to send an IRQ signal to gain the attention of the processor (IRQ 3 or 4 if it was a serial mouse and IRQ 12 if it was a PS/2 mouse). The processor used the I/O address of the display adapter to display the movement of the mouse across the screen and sent a message to the hard drive to retrieve the selected application.

When the hard drive found the appropriate information, it gave the data to the processor using either IRQ 14 or 15, depending on whether it was a primary or secondary hard drive. Many of the files necessary to run the application were stored in RAM for faster access by the processor. The cache controller, judging by the application, was able to predict which information the processor was likely to need and placed that information into the cache memory, from which the processor could retrieve it even more quickly.

When you typed the document, the keyboard used IRQ 1 to send the data to the processor. When you saved the document, the processor used the hard drive's I/O address to instruct it to store the file. When you printed the document, the processor sent the request to the printer, most likely using parallel communication.

2

Installation, Configuration, and System Optimization

I n the previous chapter, you were introduced to common components and installation and configuration procedures. This chapter focuses on devices and configurations that are more specialized and slightly more complex.

First, the chapter discusses alternative hardware configurations, including how to use more than one hard drive in the system and how to set up a SCSI system. You will also learn about peripheral devices that require more complex installation and configuration procedures, including portable-specific components. Finally, you will learn about configurations that you can perform to optimize the performance of your desktop or portable system and keep it running smoothly.

CERTIFICATION OBJECTIVE 2.01

Installing and Configuring IDE Devices

Most computers use Integrated Drive Electronics (IDE) or AT Attachment (ATA) hard and CD-ROM drive systems. The relationship between IDE and ATA is that IDE drives are built using the ATA body of standards. The terms are therefore used interchangeably. The IDE family includes IDE and Enhanced IDE (EIDE) drives. Other drives based on the ATA standards include ATAPI (typically associated with CD-ROM drives), Fast-ATA, and Ultra-ATA. Because IDE drives are built on ATA technology, the term *IDE* is often used to refer to any non-SCSI drive type (SCSI systems are discussed later in the chapter).

Because IDE drives are standardized, they can usually be recognized by the computer's BIOS. In the simplest cases, all that is needed to make a hard drive or a CD-ROM drive functional is to physically install it in the computer. However, some configurations are more complex. The following sections describe alternative drive installations, including how to configure and install multiple drives in a single system.

Master/Slave Configurations

The hard drive or CD-ROM drive controller's function is to receive commands to the drive and control the action of the drive itself. The technology incorporated in

IDE and ATA devices allows one controller to take over the function of more than one drive. This means that you can install up to two drives on a single ribbon cable. This setup is called a *master/slave configuration* because one drive's controller directs the activities of both drives. It is important to note here that most computer systems can support a mixture of IDE and ATA drives.

To create a master/slave configuration, follow the steps in Exercise 2-1.

EXERCISE 2-1

Installing Master and Slave Hard Drives

1. Determine which drive will be the master (see the "From the Classroom" sidebar for more information).

2. Locate the master/slave jumpers, which can be found on the bottom of the drive or, more commonly, on the end by the power and ribbon cable connectors. In Figure 2-1, the jumpers are located to the left of the power connector and the jumper settings are indicated by the "Standard Settings" information on the label.

FIGURE 2-1

The master/slave jumper set on a typical hard drive.

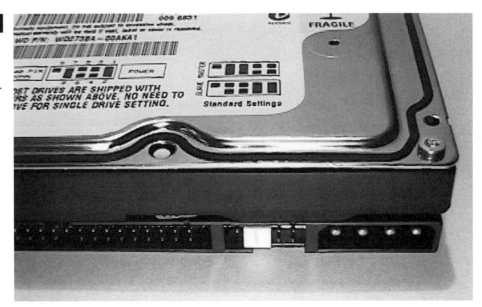

3. Use the drive label information to determine which jumper settings to use for a master or a slave configuration.

4. Set this drive as a master using the jumper(s).

5. Using the procedure explained in Chapter 1, Exercise 1-3, physically install this drive on the end of the ribbon cable and secure it to an available drive bay.

6. Using the proper jumper setting, configure the second drive as a slave.

7. Install the second drive in the middle of the ribbon cable. Your hard drive setup should look similar to the one shown in Figure 2-2. Note the position of the hard drives on the ribbon cable.

FIGURE 2-2

The finished product of a master/slave configuration.

It is important to note that, in most cases, a slave drive will work only if a master drive is present. That is, masters can function without slaves, but slaves cannot function without masters.

The master drive must be set to the master jumper setting and be installed on the end of the ribbon cable. The slave drive must be set to the slave jumper setting and be installed in the middle of the ribbon cable.

Most newer computers will detect the presence of a master/slave configuration and name the drives appropriately: Typically, the master will be drive C:, and the slave will be drive D:. However, some older computers require you to perform a drive detection. In this case, when you start the computer, enter the CMOS settings program, as discussed in Chapter 1. Select the Auto-Detect or Detect Hard Drive option (these options might have slightly different names on different computers). This choice forces the BIOS to search all drive controller connections for the presence and configuration of hard or CD-ROM drives.

Devices Per Channel

Most newer computers have two hard drive controllers. That is, the motherboard has connectors for two ribbon cables (see Figure 2-3). These controllers are termed *primary* and *secondary*. If there is only one drive present, it must be attached to the primary controller. An additional drive can be added as either a primary slave or a secondary master. It is important to note that although they are often referred to as *hard drive controllers*, these devices are not limited to controlling hard drives; they are also used to control CD-ROM drives.

If a system contains a single drive, it must be installed as a primary master. Follow the manufacturer's instructions for placement of jumpers. Typically, a secondary drive cannot work without a primary drive, and a slave drive will not work without a master.

FROM THE CLASSROOM

Choosing a Master

How do you determine which drive should be the master and which should be the slave? In many cases, it doesn't matter which is which. That is, there is no real performance difference between master and slave drives. However, as with most computer configurations, there are some exceptions.

Some operating systems require that the hard drive containing the OS itself be configured as a master. This is important to note only if you are installing drives that already contain data. If you are installing new hard drives, you don't have to worry about this; simply load the OS on the master drive after the drives are installed.

When using a mixture of old and new hard drives within the same system, set the newer drive as the master and the older drive as the slave. This setting is a good idea because newer drives can recognize and communicate with older drives, but the reverse isn't true. An older drive's controller will typically be unable to control the newer drive.

When using a hard drive and CD-ROM drive together in a master/slave configuration, always set the hard drive as the master and the CD-ROM as the slave. We use this setting because the CD-ROM's controller is unable to take control of the hard drive. Additionally, some (but not most) CD-ROM drives are designed to work as slaves, even when there is *no* master present, and they simply cannot be configured as master drives.

—*Amy Thomson, A+ Certified Technician, MOUS Master*

To add a drive to the secondary controller, simply connect the drive to a ribbon cable and attach the ribbon cable to the secondary controller port on the motherboard, ensuring that the red stripe is aligned with pin 1. There is usually no noticeable performance advantage to configuring a second drive as a secondary master rather than as a primary slave. (See the "From the Classroom" sidebar for a discussion on choosing the master or slave designation.)

FIGURE 2-3

The primary and secondary controller ports on the system board.

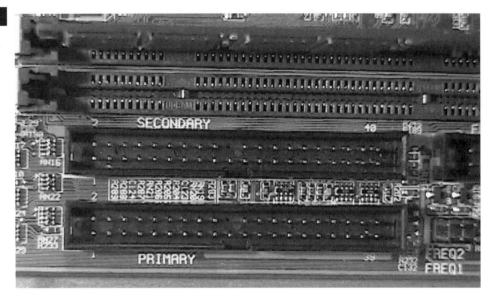

As before, the primary master receives the first available drive letter, typically C:. The remaining drives are lettered according to this order of priority: primary slave, secondary master, primary master.

on the **job**

When you add or remove a drive to or from a multidrive system, the drives are automatically relettered so that no letters are skipped. For example, suppose a system includes drives C:, D:, and E:. If drive D: is removed, the E: drive will be relabeled D: the next time the computer is started.

CERTIFICATION OBJECTIVE 2.02

Installing and Configuring SCSI Devices

Another technology standard is *Small Computer Systems Interface (SCSI)*, developed by the American National Standards Institute (ANSI). The SCSI standard applies to external devices such as printers, modems, scanners, and most other types of peripherals, and it supports internal devices such as hard and floppy drives.

SCSI systems differ from non-SCSI systems in several ways. To begin with, SCSI devices are all attached to and controlled by a SCSI controller. That is, all SCSI devices in the system are attached to the computer through the controller. The controller is actually an internal card that is installed on the motherboard. Complete the steps in Exercise 2-2 to install a SCSI controller card.

EXERCISE 2-2

Installing a SCSI Controller Card

1. Turn the computer off, remove the cover, and carry out proper ESD procedures as discussed in Chapter 4, Exercise 4-2.

2. Position the controller card upright over the appropriate expansion slot.

3. Place your thumbs along the top edge of the card and push straight down. If necessary, rock the card along its length (never side to side).

4. Secure the card to the chassis using the existing screw holes.

SCSI systems allow you to attach more devices to the computer than regular IDE systems do. IDE systems are limited to 4 drives, and the number of other devices you can attach is physically limited by the number of available expansions slots and external ports in the computer. By installing a SCSI system, you can attach 7, 15, or 31 additional devices in the computer, depending on the type of SCSI system you are using.

SCSI systems are typically much faster than non-SCSI (IDE) systems. However, SCSI systems have the disadvantage of being more expensive than IDE systems and more difficult to configure. In most cases, SCSI systems are used when speed or the ability to support a large number of devices is a priority. When cost and ease of use are factors, IDE systems are generally preferred. Currently, IDE systems are more prevalent than SCSI systems.

In all SCSI systems, the controller (sometimes called the SCSI host adapter) must be installed in the computer and assigned an IRQ and I/O address, just like any other expansion card. Other devices are attached to the controller in a *daisy-chain configuration*, in which each device attaches to the next in a long chain. Each SCSI device has two ports; one port is used to receive the cable from the device before it in the chain, and one port is used to attach to the next device in the chain. Each SCSI device is allocated a special SCSI ID rather than its own IRQ and I/O address. All communication between the computer and a SCSI device go through and are managed by the SCSI controller.

Types of SCSI Systems

Like many other computer standards, SCSI systems have evolved and improved over time. Newer SCSI standards are backward-compatible with older standards, so older devices can typically be installed in newer systems. SCSI standards and their characteristics are described in the subsections that follow. Table 2-1 provides a quick reference to SCSI types and characteristics.

TABLE 2-1   SCSI Types and Their Characteristics

Type	Bus Width	Max Throughput	Data Transfer
SCSI-1	8-bit	5MBps	SE
SCSI-2	8-bit	5MBps	SE or HVD
Fast SCSI-2	8-bit	10MBps	SE or HVD
Wide SCSI-2	16-bit	10MBps	SE or HVD
Fast Wide SCSI-2	16-bit	20MBps	SE or HVD
Double Wide SCSI-2	32-bit	40MBps	SE or HVD
Ultra SCSI-3 (Fast-20)	8-bit	20MBps	SE or HVD
Wide Ultra SCSI-3	16-bit	40MBps	SE or HVD
Ultra-2 SCSI (Fast-40)	8-bit	40MBps	HVD or LVD
Wide Ultra-2 SCSI	16-bit	80MBps	HVD or LVD
Ultra-3 (Fast-80 or Ultra 160)	16-bit	160MBps	LVD

SCSI-1

The first SCSI standard, released in 1986, was simply named *SCSI*. It became known as *SCSI-1* only when the SCSI-2 standard was released. The SCSI-1 system has an 8-bit bus, meaning it can support up to eight devices (including the controller), and it supports speeds up to 5MBps. Unfortunately, SCSI-1 did not include standardized device commands, so many early SCSI devices were not compatible with each other.

The maximum cable length in a SCSI-1 system is 6 meters. This length refers to the entire length of the SCSI chain, not the distance between each device. The use of longer cables in the system can lead to device malfunctions due to signal interference.

SCSI-2

The *SCSI-2* standard, released in 1994, includes a standardized device command set and support for more devices. It also uses more sophisticated device termination (discussed later in the chapter) and supports *command queuing*, which is the ability to send more than one command to a single device at once.

The SCSI-2 standard also introduced the implementation of *differential* (specifically, *high-voltage differential*, or *HVD*) *technology*. This term refers to the method of data transfer. Regular SCSI data transfer, called *single-ended (SE) transfer*, uses one wire to transmit each data signal. Differential SCSI sends each data signal over a pair of wires, in a manner that resists interference. Because differential SCSI is more resistant to interference, it can support much greater cable lengths than SE systems. SCSI-2 systems can use either regular or differential devices, but the two cannot exist on the same system.

The SCSI-2 standard includes several variants, so it can be the subject of some confusion. Simply put, there are five variants: SCSI-2, Fast SCSI-2, Wide SCSI-2, Fast Wide SCSI-2, and Double Wide SCSI-2. The main differences between these types are their bus widths and transmission speeds.

SCSI-2, like SCSI-1, supports an 8-bit bus and transmission speeds up to 5MBps and can support cable lengths up to 6 meters. *Fast SCSI-2* also has an 8-bit bus, but it supports double the speed (up to 10MBps) and has a maximum cable length of 3 meters for SE and 25 meters for HVD. *Wide SCSI-2* supports the traditional 5MBps, but because it has double the bus width (16 bits), its overall data transmission rate is 10MBps. *Fast Wide SCSI-2* combines the Fast and Wide technologies to yield a 16-bit bus and total transfer speed of 20MBps. Both Wide and Fast Wide SCSI-2 systems can support up to 16 devices, including the controller, and have a maximum cable length of 3 meters for SE and 25 meters for HVD.

The final variant, *Double Wide SCSI-2*, is essentially two Fast Wide systems in one. It supports a 32-bit bus and speeds up to 40MBps. However, this variant is rarely used and has been excluded from subsequent SCSI standards.

SCSI-3

The status of *SCSI-3* is a bit of a gray area. Although it is not yet finalized as a standard, many of its command sets and protocols have already been defined and are currently being implemented in available SCSI components. Therefore, SCSI-3 is not really a single cohesive standard. When people use the term *SCSI-3* or *SCSI-3 system*, they are referring to a system that incorporates the specifications that will be included in the final SCSI-3 standard.

A number of variants use the existing SCSI-3 specifications. *Ultra SCSI*, also called *Fast-20*, is an 8-bit system that can support speeds up to 20MBps. The Ultra SCSI system's bus width can be doubled to 16 bits (Wide Ultra SCSI), resulting in a total throughput of 40MBps. Like SCSI-2, Ultra SCSI can use either SE or HVD technology. Ultra SCSI supports a maximum cable length of 3 meters if four or fewer devices are attached and 1.5 meters if more than four devices are attached.

Ultra-2 SCSI, also called *Fast-40*, provides a 40MBps data throughput on an 8-bit system and 80MBps on a 16-bit system (Wide Ultra-2 SCSI). Ultra-2 marks the first use of the *low-voltage differential (LVD)* specification and the removal of support for the SE specification. Components that use LVD technology require less power to operate and can operate at higher speeds. LVD also allows Ultra-2 SCSI systems to support cable lengths up to 12 meters.

Ultra-3 SCSI, also referred to as *Fast-80* or *Ultra160*, is the latest implementation of the SCSI-3 specifications. It is available only as a 16-bit system and supports a data throughput of 160MBps. Ultra-3 SCSI systems support LVD technology only and are the first to support up to 32 devices. Its maximum cable length is 12 meters.

Address/Termination Conflicts

Each device in a SCSI system must be correctly configured so that it can communicate with the controller but will not interfere with other SCSI devices in the system. If two devices share an ID, an address conflict will occur. The controller will not be able to distinguish the conflicting devices, and it is likely that *neither* device will work. Equally important is the proper termination of the SCSI system. Improper termination can result in the total or intermittent failure of *all* devices in the SCSI chain.

The following subsections describe the proper procedures for addressing and terminating SCSI devices so that conflicts do not occur.

Addressing SCSI Devices

Although computers can support more than one SCSI system, no two devices in a *single* SCSI chain can have the same SCSI ID address. Some SCSI devices are hard-wired to use one of two or three IDs only; others might be designed to use any available ID. If the device supports Plug and Play, the system will automatically assign it an available ID address. Other devices require manual address configuration. On some devices, this configuration is accomplished via jumpers on the device itself. Other devices can be assigned an ID address electronically, using the device's ROM chip.

Some SCSI devices that require address assignment through jumpers will indicate, by label, which setting to use. However, in some cases, you will need to use the jumpers to emulate the binary equivalent of the device's ID. You must therefore be familiar with binary addressing. In short, binary uses a series of 0s and 1s to indicate the absence or presence of a value, respectively. These values double in number, starting with 1, at the rightmost digit. That is, the rightmost digit of a binary number is used to indicate the presence of a value of 1. The next digit to that is used to indicate a value of 2, the next to indicate 4, and so on.

Using this concept, the binary digit 101 indicates that the "4" value is present, the "2" value is absent and the "1" value is present. This binary's value is therefore 5 (4+1). The binary digit 1110 indicates 8 + 4 + 2. This equals 14.

Proper addressing can prove challenging, so it is best to work out an addressing "plan of action" before implementing addresses. For example, suppose a SCSI system will include a printer that *must* use ID 2, a scanner that can use either ID 2 or 4, and a modem that can use ID 4 or 5. Without knowing the address requirement of the printer, the scanner could be configured to use ID 2 and the modem to use ID 4. When it comes time to install the printer, you'll have to reconfigure the ID addresses of all other components.

The priority of ID addresses is also important. In 8-bit SCSI systems, addresses range from 0 to 7. Higher ID addresses indicate a higher priority. Because the SCSI controller is such an important part of the system, it is usually assigned ID 7.

For 16-bit and 32-bit systems, the priority of ID addresses is a bit more complex. In short, addresses increase in priority within each octet, and each successive octet has a lower overall priority than the one before it (see Figure 2-4). That is, IDs 8–15 have a lower priority than 0–7. In a 16-bit system, the order of priority, from lowest to highest, is 8, 9, 10 … 15, 0, 1, 2 … 7. Using the same principles for a 32-bit system, 7 has the highest priority, and 24 has the lowest.

exam
ⓦatch

Although you can expect some questions about SCSI IDs on the A+ exam, you don't have to memorize the priority of each address. Instead, make sure that you understand the concept behind the priority/address relationship, as explained. When you understand the reasons behind the numbering scheme, you will be able to figure out the priority of any SCSI ID address.

on the
ⓙob

This section talks a lot about the priorities given to various SCSI IDs. If two devices try to send data at the same time, the device with the highest-priority ID will be allowed to transmit, and the other device will be made to wait. Incidentally, "at the same time" means within 0.24 microseconds!

SCSI System Termination

Recall that devices in a SCSI system are chained together in a "one after the other" fashion. Signals to a device at the end of the chain must pass through all the devices in between. Because of this unique setup, special terminators, or *terminating resistors*, must be present to ensure signals at the end of the chain are absorbed rather than bounced back along the chain. In some cases, the resistor is shaped to fit into the unused second port on the last SCSI device in the chain. In other cases, the SCSI device will include an on-board terminator that is made active by using the appropriate jumper setting.

FIGURE 2-4

CSI ID priorities increase within each octet, but each successive octet has a lower priority than the preceding one.

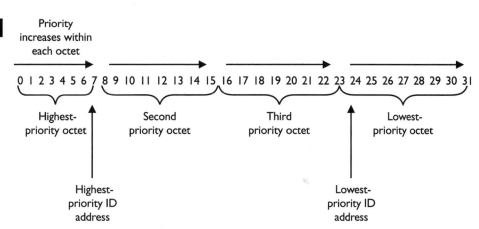

Essentially, any SCSI device that is not connected to two other devices must be at one end of the chain. If the SCSI chain is external, the last external device and the controller must be terminated. If the SCSI chain is internal only, the last internal device and the controller must be terminated. Finally, if the SCSI chain is a mixture of both internal and external devices, the last external and last internal devices on the chain are terminated.

Cabling

SCSI systems employ a variety of cable types, depending on the SCSI type, device type, and whether the device is internal or external. Furthermore, each cable type might have a different connector.

8-Bit Systems

All 8-bit SCSI systems use 50-pin cables, called *A-cables*. Internal A-cables are 50-pin ribbon cables, which resemble IDE hard drive ribbon cables (Figure 2-5). External A-cables have either 50-pin Centronics connectors (for 5MBps systems) or 50-pin high-density connectors (for greater-than-10MBps systems). Figure 2-6 shows two different A-cable connectors.

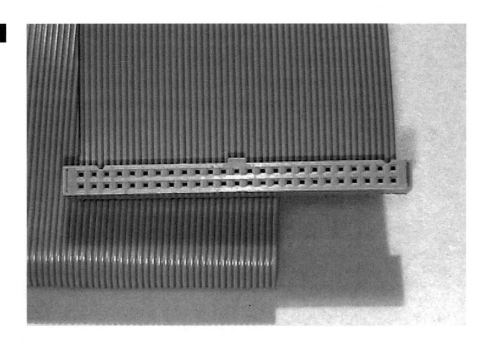

FIGURE 2-5

An internal A-cable connector.

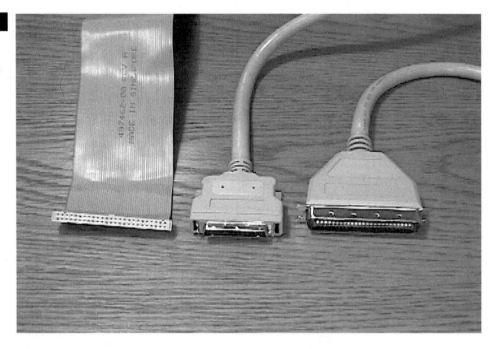

FIGURE 2-6

Internal and external A-cable connectors.

16-Bit Systems

All 16-bit systems use 68-pin cables, also known as *P-cables*. Before the introduction of the P-cable, 16-bit systems used an A-cable/B-cable combination. Internal P-cables are ribbon cables with 68-pin connections, and external P-cables have a 68-pin high-density connector.

32-Bit Systems

Although 32-bit systems are no longer supported by new SCSI specifications, you might be required to work on an older one. All 32-bit systems use a 68-pin P-cable and a 68-pin Q-cable or one 110-pin L-cable.

exam
ⓌatСh

An even larger variety of SCSI cable and connector types are available than are discussed here. The list of possible combinations is beyond the scope of this book. The information that you will be expected to know for the A+ exam is the following: 8-bit systems use 50-pin cables, 16-bit systems use 68-pin cables, and 32-bit systems use 110-pin cables. Internal cables (for any pin size) have the same type of connector as hard drive ribbon cables. External cables (for any pin size) are typically Centronics connectors in older systems and high-density connectors in newer systems.

The information in the "Installing and Configuring SCSI Devices" section has been compiled into Exercise 2-3. These are basic steps that you must perform whenever you install an external SCSI device. Read the steps carefully when performing them, because some steps are performed differently or skipped altogether for some devices.

EXERCISE 2-3

Installing External SCSI Devices

1. **Attach the device to the chain.** If the new device will be the last in the chain, use its cable to attach it to the device that is currently last in the chain. If the device will be between two existing devices, disconnect them from each other, and attach them both to the new device.

2. **Terminate the SCSI chain.** Perform this step only if the new device is at the end of the chain. If the device has an on-board terminator, select the proper jumper setting to enable it. If not, place a terminator plug in the unused port on the device.

3. **Set the SCSI ID.** If this is a Plug and Play device, the ID will be assigned automatically. Simply restart the computer, and skip the remaining steps. If the ID must be configured manually and electronically, restart the computer and run the device's Setup program (this will also load the driver, so you can skip the next step). To set the ID manually using a jumper, consult the manufacturer's documentation and make the proper jumper setting.

4. **Load the device's driver.** Restart the computer and insert the floppy disk or CD that came with the device. Run the Setup or Install program.

This section contained a great deal of information. Before you continue in the chapter, test your knowledge of the SCSI concepts by answering the following Scenario & Solution questions.

SCENARIO & SOLUTION

I want to attach 10 SCSI devices to my computer. Which type of SCSI should I use?	You need to use a type that support at least a 16-bit bus. These include any of the Wide SCSI types or the Ultra-3 SCSI-3 type.
I added a SCSI scanner to the middle of my SCSI chain. How do I terminate it?	You don't. Only devices at each end of the chain need to be terminated.
Which ID should I assign to the SCSI controller?	The SCSI controller should be assigned the ID with the highest priority. This is ID 7, regardless of how many IDs your SCSI system supports.
I added another device to the end of the SCSI chain, and now none of the devices works. What's wrong?	The new device might have an ID conflict with another device. However, since *none* of the other devices is working, it is more likely that the new device is not terminated properly or causes the chain to exceed the maximum cable length.

CERTIFICATION OBJECTIVE 2.03

Installing and Configuring Peripheral Devices

The peripherals described in this section have more complex installation and configuration requirements than the peripherals described in Chapter 1. That is, their installation and configuration go beyond simple attachment to the computer or system board. Desktop system components are discussed first, followed by portable devices.

Desktop System Components

Some of the devices described here are considered "common" because they are found in all or a majority of computers. Other components, such as those described in the USB and IEEE 1394 sections, although newer technologies, are becoming commonplace because of their improved speed and performance. Before carrying out the installation procedures described here, turn the computer off, remove the cover, and carry out proper ESD procedures as described in Chapter 4, Exercise 4-2. The installation procedures for internal components assume that you have already removed the computer case.

Display Systems

Recall from Chapter 1 that monitors must be connected to internal video cards and that the video system relies on the proper function of both components. The video card's function is to create the images that will result in the picture you see. The monitor simply displays the images sent to it by the video card.

Monitors   Monitors are not serviceable. That means that they are replaced rather than repaired when they stop functioning correctly. One reason for this is that it would typically cost more in labor and parts to fix a monitor than it would to simply buy a new one. Another reason, and probably the most important one, is that monitors can hold enough electrical charge to cause serious personal injury, even when they have been left unplugged for an extended time. When a monitor needs replacing or upgrading, turn off the computer, unplug the monitor, and replace it with the new one.

on the
Job

Monitors can hold enough charge to seriously injure you, even if they have been left unplugged. Never wear an ESD strap when working with a monitor, and never open the monitor's case.

Video Cards   If the video card must be replaced or upgraded, follow the steps in Exercise 2-4. Video cards currently come in two styles: PCI and AGP. If the system board has an AGP slot, it is preferable to use an AGP video card becasue of advanced speed and performance.

EXERCISE 2-4

Installing a Video Card

1. Position the video adapter card over the appropriate expansion slot on the system board (see Figure 2-7).

2. Place your thumbs along the top edge of the card and push straight down. If necessary, rock the card along its length (never side to side) while you apply downward pressure.

3. When the card is fully seated in the expansion slot, secure it to the computer chassis using the existing screw holes.

4. Plug the monitor into the port at the back of the video adapter card and turn it on.

5. Turn the computer on. If the video card is Plug and Play (sometimes the video card will be too new to be recognized by the OS, i.e., installing a 2001 version of a video card into a computer with a Windows 95 OS), it should be automatically detected and assigned resources, and the proper device driver should be loaded. If this is the case, skip the next step.

6. If the computer is not Plug and Play, insert the floppy disk or CD that came with the video adapter and run the Setup or Install program to load the proper device drivers and assign the appropriate system resources.

7. In Windows, right-click on the desktop and select Properties then the Settings tab.

FIGURE 2-7

The installation of a video card.

Modems

If you are installing an external analog modem, simply plug it into a COM port at the back of the computer. If the modem is Plug and Play, it will be automatically detected and configured when you turn the computer on. If it is not Plug and Play, you will have to run its Setup or Install program to load its device driver. Remember, since the modem is attached to a COM port, it will use that port's system resources (IRQ and I/O).

The installation of an internal modem is a bit more complex. Install the modem as you would any other expansion card. (You may refer to Steps 1 through 3 in Exercise 2-4.) Again, if the modem is Plug and Play, the OS will automatically configure it. However, if the modem does not support Plug and Play, you will have to configure it manually.

First, you will need to assign the modem to an available COM port, even though it is not actually physically attached to that port. Depending on the modem itself, this can be done using a jumper setting or, more commonly, electronically using a Setup program or the computer's OS. Take care not to choose a COM port whose resources are already being used by another device. For example, if COM1 is already in use, you cannot assign COM3 to the modem (COM1 and 3 share an IRQ, and COM2 and 4 share an IRQ).

Once the internal or external analog modem is properly installed and has the proper resource and device driver, it must be connected to a phone jack. Attach one end of a regular phone cable to the modem, and attach the other end to a phone jack in the wall. Before your modem can communicate with another modem, it must be configured within the OS to establish a dial-up connection. The dial-up settings include the phone number to dial and other dialing properties, such as how to get an external line or disable call waiting. This procedure is described in detail in Chapter 11.

USB Peripherals and Hubs

USB devices were described in Chapter 1 as being Plug and Play and hot swappable. This means that a USB device can be attached to the computer while the computer is in operation. The device will be immediately and automatically recognized and configured. The USB system will even provide power to most devices, such as mice, keyboards, and network adapters. However, devices such as scanners and printers must have their own power supply. To install a USB device, simply attach its USB connector into an available USB port. The maximum cable length between any two devices in a USB system is 5 meters.

Most USB-compliant computers include two ports at the back of the computer, and some system boards will even include a second built-in USB connection; therefore, two additional USB ports can be installed using a USB Motherboard header cable. As well, USB adapter cards can be installed. This means it's possible to attach up to six USB devices. How, then, can USB claim to support up to 127 devices? To create more USB ports, you can use an external *USB hub*. An external USB hub contains one cable and several (up to seven) additional ports (see Figure 2-8) and serves to increase the number of ports available for other devices. A USB hub that has its own power supply is preferable to one that doesn't. To attach a USB hub, connect its cable to an available USB port at the back of the computer (called the *root hub*) and plug it in. No additional configuration is required.

FIGURE 2-8

A USB hub provides USB ports for additional devices.

To add more USB devices, simply attach them to the USB hub. If you require even more ports, add another tier by attaching another hub to the existing one (see Figure 2-9). However, you should avoid connecting more than five hubs together, because to do so could affect device performance.

IEEE-1394

Like USB, IEEE-1394 systems support Plug and Play and hot swapping. However, IEEE-1394 is more expensive than USB and much faster (up to 400Mbps). IEEE-1394 is typically used for devices that require fast transmission of large amounts of data, such as video cameras and digital versatile disk (DVD) players.

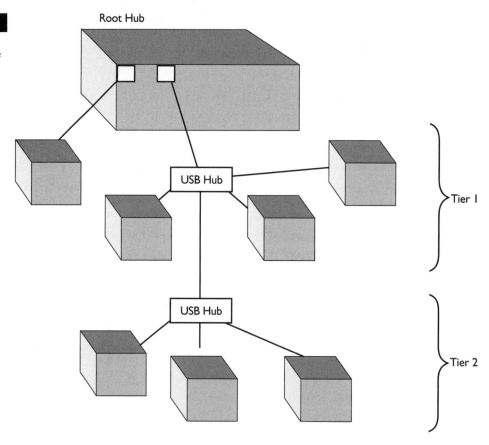

FIGURE 2-9

USB hubs can be added to make more ports available.

IEEE-1394 is often referred to as *Firewire*, the trademarked name given to Apple Computer's IEEE-1394 systems. IEEE-1394 is also referred to by other manufacturer-specific names, such as *i.link* or *Lynx*.

Firewire systems can support up to 63 external devices from a single port. Like SCSI, Firewire devices are attached in a daisy-chain (peer-to-peer) topology. No single cable in the system can exceed 4 meters. To attach an IEEE-1394 device, simply plug it into the port of the last device in the chain. The Firewire system will provide the device with power and will automatically detect and configure it.

To use Firewire, your computer must be running Windows 98 or higher, and you must have an IEEE-1394 controller. If the computer didn't come with a controller preinstalled, you can add one yourself. The controller is installed using the same procedures for installing other expansion cards. Firewire controllers are Plug and Play, so there is no need to load device drivers or configure system resources.

exam
ⓦatch

USB systems support most kinds of peripherals. IEEE-1394 (Firewire) systems support specialized high-data/high-speed devices such as video cameras and DVD players.

Portable System Components

Portable computers tend to be "what you see is what you get" (WYSIWYG) systems. In other words, because they are proprietary, they are very difficult to upgrade, and you are pretty much limited to using the components that came with the system. However, because of their compact size, many portable components, such as the keyboard and pointing device, can be difficult to use. For this reason, most portables allow you to temporarily attach easier-to-use desktop devices, for times when you are not in transit.

Keyboards

Most portable computers include a regular keyboard port in the back. To attach a regular keyboard, turn the portable off, plug in the desktop keyboard, and turn the portable back on. When the portable detects the external keyboard, it will disable the on-board keyboard.

Mouse

Most portables do not come with a mouse. Instead, they use pointing devices such as pointing sticks or touch pads. Because these devices are small and can be difficult to use, many portable computers allow you to attach a full-sized desktop mouse. Simply turn off the portable, attach the mouse to the port in the back, then restart the system.

Some portables, however, do come with a mouse. Typically, the mouse is permanently connected to the portable and can be stored in a compartment within the portable's chassis. Remove the mouse compartment's cover, and take the mouse out in order to use it.

Docking Stations

Most portable system owners use their computer while in transit but have a "base of operation," such as an office. This is typically where the user will use external devices such as keyboards, printers, monitors, and mice. The user must connect and disconnect these components every time he or she returns to or leaves the office with the portable. *Port replicators* can make this task less time-consuming by providing a permanent connection to these external devices. That is, the keyboard, monitor, and mouse (or whichever external devices the laptop is designed to access) are connected to the port replicator and left there. The user can then access them by making one connection to the port replicator rather than connecting to each device separately. Because port replicators are designed to simply replicate a portable computer's existing ports, the devices they allow you to access differ from system to system.

An *enhanced port replicator* provides the same function as a regular port replicator but also includes access to some devices that the portable would not otherwise be able to use. Typical enhanced port replicators provide access to an enhanced sound system and more PC card slots (discussed later in the chapter).

Portable system *docking stations* go even further than port replicators to allow access to *any* type of desktop component, such as printers, monitors, hard drives, and expansion slots. Simply attach the peripherals to the docking station and leave them there. When you want to access these devices, connect the portable computer to the docking station (see Figure 2-10).

Port replicators and docking stations are proprietary and can be used only with the portable for which they were designed. The method of connection and the devices supported will vary among manufacturers.

Answer the following Scenario & Solution questions to evaluate your understanding of portable system docking stations.

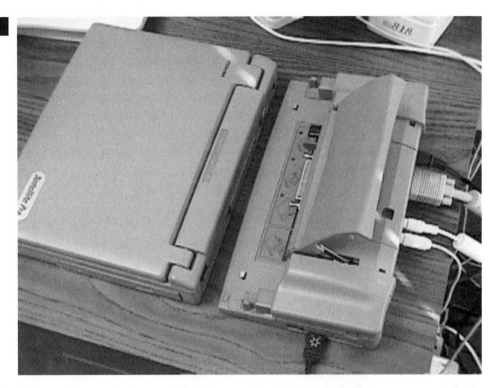

FIGURE 2-10

A portable computer and a docking station.

SCENARIO & SOLUTION

I plug my laptop into a CRT, printer, and keyboard every time I return to the office. Is there an easier way to do this?	Yes. Plug each of these devices into a port replicator and leave them there. To access the devices, simply plug your laptop into the port replicator.
When I'm in the office, I'd rather use my laptop than my desktop because it is faster. However, my desktop has access to better devices, like the printer, a scanner, a microphone, and speakers.	Your laptop might be able to use a full docking station. This device will allow your laptop to access most devices that a desktop can access.
I want to access a USB scanner with my laptop. My docking station doesn't have a USB port, but my colleague's does. How do I use my colleague's docking station?	You can't. Docking stations are designed to work with specific laptops only. You are limited to using the docking station the manufacturer has designed for your system, and you cannot access the USB scanner.

Network Interface Cards

Many computers have network interface cards (NICs), which allow them to communicate with other computers in a network (discussed in detail in Chapter 7). When they are not in transit (for example, when they are being used at the office), portable computers can also be used on a network.

To attach a portable computer to a network, you must first install a NIC. Portables allow for the easy addition and removal of expansion cards using special PC cards (the name "PC card" is actually a shortened version of "PCMCIA card," which is named after the association that introduced them). PC cards are about the size of a credit card but are slightly thicker. To use a PC card, simply insert it into the appropriate slot. To remove the card, press the ejector button. PC cards are hot swappable, so they can be added or removed while the portable is in operation.

Once the NIC has been inserted, you must attach it to a network cable. However, the connector on a network cable is much thicker than the NIC itself. For this reason, some NIC PC cards have a "flip-up" connector (see Figure 2-11). Open the connector, then attach the network cable to it.

FIGURE 2-11

A NIC PC card with an integrated network cable port.

FIGURE 2-12

A network cable
adapter (dongle)
is used to attach
the NIC PC card
to a network.

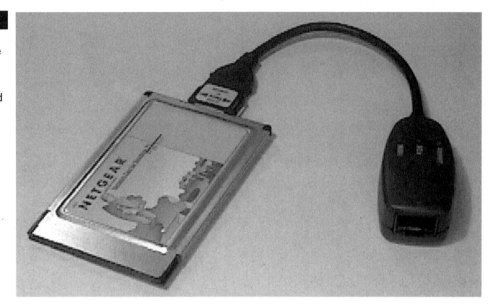

Integrated connectors are included on newer NICs only and are not available on most NIC PC cards. NICs without an integrated port require a network cable adapter, commonly called a *dongle*. One end of the dongle has a very small connector that is attached to the NIC. The other end contains a regular network (BNC or RJ-45) port, which is attached to the network cable (see Figure 2-12).

CERTIFICATION OBJECTIVE 2.04

Upgrading, Extending, and Optimizing System Performance

Most of this chapter has focused on the installation and performance of *specific* computer components. This section focuses on the performance of the computer system as a whole. In this section, you will learn how to upgrade your computer by replacing special subsystem components, such as the BIOS. You will also learn about procedures that can improve your computer's performance, such as replacing batteries, installing cache memory, and running hard drive utilities. Additionally, you will learn how to extend the abilities of your computer by installing specially designed components, such as portable system PC cards.

Desktop Computers

The procedures described here can be performed on almost all desktops. However, their relevance to portable systems is limited to the information in the "Hard Drives" and "BIOS" sections.

Memory

As you know, one function of RAM is to provide the processor with faster access to the information it needs. Within limits, the more memory a computer has, the faster it will run. One of the most common computer upgrades is the installation of more RAM.

Recall that most computers can use another type of RAM, called *cache memory*. Cache memory chips can be accessed even faster than regular RAM, so their presence can help speed up the computer. Within limits (up to 1MB), the more cache a computer has, the faster it will run. The type of cache that can be added to the computer is called Level 2 (L2) cache, and it can be installed in available slots on the motherboard.

exam
ⓦatch
Cache that can be installed on the system board is called L2, Level 2, **or** *external cache.* **Cache located within the processor itself is called** *L1, Level 1, internal,* **or** *on-board cache* **and cannot be added or upgraded (unless you replace the processor).**

Hard Drives

Throughout the operation of the computer, the hard drive will be accessed over and over again. Information will be read from, saved to, and moved from one place to another on the drive. Its operation is critical to the perceived efficiency of the computer. However, the more the hard drive is used, the less efficient it tends to become. The next two subsections describe common hard drive problems and how to resolve them.

Using Scandisk   The indexing of data on a disk is very important when that data is being saved and retrieved. Each file on the disk occupies one or more clusters, and no two files can exist on a single cluster. The first cluster on the disk contains an index of file names and locations. This index is called a *file allocation table (FAT)*. Whenever you access a file, the controller first looks it up in the FAT to determine its location on the disk, then retrieves it. Without a FAT, the hard or floppy drive would have to search every cluster until it found the requested file.

However, it is possible for the FAT to develop errors over time. *Cross-linked clusters* occur when the FAT records a single cluster as belonging to two different files. *Lost clusters* occur when a cluster containing data is not referenced in the FAT at all. Either of these errors can cause the file to be reported as missing. You can resolve these errors by running Microsoft's Scandisk utility. Scandisk searches the entire disk and compares the contents of each cluster to the information in the FAT. Scandisk then updates the FAT with the proper information about the disk's contents and file locations. Another function of Scandisk is to locate physical "bad spots" on the disk that cannot store data. Any existing data on these spots is moved, and the clusters are marked as "bad" so that no new data is stored there.

Although Scandisk can mark clusters as "bad" and retrieve information from them, it cannot repair bad clusters!

Defragmenting the Hard Drive   When files are saved to the hard or floppy drive, they are written to the first available cluster(s). Ideally, subsequent files are all saved in consecutive clusters on the disk. However, suppose a file resided on cluster 4, and another file resided on clusters 5–8. If you increased the size of the first file so that it no longer fit on one cluster, it would occupy clusters 4 *and 9*. Next, suppose you deleted the file on clusters 5–8 and replaced it with a larger file. That file would now reside on clusters 5–8 and perhaps 10 and 11. These files no longer reside on consecutive clusters and are said to be *fragmented.* Fragmentation can cause the hard or floppy drive to retrieve files more slowly, and can actually cause undue wear and tear on the drive's read/write heads.

To defragment a hard or floppy disk, you can run Microsoft's Disk Defragmenter in Windows 9x. This utility rewrites the data on the disk so that files are placed on contiguous clusters. Follow the steps in Exercise 2-5 to defragment a hard drive.

Defragmenting a Hard Drive

1. Exit all running applications, disable the screen saver, and using CTRL-ALT-DEL, one by one, turn off (end task) all running tasks, except System Tray and Windows Explorer.

2. From the Start menu, select Programs | Accessories | System Tools | Disk Defragmenter.

3. You will be presented with a Select Drive dialog box. Select the appropriate hard drive from the drop-down menu, then click OK.

4. The Defragmenter utility will begin. You can view the cluster-by-cluster details of the operation by clicking the Show Details button.

5. When the process is complete, you will be informed via a dialog box, the contents of which will vary, depending on the OS you are using. Choose to either exit the utility or defragment another disk.

Using your knowledge of hard drive utilities, answer the following Scenario & Solution questions.

SCENARIO & SOLUTION	
The computer reported a corruption error when I tried to access the floppy disk. What should I do?	Run Scandisk.
How can I speed up my hard drive?	Run Disk Defragmenter.
My computer reports that a particular file doesn't exist, but I know I saved it. What happened, and how can I find that file?	It is possible that the file exists but is not indexed properly. Run Scandisk. If the file exists, the FAT will be updated and you will be able to access it.

CPU

Some computers can support more than one type of processor. For example, the system board might be able to use a Pentium II *or* a Pentium III 400. Other computers support more than one speed for a particular type of processor. For example, the computer could support the use of either a Pentium II 400 *or* a Pentium II 450.

Always consult the manufacturer's documentation for your system board to determine which processors and speeds it supports. In most cases, you will need to configure the board for the new speed or model using a set of jumpers.

CMOS

A computer that consistently asks you for the date and time probably has a low CMOS battery. Because these batteries last only between 2 and 10 years, you are likely to have to replace a computer's battery before the computer itself becomes obsolete. To properly replace the battery, follow the steps in Exercise 2-6. Note that although this procedure cannot be followed in *all* computers, it applies to most newer computers.

EXERCISE 2-6

Replacing the CMOS Battery

1. Enter the computer's Setup program (described in Chapter 1, Firmware, CMOS) and write down all CMOS settings.

2. Turn off the computer and remove the cover, ensuring that you carry out proper ESD procedures.

3. Locate the CMOS battery on the motherboard.

4. Slide the battery out from under the retaining clip. The clip itself uses slight tension to hold the battery in place, so there is no need to remove the clip or bend it outward.

5. Note the characteristics on this battery that distinguish the bottom from the top. Install the new battery so that the bottom is in contact with the motherboard.

6. Restart the computer. Enter the system's Setup program and reset the CMOS settings you recorded in Step 1.

BIOS

Recall that the BIOS is used to translate communications between devices in the computer. The BIOS is able to do this because it contains the basic instruction set for those devices. However, if you install a device with which the computer seems unable to communicate, you might need to upgrade or replace the existing BIOS.

When to Upgrade the BIOS One way to inform the BIOS of a new device is to access the computer's CMOS settings and select the new device in the BIOS options. For example, if you upgrade the hard drive, you might need to inform the BIOS of its new type and capacity. CMOS settings are described in more detail in Chapter 5.

In some cases, however, the device might be so much newer than the BIOS that it cannot be selected from the CMOS settings. For example, if you are using an old BIOS, you can't inform it of a new 10GB hard drive, because the BIOS simply won't allow you to enter or select that size. When this is the case, the BIOS itself (not just its options) must be upgraded.

Methods for Upgrading the BIOS Flash BIOS chips can be electronically upgraded using a disk from the BIOS manufacturer. Turn the computer off, insert the manufacturer's floppy disk, and restart the computer. The disk contains a program that automatically "flashes" (updates) the BIOS so that it can recognize different hardware types or perform different functions than it could before. The BIOS retains the new information, so it has to be flashed only once.

Another way to upgrade the BIOS is to physically replace it with another. You will need to do this if the BIOS's manufacturer has stopped supporting that particular BIOS model or when it simply hasn't released a flash program with the options you need your BIOS to support. To physically replace the BIOS, locate the old BIOS chip and remove it with a chip puller. Orient the new BIOS in the same position that the old one used, then push it gently into the socket.

on the **ʘ o b**

The approach of 2000 was a busy time for replacing and upgrading BIOS chips. Many BIOSs were not designed to recognize any year later than 1999 and would have interpreted 2000 as 1900. This problem was called the Y2K bug. These BIOSs had to be flashed so that their basic instruction set included recognition of the year 2000 and later. In some computers, the BIOS was no longer supported by the manufacturer, so it couldn't be flashed. Instead, these chips had to be physically replaced.

Portable Computers

Portable computers contain several components that are not used by desktop computers. This section discusses some portable-specific devices and their functions.

Batteries

When they are not plugged into a wall outlet, portable computers get their power from special batteries. Most portable batteries are either nickel and metal hydride (NiMH) or lithium ion (LiIon). LiIon batteries use newer technology than NiMH ones and are smaller and lighter and produce more power. LiIon batteries are, however, more expensive.

Portable system batteries must be recharged from time to time, and this is the job of the AC adapter, which plugs into a regular electrical outlet. The adapter recharges the battery while the portable is operating. However, if you are not near a wall outlet when the battery's power fades, you need to replace the battery with a fully charged one.

Due to the necessity for changing the battery frequently, most portables allow easy access to it. In many cases, the battery fits into a compartment on the bottom of the computer. If this is the case, remove the battery compartment's cover, slide the old battery out, and slide the new one in (see Figure 2-13). If the battery's compartment is on the bottom, there might be a release mechanism that allows you to remove the battery. Remove the old one and insert the new one.

FIGURE 2-13

A battery located on the underside of a portable system.

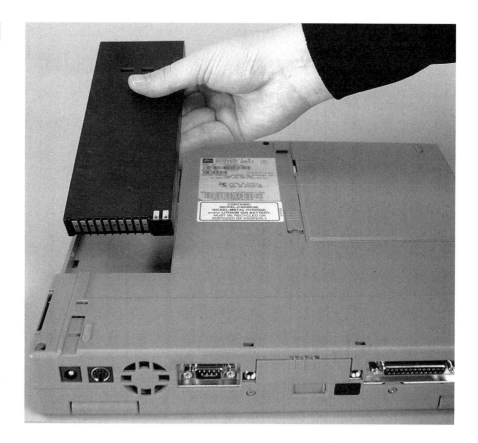

Fortunately, most portable systems give you plenty of notice before the battery is completely drained. Many systems include a power-level meter that allows you to see the battery's charge level at all times. Other systems give you a visual warning when the battery's power dips below a certain level.

Memory

Additional RAM can be added to a portable system in a number of ways. Some systems include extra RAM slots within the chassis itself. This type requires you to open the computer's case and place the RAM module in an available slot (see Figure 2-14). Because RAM modules for portables are proprietary, you cannot use them in desktop computers or in other portables.

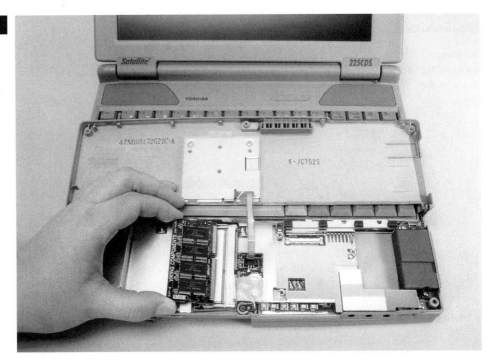

FIGURE 2-14

Installing a RAM module in a portable system.

An easier way to add more RAM to your portable is to use a memory PC card. PC cards were described earlier as being small cards that can be easily inserted in the portable to enhance or expand its abilities. In fact, PC cards originated as PCMCIA cards specifically for the purpose of adding more memory. PCMCIA stands for *Personal Computer Memory Card International Association,* a bit of a misnomer because these cards are usually used in laptops, not in PCs (desktops).

To use a memory PC card, simply insert it into the appropriate PC slot on the portable, usually located on the side (see Figure 2-15). Because memory cards are used so often, they tend to be more standardized than other portable system components. This means that you can use a generic memory PC card in your portable system.

Types I, II, and III Cards

When PC cards were first introduced, they were called PCMCIA cards and were designed strictly for adding additional memory to a portable system. PCMCIA cards

FIGURE 2-15

Installing a memory PC card.

(also called *Type I* cards) are roughly the size of a credit card (85.6mm x 54mm x 3.3mm).

Due to the popularity of these cards, the PCMCIA went on to develop another standard: PCMCIA 2.0. This standard includes the use of *Type II* cards. These cards have the same physical dimensions as Type I cards except that they are 5mm thick instead of 3.3mm. Type II PCMCIA cards are typically used for I/O devices, including network cards, modems, and sound cards.

In 1994, the PCMCIA released yet another standard, PCMCIA 2.01. This standard includes the *Type III* card, and the name was officially changed from PCMCIA card (a real mouthful) to the shortened *PC card*. Type III cards have the same length and width measurements as Type I and Type II cards but are 10.5mm thick. They are usually used for hard drive storage. The 2.01 standard also supports a wider data bus (the 32-bit Cardbus).

All PC card standards support hot swapping. A service called *socket services* runs inside the portable and detects when a PC card has been inserted or removed. When a card is inserted, another service, called *card services*, assigns the card the proper resources, such as an IRQ and I/O address. A Type III card can be used only in a

Type III slot, but Type II cards can be used in Type II or Type III slots, and Type I cards can be used in all three.

CERTIFICATION SUMMARY

Some system setups require configurations beyond what is required of most common systems. Using the proper master/slave configuration techniques, you can install up to four drives in a single system. Alternatively, you can set up a SCSI system, which, although more difficult to configure, allows you to install many more devices in the computer.

Furthermore, some individual devices require special installation or configuration or are simply too new to be considered "common." Devices such as network cards, modems, and video cards all require additional, component-specific configuration in order to work properly. However, some systems such as USB and Firewire, have emerged that allow you to install a great number of devices with little or no configuration at all.

Most computers can be optimized or enhanced by installing special components, such as cache memory or PC cards. Other optimization procedures include using disk utilities such as Disk Defragmenter or Scandisk or upgrading the system's BIOS.

TWO-MINUTE DRILL

Here are some of the key points from each certification objective in Chapter 2.

Installing and Configuring IDE/EIDE Devices

❑ Most computers support the installation of up to four hard and/or CD drives.

❑ Master drives must be configured with the proper jumper setting and are installed at the end of the drive's ribbon cable.

❑ To install a slave drive, set the jumper to the "slave" position, and attach the drive to the middle ribbon cable connector.

❑ Another master/slave configuration can be added by using the system's secondary drive controller.

Installing and Configuring SCSI Devices

❑ A SCSI system is controlled by a SCSI controller card, also called a *SCSI host adapter.*

❑ SCSI-1, SCSI-2, and SCSI-3 systems support different speeds, bus widths, and maximum cable lengths.

❑ Each device in a SCSI chain must be assigned a unique SCSI ID address.

❑ Each end of the SCSI chain must be properly terminated.

Installing and Configuring Peripheral Devices

❑ Video cards and modems require additional configuration, such as their display settings and dial-up properties, to work properly.

❑ USB systems require the use of USB hubs, a USB header cable, or USB cards to attach more than one or two devices.

❑ IEEE-1394 (Firewire) systems are similar to USB but support faster devices, such as DVD drives and video cameras.

❑ Most portables can use desktop components through the use of port replicators or docking stations.

Upgrading, Extending, and Optimizing System Performance

❏ A computer system's hard drive access speed can be increased by defragmenting the hard drive or installing cache memory.

❏ The computer's BIOS can be upgraded (flashed or replaced) to recognize new types of devices.

❏ Portable computers can use Type I, Type II, or Type III PC cards to access additional RAM, I/O devices, or storage, respectively.

SELF TEST

The following questions will help you measure your understanding of the material presented in this chapter. Read all the choices carefully because there might be more than one correct answer. Choose all correct answers for each question.

Installing and Configuring IDE/EIDE Devices

1. Which of the following statements about hard drive configurations is true?

    A. To function properly, a master drive must be accompanied by a secondary drive.

    B. The master drive must be attached to the ribbon cable using the connector that is closest to the system board.

    C. The term for a hard drive on the secondary controller is *slave*.

    D. A slave drive cannot work in the absence of a master drive.

2. You are planning to install a hard drive and a CD-ROM drive in a new system. Which of the following is typically a valid drive configuration for you to use?

    A. Install the hard drive as a primary master and install the CD-ROM as a secondary master.

    B. Install the CD-ROM as a primary master and the hard drive as a primary slave.

    C. Install the CD-ROM as either a primary master or a secondary slave.

    D. Install the CD-ROM anywhere, as long as the hard drive is a secondary master.

3. Your computer has three hard drives installed—two on the primary controller and one on the secondary controller. You are planning to install a fourth drive without changing the designations of the existing drives. Which of the following accurately describes the procedure you should follow?

    A. Enter the new drive's type and capacity in the CMOS settings, set the drive's jumper to the slave position, and install it on the available connector on the drive ribbon.

    B. Set the drive's jumper to the slave position and attach it to the ribbon cable. Restart the computer and enter the new drive's drive letter in the CMOS settings.

    C. Enter the new drive's drive letter in the CMOS settings. Set the drive's jumper to the secondary position and attach it to the ribbon cable.

    D. Set the drive's jumper to the slave position and attach it to the ribbon cable.

4. A computer has an E: drive. Assuming that all physical drives in the system have only one partition, what can you tell *for certain* about the computer?

    A. The computer has four drives installed.

    B. The C: drive is on the primary controller.

    C. The E: drive is on the primary controller.

    D. This drive is on the secondary controller.

5. Which of the following is true of master/slave hard drive configurations?

    A. Do not mix ATA and IDE drives on a single controller.

    B. The primary controller must contain drives that are technologically similar to or newer than drives on the secondary controller.

    C. Do not configure a hard drive to be CD-ROM drive's slave.

    D. Do not install drives on the secondary controller without a primary slave present.

Installing and Configuring SCSI Devices

6. You are planning to install a non-Plug and Play SCSI system controller card. Which of the following most accurately represents the proper steps in the proper order?

    A. Add the controller to the end of the existing SCSI chain and assign it an available ID address.

    B. Install the controller in an available expansion slot and assign it an IRQ and ID address.

    C. Add the controller to the end of the existing SCSI chain and assign it an available IRQ and ID address.

    D. Install the controller in an available expansion slot and assign it an ID address.

7. A customer had a properly functioning SCSI system with two internal hard drives and five external peripherals. He tells you that he added another external peripheral to the end of the chain, and now none of the SCSI devices will work. Which of the following cannot be considered a possible cause of this problem?

    A. The new device has an IRQ conflict with another peripheral device.

    B. There might be too many devices in the SCSI system.

    C. The system might not be properly terminated.

    D. The SCSI chain might be too long.

8. Refer to Figure 2-16. The maximum supported length of a mixed internal/external SCSI system cable is:

   A. The length of cable between the two ports of attached devices.

   B. The length between the far ports of attached devices.

   C. The length of the SCSI chain from the controller to the last device on either end of the chain.

   D. The length of the SCSI chain from the last device on the internal chain to the last device on the external chain.

9. Which type of SCSI system has an 8-bit bus and throughput of 40MBps and can support a maximum cable length of 12 meters?

   A. Ultra SCSI-3

   B. Wide Ultra SCSI-3

   C. Ultra-2 SCSI

   D. Ultra-3 SCSI

10. You are planning to set up a SCSI system in your computer. You want to be able to attach at least 11 devices, and you want to make the SCSI chain about 2 meters long. Which of the following SCSI types can you use?

    A. Fast SCSI-2

    B. Wide SCSI-2

    C. Wide Ultra SCSI-3

    D. Ultra-2 SCSI

FIGURE 2-16

Select the distance that constitutes the maximum cable length.

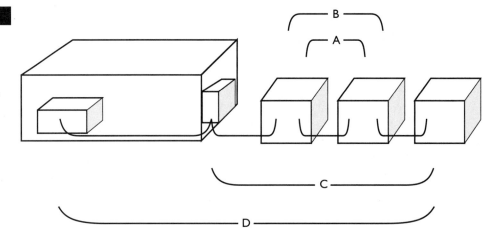

Installing and Configuring Peripheral Devices

11. As well as physical installation and resource assignment, which of the following should you configure when installing an analog modem?

    A. A dial-up connection

    B. A handshake routine

    C. An IP address

    D. Resolution settings

12. Which of the following most accurately describes the function of a USB hub?

    A. To increase the speed of the USB system

    B. To increase the number of available USB ports

    C. To allow you to use more than 127 USB devices

    D. To control the assignment of resources to USB devices

13. You are planning to add another USB device your system. What is the proper installation procedure?

    A. Turn the computer off, plug in the device, terminate the device, turn the device on, restart the computer, load the proper device driver

    B. Turn the computer off, plug in the device, turn the device on, restart the computer

    C. Plug in the device, turn the device on, load the proper device driver

    D. Plug in the device and turn it on, if necessary. (Not all USB devices have an on/off switch.)

14. A customer is planning to buy a new computer system and has asked your advice. The customer wants to use high-speed video devices but does not want a system that requires a lot of device configuration. The system should be able to handle up to 10 external devices and support hot swapping. Which type of system should you recommend?

    A. IDE/ATA

    B. SCSI

    C. USB

    D. IEEE-1394

15. Which of the following allows you to attach nearly any type of desktop component to a portable computer?

    A. Port replicator

    B. Enhanced port replicator

    C. Extended port replicator

    D. Docking station

Upgrading, Extending, and Optimizing System Performance

16. Which of the following is *not* a function of Microsoft's Scandisk utility?

    A. To restore corrupted files

    B. To resolve FAT/cluster information

    C. To fix bad sectors on the disk

    D. To remove information from bad sectors on the disk

17. Under which circumstance would you run Microsoft's Disk Defragmenter?

    A. On a set schedule

    B. When the disk reports corrupted files

    C. When the computer cannot recognize the hard drive

    D. When you accidentally delete a file

18. Your computer consistently loses its date/time setting, and you suspect the CMOS battery is at fault. Which procedure will you use to solve the problem?

    A. Replace the battery.

    B. Flash the battery using a manufacturer-provided disk.

    C. Use the computer's AC adapter to recharge the battery.

    D. Access the CMOS setting programs at startup, and select the low-power option.

19. You want to upgrade your BIOS by "flashing" it. Which procedure should you follow?

    A. Replace the BIOS chip with a newer model from the manufacturer of the original.

    B. Turn on the computer, and when you see the option to enter the system setup, press the given key combination.

    C. Insert the manufacturer's floppy disk and turn the computer on.

    D. Replace the BIOS chip with a newer model that is compatible with the system board and processor.

20. Which of the following represents a typical function of a Type II PC card?

    A. To add more memory to the computer

    B. To access a computer network

C. To provide additional power to a portable

D. To increase storage capacity

LAB QUESTION

This chapter discussed three alternative component systems: SCSI, USB, and IEEE-1394. Use the information you have learned to create a table that compares and contrasts these systems. Be sure to include information about device number, transmission speed, and installation information. You might also want to include information such as ease of use, relative expense, and other system-specific information. Use the template in Table 2-2 to complete your table.

TABLE 2-2   Lab Question Sample Table

	SCSI	USB	IEEE-1394
Maximum number of devices			
Types			
Speed			
Resources			
Additional required hardware			
Relative cost			
Device power source			
Common devices			
Communication method			
Topology (device connection method)			
Maximum cable length			
Resource configuration			
Supports hot swapping?			
Operating system			

SELF TEST ANSWERS

Installing and Configuring IDE/EIDE Devices

1. ☑ **D.** A slave drive cannot work in the absence of a master drive. In a master/slave configuration, two drives are installed on a single ribbon cable, and the master drive's on-board controller controls the function of the slave drive. If a drive is configured as a slave and there is no master present, the slave drive will not be able to communicate with the computer.

   ☒ **A**, to function properly, a master drive must be accompanied by a secondary drive, is incorrect. Master drives can be configured on either the primary or secondary controllers. Both controllers can be set up with a master/slave configuration, and the presence of a master does not necessitate the installation of a drive on the secondary controller. However, to install a drive on the secondary controller, a drive must be present on the primary controller, and to install a slave drive, a master drive must be present on the same controller. **B** is incorrect because it states that the master drive must be attached to the ribbon cable using the connector that is closest to the system board. In fact, the opposite is true. The master drive must be installed at the end of the ribbon cable, and the slave is installed in the middle (closest to the system board). **C**, the term for a hard drive on the secondary controller is *slave*, is also incorrect. The term for a hard drive on the secondary controller is *secondary*. The term *slave* is reserved for a drive that is controlled by a master drive.

2. ☑ **A.** Install the hard drive as a primary master and install the CD-ROM as a secondary master. This is the most common hard drive/CD-ROM setup. You could also install the hard drive as a primary master and the CD-ROM as a primary slave.

   ☒ **B and C** are incorrect because they suggest installing the CD-ROM as a primary master. Most OSs will work only if they are installed on a drive that is on the primary controller. Furthermore, hard drives cannot be slaves to CD-ROM drives. You can deduce from this that a hard drive must occupy the primary master position. Finally, **C** also suggests installing the CD-ROM as the secondary slave. However, slave drives must be accompanied by a master drive on the same controller. We have already determined that the hard drive cannot be on the secondary controller (**D** is incorrect for this reason). Therefore, without a master to control the secondary slave position, the CD-ROM cannot be installed there.

3. ☑ **D.** Set the drive's jumper to the slave position and attach it to the ribbon cable. Restart the computer and enter the new drive's type and capacity in the CMOS settings. In the given system, the only available position is secondary slave. Therefore, the drive must first be configured as a slave by setting the jumpers to the slave position. When this is finished, the drive is attached to the ribbon cable at the only remaining place: the middle connector on the secondary cable. Although some computers will automatically detect the new drive on startup,

others require you to enter the drive's specifications manually. When the drive is installed, restart the computer and access the CMOS settings. Enter the drive's specifications.

☒ **A** is incorrect because it suggests setting the new drive's capacity and type before it is physically installed in the computer. This should be the last, not the first, step in a hard drive installation. In fact, the BIOS won't allow you to set characteristics of a drive that doesn't physically exist in the system. **B** and **C** are both incorrect because they suggest manually entering the drive letter of the new drive. This is unnecessary because the computer will automatically letter the drives in the following order every time it is started: primary master, secondary master, primary slave, secondary slave.

4. ☑ **B.** The C: drive is on the primary controller. Recall that drives are lettered in this order: primary master, primary slave, secondary master, secondary slave. The primary master is given C:, no matter how many other drives are installed.

☒ **A** is incorrect because it states that the computer has four drives installed. Although it might indeed have four drives, you can't tell this for certain from the information given. It is also possible for this computer to have only three drives, as explained previously. **C** and **D** are both incorrect because they suggest that you can tell for certain that the drive is on one controller or another. You can tell for certain that this system has a primary master (C:). However, the other two drives might be a primary slave (D:) and a secondary master (E:) or a secondary master (D:) and a secondary slave (E:).

5. ☑ **C.** Do not configure a hard drive as a CD-ROM drive's slave. CD-ROM drives cannot control a hard drive, so they cannot be set as a hard drive's master. You can, however, set a hard drive to be a CD-ROM drive's master.

☒ **A** is incorrect because it suggests that you shouldn't install a mixture of ATA and IDE drives on a single controller. Both of these drive types are standardized and compatible with each other, so they can be installed together in a variety of configurations in a single computer. **B** is incorrect because it states that the primary controller must contain drives that are technologically similar to or newer than drives on the secondary controller. Although this is true for the master/slave relationship, it is not true for different controllers. **D** is incorrect because it states that you should not install drives on the secondary controller unless a primary slave is present. Secondary drives can be installed, regardless of the presence of a slave, as long as a primary *master* is installed. In fact, many 2-disk configurations include a primary master, secondary master, and no slaves.

Installing and Configuring SCSI Devices

6. ☑ **B.** Install the controller in an available expansion slot and assign it an IRQ and ID address. SCSI controller cards are installed like any other expansion card inside the computer. Once installed, the card must be assigned system resources, such as an IRQ address, so that the

computer can communicate with it. Finally, because the controller is part of a SCSI system, it must be assigned a SCSI ID address so that it can be identified among other devices in the SCSI chain.

☒ **A** and **C** are incorrect because they both suggest that the controller is attached to the end of the existing chain. The controller is the central element in the SCSI system, so it is installed on the system board itself. Although the controller might represent one end of the chain, it is not attached to end of an existing chain, as a peripheral SCSI device would be. **D** is incorrect because although it suggests assigning an ID address, it doesn't specify the assignment of an IRQ address. In this case, the steps given in **D** are correct but are not as complete or accurate as the steps in **B**.

7. ☑ **A.** The possibility that the new device has an IRQ address conflict with another peripheral device cannot be considered a possible cause for the SCSI system problem. SCSI devices are assigned ID addresses, not IRQ addresses. In any case, although it is true that devices cannot share a SCSI ID, this would most likely affect only the conflicting devices, not the whole chain. Furthermore, if one of the conflicting devices is the controller, it might affect the whole chain, but a peripheral device has been specified here.

☒ **B**, there are too many devices in the SCSI system, is incorrect because this might be the source of the problem. If this is a 16-bit SCSI system, it will support up to 16 devices, including the controller. However, there will be a problem if this is an 8-bit system, because 8-bit SCSI systems can support only eight devices, including the controller. Two hard drives plus the controller plus the five peripherals equals eight devices—the system's maximum. A ninth device would have to share an ID address with a device, causing that device to function improperly. If that device happens to be the controller, the entire system might not work. **C**, the system might not be properly terminated, is incorrect. The system was working properly before the addition of the new device, so you can assume that the problem lies with that device's configuration. Since the new device was installed at the end of the chain, the system's termination will have to be changed. That is, the device that used to be last in the chain will have to have its terminator disabled or removed, and the new device at the end will have to be terminated instead. **D**, the SCSI chain might be too long, is also incorrect because this might be the source of the problem. SCSI systems are limited in terms of the total length they can support from one end to the other. The addition of the new device might have caused the system to be longer than the maximum supported length.

8. ☑ **D.** The maximum cable length refers to the length of the chain from the last device on the internal chain to the last device on the external chain—that is, the total cable length in the entire SCSI system. Signals that must travel further than the recommended maximum might become so degraded by interference that they cannot be received by the intended device.

☒ **A** and **B** are incorrect because they both refer to the length between two devices, not the entire SCSI system. **C** is incorrect because it suggests that the maximum length refers to the total length on *either* side of the controller. As discussed, this length refers to the total length, including devices on *both* sides of the controller.

9. ☑ **C.** Ultra-2 SCSI has an 8-bit bus and throughput of 40MBps and can support a maximum cable length of 12 meters. It is considered "narrow" because of the 8-bit bus limitation, but it uses SCSI-3 technology to bring the speed up to 40MBps. Because Ultra-2 SCSI can use LVD data transfer, it can support cable lengths up to 12 meters.
☒ **A,** Ultra SCSI-3, is incorrect because, although this type has an 8-bit bus, it is limited to a 20MBps throughput and 1.5 meter cable length. **B,** Wide Ultra SCSI-3, is incorrect. This type has a 40MBps throughput but a 16-bit bus and maximum length of 1.5 meters. **D,** Ultra-3 SCSI, is incorrect because it has a 16-bit bus and throughput of 160MBps.

10. ☑ **B.** You can use a Wide SCSI-2 system. It is a 16-bit system and supports up to 16 devices. It also supports cable lengths up to 3 meters. Incidentally, a Fast Wide SCSI-2, Double Wide SCSI-2, or Ultra-3 SCSI system could also be used.
☒ **A,** Fast SCSI-2, is incorrect because this type of SCSI has an 8-bit bus and can support a maximum of eight devices. **C,** Wide Ultra SCSI-3, is incorrect because it is limited to a 1.5 meter cable length. **D,** Ultra-2 SCSI, is also incorrect because it can support only eight devices.

Installing and Configuring Peripheral Devices

11. ☑ **A.** When installing a modem, you should configure a dial-up connection. This will instruct the modem about connection procedures, such as which phone number to dial and how to disable call waiting.
☒ **B,** a handshake routine, is incorrect. Although modems use handshake routines when making a connection, this is a property of the modem itself, not a configurable setting that you can alter. **C,** an IP address, is incorrect because these are used for network cards, not analog modems. **D,** resolution settings, is incorrect because this type of configuration applies to video cards, not modems.

12. ☑ **B.** The function of a USB hub is to increase the number of available USB ports. Most computers that support USB include only one or two ports. To make more ports available, attach a USB hub. The hub itself attaches to an existing port and contains up to seven additional ports, to which you can attach USB devices or even more USB ports.
☒ **A,** to increase the speed of the USB system, is incorrect. USB systems are limited to about 12Mbps and cannot exceed this limit. **C,** to allow you to use more than 127 USB devices, is incorrect. Although you could physically connect more than 127 devices using a USB port, the USB system itself can use only up to 127 of them. No device will increase this limit. **D,** to control the assignment of resources to USB devices, is incorrect because this is the job of the USB controller.

13. ☑ **D.** To install a USB device, plug in the device and turn it on. The computer automatically detects the device, assigns it any resources it needs, and installs the appropriate device driver.
☒ **A**, **B**, and **C** are incorrect because they refer to turning the computer off, terminating the device, and/or loading a device driver. USB devices are hot swappable, meaning that they can be added to or removed from the system while the computer is operating. USB devices also support Plug and Play, so you do not need to install a device driver for them. Finally, USB devices do not need to be terminated, as SCSI devices do.

14. ☑ **D.** You should recommend an IEEE-1394 system. These systems (also known as Firewire) allow you to attach up to 63 external devices (64,449 if extra-port hubs are used) and support Plug and Play and hot swapping. Firewire supports speeds up to 400Mbps, so it is suited for use with high-speed devices, such as video cameras or other video equipment.
☒ **A**, IDE/ATA, is incorrect because it does not meet the customer's requirements. These systems are limited in the number of devices they can support. Although some IDE/ATA devices support Plug and Play, they do not support hot swapping. **B**, SCSI, is also incorrect. Some SCSI systems can support more than 10 devices and speeds up to 160MBps, but they typically require a lot of configuration. **C**, USB, is incorrect. USB systems meet all the customer's requests except the ability to support high-speed devices. USB systems are limited to 12Mbps.

15. ☑ **D.** A docking station allows you to attach nearly any type of desktop component to a portable computer. This is, of course, within the limits set by the manufacturer of the portable and docking station. Most docking stations remain stationary and can be connected to desktop components such as CRT monitors, printers, scanners, sound systems, and extra hard drives. When you want to access these devices with your portable computer, simply plug the portable into the docking station.
☒ **A**, port replicator, and **B**, enhanced port replicator, are incorrect because they do not allow access to the number of devices that a docking station does. Although both are used to provide quick access to some desktop components, they are limited in the devices they support. **C**, extended port replicator, is incorrect because this is not a real type of portable system component.

Upgrading, Extending, and Optimizing System Performance

16. ☑ **C.** Microsoft's Scandisk utility does not fix bad sectors on the disk. A bad sector is a "spot" on the disk that physically cannot hold data. Scandisk is simply a software utility and cannot change the physical structure of the disk.
☒ **A**, to restore corrupted files, is incorrect because this is a function of Scandisk. If part of a file resides on a bad cluster, Scandisk will attempt to remove the data from the cluster (therefore

D is incorrect) so that the file can be accessed. If all or part of the file is unreferenced in the FAT, it might also be considered "corrupted." Scandisk will read the data on the disk and ensure that references to it in the FAT are accurate (therefore **B** is incorrect).

17. ☑ **A.** You should run Disk Defragmenter on a set schedule. As files are saved, moved, and deleted, the disk can become more and more fragmented. Fragmented files take longer to retrieve than files located in contiguous clusters. Disk Defragmenter relocates cluster data so that all the clusters belonging to any one file are located close to each other.
☒ **B,** when the disk reports corrupted files, is incorrect because in this situation, you should use Scandisk. Disk Defragmenter cannot retrieve bad or lost data. **C,** when the computer cannot recognize the hard drive, is also incorrect. When this is the case, check to ensure that the drive is properly installed and that the BIOS is aware of its presence. **D,** when you accidentally delete a file, is incorrect because Disk Defragmenter does not help in "undeleting" files.

18. ☑ **A.** You should replace the battery. When the computer "forgets" the time and date, it is most likely because the CMOS battery, which normally maintains these settings, is getting low. The only solution is to replace it with a fully charged battery.
☒ **B** is incorrect because it suggests flashing the battery. This procedure applies to the upgrade of a BIOS chip, not a CMOS battery. **C** is incorrect because it suggests recharging the battery with the computer's AC adapter. Although this procedure will work with a portable system battery, CMOS batteries cannot be recharged with an AC adapter. **D** is incorrect because it suggests selecting a "low-power" option in the CMOS settings program. Any low-power setting in the CMOS settings refers to the function of the computer itself, not the CMOS battery. You cannot adjust the amount of power the CMOS chip draws from its battery.

19. ☑ **C.** To flash the BIOS, insert the manufacturer's floppy disk and turn the computer on. The computer will read the "flash" program on the disk and automatically update the abilities of the BIOS by providing it with a new instruction set.
☒ **A** and **D** are both incorrect because they suggest replacing the BIOS chip with another. The purpose of flashing a BIOS is to reprogram the existing BIOS, not to physically replace it with another. **B** is incorrect because it suggests entering the computer's system setup at startup. This procedure can be used to select different options in the existing BIOS, but it is not the procedure used for flashing (upgrading) the BIOS.

20. ☑ **B.** A typical function of a Type II PC card is to access a computer network. Type II PC cards are used for I/O operations such as for network cards, modems, and sound cards. The PC card can be inserted and removed as needed from the portable computer.
☒ **A,** to add more memory to the computer, and **D,** to increase storage capacity, are incorrect because these are the typical functions of Type I and Type III PC cards, respectively. **C,** to

provide additional power to a portable, is incorrect because portable system batteries, not PC cards, provide the portable with power.

LAB ANSWER

Table 2-3 provides the answer to the lab.

TABLE 2-3   Lab Answer

	SCSI	USB	IEEE-1394
Maximum number of devices	8, 16, or 31, including controller	127	63
Types	SCSI-1, SCSI-2, SCSI-3, and variants	Low and high speed	N/A
Speed	5, 10, 20, 40, 80, or 160 MBps	12Mbps	500Mbps
Resources	SCSI ID address	N/A	N/A
Additional required hardware	Terminator, SCSI controller	USB hub	none
Relative cost	More $$$ than IDE/ATA	≈ IDE/ATA	More $$$ than USB
Device power source	External	Supplied by system	Supplied by system
Common devices	Hard drives, printers, scanners	Any	High-speed video, DVD, digital cameras
Communication method	Parallel	Serial	Serial
Topology (device connection method)	Daisy-chain	Tiered (using hubs)	Daisy-chain
Maximum cable length	1.5, 3, 6, or 12 meters for the entire chain	5 meters between devices	4 meters between devices
Resource configuration	Manual	Plug and Play	Plug and Play
Supports hot swapping?	No	Yes	Yes
Operating system	Any	Windows 95 or higher	Windows 98 or higher

3

Diagnosing and Troubleshooting Problems

T he most common types of procedures you will perform as a computer technician are troubleshooting and resolving computer problems. The more familiar you are with the functions of the computer's components, the easier it will be for you to find the source of the problem and implement a solution. In the simplest cases, a component will simply do nothing and must be replaced. However, not all computer problems are as simple or as obvious as that one. For example, what should you do when your computer gives you a "201" error message at startup? Or if the floppy drive light comes on and won't go off?

This chapter provides you with troubleshooting techniques you can use to resolve common computer problems. It also describes the procedures you should follow in trying to determine less obvious sources of computer problems.

CERTIFICATION OBJECTIVE 3.01

Symptoms and Problems

This section presents the most common problems associated with typical computer devices and how to resolve them. Keep in mind that these are "common" problems of basic components. They do not, by any means, represent an exhaustive description of the great variety of problems you could come across as a technician. When faced with problems that do not have an obvious solution, you should follow the basic "fact-finding" steps discussed in the "Basic Troubleshooting Procedures" section of the chapter.

Please note that some of the symptoms described here can be caused by a number of different component problems. For example, suppose you turn the computer on, and nothing happens at all. This problem could be caused by a faulty processor, system board, or hard drive, or it could simply be the result of a disconnected power cable. The troubleshooting procedures described here assume that the component in question has already been determined to be the cause of the problem.

POST Audio and Visual Error Codes

When a computer is started, the BIOS performs a POST to check for the presence and status of existing components. Errors found during the POST are typically indicated by a visual error message on the screen or a series of beeps. These visual and audio error codes can differ from BIOS to BIOS, so it's best to consult the manufacturer's documentation for the meaning of each code. However, some BIOS error codes are considered "common" because they are used in most machines.

For example, most error codes in the 1** series, such as 120 or 162, indicate a problem with the system board or processor. It is rare to see a 1** error code, since most system board and processor errors are serious enough to prevent the computer from issuing the error code at all.

Memory errors detected by the POST are typically indicated by a 2** error, and keyboard errors are indicated by a 3** error. Fortunately, most visual error codes are also accompanied by a brief description of the problem. Again, consult the documentation for your specific BIOS, because these messages can often be cryptic (for example, "213: DMA arbitration time-out").

Some BIOSs use a series of beeps rather than a visual message when there is a POST error. Typically, one beep indicates that all components passed the POST. This doesn't mean that there are no problems in the computer; it simply means that none of the components has a problem that was detected by the BIOS. When the BIOS issues an audio error code, carefully count the beeps, and note whether they are long or short. Again, consult the BIOS documentation for the proper meaning of each code, because these differ from system to system. For example, one BIOS might indicate a video problem by issuing eight short beeps, while another might use one short and two long beeps.

Processor and Memory Symptoms

In most cases, processor and memory problems are fatal, meaning that when there is such a problem, the computer will not boot at all. However, you should be aware of some nonfatal error indicators. As described, 1** error codes are typical of processor problems, and 2** error codes are typical of memory problems.

If you turn on the computer and it does not even complete the POST or it does nothing at all, there might be a problem with the processor or memory. The solution to a processor or memory problem is to remove the offending component and replace it with a new one. If the error persists, there might be a problem with the slot or socket that the memory or processor uses to connect to the motherboard. In this case, the motherboard needs to be replaced.

On a final note: Some RAM errors are not reported by the computer at all. That is, if an entire memory module does not work, the computer might just ignore it and continue to function normally without it. Watch as the RAM is counted on the screen at startup to ensure that the total amount matches the capacity installed in the machine. If this amount comes up significantly short, you probably have to replace the memory module.

Mouse

A number of different symptoms are associated with mice, and they provide a common source of computer problems. Fortunately, most procedures required to resolve a mouse problem are quite simple. Let's look at two common mouse-related problems.

The Mouse Pointer Doesn't Move Smoothly on the Screen

A common mouse problem is irregular movement of the mouse pointer across the screen. Some mice even appear to hit an "invisible wall" on the screen. These symptoms indicate dirty mouse rollers. This problem is very common because, as the mouse is rolled across a desk or table, it can pick up debris, which is then deposited on the internal rollers. To clean the mouse rollers, follow the steps in Exercise 3-1.

exam
ⓦatch

The most common problem with mice is irregular movement due to dust buildup on the rollers.

EXERCISE 3-1

Cleaning a Mouse

1. Turn the mouse upside-down and remove the retaining ring (usually by twisting it counter-clockwise).

2. Slowly invert the mouse so that the ball drops into your hand.

3. If the ball itself is dirty or sticky, you can clean it with soapy water.

4. Locate the rollers inside the mouse (see Figure 3-1). There are typically two long black rollers and one small metallic roller.

FIGURE 3-1

The internal
rollers in a
typical mouse.

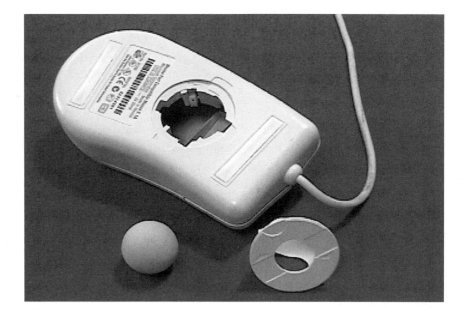

5. Use your fingers to remove the "ring" of dust from each roller, taking care not to let any material fall even further into the mouse.

6. If the rollers are sticky or if Step 5 is insufficient to clean the rollers, use a cotton swab dipped in isopropyl alcohol to clean them.

7. When you are finished, replace the mouse ball and retaining ring, ensuring that they are secured in place.

The Mouse Pointer Doesn't Move on the Screen

The mouse pointer's failure to move across the screen indicates that the computer cannot communicate properly with the mouse, so it is not receiving the appropriate signals to move the mouse pointer. One reason for this problem could be an IRQ conflict with another device. Because a serial mouse must use a COM port, it also uses that port's IRQ and I/O address. However, recall that some COM ports can share IRQ addresses. If another device attached to a COM port shares an IRQ with the mouse's COM port, the mouse will probably not work at all. If you are running

Microsoft Windows, use the Device Manger to determine if there is a resource conflict. If there is, move the offending device to a different COM port.

If the problem is not IRQ related, it might be driver related. That is, the mouse driver might be either corrupted or missing altogether. If you suspect a missing driver, you need to manually load the driver from the Setup disk that came with the mouse. If there is no driver disk, try simply restarting the computer. Most mice are Plug and Play, so the OS might automatically detect your mouse and load the appropriate driver for it at startup. If you suspect that a mouse driver exists but has become corrupted, use the Device Manager or the Mouse icon in the Control Panel to remove the existing driver. Finally, reload the driver.

Finally, an unresponsive mouse might be a symptom of a malfunctioning adapter card if it is a bus mouse. A bus mouse adapter card must be installed and configured in the same manner as other expansion cards. Ensure that it has the proper resources and that there are no conflicts. Next, ensure that the adapter card's device driver is loaded. You can also try opening the computer to ensure that the card is properly seated in the expansion slot or try replacing the card itself.

Floppy Drive Failures

There are a number of types of floppy drive failures, so there are a number of different symptoms. Fortunately, most floppy failures stem from the disk, not the drive itself. Whenever you encounter a floppy drive failure, the first thing you should do is determine whether or not the disk is at fault. The easiest way to do this is to eject the disk and insert another. If the problem goes away, the disk, not the drive, is the source of the problem. If you *must* have the information on a particular disk that's giving you trouble, try gently pulling the metal cover back and letting it snap back into place a few times, then reinsert the disk in the drive and try to access the data again. You can also try to use the disk in a different drive.

exam
ⓦatch

The disk, rather than the drive, is the cause of most floppy errors.

An "A: is not accessible" Error Message

If you put a disk in the A: drive and receive an "A: is not accessible" message, the drive cannot detect a floppy disk. The most common reason for this error is simply that no disk has been inserted in the drive or was not inserted all the way. Check to make sure that there is a disk inserted. If there is, remove the disk and try pulling the metal cover back a few times to loosen it; if the drive cannot pull the cover back, it cannot access the data on the disk.

An "Error writing to disk" Message

One of the most common symptoms of a floppy drive problem is a message stating that there is an error reading from or writing to the disk. This type of message typically indicates that the floppy drive controller is communicating properly with the computer but simply cannot access disk information. First, try to access a different disk, to rule out the original disk as the cause of the problem. If you determine that the problem is drive rather than disk related, try cleaning the drive's read/write heads.

Floppy drive cleaning kits can be purchased at many computer retail or parts stores. Typically, the kit includes a cleaning solution and what looks like a regular floppy disk. In most cases, the cleaning solution is applied to the disk, and the disk is inserted in the drive. The read/write heads are cleaned as they try to access the disk.

If the drive still cannot access a disk after cleaning, the problem lies within the drive itself, and it must be replaced.

A Floppy Drive Light That Won't Go Off

A floppy drive light that won't go off indicates that the drive's ribbon cable is attached incorrectly. Turn the computer off, remove the computer's cover, and reattach the cable the right way. Remember, the red stripe on the cable must be aligned with pin 1 on the system board and on the drive itself.

exam
Watch

A floppy drive light that comes on at startup and doesn't go out indicates a reversed ribbon cable.

An "Invalid drive" Error When Accessing the Floppy Drive

When you see this error—and any time the computer doesn't recognize the presence of the floppy drive—it means that the drive is not communicating properly with the computer. Turn the computer off and remove the cover. Make sure that the ribbon cable is present and properly and firmly attached. Next, make sure that the drive is receiving adequate power from the power supply. When you are satisfied that the drive is connected properly, restart the computer and access the CMOS settings program. Ensure that the correct floppy drive configuration is present in the BIOS settings. If the computer still does not recognize the floppy drive, the drive must be replaced with a working drive.

Use the following Scenario & Solution questions to test your knowledge about floppy drive errors.

Hard Drives

Many things can go wrong with a hard drive, each of which can result in a number of different symptoms, so it can be difficult to determine the cause of the problem. The most common symptoms are discussed here.

The Computer Will Not Boot Properly

When you start the computer, you might receive a 16** POST error message. You could also get a message stating that there is no hard drive present. Typically, these errors are not fatal, and you can boot the computer using a special boot (floppy) disk.

When you receive this error, it means that the computer doesn't recognize or cannot communicate with the hard drive. First, restart the computer and enter the CMOS settings. Ensure that the proper hard drive type is listed in the BIOS drive

SCENARIO & SOLUTION

What Should You Do If ...	Answer
You receive an "A: is not accessible" error?	Check for the presence of a floppy disk in the drive.
You receive an "Invalid drive" error?	Make sure that the drive works and is properly attached. Check to ensure that the BIOS settings match the drive type.
The floppy drive light comes on and won't go off?	Reverse the orientation of the ribbon cable in the floppy drive port.

configuration. If it is not, enter the appropriate settings, or use the system's hard drive detection option.

If the BIOS settings are correct and the drive still won't work, or if the BIOS cannot detect the hard drive, there could be a cabling problem. Open the computer and ensure that the drive has the proper master or slave driver setting and that the ribbon and power cables are attached properly and securely. You should verify that the ribbon cable itself is not the problem by replacing it with a known good one. If the cables, jumpers, and BIOS settings have been ruled out, the problem is with the drive itself, and it must be replaced.

Nothing Happens When the Computer Is Turned On

Many things can cause the computer not to turn on, including a bad power supply or system board. The problem can, however, also be caused by an improperly connected hard drive. Check the hard drive ribbon cable to ensure that the red stripe is aligned with pin 1.

The Computer Reports That There Is No Operating System

Once the BIOS has finished the POST, it looks for the presence of an OS on the hard drive. If the BIOS does not find a special OS pointer in the drive's master boot record, it assumes that no OS exists. If you haven't yet installed an OS, you must do so at that point. If an OS exists but cannot be accessed, try using the SYS command at a DOS prompt to make the drive bootable. That is, reboot the computer from the floppy drive. (This command is described in more detail in Chapter 10.) Use the command SYS C:. This command replaces the pointer in the master boot record, and the computer might be able to boot properly.

Unfortunately, most cases of a missing OS stem from the corruption or loss of essential OS files. If this is the case, you need to reload the OS. When data becomes corrupted, it might be a sign that the disk is about to fail. You should consider running Scandisk to resolve these problems. You might also want to consider replacing the hard disk before it fails completely. Before you do this, boot from a floppy disk, then try to access and save any salvageable information from the hard drive.

on the **j**ob

If Scandisk reports finding corrupted data, consider replacing the hard drive. Data becomes corrupted when it resides on a "bad" spot on the disk. It is common for a hard drive to develop a few bad clusters before it fails completely.

CD-ROM and DVD Drives

CD-ROM and DVD drives are functionally similar, so you can install or troubleshoot them using similar methods. A common problem with either of these devices is that the computer will report it can't read the disk. First, check to ensure the disk is inserted the right way. The label must be facing up, so the drive can access the data from the underside of the disk. Next, visually inspect the disk. Scratches or smudges may prevent the computer from reading the disk. Try another disk in the drive to rule out the media as the cause.

If the drive itself is the problem, check the Device Manager to ensure it has been recognized. Reload the device's driver if necessary, and check its system resources. If the problem persists, check the ribbon cable connection and jumper setting. Try the drive in another computer to pinpoint it or rule it out as the cause of the problem.

Parallel Ports

Typically, the only symptom of a failed parallel port is that the device attached to it will not work or not be detected by the computer. First, turn the device off, then back on again. Next, try restarting the computer. If there is still no response from the device, try the device in another parallel port or another computer. If the device functions properly, chances are that the original parallel port is at fault.

Check the port's resource settings in the Windows Device Manager to ensure that it is not conflicting with another device. If this is not the cause of the problem, test the function of the port using a *loopback adapter*, which, when connected to the port, can diagnose the port's ability to transmit and receive signals.

If the parallel port is faulty, it must be replaced. In older systems, the parallel port is not integrated with the system board and can be removed. If the parallel port is built into the system board, as in newer computers, you must replace the system board.

The Sound Card and Audio

The components that make up a computer audio system are the sound card, the speakers, and the supporting software. All sound system problems can be narrowed down to one or more of these components.

The Speakers Produce No Sound

The problem of speakers failing to produce sound can be caused by a number of things. First, start with the speakers themselves. Check to make sure that the volume is turned up to a sufficient level. In addition, check to make sure that they are plugged into the sound card and the proper port.

There are three ports on the sound card: microphone, sound out, and sound in. Although current sound cards and speakers come with color-coded connectors and connections, they didn't always. It is possible that the speaker is plugged into the wrong port.

If the speakers use an external power source, ensure that the power cable is properly attached and that the speakers are turned on. Try the speakers in another system to pinpoint them or rule them out as the cause of the problem.

If the speakers and the cables are not at fault, turn your attention to the audio software in the computer. Make sure that the Mute option has not been enabled and that the software-controlled volume is adjusted to a sufficient level. Try to produce sound in a number of different applications or reinstall the audio software.

If the sound card itself is at fault, check to make sure that it has the proper resources and device driver. If it does not, reassign an available IRQ, I/O address, and DMA channel, and reload the card's device driver. If the problem is still not resolved, open the computer and make sure that the sound card is properly and securely seated in the expansion slot. If the sound card itself is no longer working, replace it.

A Lot of Static Is Coming from the Speakers

Again, the symptom of speaker static might be the result of a number of problems, but it is very unlikely to be the cause of a sound card issue. First, check the volume on the speakers and the software. If the speakers are turned way up but the computer's software-controlled volume is turned down or off, the speakers transmit the only signals they are receiving—static.

The static could also be the result of a failing cable. Replace the cables with known good ones. If the static persists, it could be due to EMI. Move the speakers as far away from desktop lights, the monitor, and other interference-causing devices as you can. To rule out the speakers and cables, replace them with known working ones.

The static could also be the result of bad data in the sound file itself. Try to play a different sound file to see if the static continues. Similarly, if you are listening to a CD, try another CD.

The Computer Is Not Producing the Right Sounds

Sometimes when you play a sound file, it is played incorrectly or just makes "noise." Because the speakers only amplify and cannot alter sound signals, you can rule them out as the cause of the problem.

The problem could be in the sound file itself. Try another sound file or, if you're using a CD, replace the CD with another and try to play a sound file. If the problem is not limited to a specific sound file, try reinstalling the sound application itself.

The Monitor and Video

Like the sound system, a computer's video system contains a number of components, so it can be a bit tricky to diagnose and resolve problems. Another difficulty in resolving display problems is that you often don't see any display, so you can't see the OS or BIOS settings in order to remedy the problem.

The Computer Continues to Beep at Startup and Won't Boot Properly

This is an indication of a missing monitor or a missing or faulty video card. First, check to ensure that the monitor is properly attached to the video card. Don't worry about the monitor's power or settings, because these won't affect the computer's ability to boot. Next, check the function of the video card. Because there is no display, you can't check the resource or driver settings. You can, however, install the card in another computer to determine if it is functioning. If it is not, it must be replaced.

Complete Lack of Picture

If your monitor displays nothing at all, the first thing you should do is move the mouse or press a key on the keyboard. Many computers use screen savers or power modes that cause the screen to go blank after a specified period of time. Using the mouse or the keyboard should return the computer to its normal state.

If this action doesn't solve the problem, begin by checking the video system components. Start with the easiest component first—the monitor. Make sure that the monitor is plugged into a power outlet and is turned on. Also ensure that the brightness is set at an adequate level. Next, check the cable that attaches the monitor to the computer. In most cases, a missing or unattached cable will result in a POST error, but it is possible for this cable to come loose during operation. You can determine if the monitor is at fault by swapping it with a known good one. If the new monitor works in the system, you can assume that the original monitor is the problem. Before replacing a monitor 17" or more, you should have it checked by a trained technician. Since monitors come in larger and larger sizes, and can cost well over $1000, it would not be prudent to throw one of these out if it is possible to have it repaired at a reasonable cost.

If the monitor is not the cause, check that the video card is seated properly in the expansion slot. AGP cards, especially earlier ones, are not easily seated. Press the card firmly (not too hard) and listen for an audible click to tell you the card is seated. Later models don't seem to have this quirk. Because you cannot see the card's resources, you will not be able to determine if a configuration error is the problem. You can, however, try to install a different video card in this computer. Doing so might allow you to view the OS so that you can remove a faulty video card configuration, if it exists.

Some newer motherboards include an integrated video adapter. If this is one, look for a jumper setting to disable the on-board video and use an adapter card. If this option is not available, you need to replace the motherboard itself.

Flickering Monitor

A flickering monitor might be caused by a faulty monitor. Replace the monitor with another to see if the problem still exists. Flickering can also be caused by an inappropriate *refresh rate* setting. The refresh rate configures how often the display gets "repainted." If the rate is too low for the video system you are using, it can cause the display to flicker. Access the Control Panel's Display icon, and choose a different refresh rate.

Screen Elements Are Repeated Over and Over Again, All Over the Screen

Repeated screen elements are more common in older video systems. This problem is due to the use of an improper resolution setting for your video system. This setting results in multiple copies of the same image, including the mouse pointer, all over the screen. To solve this problem, enter the Display settings and reduce the resolution setting. This task can be cumbersome because more than one mouse pointer appears on the screen, making it nearly impossible to tell which is the real one. To navigate through the appropriate screens, it is suggested that you use the keyboard.

Modems

External modems are much easier to diagnose than internal modems. That is because they typically have indicator lights that can inform you of their status, and it is easier to see if they are plugged in properly. However, other than internal adapter problems, both types of modems can display a number of symptoms.

A "No Modem Is Present" Message

Display of a message indicating that no modem is present means that the computer doesn't recognize the modem or can't communicate with it. If the modem is external, make sure that it is properly plugged into a serial port. You can test the cable by swapping it with a known good one, and you can test the serial port by attaching and configuring a known working device. Most external modems have an external source of power. Make sure that the power cable is properly attached and that the power switch is turned on. The modem should display a "power on" light.

You should also make sure that the modem has been assigned the appropriate resources. If the modem is external, make sure that the COM port to which it is attached doesn't have a resource conflict. If the modem is internal, make sure that it has been assigned to a COM port that is both available (doesn't have a device attached) and has resources that are not in conflict with another device. If this is not the source of the problem, check for the presence of the modem's device driver. If it hasn't been properly loaded, run the modem's Setup program or install the driver using the Windows Device Manager. If you suspect that the driver is present but corrupted, uninstall, then reinstall it.

This problem can also be caused by incorrect dial-up properties. That is, your dial-up software might be configured to use an incorrect or nonexistent modem. Check the dial-up settings and ensure that the proper modem and modem type are selected.

Finally, if the modem is internal, open the computer and ensure that the modem is properly seated in the expansion slot. If the modem itself (internal or external) is found to be at fault, replace it.

A "No Dial Tone" Message

If your screen displays a message saying that your modem does not detect a dial tone, you should first ensure that the cable is properly attached to both the modem and the jack. Try unplugging the cable from the jack, then plugging it in again.

Next, you can test the cable by swapping it with a known good one. This problem might also be the cause of a bad phone line. Plug a phone into the suspect jack and pick up the handset, as normal. If there is no dial tone, the problem is with the line itself. If there is a dial tone, the problem is most likely the modem cable.

The Modem Dials But Cannot Make a Connection

A modem's failure to connect is usually caused by problems incurred during the handshake phase of the communication process. The first step in a modem handshake is that the receiving (answering) device sends a guard tone to indicate that it is indeed a modem (and not a person or a fax machine). If the dialing modem doesn't receive a guard tone, the connection will be dropped. Check the phone number you are dialing; you might mistakenly be dialing a regular household or fax number.

Another step in the handshake process is for both modems to agree on a transmission speed. If the two modems don't have a single compatible speed, the connection will be dropped. For instance, suppose your modem is able to operate 28.8Kbps or lower, and the modem at the other end is able to operate only at 36.6Kbps. The modems do not have a common transmission speed, so the connection will not continue.

The inability to make a connection can also indicate that there is a lot of interference on the line. You can test for this by listening for line "static" using a regular phone. If static is present, the problem must be resolved by the phone company.

The Modem Drops the Connection During Operation, Usually at Random

The main reason for an otherwise functioning modem to suddenly drop the connection is that it has been interrupted by another call. If your phone line has call waiting, ensure that it has been disabled in the modem's dial-up configuration. This problem can also occur if the modem shares a phone line with a regular phone or fax machine. If the phone is picked up during a modem session, the modem connection will be dropped.

The Modem Appears to Receive "Garbage"

Random "garbage," or invalid characters, are typically the sign of a noisy line. That is, static (EMI) on the line is being interpreted by the modem as valid data. Try using another line, moving EMI-causing devices out of the way, or contact the phone company.

In more serious cases, all the data received by the modem can appear garbled. This means that the modem is interpreting every bit of data incorrectly and is probably using different communication standards than the modem at the other end. Disconnect, then try again; the handshake might be successful a second time. If it is not, ensure that dial-up settings, such as baud rate and parity, match those of the other modem.

BIOS

If the BIOS has a nonfatal error, you will be notified at startup by a series of beeps or a visual message indicating that there is a BIOS checksum failure. This means that the BIOS chip did not pass the POST. If this is the case, replace the BIOS.

If the BIOS fails during the computer's operation, you will notice immediately because the computer will no longer be able to communicate with its peripherals. Most notably, the video system will shut down and the screen will go blank. However, because the BIOS is responsible for the proper function of every other component, it might not be obvious as the cause of the problem. In the case described here, you would most likely attempt to troubleshoot the video system itself before you came to the conclusion that the BIOS was at fault.

Motherboards

In many cases, when a motherboard fails, it causes a fatal error that prevents the computer from booting properly. However, if the BIOS is able to run a POST, it might report a problem with the motherboard as a 1** error. Unfortunately, as with a BIOS failure, no one symptom or set of symptoms can immediately be used to pinpoint the motherboard as the point of failure.

A faulty motherboard can cause a great number of different symptoms to occur and can even cause it to appear that a different component is at fault. This is because a problem on the motherboard could be localized in one particular area, such as a single circuit or port, causing a failure of a single device only. For example, if the video card's expansion slot on the motherboard stops working, it will appear that there is a problem with the display system itself. In this case, you are likely to discover the motherboard as the point of failure only after checking all other components in the video system.

When there is a problem with the motherboard, the only solution is to replace it. However, because of the difficulty and expense of replacing the motherboard, this should be done only when every other possibility, including the BIOS chip, has been examined.

on the **Job** *Due to the difficulty and expense involved in replacing a motherboard, it (and the processor) should be the last components that you suspect. Test all other affected components before determining that the motherboard is at fault.*

Universal Serial Bus

Recall that USB devices are hot swappable and support Plug and Play. Because so much of a USB device's operation depends on the function of the USB controller, this is where a majority of USB-related problems lie. It is possible, however, for a USB device itself to fail. Some of the most common USB problems are discussed here.

The USB Device Doesn't Seem to Get Power

Most devices get their power from the USB system or, more specifically, from the root or external hubs. First, if the device has a power switch or button, make sure it's turned to the on position. Next, make sure that the cable is securely connected. If this is a new installation, check the documentation and packaging to be sure an external power cord hasn't been overlooked. You should also check to make sure that the device is plugged into the proper type of hub. "Low-powered" USB devices can be plugged into any type of USB hub, but "high-powered" devices (which use over 100 milliamps) must be plugged into self-powered USB hubs only.

The USB Keyboard Won't Work

The keyboard's drivers and resources are typically controlled by the BIOS. When you install a USB keyboard, the BIOS must be informed so that it will hand control of the keyboard to the USB system. Enter the CMOS settings at startup and ensure that the USB keyboard option is turned on. If this option doesn't exist and you still want to use the USB keyboard, you might need to upgrade the BIOS or the computer itself.

USB Device Is "Unknown" Message, or the Device Won't Work

A message stating that the USB device is unknown or the device simply won't work means the computer cannot communicate with the device. First, make sure that the device is properly attached and is receiving power, and try switching it to another port. Make sure that the device's cable is not longer than 5 meters. Although most USB devices are Plug and Play, a few require proprietary drivers. Make sure that a driver is loaded for this device.

Check to make sure that the device is using the proper communications mode. On startup, the USB controller assigns an ID to all devices and asks them which type of data transfer (interrupt, bulk, or continuous) they will use. If a device is set to use the wrong type of transfer mode, it will not work. Finally, check the device itself by swapping it with a known good one.

None of the USB Devices Will Work

If none of the USB devices work, you could have a problem with the entire system or the USB controller. First, make sure that your OS is USB compliant, such as Windows 98 or 2000. Next, make sure that the number of devices does not exceed 127 and that no single cable length exceeds 5 meters. The USB system is also limited to five tiers or five hubs in a single chain. Check the cable length and cable connections, especially from the root hub to the first external hubs. A loose connection will prevent all devices on the external hub from functioning.

If the problem isn't in the USB physical setup, turn your attention to the USB controller. Make sure that a proper driver has been loaded for it and that it does not have an IRQ or I/O conflict with another device. You should also check the BIOS for USB support, to determine if you can use USB in this system.

Complementary Metal Oxide Semiconductor

Problems stemming from the CMOS include lost or incorrect settings. Lost settings occur when the CMOS battery begins to lose power. You will generally be informed of this problem by a 1** error message at startup or by a prompt to enter the correct time and date. When this is the case, replace the battery.

Incorrect CMOS settings can have many incarnations because there are CMOS settings for a great variety of system elements, including hard drives, floppy drives, the boot sequence, keyboard status, and parallel port settings. The incorrect setting will be manifested as an error relating to that particular device or function, so it can be difficult to pinpoint the CMOS as the source of the problem. However, when you need to change or update the CMOS, enter the CMOS settings at startup, make the appropriate change(s), save the new setting(s), and restart the computer.

Power Supplies and Fans

Power supplies can experience total or partial failures, resulting in inconsistent or displaced symptoms. However, you can identify a few "common" symptoms of power supply failure to pinpoint the problem; those symptoms are discussed here. When the power supply fails, it must be replaced. Never try to open or repair a power supply, because it can hold enough charge to seriously injure you.

on the
Job

Like monitors, power supplies can cause serious personal injury. Never open the case of a power supply!

Nothing Happens When the Computer Is Turned On

There are a few things that can cause lack of any activity at system startup, such as a bad processor or memory, but the most likely suspect is the power supply. When the power supply stops working, so does the computer's fan, which is typically the first thing you hear when you turn the computer on. Check to make sure that the power supply is properly connected to an electrical outlet. In addition, check the power selector (on the back of the computer between the power cord connection and the on/off switch) to ensure that it has the right setting for your geographic region (North American [115] or European [230] voltage).

You should also check to ensure the P8, P9, and other power cables are properly attached to necessary devices, including the computer's power button. If the power supply doesn't work, replace it.

The Computer Turns On But There's No Fan

If your computer turns on but you don't hear the sound of the computer's fan, save your work and turn the computer off immediately. The power supply's built-in fan draws air into the computer to keep the components from overheating. If the fan isn't working, you can cause serious damage by running the computer.

Once the computer is off, you should try cleaning the fan itself, using the procedures described in Chapter 4. Because the fan draws air, it can also draw dust, lint, or hair that can cause the fan to stop rotating. If cleaning doesn't resolve the problem, you must replace the entire power supply.

exam
Watch

If the power supply's fan stops working, you must replace the entire power supply, not just the fan.

The Computer Behaves Sporadically or Reboots Itself

Sporadic behavior or self-booting is typical behavior from a computer with a bad power supply. If the power supply is providing power to only some devices, the computer will behave irregularly; some devices will seem to work, while others will work only part of the time or not at all. Check to make sure that the P8, P9, and all other power connectors are properly attached.

If the power supply's fan is broken, the computer's components will also behave strangely. Overheated components might work sometimes but not others, and very commonly, an overheated computer will simply shut itself off or spontaneously reboot. Try cleaning the power supply fan. If this doesn't solve the problem, replace the power supply.

Slot Covers

Believe it or not, the removable slot covers at the back of the computer are not there solely to tidy up the appearance of the computer. They serve to keep dust and other foreign objects out of the computer. If you leave the slot covers off, you run the risk of allowing dust to settle on the internal components, especially the empty expansion slots (which are notoriously difficult to clean). Removal of the slot covers can also cause the computer to overheat. The computer is designed so that the devices expected to generate the most heat are in the fan's "line of fire." If the slot covers are left off, the air's path through the computer could be changed or impeded, resulting in improper cooling of the components inside.

The Fan Is Noisy

There are more cooling fans inside a computer than the one on the power supply. Today's computers have one (slot) or two (SEC) cooling fans on the CPU. There can also be one or more strategically placed cooling fans inside the case.

When a fan begins to wear out, it makes a whining or grinding noise. When this happens, replace the fan, unless it is inside the power supply. In that instance, replace the entire power supply. Opening the power supply is dangerous and time spent on such a repair is more valuable than the replacement cost of a power supply.

Hard Drive Address Translation

Address translation involves translating the actual addresses on a hard drive into addresses that the BIOS can use. Address translation typically occurs on older systems that cannot access over 528MB of hard drive space. One type of address translation is called *logical block addressing (LBA)*. Here's how it works: In older hard drives, each sector is identified by its *cylinder, head, and sector (CHS)* address (a sort of 3-D grid), and there is no support for addresses over 528MB. Using LBA, each sector is identified by a linear numerical value from 0 to 8.4GB (or the hard drive's total capacity, whichever is lower). When the BIOS asks for a CHS address, it is translated into the actual hard drive sector's number.

To use drive translation, both the BIOS and the hard drive must support its use. BIOS chips that support translation are called *enhanced*. Next, the proper translation mode must be selected in the BIOS options. *Normal* mode is the nontranslation mode. *LBA mode* and *large mode* (also called *enhanced mode*) both provide address translation, but they use different addressing methods. LBA mode is typically faster, but large mode has the advantage of being supported by all EIDE hard drives.

You should never enable or disable address translation on a drive that already contains data, because the data could be lost. If you cannot enable translation, check to see if your BIOS supports this feature. If you aren't using an *enhanced BIOS*, you will not be able to use translation. Furthermore, you might not have these options if your BIOS is fairly new. New BIOS chips are able to communicate with hard drives of nearly any capacity and do not need large or LBA mode to do so.

Before you continue in the chapter, test your knowledge of basic symptoms by answering the following Scenario & Solution questions.

SCENARIO & SOLUTION

How do I replace a bad integrated parallel port?	If the parallel port is integrated with the motherboard, you must replace the motherboard.
The computer continually asks me for the time at startup. What should I do?	Replace the CMOS battery.
What should I do with a computer that keeps rebooting itself?	Replace the power supply.
What should I do when the mouse pointer doesn't move smoothly on the screen?	Clean the mouse.

Troubleshooting Tools

In order to be completely prepared for any on-site computer problem, you would have to equip yourself with every type of cable, connector, battery, or driver that any component might need. Since you can't do this, you should stick to the basic troubleshooting tools, utilities, and devices described here.

Toolkits

Most computer toolkits include an array of Phillips, flathead, and Torx screwdrivers of varying sizes. You should keep the most popular sizes of each. It might also be helpful to include an extractor, also called a *parts grabber.* These are useful for retrieving dropped objects, such as jumpers or screws, from inside the computer. Your toolkit should also include a flashlight for peering into dark places and a small container for holding extra screws and jumpers (a film case should work).

Multimeters

Some toolkits come with a multimeter. If not, you should get one separately. *Multimeters* are used to measure the resistance, voltage, and/or current within computer components. They are most commonly used to determine connectivity between two components. For example, if a circuit or cable is measured as having infinite resistance, it means that there is a break somewhere in the line. A multimeter can also be used to ensure that the power supply is generating the appropriate voltage or that a motherboard component is receiving the proper current.

Software Tools

One of the most useful tools you can bring with you to a customer's site is a startup (boot) disk. A boot disk will allow you start the computer in a state of minimal devices and files, so that you can locate an offending device or file before it is loaded and causes the computer to halt or crash. (See Chapter 9 for details on creating a startup disk.) Other software tools that you should have include antivirus software, diagnostic utilities, and data recovery utilities.

FROM THE CLASSROOM

Tools You Can Do Without

You might come across some tools on the market or included in a toolkit that you really should avoid. To begin with, you should never use a magnetized screwdriver when repairing a computer. Remember, lots of computer components rely on magnetic storage. If you use a magnetized screwdriver around the hard drive, for example, you could inadvertently wipe it clean of its data. Many technicians use magnetized screwdrivers to retrieve small parts that get dropped inside the computer. Instead, you should use what is commonly (and not very poetically) referred to as a *parts grabber*. This is a pen-sized tool with a plunger at one end. When you press the plunger, small, hooked prongs are extended at the other end.

If you absolutely have to magnetize your screwdriver, rub it against the computer's internal speaker. The screwdriver will be magnetized for only a short time, thus reducing the risk of accidentally erasing magnetically stored data.

Another tool to avoid is the two-pronged IC extractor, also known as a *chip mangler*. These are shaped like tweezers and are designed for pulling chips off the motherboard. However, with the force of your hand localized to only two points on the chip, it is easy to cause damage to the chip. For this reason, you should also avoid using pliers to extract chips. The only chip pullers you should use have one prong that fits between *each* row of the chip's pins, evenly distributing the pressure applied by your hand.

Another chip-mangling device is the *chip inserter*. This device is placed on top of a chip on the motherboard. By pressing the plunger at the other end of the device, you can insert the chip into its sockets. However, because you can't feel how much pressure you are exerting or whether the chip is lined up properly, it is easy to break or bend the pins. Instead, you should use your fingers or thumb to gently push the chip into its socket.

—Amy Thomson, A+ Certified Technician,
MOUS Master

CERTIFICATION OBJECTIVE 3.02

Basic Troubleshooting Procedures

As you know, to resolve any computer problem, you must first determine its source. However, in many cases, the computer can behave in a way that does not easily lead you to the device that is causing the trouble. In these cases, you need to use a combination of the computer's symptoms and its history as well as information from the computer's user.

All computer problems can be resolved. Sometimes this resolution includes adjusting configurations or replacing a component. It can even include replacing the computer altogether. However, before you can make this determination, you must be able to locate the source of the problem. The following discussions describe where to look for the information you need before you can begin troubleshooting.

Information Gathering

In many cases, as a technician, you will be expected to troubleshoot computers that you do not regularly use. That is, you might be called into a client's office or have an unfamiliar computer brought to you for repairs. The first step is to gather as much information as you can about the computer itself and its peripherals, applications, and history.

Customer Environment

If you are performing on-site troubleshooting, notice your surroundings. They might give you a clue as to a problem's cause, and if you notice potential trouble, you can help to prevent future problems.

Take notice of the room's environment, such as the temperature. Most computer components do not work well in the presence of heat. Furthermore, very high or low humidity can cause condensation or electrostatic discharge, respectively, both of which can lead to problems. A safe humidity level is between 50 and 80 percent. You should also be aware of nearby devices that could cause EMI.

Look at the way components are plugged into wall outlets and determine if the outlets are overburdened by too many plugs. Take note of the way cables are arranged. For example, do people have to step over the cable to the printer? Such a setup can lead to a loose cable connection.

Finally, you should notice the way that people use the computer. Although you are not on-site to tutor people in application or shortcut use, it might help you to notice rough handling of the equipment. If the user "bangs" on the keys, you will have a good clue as to the cause of a faulty keyboard. In addition, some users tend to triple- and quadruple-click icons on the screen in an attempt to hurry things along. This practice can lead to computer lock-ups.

Symptoms and Error Codes

One of the best guides in determining the cause of a problem is the user who was working on the computer when the failure occurred. After taking note of the environment, your first question to the user should be, "What happened?" This question will prompt the user to tell you about the problem—for example, "The printer won't work." Ask about other problems: Do other devices work? The answers you receive can tell you a great deal. If no other devices work, you know you are dealing with a more serious device-independent problem. Ask about the device's history. Did this device ever work? If the user tells you that the device was just installed, you have a very different task ahead of you than if the user tells you it worked fine all day until now.

If the user complains of an error code, ask for as much detail about the error as possible. If the user can't remember, try to recreate the problem. Again, ask if this is a new or old error message, and ask if the computer's behavior changed after the error. For example, the computer might issue a warning that simply informs the user of some condition. These types of messages might not affect performance. If the error code points to a device, ask the device-related questions we've already mentioned. For example, the error message might have stated that the floppy disk couldn't be accessed.

Problem Situation

When you have determined what the problem is (its symptoms, not its cause), you need to get some basic history from the user. Ask if the problem occurred at random or in response to a user action. An error that occurs "out of the blue" is a different matter from an error that occurs every time the user tries to use the scanner, for example.

Try to replicate the problem. That is, if the user says the printer won't work, ask her to send another print job. Watch closely as the user performs the task. Take note of any error messages or unusual computer activity that she might not have noticed. Your observation will also give you a chance to see the process from beginning to end. For example, if the user is trying to print an image, watching her perform the task might allow you to see a problem such as incorrect printer selection or the absence of an entry in the Number of Pages field. You should also note the way the user performs the task, to determine if it is being performed properly. For example, a CD-ROM drive error could be the result of the user trying to copy a file onto a nonwritable CD.

When the user tries to replicate the problem, the original problem might not recur. In this case, it is likely that there was another process preventing the action from taking place. For instance, if the user tries to access a newly inserted CD before the CD-ROM drive has had a chance to spin up, an error will occur. The next time the user tries to access the CD, there will be no problem.

on the
() o b

Be very aware of your personal interactions with the user at this point. These problems are a common occurrence, and a user's initial reaction is often embarrassment.

You should also find out about any recent changes to the computer or the surroundings. For example, ask if a new component or application has recently been installed. If one has, ask if the feature or device has worked at all since the new installation. The answer to this question could lead you to important information about application or device conflicts. For example, if the user tells you that the sound hasn't worked ever since a particular game was loaded, you can suspect that the two events—the loading of the new game and the sound failure—are related.

Pinpointing the Hardware or Software

The information that you gather from the user might be enough to pinpoint the cause of the problem. If it's not, you need to narrow down the search even further by determining if the problem is hardware or software related. In the remaining sections, a hardware problem is considered to include the device as well as its resources, configuration files, and device drivers. Software problems include applications, OSs, and utilities.

One of the quickest ways to determine if the hardware or the software is at fault is to use the Windows Device Manager. Any conflicting or "unknown" devices will be indicated here. If the Device Manager offers no information about problems, it doesn't mean that there isn't a hardware problem; it means only that Windows hasn't recognized one.

Most hardware devices can be used by a number of applications, and vice versa. Therefore, you can narrow the search by trying to access more than one type of device from the suspect application or using more than one application to access the suspect device. Suppose, for example, that a user was unable to scan an image into a particular word processor. Use a different application to access the scanner. If it works, you can conclude that the scanner is physically sound and turn your attention to the configuration or reinstallation of the original application. If, however, the scanner does not work in another program, use the original program to access another device, such as the printer.

Continue combining applications with hardware devices to try to rule out one or the other. Keep in mind that this method will not always lead you to a definitive conclusion. For example, suppose a printer can't be accessed by any application. Although it would appear that the printer is at fault, it might be that it is simply not set as the default printer. This is a software, not a hardware, problem.

Troubleshooting, Isolation, and Problem Determination Procedures

Once you have followed these procedures and determined the device or subsystem at fault, you should restart the device or computer. In many cases, restarting the computer releases resources that a device or application needs to use but that are being tied up by another device or application. Restarting the computer also forces the computer to reestablish the presence of existing devices and clear information out of its memory.

Hardware Problems

If restarting the computer doesn't solve the problem, determine if this symptom is familiar to you. For example, if you know the mouse connection often comes loose from a particular computer, you should look there first when the mouse stops working. If the problem is unfamiliar to you, use the information in this section to help you further narrow your search.

Always check the connection of a device to the computer, and make sure that the device is properly configured to use system resources and a driver. If the answer is not apparent, you need to focus your search on the components of the failed system or subsystem. For example, if there is no computer display, there is no need to check the components of the sound system.

When examining a subsystem, always start with the parts that are easiest to access or to see. In the example of a nonfunctioning display, check the monitor before you take the computer apart to check the adapter card. For any subsystem, start with the most accessible part and work your way into the computer. A good knowledge of the system's components, as described in Chapters 1 and 2, will help you determine which devices belong to which subsystems. It is especially important to note whether the device is local or accessed through the network. A problem using a printer, for example, could actually be caused by the computer's inability to make a network connection.

If everything in the current system *appears* to be okay (in other words, everything is powered on and properly attached and there are no resource conflicts), suspect the devices themselves. To identify or rule out a device as the cause of the problem, swap it with another. Take a spare component (one that you know functions correctly) and use it in place of the suspect component. If the new component works, you have discovered the problem.

If the new component doesn't work, there must be a problem elsewhere. In this case, don't assume the original component works; it, plus another component, could have failed at the same time. You can install the original component in another system to determine its functionality. For example, assume that a video system has a bad adapter card *and* a bad monitor. You swap the monitor with another and get no response, so you assume that the monitor is not the cause of the problem and reattach it. When you get the adapter working, there is still no video, because you are using the original bad monitor. Always swap one component at a time. To take another example, suppose that a computer can't use a particular scanner. You switch ports, swap the cable, and swap the scanner, all at the same time. If the computer is then able to scan correctly, you will not be able to determine whether it was the port, the cable, or the scanner that caused the problem in the first place.

Again, working your way into the computer, swap out each component with a working one. This includes the problematic device itself and any cables attached to it. If the device is external, try plugging it into another port or try attaching a different device to the suspect port. If the device is internal, switch it to another expansion slot.

If you have tested the attachment and configuration of each device and still have not solved the problem, look at the underlying hardware within the computer itself. That is, test components that are responsible for the computer's performance as a whole, including the BIOS, the CMOS battery, the processor, RAM, and the system board.

exam
ⓦatch

Many things can go wrong with computer components, and the A+ exam will test your ability to determine the causes of these problems. The best thing you can do to prepare yourself is to become very familiar with the functions of the computer's components as well as which components make up different subsystems. Next, when you're diagnosing a problem, remember that you should always start with the easiest, most accessible components and work your way into the computer. Finally, remember to always swap suspect components with known working ones.

Software Problems

If you have determined that the problem is software related, and rebooting the computer didn't solve the problem, you should turn your attention to the configuration of the application. Most applications or utilities include a Preferences, Tools, or Options feature, through which you can configure its operation and the devices it can access.

You can also try uninstalling the application, then reloading it. Some application installations contain errors that affect only one or a small number of its functions. Use the Uninstall utility that came with the application, or use the Windows Uninstall utility.

Check to make sure that the computer meets the application's minimum requirements. It is possible that the computer simply will not support the application. Check the application manufacturer's Web site for patches and updates. Perhaps this user is experiencing a problem caused by a flaw in the application itself. Most manufacturers release patches that can remedy discovered problems.

The information in this section has been compiled into Exercise 3-2. Follow these steps when troubleshooting a hardware problem.

EXERCISE 3-2

Troubleshooting a Hardware Problem

1. Gather as much information from the customer as you can, including symptoms, error messages, computer history, and action at the time of the failure.

2. Try to reproduce the problem, taking note of any error messages or unusual system activity.

3. Determine whether the problem is hardware or software related. Do this by watching error messages, using the Device Manager, and accessing the hardware using a variety of applications. The remainder of this exercise assumes that the problem is hardware related.

4. Start with the most accessible component in the affected subsystem, making sure that it has power and is properly connected.

5. Check the resources of the device and ensure that a device driver has been loaded for it.

6. Test the device by using it in another computer or by using a known working device in its place.

7. Continue testing and checking all components in the subsystem, working your way into the computer.

8. Finally, test the computer's most basic components, such as the BIOS, system board, memory, and processor.

Now that you are familiar with basic troubleshooting techniques, try to answer the following Scenario & Solution questions.

SCENARIO & SOLUTION

How can I determine if a monitor has gone bad?	Try it in a working system.
What should I do if an application has been incorrectly installed?	Uninstall, then reinstall it.
My sound system is bad. Where should I start to look for the problem?	Start with the speakers, and work your way into the computer.

CERTIFICATION SUMMARY

As a computer technician, you will be required to locate and resolve the source of computer problems. If you have a good knowledge of the functions of the computer's components, you will be able to more quickly troubleshoot problems that occur. However, there are other telltale signs of failed components. For example, you can use POST error codes to determine the cause of a problem. Although the troubleshooting procedures differ from component to component and even for different problems within the same component, a majority of the procedures involve cleaning the component, ensuring that it is properly attached to the computer, and finally, replacing the component.

Unfortunately, not all computer problems are easy to diagnose, and it could take some time for you to find the offending device or application. When trying to determine a problem's source, gather as much information about the problem as you can, and try to reproduce the problem. Next, determine if this is a hardware or a software problem. If it is a software problem, check the application's configuration or try uninstalling, then reinstalling it. If the problem is hardware related, identify the components that make up the failing subsystem. Starting with the most accessible component, check for power and proper attachment to the computer. Check the device's configuration and presence of a device driver. Finally, swap suspected bad components with known good ones.

Remember that every problem has a resolution, whether it is simply reattaching a loose cable, changing an application's settings, or replacing entire subsystems. As a computer technician, you have the responsibility for determining which course of action is the most appropriate for each computer problem you face.

TWO-MINUTE DRILL

Here are some of the key points from each certification objective in Chapter 3.

Symptoms and Problems

❑ POST error codes, such as 1**, 2**, and 3**, can indicate system board, memory, or keyboard failures, respectively.

❑ Most system board, processor, and memory errors are fatal, meaning that the computer cannot properly boot up.

❑ The most common mouse problem is irregular movement, which is resolved by cleaning the internal rollers in the mouse.

❑ A hard drive that begins to develop corrupted data should be replaced before all the information stored on it is lost.

❑ When troubleshooting a video or audio problem, start with the most accessible component, and check to ensure that it is getting power and is properly connected to the computer.

❑ When resolving modem errors, make sure that the modem is properly attached and configured and that there is a connection to the phone jack and a good dial tone.

❑ Motherboard errors can be the most difficult to pinpoint and, due to the cost and effort involved in replacement, should be the last device you suspect when a subsystem or the entire computer fails.

❑ Never open the power supply or try to replace the fan; rather, replace the entire power supply when the fan stops working.

Basic Troubleshooting Procedures

❑ When faced with a computer problem, gather information from the customer, such as what the problem is, what happened before the problem occurred, and what, if anything, has changed recently in the computer.

❑ Determine whether the problem is hardware or software related by accessing suspect devices with more than one type of application, and vice versa.

❑ To resolve software problems, check the software's configuration and its minimum requirements, then try to reinstall it.

❑ To resolve a hardware problem, first identify and test the components that belong to the affected subsystem.

❑ Always check to ensure that a failed device has power and is connected to the computer.

❑ Verify a suspect component's status by trying to use it in another computer or by replacing it with a known working component.

❑ Check the configuration of a failed device to ensure that it does not have a resource conflict with another device.

SELF TEST

The following questions will help you measure your understanding of the material presented in this chapter. Read all of the choices carefully because there might be more than one correct answer. Choose all correct answers for each question.

Symptoms and Problems

1. Which component is typically associated with a 3** BIOS error code?

    A. The motherboard

    B. The keyboard

    C. The processor

    D. RAM

2. Which of the following symptoms is not a typical symptom of a RAM error?

    A. The POST cannot be conducted.

    B. When you turn the computer on, nothing happens.

    C. The system reports that there is no operating system.

    D. The BIOS reports a 2** error.

3. A user complains that the mouse pointer does not move smoothly across the screen. Which of the following is most likely to remedy the problem?

    A. Reinstalling the mouse driver

    B. Ensuring that the mouse cable is connected securely to the computer

    C. Ensuring that there are no IRQ conflicts between the mouse and another device

    D. Cleaning the mouse

4. Which of the following should you do first when you receive the error shown in Figure 3-2?

    A. Make sure that there is a floppy disk in the drive.

    B. Ensure that the floppy ribbon cable is attached properly.

    C. Make sure that the floppy drive is properly configured in the BIOS settings.

    D. Clean the floppy disk.

A typical error
message.

5. You have just finished building a computer. You notice that when you turn the computer on, the floppy drive light comes on and won't go off. What should you do?

A. Insert a different disk into the drive.

B. Reverse the ribbon cable on the drive.

C. Swap the drive with another one.

D. Nothing.

6. When you tried to access a hard drive, you received an "Invalid Drive" error. Which of the following can you rule out as the cause of this error?

A. The hard drive

B. The BIOS

C. The ribbon cable

D. Corrupted files

7. When the computer is started, it displays a "Missing Operating System" error. Which command can you use to make the drive bootable?

A. BOOT

B. BOOT OS

C. SYS

D. SYSTEM

8. A user complains that when he plays a CD in the computer, the music is accompanied by a lot of static. All the following are possible causes of this problem *except*:

A. The speaker cables

B. The speaker volume

C. The CD

D. The monitor

9. Which of the following might be responsible for your modem producing random "garbage" or meaningless characters?

    A. A missing device driver

    B. An improper resource (IRQ or I/O) configuration

    C. A failed or improper modem handshake

    D. Static on the phone line

10. A customer complains that the computer spontaneously reboots and sometimes will not start at all. Furthermore, even when the computer does start, there's not as much noise as usual. Which device is most likely causing these problems?

    A. The power supply

    B. The system board

    C. The processor

    D. The RAM

Basic Troubleshooting Procedures

11. You have just arrived at a customer's office to perform on-site troubleshooting for a faulty sound system. Which of these environmental indicators could be the cause of the problem?

    A. The room is humid.

    B. The room is cool.

    C. Only 3 out of 15 people are using the network.

    D. The lights are off in the room.

12. You are trying to resolve a video problem. The screen is blank, and you are fairly certain that the monitor itself is bad. Which of the following should you do first to verify your suspicion?

    A. Make sure that the monitor's driver is properly installed.

    B. Ensure that the video adapter is properly configured.

    C. Ensure that the monitor does not have an IRQ conflict with another device.

    D. Swap the monitor with a known working one.

13. A document was created in a word processing application but will not print properly. After ensuring that the printer has power and a proper connection to the computer, what is the next thing you should do?

    A. Use the same application to access the scanner.

    B. Reload the printer's device driver.

    C. Try to print from another application.

    D. Reinstall the word processor.

14. In troubleshooting a display problem, you swapped the monitor with a known good one, but this did not resolve the problem. What should you do next?

    A. Reattach the original monitor to the computer.

    B. Make sure that the cable from the monitor to the video card is connected tightly.

    C. Ensure that the adapter card is properly seated in the expansion slot.

    D. Swap the adapter card.

15. A user has complained that she can't print from a particular word processor application or a certain graphics program. However, the spreadsheet program prints fine. Assume that this is a network printer. Which of the following is the likely cause of this problem?

    A. The configuration of the word processor and graphics programs

    B. The printer's device driver

    C. The printer itself

    D. An improper network configuration

16. When your computer's sound system was first installed, it worked fine. Now it produces no sounds at all. Which of the following should you check first?

    A. The sound card's configuration

    B. The speaker's configuration

    C. The sound card itself

    D. The speaker itself

17. Assume that a computer has a functioning display system. Which of the following represents the proper order of steps you should perform to most efficiently determine the source of a hardware problem on the computer?

    A. Try to reproduce the error, gather information about the problem, swap the device with a known good one, and check the device's configuration.

    B. Gather information about the problem, try to reproduce the error, swap the device with a known good one, and check the device's configuration

    C. Gather information about the problem, try to reproduce the error, check the device's configuration, and swap the device with a known good one.

    D. Check the device's configuration, gather information about the problem, try to reproduce the error, and swap the device with a known good one.

18. When a user tries to save to the hard drive in a particular application, the computer locks up. Otherwise, the application works normally. Assume that the computer has only one hard drive installed. Which of the following can you rule out as the cause of the problem?

   A. The hard drive's configuration

   B. An improper installation of the application

   C. An improperly written application

   D. Insufficient system requirements

19. You played a game on the computer about an hour ago and closed the game when you were finished. In the meantime, you opened a word processor, sent a print job to the printer, and then closed the application. When you tried to restart the game, nothing happened. Which of the following should you do first?

   A. Obtain a manufacturer's patch for the game

   B. Troubleshoot the printer

   C. Restart the computer

   D. Reinstall the game

20. A customer has complained of an error message regarding the scanner but cannot remember the wording of the error message that appeared. Which of the following should you do next?

   A. Restart the computer.

   B. Have the user try to replicate the problem.

   C. Check the scanner's configuration.

   D. Swap the scanner with a known good one.

LAB QUESTION

A customer has complained about a problem in playing a music file. He tells you that the computer seemed to run the file, but no sound was produced, even though it worked properly yesterday. Although you don't know it at first, the problem is that the sound card's expansion slot has failed because of a broken circuit. Describe the steps you will perform, in the proper order, to determine that this is the cause of the problem. Also discuss how you will resolve the problem.

SELF-TEST ANSWERS

Symptoms and Problems

1. ☑ **B.** The keyboard is typically associated with a 3** BIOS error code. When the computer is started, the BIOS performs a POST, which checks for the presence and function of certain components. If a keyboard error, such as a missing cable or stuck key, is detected, the BIOS typically reports a 3-series error code.

   ☒ **A**, motherboard, and **C**, processor, are incorrect because these errors, if detected by the BIOS, are typically indicated by a 1** error code. **D**, RAM, is incorrect because memory errors are typically associated with a 2** error code.

2. ☑ **C.** The system reports that there is no operating system. The OS resides on the hard drive and, following the POST, the BIOS looks for the OS and gives it control. If the computer reports a missing OS, it means that one doesn't exist on the hard drive, it cannot be read from the hard drive, or that the computer cannot communicate with the hard drive. It is very unlikely that you would receive this particular message if there were a memory error.

   ☒ **A**, **B**, and **D** are incorrect because these are all typical symptoms of bad memory. If the memory has totally failed, the BIOS cannot conduct or complete the POST and might not be able to even initiate the processor. This might make it appear that the computer does absolutely nothing when it is turned on. Noncritical memory errors can be indicated by a 2** error code.

3. ☑ **D.** Cleaning the mouse is most likely to remedy the problem of a mouse pointer that doesn't move smoothly on the screen. As a mouse is moved, its ball can pick up dust and other particles and deposit them on the internal rollers. Buildup on the rollers causes them to move erratically, resulting in a mouse pointer that "jerks" around on the screen. Remove the mouse's retaining ring and ball, then remove the buildup from the rollers.

   ☒ **A**, reinstalling the mouse driver, is incorrect because if the mouse does not have a proper driver, it won't work at all. Driver problems for any device will cause that device to stop functioning altogether or to work sporadically. In this case, the mouse is not working sporadically (sometimes working and sometimes not), it is just not moving smoothly. **B**, ensuring that the mouse cable is connected securely to the computer, is also incorrect. If the mouse connector is not plugged into the computer, there will be no response from the mouse at all. If the mouse connector is loose, the operation of the mouse could be sporadic. That is, the mouse might work at some times and not at others. However, it would be extremely rare for a loose mouse connection to continuously make and break contact with the computer fast enough for it to appear that the mouse was working but not moving smoothly. **C**, ensuring that there are no IRQ conflicts between the mouse and another device, is also incorrect. If the mouse has a resource conflict with another device, the mouse either will not work at all or will work only when the other device is not being used. Again, the problem in this case is not a mouse that works sporadically but one that does not move smoothly.

4.   ☑   **A.** Make sure that there is a floppy disk in the drive. This error indicates that the drive did not detect a disk. The most common reason for receiving this error is simply that a disk hasn't been inserted or was not inserted all the way.

☒   **B**, ensure that the floppy ribbon cable is attached properly, and **C**, make sure that the floppy drive is properly configured in the BIOS settings, are both incorrect. You should suspect a ribbon cable or BIOS setting problem only if the computer cannot communicate with the floppy drive. However, the error shown here is used to indicate that the drive searched for but did not detect a disk. If the drive can look for and report the absence of a floppy disk, the drive itself must be able to communicate with the computer. **D**, clean the floppy disk, is incorrect because although this message is used to indicate a problem accessing the disk, you will not solve the problem by trying to clean the disk. The disk's surface contains very small magnetic charges that would most likely be removed as soon as you touched it. Never touch the surface of a disk. It is floppy *drives*, not disks, that can be cleaned.

5.   ☑   **B.** You should reverse the ribbon cable on the drive. A floppy drive light that comes on and won't go out is a sure indicator of a ribbon cable that has been reversed in the drive's port. Make sure that you align the cable's red stripe with pin 1 on the floppy drive's port.

☒   **A**, insert a different disk into the drive, is incorrect because this error will occur at startup, with or without a disk present in the drive. It is caused by a reversed ribbon cable and is totally unrelated to the presence or integrity of a floppy disk. **C**, swap the drive with another one, is incorrect because, although the drive won't work properly in this condition, there is nothing wrong with the drive itself. Simply reverse the ribbon cable, and the drive will work normally. **D** is incorrect because it suggests that you should do nothing in this case. However, when the stated condition occurs, the ribbon is on backward, and the drive will not work. This is a condition that must be remedied in order to use the floppy drive.

6.   ☑   **D.** You can rule out corrupted files as the cause of an "Invalid Drive" error. When you access the hard drive, the computer first checks for its existence, then tries to access information on it. If the computer cannot find or communicate with it, you will receive the error message. The computer has not even attempted to read the information on the drive yet, so the integrity of the data cannot be the cause of the problem. In this case, you must focus on reasons that the drive itself is not being recognized.

☒ **A,** the hard drive, **B,** the BIOS, and **C,** the ribbon cable, are all incorrect because these are all possible causes of the error. Again, the error message indicates that the computer doesn't know about the existence of the drive or can't communicate with it. Reasons for this can include a bad drive; a faulty, loose, or disoriented cable; or an improper hard drive configuration in the system BIOS.

7. ☑ **C.** You can use the SYS command to make a drive bootable. The drive's OS could be considered "missing" because it doesn't exist or because one or more critical system files are missing or corrupted. Using the SYS command, you can get the computer to a point at which you can at least read the files on the drive and determine the cause of the problem or move important data to another place.
☒ **A,** BOOT, **B,** BOOT OS, and **D,** SYSTEM, are all incorrect because they are not real DOS commands.

8. ☑ **B.** The speaker volume is not a possible cause of the static problem. If the user can hear *anything* coming from the speakers, including static, the volume must be at a sufficient level.
☒ **A,** the speaker cables, is incorrect because if they are old, cracked, too long, or not shielded, they might be susceptible to EMI, a major cause of static. **C,** the CD, is incorrect because this too could be the cause of the static. If the CD is dusty, dirty, or contains scratches or flaws, stray or incorrect data can be read from it, sounding like static. **D,** the monitor, is also incorrect. Speakers that are exposed to EMI produce will static. The monitor is one of the greatest sources of EMI in the entire computer system. For this reason, you should keep the speakers as far away from the monitor as possible.

9. ☑ **D.** Static on the phone line can be responsible for causing the modem to produce random garbage characters. The computer tries to interpret the static as real data. The meaningless characters you see are the modem's interpretation of this "data."
☒ **A,** a missing device driver, and **B,** an improper resource configuration, are both incorrect. Both of these cause the modem to not work at all (or to work sporadically, in the case of a resource conflict). **C,** a failed or improper modem handshake, is also incorrect. During the modem handshake, the two modems determine the rules of communication. If this part fails or is misinterpreted by one modem, all the data transmitted, not just a random character here and there, will appear meaningless.

10. ☑ **A.** The power supply is most likely causing the problems. When a power supply begins to fail, it often manifests itself in a number of different, sporadic symptoms. If the power supply's fan stops working, the computer will overheat and spontaneously reboot itself. If the components are still hot when the system is restarted, the computer will likely do nothing. The computer will also do nothing on startup if the power supply is not providing adequate voltage to the

motherboard. Finally, the computer normally issues many noises at startup: counting RAM, spinning up and accessing the hard drive, and the like. However, the most prominent sound is the power supply's fan. If this noise is absent, it is likely that the fan is not working and that the power supply must be replaced.

☒ **B**, the system board, **C**, the processor, and **D**, the RAM, are all incorrect. Although failure of each of these components can result in a nonresponsive computer at startup, they cannot cause all the problems mentioned. For example, although the computer makes noise as it counts the RAM, this is usually only a 2- or 3-second operation, and a RAM failure typically will not cause the computer to reboot. Although an overheated processor can cause the computer to spontaneously reboot, it does not make the noise that you hear when you start the computer.

Basic Troubleshooting Procedures

11. ☑ **A.** The room is humid. High humidity can cause condensation to form on computer components, which can lead to their failure. The humidity should be kept below 80 percent.

☒ **B**, the room is cool, is incorrect because it is warm, not cool, air that can lead to component failure. Note that although most components will fail in extreme cold, it is highly unlikely that an office would be kept at such a temperature. In any case, in this situation, the room is cool, not cold. **C**, only 3 out of 15 people are using the network, is also incorrect. Sound systems do not run from the network, so they would be unaffected by the amount of network traffic. Furthermore, 3 out of 15 people accessing the network is a relatively low number, and in this case, you should expect faster, not slower, access to network devices. **D**, the lights are off, is incorrect. In most cases, the status of the room lights will have no effect on the function of a sound system. In some rare cases, however, they could cause EMI, which can alter the computer's behavior. If anything, there should be fewer problems with the computer when the lights are off than when they are on.

12. ☑ **D.** The first thing you should do is swap the monitor with a known working one. If the second monitor works, you will have pinpointed the original monitor as the source of the problem. If the second monitor doesn't work, you can be fairly certain that the monitor isn't causing the problem. (You should test the original nonworking monitor with another machine to make sure.)

☒ **A**, make sure that the monitor's driver is properly installed, is incorrect. Although monitors do require drivers, if the screen is blank, you will not be able to see whether the driver exists or not. **B**, ensure that the video adapter is properly configured, is also incorrect for this reason. Furthermore, although the video adapter can be the cause of a video problem, you have already narrowed down the monitor as the cause. Adjusting the adapter will have no effect on the function of the monitor itself. **C,** ensure that the monitor does not have an IRQ conflict with another device, is incorrect because monitors do not have IRQ addresses. Even if they did, you cannot see the OS in this case, so you cannot see the monitor's configuration.

13. ☑ **C.** In this case, the first thing you should do is try to print from another application. This is the fastest way to determine if the printer or the application is at fault. If the second application can send a print job, the original application might need to be reconfigured or reinstalled.

   ☒ **A,** use the same application to access the scanner, is incorrect. Although you might end up performing this procedure, it shouldn't be the first thing you do. Suppose you did, and the application was able to access the scanner; this would tell you nothing about the printer. You would still be left not knowing whether the printer itself or its configuration in the application was at fault. **B,** reload the printer's device driver, and **D,** reinstall the word processor, are also incorrect. These steps could eventually be required to resolve the problem, but remember, always start with the easiest and most basic troubleshooting procedures first. Suppose that the original application was at fault in this case. If you went ahead and uninstalled, then reloaded, the printer driver, you would have performed a time-consuming procedure for nothing. Alternatively, if the printer itself or its configuration were at fault, you would have reinstalled the application with no effect.

14. ☑ **B.** You should make sure the cable connection is tight. Remember, when diagnosing a hardware problem, start with the outermost components and work your way into the computer. After the monitor, the cable is the next component in the video system.

   ☒ **A,** reattach the original monitor to the computer, is incorrect because both the monitor and another component might be at fault. Use the monitor that you know is functioning until you can get the video system working, then reattach the original monitor. **C,** ensure that the adapter card is properly seated in the expansion slot, and **D,** swap the adapter card, are incorrect because they both involve opening the computer and are more time-consuming than a simple cable swap. Always rule out easily installed components before you take the computer apart.

15. ☑ **A.** The configuration of the word processor and graphics programs is the most likely cause of the problem. You should check that these programs are configured to print to the correct printer, using appropriate buffer sizes, resolutions, and any other print job-related application settings.

   ☒ **B,** the printer's device driver, **C,** the printer itself, and **D,** an improper network configuration, are all incorrect because these would all lead to the inability to print from any program. Recall, however, that in this case, the user can print from a spreadsheet program. This situation indicates that the printer is working and that the computer can access it.

16. ☑ **D.** You should check the speaker itself. Ensure that it is receiving power and that the volume is turned up to a sufficient level. In addition, make sure that the cables are properly attached and that the speaker is not near any EMI-causing devices. These should be the first steps, since the speaker is the easiest component in the sound system to access (and the most likely to fail).

☒ **A,** the sound card's configuration, is incorrect. Since the sound system worked at one time, you can assume that the sound card was properly configured. Although the configuration might have become corrupt and caused this problem, it is more time-consuming to reconfigure the sound card than it is to physically check the speaker for power, volume, and connectivity. **B,** the speaker's configuration, is incorrect. Speakers simply amplify signals from the sound card and do not need to communicate with other components in the computer. Therefore, the speakers do not need computer resources or drivers. **C,** the sound card itself, is incorrect because this is a more time-consuming procedure than testing the speakers. Because the sound card is internal, checking it requires you to shut down the computer and take it apart.

17. ☑ **C.** Gather information about the problem, try to reproduce the error, check the device's configuration, and swap the device with a known good one. Whenever you troubleshoot a hardware problem, first gather as much information as you can: What is the problem, were there any error messages, has anything changed within the computer? This should be the first step because the answers to these questions could tell you enough to pinpoint the problem's source. If they do not, try to reproduce the error. The device might work this time. This step might also give you a chance to note error messages or unusual system activity. Next, check the configuration of the device to ensure that it has the proper system resources and a valid device driver. If these steps don't resolve the problem, suspect the device itself, and try another in its place.

☒ **A, B,** and **D** are all incorrect because they list the troubleshooting steps in the wrong order. Although the steps can physically be performed in any order, it is not efficient to do so. For example, if an error points to a missing floppy disk, you will have wasted a lot of time by replacing the drive itself first.

18. ☑ **A.** You can rule out the hard drive's configuration as the cause of this problem. If the computer was configured incorrectly, the application would not work at all and the computer might not even boot properly. Therefore, you must turn your attention to the application itself as the cause of the problem.

☒   **B,** an improper installation of the application, is incorrect because this might be the cause of the problem. If the application was installed with missing, misplaced, or corrupt files, certain functions of the application (including its ability to save files) might be disrupted. If this is the case, uninstall, then reinstall the application. **C,** an improperly written application, is also incorrect. If the application contains flaws (bugs), it might not perform certain actions properly. If this is the case, it means that the problem is in the application's code. Check for manufacturer updates or patches to resolve the problem. **D,** insufficient system requirements, is also incorrect because this might be causing the problem. If the system's processor or memory capacity is insufficient to run the application, the computer might respond by being unable to fulfill a particular request, causing the computer to lock up.

19.   ☑   **C.** You should restart the computer. In some cases, applications can use computer resources, such as memory or processor time, and not release them, even when the application is closed. By restarting the computer, you will remove the application from memory and/or cause it to release any system resources.
☒   **A,** obtain a manufacturer's patch for the game, and **D,** reinstall the game, are incorrect because these procedures are typically used when an application contains corrupt or improper instructions. Since the game worked originally, this is not likely the case. Furthermore, it is typically more time-consuming to install a patch or reinstall an application than it is to reboot the system. **B,** troubleshoot the printer, is incorrect. The printer is also an unlikely suspect in this case. Again, although it is not impossible for the printer to be the cause of this problem, troubleshooting the printer is more time-consuming and less likely to resolve the problem than simply restarting the computer.

20.   ☑   **B.** You should have the user try to replicate the problem. This will allow you to take note of the error message when it is displayed. It will also allow you to ensure that the user is following the proper procedures, check for configuration settings, and note any unusual system activity. These might all quickly and effectively allow you to determine or narrow down the cause of the problem.
☒   **A,** restart the computer, is incorrect. Although you could end up restarting the computer later, this step by itself will not allow you to see the error message. **C,** check the scanner's configuration, and **D,** swap the scanner with a known good one, are both incorrect. Again, although you could end up performing these procedures at some point, they should not be the first things you do in this case. You will have wasted quite a bit of time if you reconfigure or replace the scanner when the error message clearly stated that the scanner was simply not turned on.

LAB ANSWER

1. On arrival at the customer's site, take note of potential problem-causing factors, such as the temperature and the humidity.

2. Ask the customer about the computer's history. For example, ask whether this has occurred before or if a new device or application has been installed.

3. Have the customer try to play the sound file again. Watch for irregular system activity, the presence of error messages, and other on-screen indicators, such as a visual volume control on the screen.

4. Check that the speakers are receiving power and that the volume is set at a sufficient level. (You might choose to do this before the previous step, since it is so easy and quick to check.)

5. Make sure that the speakers are securely connected to the sound card.

6. Try to play a different sound file to determine if the original sound file is corrupt. In this particular case, the second sound file should cause the same result as the first.

7. Try to play a sound file in a different application. Do not use the original sound file, because both the file and the original application file could be at fault. Again, considering the actual cause of the problem, the result should be the same. This indicates (but does not prove) that the original application and sound file are not at fault.

8. Restart the computer, then try to have the system produce sound again. This might resolve the problem if the sound card's configuration was improperly loaded the first time or if another application is using a resource the sound card or application needs.

9. At this point, you should have determined that this is a hardware, not a software, problem. Swap the speakers with known good ones.

10. Swap the speaker cables with known good ones.

11. Check the configuration of the sound card. Look for a resource conflict or a bad or missing driver. If you are using Windows 9x or 2000, you can use the Device Manager. Given the actual cause of this problem, you should see nothing to indicate a configuration error. However, you might want to remove the sound card's driver, then reinstall it, just to rule it out as the cause.

12. Turn the computer off, remove the case, and ensure that the sound card is properly seated in the expansion slot.

13. At this point, you can either try to install the card in another expansion slot or swap the sound card with a known working one. If you swap the card first, turn the computer back on, configure it, then try to play a sound file. If you try the card in another slot first, you will have located the source of the problem (the expansion slot).

14. To determine why the slot has failed, you can use a multimeter to test its ability to receive signals. In this case, you would find that the bad circuit offers infinite resistance, indicating a break in the circuit.

15. To resolve this problem, you can continue to use the original sound card in an alternate expansion slot. However, if you need all the other slots for other components, you will probably end up replacing one of the devices with an external one (to free up a slot) or replacing the entire motherboard.

4

Power Protection and Safety Procedures

Y ou should now be familiar with proper installation and configuration procedures for many computer devices. You should also be familiar with determining when components need to replaced or reconfigured. In this chapter, you will learn about procedures you can perform to prevent problems from occurring in the first place. You will also learn about procedures you should follow so that you do not cause damage to computer components or cause harm to yourself or the environment.

CERTIFICATION OBJECTIVE 4.01

Preventive Maintenance Products and Procedures

Regular cleaning of computer components can extend a computer's life. For example, by regularly cleaning the power supply fan, you can ensure that it is able to properly cool the computer's internal components. Regular cleaning can also help stop problems before they start, as in dust build-up inside a mouse.

Giving a computer a regular cleaning also gives you a good opportunity to inspect the computer's components and determine if the potential for a problem exists. For example, while cleaning the system, take note of loose components or connections and tighten them up. You should also look for frayed or cracked cables and replace them, even if they have not yet caused a problem.

Liquid Cleaning Compounds

Before using a liquid cleaner on any device, make sure that the computer is off and that the component is completely dry before you turn the computer on again. In addition, note that you should stick to the procedures discussed within this section. That is, do not use a type of liquid cleaner on a device other than the ones discussed here. For example, if you were to use water rather than alcohol on the floppy drive, you might cause permanent damage to it.

Some computer components, such as a mouse ball, the mouse casing, and the case on the monitor and computer itself, can be cleaned using *mild,* soapy water or a damp (not wet) cloth. In short, most plastic external coverings in the computer system can be cleaned this way. Make sure that no liquid drips on the components.

If the keyboard is sticky, you can clean it with plain, distilled water. Make sure that you unplug the keyboard from the computer, and make sure that the water contains no impurities such as soap or iron. Ensure that the keyboard is entirely dry before reattaching it to the computer.

Some devices are harmed by water and/or soap and should be cleaned with denatured (isopropyl) alcohol. For example, the cleaning liquid that comes in most floppy drive cleaning kits is alcohol. You can also use alcohol to clean any residue on a mouse roller that you can't remove with your fingers.

Finally, you can use regular glass cleaner to clean the screen on a CRT monitor. Follow the steps in Exercise 4-1 to properly clean a monitor.

on the **ᵾob**   *Never use glass cleaner on an LCD.*

EXERCISE 4-1

Cleaning a Monitor

1. Shut down the computer.

2. Turn the monitor off and unplug it from the electrical outlet.

3. Spray a small amount of glass cleaner on a clean cloth or paper towel.

4. Use the cloth to rub fingerprints or other smudges off the monitor screen. Be careful not to let any cleaner drip.

5. Allow the glass cleaner to completely evaporate (about a minute).

6. Plug the monitor back in and turn it on.

Cleaning Contacts and Connectors

It's a good idea to check your system's contacts to make sure that they are establishing a good connection. Bad connections can lead to malfunctioning components. One way to remove buildup is to use isopropyl alcohol on a cotton swab to clean the contacts. You can also use a plain white pencil eraser to remove buildup or corrosion. Do not use a standard pink eraser or an ink eraser, as they are too abrasive.

Removing Dust and Debris from the System

One of the most common reasons to clean a computer is to remove dust buildup. Recall that the power supply's fan draws air into the computer and distributes it over the internal components. It can do the same thing with dust. Because dust can cause ESD (Electrostatic Discharge) and can lead to overheated components, it's important to clean the inside of the computer regularly. Places to pay particular attention to include the system board, the bottom of the computer chassis, and especially the fan itself.

One of the easiest ways to remove dust from the system is to use compressed air to blow the dust out. Compressed air comes in cans that are roughly the size of spray-paint cans. Typically, a liquid at the bottom of the can compresses the air and forces it out when you depress the can's nozzle. If you turn the can upside-down, you can cause the liquid to be released. Avoid doing so; the liquid can cause freeze burns on your skin and damage the computer's components. You should also be aware of where the dust is being blown. That is, make sure that the dust is not being blown from one component only to settle on another. You can also used compressed air to blow dust out of the keyboard, expansion slots, and ports.

Another common method for removing dust is to vacuum it out. This has the advantage of removing dust without allowing the dust to settle elsewhere. It is best to use a special hand-held vacuum, which will allow you to get into smaller places and clean the computer without accidentally hitting and damaging other internal components. Remove the nozzle from inside, and move the vacuum cleaner away from the computer before turning it off.

Finally, you can use a lint-free cloth to wipe off dusty surfaces. Avoid using the newer dust cloths that work by "statically attracting" dust. Remember, static is harmful to the computer.

exam
ⓦatch

Compressed air is more effective in cleaning places that are hard to get at, but vacuums cause less mess.

Now that you are familiar with common cleaning compounds and procedures, you should be able to answer the following Scenario & Solution questions.

SCENARIO & SOLUTION

What should I use to clean the monitor's screen?	Use glass cleaner. Spray the cleaner on a cloth, not directly on the monitor.
How can I remove dust from the computer?	Vacuum it, or use compressed air to blow it out.
What should I use to remove dirt from the computer case?	Use mild, soapy water on a damp (not wet) cloth.

FROM THE CLASSROOM

Cleaning the Keyboard

Many computer users tend to eat while they use the computer. They also tend to drink, use erasers, shuffle papers, or pick lint off themselves while at the computer. The poor keyboard is usually an unfortunate witness to all these activities, and its design allows it to hold more dust, crumbs, hair, and other gunk than any other device. Keyboards, therefore, typically require a lot of cleaning, and because the debris can be hard to get at, you might need to use some creative cleaning techniques.

If the keyboard is sticky, you can clean it with water; it won't harm the keyboard as long as the water doesn't contain impurities and the keyboard is not plugged into the computer while it's still wet. You can even clean your keyboards in the dishwasher! Make sure that the water is free of iron and other minerals. Never use soap when you do this. Furthermore, don't leave the keyboard in the machine for the dry cycle; the heat can cause damage, so let the keyboard air-dry overnight.

Another good way to clean the keyboard is to simply turn it upside-down and shake it. You'll probably be surprised at the amount of stuff that falls out. If this doesn't do the trick, use a can of compressed air to blow debris out of the keyboard, or use a small hand-held vacuum. Some types of crud can be stubborn, and you could end up having to remove each keycap to properly clean the keyboard. Use a flathead screwdriver to pry the keycap(s) off. (Make sure that the computer is off before you do so.) To replace a keycap, simply orient it the right way and snap it into place. Be careful of the Spacebar; it sometimes contains springs that can fly out and disappear. Taking the keyboard apart like this can be very time-consuming, so it should really be a last resort.

—Amy Thomson, A+ Certified Technician, MOUS Master

CERTIFICATION OBJECTIVE 4.02

Power Protection and Safety Procedures

The computer's supply of power is an important consideration when performing maintenance or troubleshooting procedures. The safety of the computer's components is important, and you must ensure that the computer is receiving a safe and steady power supply. Failure to do so can result in lost work, corrupted files, and physically damaged components. Your personal safety is also an important issue. Many of the things that make a computer function properly, such as high voltage and lasers, can cause you harm. You must also keep the safety of the environment in mind. Computers contain many components that, if disposed of improperly, can contaminate the ground, water, or other parts of the environment. Finally, you must protect the safety of computer components, whether they are installed in the computer, in transit, or in storage.

Power Protection

Many things can go wrong with the power supply to your home or office. The power could suddenly decrease, increase, or be cut off altogether. The power can also contain noise, due to EMI (Electromagnetic Interference). To keep your computer functioning properly, you need to be able to recognize signs of power problems and make the proper use of devices that can help control the flow of electricity.

Determining the Signs of Power Issues

A common power problem is a temporary reduction in the amount of electricity to your home or office. In these cases, the power is not totally cut off but can sag to levels that will harm your computer's components, especially when the power returns to its normal level. These power reductions are referred to as *brownouts* because they tend to make regular lights go very dim (but not out).

A *blackout* occurs when the power is totally cut off. Blackouts can last from less than a second to several hours, depending on the source of the problem. When a blackout occurs, the computer loses all power, and you will lose any information that you haven't saved. Furthermore, if the computer is in the middle of saving, moving, or deleting a file when the power goes out, it is likely that that file will become corrupted or missing. The sudden loss of power can also result in the accumulation of temporary files that would have been automatically deleted if the computer had been shut down normally.

Another danger with a blackout is what happens to the computer when the power suddenly comes on again. Most newer computers are designed to come back on only if the power button is pushed again. However, older computers might automatically come back on when the power is restored, resulting in a harmful power surge. When the power goes out, you should always turn the computer and monitor off, or better yet, unplug them.

Power surges occur not only when the power is restored. The regular supply of electricity can contain temporary dips and increases. These increases are *power surges*. Like brownouts, power surges are temporary and are not typically very extreme. In fact, you might not even notice when a power surge occurs. However, if the lights become brighter or if electrical devices begin to make more noise than usual, these issues could be due to a power surge. Power surges can be very harmful to computer components. Recall that the power supply not only converts electricity from AC to DC, but it also drops the overall voltage from 110–120 to only 3–12 volts. The power supply does this by using resistors to shield a certain amount of excess voltage. If there is a power surge, however, the total voltage could be more than the resistors can shield, resulting in a higher voltage within the computer itself.

A *power spike* is more extreme than a power surge and typically does not last as long. Due to their extreme nature, power spikes are much more likely to damage computer components.

The electrical supply can also contain interference due to the presence of high-voltage equipment in the area or very long cables. (The longer a cable, the more susceptible it is to EMI.) Current that contains EMI is referred to as *noisy* or *dirty* and can cause problems in the computer because the noise can result in dips and increases in the amount of electricity reaching the computer. Noisy power lines can also create magnetic fields, which can be damaging to magnetically stored data.

Preventing Power Problems

An uninterruptible power supply (UPS) can be used to prevent or remedy some or all of the above power issues. A typical UPS has a battery that provides temporary backup power in the case of a blackout. This backup gives users enough time to properly save their work and safely shut their computers down in the event of a power loss. One type of UPS is a *standby power system (SPS)*, which is attached to the computer. The UPS enables its battery power when it detects a loss of electricity. Unfortunately, there can be a brief lapse in power during the time it takes for the UPS to detect a power problem and switch to battery power.

A more expensive but more efficient type of UPS is an *online UPS*, which is located between the computer's power supply and power supply (electrical outlet) from the electric company. Incoming power keeps the UPS battery charged, and all power to the computer comes from the battery. When the power goes out, the UPS simply continues to provide the computer with power from the battery's reserve. This means there is no "break" in the power, as there is in an SPS.

To prevent problems resulting from power surges and power spikes, you can use a *suppressor*. Suppressors are designed to "smooth out" the flow of electricity by removing excess voltage caused by power surges and spikes. Suppressors are available as individual devices or integrated with a UPS.

To combat noisy or dirty current, you should use a *noise filter*. Noise filters are designed to condition the flow of electricity by removing EMI. Like suppressors, noise filters can be used as individual devices or as part of a UPS.

exam
ⓦatch

You should know the differences between the functions of these devices: UPSs provide backup power, suppressors smooth out surges and spikes, and noise filters remove EMI. A UPS can also come with an integrated suppressor and/or noise filter.

Test your knowledge of power protection devices before continuing in the chapter. Please refer to the following Scenario & Solution.

SCENARIO & SOLUTION

Which device can absorb excess power?	A suppressor.
What can I use to remove EMI from the power source?	A noise filter.
What should I use to provide backup battery power?	A UPS.
How can I prevent problems from blackouts, surges, and EMI, all at the same time?	Get a UPS that has an integrated suppressor and noise filter.

Personal Safety Procedures

The power used by the computer, especially the power found in the computer's high-voltage devices, is enough to cause injury or death. Some computers also use lasers. You must always be aware of the potential for injury when working with the devices described here.

Lasers

Computers use lasers to read information from CD-ROMs, and some printers use lasers in creating printout images. The Level 3 lasers used for these purposes aren't enough to burn you, but they can cause eye damage if you look straight at them. Most CD-ROM drives and laser printers are designed to stop functioning as soon as their cases are opened or removed. However, you should never tamper with the laser device or try to make it work without its case or cover.

High-Voltage Equipment

Most of a computer's components run on very low voltage ($\pm$3v to $\pm$12v DC). However, some components require higher voltage to function properly and can store enough voltage to cause personal injury, such as burns. Two common high-voltage devices, the power supply and the monitor, are described in the following sections. However, always be aware of other potentially high-voltage equipment, such as the power supply in a printer. High-voltage devices are typically indicated by a high-voltage warning label. When working with these types of devices, unplug them, never open them up, and always remove your ESD strap.

Power Supplies   Always unplug the power supply from the wall outlet when you are working inside the computer. Even when turned off, the power supply can conduct electricity. Some technicians prefer to leave the power supply plugged in while they work on the computer to allow static to bleed away from the computer into the wall outlet's ground wire. However, there are safer methods for removing static (discussed later in this chapter), so there is no need to leave the power supply plugged in.

As discussed previously, the power supply itself is able to store electrical charges for long periods of time, even when it has been unplugged. Never open the power supply's case, and never wear an ESD wrist strap when replacing or handling the power supply. ESD straps are designed to bleed static charges away from the computer, through your body. If worn near a power supply, the strap could conduct high-voltage electricity as well as static charges. These high voltages are enough to harm you.

Cathode Ray Tubes   Like power supplies, CRT monitors are considered high-voltage equipment and can store a harmful electrical charge, even when they are unplugged. Never open a CRT case, and never wear a wrist strap when working with a CRT.

exam
ⓦatch   *Power supplies and CRT monitors are high-voltage equipment. Never open them, and never wear an ESD strap while working with them.*

Environmental Safety Procedures

Many of the computer's components—such as monitors, which may contain lead, and system boards, which may contain mercury—are harmful to the environment. These items, as well as the ones discussed in the following sections, must be recycled or disposed of in the proper manner (in other words, not placed in landfills).

Batteries

Many batteries contain environmentally hazardous materials, such as lithium, mercury, or nickel-cadmium. Therefore, they cannot be placed in landfills lest they contaminate the ground or nearby water. Many communities have special recycling depots that accept batteries, to be recharged, reused, or properly processed so that they do not introduce harmful elements to the environment. Many communities also conduct hazardous material pickups once a month, in which you can hand over all toxic materials, such as batteries and paint, for proper disposal.

Toner Kits and Cartridges

Printer toner cartridges also provide a potential environmental hazard, simply due to their large numbers and the space they can take up in a landfill. For this reason, they should not simply be thrown away. Fortunately, most toner cartridges are reusable. That is, many companies will buy back used toner cartridges, then refill and resell them.

Chemical Solvents and Cans

Chemical solvents designed for the computer are just as hazardous to the environment as noncomputer-related chemical solvents. They must be disposed of in a similar manner. Look for a hazardous material pickup in your area.

Material Safety Data Sheet

Whenever you are unsure of the proper disposal procedures for a component, look for its *material safety data sheet (MSDS)*. An MSDS is a standardized document that contains general information, ingredients, and fire and explosion warnings as well as health, disposal, and safe transportation information about a particular product. Any manufacturer that sells a potentially hazardous product is required to issue an MSDS for it. If an MSDS didn't come with a particular component, contact the manufacturer or search for it on the Internet. A number of Web sites, including sites sponsored by Cornell University (*http://msds.pdc.cornell.edu/msdssrch.asp*) and Vermont Safety Information Resources Inc. (*http://siri.uvm.edu/*), contain large repositories of MSDSs.

Component Safety Procedures

You should now be familiar with the procedures for preventing harm to the computer's power supply, yourself, and the environment. It is also important to know how to protect the computer's delicate components from harm. This section focuses on some potential dangers to these components and how you can protect them.

Electrostatic Discharge

One of the most prevalent threats to a computer component is ESD, also known as *static*. Static is all around us, especially when the humidity is low. When you put on a jacket that makes the hair on your arm stand up or when you rub a balloon on your hair to make it stick it to the wall, you are encountering static electricity. When you touch a light switch and receive a jolt, you are experiencing a static discharge. ESD is caused when two objects of uneven charge come in contact with one another. Electricity has the property of traveling to areas with lower charges, and the static shock that you feel is the result of electrons jumping from your hand to the metal screw in the light switch plate. The same process can occur within the computer. If your body has a high electric potential, electrons will be transferred to the first computer component that you touch.

What ESD Can Do   If an ESD charge is very low, it might not cause any damage to the computer. However, recall that most computer components are designed to receive voltages of ±12 or less. Most static electricity has a much higher voltage: up to 3000 volts if you can feel the discharge and up to 20,000 volts if you can see it! These voltages are enough to damage the circuits inside the device and render it inoperable.

Most static discharges are above 1000 volts, but it takes a charge of only about 30 volts to destroy a computer component!

Because it takes such a small charge to damage a computer component, you might be unaware of its occurrence. This is referred to as *hidden ESD*. Hidden ESD can also come from a dust buildup inside the computer. Dust and other foreign particles can hold an electric charge that slowly bleeds into nearby components. Hidden ESD can cause more serious problems than ESD that you can feel. For example, if hidden ESD has damaged a component, you will be unaware of it until that device begins to malfunction. Because you weren't aware of the ESD damage when it occurred, it could be difficult for you to pinpoint the problem.

When ESD causes the immediate malfunction of a device, it is considered *catastrophic*. When ESD causes a gradually worsening problem in a device, it is referred to as *degradation*. As unlikely as it might seem, catastrophic damage can be less harmful to the system than degradation. When a device suffers catastrophic damage, the result is immediate and typically quite obvious, so the device will most likely be replaced right away. Degradation, on the other hand, can cause a component to malfunction sporadically, sometimes working and sometimes not. This makes it harder to pinpoint the problem, so the problem itself can persist for a longer period of time. Additionally, a total failure of one component will typically not affect the usability of other components. However, degradation can cause a component to fail in ways that also result in the failure of other components.

Common ESD Protection Devices

There are many ways to prevent ESD from damaging the computer. First, ESD is typically caused by low humidity. Always keep the room's humidity between 50 and 80 percent (but no higher than 80 percent or condensation could form).

You should also use special ESD devices, such as ESD wrist or ankle straps. ESD straps have a cuff that fits around your wrist or ankle and are designed to bleed static charges away from the computer via your body. Some ESD straps have an alligator clip that is attached to a grounded, metal object, such as a table leg. Other straps have a single prong that is plugged into the ground wire in a regular wall outlet. Make sure that you read the directions for your particular strap, and make sure that you know which part of the wall outlet contains the ground wire.

exam

ⓦatch

For your own safety as well as your success on the A+ exam, make sure that you know which plug is for the ground wire. It is the round one in the outlet. Never try to plug an ESD strap into either of the two "slots" on the outlet—they contain electricity!

ESD mats look like vinyl placemats but have a wire lead and an alligator clip. Their function is similar to that of an ESD strap and can be used as a safe place to put expansion cards or other internal components that you have removed from the computer. Before you pick up a loose computer component, discharge any static electricity in yourself by touching something metal, such as a table leg or chair. This will prevent electrons in your body from being passed onto the device.

Another way to combat ESD is to use antistatic spray. ESD spray is commercially available and is typically used to remove static from your clothes. However, you can use it to remove static from yourself, from the carpet, and from your work area, to protect computer components.

on the

ⓙob

Never spray antistatic spray directly on a computer component. If you use the spray on your work surface, make sure that it is completely dry before setting components down on it.

ESD can cause a lot of damage to your computer unless you are knowledgeable about dealing with it and take proper precautions. Test your knowledge by answering the following Scenario & Solution questions.

SCENARIO & SOLUTION

When should I use an ESD strap?	Use a strap whenever you perform repairs or maintenance on the computer, except on the monitor or power supply.
Which kind of ESD is usually most damaging to the system?	Degradation is most damaging. This type of ESD can cause a device to fail gradually so that it can affect other components and is hard to troubleshoot.
What ESD devices are available?	ESD wrist and ankle straps drain static from the computer, through your body. Antistatic spray inhibits the buildup of static, and ESD mats offer a good place to put components when they are temporarily out of the computer.

Situations That Could Present a Danger or Hazard

As well as low humidity, a number of other situations can lead to problems with ESD. First, you should be aware of what you are wearing. You should always wear rubber-soled shoes when working on the computer, and avoid wearing clothes that attract static. Furthermore, you should remove your rings and other jewelry, to prevent causing an electrical arc. Never wear an ESD strap near a high-voltage device; you can injure yourself if you do. Finally, never touch a high-voltage device and another component at the same time, because your body can conduct electricity from the high-voltage device into the other component.

The procedure in Exercise 4-2 will lead you through the process of protecting your workspace, and the computer, from ESD damage.

EXERCISE 4-2

ESD-Proofing Your Workspace

1. Maintain the room's humidity between 50 percent and 80 percent.

2. Spray your clothing and the work area with antistatic spray. Do not directly spray the computer or its components.

3. Place an ESD mat (for setting components on) on the workspace and attach its alligator clip to something stationary and metal, such as the leg of a table.

4. Remove all jewelry, including rings.

5. Put an ESD strap around your wrist or ankle, and attach the other end to a stationary metal object (if it has an alligator clip) or plug it into the wall outlet's ground wire (if it has an outlet prong).

Proper Storage of Components

Whenever you remove a component from the computer, it becomes susceptible to damage from external sources. Therefore, you must ensure that components are properly protected when they are placed in storage. Always store computer components in a cool, dry place (but not dry enough to harbor static buildup). Heat can damage a component's circuits and cause magnetically stored data to be lost. Furthermore, damp environments can cause condensation to form, leading to corrosion, or can cause the component to short-circuit when it is reinstalled in the computer.

You should also make sure that components, especially those that use magnetic storage, are kept safely away from high-voltage devices, EMI-causing devices, and other sources of magnetism. Internal components should always be placed in ESD bags before they are stored or transported. ESD bags are designed to move static from the inside of the bag to the outside, keeping the components inside safe.

Many technicians place components on the ESD bag they're removed from. This can cause damage, and should not be done unless specifically instructed to do so by the manufacturer. (Some system board manufacturers instruct you to place the motherboard on the ESD bag it came in.) Some ESD bags work by moving static charges from inside the bag to the outside, and by placing a component on one of these bags, it can be exposed to harmful static.

On a final note, never store computer batteries for extended periods of time. Battery casings are notorious for corroding, allowing the chemicals inside to leak or explode out. This can cause a large mess, destroy nearby components, and cause skin burns if you touch it.

CERTIFICATION SUMMARY

This chapter focused on ways to prevent computer problems and how to protect the computer, the environment, and yourself from harm. One of the most effective ways to stop problems before they start is to clean the computer often. Cleaning can prevent damage due to overheating, reverse the progression of a problem before it becomes noticeable, and give you a good chance to inspect the computer's internal components for signs of wear and tear.

Some components, such as plastic casings, can be cleaned with mild, soapy water. Others, such as floppy drives or mouse rollers, require the use of isopropyl alcohol. Always check with the manufacturer for proper cleaning instructions, and never use a liquid cleaner on a device for which it was not intended.

You can also help prevent computer problems by conditioning and "smoothing out" the power source. By using a UPS, suppressor, and/or noise filter, you can remove or minimize problems caused by power outages, surges, or EMI.

Always be aware of potential environmental and personal hazards. Always dispose of computer components properly. You can check the component's MSDS for proper disposal instructions. You should also be aware of components that use high voltage or lasers, such as the monitor, power supply, and CD-ROM drive. Finally, handle components carefully when you store them. Keep them out of hot or damp places, and keep magnetic storage devices away from EMI-emitting devices.

✓ TWO-MINUTE DRILL

Here are some of the key points from each certification objective in Chapter 4.

Preventive Maintenance Products and Procedures

❑ Cleaning the computer can help you prevent problems and replace worn-out components before they stop working.

❑ Use mild, soapy water to clean the mouse ball and plastic casings.

❑ Clean a sticky keyboard with distilled water.

❑ Use isopropyl alcohol to clean mouse rollers and floppy drives.

❑ Use regular glass cleaner to remove smudges and fingerprints from the glass screen on a CRT monitor (but not on an LCD).

❑ Check all connections to ensure that there is no corrosion or other buildup.

❑ Use a plain white eraser or isopropyl alcohol to clean contacts.

❑ Use compressed air or a vacuum to remove dust from the fan and the inside of the computer.

Power Protection and Safety Procedures

❑ Use a UPS to provide backup power in the event of a brownout or blackout.

❑ Suppressors can be used to absorb excess voltage.

❑ Noise filters "condition" the electrical supply by removing EMI.

❑ Monitors and power supplies are considered high-voltage equipment and should never be opened.

❑ Many computer components, such as batteries, contain harmful substances and must be disposed of properly.

❑ Clean the computer often and use ESD straps and mats to reduce the possibility of ESD damage.

❑ Always store computer components in ESD bags, and place them in cool, dry places.

SELF TEST

The following questions will help you measure your understanding of the material presented in this chapter. Read all the choices carefully because there might be more than one correct answer. Choose all correct answers for each question.

Preventive Maintenance Products and Procedures

1. Which of the following is the most effective device for cleaning the internal rollers in a mouse?

   A. An eraser

   B. Isopropyl alcohol

   C. Mild, soapy water

   D. Distilled water

2. Which of the following can you clean with mild, soapy water?

   A. The mouse ball

   B. The monitor screen

   C. The keyboard

   D. Connectors

3. A user has complained that the keys are sticking on her keyboard. Which of the following should you do?

   A. Clean the keyboard with compressed air.

   B. Soak the keyboard in mild, soapy water.

   C. Clean the keyboard with isopropyl alcohol.

   D. Put the keyboard in the dishwasher.

4. Which of the following should you avoid using to clean a keyboard?

   A. Compressed air

   B. Water

   C. An eraser

   D. A vacuum

5. There are fingerprints all over your monitor, so you have decided to clean it. Which procedure should you follow?

   A. Turn the monitor off and unplug it from the wall outlet. Spray the screen with glass cleaner, then wipe it off. Wait for the screen to dry, then plug the monitor back in and turn it on.

   B. Turn the monitor off and unplug it from the wall outlet. Wipe the screen with mild, soapy water. When the screen is dry, plug the monitor back in and turn it on.

   C. Use a dry, lint-free cloth to wipe the screen clean of fingerprints.

   D. Ensure that no power is going to the monitor. Apply glass cleaner to a paper towel and wipe the screen with it. Wait for the screen to dry, then use it normally.

6. When checking a malfunctioning sound card in an early Pentium system, you find a buildup of corrosion on the contacts. What do you do?

   A. Use a small white eraser to clean the connector.

   B. Soak the connector in distilled water.

   C. Use a cotton swab soaked in mild, soapy water.

   D. Use a can of compressed air to blow the debris out of the connector.

7. When you turn on your computer, you notice that the fan is not spinning as quickly as usual. What is the first thing you should do?

   A. Replace the fan.

   B. Use compressed air to clean the fan.

   C. Replace the power supply.

   D. Use isopropyl alcohol to clean the fan.

8. Which of the following statements is true regarding the use of compressed air or a vacuum to remove dust from a computer?

   A. Vacuuming is generally messier than using compressed air.

   B. Vacuums make it easier to get into smaller places.

   C. Compressed air has the potential to cause personal injury.

   D. You are more likely to damage a component using compressed air.

9. Which of the following is not a benefit of regularly cleaning the computer?

   A. Reducing the probability of ESD

    B. Preventing the overheating of components

    C. Allowing you to determine the voltage output of the power supply

    D. Allowing you to determine the presence of improper connections

10. You are vacuuming the computer and you come across a cable on which the outer shield is cracked, but the internal wires are still intact. Which of the following should you do?

    A. Pay close attention to the behavior of the computer so that you can tell when to replace the cable.

    B. Use electrical tape to patch the cable.

    C. Replace the cable.

    D. Nothing.

Power Protection and Safety Procedures

11. ESD can be harmful to which of the following?

    A. People

    B. Expansion cards

    C. The computer's power supply

    D. The environment

12. Which device can be used to protect the computer from electrical power surges?

    A. An ESD strap

    B. A suppressor

    C. A noise filter

    D. A standby power UPS

13. A customer is complaining that the power in the office sometimes surges, sometimes causes blackouts, and has EMI. What single device can you recommend to help the most in this situation?

    A. A noise filter

    B. A suppressor

    C. A UPS

    D. A backup battery

14. Which type of UPS is most effective?

A. An SPS because it generates battery power longer than an online UPS

B. An online UPS because it prevents lapses in the power supply when a blackout occurs

C. An SPS because it provides battery power more immediately during a blackout

D. An online UPS because it will draw less power from the electrical source than an SPS

15. Which of the following is not considered a high-voltage device?

A. A printer power supply

B. A computer power supply

C. A monitor

D. A CMOS battery

16. You are planning to replace the internal sound card in your computer. Which of the following describes the proper safety precautions you should take?

A. Unplug the computer, spray your workspace with antistatic spray, put an ESD strap on, open the computer, remove the card, and place it on an antistatic bag.

B. Unplug the computer, place an ESD mat on your work surface, open the computer, put an ESD strap on, spray the sound card with antistatic spray, and replace the card.

C. Put an ESD strap on, place an ESD mat on your work surface, unplug the computer, spray the computer with antistatic spray, open the computer, remove the card, and place it on the ESD mat.

D. Place an ESD mat on your work surface, unplug the computer, put an ESD strap on, open the computer, remove the card, and place it on the ESD mat.

17. Why should you recycle printer toner cartridges?

A. Because they contain acids that can cause personal injury

B. Because they contain chemicals that can contaminate the nearby soil or water supply

C. Because they contain hazardous materials that can contribute to the depletion of the ozone layer

D. Because they are sold in very large numbers

18. You just installed a new video card, but it doesn't work. You remember feeling a little shock when you picked the card up. What is the likely cause of the video card problem?

A. Catastrophic ESD

    B. Degradation

    C. Hidden ESD

    D. Sudden ESD syndrome

19. Computers in a particular office have been experiencing an unusually high occurrence of ESD damage. Which of the following is most likely to reduce the occurrence of ESD?

    A. Raise the temperature of the room.

    B. Lower the temperature of the room.

    C. Raise the humidity of the room.

    D. Keep the lights as dim as possible.

20. In which type of environment should you store a hard drive?

    A. Cool and damp

    B. Cool and dry

    C. Warm and damp

    D. Warm and dry

LAB QUESTION

While at a friend's place, you notice the following things:

- He often eats while using the computer.
- He has a pet cat.
- The lights flicker when he turns the speakers on.
- He has a habit of rubbing his feet on the floor.
- There are floppy disks stacked near the monitor.

From this information, what types of problems might you expect to occur? How can you prevent or resolve these problems?

SELF-TEST ANSWERS

Preventive Maintenance Products and Procedures

1. ☑ **B.** You should use isopropyl alcohol to clean the internal rollers in a mouse. First, you can try to remove debris using your fingers. If this doesn't work, apply some alcohol to a cotton swab and rub the debris off. Ensure that none of the debris falls into the mouse.

   ☒ **A,** an eraser, is incorrect because, although this could help remove roller buildup, it is not as effective as alcohol, and it is likely that shavings from the eraser will be deposited on the rollers or other internal areas of the mouse. **C,** mild, soapy water, and **D,** distilled water, are incorrect. These are not as effective in this case as alcohol and could damage the mouse.

2. ☑ **A.** You can clean the mouse ball with mild, soapy water. Remove the ball from the mouse, clean it, rinse it thoroughly, and make sure it is completely dry before replacing it in the mouse. As long as you follow this procedure, you don't have to worry about water dripping onto other parts of the mouse, as it would if you used water to clean the rollers.

   ☒ **B,** the monitor screen, is incorrect. The screen is made of glass, and soapy water is likely to leave a visible residue. You should use glass cleaner on the monitor screen. **C,** the keyboard, and **D,** connectors, are incorrect. Although mild, soapy water could make them appear clean, there is a chance that a buildup of soap will be left behind when the keyboard or connector dries. This can lead to sticky keys or poor connections.

3. ☑ **D.** Put the keyboard in the dishwasher. As long as the water doesn't have soap or mineral impurities in it, this practice is perfectly safe. In addition, don't leave the keyboard in the machine for the "dry" cycle. You could also clean the keyboard by soaking it in distilled water. Make sure that the keyboard is completely dry before reattaching it to the computer.

   ☒ **A,** clean the keyboard with compressed air, is incorrect because, although this will remove dust, it will not remove sticky residue. **B,** soak the keyboard in mild, soapy water, is incorrect because soap residue can be left on the keyboard, causing the keys to remain sticky. **C,** clean the keyboard with isopropyl alcohol, is incorrect because the alcohol could react with the plastic and will likely evaporate before it can rinse away the sticky residue.

4. ☑ **C.** You should avoid using an eraser to clean a keyboard. When erasers are used, parts of the eraser tend to come off as small shavings. These can get under the keys, causing more problems.

   ☒ **A,** compressed air, and **D,** a vacuum, are incorrect because these are both good methods to use for removing dust or other loose debris from the keyboard. **B,** water, is incorrect because it can be used to clean the keyboard when there is a sticky residue.

5. ☑ **D.** To clean fingerprints from a monitor, ensure that no power is going to the monitor. Apply glass cleaner to a paper towel and wipe the screen with it. Wait for the screen to dry, then use it normally. You should always make sure that there is no power by turning the monitor off and unplugging it. The monitor contains high voltage, and you will be applying liquid to it. Always spray the glass cleaner on the paper towel, not on the screen itself. This prevents stray spray from getting into places it shouldn't and prevents drips. When the screen is clean and dry, plug it in and use it as you normally would.
☒ **A** is incorrect because it suggests spraying the glass cleaner directly on the screen. Again, you should avoid this practice because it could allow spray to get into places it shouldn't and can result in dripping. **B** is incorrect because it suggests using mild, soapy water. However, as with regular glass, if soapy water is used on the screen, it could leave streaks and a soap buildup. **C** is incorrect because it suggests using a dry, lint-free cloth to clean the screen. Although safe, this procedure will be ineffective for removing fingerprints.

6. ☑ **A.** You should use a small white eraser to the clean the contacts. This is a relatively effective way to remove corrosion. Ensure, however, that eraser shavings don't fall into the computer.
☒ **B**, soak the connector in distilled water, is incorrect. Not only is this an ineffective way of removing corrosion, but it could also lead to more corrosion. **C**, use a cotton swab soaked in mild, soapy water, is incorrect because this can lead to soap residue on the connector. This residue could prevent a good connection and could add to the buildup of corrosion. **D**, use a can of compressed air, is incorrect. Although effective for removing dust, compressed air is not effective in removing corrosion, which is typically caked on.

7. ☑ **B.** You should use compressed air to clean the fan. The fan could be spinning slowly because a buildup of dust is preventing it from spinning at its regular speed. Turn the computer off, and use the compressed air to blow the dust out of the fan. Make sure that you blow the dust away from, not into, the computer.
☒ **A** and **C** are both incorrect because they suggest replacing parts. Although this might be the solution, you should try cleaning the fan before you replace a component. If cleaning it solves the problem, you will have saved time and money. Note that you should never carry out the procedure in **A** (replace the fan). The fan is part of the power supply, and when it stops working, you must replace the whole power supply. Never open the power supply. **D** is incorrect because it states that you should use isopropyl alcohol to clean the fan. The fan is housed within the power supply, which is a high-voltage device. Always keep all liquids away from it.

8. ☑ **C.** Compressed air has the potential to cause personal injury. Compressed air cans contain a pressurizing liquid that can cause skin burns if released. Never hold a compressed air can upside-down, and don't shake the can before spraying.

☒ **A,** vacuuming is generally messier than using compressed air, is incorrect. When you vacuum the computer, the dust is deposited in the vacuum, away from the computer. When you use compressed air, the dust can be deposited everywhere. When using compressed air, you must be very careful not to blow dust from one component onto another. **B,** vacuums make it easier to get into smaller places, is also incorrect. The thin nozzle on a compressed air can creates an air stream that can get into every nook and cranny of the computer. Vacuums (even hand-held ones) are much bulkier and might not be able to get into small places. **D,** you are more likely to damage a component using compressed air, is incorrect. Although it is possible to damage a component by applying pressurized air to it, you are more likely to damage a component by accidentally hitting it with the vacuum.

9. ☑ **C.** Cleaning the computer will not allow you to determine the voltage output of the power supply. Cleaning involves removing dust from the computer and visually inspecting connections and cables. Determining the power supply's voltage output requires the use of voltage testing with a voltmeter or multimeter.

☒ **A,** reducing the probability of ESD, is incorrect because this is a good reason to clean the computer. Dust can hold a static charge that can bleed into components over time, resulting in ESD damage. By removing the dust, you can remove this risk. **B** is incorrect because it suggests that cleaning the computer can't help prevent components from overheating. By removing dust from components, you can ensure that they are cooled properly, and by keeping the fan clean of dust, you can ensure that it rotates as fast as is necessary. **D** is incorrect because it suggests that determining the presence of improper connections is not a benefit of cleaning the computer. However, part of cleaning the computer is checking the connections for corrosion and to ensure they are securely attached.

10. ☑ **C.** You should replace the cable. Even though the cable appears to work now, whatever caused the crack to occur could still be at work and cause the cable to fail altogether. Replace the cable as soon as you find the problem, since you already have the computer taken apart.

☒ **A** is incorrect because it states that you should pay close attention to the behavior of the computer so that you can tell when to replace the cable. This is not a good idea because the eventual failure of the cable could cause more serious problems than a lack of signal to the intended device, such as a power arc or improper data, resulting in harmful component behavior or lost data. **B,** use electrical tape to patch the cable, is incorrect because this is an incomplete solution. This could provide only a temporary fix for the problem. Furthermore, corrosion might have already started on the exposed wires. They should be replaced, not patched. D is incorrect because it suggests you should do nothing about the cable. However, it is not normal for a cable to have a cracked shield. You should replace it right away to prevent it from causing problems.

Power Protection and Safety Procedures

11. ☑ **B.** ESD is harmful to expansion cards. It is also harmful to other computer components such as the system board, processor, and RAM modules. These devices are used to receiving between ±3v and ±12v DC. However, the voltage produced by ESD can be tens of thousands of volts.

    ☒ **A,** people, is incorrect. Although ESD might be enough for you to feel a small shock, it is not harmful. **C,** the computer's power supply, is also incorrect. The power supply is a high-voltage device that is not affected by the relatively low current of a static discharge. **D,** the environment, is also incorrect. ESD occurs when electrons move from an area of high electrical potential to an area of low electrical potential. It has no effect on the air, ground, or water.

12. ☑ **B.** A suppressor can be used to protect the computer from electrical power surges. Power surges can damage the computer's components. Suppressors are able to remove excess voltage from the power during surges.

    ☒ **A,** an ESD strap, is incorrect because this is used to drain static charges from the computer's components, not to prevent damage due to power surges. **C,** a noise filter, is incorrect because its function is to remove EMI and other "noise" from the incoming power supply to the computer. **D,** a standby power UPS, is incorrect because this device is used to provide temporary battery power to the computer in the event of a power lapse or blackout.

13. ☑ **C.** A UPS can help the most in this situation. A UPS contains a backup battery system; some also have an integrated noise filter and suppressor. One of these all-in-one units can prevent problems stemming from power surges, blackouts, and EMI.

    ☒ **A,** a noise filter; **B,** a suppressor; and **D** a backup battery, are all incorrect. Each of these devices is available independently of the others, but each remedies only one of the three power issues. All three issues can be resolved by purchasing a UPS that contains battery backup, a suppressor, and a noise filter all in one unit.

14. ☑ **B.** An online UPS is the most effective because it prevents lapses in the power supply when a blackout occurs. Online UPSs are attached between the computer and the wall outlet. All power from the wall outlet is converted by the UPS into battery power. This battery supplies the computer with power. When the power goes out, the battery continues to work normally,

drawing power from its reserve. There is no momentary lapse in power while the UPS switches from regular power to the battery, as there is in an SPS.

☒ **A** is incorrect because it suggests that an SPS can provide power for a longer amount of time than an online UPS. In many cases, the performance of an online UPS is superior to that of an SPS. In any case, short- and longer-term battery power is available for both UPS types, depending on the model and how much you are willing to spend. **C**, an SPS because it provides battery power more immediately during a blackout, is incorrect. As explained, an SPS causes a lapse in power during the switch from regular to battery power. An online UPS always supplies the computer with battery power and continues to do so during a power outage. **D** is incorrect because it suggests that an online UPS is most effective because it will draw less power from the electrical source than an SPS. There is no significant difference between an SPS and online UPS in terms of the amount of electricity they draw from the wall outlet. Even if there were, it would have little or no effect on the operation of the computer, as long as the UPS still produced the proper voltage.

15. ☑ **D.** A CMOS battery is not considered a high-voltage device. This means it doesn't contain enough voltage to harm you. It could, however, contain chemicals or other elements that can burn your skin, so you should never open a battery. You must also dispose of batteries properly so that they do not cause environmental damage.

☒ **A**, a printer power supply; **B**, a computer power supply; and **C**, a monitor, are all incorrect because they are all considered high-voltage equipment. This means that they hold enough charge to seriously injure you. Never open the case of a high-voltage device, and never wear an ESD strap when working around one.

16. ☑ **D.** When replacing the sound card, you should place an ESD mat on your work surface, unplug the computer, put an ESD strap on, open the computer, remove the card, and place it on the ESD mat. The ESD mat, when properly grounded, provides a good place to put components when you remove them from the system. As with all electrical equipment, you should unplug the computer before you open it. The ESD strap will help prevent you from causing ESD when you touch the components in the computer.

☒ **A** is incorrect because it suggests placing the removed component on an antistatic bag. However, these bags work by removing static buildup from the inside and placing it on the outside of the bag. It is possible to cause ESD damage by exposing a component to this static buildup. **B** and **C** are incorrect because they suggest spraying the sound card or the computer with the antistatic spray. This liquid can harm computer components and should never be sprayed directly on them. Furthermore, you should never apply liquid of any kind to the computer's high-voltage power supply.

17. ☑ **D.** You should recycle printer toner cartridges because they are sold in very large numbers. Most computer users go through toner cartridges fairly quickly. It is better to recycle them and keep them out of landfills due to the amount of overall space they would take up if they were thrown away every time they were emptied. This is the same principle as that of recycling bottles and cans; they are not harmful to the environment per se, except that they take up space in landfills and can be better used if they are recycled.

☒ **A, B,** and **C** are all incorrect because they suggest that toner cartridges contain harmful acids, contaminating chemicals, and materials that can deplete the ozone layer, respectively. Toner cartridges do not contain any of these elements.

18. ☑ **A.** The likely cause is catastrophic ESD. The term *catastrophic ESD* refers to ESD damage that causes immediate and total failure of the affected component. The only solution is to replace the video card.

☒ **B,** degradation, is incorrect because this refers to gradual ESD damage over time. **C,** hidden ESD, is incorrect because this refers to ESD damage that you are unaware of, such as that being caused by a dust buildup. However, the shock you felt was almost certainly ESD. **D,** sudden ESD syndrome, is not a real term.

19. ☑ **C.** Raising the humidity of the room could help reduce the occurrence of ESD. Although many things contribute to ESD, one of the most significant is low humidity. Keep the room's humidity between 50 percent and 80 percent.

☒ **A** and **B** are incorrect because they suggesting altering the temperature of the room. However, humidity is a more likely contributor to ESD than temperature. **D,** keep the lights as dim as possible, is incorrect because although the presence of lights could cause EMI, it will not cause ESD.

20. ☑ **B.** You should store a hard drive in a cool and dry environment. Components must stay cool to work properly, and dry air is less likely to cause corrosion. Note that although dry air can contribute to ESD, a hard drive in storage will not just "develop" ESD. However, if the room is dry, make sure that you discharge static from yourself before touching the drive.

☒ **A,** cool and damp, is incorrect because damp air can lead to corrosion. **C,** warm and damp, and **D,** warm and dry, are both incorrect because a warm environment could cause the hard drive to lose its data.

LAB ANSWER

Obviously, your friend has some unsafe habits and should be warned about the possible results. If your friend eats at the computer, there is a likelihood of crumbs falling into the keyboard. If this happens, some of the keys might not depress all the way when pressed due to crumbs stuck underneath them. This problem can be resolved by turning the keyboard upside-down and shaking it. You could also clean the keyboard by blowing the crumbs out with compressed air or vacuuming them out. You might have to remove some of the keycaps to get at the material underneath them.

It is also possible for drinks to spill into the keyboard. When the liquid dries, it can leave a sticky residue. This can result in keys that stick when they are pressed. You can remedy this problem by soaking or rinsing the keyboard in distilled water.

If there are crumbs and liquid in the keyboard, there could also be some on the work surface on which the computer sits. These crumbs can be picked up and deposited into the mouse. You can remove the mouse's retaining ring and ball to clean it.

Your friend also has a cat, which means there could be loose fur present. As well as getting into the keyboard and mouse, fur can be drawn in by the power supply fan and deposited inside the computer. Using proper safety procedures, open the computer and used compressed air or a vacuum to remove fur and dust.

The fact that the lights flicker whenever your friend turns the speakers on could mean that the two are located too close to one another. If the speakers can affect the lights, there is a good chance that the lights are affecting the speakers with EMI. Move the two as far from each other as possible. Furthermore, flickering lights indicate an unsteady supply of power. Your friend might want to consider using a UPS that will smooth out the dips and increases in the power supply.

If your friend has a habit of rubbing his feet on the floor, he may be generating static. When he touches the computer or a floppy disk, he could cause ESD and damage the component. Antistatic spray on the floor and your friend's clothing could help prevent this problem.

Recall that floppy disks (and all magnetic storage) are susceptible to damage from EMI. Also recall that the monitor can produce EMI. It can therefore be unsafe to place the two near each other, because doing so could erase the data on the floppy disks. The disks should be moved as far away from the monitor and other EMI-causing devices as possible or placed in a shielded case.

5

Motherboard, Processors, and Memory

Y ou should already be familiar with the roles of the processor, RAM, the motherboard, and CMOS in the computer system. This chapter takes an in-depth look at the characteristics and specifications of each of these complex devices. Common processors in the Intel lineup are examined in terms of their abilities and differences. Various types of RAM are also discussed, as are rules you must follow regarding which types of RAM you can use in your system. The motherboard, including different form factors and designs, is discussed. Finally, the chapter finishes up with a description of basic CMOS settings and how these settings can alter the performance of the computer.

CERTIFICATION OBJECTIVE 5.01

Popular CPU Chips

There are many CPU manufacturers, including AMD, Cyrix, and Intel. Over time, these manufacturers have released a number of processor models, ranging from the 8086 (released in 1978) to the currently popular Pentium III and AMD Athlon. Beginning in 1995, AMD, Cyrix, and Intel began to seriously compete with one another, releasing processors at roughly the same times. The following subsections discuss the common processors, beginning with what are termed *fifth-generation processors.*

Pentium (586)

The Intel Pentium processor was first released in March 1993. It was the first *superscalar* processor, meaning that it was capable of parallel processing. This meant that two sets of instructions could be processed at the same time. Pentium processors support speeds of 60, 66, 75, 90, 100, 120, 133, 150, 166, and 200MHz. Pentiums 60 and 66 have a 273-pin PGA design and fit into "Socket 4" on the motherboard. These earlier processors contained around 3.1 million transistors and used 5vDC. Pentiums 75–200 are 296-pin staggered PGAs that use Socket 7. The Pentium 75–133MHz processors have 3.2 million transistors, and Pentium 150–200MHz processors have 3.3 million transistors. All Pentiums over 66MHz use 3.3vDC and can use either a passive heat sink or a fan (an active heat sink).

All Pentium processors have a 64-bit data bus, meaning that the processor can receive or transmit 64 bits at a time. They also have a 64-bit register (internal data bus), which is the on-board storage area in the processor. The Pentium processor has a 32-bit address bus, which means that it can address up to 4GB of memory.

Pentium processors include 16KB of on-board, integrated cache memory. This type of memory is often referred to as L1, or Level 1, cache. They are also able to access between 256KB and 512KB of motherboard (L2) cache. See the "From the Classroom" sidebar on page 197 for more information about L1 and L2 cache.

Pentium Pro

The Pentium Pro processor was released in November 1995 and was designed for use on servers rather than regular desktops. The Pentium Pro supports speeds of 150, 166, 180, and 200MHz. Its form is a 387-pin dual staggered PGA, and it uses socket 8 on the motherboard.

The Pentium Pro contains approximately 5.5 million transistors and uses 3.3vDC (3.1 for the 150MHz). Due to the increased number of transistors, Pentium Pro chips require an on-board fan. That is, they generate too much heat to use a passive heat sink.

Like the Pentium, the data bus of a Pentium Pro is 64 bit, and the register size is 32 bit. However, the Pentium Pro has a larger address bus, at 36 bits. This allows it to address up to 64GB of RAM. It also has a 16KB L1 cache, but it has an on-board L2 cache that runs at the same speed as the processor. The Pentium Pro can support between 256KB and 1MB of L2 cache.

AMD K5

Also released in 1995 was the K5 processor, designed by AMD. This processor supports speeds of 75, 90, 100, and 116MHz. It contains 4.3 million transistors and uses 3.52vDC. The K5 processor has a 296-pin PGA design and uses Socket 7. It also requires an active heat sink (fan). Like the Pentium, the K5 has a 64-bit data bus, a 32-bit register, and a 32-bit address bus. It is therefore able to address up to 4GB of RAM. The main difference between the Pentium and K5, other than the supported speeds, is the use of L1 cache. The Pentium supports up to 512KB; the K5 supports only 8KB.

Cyrix MI

The third competitor of note is Cyrix, which, in 1995, released its MI ("M One") processor. It supports 100–150MHz speeds and comes in a 296-pin PGA design. This processor has about 3 million transistors and uses 3.3vDC. Like other fifth-generation processors (Pentium and AMD K5), the Cyrix MI processor has a 64-bit data bus, a 32-bit register, and a 32-bit address bus. The MI includes 16KB of L1 cache.

Pentium with MMX Technology

In January 1997, Intel released a processor similar to the Pentium but with an improved instruction set (MMX) for handling graphics and other multimedia. All Pentium-family processors released since this Pentium with MMX technology include the MMX instruction set. The Pentium with MMX supports 166, 200, and 233MHz speeds and uses the same 296-pin staggered PGA form as a regular Pentium. The Pentium with MMX uses 3.3vDC externally, but because it uses only 2.8vDC internally, it must use a special Socket 7 that supplies the appropriate voltage. This processor contains 4.5 million transistors and can use either a passive heat sink or a fan.

The Pentium with MMX has the same data bus (64 bit), register size (32 bit), and address bus (32 bit) as the Pentium. It is also able to access up to 4GB of RAM, 32KB of L1 cache, and either 256KB or 521KB of motherboard L2 cache.

Pentium II

The Pentium II processor, released in May 1997, marks a radical form change from previous Intel processors. The Pentium II includes 512KB of on-board L2 cache, so the form was changed from the PGA to the much larger single-edge contact (SEC). SEC processors (242 pin) are attached to the motherboard via a Slot 1 connector.

The Pentium II introduced a number of new characteristics, such as its support for speeds of 233, 266, 300, and 333MHz. It contains approximately 7.5 million transistors, so it must use a special cooling fan. It uses 3.3vDC and includes 32KB of L1 cache. Like other processors in the Pentium family, the Pentium II has a 64-bit data bus and a 32-bit register. However, like the Pentium Pro, it has a 36-bit address bus, so it can use up to 64GB of RAM.

AMD K6

Around the time of the Pentium II processor's release, AMD released its own sixth-generation processor, the K6. This processor supports speeds from 166–266MHz. It has around 8.8 million transistors and uses 3.3vDC. Like previous AMD processors, the K6 is a 296-pin PGA and uses Socket 7 to attach to the motherboard. As with most processors, the K6 has a 64-bit data bus, a 32-bit register, and a 32-bit address bus. It also includes between 256KB and 1MB of L1 cache, but it does not include an on-board L2 cache.

Cyrix MII

Also released in 1997 was the Cyrix MII processor, which supports speeds of 150, 166, or 187MHz. It contains 6 million transistors, uses 3.3vDC, and has a 296-pin PGA form. Although its data bus, register, and address bus match that of the K6, the MII contains only 64KB of L1 cache.

Pentium III

The Pentium III (PIII) processor was released in March 1999. It includes advanced multimedia (MMX) instructions, called *single instruction multiple data (SIMD)* technology. Its first variant, referred to as simply Pentium III, has 512KB in on-board L2 cache and uses a 100MHz system bus. The second Pentium III variant is the Pentium III B, the main improvement of which is that it uses a 133MHz system bus. The final PIII variant is the Pentium III E. The PIII E processor uses 256KB of on-board *advanced transfer cache (ATC)*. ATC is simply a new technology that can increase performance by about 25 percent. Pentium III processors range in speeds from 450MHz to 1.13GHz and can include either, neither, or both of the E and B technologies.

Pentium III processors are available in two forms. The first form was a 242-pin SEC, and later, the PIII was released as a 370-pin PGA. The PIII SEC can use a regular Slot 1, as long as the slot supports 2.0vDC, and the PIII PGA uses a PGA370 ZIF. Pentium III processors contain 9.3 million transistors and have integrated fans. Like most processors in the Pentium family, the PIII has a 64-bit data bus, a 32-bit register, a 36-bit address bus, and support for 64GB of memory. The PIII also includes 32KB of L1 cache.

AMD Duron and Athlon

Other seventh-generation processors (along with the PIII) are the Duron processor, released by AMD in 1999, and the Athlon, released in 2000. The Duron supports speeds between 700 and 800MHz; the Athlon gives the PIII a run for its money with support for 850MHz–1.2GHz and 128KB of L1 cache.

The preceding subsections contain a good deal of very specific information about popular processors. However, because Intel processors are the most commonly used, you can expect to see more reference to them than the other processor types on the A+ exam. The information that you should concentrate on for the A+ exam is summarized in Table 5-1.

TABLE 5-1	Intel Pentium Processors

	Pentium	Pentium Pro	Pentium MMX	Pentium II	Pentium III
Form	273- or 296-pin PGA	387-pin PGA	296-pin PGA	242-pin SEC	242-pin SEC or 370-pin PGA
Socket	4, 5, or 7	8	7	Slot 1	Slot 1 or PGA370
Voltage (vDC)	3.3 or 5	3.1 or 3.3	3.3	3.3	2
Speeds	60–200MHz	150–200MHz	166–233MHz	233–333MHz	450MHz–1.13 GHz
L1 cache (KB)	16	16	32	32	32
L2 cache	256–512KB on motherboard	256–1MB on-board	256–512KB on motherboard	512KB on-board	256–512KB on-board
Notes	First to use parallel processing	Designed for servers	Enhanced multimedia	First to use SEC form	SIMD instruction set

FROM THE CLASSROOM

Isn't "On-Board L2 Cache" an Oxymoron?

Traditionally, L1 cache is located within the processor (on-board), and L2 cache is located on the motherboard. However, some newer processors (Pentiums Pro, II, and III) include L2 cache that is said to be "on board." This means that it is included with the processor itself. However, L1 cache is actually *part of* the processor, and on-board L2 cache is external to the processor but housed within the same casing. That is, the processor and external cache have been bundled together in a convenient package. So, for example, when you pick up a Pentium II, you are actually holding the processor (which has L1 cache) and the L2 cache.

The reason for including L2 cache in the processor package is to speed it up. L2 cache

that is located on the motherboard is limited to the system bus speed (around 133MHz at best; compare that to the actual speed of the processor). By removing the L2 cache from the motherboard and placing it within the processor, it is able to run at the processor's speed.

Due to the popularity in this design, the term *Level 3 cache* has emerged. Now, in many cases, L1 refers to the processor's internal cache, L2 refers to the cache located external to the processor but within the processor package, and L3 refers to cache located on the motherboard (what used to be referred to as L2).

—Amy Thomson,
A+ Certified Technician, MOUS Master

exam
Ⓦatch
There are a great many differences between processors in the Pentium family. However, you should concentrate on the characteristics listed in Table 5-1.

It is fairly easy to identify an Intel processor by its physical shape and markings. However, you can also identify the processor without opening the computer. If you are using Microsoft Windows, follow the steps in Exercise 5-1 to find out what type of processor your computer is using.

EXERCISE 5-1

Identifying Your Processor

1. Right-click the My Computer icon.

2. Select Properties.

3. Read the information in the General tab. Use the data in Table 5-2 to determine your processor type.

TABLE 5-2	If You See This ...	Your Processor Is ...
Intel Processor Family and Model Numbers	Intel, x86 Family 5	Intel Pentium
	Intel, x86 Family 6 Model 1	Intel Pentium Pro
	Intel, x86 Family 6 Model 3	Intel Pentium II
	Intel, x86 Family 6 Model 5	Intel Pentium II
	Intel, x86 Family 6 Model 6	Intel Pentium II
	Intel, x86 Family 6 Model 7	Intel Pentium III
	Intel, x86 Family 6 Model 8	Intel Mobile Pentium III

CERTIFICATION OBJECTIVE 5.02

Random Access Memory

The primary function of RAM is to provide a temporary storage place for information about devices and applications. However, there are many types of RAM with which you should be familiar. This section discusses the many incarnations of RAM as it has been developed and refined over time. This section also discusses important factors to consider when installing or upgrading the RAM in a computer system. That is, there are guidelines you must follow about the type of RAM, the type of package, and the amounts of RAM that you install in a particular system. These concepts are revisited in Chapter 9, Memory Management.

Types of RAM

RAM is not all the same. Over time, RAM technology has improved, changed form, and been used for specialized components. The most common types of RAM are discussed here.

SRAM

Static RAM (SRAM) was the first type of RAM available. SRAM can be accessed at approximately 10 nanoseconds (ns), meaning that it takes about 10ns for the processor to receive requested information from SRAM. The structure of SRAM chips limits them to a maximum data capacity of 256KB. Although SRAM is very fast compared with DRAM, it is also very expensive. For this reason, SRAM is typically used only for system cache.

DRAM

Dynamic RAM (DRAM) was developed to combat the restrictive expense of using SRAM. DRAM chips provide much slower access than SRAM chips but can store several megabytes of data on a single chip (hundreds of megabytes if they are packaged together on a module). Every "cell" in a DRAM chip contains one transistor and one capacitor to store a single bit of information. This design makes it necessary for the DRAM chip to receive a constant power refresh from the computer, preventing the capacitors from losing their charge. This constant refresh can make access even slower and causes the DRAM chip to draw more power from the computer than an SRAM chip. Because of its low cost and high capacity, DRAM is used as "main" memory in the computer.

The term *DRAM* is typically used to describe any type of memory that uses the technology just described. However, the first DRAM chips were very slow (~80–90ns), so faster variants have been developed. The list is quite large and includes fast-paged RAM, EDO RAM, SDRAM, RDRAM, SDLRAM, and BEDO RAM. As computer systems improve, the list of DRAM technologies continues to grow. However, EDO, SDRAM, RDRAM, and DDR RAM are currently the most common, so they are described here.

EDO RAM

Extended data out (EDO) RAM improves on traditional DRAM by performing more than one task at a time. When one piece of data is being sent to the processor, another is being retrieved from the RAM module. While that piece of data is being transferred, the EDO RAM is looking for the next piece to retrieve for the processor. This process enables the chip's data to be accessed at about 60ns. EDO RAM chips can be used only in a computer system whose processor and motherboard support its use.

SDRAM

Synchronous dynamic RAM, or *SDRAM,* is about twice as fast as EDO RAM because it is able to run at the speed of the system bus (up to 100–133MHz). However, as faster system bus speeds are developed, EDO and SDRAM are being replaced with other, faster types of DRAM, such as RDRAM and DDR RAM. Like EDO RAM, SDRAM can be used only in systems that support it.

RDRAM

RDRAM is an acronym for *Rambus Dynamic RAM* and gets its name from the company that developed it, Rambus, Inc. RDRAM uses a special Rambus channel that has a data transfer rate of 800MHz. The channel width can be doubled, resulting in a 1.6GHz data transfer! RDRAM can be used only in computers with special RDRAM channels and slots. RDRAM is fairly new, so you shouldn't expect to see it in computers that were manufactured before 1999.

DDR RAM

Double data rate (DDR) RAM doubles the rate of speed at which standard SDRAM can process data. That means DDR is roughly twice as fast as standard RAM.

Currently, the standards available for DDR RAM are PC1600 and PC2100. This new labeling refers to the total bandwidth of the memory, as opposed to the old standard, which listed the speed rating (in MHz) of the SDRAM memory—in this case, the PC66, PC100, and the PC133.

VRAM

Video RAM (VRAM) is a specialized type of memory that is used only with video adapters. The video adapter is one of the computer's busiest components, so, to keep up with video requirements, many adapters have an on-board miniprocessor and special video RAM. The adapter can process requests independently of the CPU, then store its results in the VRAM until the CPU retrieves it. VRAM is much faster than EDO RAM and is capable of being read from and written to at the same time. The result is better and faster video performance. Because VRAM includes more circuitry than regular DRAM, VRAM modules are slightly larger.

The term *Video RAM* refers to both a specific type of memory and a generic term for all RAM used by the video adapter (much like the term *DRAM*, which is often used to denote all types of memory that are dynamic). Faster versions of video memory have been introduced, including WRAM.

WRAM

Window RAM (WRAM) is another type of video RAM but provides faster access than VRAM. It uses the same dual-ported technology that allows devices to read and write data to the video memory at the same time. The term "window" refers to its ability to retrieve large blocks (windows) of data at one time.

Physical Characteristics

The RAM types discussed so far can have many different physical forms. Your system must support both the technology and form of a memory module. The system must also support the data width of the memory as well as its method of error correction. The following subsections describe some common physical forms of memory modules and other characteristics that distinguish one module from another.

Single Inline Memory Modules

The first memory chips were *dual inline package (DIP)* chips, which were inserted directly onto the motherboard. However, as discussed in Chapter 1, their structure made them prone to "chip creep." Single inline memory modules (SIMMs) were developed to combat the loosening of memory chips and to recover space on the motherboard.

SIMMs are available in 30-pin and 72-pin forms. Thirty-pin SIMMs are 8 bit, meaning that data can be transferred into or out of the module 8 bits at a time. Seventy-two-pin SIMMs are 32 bit. Because SIMMs are older technology, they are typically used for fast-paged and EDO RAM. You are not as likely to find a SIMM with SDRAM, since dual inline memory modules (DIMMs) were the prevalent form when SDRAM was introduced.

Dual Inline Memory Modules

DIMMs look similar to SIMMs but are slightly longer and are installed into a different type of slot. DIMMs have two rows of connectors, equaling 168 connectors in all, and are 64 bit. DIMMs are likely to contain either EDO RAM or SDRAM simply because those technologies were common when DIMMs were introduced.

Rambus Inline Memory Module

The *Rambus Inline Memory Module (RIMM)* is designed specifically for use with Rambus memory. RIMMs look just like DIMMs but have 184 connectors. They are also more proprietary and less common than SIMMs and DIMMs. RIMMs are 16 bit.

Memory Banks

The *bit width* of a memory module is very important; the term refers to how much information the processor can access from or write to memory in a single cycle. A *memory bank* represents the number of memory modules required to match the data bus width of the processor.

For example, a Pentium II processor has a 64-bit data bus. In this computer, one 64-bit DIMM would make one memory bank. Two 32-bit SIMMs are required to make one memory bank, and four 16-bit RIMMs are in one memory bank. You must ensure that the computer contains at least one full memory bank, or it will not even boot.

exam
Ⓦatch

A memory bank refers to a match between the processor's data bus width and RAM's bit width. If you are using a 64-processor, one 64-bit DIMM makes a full bank, and four 16-bit RIMMs make a full bank. The term memory bank does not refer to the slots used to attach the RAM modules to the motherboard.

When dealing with processors from the Pentium family, it is not difficult to determine how much memory you need to create a full bank, since they are all 64-bit processors. However, you might have to work with older processors and older types of RAM. Use the formula in Exercise 5-2 to figure out the number of memory modules you need to install in your computer.

EXERCISE 5-2

Calculating the Memory Bank Size

1. Determine the data bus width of the processor in your computer (16 bit for a 386SX, 32 bit for a 386DX or 486, 64 bit for the Pentium family).

2. Determine the bit width of the memory module. Thirty-pin SIMMs are 8 bit, 72-pin SIMMs are 32 bit, DIMMs are 64 bit, and RIMMs are 16 bit.

3. Divide the processor's data bus width (Step 1) by the memory's bit width (Step 2). The number you get is the number of memory modules you must install to create one full bank.

Parity and Nonparity Chips

One type of error checking used with memory is called *parity*. In parity, every byte of data is accompanied by a ninth bit (the parity bit), which is used by the receiving device to determine the presence of errors in the data. There are two types of parity: odd and even. In *odd parity*, the parity bit is used to ensure the total number of 1s in the data stream is odd. For example, suppose a byte consists of the following data: 11010010. The number of 1s in this data is 4, an even number. The 9th bit will be a 1, to ensure that the total number of 1s is odd: 110100101.

Parity is not failure-proof. Suppose the above data stream contained two errors: 101100101. If the computer was using odd parity, the error would slip through (try it; count the 1s). However, parity is a quick routine and does not inhibit the access time of memory the way a more sophisticated error-checking routine would.

Some memory modules use parity. These modules include an extra bit for parity for every 8 bits of data. Therefore, a 30-pin SIMM without parity is 8 bit and with parity is 9 bit. A DIMM without parity is 64 bit. With parity, the DIMM has 8 extra bits (one parity bit for every 8 data bits). Therefore, a DIMM with parity has 64 + 8 bits = 72 bits. If your system supports parity, you must use parity memory modules. You cannot use memory with parity if your system does not support it.

on the
()ob

Memory with parity checking is becoming less and less common in newer systems. The majority of today's computer systems do not support memory that uses parity.

Test your knowledge of the memory concepts in this section by answering the following Scenario & Solution questions.

SCENARIO & SOLUTION

Which types of memory packages are available?	SIMM, DIMM, and RIMM.
How many DIMMs make a full bank in a Pentium-class computer?	The processor's data bus and the DIMM are both 64 bit.
What is the parity bit for the data stream 10110110 if the RAM uses odd parity?	0. The parity bit in this case is a 1 or 0 to ensure that the total number of 1s is odd. There are five 1s in this data stream, so the parity bit is 0.
What does *dual ported* mean?	This term refers to the ability of the computer to read from and write to memory at the same time. This is a characteristic of VRAM and WRAM.

CERTIFICATION OBJECTIVE 5.03

Motherboards

As you now know, the type and amount of memory you install depends on the type of processor you are using. You must follow specific guidelines or the computer will not work. The same is true for motherboards. That is, you cannot install just any type of processor or memory in the motherboard and make it work. There are several motherboard forms, each with different layouts, components, and specifications. Most motherboards are restricted to using only a few types of processors and memory.

This section focuses on types of motherboards and their typical integrated components. You will also learn about the differences between the motherboard's communication buses and the types of systems they allow you to use. However, all motherboards are unique in terms of the type of slots, memory, and processor they support. In other words, you cannot tell which components a motherboard supports solely by knowing which type of motherboard it is. Therefore, you must always check with the manufacturer's documentation before you upgrade or install a processor or memory.

Types of Motherboards

Although motherboards can vary from computer to computer, there are two common forms: the AT and ATX. Their sizes, typical components, and prevalence are discussed here.

Full and Baby AT

Advanced Technology (AT) motherboards were introduced in 1984 (around the time of the Intel 80286 processor). They measure approximately12 inches by 13 inches and typically support 80286 or older processors, 5.25 inches floppy drives, and 84-key keyboards. A smaller version of the AT motherboard, typically measuring around 8.5 inches by 13 inches was later released. This form was called the Baby AT, and the original form became known as the Full AT. The two AT motherboards are similar in layout, but the Full AT motherboard is now practically obsolete, and the Baby AT motherboard is still being used by some manufacturers. Depending on when it was manufactured, Baby AT motherboards might contain SIMM and/or DIMM memory slots and 80386, 80486, or Pentium processor slots. Baby AT motherboards also use the 3.5 inches floppy drive rather than the older 5.25 inches.

AT motherboards can be identified by the fact that the parallel and serial ports are not integrated with the keyboard; rather, they are installed in an empty chassis slot and attached to motherboard ports via small ribbon connectors. Other identifying characteristics of the AT motherboard are the placement of the processor socket near the end of the expansion card slots, the use of a DIN-5 keyboard connector, two power connector ports (for P8 and P9 connectors), and support for ±12 and ±5vDC only.

on the **job**

Some manufacturers are still using the Baby AT motherboard for new computers. Therefore, although it is rare, you might find this form with support for newer processors and support for USB and/or IEEE-1394.

ATX

The *ATX motherboard* was released by Intel in 1996 and is the most commonly used form in new PCs. *ATX* is not an acronym but is the actual trademarked name of the motherboard form. The ATX form is the same size as a Baby AT motherboard but has a different orientation and layout (see Figure 5-1). Note that the processor is located further from the expansion slots, and the hard drive and floppy drive connectors are located closer to the bays on the chassis.

e x a m
ⓦ a t c h

Although there are many variants, most of today's computers are based on the ATX motherboard.

FIGURE 5-1

The ATX
motherboard.

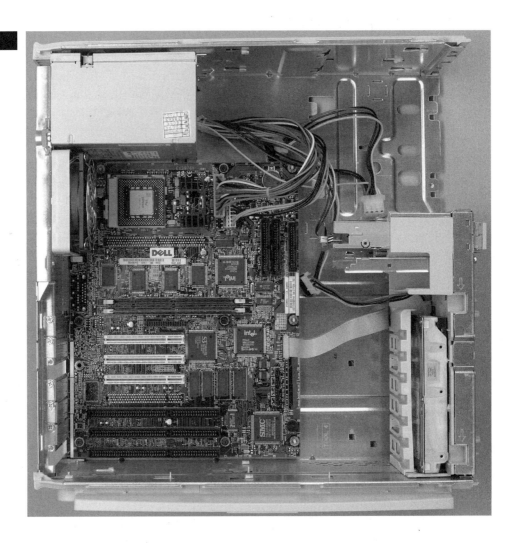

The ATX motherboard also includes integrated parallel and serial ports (I/O ports) and a Mini-DIN-6, rather than a DIN-5, keyboard connector. The ATX motherboard's power supply uses a single motherboard connector and supplies voltages of ±12, ±5, and +3.3vDC. Again, depending on when it was manufactured, an ATX motherboard can contain SIMM and DIMM memory slots; support for BIOS-controlled power management; 80386, 80486, or Pentium-class processor sockets; and support for USB.

Test your knowledge of motherboard concepts by answering the next Scenario & Solution questions.

Bus Architecture

The term *bus* is used to refer to pathways that signals use to travel from one component to another in the computer. There are many types of buses, including the processor bus, which is used by data traveling into and out of the processor itself. This bus type was described earlier in the "Popular CPU Chips" section. The address and data buses described there are both part of the processor bus. Another type of bus is the *memory bus*, which is located on the motherboard itself and is used by the processor to access memory.

The following subsections focus on various types of I/O buses, the paths between the processors, and I/O components such as peripherals and drives. You can access a motherboard's I/O bus by installing expansion cards into the appropriate expansion slots. Common expansion card types are shown in Figure 5-2.

SCENARIO & SOLUTION

How do ATX motherboards differ from Baby AT motherboards?	ATX motherboards include 3.3vDC, have integrated I/O ports, and include a Mini-DIN-6 keyboard connector, to name a few differences.
What is the most commonly used motherboard form?	The ATX.
Which motherboard form is typically the largest?	The Full AT, which measures 12 inches by 13 inches.

FIGURE 5-2

ISA, PCI, and
VESA (bottom)
expansion cards.

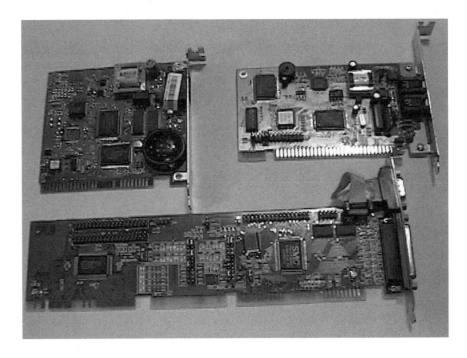

ISA

The first type of I/O bus was the *Industry Standard Architecture (ISA)* bus. This is an 8-bit bus, meaning that data can travel 8 bits at a time between devices. Later, in 1984, a 16-bit ISA bus was developed. Both the 8-bit and 16-bit ISA buses run at 8.3MHz.

Although some expansion cards (such as most sound or modem cards) require only 8 or 16 bits, the ISA bus is becoming obsolete. Current motherboards carry only one ISA slot, and most of the newer motherboards no longer include any ISA slots. For those motherboards that still have them, the 8-bit and 16-bit slots are different sizes, but an 8-bit card can be used in a 16-bit slot. That is, the 8-bit card uses only the first half of the slot's connectors.

EISA

Extended ISA (EISA) bus architecture was developed after 16-bit ISA and offers a 32-bit data width and bus speed of 8.3MHz. EISA slots on the motherboard look just like 16-bit ISA slots. The difference, however, is that EISA slots have two rows of connectors, one deeper than the other. The EISA expansion card has two corresponding connector lengths. EISA slots are backward compatible with 8-bit and 16-bit ISA expansion cards. That is, you can use an EISA, 8-bit ISA, or 16-bit ISA card in an EISA slot.

Today, EISA slots are not as common as ISA slots, since faster (and wider) 32-bit architectures have been developed. You are unlikely to find an EISA slot on a motherboard designed for an 80486 or newer processor.

VESA Local Bus

The *VESA Local Bus (VL-Bus)* was developed in 1992 by the Video Electronics Standards Association (VESA). It was designed specifically for use in the 80486 processor, to improve video performance. Unlike its predecessors, the VESA bus is not limited to using the regular I/O expansion bus. Rather, the VESA bus provides a direct channel between the VESA card and the processor (called a *local bus*). The VESA bus can run at speeds up to 33MHz.

Like EISA, the VL Bus is a 32-bit bus. VESA slots are actually 16-bit ISA slots with an extra brown slot at the end. VESA video cards are therefore very long and, unfortunately, prone to coming loose. VESA slots are backward compatible with ISA cards, meaning that you can use a VESA, 8-bit ISA, or 16-bit ISA card in a VESA slot. As well as video cards, VESA slots are sometimes used for hard drive controllers.

PCI

The most common bus architecture in new computers is *Peripheral Component Interconnect (PCI)*. It was released in 1993 and is typically found in 80486 and newer systems. The PCI bus is 32 bit and can run at half the processor's memory bus speed. Although it is considered a "local" bus, it is not limited to the 80486 processor the way VESA architecture is.

PCI slots are smaller than ISA slots and are typically white. PCI cards and slots are not compatible with those of other bus architectures. Although PCI was initially developed for video cards, PCI cards are also available for video, networking, and SCSI controllers, among other peripherals.

on the **job**

A 64-bit, 66MHz PCI standard has been developed but is not being widely implemented. Instead, it has been used as the foundation for the AGP architecture, described in the following section.

AGP

AGP stands for *accelerated graphics port* and is a relative newcomer to the computer industry. AGP is a local bus and was designed only for video. This architecture is typically considered a "port" rather than a bus because it consists of a direct link between the processor and the video card only. AGP is 32 bit and can run at the speed of the processor's memory bus.

AGP slots look very similar to PCI slots, but they are not compatible with PCI cards. To use AGP, the system's chipset and motherboard must support it. The AGP architecture also includes an AGP controller, which is typically a small, green chip on the motherboard itself.

exam
⑩atch

The most common bus architectures in today's computers are ISA, PCI, and AGP. Almost all computers contain expansion slots for each of these bus types.

Expansion cards are all installed using the same procedure, regardless of the slot type. Use the installation procedure outlined in Exercise 5-3.

EXERCISE 5-3

Installing an Expansion Card

1. Turn the computer off, and ensure that you carry out proper ESD procedures.

2. Position the controller card upright over the appropriate expansion slot.

3. Place your thumbs along the top edge of the card and push straight down. If necessary, rock the card along its length (never side to side).

4. Secure the card to the chassis using the existing screw holes.

USB

As discussed in Chapters 1 and 2, the Universal Serial Bus, or USB, offers a bandwidth of 12Mbps for USB 1.1 and a design data rate of 480Mbps for USB 2.0, and is used to connect up to 127 external devices. The USB controller itself (if it is not integrated) is installed in a PCI expansion slot. It supports both Plug and Play and hot swapping.

PC Card and PCMCIA

Recall from Chapter 2 that PC Cards, which were designed for use in portable computers, come in several types. Type I and Type II cards (also referred to as *PCMCIA cards*) are 16bit. Type III cards are 32 bit. Each PC card slot is backward compatible, meaning that you can insert a Type I or II card in a Type II slot, and you can insert all three card types into a Type III slot.

IDE

The preceding I/O bus architectures are used for attaching video or peripheral cards to the computer. IDE devices, such as hard drives and CD-ROM drives, also use the system's I/O bus. However, recall from Chapter 2 that there are several drive interface standards, including the IDE and ATA families (collectively referred to as *IDE*).

Older ATA or IDE hard drives are 16 bit, so whether they require a controller card or have a controller card that is integrated with the motherboard, they use the 16-bit ISA bus. Faster standards, such as Ultra DMA, ATAPI, and EIDE require the use of a local bus, such as the 32-bit VESA or PCI architectures.

SCSI

When installing a SCSI system, you must use a system controller that will at least meet the bit width of the SCSI system you are installing. For example, a Wide SCSI-2 system requires at least a 16-bit ISA bus because it is a 16-bit SCSI system (refer to Chapter 2 for SCSI system bus widths). Additionally, you must consider the speed of the SCSI system. The ISA bus is limited to 8MBps, so it is sufficient for use with SCSI 1 or regular SCSI 2, which run at a maximum of 5MBps. However, if you plan to use any other SCSI system, consider using a SCSI controller designed for a local bus architecture, such as VESA or PCI.

You should now be familiar with common bus architectures and their characteristics. Test your knowledge before continuing in the chapter by answering the following Scenario & Solution questions.

SCENARIO & SOLUTION

What are the most common bus architectures used today?	ISA, PCI, and AGP.
Which slots can I use to install an 8-bit ISA card?	8-bit ISA, 16-bit ISA, EISA, and VESA.
Which bus architecture should I use to connect an IDE drive interface?	The IDE interface is 16 bit, so you should use a bus type that is 16 bit or wider. You should use a local bus to take advantage of the IDE drive's speed.

CERTIFICATION OBJECTIVE 5.04

Complementary Metal-Oxide Semiconductor Settings

Most computer systems (especially newer ones) allow you to customize the settings of a number of motherboard components. This is done by selecting options within the CMOS settings program. Literally hundreds of CMOS settings are available in different computers; only the most common ones are discussed here.

To access the computer's CMOS settings, watch the computer screen at startup. Following the POST, a message appears, indicating the proper key sequence you should use to enter the CMOS settings program. This key combination varies among computers but is typically F2, Del, or Ctrl + Alt + Esc. In most systems, the message will appear for only 3 to 5 seconds. You must use the indicated key combination within that allotted time.

Note also that CMOS settings programs are designed differently. Some allow you to use the mouse and some the keyboard only. Furthermore, the names of the settings might be slightly different. Use the program's Help feature for information about how to navigate through the program and save or discard your changes. It's a good idea to make notes about the current CMOS settings before you change them, in case you need to change them back. Although this won't work in all computers, you can try the procedure in Exercise 5-4 to print the CMOS settings.

EXERCISE 5-4

Backing Up the CMOS Settings

1. Restart the computer using the Ctrl + Alt + Delete key combination (do not use the reset or power buttons to do this).

2. Enter the CMOS settings program using the specified key combination.

3. Press the Print Screen key on the keyboard to print the current screen. Although this will not work in all systems, it could provide you with a handy hard copy of the CMOS settings.

4. Use the Print Screen key on each screen of the CMOS settings program. If this procedure doesn't work on your computer, you can purchase a third-party CMOS backup program or resort to using pen and paper to write a copy of the settings.

Printer Parallel Port

You can use the CMOS settings to configure the IRQ and I/O addresses of the system's parallel port(s). In newer computers, however, most parallel ports support the IEEE-1284 standard, meaning that they are Plug and Play, so they are configured automatically by the OS.

You can also use the CMOS settings to set the parallel port mode. For example, many parallel ports run in *unidirectional mode* by default. This means that peripheral devices attached to the port can receive but cannot send data. This mode might be referred to in the CMOS settings as "Transfer only." However, some parallel devices are designed to send communication signals back to the computer. These devices require a *bi-directional mode* (also called Standard mode on some machines).

Newer devices may take advantage of faster IEEE-1284 bi-directional modes, called ECP or EPP modes. *Enhanced capability port (ECP) mode* allows access to DMA channels and is approximately 10 times faster than regular bi-directional mode. ECP mode is used for printers and scanners. *Enhanced parallel port (EPP) mode* offers the same performance as ECP but is designed for use with parallel devices other than printers and scanners.

Another CMOS parallel port setting is *enable/disable*. You can use this feature to instruct the computer to use or ignore the parallel port. It can be useful to temporarily disable the port when troubleshooting or if the port is in conflict with another component. You might also need to disable the on-board parallel port if it has stopped working. Disabling it will allow you to install another (nonintegrated) parallel port.

COM/Serial Port

Like the parallel port, you can use the CMOS settings to configure the IRQ and I/O address of the COM port(s). However, in newer systems, this is accomplished by the OS. You can also use the CMOS settings to enable or disable the COM port.

Floppy Drive

The CMOS settings program contains options for the configuration and use of the floppy drive. You can enable or disable the use of the motherboard's integrated floppy disk controller by selecting the appropriate option. You might want to disable the controller so that you can use an expansion controller card instead. You can also configure the floppy drive controller so that it cannot be used to boot the computer. You might want to do so to prevent boot sector viruses from affecting your computer or to speed up the overall boot sequence if you don't plan to boot from floppy disk. If you later find you need to boot from the floppy drive, simply change the CMOS settings accordingly.

You can also use the CMOS settings to configure individual floppy drives on the controller. If the floppy drive type is not automatically selected by the BIOS, use the CMOS to select the proper setting: 360KB, 720KB, 1.2MB, 1.44MB, or 2.88MB, depending on the type of drive you are using.

Hard Drive

You can use the CMOS settings to set the type and capacity of each hard drive installed in the system. You should set the type to Auto, if this option is available. This setting instructs the BIOS to read the type and capacity from the drive itself. However, older systems might require you to manually enter the type and capacity (tracks, sectors, and cylinders) of each drive. You can also use the Autodetect feature to force the BIOS to search for and reidentify all hard drives in the system. This option is typically used when a slave or secondary drive has been added to the system or when the hard drive has been upgraded.

Memory

As discussed in previous chapters, RAM capacities do not have to be configured. RAM is simply installed in the computer and automatically counted by the BIOS at startup. However, you can use the CMOS settings to enable or disable the memory's ability to use parity error checking. You can use this setting only if the RAM supports parity. If you enable the CMOS parity option but are not using memory that supports parity, the computer will not boot properly. You can also use the CMOS settings to turn the memory "tick sound" off. This is the sound you hear when memory is being counted by the BIOS at startup. Some systems even let you manually set the speed and timing of the existing RAM so that all modules match. This option is typically found only in older machines.

exam
ⓦatch   *RAM capacity is counted at startup, not configured in the CMOS settings.*

Boot Sequence

The Boot Sequence CMOS setting relates to the order in which the BIOS will search devices for an OS. The default setting on most computers is A:, C:, CD-ROM. You can change this order so that the computer looks first on the hard drive or CD-ROM. This is particularly helpful in keeping boot sector viruses from infecting the computer, when you are troubleshooting, and when you are installing an OS for the first time. For example, many OS CDs contain enough instructions to boot the computer and install the OS, even without a boot (floppy) disk or a minimal OS on the hard drive.

Date and Time

You can use the CMOS settings program to set the computer's real-time clock. The date and time that you set here will be used by the OS, as well as any applications that are date or time aware. You can also set the date and time using the Windows OS. If you change the date and time in the CMOS, it will automatically be updated in the OS, and vice versa.

Passwords

Most CMOS settings programs allow you to set passwords on the computer itself. A user password can be set to allow or restrict the booting of the system. That is, if booting is enabled, the proper password must be entered for the computer to finish booting. A supervisor password can be set to allow or restrict access to the CMOS settings program itself or to change user passwords. Some systems (typically newer ones) include both password options; older systems typically include only supervisor-type passwords, required to both boot the system and enter the CMOS settings program.

You must be especially careful with supervisor passwords. If you forget the CMOS password, you can't even get into the CMOS program to change or disable the password. Fortunately, most systems that have the CMOS password feature include a "clear password" jumper on the motherboard. If you forget the CMOS password, you can open the computer and set the jumper so that the password is removed. If there is no jumper for clearing the password, you can clear the entire contents of the CMOS by temporarily removing the battery. This is, however, a last resort, since you will use all but the default settings.

Plug-and-Play BIOS

If the BIOS is Plug and Play, the CMOS settings program will probably include some options for configuring it. One option is Plug and Play Operating System. When enabled, this setting informs the BIOS that the OS will configure Plug-and-Play devices. If this option is disabled, these devices will be configured by the BIOS itself. Another Plug-and-Play option allows you to enable or disable the BIOS's configuration of Plug-and-Play devices.

CERTIFICATION SUMMARY

This chapter focused on detailed characteristics of CPUs in the Pentium family, motherboard forms, memory types, and CMOS settings. These components are all interrelated, and it is important for you to understand which CPUs can work with which types of memory. Furthermore, you must use a motherboard that supports the CPU and RAM and ensure that the CMOS will support the installed components. A good knowledge of these concepts is especially important when you are repairing or upgrading a computer system.

For example, by knowing the CPU's memory address width, you will know the maximum RAM capacity it can access. In addition, by knowing the CPU's data bus width, you will know how many RAM modules you must install at a time to create a full memory bank. Before purchasing a motherboard, ensure that it has the proper RAM and CPU slots and that the CMOS settings are appropriate for your needs.

TWO-MINUTE DRILL

Here are some of the key points from each certification objective in Chapter 5.

Popular CPU Chips

❑ Processors in the Pentium family include the Pentium, Pentium Pro, Pentium with MMX, Pentium II, and Pentium III.

❑ Pentium II and Pentium III processors connect to the motherboard using Slot 1, and other Pentium processors use sockets.

❑ Pentium Pro, Pentium II, and Pentium III processors include on-board L2 cache.

Random Access Memory

❑ SRAM is very fast, very expensive, and used for L2 cache in most systems.

❑ DRAM is slower than SRAM but is less expensive and has a higher capacity and is used as main memory in the computer.

❑ You must install SIMMs, DIMMs, and RIMMs in full memory banks so that their total bit width matches the width of the processor's data bus.

❑ Some memory modules use an error-checking method called odd or even parity.

Motherboards

❑ The most common type of motherboard in current computers is the ATX form factor, which includes 3.3vDC support, Mini-DIN-6 keyboard connectors, and a single P1 power connector.

❑ The most common type of bus architectures are ISA, PCI, and AGP.

❑ VESA, PCI, and AGP bus architectures are considered "local" because they connect more directly with the processor.

❑ When using a drive interface, such as IDE or SCSI, use a bus architecture that supports the interface's bit width and use a local bus architecture for faster devices.

Complementary Metal-Oxide Semiconductor Settings

❑ The CMOS settings program allows you to alter the behavior and configuration of many of the system's components.

❑ Parallel ports can be set to unidirectional, bi-directional, ECP, or EPP mode.

❑ You can use the CMOS settings to disable or enable the I/O ports, floppy drive, hard drive, or Plug-and-Play support.

❑ The CMOS settings program allows you to set the time and date, user passwords, and boot sequence.

SELF TEST

The following questions will help you measure your understanding of the material presented in this chapter. Read all of the choices carefully because there might be more than one correct answer. Choose all correct answers for each question.

Popular CPU Chips

1. What is the data bus width of all Pentium-class processors?

   A. 32 bit

   B. 36 bit

   C. 64 bit

   D. Pentium processors have different data bus widths

2. While shopping for computer components, you come across a motherboard that has a Socket 8. Which type of processor can you install on this motherboard?

   A. Pentium

   B. Pentium Pro

   C. Pentium with MMX

   D. Pentium II or III

3. Your computer is a Pentium MMX with 2GB of RAM. You plan to add more memory to the system, but you don't want to add more RAM than the processor can access. How much more memory should you add?

   A. None

   B. 2GB

   C. 30GB

   D. 62GB

4. How does a Pentium II processor attach to the motherboard?

   A. Socket II

   B. Socket 9

   C. Slot 1

   D. The processor is integrated

5. Which of the following processors is available in versions E or B and uses SIMD technology?

   A. Pentium Pro

   B. Pentium with MMX

   C. Pentium II

   D. Pentium III

Random Access Memory

6. What is the maximum capacity of an SRAM chip?

   A. 256KB

   B. 512KB

   C. 1MB

   D. 64MB

7. Which of the following statements is true regarding DRAM and SRAM?

   A. DRAM is used as main memory because it is cheaper than SRAM.

   B. SRAM is used as main memory because it is faster than DRAM.

   C. DRAM is used as cache memory because it is available in higher capacities than SRAM.

   D. SRAM requires a constant power refresh.

8. A customer is planning to add more RAM to her computer system and has asked your advice. The computer is a Pentium and already has 2GB of memory in DIMM form. She wants to add 4GB of RDRAM but was told that her computer probably wouldn't support it. What do you tell her?

   A. RDRAM is intended for use by video cards, not processors.

   B. She has already reached the RAM capacity for her system.

   C. RDRAM is not supported by the processor in this case.

   D. Go ahead and add the RDRAM.

9. You are building a new Pentium III computer, and you have installed two RIMMs, totaling 6GB of memory in two of the four slots. However, the computer will not boot. Which of the following could be the problem?

   A. The processor cannot access the memory type.

   B. The memory capacity is too low for the processor.

C. The memory capacity is too high for the processor.

D. There are not enough modules installed.

10. A computer uses odd parity. What is the parity bit for the data stream 10110010?

A. 0

B. 1

C. 01

D. Computers do not use odd parity

Motherboards

11. Which is the most commonly used motherboard form in currently manufactured computers?

A. Baby AT

B. AT

C. Full ATX

D. ATX

12. You are planning to purchase an 8-bit internal modem for your Pentium II computer. Which type of expansion slot is it most likely to use?

A. 8-bit ISA

B. 16-bit ISA

C. PCI

D. AGP

13. You are rebuilding a computer that has only VESA slots (a rare case indeed!). Which types of expansion cards can you install in the computer?

A. VESA only

B. 8-bit ISA, 16-bit ISA, and VESA

C. EISA and VESA

D. 8-bit ISA, 16-bit ISA, EISA, and VESA

14. Which of the following are considered "local" bus architectures?

A. ISA, VESA, and PCI

B. EISA, VESA, and PCI

C. VESA, PCI, and AGP

D. AGP only

15. Which type of PC Card supports a 32-bit data transfer?

A. Type III only

B. Types II and III only

C. Types I, II, and III

D. Type II only

Complementary Metal-Oxide Semiconductor Settings

16. You have just installed a *new* printer in your new computer. However, when you try to print, you receive a "Port Mode" error. Which port mode does the printer most likely require?

A. Output only

B. Bi-directional

C. ECP

D. EPP

17. Which of the following is not a valid CMOS memory setting?

A. Enable/disable tick sound

B. Capacity

C. Enable/disable parity

D. RAM speed/timing

18. You have just changed the Boot Sequence option in the CMOS settings program. Which of the following will be altered by this change?

A. The order in which the BIOS searches the drives for an OS.

B. The location of the BIOS's boot instructions.

C. The order in which the system's bootable drives will be lettered.

D. The order in which the POST will be conducted.

19. A particular computer's CMOS is set so that a password is required to boot the computer and enter the CMOS settings program. However, the user has forgotten the password. What can you do to remedy the problem?

   A. Use the supervisor password to clear the user password.

   B. Boot from the floppy disk, then look up the user's password in the CMOS.

   C. Remove, then reinstall, the CMOS battery.

   D. Open the computer and use the password jumpers to determine the current password.

20. Which of the following Plug-and-Play options can you use in the CMOS settings program?

   A. Inform the BIOS of Plug-and-Play devices in the system.

   B. Instruct the BIOS to perform an immediate search for all Plug-and-Play devices in the system.

   C. Set the IRQ addresses of Plug-and-Play devices in the system.

   D. Inform the BIOS of a Plug-and-Play OS.

LAB QUESTION

Your current computer has the following specifications:

- Pentium 60
- Baby AT motherboard
- Four 72-pin SIMMs, totaling 4GB of RAM, odd parity

You have decided to upgrade the computer to a Pentium II 300. However, based on your reading of the information in this chapter, you know that you cannot simply buy a new processor and install it in the system. Which other components will you likely have to replace? What new features will the upgraded computer have?

SELF-TEST ANSWERS

Popular CPU Chips

1. ☑ **C.** All Pentium-class processors have a 64-bit data bus. This means that 64 bits can enter or leave the processor at a time.

    ☒ **A,** 32 bit, is incorrect. Older processors have 32-bit data buses, but all Pentiums have 64 bits. Pentiums do, however, all have a 32-bit register (internal bus). **B,** 36 bit, is incorrect. No Intel processor has a 36-bit data bus, although some Pentium-class processors have a 36-bit memory address bus. **D** is incorrect because it states that Pentium processors have different data bus widths. Although they do differ in memory address bus width, they *all* have the same data bus width: 64 bits.

2. ☑ **B.** You can install a Pentium Pro on this motherboard. Socket 8 is designed for a 387-pin dual staggered PGA. The Pentium Pro is the only processor that uses this form.

    ☒ **A,** Pentium, is incorrect because this processor uses Socket 4, 5, or 7 but not 8. **C,** Pentium with MMX, is incorrect because this processor also uses Socket 7. **D,** Pentium II or III, is incorrect because these processors do not use sockets at all. Instead, they connect to the motherboard using Slot 1.

3. ☑ **B.** You should add 2MB of RAM. The Pentium with MMX has a 32-bit address bus, so it can access a maximum of 4GB of RAM. Since there is already 2GB, you can add only 2GB more and still remain within the processor's capacity. Note that you can physically install more memory, but the processor will behave as though it wasn't there.

    ☒ **A,** none, is incorrect because the Pentium MMX is not limited to 2GB. **C,** 30GB, is incorrect because this would total 32GB of RAM, 28GB more than the processor can access. **D,** 62GB, is incorrect because it would bring the total RAM capacity to 64GB, which is 60GB more than the processor can access. Note, however, that this is a legitimate RAM capacity for a Pentium Pro, Pentium II, or Pentium III.

4. ☑ **C.** Pentium II processors attach to the motherboard using Slot 1. Pentium II and Pentium III processors have an upright SEC design that requires a different connector than earlier processors.

    ☒ **A,** Socket II, and **B,** Socket 9, are incorrect because no Intel processors use either of these. Furthermore, Pentium II processors use slots, not sockets. **D,** the processor is integrated, is incorrect. None of the Pentium-class processors is integrated with the motherboard.

5. ☑ **D.** The Pentium III is available in versions E or B and uses SIMD technology. The E version includes the use of advanced transfer cache (ATC), and the B version can be used with a 133MHz system bus rather than the traditional 100MHz. The Pentium III's SIMD technology allows it to carry out advanced multimedia instructions.

☒ **A,** Pentium Pro, **B,** Pentium with MMX, and **C,** Pentium II, are incorrect because they were all developed before the creation of the technology used in the E and B variants and SIMD instructions.

Random Access Memory

6. ☑ **A.** The maximum capacity of an SRAM chip is 256KB. Its technology precludes it from supporting higher capacities in a single chip. DRAM, on the other hand, is able to support much larger capacities.
☒ **B,** 512 KB, **C,** 1MB, and **D,** 64MB, are all incorrect. SRAM chips cannot be made to hold more than 256KB.

7. ☑ **A.** DRAM is used as main memory because it is cheaper than SRAM. It also supports higher capacities than SRAM. However, DRAM draws more power from the computer because it requires a constant refresh, and it is not nearly as fast as SRAM.
☒ **B** is incorrect because it states that SRAM is used as main memory because it is faster than DRAM. Although it is true that SRAM is faster, it is not used as main memory due to its expense and its relatively low capacity per chip (256KB). **C,** which states that DRAM is used as cache memory because it is available in higher capacities than SRAM, is also incorrect. SRAM is used as cache memory because of its speed. Although SRAM is limited in capacity, most systems do not improve when more than 1MB of cache is added. Therefore, the high capacity of DRAM is irrelevant for use as cache memory, and its slow speed makes it a poor cache memory type. **D,** SRAM requires a constant power refresh, is incorrect. It is DRAM that requires a constant refresh.

8. ☑ **C.** RDRAM is not supported by the processor in this case. RDRAM uses special RIMM slots that weren't yet available when motherboards were being designed for the Pentium processor. Due to the timing of the release of these two technologies, it is very unlikely that a motherboard would have been manufactured that supported a processor that old and a RAM technology that new.
☒ **A** is incorrect because it says that RDRAM is intended for use by video cards, not processors. RDRAM is actually a type of system RAM, not a video RAM technology. **B** is incorrect because it suggests that the computer already has the maximum accessible RAM capacity. However, Pentium processors have a 32-bit memory address bus, so they can access up to 4GB of RAM. **D** is incorrect because it suggests telling her to install the RDRAM. However, as discussed, the motherboard probably doesn't support RDRAM, and it is unlikely that the appropriate RIMM slots are even present.

9. ☑ **D.** There are not enough modules installed. The RAMBUS channel requires that all sockets be populated with either a RIMM (at least one) module or a C-RIMM. In this case,

you would have to add two C-RIMMS to the empty slots.

☒ **A** is incorrect because it suggests that the processor cannot access the memory type. However, the Pentium III and RIMM memory (RDRAM) were released at roughly the same time and are compatible. The motherboard would not support a processor and memory type that cannot be used together. **B**, the memory capacity is too low for the processor, is incorrect. Although computers must have a certain minimum capacity of RAM to boot properly, it is well below 6GB. **C** is incorrect because it suggests that the memory capacity is too high for the processor. The Pentium III processor can access up to 64GB of memory. Furthermore, if too much memory is installed, the excess will simply be ignored. It will not prevent the computer from booting.

10. ☑ **B.** The parity bit in the data stream 10110010 is 1. In odd parity, the parity bit is used to ensure that the total number of 1s is odd. This data stream contains four 1s. The parity bit is set to 1, bringing the total number of 1s to five (odd parity).

☒ **A**, 0, is incorrect because this would result in an even number of 1s (four). **C**, 01, is incorrect because it suggests that the parity bit is 2 bits long. However, a parity bit is just that—1 bit. **D** is incorrect because it states that computers do not use odd parity. Not all computers use parity. However, in those that do, odd parity is the most common type.

Motherboards

11. ☑ **D.** The ATX is the most commonly used motherboard in computers being manufactured today. The ATX motherboard, unlike its predecessors, supports 3.3vDC and Mini-DIN-6 keyboard connectors and has integrated parallel and serial ports.

☒ **A**, Baby AT, and **B**, AT, are both incorrect. The term *AT* is typically used to refer to the Full AT or both Full and Baby AT forms. These forms are older and are used much less frequently than the ATX form. AT motherboards typically do not have integrated I/O ports and do not support 3.3vDC. Note that although some manufacturers continue to use upgraded Baby AT motherboard forms, they are not nearly as common as the ATX form. **C**, Full ATX, is incorrect because this is not a real motherboard form. The word *Full* is used to distinguish the original AT form from the newer, smaller Baby AT form.

12. ☑ **B.** The 8-bit internal modem is most likely to use a 16-bit ISA slot. Most computers, even new ones, include one or several 16-bit ISA slots. These slots are backward compatible, meaning that they can support an 8- or 16-bit ISA card.

☒ **A**, 8-bit ISA, is incorrect because the computer is a Pentium II. Eight-bit ISA cards can use 16-bit ISA slots, so the 8-bit ISA slot is obsolete in newer computers. **C**, PCI, is incorrect. Most new computers contain PCI slots for fast 32-bit devices, but they also contain 16-bit ISA slots for slower 8- or 16-bit devices. It is unlikely that a manufacturer would design a modem to "waste" a PCI slot when an ISA slot would suffice. **D**, AGP, is incorrect because these slots are designed for video cards only.

13. ☑ **B.** You can install 8-bit ISA, 16-bit ISA, and VESA cards in a VESA slot. The VESA slot is in fact a 16-bit ISA slot with an addition at the end.

☒ **A**, VESA only, is incorrect because VESA slots are backward compatible with 8-bit and 16-bit ISA cards. **C** and **D** are incorrect because EISA and VESA are not compatible. EISA cards contain two connector lengths, designed to be inserted into an EISA slot that has two socket depths. However, recall that a VESA slot is simply a 16-bit ISA slot with an addition. Although an EISA slot can hold a 16-bit ISA card, an ISA slot cannot hold an EISA card.

14. ☑ **C.** VESA, PCI, and AGP are all considered "local" bus architectures. This means that they are not limited to the traditional I/O system bus but can access the processor's memory bus or the processor itself directly. Local buses typically run much faster than the standard I/O system bus.

☒ **A**, ISA, VESA, and PCI, and **B**, EISA, VESA, and PCI, are incorrect. The concept of a local bus did not exist until the VESA architecture, which was released *after* the ISA and EISA architectures. **D**, AGP only, is incorrect because the VESA and PCI architectures are also local.

15. ☑ **A.** Type III is the only PC Card that supports a 32-bit data transfer. It is also backward compatible, so some Type III cards are 16 bit, and 16-bit Type I and Type II cards can be used in a Type III socket.

☒ **B, C,** and **D** are all incorrect because they suggest that Type I and/or Type II cards support a 32-bit data transfer. They are, in fact, limited to 16 bits.

Complementary Metal-Oxide Semiconductor Settings

16. ☑ **C.** The printer most likely requires ECP mode. ECP mode is newer and faster than output only or bi-directional and is used most commonly for newer printers.

☒ **A**, output only, is incorrect because this is an older mode used with printers that can only receive data from the computer. Most newer printers also require the ability to send data to the computer. **B**, bi-directional, is incorrect because this mode uses older technology. Again, since the printer is new, it most likely takes advantage of newer port technology. **D**, EPP, is incorrect. EPP uses technology similar to ECP, but it is used for parallel devices other than printers and scanners.

17. ☑ **B.** The capacity is not a valid CMOS memory setting. RAM is automatically counted on startup, and you cannot configure the system to use more or less RAM than what is actually available.

☒ **A**, enable/disable tick sound, is incorrect because this is a common memory setting within the CMOS settings program. This option allows you to turn on or off the sound of the memory count at startup. **C**, enable/disable parity, is also incorrect. In systems that use memory parity, you can choose to disable or enable it. **D**, RAM speed/timing, is incorrect because, although rare, this is a valid CMOS setting on some systems (typically older ones).

18. ☑ **A.** If you change the boot sequence, you alter the order in which the BIOS searches the drives for an OS. On startup, the BIOS performs a POST, then searches for a valid OS. When one is found, the BIOS hands it control of the remainder of the boot process. In many computers, the BIOS will first search the A: drive, then the C: drive, and finally the CD-ROM drive.

 ☒ **B,** the location of the BIOS's boot instructions, is incorrect. The BIOS's boot instructions are always stored on the CMOS chip, and you cannot alter their location. **C**, the order in which the system's bootable drives will be lettered, is also incorrect. On most systems, the floppy drives will be given A: and B: labels (if a second floppy drive exists), and the hard drives will be given letters starting with C:. Although some utilities and OSs allow you to change these letters, you cannot do so in the system's CMOS settings program. **D**, the order in which the POST will be conducted, is incorrect because you cannot alter this order.

19. ☑ **C.** You can remove, then reinstall, the CMOS battery. This will erase all nondefault settings in the CMOS. However, use this as a last resort, because you will need to reconfigure the CMOS. Incidentally, you could also try looking for a "clear password" jumper on the motherboard.

 ☒ **A** is incorrect because it suggests using the supervisor password to clear the user password. In this computer, there is one password for both booting the computer and accessing the CMOS program. You cannot even get into the CMOS program without the proper password. Note, however, that some computers have two separate passwords. A user password is required to boot the computer, and a supervisor password is required to enter the CMOS settings. This, unfortunately, is not one of those computers. **B** is incorrect because it suggests that you can look up the password in the CMOS settings if you boot from a floppy disk. Without the proper password, you cannot boot from any device, including a floppy disk. Furthermore, the ability to boot from a floppy disk is completely unrelated to the ability to read CMOS settings. **D**, open the computer and use the password jumpers to determine the current password, is incorrect. Although some systems include a jumper that allows you to erase the password, no system includes a jumper that indicates the password.

20. ☑ **D.** You can use the CMOS Plug-and-Play options to inform the BIOS of a Plug-and-Play OS. If one exists, the BIOS will let it configure Plug-and-Play devices. If not, the BIOS will configure the devices itself.

 ☒ **A**, inform the BIOS of Plug-and-Play devices in the system, is incorrect. The whole concept of a Plug-and-Play BIOS is that the BIOS will automatically detect those devices. Therefore, they do not have to be manually entered. **B**, instruct the BIOS to perform an immediate search for all Plug-and-Play devices in the system, is also incorrect. The BIOS will automatically search for these devices at startup. The immediate search for devices refers to the Autodetect feature that can be used to force the BIOS to search for all existing hard drives in the system. **C,** set the IRQ addresses of Plug-and-Play devices in the system, is incorrect. Again, a Plug-and-Play BIOS will detect and configure Plug-and-Play devices automatically. This means there is no need to set the IRQs manually.

LAB ANSWER

As well as a new processor, you will have to purchase a new motherboard. Although some motherboards will support a range of speeds for a particular processor model, they include only one type of slot or socket, so they only support one model type. Pentium 60 processors use Socket 4, but Pentium II processors require Slot 1. The motherboard you purchase will most likely have to be an ATX form, because Baby AT forms are becoming exceptionally rare. In fact, almost all new computers use ATX rather than Baby AT forms.

If you are buying an ATX motherboard, you will also have to replace the power supply. The Pentium processor uses 5vDC, but the Pentium II requires 3.3vDC. Furthermore, AT motherboards use separate P8 and P9 connectors, whereas ATX motherboards use a single P8/P9 connector. You might also have to replace the keyboard. Baby AT motherboards typically include DIN-5 keyboard connectors, but ATX motherboards have Mini-DIN-6 keyboard connectors.

The fact that you are buying a new motherboard could also mean that you cannot use the memory SIMMS that you currently have. Most new computers do not support parity, and due to the age difference between the two technologies, it is unlikely that a motherboard designed for a Pentium II would include SIMM slots. The new motherboard is more likely to include DIMM or RIMM slots. Even if you can use your old SIMMs, they are likely to support older RAM types, such as EDO RAM, whereas the new motherboard is likely to support newer, faster types, such as SDRAM or RDRAM. In any case, you might end up buying more RAM for your computer, since the Pentium II supports up to 64GB of memory.

The new motherboard/processor combination might allow you to use more advanced technologies, such as Plug-and-Play BIOS, AGP bus architecture, or USB. In fact, you might find that some of your older devices, such as your video card, cannot be installed in the new system.

In summary, you can probably keep components such as the monitor, modem, sound card, hard drives, floppy drive, and mouse. Most of the other components will either not physically fit into the computer or will not be recognized by the new BIOS or processor.

6

Printers

O ne of the most commonly used computer peripherals is the printer. Because there are many types of printers, and because they will comprise a large portion of your troubleshooting efforts, this entire chapter is devoted to them. This chapter discusses various printer types as well as how they work. It also introduces you to common printer problems, troubleshooting techniques, and preventive maintenance procedures that can help you keep the printer working properly.

CERTIFICATION OBJECTIVE 6.01

Basic Printer Concepts

The best tool you can have to properly care for and troubleshoot printers is a good understanding of how they work and how to properly set them up. If you know the functions of a printer's components, you will more easily be able to determine the cause of problems when they occur. A good understanding of configuration and setup procedures will allow you to make the printer accessible to the users who need it.

Types of Printers

Over time, printer technology has improved to the point at which they can produce photo-like images. However, a number of printer technologies are still in use, due to cost and quality differences between them. The three most common printer technologies—dot matrix, inkjet and bubblejet, and laser—are discussed here.

Dot Matrix Printers

Dot matrix printers are the "original" type of printer, and have been around for a long time; however, they are no longer readily available, except for business use in printing receipts and the like. Dot matrix printers are so named because they use a matrix of pins to create dots on the paper. Each pin is attached to a *solenoid*, which, when activated, forces the pin toward the paper. As the *print head* (which contains the pins) moves across the page, different pins are forced forward to strike a printer *ribbon* against the paper. Because of this action, dot matrix printers fall into the *impact printer* category. Furthermore, because their printouts are created line by line, dot matrix printers are also considered *line printers*.

Dot matrix printers typically use a *continuous form feed* to move special paper through the printer. A continuous form feed (also called a *tractor feed*) comprises two wheels, one on either side of the paper. Each wheel contains "spokes," or sprockets, that fit into corresponding holes at each edge of the paper. As the wheels turn, the paper is pulled through the printer. The perforated sides of the paper can be removed once the printout is complete, and the pages can be removed from each other or left attached to each other in a continuous string of pages.

Because of the print process they use, dot matrix printers do not provide very good resolution. That is, text and images can appear grainy, and if you look closely at a dot matrix printout, you will be able to see each individual printed dot. Furthermore, dot matrix printers are limited in their ability to use color. Most of these printers can use one printer ribbon only. This ribbon is typically black, but another color can be substituted. Some dot matrix printers are capable of using ribbons with more than one (up to four) colors, while some are capable of using more than one (up to four) printer ribbon. However, they are not capable of producing as many color combinations as other printer types.

One advantage of dot matrix printers is that they are relatively inexpensive. Additionally, because they are impact printers, they can be used for making carbon duplicate or triplicate forms. Because of their simple design, dot matrix printers are also typically easier to troubleshoot than other printer types.

Inkjet and Bubblejet Printers

Inkjet printers (see Figure 6-1) use ink in cartridges, rather than ribbons, to create text or graphic printouts. The ink cartridge in an inkjet printer contains a small pump, which forces ink out of the reservoir, through a nozzle, and onto the page. Inkjet printers create printouts line by line, so they are considered line printers, but their print mechanisms do not make contact with the page, so they are considered *nonimpact printers.* Inkjet printers provide much better resolution than dot matrix printers, and are capable of using colored ink. Unlike dot matrix printers, inkjets can combine basic colors to produce a wide range of colors. Inkjet printers are not nearly as loud as dot matrix printers and are much faster. As you might expect, inkjet and bubblejet printers, because of their ability to print in color, are most popular with consumers and end users.

A variant of the inkjet printer is the *bubblejet printer.* Bubblejets resemble inkjets, but their ink cartridges contain heating elements rather than pumps. When the element is heated, the ink expands and forms a bubble of ink on the nozzle. When

An inkjet printer.

the bubble becomes large enough, it "bursts" onto the paper and creates a dot of color. Although this process sounds messy, bubblejets actually provide better printouts than the original inkjets. Generally, the term *inkjet* is used to refer to all printers that use ink (inkjets, bubblejets, and deskjets).

Inkjet printers typically use *friction-feed* rollers to move the paper through the printer. In friction feed, a stack of pages is kept in a feeder tray. A rubber or plastic roller uses friction to grab the top page and pull it into the printer. Some advantages to this type of feed are that you don't have to worry about lining up the page perforations or the holes and sprockets, and you don't have to separate pages from one another when the printout is finished. Unlike tractor-feed printers, friction-feed printers can be used to print on paper that has an irregular shape or size. You can even print on envelopes and cards.

Laser Printers

Laser printers are perhaps the most commonly used printers in office environments. They also provide the best quality and have the most complex structure and process. A laser printer is shown in Figure 6-2. Because there are many components in a laser printer, many things can go wrong. This section provides a description of the laser print process. The more familiar you are with it, the easier it will be for you to discover and troubleshoot problems.

FIGURE 6-2

A typical laser
printer.

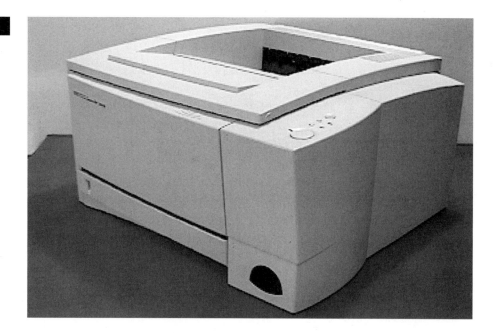

The Laser Print Process Although some laser printers use slightly different processes, the one described here is the generally accepted order of events. Note that these events occur in cycles, so it is not as important to know which step is first or last; rather, it is *order* of events that is important. For example, some sources list the charging step as the first, while others list the cleaning step as the first. For the purposes of this discussion, we'll consider the charging step first.

1. **Charging** In the charging step, the printer's *high-voltage power supply (HVPS)* conducts electricity to the *primary corona wire*, which in turn passes the voltage on to the printer's *drum*. This voltage is typically around –5000vDC.

2. **Writing** The photosensitive drum now contains a very high negative charge. In the writing step, the printer's *laser* begins to move along the drum, creating the image that will eventually appear on the printout. Because the drum is *photosensitive*, each place that the laser touches loses most of its charge. By the end of the writing step, the image exists at around –100vDC, while the rest of the drum remains charged to –5000vDC.

3. **Developing** In this stage, the cover on the printer's *toner cartridge* is opened. The toner itself contains small particles that are attracted to the less negatively charged (–100vDC) areas of the drum. By the end of this stage,

the drum contains a toner-covered image (in the shape of the final printout), and the remainder of the drum remains at −5000vDC.

4. **Transferring** At this point, the paper begins to move through the printer, past the drum. The *transfer corona wire* is responsible for applying a small positive charge to the paper as it passes through. This positive charge "pulls" the negatively charged toner from the drum onto the paper.

5. **Fusing** The only thing holding the toner to the paper at this point is electrical charges. The toner itself contains resin, which melts when heated. As the paper leaves the printer, it passes through a set of *fusing rollers*, which have been heated by a *fusing lamp*. The heat on the rollers causes the toner to melt, or *fuse*, to the paper.

6. **Cleaning** When the printout is complete, a rubber *cleaning blade* moves along the drum to remove residual toner. The toner is then deposited into a small reservoir. Next, one or more *erasure lamps* come on, exposing the drum to light. Because the drum is photosensitive, it loses any remaining charge when the light touches it. The printer is now ready to create another image.

exam
Watch
Make sure that you are familiar with the laser print process. Knowing this process will help you determine which component is at fault when there is a problem.

Now that you are familiar with the laser print process, test your knowledge by answering the following Scenario & Solution questions.

SCENARIO & SOLUTION

What is the function of the laser in a laser printer?	To reduce the drum's charge in areas that will later hold toner.
How does the image get from the drum to the paper?	The transfer corona wire applies a positive charge to the paper. As the paper passes the drum, the negatively charged toner is attracted to the page.
How is the drum cleaned?	A cleaning blade removes residual toner from the drum, and an erasure lamp removes any remaining charge from the drum.
What makes the toner stick to the paper?	The toner contains resin, which is melted onto the paper when it passes through the heated fusing rollers.

The laser printer is considered a nonimpact printer, and since it creates printouts one page at a time (rather than one line at a time), it is also considered a *page printer*. Laser printouts do not use dots of color, so they are typically able to provide excellent resolution. They are also able to blend colors into practically any shade. In a color printer, the writing and developing stages take place four times (once for each basic color—red, green, blue, and yellow) before the image is transferred to the paper. Like inkjet printers, laser printers typically use friction feed to move the paper through the printer. However, there is typically more than one set of rollers within the laser printer, to keep the page moving smoothly until it is ejected. Laser printers are the quietest and fastest printers, but they are also the most expensive type.

As a technician (and to become A+ certified), you are expected to know the basic differences between printer types. Test your knowledge of these concepts by answering the following Scenario & Solution questions.

Types of Printer Connections and Configurations

There are a number of different ways to access a printer. For example, you can configure a printer so that it is attached directly to the computer or attached

SCENARIO & SOLUTION

What type of medium does each printer type use to create images?	Dot matrix printers use ink ribbons, inkjet printers use ink, and laser printers use toner.
What is an impact printer?	An impact printer is one that uses physical impact to create images, such as the pins on a dot matrix printer.
What are two types of nonimpact printers?	Inkjet and laser printers do not "strike" the print medium onto the page, so they are considered nonimpact printers.
What is a line printer?	A line printer is one that creates an image one line at a time. Dot matrix and inkjet printers are line printers.
Is the laser printer a line printer?	No. The image is created one page at a time, not one line at a time. The laser printer is therefore considered a page printer.
What is the difference between a true inkjet printer and a bubblejet printer?	An inkjet printer uses a small pump to spray ink on the paper. A bubblejet printer uses heat to cause ink bubbles to burst onto the paper.

indirectly through a network. You can also configure the printer so that it is accessible to only one person or to an entire network of people. Some of the common printer setups are described in this section.

Parallel Printers

The most common way to attach a printer to a computer is through the computer's parallel (LPT) port. In fact, most parallel ports can be set to transmission modes designed specifically for use with printers (for instance, ECP mode). To connect a printer in this way, attach the parallel cable to the printer and the computer. The end that attaches to the printer is typically a 36-pin Centronics connector; the end that attaches to the computer is a DB-25 connector. It is suggested that you do not use a parallel cable longer than 6 feet, because longer cables are more susceptible to errors caused by EMI.

You must also attach the printer's power cable to a wall outlet or other source of power. If the printer is Plug and Play, the OS will detect it on startup and load a device driver for it. If the printer is not Plug and Play, you will need to manually load a driver for it. Insert the disk that came with the printer and run the Setup or Install program. Because the printer is attached to the parallel port, it will use that port's IRQ and I/O address assignments.

USB Printers

More and more printers are being manufactured to support USB connections. As described previously, to attach a USB printer, simply plug it into a USB external or root hub. There is no need to even turn the computer off. If the printer requires an external power supply, plug the printer into a power source. Most USB devices support Plug and Play. If the USB printer does not, load its driver using the Setup or Install program that came with the printer.

Network Printers

There are two ways to access a printer on a network. The first is to use a true network printer. This type of printer contains a network interface card (NIC) and is configured in the same manner as other computers on the network. (You'll find more on this topic in Chapter 7.) The printer itself contains a user interface, typically a small keypad, for configuration.

on the **job**

Printers are the most commonly accessed network resources and are the cause for a majority of network-related trouble calls.

Another way to network a printer is to configure it as a *shared resource*. Shared printers are attached to a computer's parallel, USB, or other port, as described in the preceding subsections. The printer is then shared with other users, in the same manner that files and other resources can be shared on the network. In this type of setup, the printer can be accessed only via the network if the computer to which it is attached is turned on and has network access. This computer, incidentally, is called the *print server*. Follow the steps in Exercise 6-1 to make a local printer accessible on a Windows network.

EXERCISE 6-1

Configuring a Printer as a Shared Resource

1. Determine which computer on the network will act as the print server (the computer that the printer will be attached to).

2. Turn the computer off, and attach the printer.

3. Connect the printer to a power source.

4. Turn the computer on and load a device driver for the printer, if required.

5. Double-click the My Computer icon.

6. Double-click Printers.

7. Right-click the printer you want to share, then select Properties.

8. Select the Sharing tab (the default setting should be "Not Shared").

9. Select the Shared option and enter the share name (the name that will identify this printer to other users).

10. Click OK. Other users should now be able to access this printer through the Network Neighborhood. See Chapter 7 for more information on how to access a shared printer.

exam
Watch

A network printer is different from a printer that is shared on a network. A true network printer has a NIC and is configured as a separate node on the network. A shared printer is attached to a computer on the network and can be accessed only if that computer is turned on and is on the network.

CERTIFICATION OBJECTIVE 6.02

Care, Service, and Troubleshooting

There are a great number of moving parts in printers, and because of the frequency at which they are used, moved, and reloaded with paper, ink, or toner, they are prone to developing problems. The following subsections are designed to introduce you to common problems and their resolutions as well as procedures you can use to care for the computer and prevent the occurrence of problems.

Feed and Output

A common printer problem is related to the mechanics of the paper-feed process. If there is too much paper in a friction-feed paper tray, more than one page can be fed through the printer at a time. The extra page can cause problems with the print process itself and can cause jams within the printer. The same can happen if there is static within the pages. Static can cause the pages to stick together so that they are not pulled through the printer one at a time. To avoid multiple-page feeding problems, reduce the amount of paper you place in the tray, and use your thumb to "riffle," or quickly separate, the pages before you load them into the paper tray.

Another friction-feed printer problem occurs when no pages are fed into the printer. This is more common in inkjet printers, which have an upright paper tray. If the stack of paper is too small, the friction rollers might not be able to make contact with the top page.

Tractor-feed printers are notorious for feeding paper incorrectly through the printer. The problem is not usually in getting the paper through but in lining the paper up properly. Recall that these feed mechanisms require special paper, in which each piece of paper is attached to the page before it, much like in a roll of paper towel. If the roll of paper is not lined up properly, the text that is supposed to be on one page could actually be split over two pages. When this is the case, continue advancing the roll of paper until it is properly aligned.

Paper Jams

Many things can cause a paper jam, such as improperly fed pages, pages that are too thin, static, dust build-up, or worn printer components. You will typically be informed of a paper jam because the printer will stop the current print job. You might see an error message on the printer itself or on your computer screen. Most printers will not resume operation until the jam is completely cleared.

When a printer experiences a paper jam, the first thing you should do is lift the cover. Look for the paper, and if it is visible, gently try to remove it. Don't pull too hard, because you could end up ripping the page, and the smaller pieces left inside the printer will be even harder to get out. Some printers, typically laser printers, include levers that you can release to more easily remove jammed paper. When removing jammed paper, always pull in the direction that the paper normally travels through the printer. Pulling the other way could damage rollers and other internal components.

If the printer continues to jam often, try using a different paper weight. Printers typically require a particular weight of paper, and if you use paper that is too thin or too thick, jams can occur. If the paper itself is not the problem, try cleaning the printer of dust and other build-up (techniques are discussed at the end of the chapter). If the printer continues to experience paper jams, you might need to replace the feed rollers.

Print Quality

Any time the printer produces a poor-quality image should be considered a problem. Most quality-related problems are easily resolved by replacing ink, toner, or laser printer drums. However, quality problems can be caused by failures within the device's print process. This is where your knowledge of the inkjet and laser print processes will come in handy. Let's look at some common problems related to quality.

exam ⓦatch

The most common procedure you will need to carry out for printers is the replacement of toner or ink cartridges.

The Printer Produces Blank Pages

If a dot matrix printer produces blank pages, pay attention to the sound coming from the printer itself. If you cannot hear the pins striking the page, try replacing the print head. If the pins are striking the page but there is a blank printout, there

FROM THE CLASSROOM

Patience, Patience, Patience

Some users tend to "pull" paper through as it is exiting the printer. However, the paper is ejected at precisely the rate at which the image is created, so pulling the paper can cause gaps in the printed text or image.

Pulling the paper through can also cause small tears in the paper. The result is that small particles or larger pieces of the page can be left behind in the printer. If they are left in the paper path, they can impede the passage of subsequent pages, resulting in a paper jam. Even worse, they can build up near moving components, limiting their range of motion and causing premature wear and tear.

Finally, by pulling the paper, you can end up forcing the printer's rollers to rotate more than they should. This is typically accompanied by a grinding noise akin to nails on a chalkboard. The result can be stripped components, burnt-out motors, and undue wear and tear. Be patient. Pulling paper through the printer to speed up image creation isn't any more effective than pressing an elevator button over and over again to make the elevator arrive more quickly.

—Amy Thomson, A+ Certified Technician,
MOUS Master

is a ribbon problem. First, check to ensure that the ribbon is lined up with the print head. If the ribbon gets accidentally pulled above or below the print head, no image will be created on the page. If the ribbon is already lined up properly, you should suspect that the ribbon is worn out. You can resolve the problem by replacing the ribbon.

If an inkjet printer produces blank pages, the likely suspect is the ink cartridge. Use the printer's software utility to determine the amount of ink left in the cartridge. If no such utility came with the printer, remove the cartridge and gently rock it back and forth to determine if there is ink present. If there is not, replace the cartridge. If there is ink, the problem could be a clogged nozzle. Follow the printer manufacturer's instructions for cleaning the printhead/printer cartridge(s) with the provided software. To clean manually, use a clean foam-rubber swab or lint-free cloth slightly dampened with distilled water, again following manufacturer's instructions.

There are several possible causes of blank pages produced by a laser printer. To begin with, check the toner. If the cartridge is empty, replace it. If it is not empty, try replacing the drum. Sometimes drums become unable to hold a charge after time (in some laser printer models, the toner and drum come as an integrated unit). If this does not resolve the problem, use your knowledge of the print process itself. A blank page means a failure of the toner to be attracted to the paper. Perhaps the laser did not discharge areas of the drum. It could also be that the transfer corona wire (or underlying HVPS) did not apply a positive charge to the paper. Unfortunately, these components are difficult to replace, and you could end up sending the printer to a repair shop that specializes in laser printers. Fortunately, almost all laser print problems are resolved by changing the toner and/or drum.

Random Speckles on the Page

If any type of printer produces a page with speckles or blotches on it, try cleaning the printer. Ribbon ink, cartridge ink, and toner can be deposited within the printer itself and transferred onto the paper as it passes through the printer. Cleaning procedures are discussed later in the chapter.

Repeated Speckles or Blotches

Repeated speckles are those that appear at regular intervals on each page or down the entire length of a page. Again, for any printer type, try cleaning the printer first, paying particular attention to the feed rollers.

If there are repeated speckles in a laser printout, suspect the drum. If there is a small nick in the drum, toner will collect there and be transferred onto each page. In addition, during the cleaning step, some drums lose their ability to drop their charge. In either case, replacing the drum should solve the problem.

Printout Contains a Faint Image of the Last Printout

A *ghosted image* occurs when an image from a previous printout appears on subsequent printouts. This phenomenon occurs only in laser printers and indicates a failure of the cleaning process. The drum, as explained, might have lost the ability to drop its charge in the presence of light. Replace the drum to try to resolve the problem. If the drum is not the cause, it could be either the cleaning blade or the erasure lamps. Again, these components are not easy to replace, so you will probably have to send the printer back to the manufacturer or to a specialized printer repair shop.

The Printout Uses the Wrong Colors

Assuming this is not an application-related setting, a problem with incorrect colors is almost exclusively limited to inkjet printers. If the nozzle on one or more of the colors on a color ink cartridge gets clogged, the colors may come out "dirty" or might not be produced at all. Use isopropyl alcohol on a cotton swab to remove dried ink and unclog the nozzles. Another possible cause of this problem is the level of ink. If one color in the color cartridge gets low, the proper shades will not be produced. To resolve this problem, replace the cartridge.

The Printout Is Smudged

If a dot matrix printer produces a smudged printout, check the pins on the print head. Stuck pins can cause printouts to have a smudged appearance as they drag across the page. If this is the case, replace the print head.

If the printer is an inkjet, the smudges are most likely the result of something touching the printout before the ink has had a chance to dry. However, if the problem persists, try cleaning the printer. If this doesn't resolve the problem, it could indicate worn-out cartridge nozzles. Simply replace the ink cartridge.

Smudged laser printouts are usually the result of a failed fusing process. You might need to replace either of the fusing rollers or the halogen lamp.

The Printer Is Producing "Garbage"

Garbage characters in the printout indicate a communication problem between the computer and printer. First, make sure to select the right printer in the Print dialog box. If more than one printer driver is installed, it is possible another printer has inadvertently been selected, which will produce garbage. Next, make sure that the cable is firmly and properly attached. Try turning the printer off, then back on. Restarting the computer could also solve the problem. Next, check the printer's resources. Make sure that a proper driver has been loaded. If you suspect the driver is corrupt, remove it, then reload it. In addition, ensure that the printer has been assigned the proper IRQ and I/O address. If this is a parallel port, you will need to check the resources of the port itself.

If there is more than one printer port on the computer (LPT1 & 2 or multiple USB ports), try the printer in another port or with another computer. Look at the printer settings in the OS to ensure that the attached printer matches the type selected in the printer settings area. Finally, this problem could be the result of insufficient printer memory. You can test this hypothesis by trying to print a very small document. If it works, there is a good chance that the original document was too large for the printer's memory. You can add more RAM to the printer using the same modules that the computer uses (SIMMs or DIMMs).

e x a m
ⓦat c h

Whenever you are faced with an unfamiliar print-quality problem in a laser printer, replace the drum. If this does not solve the problem, use your knowledge of the laser print process to determine which step (and therefore, which component) has failed.

Errors

As with computers, printers are associated with a great variety of error messages. Furthermore, printers often come with their own configuration and monitoring utilities, each with proprietary error messages. Some of the more common errors are described here. Note that these messages could appear on the computer screen or, if you are using a laser printer, on the printer's console. Some of these messages are generated by the OS. Any time you receive a printer error message that you do not understand, check the message or error code number in the manufacturer's documentation.

on th e
ⓙo b

If your printer is reporting an error that is not documented by the manufacturer, check the Internet. Most printer manufacturers have Web sites with frequently asked questions (FAQs), troubleshooting forums, or lists of error codes and their meanings.

Paper Out

This message indicates that there is no paper in the printer. If the printer uses a tractor feed, you will need to lift the printer lid, feed the first sheet of the new stack through the paper path, and line up the holes with the feed wheels. As this procedure differs among systems, consult the manufacturer's documentation.

If you are using a tray-style friction-feed printer such as that used by laser printers and some inkjet printers, simply pull out the appropriate paper tray. Insert a stack of paper, then close the tray all the way. The error message should go away on its own. If you do not close the tray all the way, a "Tray Open" or "Close Tray" message might appear. If the printer uses an upright friction feed, such as those used in inkjet printers, follow the steps in Exercise 6-2 to add more paper.

EXERCISE 6-2

Adding Paper to an Upright Friction-Feed Printer

1. Release the tray lever at the back of the printer. This will cause the paper tray to drop slightly away from the friction rollers.

2. Place a small stack of paper in the tray, using the paper guides.

3. Engage the tray lever. This will bring the paper closer to the feed rollers.

4. The printer might automatically detect the paper and continue the print job. If not, look for and press the Paper Advance button on the printer. This instructs the printer to detect and try to feed the paper.

The "Paper out" message could appear even if there is paper in the tray. Again, if the paper gets too low to be "grabbed" by the feed rollers, the printer will behave as though there is no paper there. If this is the case, remove the paper, then reinsert it in the tray or add more paper to the current stack.

I/O Error

This error can take many forms, including "Cannot communicate with printer" or "There was an error writing to LPT#." This message is typically reported by the OS, and it indicates that the computer cannot properly communicate with the printer. Start by ensuring that the printer is turned on. If it is not, turn it on, then try to print. You might need to restart the computer, to ensure that it redetects the presence of the printer.

Next, make sure that the printer cable is firmly and properly attached to both the printer and the computer. Make sure that a proper driver has been loaded. If you suspect that the driver is corrupt, remove it, then reload it. In addition, ensure that the printer has been assigned the proper IRQ and I/O address. If this is a parallel port, you will need to check the resources of the port itself.

Try the printer in another port or with another computer. Furthermore, look at the printer settings in the OS to ensure that the attached printer matches the type selected in the printer settings area.

Incorrect Port Mode

Again, this error message may be worded differently, but it indicates that the parallel port to which the printer is attached is using the wrong mode. This message usually appears on the computer rather than on the printer. Enter the computer's CMOS settings and change the printer to the proper mode (unidirectional, bidirectional, ECP, or EPP). Consult the manufacturer's documentation for the correct mode (the error message itself might indicate the proper mode).

No Default Printer Selected

This is a Windows-generated error, indicating that no printer has been installed or that Windows has not been informed of a default printer to use. As well as running the printer's Setup program, some printers require that you set the printer up in the Windows Printers folder. Double-click My Computer, then double-click Printers. Right-click the icon of the printer you want to set as the default, then select Set as Default. If no printers are listed in the Printers folder, double-click the Add Printer icon, then follow the on-screen installation steps.

Toner Low

The "Low toner" message applies to laser printers only. It typically appears well before the toner is completely gone, as a sort of early warning. The computer should continue to print normally. You can make the error message go away by removing the toner cartridge and *gently and slowly* rocking the cartridge back and forth. This will resettle the toner. Note, however, that this is not a solution to the problem. The reason for the error is to warn you to replace the toner cartridge soon. Most laser printers will not work at all if the toner cartridge is empty.

If the printer is an inkjet, an "Ink low" message could appear or an ink level bar be displayed. Replace the cartridge.

on the
job

When ink cartridges get low, you should replace rather than refill them. When you buy an ink cartridge, it comes with a new pump/heating element and new nozzles. By refilling an old cartridge, you will be reusing old, possibly worn-out components.

Use the information in the preceding troubleshooting sections to answer the following Scenario & Solution questions.

SCENARIO & SOLUTION

My laser printer produces the same blotch over and over again. What should I do?	Clean the printer, especially the rollers. If this doesn't work, replace the drum.
My inkjet printer is producing smudged printouts. Why?	There is probably something coming in contact with the page before the ink has had a chance to dry.
What is a "ghosted" image?	It is an image from a previous printout that appears on subsequent printouts. This appears in laser printers only. Replace the drum. If this doesn't work, replace the cleaning components.
Why does my printout contain the wrong colors?	You are probably using an inkjet printer that is low in a particular color or has a clogged cartridge nozzle.

Safety Precautions

You should follow several safety procedures whenever you work with or around a printer. To begin, printers have lots of moving parts. Don't let long hair, clothing, jewelry, or other objects near the feed or exit rollers. Furthermore, don't try to operate a printer with the cover off. The cartridge in an inkjet printer and the print head in a dot matrix printer move back and forth quickly across the page, and it is possible to get your hands or other objects in the way. This can harm you and the printer's components.

You must be especially careful when working around laser printers. They contain lasers that can cause eye damage. Fortunately, most printers do not work once their covers are raised. A more common printer-related injury is caused by the fusing equipment. The fusing lamp can generate around 200°F! Any time you open the laser printer to replace the drum or cartridge or to clear a paper jam, give the printer ample time to cool down.

Preventive Maintenance

Again, because of the frequency with which printers are used, they require steady maintenance. Fortunately, the procedures are easy. The best thing you can do to prolong the life of a printer and prevent problems from occurring is to clean it regularly. In all printers, small particles of paper can get left behind and cause a potentially harmful build-up. This build-up can hold static, which can in turn damage components through ESD or cause pages to stick together. Removing build-up will also keep the paper path clear, thus reducing paper jams and ensuring that the motion of moving parts is not inhibited. You can remove dust and particle build-up using compressed air or a vacuum. As you clean the printer, be on the lookout for small corners of paper that might have been left behind during the print process or when a paper jam was cleared.

exam
Ⓦatⅽh
The most important preventive maintenance procedure for a printer is regular cleaning.

If the printer is an inkjet, you should look for and remove ink from the inside of the printer. Ink can leak or get smudged off the paper. As the ink dries, it can cause moving components or paper to stick. Laser printers can accumulate toner. Empty the toner reservoir regularly, and remove other excess toner using a paper towel or cotton swab.

You can also help prevent paper jams and component wear and tear using the proper paper for your printer. If you have ever felt typewriter paper and printer paper side by side, you noticed weight and thickness differences. Using the wrong paper can lead to paper jams and cause undue wear on the printer's components.

CERTIFICATION SUMMARY

The focus of this chapter was the components, procedures, troubleshooting, and maintenance procedures for common printer types. The type of printer that a user chooses to work with depends on its expense, resolution, speed, and ability to produce colors. Dot matrix printers are the least expensive, but they also provide the lowest quality. Laser printers, the most expensive, can provide excellent printouts and are the most common type used in offices. For this reason, you are likely to deal with laser printers more frequently than with other printer types.

By understanding a laser printer's print process, you will more easily be able to pinpoint and resolve problems. For example, if you know the components involved in the fusing process, you will be able to determine which components need replacing when the fusing process fails. Furthermore, by regularly cleaning the printer, regardless of its type, you can extend the life of the printer and prevent potential problems from occurring.

TWO-MINUTE DRILL

Here are some of the key points from each certification objective in Chapter 6.

Basic Printer Concepts

❏ Dot matrix printers are impact printers because they create images by striking an array of pins against the page.

❏ Inkjet printers use a small pump to spray ink on the page, and bubblejet printers use heat to place bubbles of ink on the page.

❏ Laser printers use a drum to transfer toner to the page.

❏ Dot matrix and inkjet printers are line printers; laser printers are page printers.

❏ The six steps in the laser print process are charging, writing, developing, transferring, fusing, and cleaning.

❏ Printers can be attached locally to a computer using a parallel or USB connection.

❏ True network printers contain a NIC and are stand-alone network devices.

❏ Regular local printers can be shared on the network as long as the print server is turned on and has network access.

Care, Service, and Troubleshooting

❏ Tractor feeds use sprocketed wheels to pull a continuous roll of paper through the printer, while friction feeds use rubber or plastic rollers to pull single pages through.

❏ Paper jams can be caused by pages sticking (due to static), worn-out feed mechanisms, particle build-up, or using the wrong paper weight.

❏ Blank pages are usually resolved by replacing the printer's ribbon, ink cartridge, toner cartridge, or drum.

❏ If a printer produces a repeated blotch, clean the printer; if it is a laser printer, replace the drum.

❑ Ghosted images are caused by a failure of the laser printer's cleaning step and can usually be resolved by replacing the drum.

❑ If the printer produces garbled text or cannot be found by the computer, the computer is not communicating properly with the printer.

❑ The most important preventive maintenance procedure you can carry out on a printer is regular cleaning.

SELF TEST

The following questions will help you measure your understanding of the material presented in this chapter. Read all of the choices carefully because there might be more than one correct answer. Choose all correct answers for each question.

Basic Printer Concepts

1. Which type of paper feed uses a continuous roll of paper?

    A. Tractor feed

    B. Friction feed

    C. Roller feed

    D. Dot matrix feed

2. Which of the following printer types contains a heating element within the cartridge?

    A. Dot matrix

    B. Inkjet

    C. Bubblejet

    D. Laser

3. Which of the following does a dot matrix printer use to create printouts?

    A. Ink cartridge

    B. Ribbon

    C. Paint

    D. Toner

4. Which of the following statements about bubblejet printers is accurate?

    A. Inkjet printers typically produce better-quality printouts than bubblejets.

    B. Both are the least expensive types of printer.

    C. Inkjet printers are line printers, and bubblejets are page printers.

    D. Bubblejet printers create images by allowing bubbles of ink to burst onto the paper.

5. A user has removed the primary corona wire from a laser printer. Assuming the printer will still work, which step will fail?

    A. Transferring

    B. Fusing

C. Charging

D. Cleaning

6. During which step of the laser print process is the laser used?

A. Charging

B. Writing

C. Developing

D. Fusing

7. You suspect that a laser printer is not properly performing the cleaning step. Which component might be responsible?

A. Primary corona wire

B. Erasure lamp

C. Laser

D. Fusing lamp

8. What is the purpose of a laser printer's transfer corona wire?

A. To apply toner to the drum

B. To apply toner to the paper

C. To apply a charge to the drum

D. To apply a charge to the paper

9. A user is planning to connect a parallel printer to the computer and wants your advice on cable length. What do you tell the user?

A. Cable length doesn't matter.

B. Keep the cable under 6 feet to avoid EMI.

C. Keep the cable over 6 feet to ensure proper communication timing.

D. Keep the cable under 25 feet to speed communication.

10. A company has one laser printer, which is attached to the secretary's parallel port. However, other users would like to access the printer. Which is the most efficient and cost-effective solution?

A. Have users e-mail their documents to the secretary for printing.

B. Have users physically move the printer to their computers when they want to print.

C. Share the printer as a network resource.

D. Have the company buy a network printer.

Care, Service, and Troubleshooting

11. You are troubleshooting a printer for which the paper-feed mechanism is experiencing problems. Which of the following can you rule out as the cause?

    A. Improper communication between the computer and printer

    B. Static

    C. Not enough paper in the tray

    D. Wrong paper weight

12. The printer at your office has recently started experiencing paper jams. They seem to be occurring quite frequently. Which of the following should you do first?

    A. Try a different type of paper.

    B. Replace the printer.

    C. Replace the feed rollers.

    D. Replace the transfer corona wire.

13. A bubblejet printer is producing blank pages. Which of the following is *least* likely to be the cause of the problem?

    A. The cartridge nozzles are dirty.

    B. The printer is dirty.

    C. The cartridge is empty.

    D. The heating element is not working.

14. What is the first thing you should do when a printer produces random blotches on the page?

    A. Replace the ribbon, ink, or toner cartridge.

    B. Replace the drum.

    C. Clean the printer.

    D. Check the communication between the computer and printer.

15. A customer tells you that the printer is creating printouts that contain images left over from previous printouts. From this information, you can verify *all but* which of the following?

    A. This is a laser printer.

    B. There has been a failure in the cleaning step.

    C. This problem can be resolved by replacing the drum.

    D. This is a "ghosted" image.

16. A printer is producing garbled printouts, with characters that don't make any sense. Which of the following is true?

   A. There was a failure during the writing step.

   B. The printer should be cleaned.

   C. There is a communication problem between the computer and the printer.

   D. The printer cable should be replaced.

17. Which component are you most likely to replace in a laser printer?

   A. The toner/drum assembly

   B. The feed rollers

   C. The parallel cable

   D. The paper tray

18. Which type of printer is most likely to produce a printout with the wrong or "dirty" colors?

   A. Dot matrix

   B. Inkjet

   C. Laser

   D. A parallel printer with a cable over 6 feet

19. A color laser printer recently displayed a "Yellow toner low" error message. However, you do not have a replacement toner cartridge at the moment. What should you do?

   A. Stop using the printer until you can replace the cartridge.

   B. Refill the cartridge with the toner in the reservoir used to store excess toner from the cleaning step.

   C. Continue using the printer, but don't print documents or images that contain yellow.

   D. Remove the yellow toner cartridge, gently rock it back and forth, then place it back in the printer.

20. Which of the following is most likely to prevent printer problems?

   A. Regularly recharging the power supply

   B. Regularly replacing the feed rollers

   C. Regularly cleaning the printer

   D. Giving the printer a two-day rest

LAB QUESTION

Use the information within this chapter to describe the laser print process. Discuss how this information can be used to troubleshoot printer problems. For example, make correlations between particular problems and the likely component or process at fault.

SELF TEST ANSWERS

Basic Printer Concepts

1. ☑ **A.** A tractor feed uses a continuous roll of paper. The roll of paper resembles a roll of paper towel, with a perforated line between each sheet. A row of holes runs down each side of the entire roll. These holes are lined up with sprocketed wheels, which pull the paper through the printer.

   ☒ **B,** friction feed, is incorrect because this type of feed uses rubber or plastic rollers to "grab" individual sheets of paper. **C,** roller feed, and **D,** dot matrix feed, are both incorrect because they are not real paper-feed types.

2. ☑ **C.** Bubblejet printers contain a heating element within the cartridge. When this element is heated, it causes the ink in the cartridge to expand and form a small bubble on the cartridge's nozzle. When the bubble gets big enough, it bursts onto the paper.

   ☒ **A,** dot matrix, is incorrect because this type of printer uses pins to strike a ribbon against the paper. Dot matrix printers do not use cartridges or heating elements. **B,** inkjet, is incorrect because this printer uses a pump within the ink cartridge to spray ink onto the page. **D,** laser, is incorrect because this type of printer does have heating components, which are used during the fusing process. However, this is a fusing lamp, not a heating element, and it is not contained within the printer's toner cartridge.

3. ☑ **B.** Dot matrix printers use a ribbon to create printouts. The ribbon contains ink, which is transferred to the page when the pins strike the ribbon against the paper.

   ☒ **A,** ink cartridge, is incorrect because this is used by inkjet and bubblejet printers, not dot matrix printers. **C,** paint, is incorrect because no mainstream printers use paint. **D,** toner, is incorrect because this is used by laser printers (and photocopiers).

4. ☑ **D.** Bubblejet printers create images by allowing bubbles of ink to burst onto the paper. When the ink inside the cartridge is heated, it expands, forcing a bubble of ink onto the cartridge nozzle. The bubble continues to expand until it bursts onto the page.

   ☒ **A,** inkjet printers typically produce better-quality printouts than bubblejets, is incorrect. Although bubblejet technology sounds messier than inkjet technology, bubblejets are typically able to produce better images than inkjets. **B** is incorrect because it suggests that inkjet and bubblejet printers are the least expensive types. Of the printers discussed in this chapter, dot matrix printers are the least expensive, laser printers are the most expensive, and inkjet and bubblejet printers are between the two in terms of expense. **C,** inkjet printers are line printers, and bubblejets are page printers, is also incorrect because both types create images line by line, so they are line printers. Laser printers are page printers.

5. ☑ **C.** The charging step will fail. The purpose of the primary corona wire is to apply a very high negative charge to the printer's drum. Without the primary corona wire, the drum will not be charged.

   ☒ **A**, transferring, is incorrect because the transfer corona wire, not the primary corona wire, is used in this step. **B**, fusing, is also incorrect because the fusing step uses a very hot fusing lamp to heat the fusing rollers. The heat causes the toner to fuse to the page as it passes through the rollers. **D**, cleaning, is incorrect because this step uses a cleaning blade and erasure lamps, not the primary corona wire.

6. ☑ **B.** The laser is used in the writing step. Prior to this step, the printer's drum has been given a very high negative charge. In the writing step, the laser draws the image that will be printed. The areas that the laser touches lose most of their charge, and these represent the areas to which toner will be attracted in the developing stage.

   ☒ **A**, charging, is incorrect because the primary corona wire is used in this step. **C**, developing, is incorrect because in this step, the toner is released from the cartridge and attracted to the drum. The laser is not used in this step. **D**, fusing, is also incorrect because in this step, the fusing rollers are heated so that the toner will fuse to the page as it exits the printer.

7. ☑ **B.** If the cleaning step is not being performed properly, the erasure lamp could be responsible. The cleaning step occurs in two stages. First, a cleaning blade removes excess toner from the drum, then an erasure lamp comes on and removes any residual charge from the drum.

   ☒ **A**, primary corona wire, is incorrect because this component is used in the charging step to apply a high negative charge to the drum. **C**, laser, is incorrect because this is used in the writing step to discharge areas of the drum that will later hold toner. **D**, fusing lamp, is incorrect because this is used to heat the fusing rollers so that the toner is fused (melted) to the page during the fusing step.

8. ☑ **D.** The purpose of a laser printer's transfer corona wire is to apply a charge to the paper. During the transferring step, the transfer corona wire applies a positive charge to the paper so that the negatively charged toner will be attracted to it as the paper moves past the drum.

   ☒ **A**, to apply toner to the drum, and **B**, to apply toner to the paper, are incorrect. Toner is not *applied* during the laser print process; rather, toner is electrostatically attracted to either the drum or the paper. **C**, to apply a charge to the drum, is incorrect because this is the function of the primary corona wire.

9. ☑ **B.** Tell the user to keep the cable under 6 feet to avoid EMI. Parallel cables longer than 6 feet are susceptible to interference and data corruption and loss.

   ☒ **A**, cable length doesn't matter, is incorrect because parallel cables over 6 feet (and serial cables over 25 feet) can experience EMI-related problems. **C**, keep the cable over 6 feet to ensure proper communication timing, is incorrect because the cable should be kept *under* 6 feet, not *over* 6 feet. Furthermore, the length of the cable is unrelated to the timing of the communication. **D**, keep the cable under 25 feet to speed communication, is incorrect because although it takes data longer to travel long cables than short ones, there is no *noticeable* difference to the user. Furthermore, the cable should be kept under 6 feet, not 25.

10. ☑ **C.** The most efficient and cost-effective solution listed is to share the printer as a network resource. The printer can remain attached to the secretary's desktop PC, but others will be able to send print jobs to it.

☒ **A** is incorrect because it suggests getting users to e-mail their documents to the secretary and having the secretary open and print the files. This is not an efficient solution; printing other people's documents will most likely interrupt the secretary's work and take up unnecessary time. **B**, have users physically move the printer to their computers when they want to print, is also incorrect because although this solution will work, it is not very efficient. It is time-consuming to reattach a printer over and over again each time someone wants to print. Furthermore, the excess transportation of the printer could cause it premature wear and failure. **D**, have the company buy a network printer, is incorrect because it is not a cost-effective solution. The company already has a printer that can be accessed through the network, even though it is not a true network printer (one with a NIC). In this case, there is no benefit associated with buying and networking another printer.

Care, Service, and Troubleshooting

11. ☑ **A.** You can rule out improper communication between the computer and printer as the cause of this problem. The paper-feed mechanism is under the direction of the printer itself, not the computer. Poor communication between the two will not result in improper paper feeding.

☒ **B**, static, is incorrect because this can cause pages to stick together so that they are fed into the printer two or more at a time. **C**, not enough paper in the tray, is also incorrect because if there is not enough paper in the tray, the friction rollers might not be able to "grab" the top sheet. **D**, wrong paper weight, is incorrect because this might be the cause of the feeding problem. If the paper is too thick for the printer, it might not fit into the paper path. If it is too thin, more than one page can be fed at a time, or the page might not be fed at all.

12. ☑ **A.** You should try a different type of paper. If the printer has just recently started experiencing paper jams, it indicates that something has recently changed within the printer. The paper you are using might be the wrong weight. Using a different paper weight could solve the problem. Incidentally, cleaning the printer could also resolve the problem.

☒ **B**, replace the printer, is incorrect because, in this case, there is probably nothing wrong with the printer that can't be replaced or otherwise resolved. Replacing the printer as a first measure would most likely be an unnecessary step. **C,** replace the feed rollers, is incorrect because although this might be the ultimate resolution to the problem, it shouldn't be your first step in this case. Changing the paper type is much simpler and faster and more likely to resolve the problem than taking the printer apart to change the feed rollers. **D,** replace the transfer corona wire, is incorrect because this component is used to charge the paper as it passes through the printer. It is unrelated to the mechanism used to move the paper through the paper path.

13. ☑ **B.** The least likely cause of blank inkjet printouts is that the printer is dirty. Dust or ink build-up in the printer can cause paper jams and smudged printouts, but it will not cause blank printouts.
☒ **A,** the cartridge nozzles are dirty, is incorrect because that might be the cause of the problem. If the nozzles get dirty, they can become clogged so that no ink can get from the cartridge onto the page. **C,** the cartridge is empty, is incorrect because this might be the cause of the problem. If there is no ink in the cartridge, there is no medium with which to create the printout. **D,** the heating element is not working, is incorrect because if the heating element in a bubblejet ink cartridge stops working, the ink cannot expand and form the bubbles that will eventually create the image on the page. To replace the heating element, simply replace the ink cartridge.

14. ☑ **C.** When a printer produces random blotches, the first thing you should do is clean the printer. In any printer type, these blotches or speckles are most likely caused by excess ink or toner deposits inside the printer.
☒ **A,** replace the ribbon, ink, or toner cartridge, is incorrect because the problem in this case is not a lack of toner or ink but the presence of excess toner or ink. **B,** replace the drum, is incorrect because this might resolve the problem of repeated speckles in a laser printer, but it is typically not the cause of random blotches. **D,** check the communication between the computer and printer, is incorrect. Communication problems result in garbled printouts or no printouts but are not responsible for causing blotches on a printout.

15. ☑ **C.** You cannot verify that the problem can be resolved by replacing the drum. Although that might be a solution to the problem, it is not the only possibility. In this case, the cleaning blade or erasure lamps might need to be replaced.
☒ **A,** this is a laser printer, is incorrect because you can verify this fact from the information given because laser printers are the only type that experience the stated problem. **B,** there has been a failure in the cleaning step, is incorrect because this problem is caused when toner or a residual charge is left on the drum during subsequent printouts. It is the job of the cleaning step to remove the toner and charge. **D,** this is a ghosted image, is incorrect because that is the proper name for this type of printout.

16. ☑ **C.** There is a communication problem between the computer and the printer. Whenever the printer produces garbled or nonsensical printouts, it received the wrong or incomplete instructions from the computer or it interpreted those instructions incorrectly. All of these are communication problems.

    ☒ **A**, there was a failure during the writing step, is incorrect because a failure during the laser printer's writing step is likely to result in a blank or incomplete printout. The writing step simply draws the printed image that it is instructed by the printer to draw. The writing step is not responsible for interpreting signals from the computer. **B**, the printer should be cleaned, is incorrect because a dirty printer can cause paper jams or blotches, but it will not cause the wrong characters to be printed. **D**, the printer cable should be replaced, is incorrect because this is just one of many issues that could be responsible for the communication problem. For example, the printer might have a corrupted driver, have a resource conflict, or be different from the printer that Windows has been configured to use.

17. ☑ **A.** You are most likely to replace a laser printer's toner/drum assembly. The toner cartridge will eventually run out of toner and need to be replaced. In many printers, the toner and drum are an integrated unit.

    ☒ **B**, the feed rollers, **C**, the parallel cable, and **D**, the paper tray, are all incorrect because although these components do require replacing in some printers, it is rare for them to fail. Therefore, they are not replaced nearly as often as toner/drum assemblies.

18. ☑ **B.** An inkjet printer is the most likely to produce a printout with the wrong or dirty colors. This is typically caused by low levels of one of the basic ink colors or by dirty, semiclogged cartridge nozzles. The solution is usually to clean the nozzles or replace the cartridge.

    ☒ **A**, dot matrix, and **C**, laser, are incorrect because although they can produce the wrong colors, they are less likely to do so than an inkjet printer. Furthermore, dot matrix and laser printers are not likely to produce "dirty" colors. **D**, a parallel printer with a cable over 6 feet, is incorrect because a parallel cable over 6 feet can cause EMI-related problems, but these will tend to be in the form of garbled printouts or other communication problems. It would be very rare for a cable to cause a printout that had the proper content but the wrong colors.

19. ☑ **D,** you should remove the yellow toner cartridge, gently rock it back and forth, then place it back in the printer. This action could settle the toner so that the error message temporarily goes away. Incidentally, most printers allow you to keep printing, even with this error displayed. That is because the "Toner low" message is a warning, designed to inform you to replace the cartridge before it is completely empty.

    ☒ **A**, stop using the printer until you replace the cartridge, is incorrect because again, this message is a warning, not a fatal error. Continue using the printer, but be aware that some of the colors might not appear in the proper shade. **B**, refill the cartridge with the toner in the reservoir used to store excess toner from the cleaning step, is incorrect because although this might work in a black laser printer, it will not work in a color printer. Recall that the drum in a laser printer contains all four toner colors for each color printout. When the excess toner is cleaned from the drum, the colors are not separated. Therefore, in this printer, the toner reservoir contains toner for all four colors. **C**, continue using the printer, but don't print documents or images that contain yellow, is incorrect because this message is a warning, given before the toner drops below levels that would affect the printer's performance. Go ahead and use yellow, but replace the cartridge as soon as colors start to come out incorrectly. Incidentally, it would be nearly impossible to avoid printing images that contain yellow. Laser printers use nearly infinite combinations of colors, and it is extremely difficult to tell if yellow has been used in some color combinations.

20. ☑ **C.** Regularly cleaning the printer is most likely to prevent printer problems. Build-up inside the printer can cause ESD, block the paper path, and cause moving components to wear out. By cleaning the printer, you can also remove excess ink or toner that can produce stray marks on printouts.

☒ **A**, recharging the power supply, is incorrect because printer power supplies do not need to be recharged. **B**, regularly replacing the feed rollers, is incorrect because it is rare for these rollers to fail, so replacing them on a regular basis is unlikely to prevent future problems. **D**, giving the printer a two-day rest, is incorrect because printers do not need to "rest" and do not perform better after being left idle for a period of time.

LAB ANSWER

In the charging step of the laser print process, the HVPS charges the primary corona wire to approximately -5000vDC. This charge is passed on from the primary corona wire to the photosensitive drum. This high charge represents areas of the drum that will not contain toner. A totally black printout can result from an HVPS or primary corona wire failure.

In the next step, writing, the laser draws (writes) the document or image to be printed on the surface of the drum. All areas that are touched by the laser are reduced in voltage to about -100vDC. These areas attract toner. If the laser does not perform its function or if the drum does not hold the proper -100vDC charge, the entire drum will remain at -5000vDC. If this is the case, the drum will not attract toner to the proper areas, and the result will most likely be a blank printout. In the developing step, the toner cartridge is opened, and toner is attracted to the -100vDC areas of the drum. Again, if the charging step has failed, toner could be attracted to the entire drum, resulting in a black printout. If the writing step has failed, the drum might not attract any toner. The result would be a blank printout. If, in the developing step, there is no toner in the cartridge or if the cartridge fails to open, no toner will be attracted to the drum. Again, the result would be a blank printout.

Next, the paper begins to move through the printer. This is the beginning of the transferring step. The HVPS applies a positive charge to the transfer corona wire, which in turn applies a positive charge to the paper. As the paper passes the drum, the negatively charged toner is attracted from the drum onto the paper. If the HVPS or transfer corona wire fails during this step, the toner will remain on the drum, rather than being attracted to the paper. The result will be a blank printout. In the fusing process, a fusing lamp applies very high heat to the fusing rollers. As the page passes through the rollers, the toner is melted (fused) onto the paper. If the fusing procedure fails, the printout will contain loose toner powder and will most likely be smudged.

Finally, during the cleaning process, a cleaning blade removes the excess toner from the drum and deposits it into a toner reservoir. A series of erasure lamps are then activated, removing any excess charge from the drum. If the cleaning blade does not work, leftover toner will remain on the drum and be transferred to the next printout. This results in a ghosted image. If the erasure lamps do not properly discharge the drum, toner can be attracted to the wrong areas during subsequent developing steps. Again, the result is a ghosted image.

7

Basic
Networking

N etworks provide home users and business people with the ability to share files, resources, and mail, almost instantly, as though they resided locally on the user's computer. Computer networks have become so important in some settings that they provide the basis for nearly all business transactions. Networks make it possible to share documents and images with people all around the world, literally at the click of a mouse.

Computer networking is a very broad topic. There are many types of networks, from simple peer-to-peer ones to huge intranets and even the Internet itself. Each type of network can employ a different combination of network OS, cabling, protocols, and security measures. These combinations are known as the network's *architecture*. In fact, CompTIA's Network+ certification is based entirely on networking concepts and network architectures. Obviously, a discussion of the full spectrum of network details and specifications is too broad in scope to be contained in this chapter. However, as a computer technician, you should be aware of basic networking concepts so that you can troubleshoot minor problems on networks that have already been established. This chapter focuses on basic concepts of physical networks; Chapter 11 focuses on network protocols and how to configure Windows for network access.

CERTIFICATION OBJECTIVE 7.01

Networking Concepts

To properly maintain and troubleshoot a network, you must first be familiar with basic network concepts such as physical layout, cable types, and protocols. The combinations of these factors can be implemented in hundreds of different arrangements. The most common types of each are discussed in this section.

Topologies

The term *network topology* refers to the physical layout of computers and other equipment in the network. The most commonly used topologies are star, bus, and ring. The characteristics, special equipment, and advantages and disadvantages of each are discussed here.

Star Topology

Star networks consist of computers that are all attached to a network device called a *hub* (see Figure 7-1). The hub's job is to receive signals (called *data packets*) from one computer, and relay them to all other attached computers. The computer to which a packet is addressed opens and reads the data. All other computers attached to the hub ignore the packet.

Star networks do not always appear like the one in Figure 7-1 when they are implemented. It might be inconvenient to place a hub and cables in the middle of an office. In most implementations, the hub will be placed on one side of the room, with the cables running under tables or desks to the hub. In these cases, the topology doesn't physically resemble a star but is still considered a star topology.

One advantage to implementing a star network is that if a single computer goes down, the rest of the network is not affected. The same is true for the cables. No single cable in a star network can cause the downfall of the entire network. This type of arrangement also makes it easy to add new computers to the network (this

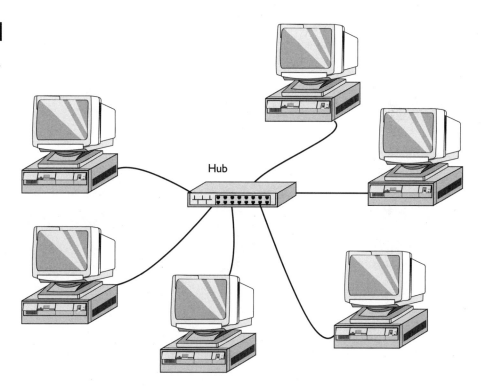

FIGURE 7-1

In a star network, computers are attached to a central hub.

Hub

is called *scalability*). The new computer can be set up in any free space and its cable attached to any available hub port.

One disadvantage of this type of network is the extra expense of the hub itself. Furthermore, the hub can provide a single point of failure for the entire network. That is, if the hub goes down, the entire network will fail. Another disadvantage is the method of data relay. Recall that when the hub receives data from any computer, it sends it to all other computers. This is called a *network broadcast*, and it can cause enough unnecessary network traffic to result in slow data transmission, especially in networks with a large number of computers. Finally, star networks allow only one computer to transmit at a time.

Bus Topology

In a *bus topology*, each computer is connected to a cable backbone (see Figure 7-2). In most cases, the backbone itself is a series of connected cable segments. At each junction in the backbone is a three-way T-connector that also attaches to a computer in the network. When one computer sends data, the packet travels along the backbone. Each computer examines the packet, but only the computer to which the packet is addressed will accept it. To prevent data from "bouncing" back and

FIGURE 7-2   In a bus topology, each computer is attached to a cable backbone.

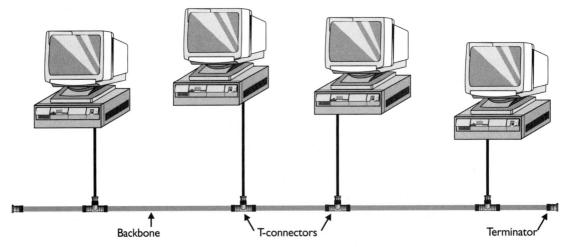

Backbone   T-connectors   Terminator

forth from one end to the other, a 50ohm terminator must be attached to each end of the backbone.

Another method of creating a bus network is to use a single length of cable for the entire backbone and to attach each computer using a vampire tap. A *vampire tap* contains prongs that are used to pierce the backbone cable and make contact with the wires inside. However, these devices are more difficult to use than T-connectors and are more prone to failure, and the single length of backbone is more difficult and costly to replace than a single backbone segment. A bus network that uses vampire taps must still be terminated at both ends.

The bus network is by far the simplest topology to implement, requires no special additional network equipment, and uses less cable than a star topology. However, bus networks allow only one computer to send data at a time. Bus networks are not easily scaled, meaning that it is more difficult to add another computer to the network than with other topologies. The failure of a computer on a bus network will not affect the other computers, but if there is a break in the backbone, the entire network will fail. The entire network will also fail if it is not properly terminated.

Ring Topology

In a *ring network*, each computer is attached to the next in a circle formation (see Figure 7-3). Each computer therefore has two network ports—one for the incoming cable and one for the outgoing cable. Data always travels in one direction in a ring network. When one computer sends data, that data is received by the next computer in line. That computer reads the packet address and passes the packet on. This process continues until the packet reaches its destination.

One advantage of a ring network is that more than one computer can send data at a time. Furthermore, as a packet travels around the ring, it is examined and regenerated at full strength by each computer until it reaches its destination. This means that ring networks experience very little signal loss (called *attenuation*).

Disadvantages of a ring topology are its expense and the relative difficulty of setting them up. Ring networks also have many points of failure. If any computer in the ring goes down or if there is a break in any of the cables, the entire network will fail.

exam
ⓦatch

Understanding how data is passed on a particular topology is a key to understanding the effect if a single computer or cable on the network fails.

FIGURE 7-3 In a ring topology, each computer is attached to the next in a circle formation.

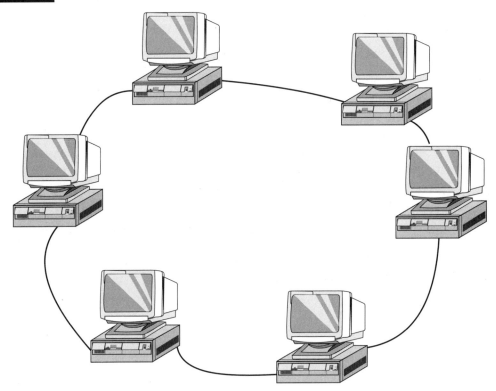

Before you continue in the chapter, answer the following Scenario & Solution questions to test your knowledge of network topologies.

SCENARIO & SOLUTION

How is a star network arranged?	Each computer is attached to a single hub using a separate cable.
What are the advantages of a bus network?	It is simple to implement and uses less cable.
Which topology has the highest number of potential failure points?	A ring. If any cable or computer fails, the entire network will go down.
How many computers can transmit on each type of topology?	Star and bus topologies are limited to one transmission at a time; ring topologies are not.

Protocols

A network's protocol is the "language" it uses for data transmission. The protocol includes the rules for communication, packet size, addressing, and ability to be routed. Computers on a network cannot communicate with other computers unless they are using the same protocol. The three most common protocols on Windows-based systems are TCP/IP, NetBEUI, and IPX/SPX.

TCP/IP

Transmission Control Protocol/Internet Protocol (TCP/IP) is by far the most common protocol on internal networks and is the protocol of the Internet. TCP/IP requires more configuration than other protocols but is the most robust, can be used on very large networks, and is routable. The term *routable* refers to the ability to send data to other subnetworks, typically connected by a bridge or router. TCP/IP allows for cross-platform communication. That means that computers using different OSs (such as Windows and Unix) can send data back and forth, as long as they are both using TCP/IP. Each computer in a Windows TCP/IP network must be configured with a computer name and workgroup (or domain) and a unique IP address. An *IP address* is a 128-bit address that is indicated by four numbers from 0–255, each separated by a period. An example IP address is 238.14.82.31.

exam
ⓦatch

TCP/IP is the most common protocol and is the only one that allows networks to access the Internet.

NetBEUI

NetBEUI stands for *NetBIOS Extended User Interface* and can be used only in small networks. It requires no address configuration and provides faster data transfer than TCP/IP. Each Windows computer in a NetBEUI network is configured only with a computer and workgroup name. However, NetBEUI's cross-platform support is limited to Windows and other Microsoft OSs. Furthermore, NetBEUI is not routable and not robust in unstable networks.

on the
ⓞ ob

The NetBEUI protocol is good if you are creating a very small internal network at the office or at home. NetBEUI is included with Windows, so literally, all that is required is that you connect the computers, elect to use the protocol, and assign a computer name to each computer. It's free and its extremely easy to implement.

IPX/SPX

IPX/SPX stands for *Internetwork Packet Exchange/Sequenced Packet Exchange*. It is designed specifically for use with the Novell NetWare OS. It is routable and otherwise similar to TCP/IP, except that it has limited cross-platform support and cannot be used on the Internet.

Cabling

There are many types of network cables, but the most common fall into one of three categories: twisted-pair, coaxial, and fiber-optic. Their characteristics, advantages, and common implementations are discussed here.

Twisted-Pair Cable

Twisted-pair cable is the most popular cable type for internal networks. These cables are so named because the cable contains pairs of wires that are twisted around each other. These twists help "boost" each wire's signals and make them less susceptible to EMI. Additionally, twisted-pair cables may be shielded. *Shielded twisted-pair (STP) cables* contain an extra insulating layer that helps prevent data loss and block EMI. Due to the expense of STP cables, *unshielded twisted-pair (UTP) cables* are actually used more often.

There are several standards for twisted-pair cables, each with a different number of wires, speed, and implementation. These standards are often referred to as *CAT #*—for example, CAT3 or CAT4 (*CAT* is short for *category*). CAT5, a type of UTP, is the most common twisted-pair cable. Table 7-1 presents a summary of twisted-pair cable offerings.

TABLE 7-1	Type	Speed	Common Use
Twisted-Pair Cable Standards	CAT1	1Mbps	Phone lines
	CAT2	4Mbps	Token Ring networks
	CAT3	16Mbps	Ethernet networks
	CAT4	20Mbps	Token Ring networks
	CAT5	100Mbps	Ethernet networks

Twisted-pair cables can be identified by their use of RJ-45 connectors, which look like regular phone connectors but are slightly larger. This type of cable is most commonly implemented in star networks.

Coaxial Cable

Coaxial cables (*coax* for short), which are used to connect televisions to cable outlets, are also used in bus networks and, to a lesser degree, in star networks. Coax cables contain a single copper wire surrounded by an insulating layer and have BNC connectors. Coax cables are less susceptible to interference than STP or UTP cables, so they can typically be used in longer lengths.

Coaxial cable is often categorized as either Thinnet or Thicknet. *Thinnet cable* is physically thinner and has a lower throughput rate. *Thicknet* is thicker, and because it is better shielded, it can be used for longer distances.

on the
job

Thicknet is physically harder to work with than Thinnet because it is thicker and less pliable than Thinnet. This makes it difficult to bend the cable to go around corners or tuck behind desks.

Fiber-Optic Cable

Fiber-optic cable, or *fiber* for short, is not commonly used within local area networks (LANs) but is often used to join separate networks over long distances. Fiber transmits light rather than electrical signals, so it is not susceptible to EMI. It is capable of faster transmission than other types of cable, but it is also the most expensive. Fiber-optic cable is most commonly implemented in ring networks but can also be used in ring and bus topologies.

exam
Watch

In most implementations, twisted-pair is used in star networks, coax is used in bus networks, and fiber-optic is used in rings.

Network Access

Network access refers to the method that computers use to determine when they can communicate, how messages are transferred, and what to do in the case of a data collision. The two most commonly implemented access methods are CSMA/CD and token passing.

CSMA/CD

CSMA/CD stands for *carrier sense multiple access/collision detection*. In this access method, when a computer wants to send a data packet, it first "listens" to the network to determine if another transmission is already in progress. If there is another transmission, the computer waits, then listens again. When there is no other network activity, the computer sends its data packet. However, if another computer has sent a packet at the same time, a collision will occur.

When the collision is detected, both computers stop transmitting, wait a random amount of time, then begin the listening/transmitting process again. This procedure is carried out until the data is properly transmitted. On large networks, the number of collisions can be quite high, so it can take a number of tries until a computer can send its packet. CSMA/CD is the most common LAN access method.

Token Passing

Token passing is less common but much more orderly than CSMA/CD. In this access method, one computer in the network generates an electronic signal, called a *token*. The token is passed from computer to computer on the network. If a computer receives the token but has no data to transmit, it simply passes the token along. If the computer does have data to transmit, it places the data behind the token, then sends them both to the next computer in line. A computer cannot transmit data until it receives an "empty" token (one with no data packet attached).

When a token is accompanied by data, its address is examined by each computer, then sent along again until it reaches its destination. The destination computer examines the token, removes the data packet, and then sends the empty token around again. Unfortunately, if there is a lot of network traffic, it could take a very long time for a computer to get an empty token so that it can transmit its data. For this reason, token passing is typically used only on smaller networks.

Because computers can transmit only if they have the token and because there is only one token per network, there is no chance of a data collision. However, the token itself can get lost in the network, or a computer could hang on to the token without resending it. In either case, network traffic is halted until the token is regenerated.

Full- and Half-Duplex Transmission

In computer terms, data can be unidirectional or bi-directional. In unidirectional communications, data can travel in one direction only. This type of communication

FROM THE CLASSROOM

It's Your Turn ... No, Wait, It's My Turn

The CSMA/CD and token passing access methods are not unlike common human social practices. CSMA/CD is especially similar to our everyday rules of conversation. Recall that in CSMA/CD, each computer listens to the network, and if it detects no traffic, it sends its data. If there is a collision between two computers, both stop transmitting, wait a random amount of time, then try again. Isn't that just like our conversations with each other? Typically, if you are listening to someone speak, you are not trying to talk, and vice versa. However, when both people try to talk at the same time, both of you will most likely stop, wait a random amount of time, and then one of you will try again.

Recall that in token passing, computers cannot transmit data until they receive the token. You might have seen this practice in real life among groups who use a "talking stick." In some cultures, as a way of ensuring that everyone gets a chance to speak, a talking stick or other symbolic object is passed around among the people present at a gathering. No one may speak until he or she is holding the talking stick. Just like in computer networks, this is an orderly type of communication, but overall communication can take longer as the stick (or token) is being passed around. This type of communication can also mean longer waiting times before individuals get their turn.

—*Amy Thomson,*
A+ Certified Technician, MOUS Master

is used in ring networks. In bi-directional communications, data can travel in either direction. The term *half-duplex* indicates that data can travel in either direction but only in one direction *at a time*. In *full-duplex* communications, data can travel in both directions *at the same time*.

Ways to Network PCs

By combining topologies, cable types, protocols, access methods, and other network variables, it is possible to come up with hundreds of different network architectures. There are, however, a few standardized combinations, as described in this section.

802.3 (Ethernet)

The Ethernet standard, developed by IEEE, is by far the most common. Also known as IEEE 802.3, this type of network combines CSMA/CD access with half-duplex communication and supports transmission speeds of either 10Mbps or 100Mbps. Ethernet networks can use twisted-pair, coax, or fiber-optic cable and can use bus or star topologies. You must use a special Ethernet NIC to access an Ethernet network.

Ethernet networks are often referred to by their speed, channel type, and cable type. For example, the term *10BaseF* indicates a 10Mbps network that uses one (base) channel and fiber-optic (F) cable. 100BaseT is a 100Mbps Ethernet network that uses twisted-pair. Table 7-2 contains Ethernet types and their characteristics.

exam
ⓦatch

Ethernet networks are identified by this configuration: (speed)Base(cable). The 10 or 100 at the start of the configuration signifies the speed in Mbps, and the letter or number at the end indicates the cable type (T = twisted-pair, 2 = Thinnet, 5 = Thicknet, and F = fiber).

Token-Passing Networks

Token-passing networks are those that use the token-passing access method. There are several IEEE-defined standards for token passing, including Token Ring, Token Bus, and Fiber Distributed Data Interface (FDDI). Token-passing networks can use star, ring, or bus topologies and coax, twisted-pair, or fiber-optic cabling. For each token-passing network type, you must install the proper type of NIC.

TABLE 7-2   Ethernet Types and Characteristics

Type	Speed	Cable	Maximum Cable Length	Topology
10BaseT	10Mbps	Twisted-pair	100m	Star
10Base2	10Mbps	Coax (Thinnet)	185m	Bus
10Base5	10Mbps	Coax (Thicknet)	500m	Bus
10BaseF	10Mbps	Fiber-optic	2000m	Star
100BaseTX 100BaseT4	100Mbps	Twisted-pair	100m	Star
100BaseFX	100Mbps	Fiber-optic	412m	Star

Token Ring networks are based on the IEEE 802.5 standard and have transmission rates of either 4Mbps or 16Mbps. They use twisted-pair cable and half-duplex communication. Although Token Ring networks may actually have a physical ring topology, it is more common for them to have a star topology. In either case, the token travels from one computer to the next, in order, in a conceptual ring. This type of network uses a multiple access unit (MAU) instead of a hub. See Figure 7-4 for an illustration of a conceptual ring on a physical star topology.

exam
ⓦatch

Token Ring networks with a star topology use a MAU, not a hub.

Another type of token-passing network is Token Bus. This network, based on IEEE standard 802.4, is similar to Token Ring but uses a coax bus topology rather than a twisted-pair ring or star. A Token Bus network can transmit at 4Mbps only.

FDDI networks use the FDDI standard, which was developed by ANSI and based on the IEEE 802.5 Token Ring standard. FDDI networks use a fiber-optic dual-ring structure and are capable of transmitting up to 100Mbps.

Dial-Up Networks

A *dial-up network* connection uses a modem rather than a network card and uses regular phone cables instead of network cables. In a dial-up connection, one computer must be configured to dial the host computer, and the host computer

---

FIGURE 7-4

A conceptual ring on a physical star network.

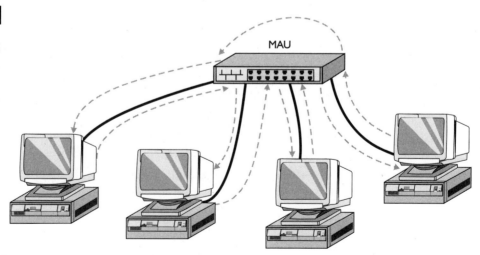

MAU

must be configured to permit dial-up access. Once a dial-up connection has been established, the two computers can communicate as though they were part of a LAN. If the host computer is already part of a LAN, the dial-up connection can be used to allow remote access to it.

Direct Cable Connection

It is possible to network two PCs simply by connecting them via their parallel or serial ports. Direct cable connections require special cables with different pinouts so that the send wires on one computer match the receive wires on the other computer. This is called a *cross-over cable*. Although this type of connection provides relatively fast data transmission, it is limited to two computers only, and distances are limited to 25m for a serial connection and 8m for a parallel connection. To configure a direct cable connection in Windows 98, follow the procedure in Exercise 7-1. This exercise describes how to first configure the host, then the guest machine.

EXERCISE 7-1

Configuring Windows 98 Computers for a Direct Cable Connection

1. Click Start, then select Programs | Accessories | Communications | Direct Cable Connection. If you do not see Direct Cable Connection in the Communications menu, use the Add/Remove Programs utility to install it.

2. The Direct Cable Connection Wizard will open. Select Host, then select Next.

3. You will be prompted to select a computer port to use for the connection. Select the appropriate port. Plug the cable in, and click Next.

4. You will be prompted to configure the computer to use File and Printer Sharing, if it has not already been set up. Click File and Printer Sharing.

5. The Network dialog box will open. Click File and Print Sharing, then elect to allow access to both files and printers. Click OK, then click OK again. If you have made a change in the network dialog box, you will need to restart your computer.

6. Click Next in the Direct Cable Connection Wizard.

7. In the final screen, you can choose to force guests to use a password to access the host computer. To do so, enable the "Use password protection" option, then click Set Password. Enter the password, and click OK.

8. Click Finish.

9. To configure the guest computer, start the Direct Cable Connection Wizard and select Guest rather than Host.

10. Select the port, then click Next.

11. Click Finish.

12. The two devices should be able to "see" each other in Network Neighborhood.

Infrared Networks

Computers can also be networked using *infrared communications*. There are several ways to do this, including direct cable connection, in which two computers can be networked as long as their IrDA ports are properly configured and are facing each other (see Chapter 1 for more information about IrDA devices). A more recent implementation of infrared access is the IEEE 802.11 standard. This standard specifies an Ethernet network that uses infrared rather than network cables and can transmit up to 20Mbps.

Now that you are familiar with some basic networking concepts, test your knowledge by answering the following Scenario & Solution questions.

SCENARIO & SOLUTION

What is a 10BaseT network?	This nomenclature indicates an Ethernet network. The *10* signifies the speed in Mbps, and the *T* means the network uses twisted-pair cabling.
Which types of networks use token passing?	Token Ring, Token Bus, and FDDI.
Which type of cable is the most common?	Twisted-pair.
What is the most popular network protocol?	TCP/IP.

CERTIFICATION OBJECTIVE 7.02

Network Setup and Troubleshooting

The actual implementation of a network is a very large and complex task. It requires intensive preplanning in terms of design, access, security, fault tolerance, and scalability issues, on top of the physical implementation of the protocols, topologies, and access methods described already in this chapter. This job is typically the domain for computer network specialists. However, there are some relatively common and simple network problems that you will be able to resolve without complete training as a network specialist. These troubleshooting issues, as well as procedures for configuring a computer to join a network, are described in this section.

Installing and Configuring Network Cards

As we discussed, most networks require the installation of NICs in each computer. The purpose of the NIC is to translate the computer's data into signals that can travel on the network and to take care of actually sending and receiving network traffic. As well as configuring the computer's NIC with the proper driver and system resources, you must also configure the computer with the settings it will need to join the intended network. The physical installation of a NIC is a relatively simple matter that includes physically attaching it to the motherboard, then loading its Setup or Install program (unless it is Plug and Play).

The next step is to configure the NIC to use the proper protocol. In Windows, these protocols include TCP/IP, NetBEUI, and IPX/SPX. The computer must be given a unique address and/or name, and it might need to be configured to join a particular workgroup or domain. The process for configuring an Ethernet card to use TCP/IP in Windows 9x is described in Exercise 7-2. This exercise assumes that the Ethernet card has already been installed and configured to use the proper system resources.

EXERCISE 7-2

Configuring an Ethernet Card for TCP/IP

1. Open the Windows Control Panel and double-click Networks. Ensure the Configuration tab is displayed.

2. Select the TCP/IP protocol from the list, then click Properties. If TCP/IP does not appear in the list, proceed with steps 2a through 2c to add it.
   2a: If TCP/IP is not in the list, click Add.
   2b: Select Protocol and click Add.
   2c: Select Microsoft from the Manufacturers list and select TCP/IP from the Protocols list. Click OK.

3. Select the Specify an IP Address Option.

4. Enter the IP Address and Subnet Mask for the network adapter (you can obtain these from the network's administrator).

5. Click OK.

6. Click the File and Print Sharing button. If desired, select the options to give others access to your files and/or printer, then click OK.

7. Select the Identification tab.

8. Enter a unique Computer Name and the name of the Workgroup that this computer will join on the network.

9. Click OK. You will be prompted to restart your computer. None of the new network settings will take effect until the computer is restarted.

Increasing Bandwidth

A network's *bandwidth* is the amount of data that can transmitted on the network at one time. For example, a 10Base2 network has a bandwidth of 10Mbps. If a network is perceived to be slow, increasing the bandwidth can improve its speed. That is, the more data that can be sent at once, the faster transmissions will be delivered from beginning to end and the faster the network will run overall.

In many cases, you can increase the bandwidth by upgrading the network's components. For example, you can replace 10Mbps cards with 100Mbps cards. You might also need to upgrade the cable types—for example, from CAT3 to CAT5—to support the new speed. The entire network will run at the speed of the hub or MAU (if one exists) or the speed of the cable, whichever is slower. If a single NIC supports a lower speed than all other network components, the network will be unaffected except in communications with that NIC. For example, suppose that an entire network supports 100Mbps, except for a NIC that supports only 10Mbps. All communications to or from that NIC will run at 10Mbps. All other communications will run at 100Mbps.

Finally, recall that most networks are *baseband*, meaning they use one of the cable's channels to transmit data. Some network technologies, such as 1000BaseT, can use more than one channel on a single cable. This is called *broadband*, and it is the same technology that allows a television cable to provide more than one channel.

Loss of Network Connectivity

When you suspect that a computer is not on the network, first check the Windows Network Neighborhood. Under normal conditions, all other computers that can be accessed in the current workgroup will be listed. If a computer cannot access the network, the Network Neighborhood window will open and a message will appear, stating "Unable to Browse Network." If this is the case, check the NIC itself. Most NICs indicate network connectivity with an indicator light. Check the cable by swapping it with a known good one. Try to restart the computer, and ensure that the proper network name and password are entered, if necessary.

If these procedures don't work, check the configuration of the NIC in Network Settings. Make sure that it is configured with the proper workgroup, and ensure that it is not using a conflicting IP address. You should also check the NIC's driver and use of system resources. As a last resort, replace the NIC.

on the **Job**

As with other hardware troubleshooting methods, start by trying to replicate the problem, then restart the computer. Pinpoint a hardware-related network problem by checking the outermost, most accessible components first, then working your way in.

Loss of Data

Because NICs use error checking, it is rare for data to get lost en route. However, many networks use servers that store users' data. A *server* is a computer that controls network access or provides resources to a network, such as a printer, application, or storage space. It is very important in these cases to ensure that data is available if the server temporarily goes down or to ensure that data is not permanently lost if the server is not recoverable. There are several techniques for preventing loss of data in the event of a server failure. Data-loss prevention techniques provide *fault tolerance* to the network, meaning that the network can tolerate a failure and continue to function even if there is a failure.

Tape Backups

Servers can be configured to automatically and regularly back up their entire contents to tape. For example, if a server performs a nightly backup, it makes a copy of all data that was saved on the server earlier that day. Then if the server fails, the current day's data will be lost, but all files created previously can be recovered from the tape.

Mirroring

Many networks employ backup servers that take over the function of the primary server if it fails. This is called server *mirroring*, and it involves saving all data to both the primary and backup servers. If the main server fails, the backup server can take over its function, and users might never even know the problem occurred. Unfortunately, the process of saving all data twice can be time consuming and might make the network appear slow.

Clustering

Another way to prevent data loss is to spread data over more than one server so that data and services can be accessed, even if the original server loses its data. This type of strategy is called server *clustering*. As well as providing fault tolerance, clustering also provides *load balancing*, which means that the workload is divided (balanced) between two or more servers.

Use the following Scenario & Solution questions to test your knowledge of the fault-tolerance methods described in the previous sections.

SCENARIO & SOLUTION

What is fault tolerance?	Fault tolerance is the ability of a network to continue functioning, even when there is a failure among one of its components.
What are common data-loss prevention techniques?	Server mirroring, server clustering, and tape backups.
Which fault-tolerance method provides load balancing?	Clustering, which divides work between two or more servers, provides load balancing.

Network Slowdown

Many things, including reduced bandwidth or excessive traffic, can result in network slowdowns. The very nature of some networks makes them prone to slow data transmission. For example, recall that in a token-passing network, a computer cannot transmit until it has an empty token. If there is a lot of traffic on the network, it could take a long time before the computer gets the empty token. The reason for this delay will not be apparent to the user, however. To the user, it will simply appear that the data is taking a long time to get to its destination.

Furthermore, recall the function of a hub. When a computer sends data, the hub receives it, then retransmits it to all other computers. On a 16-port hub, this means that 14 packets were sent out unnecessarily (16 minus the sending and receiving computers). This extra traffic can cause more collisions, which ultimately results in slower data transfer.

If the network experiences a single busy period, there is little you can do to resolve the problem. However, if a network gradually gets slower and slower over time, it could be that there is too much traffic for the network's capabilities, and the network will have to be split up or upgraded. Furthermore, if there is a lot of interference, there could be many data errors, which result in the resending of entire data packets. Again, this situation raises the total amount of traffic on the network and slows down its overall performance.

CERTIFICATION SUMMARY

The field of networking is very large and diverse. However, as a computer technician, you should be familiar with basic network terminology and network arrangements. For example, you should be able to recognize a star, bus, or ring topology and be familiar with the cable types they employ, as well as the advantages and disadvantages of each. You should also understand the differences between common network protocols, from the very simple NetBEUI to the more complex protocol of the Internet, TCP/IP.

The combination of these factors makes up the network's architecture. The 10BaseT Ethernet standard, for example, employs CSMA/CD 10Mbps access on a star network and typically uses CAT5 twisted-pair cabling. A Token Bus network uses 4Mbps token passing on a coaxial cable bus network. Knowing the characteristics of each network component or factor will help you make decisions about the type of network to deploy and will also help you pinpoint and resolve networking problems.

TWO-MINUTE DRILL

Here are some of the key points from each certification objective in Chapter 7.

Networking Concepts

❑ Computers are connected to a hub in a star topology, to a main backbone in a bus topology, and to each other in a ring topology.

❑ The TCP/IP protocol is the most common, most difficult to configure, and the protocol of the Internet.

❑ The NetBEUI protocol is simple to implement but is not routable.

❑ The most common twisted-pair cable is CAT5, which can transmit up to 100Mbps.

❑ Twisted-pair cable can be shielded or unshielded and uses an RJ-45 connector.

❑ Coaxial cable is more shielded than STP, contains a single copper wire, and uses a BNC connector.

❑ Fiber-optic cable transmits light signals, and although it can transmit faster and at longer distances, it is not popular, due to its expense.

❑ In CSMA/CD access, each computer is free to transmit as long as no other computer is also transmitting.

❑ Ethernet networks, such as 10BaseT or 100BaseFX, use CSMA/CD and can transmit data at either 10Mbps or 100Mbps.

❑ Token-passing networks support 4Mbps or 16Mbps, and computers can communicate only if they have the network's empty token.

Network Setup and Troubleshooting

❑ A computer's NIC (for example, Ethernet or Token Ring) must support the type of network it is joining.

❑ The NIC must be configured for use by the computer and is also configured to communicate on the network.

❑ Network communications can occur only as fast as the slowest involved element, such as the NIC, hub, or cable.

❑ Some network servers use mirroring or clustering to prevent or reduce data loss in the event of a server failure.

❑ Network slowdowns can be caused by interference, heavy traffic, or insufficient equipment.

SELF TEST

The following questions will help you measure your understanding of the material presented in this chapter. Read all of the choices carefully because there might be more than one correct answer. Choose all correct answers for each question.

Networking Concepts

1. A network consists of five computers attached to a hub. There is a break in one computer's network cable. How will this break affect the network?

   A. The entire network will fail.

   B. Only the computer attached to the faulty cable will be unable to access the network.

   C. Only computers that were booted before the computer with the faulty cable will be able to access the network.

   D. Only computers that were booted after the computer with the faulty cable will be able to access the network.

2. Which of the following points of failure will affect the connectivity of an entire star network?

   A. A single computer

   B. A single cable

   C. The backbone

   D. The hub

3. Which type of network uses terminators and T-connectors?

   A. Bus

   B. Star

   C. Ring

   D. FDDI

4. A computer in a ring network won't boot properly. What effect will this have on the network?

   A. The entire network will fail.

   B. Only the failed computer will be unable to access the network.

   C. All computers located after the failed computer will be unable to access the network.

   D. All computers located before the failed computer will be unable to access the network.

5. Which protocol requires that each computer have a unique 128-bit address?

    A. TCP/IP

    B. NetBEUI

    C. IPX/SPX

    D. All of the above

6. Your company has a large network, and due to increased traffic, you have decided to split the network into two connected subnetworks. Which of the following protocols must you avoid using?

    A. TCP/IP

    B. NetBEUI

    C. IPX/SPX

    D. You can use any of the above

7. Which network cable type has a maximum speed of 16Mbps?

    A. CAT2

    B. CAT3

    C. CAT4

    D. CAT5

8. Which of the following is the most common type of cable used in bus networks?

    A. CAT5

    B. STP

    C. Coaxial

    D. Fiber-optic

9. Which of the following most accurately describes the CSMA/CD network access method?

    A. An electronic signal is constantly passed around the network, and no computer can transmit until it receives the signal.

    B. A central device polls each computer in order, asking if the computer has any data to transmit.

    C. When a computer wants to transmit, it interrupts the network's central device and is given a transmission priority.

D. When a computer wants to transmit, it first listens for traffic. If a data collision occurs, each transmitting computer waits a random amount of time, then retransmits.

10. A customer has set up a twisted-pair star topology and wants to implement a Token Ring standard. What do you tell the customer?

A. They must first change the topology to a ring.

B. They must first change the cable type to fiber-optic.

C. They must change the topology to a ring and change the cable type to fiber-optic.

D. Tell the customer the Token Ring standard can be implemented on the current topology.

11. A customer has called about a network problem. When asked, the customer tells you that it is a 10Base5 network. What can you tell about this network without even seeing it?

A. It supports a maximum cable length of 185m.

B. It uses token passing.

C. It has a bus topology.

D. It uses twisted-pair cabling.

12. A customer works at an office that uses an Ethernet network, but she cannot remember the network's supported maximum speed. What do you tell the customer?

A. The network's speed is 4Mbps.

B. The network runs at 4Mbps, 10Mbps, or 16Mbps.

C. The network runs at either 10Mbps or 100Mbps.

D. The network runs at 4Mbps, 10Mbps, 16Mbps, or 100Mbps.

13. Which of the following network connections requires a cross-over cable?

A. Ethernet

B. FDDI

C. Dial-up

D. Direct cable connection

Network Setup and Troubleshooting

14. When configuring a computer for network access, the computer name must:

A. Be unique

B. Match the names of the other computers on the network

C. Match the computer's IP address

D. Be entered only if you are using the NetBEUI protocol

15. Which of the following are required to properly configure a computer to use the NetBEUI protocol?

A. Computer name

B. Workgroup name and IP address

C. Subnet mask and computer name

D. Subnet mask and IP address

16. One computer on a Token Ring network has a 4Mbps NIC. All other network components, including NICs, MAUs, and cables, support 16Mbps. What effect will the slower NIC have on the network?

A. The entire network will run at 4Mbps.

B. All devices will be able to communicate except the 4Mbps NIC.

C. When communicating with the 4Mbps NIC, communications will run at 4Mbps; otherwise, the network will run at 16Mbps.

D. No computer will be able to access the network.

17. A user has called you and complained that he cannot get his computer on the network. You tell him to open the Windows Network Neighborhood. Which of the following will occur in support of the user's claim?

A. All computers within the user's workgroup will be displayed.

B. The Network Neighborhood window will not open.

C. A message stating "Unable to browse network" will be displayed.

D. The Network Neighborhood window will contain the text "Network Access Not Configured."

18. What is the purpose of mirroring a network server?

A. To speed up network activity

B. To provide fault tolerance

C. To provide load balancing

D. To increase bandwidth

19. Which type of fault tolerance method provides load balancing?

    A. Mirroring

    B. Tape backups

    C. Clustering

    D. All of the above

20. Your company is growing, and your 100BaseTX network has been getting consistently slower over the past month. A coworker has stated that the problem is being caused by the hub. How might the hub be responsible?

    A. The hub might not support 100Mbps.

    B. The hub might be causing excess network traffic.

    C. The hub might be unable to find all the computers on the network.

    D. The hub cannot be responsible.

LAB QUESTION

One of your clients owns a company that currently uses a 4Mbps Token Ring network. The network uses a star topology and CAT3 cabling. The company has been growing, and its owner would like to upgrade the network to the Ethernet standard. Your client has asked what the options are. In a few paragraphs, discuss Ethernet options as well as the network components that must be added, replaced, or upgraded. Discuss the advantages, disadvantages, and performance of each option. Supply as much information as you can so that the customer can make an informed decision.

1. DIMM memory sockets
2. Secondary EIDE channel connector
3. Microprocessor
4. Power supply
5. Power input connector
6. Battery socket
7. 3.3-V power input connector
8. Diskette drive interface connector
9. Primary EIDE channel connector
10. Control panel connector
11. System board jumpers
12. ISA expansion-card connectors
13. PCI expansion-card connectors

The inside of the typical IBM personal computer, showing the most vital system components such as the microprocessor, power supply, expansion cards, drive controllers, and memory sockets. Expansion cards, floppy and hard drive cables, as well as the drives themselves have been omitted for a clear view of the motherboard. Every component seen here will be tested on the exam, in addition to other components that are not shown here: hard drives, CD-ROM drives, and tape drives. For the exam, you will be expected to know the characteristics of each component of a standard computer system, and how to diagnose and resolve problems related to each.

A Typical Motherboard

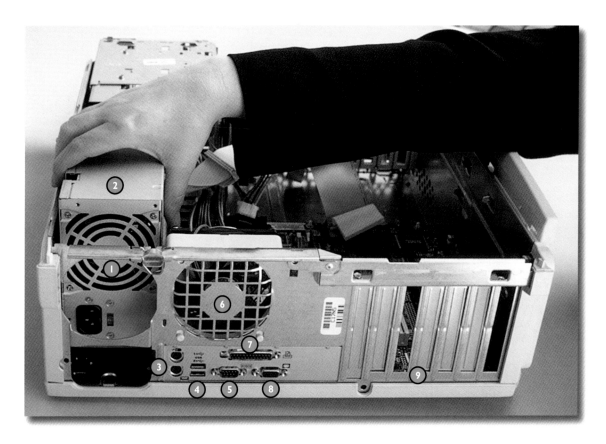

The installation of a power supply in an IBM compatible computer. Most power supplies are removed with four screws on the rear of the power supply. Repair of a power supply should be performed by a skilled technician with the necessary training and equipment to work on power supplies. The replacement of a power supply should occur immediately if the fan stops functioning because the power supply can overheat and destroy the entire computer. For the exam, you will need to understand the symptoms of a failing power supply.

1. Power supply cooling fan
2. Power supply
3. Keyboard and PS/2 mouse connectors
4. USB ports
5. Serial port
6. Cooling fan
7. Parallel port
8. Monitor port
9. Slot covers

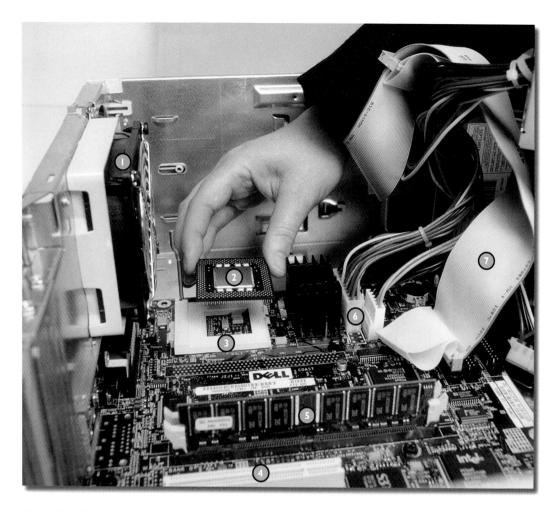

1. Cooling fan
2. CPU (processor) central processing unit
3. Processor socket
4. PCI expansion slot
5. 168-Pin DIMM memory
6. Power supply connectors
7. IDE flat data ribbon cable

Installation of a microprocessor in a computer. Notice how the lever in the processor socket is in the raised position. Once the processor is placed in the socket, you then lower the lever to lock the processor in place. To free the processor, you simply raise the lever. This is known as a Zero Insertion Force (ZIF) socket, and not all motherboards are equipped with this type of socket. For the exam, you most likely will not have to worry about the ZIF socket, but you will need to know about the various types of processors on the market. You will need to know the characteristics of each processor, such as the width of the data bus and address bus, and the register size.

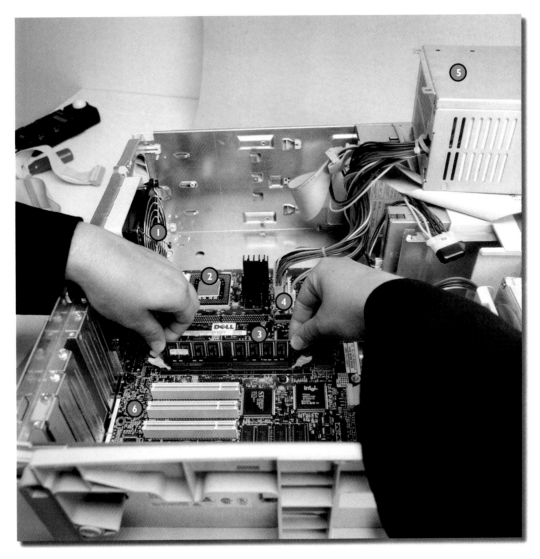

Installation of 168-pin DIMM memory in a computer. With DIMM memory, the module is inserted straight up and down, unlike the insertion method of SIMM memory, which is inserted at a 45 degree angle and then clicked into place when the memory is in the upright position. The notches on the DIMM memory module will lock into place with the keys located on the socket. For the exam, you will need to know the various types of memory available, including ROM, RAM, DRAM, and SRAM, and the characteristics of each.

1. Cooling fan
2. Central processing unit
3. 168-Pin DIMM memory
4. Power supply connectors
5. Power supply
6. PCI expansion slots

Installation of a floppy disk drive in the front bay of an IBM compatible computer. The floppy drive is 3.5 inches in size. Most computers have bays for two 3.5 floppy drives located on the front of the computer. The 5.25-inch bays are used for CD-ROM drives and tape drives. For the exam, you will need to know how to troubleshoot the floppy disk drive subsystem, which includes the media, floppy drive, cable, and the controller.

1. CD-ROM drive
2. Additional CD-ROM or tape drive bay (5.25-inch size)
3. Floppy disk drive bays (3.5-inch size)
4. Floppy disk drive

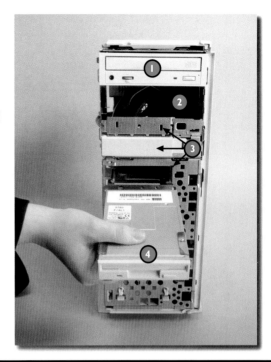

A printer motor used to move the paper through the printer. There are a few motors located in a printer—the main drive, paper feed, and transport motor. Every manufacturer uses different types of motors in varying places throughout the printer, so you must consult your vendor's documentation when replacing or servicing a printer motor. For the exam, you do not need to know about the motor specifically, but you should know what the effect will be on the print quality when a printer motor has failed.

1. Printer motor
2. Paper feed frame

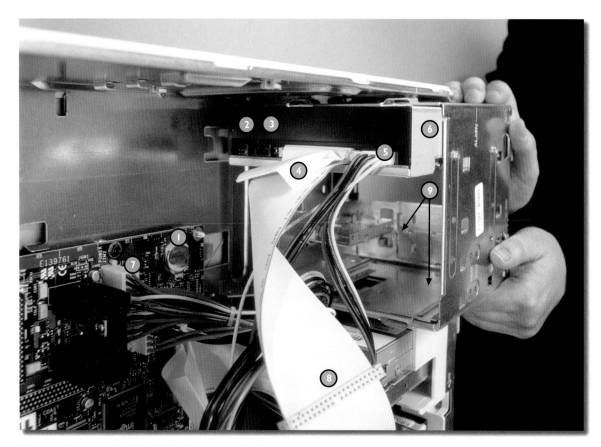

The installation of a CD-ROM drive in an IBM compatible computer. The illustration shows the back of the CD-ROM drive which contains the connector for the 40-pin IDE cable, the power connector, sound card connector, and the master/slave jumpers. You can look down the length of the IDE cable and see another 40-pin connector for attaching another CD-ROM drive or hard drive in a master/slave configuration. For the exam, you should know the connectors and cables used in IDE devices such as hard drives and CD-ROM drives.

1. CMOS battery
2. Master/slave jumpers
3. Sound card connector
4. IDE cable
5. Power cable
6. CD-ROM drive
7. Power supply connectors
8. Additional connector for another IDE device
9. Additional CD-ROM or tape drive bays (5.25-inch size)

An example of replacing an ISA sound card in an IBM compatible computer. Expansion cards are installed with a slight rocking motion with a firm grip on both ends of the card. You can see it is standard for motherboard vendors to color the ISA slots black and the PCI slots white. For the exam, you will need to know the differences between ISA, EISA, MCA, and PCI, and the characteristics of each.

1. Floppy disk drive cable
2. ISA sound card
3. ISA expansion slots
4. PCI expansion slots
5. 168-Pin DIMM memory
6. Additional 168-pin DIMM memory socket

1. Configuration jumpers
2. Floppy disk drive cable
3. Jumper configuration settings

A view of configuration jumpers on a motherboard. Most motherboards have jumpers to configure internal processor speed and external bus speed. These settings are usually stamped on the motherboard in white, as seen in the illustration. If you do not configure these jumpers correctly, you could overclock your processor causing it to burn up; if you underclock the processor, you might not be utilizing the processor to its full potential. For the exam, you probably won't be asked about jumpers on the motherboard, but you will be asked about the data bus, address bus, and register size of the various processors on the market.

Installing an IDE hard drive in an IBM personal computer. From the illustration, you can see the 40-pin IDE connector on the hard drive and the 40-pin ribbon cable. When you are installing a hard drive in a system, you have the ability to make the hard drive the master of its own controller, or to configure the hard drive in a master/slave relationship with another device, such as another hard drive or CD-ROM drive. The exam will test your knowledge of configuring a hard drive using the CMOS SETUP program.

1. ISA expansion slots
2. PCI expansion slots
3. 168-Pin DIMM memory
4. Cooling fan
5. 40-Pin IDE cable
6. 3.5-Inch floppy disk drive
7. 40-Pin IDE connector
8. Power cable
9. Hard disk drive

An internal modem, which has visible jumpers in red for configuring COM port assignments. The illustration also shows a sticker on a chip, which details the various jumper settings to configure the COM port settings. The modem also includes RJ-11 connectors for connecting to the phone line and to the telephone. The exam will test your knowledge of the standard COM ports and IRQs for configuring modems.

1. Com port setting jumpers
2. Jumper diagram
3. Telephone and phone line connectors

Twisted-pair coaxial cabling with an RJ-45 connector. Coaxial cable is resistant to the interference and signal weakening that other cabling, such as unshielded twisted-pair (UTP) cable, can experience. In general, coax is better than UTP for connecting longer distances and for reliably supporting higher data rates with less sophisticated equipment. For the exam, you should know the type of connector used with UTP cabling.

1. Twisted-Pair cabling
2. RJ-45 connector

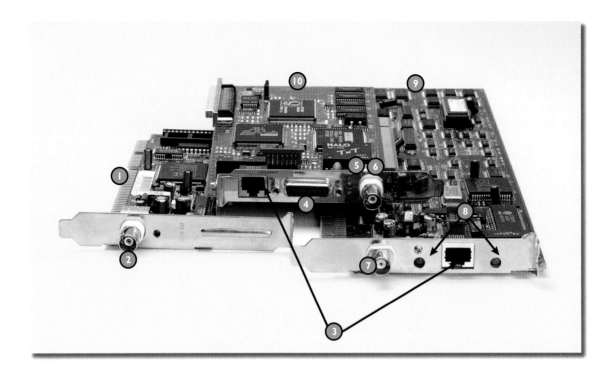

Various network interface cards with support for coax, twisted-pair, and AUI. The network interface card on the left has only one interface for a coax BNC connector. The network interface card on top has an interface for a coax BNC connector, an AUI connector, and a UTP RJ-45 connector. The network interface card on the right has an interface for a coax BNC connector and a UTP RJ-45 connector. Both the top and right network interface cards have power and link lights also. For the exam, you should know what interfaces are available on network interface cards, and the common resources, such as IRQ and I/O address, used for network cards.

1. Coaxial network interface card
2. Coaxial connector
3. Twisted-Pair connectors
4. AUI connector
5. Link and power lights
6. Coaxial connector
7. Coaxial connector
8. Link and power lights
9. Combo network card with twisted-pair and coaxial support
10. Combo network card with twisted-pair, coaxial, and AUI support

Various Network Interface Cards with Coaxial, Twisted-Pair, and AUI Support

A typical printer's system board that consists of the logic required to operate the printer. Every manufacturer uses different types of logic boards in varying places throughout the printer, so you must consult your vendor's documentation when replacing or servicing the logic board. For the exam, you do not need to know about the logic board specifically, but you should know what the affect will be on a printer if the logic board is faulty and needs to be replaced.

1. Power input
2. Centronics port

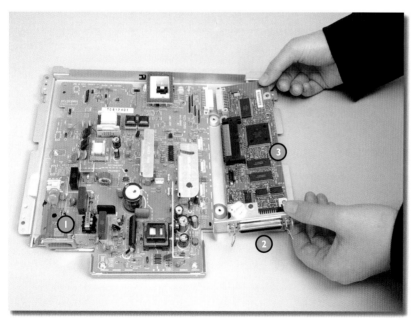

A printer's sublogic board which works in conjunction with the primary printer system board that enables you to replace or upgrade the capability of the sublogic board. Most printer sublogic boards allow you to change the port, such as replacing the Centronics port. For the exam, you should be able to identify the characteristics of parallel ports on a computer, such as ECP, EPP, and Bi Directional printer ports.

1. Power input
2. Centronics port
3. Add-on adapter card with parallel (Centronics) port

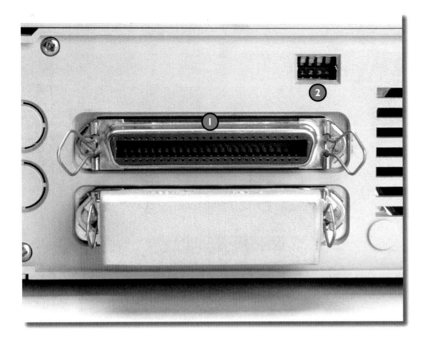

A device with external SCSI interfaces. This particular device uses a 50-pin Centronics SCSI connector, which is nearly identical to the Centronics printer cable connector. Also visible is the SCSI address ID jumper, which enables you to configure a SCSI device for a particular SCSI ID from 1–4. There are eight available addresses for SCSI IDs, with seven usually being reserved for the SCSI adapter itself. The exam will test your knowledge of the various SCSI connectors that are available.

1. Centronics 50-pin
   SCSI connector
2. SCSI address ID jumpers

SCSI Port

The types of Small Computer Systems Interface (SCSI) connectors available. The top SCSI connector is a 50-pin high-density connector. The middle SCSI connector is a 68-pin high-density connector. The bottom connector is a Centronics 50-pin connector, not to be confused with a Centronics printer connector, which looks almost identical. For the exam, you need to know the types of SCSI connectors presented here.

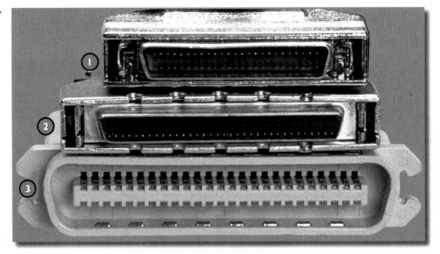

1. 50-Pin high-density SCSI
2. 68-Pin high-density SCSI
3. Centronics 50-pin SCSI

Various SCSI Connectors

A notebook computer combination cable with support for twisted-pair and coaxial cable. This unit plugs into the PCMCIA network interface card located inside the PC card bay of the notebook computer (not shown). As a travelling network technician, it's a good idea to have a combination cable like the one shown so you can connect to both a coaxial or twisted-pair network with the same PCMCIA network card. For the exam, you should know what interfaces are available in a network adapter such as this.

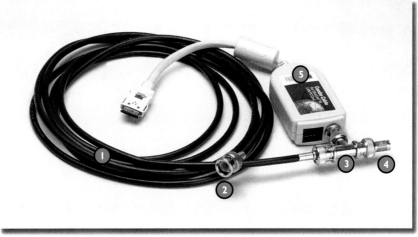

1. Thinwire 10Base2 coaxial cable
2. BNC connector
3. BNC connector
4. Terminator
5. Combination twisted-pair/ coaxial dongle

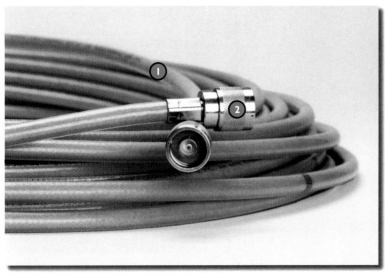

A thickwire (10Base5) cable with a BNC connector. Thicknet is extremely bulky and difficult to work with, therefore it is rarely used. Thickwire cabling is used as a network backbone or a connection between two different hubs or routers. For the exam, you should know the type of connector used with UTP cabling.

1. Thickwire (10Base5) coaxial cable
2. BNC connector

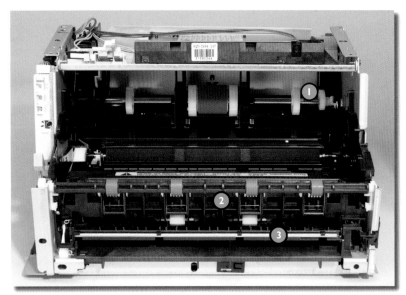

The front view of a printer roller assembly showing the numerous rollers and gears associated with a modern printer. The only internal components of a printer that you will have to be familiar with for the exam is the laser printer and the laser printing process. These components include the primary corona wire, cleaning blade, transfer corona, and the photosensitive drum. Each laser printer component is responsible for a phase during the printing process.

1. Pickup roller assembly
2. Delivery assembly
3. Separation assembly

A side view of the printer roller assembly with a view of the numerous gears involved in the printing process. From the illustration, you can see how the pickup roller assembly is removable and can be replaced in the event it becomes defective. For the exam, the only components of the printing process you should be familiar with are those of the laser printer. In addition, you should know the various phases of the laser printing process, such as the cleaning, charging, writing, developing, transferring, and fusing phase, and what occurs during each of the phases.

1. Pickup roller assembly

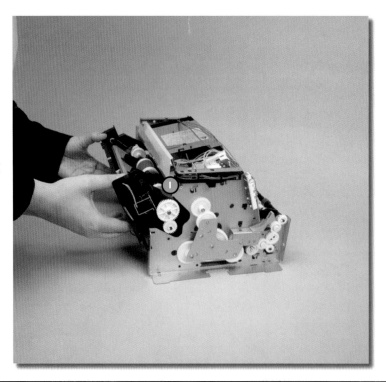

1. Power supply cooling fan
2. Cooling fan
3. Power input
4. PS/2 mouse connector
5. Keyboard connector
6. USB ports
7. Serial port
8. Parallel port
9. Monitor port

The back of a computer, illustrating the power supply and common connectors found on a personal computer. You can see the cooling fan for the power supply in addition to the CPU's cooling fan. The illustration also shows a PS/2 mouse connector, Mini-DIN keyboard connector, two USB ports, and a parallel, serial, and monitor port. For the exam, you should be able identify the physical characteristics of a serial or parallel port.

Installing memory modules in a portable notebook computer. Although most notebook computers are different, the illustration shows one method of upgrading the memory in a notebook computer. For the exam, you will not need to know anything memory-related on a notebook computer. You will need to know about memory in general, including the types of memory chips available, such as the difference between SIMMs and DIMMs.

1. Memory module
2. Contacts

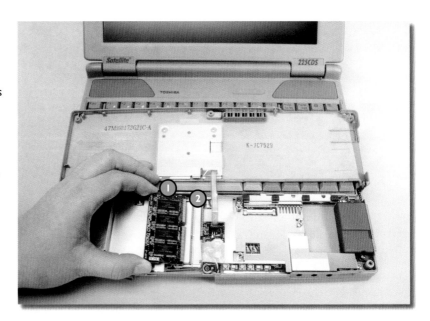

A side view of a printer's rollers and gears. You can see the complex innerworkings of a printer and how you need to provide continual routine preventative maintenance on the printer to keep the rollers and various mechanical devices working correctly. For the exam, you should know how to clean and maintain a dot matrix, ink jet, and laser printer.

SELF-TEST ANSWERS

Networking Concepts

1. ☑ **B.** Only the computer attached to the faulty cable will be unable to access the network. In a star network, each computer has its own cable, which is attached to the hub. One computer's cable will not affect the performance of other computers.

   ☒ **A,** the entire network will fail, is incorrect. The only single point of total network failure on a star network is the hub. That is, if the hub stops functioning, no computer will be able to access the network. **C** and **D** are incorrect because they suggest that only computers booted before or after the computer with the bad cable will be affected. First, only the computer attached to the bad cable will be affected. Furthermore, in networks in which one computer's failure results in the failure of other systems, the order in which the computers booted is irrelevant.

2. ☑ **D.** The hub is a point of failure that will affect an entire star network. All computers in a star network are attached to the hub. If the hub stops functioning, the computers will have no method of communication. Therefore, if the hub fails, the entire network will fail.

   ☒ **A,** a single computer, and **B,** a single cable, are incorrect. In a star network, each computer has its own cable and is connected to the hub independently of the other computers. The failure of a single computer or cable does not affect other machines on a star network. **C,** the backbone, is incorrect because star networks do not have backbones. Backbones are implemented in bus networks.

3. ☑ **A.** A bus network uses terminators and T-connectors. Bus networks consist of a coaxial cable backbone, which must be terminated with a 50ohm terminator at each end, to prevent signal "bouncing." Each computer in a bus network is attached to the backbone via a T-connector or, in some cases, a vampire tap.

   ☒ **B,** star, is incorrect because it does not use terminators or T-connectors. Instead, each computer is attached to a hub. **C,** ring, is also incorrect. In a ring network, each computer is attached to the next in a circular daisy-chain fashion. **D,** FDDI, is incorrect because this is a network standard that uses token passing on a fiber-optic double-ring topology.

4. ☑ **A.** The entire network will fail. In a ring network, each computer is connected to the next. All network traffic must go through each computer and be retransmitted until it reaches its destination. If one computer cannot access the network, is turned off, or will not boot properly, the network will not function.

   ☒ **B** is incorrect because it states that only the failed computer will be unable to access the network. Although this is true in a star or bus network, the structure of a ring network is such that a single point of failure anywhere in the network will result in a total network failure. **C** and **D** are incorrect because they suggest that only certain computers, located before or after the failed computer, will not be able to access the network. Again, because of the ring's structure, all computers will fail. Furthermore, because of its ring topology, all computers could be said to be before or after the failed computer.

5. ☑ **A.** TCP/IP requires that each computer have a unique address. This is the computer's Internet Protocol (IP) address, and it identifies the computer on the network, between connected networks, or the Internet.

   ☒ **B,** NetBEUI, is incorrect because it requires a unique computer name and common domain or workgroup name only. **C,** IPX/SPX, is incorrect because this protocol requires a simple network address, not a 128-bit address. For this reason, **D,** all of the above, is also incorrect.

6. ☑ **B.** You must avoid using the NetBEUI protocol. NetBEUI is effective only on small networks and is not routable. That means that computers using NetBEUI cannot communicate with computers on other subnetworks, even if they are physically connected.

   ☒ **A,** TCP/IP, and **C,** IPX/SPX, are incorrect because, depending on the network's needs, you could potentially use either of these protocols. They are both routable, meaning that they can both be used to access computers on connected subnetworks. **D** is incorrect because it states that you can use NetBEUI, TCP/IP, or IPX/SPX. Again, this is incorrect because you cannot use NetBEUI.

7. ☑ **B.** CAT3 has a maximum speed of 16Mbps. It is frequently used in 10Mbps Ethernet networks.

   ☒ **A,** CAT2, is incorrect because this cable type supports a maximum of 4Mbps. It is typically used only in token-passing networks such as the Token Bus or 4Mbps Token Ring. **C,** CAT4, is incorrect because it supports a maximum speed of 20Mbps. It is typically used in 16Mbps Token Ring networks. **D,** CAT5, is incorrect because its maximum speed is 100Mbps. It is typically used in 100Mbps Ethernet networks.

8. ☑ **C.** Coaxial cable is the most common type of cable used in bus networks. It is typically used to create the bus network's backbone. In most bus networks, small segments of coax cable are attached using T-connectors, which also connect to individual computers.

   ☒ **A,** CAT5, is incorrect because this is a type of UTP that is not commonly found in bus networks. Rather, CAT5 is usually implemented in star networks. **B,** STP, is also incorrect for this reason. STP is a type of twisted-pair cable that is typically used in star topologies. **D,** fiber-optic, is incorrect because this type of cable is not used as commonly in bus networks as coax cable. Fiber is more often found in ring networks.

9. ☑ **D.** In CSMA/CD, when a computer wants to transmit, it first listens for traffic. If a data collision occurs, each transmitting computer waits a random amount of time, then retransmits. In other words, when the computer detects that the line is clear, it will transmit its data, listening all the time for collisions. If another device transmits at the same time, both devices will stop transmitting, then try to resend the data after a random period of time.

☒ **A** is incorrect because it suggests that computers will not transmit until they have received a special network signal. This is a description of token passing. The electronic token continues to move from one computer to another, and no computer can transmit without first having the token. **B** is incorrect because it suggests that a network device checks each computer to determine if it has data to send. This is a description of polling. **C** is incorrect because it suggests that networked computers use interrupts to receive a transmission priority. Although this is true of the relationship between computer components and the processor, it does not apply to network access.

10. ☑ **D.** Tell the customer the Token Ring standard can be implemented on the current topology. Although Token Ring networks use a conceptual ring, in which each device passes an electronic token from one computer to another, this standard can be implemented on a star network. In fact, due to its relatively low occurrence of single-point failure, the star is the most common topology for Token Ring networks. In this setup, a computer will receive the token, then pass it on to the hub, where it is sent to the next computer.

☒ **A,** which suggests that the network must have a ring topology, is incorrect. As explained, a conceptual ring network does not have to exist on a physical ring. **B** is incorrect because it suggests that the cable must be changed to fiber-optic. Although fiber-optic cable can be used in FDDI token-passing networks, it is not required for Token Ring networks. In fact, the Token Ring standard specifies the use of twisted-pair only. **C** is incorrect because it suggests changing both the topology and the cable type. Again, in this case, the customer can use the existing cable and topology.

11. ☑ **C.** This network has a bus topology. The term *10Base5* indicates an IEEE Ethernet standard that uses Thicknet coax cable arranged in a bus topology.

☒ **A** is incorrect because it states that the network supports a maximum cable length of 185m. Because the 10Base5 standard uses Thicknet coax, it actually supports up to 500m cable lengths. **B,** it uses token passing, is incorrect because as an Ethernet standard, it uses CSMA/CD. **D,** it uses twisted-pair cabling, is incorrect. Again, the *5* in *10Base5* indicates Thicknet coaxial cable.

12. ☑ **C.** You should tell the customer that the network runs at either 10Mbps or 100Mbps. These are the two standard speeds for Ethernet networks. As an aside, newer Ethernet standards support 1Gbps, but these are rare. You are probably safe in guessing that this network runs at either 10Mbps or 100Mbps.

    ☒ **A, B,** and **D** are all incorrect because they suggest that the network can run at a maximum speed of 4Mbps and/or 16Mbps. However, these are the maximum supported speeds for Token Ring networks, not Ethernet networks.

13. ☑ **D.** A direct cable connection requires a cross-over cable. In a direct cable connection, two computers are attached directly to each other through their serial or parallel ports. The cable's wires must be altered so that the send wires on one computer are aligned with the receive pins on the other computer. This cable is therefore called a cross-over cable.

    ☒ **A,** Ethernet, is incorrect because this type of network requires regular twisted-pair, coax ,or fiber cabling. **B,** FDDI, is incorrect because this requires regular fiber-optic cables. **C,** dial-up, is incorrect because this type of connection requires a modem and a phone line.

Network Setup and Troubleshooting

14. ☑ **A.** The computer name must be unique. The computer name is the name that identifies your computer to other users on the network.

    ☒ **B** is incorrect because it states that the computer name must match the names of the other computers on the network. This is true of domain or workgroup names, but not computer names. **C,** match the computer's IP address, is also incorrect. IP addresses are required only for computers that use TCP/IP. If the computer does require an IP address, it does not have to match the computer name, and in fact, the computer name should be easy to recognize and be different from the IP address. **D** is incorrect because it states that the computer name is entered only if you are using the NetBEUI protocol. The TCP/IP, IPX/SPX, and NetBEUI protocols all require the entry of a computer name.

15. ☑ **A.** All that is required to properly configure a computer to use the NetBEUI protocol is a computer name. The NetBEUI protocol is the simplest to configure, and since it is not routable, there is no need (and no way) to enter complex configuration information.

    ☒ **B, C,** and **D** are all incorrect because they contain elements that are required to configure TCP/IP only. NetBEUI does not require a workgroup name or IP address, because the protocol allows the computer to communicate with only one workgroup (it is not routable). Subnet masks are required only when an IP address is being configured, so they are not entered in a NetBEUI configuration.

16. ☑ **C.** In this case, when communicating with the 4Mbps NIC, communications will run at 4Mbps; otherwise, the network will run at 16Mbps. In other words, the network will support 16Mbps. However, all transmissions sent by the 4Mbps NIC will be sent at 4Mbps only. Furthermore, data can be received by this NIC at 4Mbps only. When a faster NIC tries to communicate with it, the 4Mbps NIC will "miss" most of the data and have to continually ask the faster NIC to resend it.

☒ **A,** the entire network will run at 4Mbps, is incorrect. This is not a case of the network being as slow as its slowest component. Although that might be the case if the MAU or cables supported only 4Mbps, the slower NIC will not affect transmissions in which it is not involved. **B** is incorrect because it suggests that the slower NIC will not be able to access the network. As long as it supports the proper protocol, it will be able to communicate with other devices. **D** is incorrect because it suggests that the network won't work at all. Again, the network will function, and transactions that do not involve the slower NIC will be unaffected by its speed.

17. ☑ **C.** A message stating "Unable to browse network" will be displayed. This error message indicates that the current computer does not have network access.

☒ **A** is incorrect because it states that all computers within the user's workgroup will be displayed. Such a list, however, will be displayed only if the user's computer *does* have network access. **B,** the Network Neighborhood window will not open, is incorrect because the computer will open the window and attempt to locate another computer on the network before the error message appears. **D** is incorrect because it suggests a "Network Access Not Configured" message will appear in the Network Neighborhood window. This is not a valid Windows message.

18. ☑ **B.** The purpose of mirroring a network server is to provide fault tolerance. A mirrored server is a type of backup server that contains the same data as the primary, or main, server. All data that is stored on the main server is also stored on the mirrored server. If the primary server fails, the mirrored server will simply take over, and no data will be lost.

☒ **A,** to speed up network activity, is incorrect because the time it takes to write all data twice can actually result in a slower network. **C,** to provide load balancing, is also incorrect. *Load balancing* refers to dividing tasks up equally among servers so that one server is not doing all the work. However, in a mirrored server, all work is actually being done twice. The mirrored server doesn't take any of the workload off the primary server. **D,** to increase bandwidth, is incorrect because keeping a duplicate copy of server data is unrelated to the speed at which computers can communicate with one another.

19. ☑ **C.** Clustering provides load balancing. In clustering, data is split up and saved on two or more servers so that if one server fails, the other(s) can continue to provide files and services. Because the workload is divided among servers, clustering also provides load balancing.

    ☒ **A,** mirroring, is incorrect. Although mirroring does provide fault tolerance, it works by writing all data twice—once to the primary server and once to the backup, or mirrored, server. Each server must therefore do a full share of work. **B,** tape backup, is also incorrect. Creating scheduled tape backups of server data provides fault tolerance but does not take any of the server's regular workload. Therefore, this method does not provide load balancing. For these reasons, **D,** which suggests that all methods provide load balancing, is incorrect.

20. ☑ **B.** The hub might be causing excess network traffic. When a computer on a hub transmits data, the data is received by the hub, then retransmitted to all other computers on the network. This is called *broadcasting*, and it can result in excessive network traffic. Since your company is growing, it is likely that there are more computers on the network, so the hub is generating even more unnecessary traffic than before.

    ☒ **A,** the hub might not support 100Mbps, is incorrect. If the hub supports a slower speed, it will result in slower network activity. However, the problem has been worsening gradually over time. If the hub did not support 100Mbps, it would have caused slow network traffic from the beginning, not gradually over the period of a month. **C** is incorrect because it states that the hub might be unable to find all the computers on the network. The hub does not "look" for computers; it simply retransmits data to all network cables that are attached to a hub port. The hub itself does not read the destination address on data packets, so it does not need to find the network's computers. **D** is incorrect because it suggests that the hub cannot be responsible for the network slowdown. While the hub *might* not be the cause, it is certainly a likely candidate.

LAB ANSWER

The simplest option to implement in this case is 10BaseT. The existing topology can be used, and because CAT3 cables support up to 16Mbps, the existing cables can be used as well. However, the NICs will have to be replaced, and the network's MAU will have to be replaced with a hub. This network will run at 10Mbps, and cable lengths will be limited to 100m.

The network could also be converted to 10Base2 or 10Base5. The advantage in this conversion is longer cable lengths (185m and 500m, respectively). However, to implement either of these options, the NICs must be replaced, and the cable must be changed from CAT5 to coaxial. Furthermore, these networks will require 50ohm terminators, and the topology must be changed from star to bus.

This option is not recommended, because it requires much more work and expense than 10BaseT but will provide the same speed (10Mbps).

If the network is converted to 10BaseF, the network will run at 10Mbps and support cable lengths up to 2000m. The existing topology (star) can be used, but the cables will have to be replaced with fiber-optic, and the MAU will have to be replaced with a hub. Again, this option is not recommended, because it requires more effort than 10BaseT but will still provide only 10Mbps access.

If the customer wants an even faster network, the 100BaseTX or 100BaseT4 standards can be implemented. Like 10BaseT, this would require the replacement of the Token Ring NICs with Ethernet NICs, and the MAU must be replaced with a hub. Although the existing topology (star) can be used, the CAT3 cables will not support the new speed. In this case, they should be upgraded from CAT3 to CAT5.

Another 100Mbps option is the 100BaseFX standard. The existing topology can be used, but again, the MAU and NICs must be replaced. Like the 100BaseTX or 100BaseT4, the 100BaseFX requires the replacement of the network cables—in this case, to fiber-optic. This type of network requires no more effort than the 100BaseTX or 100BaseT4 but is likely to cost more, since fiber-optic cabling is significantly more expensive than twisted-pair. However, the network will be less susceptible to interference and will support cable lengths over 400m.

Part II

A+ Operating Systems Technologies

8

Operating System Fundamentals

T he remainder of this book is focused on the A+ Operating System Technologies exam. This exam tests your knowledge of Windows 95, Windows 98, and Windows 2000 as they relate to installation, configuration, troubleshooting, and networking procedures. This chapter describes the basics of these OSs, including their functions, main characteristics, system files, and file and disk management.

CERTIFICATION OBJECTIVE 8.01

Operating System Functions and the Windows Family

There are two distinct OS types in the Windows family. Although Microsoft intended the Windows 9x line, which includes Windows 95 and Windows 98, and Windows ME, for home use, it has also been adapted for small businesses and corporate desktops for many years. The Windows 2000 OS is part of the NT lineup and is typically used in business networks. The following subsections describe the basic functions and characteristics of each OS as well as how they differ from each other.

Major Operating System Functions

The primary function of any OS is to provide a user interface. In other words, the OS allows the user to enter commands and is responsible for translating those commands into requests that the computer can understand. The OS is also responsible for displaying the results of those requests to the user.

Another important function of an OS is to manage the computer's files in an organized manner. The OS keeps track of the functions of particular files and calls or runs those files when they are needed. Furthermore, the OS is responsible for maintaining file associations so that files are launched in the proper applications.

Finally, the OS is also responsible for managing the computer's disks. That is, the OS keeps track of which disk is associated with a particular drive letter. The OS is also responsible for creating and using the disk's cluster, FAT structure, and file system.

Common Windows Components

The Windows 9x and 2000 OSs provide a graphical user interface (GUI) that the user can navigate using either a mouse or keyboard. The main Windows screen is called the *desktop* because it is intended to resemble an actual desk. The Windows 98 desktop is displayed in Figure 8-1.

The desktop contains several graphics, called *icons*. These icons can represent applications, folders, or navigation tools. Applications and folders can be launched or opened by double-clicking the appropriate icon.

The *taskbar*, typically located at the bottom of the desktop, contains the Start menu, a button for each running application, and the time of day. You can switch between open applications simply by clicking the appropriate taskbar button. Depending on its configuration, the taskbar can also contain device status meters

FIGURE 8-1 The Windows 98 desktop.

and buttons for launching applications. The Start menu itself, shown in Figure 8-2, provides access to Windows Help, configuration options, and most of the computer's applications.

Windows 9x and 2000 also include *shortcut menus* that, when enabled, provide you with quick access to task-specific features. For example, the desktop's shortcut includes options for arranging icons, creating new files and folders, and configuring the appearance of the desktop itself. The taskbar's shortcut menu provides you with a list of tasks and configuration options related to the taskbar. To open an element's shortcut menu, right-click the element.

Windows OSs support *multitasking*, which is the ability to run more than one application or utility at once. This feature is very handy if you are using information from one application to create a file in another application. As you can see in Figure 8-1, the taskbar shows that the computer has an open folder (A+) and is running Netscape Navigator and Adobe Acrobat.

Another common feature of the Windows OSs is the use of My Computer and Windows Explorer to view, move, rename, copy, or delete files and folders. When files are deleted, they are placed in the Recycle Bin. Files are not truly deleted until the Recycle Bin is emptied. This makes it possible for you to recover files that were deleted by accident.

FIGURE 8-2

The Windows 98
Start menu.

Contrasts Between Windows 9x and Windows 2000

The main difference between the Windows 9x and Windows 2000 OSs is in their configuration. Windows 9x can be networked with other computers in a peer-to-peer configuration, as well as with a server-based network. In the peer-to-peer network, resources are shared, and users must supply passwords to access certain resources or files. This is called *share-level security.*

Windows 2000, on the other hand, is a true server-based *network operating system.* This means that it enables a single server to manage computers on a network and provide or deny access based on user privileges. This is called *user-based security.* Users must enter the proper passwords before they can even access their computers, and restricted resources appear nonexistent to the user. Contrast this with share-level security, whereby a user can access a restricted resource if the user happens to guess the password. Windows 2000 is available in workstation and server editions, depending on its role in the network.

on the Job

Windows 2000 is not really intended for home users. It supports business hardware, uses a great amount of computer resources, and is quite expensive. It is aimed as business use. Microsoft has released a 2000 version of the Windows 9x line for home users, called Windows Millennium (Windows Me). As well, Windows XP Professional (for business) and Windows XP Home were released in October 2001. Although these latest releases won't be on the CompTIA certification test, the technician should be prepared to encounter both on the job.

All three Windows OSs (95, 98, and 2000) support Plug and Play, but whereas Windows 9x supports home user-type devices, Windows 2000 supports business-type devices. For example, Windows 9x has extensive support for video cards, sound cards, and game ports. Windows 2000 is more likely to support devices such as card readers, NICs, and scanners.

Other differences, such as memory usage, on-the-fly partitioning, and file systems, are discussed later in the chapter. If you are unsure of the OS you are using, watch the computer at startup. A Windows splash screen will appear before the OS is completely loaded, indicating the OS type. You can also determine which OS you are using by clicking the Start button on the taskbar. The OS name will appear along the left-hand side of the pop-up menu. If you want more details about the OS version and edition, follow the steps in Exercise 8-1.

EXERCISE 8-1

Determining the Operating System Type

1. Right-click the My Computer icon.

2. Select Properties from the shortcut menu that appears. The System Properties dialog box will appear.

3. Ensure that the General tab is displayed. The OS version and edition are listed under System:.

CERTIFICATION OBJECTIVE 8.02

System Files and Utilities

System files are files that the OS requires in order to function properly. Each system file has a function that alters, manages, or runs part of the OS itself or other system files. Contrast this with an *application file,* such as a saved game, document, or image file. The existence of an application file will not alter the behavior of the OS. You can change, create, or delete a nonsystem file without affecting the performance of the computer.

In most cases, a deleted, missing, or corrupt system file will result in an improperly functioning OS feature or could lead to an OS that will not function at all. A good knowledge of the Windows OS system files and their functions will allow you to pinpoint and resolve OS problems based on the behavior of the computer or on the error messages you receive.

Several types of system files are discussed in the following subsections. First, the system files specific to Windows 9x are discussed, followed by system files specific to Windows 2000. Memory management files are described, as are command-line interface files.

Many of the OS system files are location-dependent. That is, they will not be loaded and properly executed if they are not in a specific location. For this reason, and to keep them from being accidentally deleted, most system files are *hidden.* This means that they will not be displayed in the My Computer or Windows Explorer navigation windows. To view system files, follow the steps in Exercise 8-2.

EXERCISE 8-2

Viewing System Files

1. Double-click the My Computer icon.

2. Click the View menu, and select Folder Options.

3. Select the View tab.

4. Under Hidden Files, select the Show All Files option.

5. Click OK. All files that are listed as system and/or hidden files will now appear, but hidden files will be "grayed out" to indicate their status.

Windows 9x

Some of the Windows 9x system files listed here are required to properly boot the computer and run the OS. Others exist as *legacy files*, to provide backward compatibility with older applications (see the From the Classroom sidebar on page 319). There are hundreds of system files in the Windows 9x OS, but you don't need to be familiar with all of them. The ones that tend to crop up in installation and troubleshooting procedures are the boot files and configuration files, explained in the following sections. Also discussed here are Windows 9x utilities for configuring or managing system files.

e x a m
Ⓦa t c h

Make sure that you are familiar with the role of all these files as well as whether they are required and where they are located.

IO.SYS

The IO.SYS file is responsible for organizing and conducting the early stages of the Windows 9x boot process. It is responsible for finding and loading other system files and checking to ensure that those files contain the proper settings. IO.SYS also provides the OS with details about the hardware installed in the computer. IO.SYS is a required system file, and its role in the boot process is described in more detail in Chapter 9. To function properly, IO.SYS must be located on the root directory (for example, C:).

MSDOS.SYS

In Windows 9x, the MSDOS.SYS file contains startup configuration parameters, such as which OS to use by default if more than one OS is installed on the system (a multiboot configuration). This file must be located in the root directory. MSDOS.SYS also contains the location of required boot files, the default boot mode, and the presence and display time for the Windows startup screen (the one that says "Starting Windows"). The MSDOS.SYS file's role in system startup is explained in more detail in Chapter 9.

on the job

MSDOS.SYS plays a very different role in Windows 9x than in DOS. In DOS, MSDOS.SYS is not user editable and is responsible for translating requests between the user and the hardware. In Windows 9x, IO.SYS takes over that function, and MSDOS.SYS has been changed to an editable boot configuration file.

WIN.COM

The last operation of the Windows 9x IO.SYS file is to locate and run WIN.COM. This file is responsible for conducting the remainder of the Windows 9x OS startup. WIN.COM is located in the WINDOWS folder, and its role in system startup is explained in more detail in Chapter 9.

SYSTEM.DAT

The bulk of Windows 9x application, user, and hardware settings are stored in a large database called the Windows *registry*. The registry is actually composed of two files: USER.DAT and SYSTEM.DAT. SYSTEM.DAT contains settings about the computer's hardware, such as drivers, resources, and configuration data.

SYSTEM.DAT is so important to the function of Windows 9x that every time you shut down the computer, a backup copy of the file is made. This backup copy, called SYSTEM.DA0 (that's a zero, not the letter "O") will be used at startup if the original SYSTEM.DAT file is missing or corrupted. SYSTEM.DAT must be located in the WINDOWS folder.

USER.DAT

The other half of the Windows registry, USER.DAT, contains user-specific information such as installed applications, file associations, color settings, and passwords. Every user profile on the computer is represented individually in the USER.DAT file. Like the

SYSTEM.DAT file, USER.DAT is located in the WINDOWS folder and is backed up each time the computer is properly shut down. The USER.DA0 file will be used if there is something wrong with the USER.DAT file.

SYSTEM.DAT and USER.DAT are Windows registry files and are the heart of the OS.

SCANREG

Windows 98 includes the file SCANREG.EXE, which is a registry backup utility. This utility runs in the Windows background and backs up the registry each time the computer is started. If you want to manually back up the registry, run SCANREG /BACKUP from the Windows Run line. The registry files will be saved in the Windows\Sysbackup folder by default. To use the Run command line, click the Start menu, then select Run. Enter the appropriate command (in this case, SCANREG) in the Open text field, then click OK.

To use a backed-up copy of the registry, you must access a DOS command prompt. That is, start the computer from a DOS boot disk or select Shutdown and Restart in MS-DOS mode. At the DOS command prompt, enter the command **SCANREG/RESTORE**. The last five backup copies of the registry will be displayed. Select the appropriate copy.

REGEDIT.EXE

During normal operation, the registry is automatically updated when you load, move, or delete an application or when you change the computer's configuration using Windows configuration utilities (such as the Control Panel). However, it is possible to open and manually edit the registry using the *registry editor*. The registry editor is a file called REGEDIT.EXE, and it can be launched by entering REGEDIT in the Windows 9x Run line.

The registry editor, shown in Figure 8-3, organizes the registry database into six *Hkeys* but does not identify to which .DAT file each entry belongs. Entries are displayed in a tree structure on the left, and the selected entry's values are displayed on the right. When you double-click an Hkey, its subkeys are displayed. There can be several levels and sublevels within a single Hkey, so it can be difficult to find the proper entry. Furthermore, many subkeys throughout the registry can have the same name. This makes it even more difficult to navigate the database. Fortunately, the registry editor includes a Find feature that can locate entries for you.

FIGURE 8-3

The Windows 9x
Registry Editor.

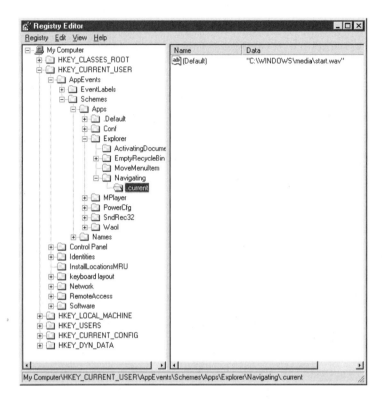

on the
job

Each entry in the registry is known as a key, and its representation in the
registry editor is known as its handler (thus the term Hkey).

When you modify, create, or remove an entry, it is saved automatically and
immediately. A single change to the registry can cause fatal OS errors, so you should
never use this method unless you are absolutely sure about what you are doing. It is
best to stick to the Windows configuration utilities when you make a change.

WIN.INI

In older OSs, the WIN.INI file, rather than the USER.DAT file, is used to store
application settings. Some older applications are designed to use the WIN.INI file
and cannot even recognize the newer USER.DAT file. Without access to the
WIN.INI file, these applications will not function properly, so Windows 9x includes
WIN.INI for backward compatibility. Typical settings in the WIN.INI file include

the registered fonts, icons, and display settings, such as colors and window border thickness. WIN.INI is located in the WINDOWS folder.

SYSTEM.INI
Like WIN.INI, SYSTEM.INI is located in the WINDOWS folder and is typically used in older (pre-Windows 95) OSs. It stores data about the system's hardware, such as device drivers and configuration settings. It is included in Windows 9x to allow older 16-bit applications to access the system's hardware.

CONFIG.SYS
The CONFIG.SYS file, originally used in MS-DOS, is even older than the WIN.INI and SYSTEM.INI files and is used to load device drivers and configure memory usage. CONFIG.SYS is included in Windows 9x to retain backward compatibility with devices and applications that can run properly only if they have access to the CONFIG.SYS file. CONFIG.SYS must be located in the root directory to be properly processed.

AUTOEXEC.BAT
The AUTOEXEC.BAT file, found in the root directory, is typically used in conjunction with the CONFIG.SYS file and contains application or environment settings. For example, color settings or the command to automatically launch a particular application can be found in the AUTOEXEC.BAT file. Again, this file is included in Windows 9x for backward compatibility.

exam
ⓦatch

SYSTEM.DAT and USER.DAT are required in Windows 9x. SYSTEM.INI, WIN.INI, CONFIG.SYS, and AUTOEXEC.BAT are not required but are included for backward compatibility with older applications and devices.

SYSEDIT
The legacy configuration files discussed here can be opened and modified in any Windows text editor, such as Notepad. However, Windows 9x includes a utility called the System Configuration Editor that allows you to view and modify all these files at once. To launch the System Configuration Editor, type **SYSEDIT** in the Windows Run line. The WIN.INI, SYSTEM.INI, AUTOEXEC.BAT,

CONFIG.SYS, and PROTOCOL.INI files will be displayed (see Figure 8-4). You can modify each of these files as though it had been opened individually.

MSCONFIG

Windows 98 includes a System Configuration Utility that allows you to modify legacy configuration files without having to alter the files directly, as in the Sysedit utility. To launch the System Configuration Utility, enter **MSCONFIG** in the Windows Run line. A dialog box similar to the one shown in Figure 8-5 will appear.

Using this utility, you can elect to process all, none, or some of the system's legacy configuration files. By selecting a specific file's tab, you can also elect to process or ignore individual command lines. Using the MSCONFIG utility is much safer than using SYSEDIT, because it does not allow you to edit the configuration files directly. This means that you cannot accidentally cause a fatal error by modifying or deleting the wrong entry.

FIGURE 8-4

The Sysedit utility allows you to modify legacy configuration files.

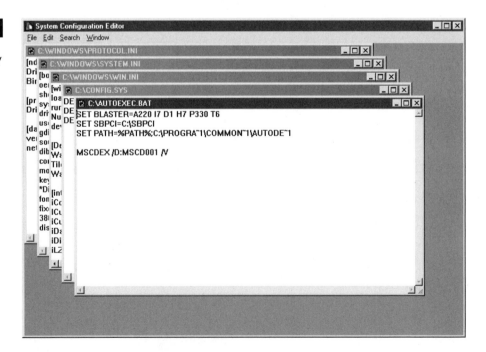

FIGURE 8-5

The Windows 98
System
Configuration
utility.

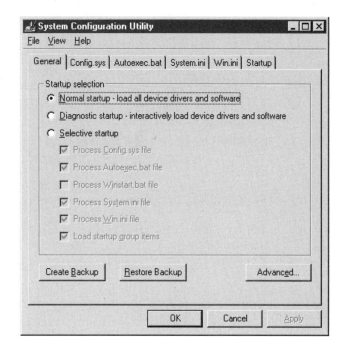

Control Panel

As mentioned previously, the Windows 9x Control Panel provides you with a safe
way to configure many of the system's configuration settings. To access the Control
Panel, double-click My Computer, then double-click Control Panel, or select Start |
Settings | Control Panel. As you can see in Figure 8-6, a typical Control Panel
includes applets for configuring the keyboard, the mouse, and network and
date/time settings, among other things. To open an applet, double-click its icon,
make the necessary changes, then click OK. The registry will be automatically and
safely updated with your changes.

exam
Watch

*If you want to edit the registry directly, use the Registry Editor. If you want to
edit the registry safely, use the Control Panel.*

Device Manager

The Windows 9x Device Manager provides you with a single location to view and
modify hardware configurations. To access the Windows 9x Device Manager,
right-click My Computer, then select Properties. The System Properties dialog box

FIGURE 8-6

The Windows 9x
Control Panel.

will open. Select the Device Manager tab. A window similar to the one shown in Figure 8-7 will be displayed.

All hardware devices attached to the system are categorized and listed in this dialog box. To view a device, double-click its device category. You can view a device's system resource configuration by selecting it, then clicking Properties. The device's IRQ, I/O address, and/or DMA allocation will be displayed. You can also view, remove, or reload the device's driver.

If you suspect a hardware configuration problem, you can use the Device Manager to determine its cause. Devices that are not recognized by Windows or that are improperly configured will be accompanied by a warning symbol (a yellow question mark and/or a yellow exclamation point). For example, you can see this warning symbol next to the PCI Communication Device in Figure 8-7.

HWiNFO

HWiNFO is a hardware detection utility for Windows 9x and 2000. It is similar to the Device Manager but provides more detail about components, such as the

FIGURE 8-7

The Windows 98
Device Manager.

capacity, speed, and manufacturer of RAM, hard drives, printers, and ports. HWiNFO is not included with Windows but can be downloaded from REALiX at www.hwinfo.com. The HWiNFO utility can be run at any time during the operation of the computer. First, the utility completes a hardware detection phase, then it displays the results in a window similar to the one shown in Figure 8-8.

This utility includes a *log file*, which allows you to log the current system settings and track them over time. HWiNFO also performs benchmark tests on the processor and memory. This means that the utility tests their speed and capacity, then compares the results with those of components built by other manufacturers. HWiNFO also allows you to monitor the temperature of the CPU and motherboard. Although HWiNFO can be used in either Windows 9x and 2000, it is really designed for the NT platform, so some features might not be available in Windows 9x.

Automatic Skip Driver

When the computer starts up, the Windows 9x device drivers are loaded with the OS. However, if a driver is missing, corrupt, or incompatible with the OS, it could prevent the OS from loading, even if the driver is not for a critical device (such as the video card). To help prevent drivers from halting the system, Windows 98

FIGURE 8-8

The HWiNFO
utility.

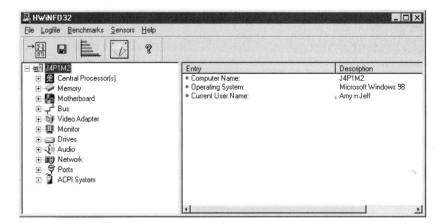

includes a utility called Automatic Skip Driver (ASD). This utility automatically
detects potential driver problems and configures the computer to skip over them
at startup. When this is the case, the driver will not be loaded, but the OS will
otherwise start up normally, allowing you to troubleshoot the problem.

The ASD utility runs automatically in the Windows background. To view ASD
results, you must run ASD.EXE. That is, enter **ASD** at the Windows 98 Run line or
select Start | Programs | Accessories | System Tools | System Information. You can
access ASD from the Tools menu of the System Information window. ASD will
report all drivers that it has disabled and give you an opportunity to re-enable them.

WSCRIPT

Windows includes a Windows Scripting Host, which allows you to create and
use non-native (non-DOS) scripts such as Visual Basic, Java, and Perl. The
WSCRIPT.EXE utility runs in the background and allows you to view, run,
or modify non-Windows scripts using Windows tools such as the Notepad.

Most of the time, you will be totally unaware of the Scripting Host because it
simply runs in the background. However, you can use the WSCRIPT command to
modify the behavior of scripts. Enter **WSCRIPT** at the Windows Run line. Here,
you configure the scripting host to automatically shut down long or indefinite
scripts after a specified period of time.

Before continuing in the chapter, test your familiarity with Windows system files
by answering the following Scenario & Solution questions.

SCENARIO & SOLUTION

	Which configuration files are typically associated with…		How can you modify them…	
	Devices?	Applications?	Directly?	Safely?
Windows 9x	SYSTEM.DAT	USER.DAT	REGEDIT.EXE	Control Panel
Legacy applications	SYSTEM.INI	WIN.INI	SYSEDIT.EXE	MSCONFIG

FROM THE CLASSROOM

A Legacy of Problems

Windows 9x and 2000 are 32-bit OSs, meaning that the OS code can be accessed 32 bits at a time. Applications written for these OSs are also 32 bit. Thirty-two-bit applications have better memory usage, access the hardware differently, and cause fewer lock-ups than older, 16-bit applications.

However, many users want to be able to run 16-bit applications with newer OSs. For this reason, Windows 9x OSs include legacy configuration files so that these older applications can be used. For example, applications written around the time of Windows 3.1 were likely designed to access the SYSTEM.INI configuration file and

know nothing about the Windows registry. Without the SYSTEM.INI file, the application could not run in Windows 9x.

Unfortunately, these older programs can still cause problems in newer OSs, such as device hogging and computer lockups. However, Windows 9x is the home user's OS, and most home users cannot afford to upgrade their software every time they upgrade the OS. The NT lineup, on the other hand, is designed for business use. Windows 2000 provides much less support for legacy applications, and it does not use the older configuration files found in the Windows 9x OSs.

—Amy Thomson, A+ Certified Technician, MOUS Master

Windows 2000 System Files

Windows 2000 uses many of the same system files as Windows 9x. For example, it relies on the use of a Windows registry. However, Windows 2000 does not support the same level of backward compatibility as Windows 9x. Therefore, SYSTEM.INI and WIN.INI are not present in Windows 2000. The AUTOEXEC and CONFIG files exist in Windows 2000 as AUTOEXEC.NT and CONFIG.NT. Windows 2000 also has some utilities in common with Windows 9x, such as the Control Panel and Windows Scripting Host. Other system files unique to Windows 2000 are described in the following subsections.

BOOT.INI

The BOOT.INI file is used by Windows 2000 if the computer contains more than one OS. This is referred to as a *dual-boot configuration*. When a dual-boot machine is started, you must select which OS to use. The BOOT.INI file is responsible for displaying the OS choices at startup. It also contains the location of each OS so that the computer knows where to look for the selected one. Once an OS has been selected and found, the function of BOOT.INI is complete.

NTLDR

The function of the NTLDR file is similar to that of IO.SYS in Windows 9x. The NTLDR file is used to coordinate the system's startup procedure and is responsible for locating and initializing other required startup files. NTLDR's role in the Windows 2000 startup process is explained in more detail in Chapter 9.

NTDETECT.COM

This file is also part of the Windows 2000 boot process. Once NTLDR is initialized, it finds and initializes the NTDETECT.COM file. NTDETECT is responsible for gathering information about the hardware that currently exists in the system. This information is reported back to NTLDR, which writes the information in the Windows registry.

NTBOOTDD.SYS

This file's only purpose is to allow Windows 2000 to boot from a SCSI device. If required, it is located and initialized by NTLDR.

REGEDT32

Windows 2000 includes two registry editors: REGEDIT.EXE (the same one used in Windows 9x) and REGEDT32. Unlike REGEDIT, the REGEDT32 version displays each subtree in a separate window and allows you to enter key values larger than 256 characters. REGEDT32 also allows you to set security restrictions on keys, subkeys, or individual values so that they can be modified only by authorized users. On a final note, REGEDT32 does not have REGEDIT's ability to set bookmarks and has a less powerful search feature.

Computer Management

Windows 2000 includes a Computer Management console, which contains configuration utilities for the system's printers, security, and disk management, among other things. To open Computer Management, click Start, then select Programs | Administrative Tools | Computer Management. A window similar to the one in Figure 8-9 will be displayed.

The Computer Management utility provides you with a safe way to view and configure system resource allocation, disk usage, group security, configuration of hardware devices, application settings, password settings, and storage devices, among

FIGURE 8-9

The Windows 2000 Computer Management window.

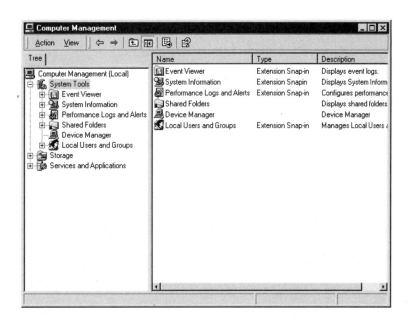

other things. When you make a change in the Computer Management utility, the registry is automatically updated.

Memory Management Files

The first PCs could access only 1MB of RAM, which was sufficient for the applications of the time. However, as technology improved, the 1MB limit became a hindrance as applications were developed that required more than the allotted memory space. Several memory management utilities were developed to allow these older computers to access more memory, and some of these utilities are still used today. These files, as well as their common implementations, are described here.

Conventional Memory

The first 640KB of RAM have traditionally been used for running applications and the OS itself (DOS). This memory area was originally called *system memory*.

Upper Memory

The remaining 384KB of memory were set aside (reserved) for device drivers. Applications could not access this memory space, even if it wasn't being entirely used by the system. This memory space was initially termed *reserved memory*.

Extended and High Memory

When the Lotus 1-2-3 spreadsheet application was released, users often found that it required more than 640KB of memory. To resolve the 1MB memory barrier problem, Lotus, Intel, and Microsoft joined forces and developed the LIM memory specification. In this specification, system memory was renamed *conventional memory* and reserved memory was renamed *upper memory*.

More important, however, was the development of a memory manager that would allow applications to use memory over 1MB (called *extended memory*). This manager, a file called HIMEM.SYS, could also be used to load the OS into the first 64KB of extended memory, an area called *high memory*.

To use the extended memory specification (XMS), HIMEM.SYS must be referenced in the CONFIG.SYS file, as shown here:

```
DEVICE=C:\DOS\HIMEM.SYS
DOS=HIGH
```

The first line instructs the computer to locate and initialize the HIMEM.SYS file, thus enabling the extended memory area. The second line is used to load DOS into the high memory area (HMA).

Expanded Memory

At the time of the LIM specification release, many users still had older Intel 8088 and 80286 computers, which, because of the small memory address bus, simply could not be made to access memory over 1MB. For these individuals, the LIM specification included an expanded memory manager that could "trick" the processor into using extended memory. A file called EMM386.EXE is able to swap pages of memory between extended memory and upper memory. In other words, when the processor requests data that is located in extended memory, EMM386.EXE retrieves the information, then places it in upper memory, which is accessible to the processor. This process is also known as *paging.*

EMM386.EXE also enables programs to use upper memory as system memory. In other words, upper memory is no longer reserved for device drivers but can be accessed by regular applications. To enable the expanded memory specification (EMS), the EMM386.EXE file must be referenced in CONFIG.SYS, as shown here:

```
DEVICE=C:\DOS\HIMEM.SYS
DEVICE=C:\DOS\EMM386.EXE
DOS=HIGH,UMB
```

The last line instructs the computer to load as much of DOS into high memory as it can and to load whatever is left over into upper memory (Upper Memory Banks = UMB). The EMM386.EXE reference in the CONFIG.SYS file must come *after* the reference to HIMEM.SYS. This is because expanded memory relies on the existence of the extended memory area.

Fortunately, Windows 9x and 2000 are able to manage memory without the use of the memory managers described previously. That is, these Windows OSs can load any type of data (application, system, drivers) into any available memory blocks. However, Windows 9x retains the ability to use these files for backward compatibility with older applications and requires HIMEM.SYS during startup. Windows 2000, which has removed virtually all sources of backward compatibility for memory management, does not use these memory management files.

Before you continue, use the following Scenario & Solution questions to test your knowledge of the memory concepts presented in the previous sections.

SCENARIO & SOLUTION

What is extended memory?	All memory above 1MB.
What is expanded memory?	A routine that swaps memory between extended and upper memory so that it may be accessed by the processor.
What is the function of HIMEM.SYS?	To enable access to extended memory and load DOS into high memory.
What is the function of EMM386.EXE?	To enable expanded memory and to use upper memory as though it were conventional memory.

Virtual Memory

When the computer runs out of RAM, it uses space on the hard drive to temporarily store data. This is called *virtual memory*. Accessing files on the hard drive is much slower than accessing files in RAM, but using virtual memory can prevent the computer from running out of temporary storage space and experiencing out-of-memory errors.

The space on the hard drive used for virtual memory is called a *swap file*. In Windows 9x, the swap file is called WIN386.SWP. The Windows 2000 swap file is called PAGEFILE.SYS. Whenever the processor requests data that is not in RAM, a *page fault* occurs. Whenever a page fault occurs, the virtual memory manager looks on the swap file for the requested data, then moves it into RAM for the processor to access. In some cases, the computer can spend all its time moving data between RAM and the swap file. This process is called *thrashing*, and the result is a computer that "freezes up," even though there appears to be excessive disk activity.

You can disable the swap file in Windows 9x using the Performance tab in the System Properties dialog box (access System in the Control Panel). However, by disabling it, you run the risk of not being able to run many applications because out-of-memory errors might occur. Additionally, you can change the swap file's size in either Windows 9x or 2000. However, this practice is not recommended. Windows is designed to expand or decrease the size of the swap file as needed. By setting a specific size, you might be setting it too low so that you run out of virtual memory or too high so that it takes up disk space that could be used for other things.

Command-Line Files

Windows 9x and 2000 include a DOS command shell, which enables you to run commands from a DOS prompt. Additionally, Windows 9x includes a DOS mode, in which the computer can be restarted with DOS-only components. To open a DOS shell, enter **COMMAND** on the Windows Run line. Additionally, you can run any of the DOS commands that follow by entering them on the Windows Run line. A DOS shell will open automatically and run the command. To run in DOS mode, select Shutdown, then Restart in MS-DOS Mode from the Windows 9x Start menu.

As a technician, you might be required to use DOS commands when troubleshooting a computer that won't load Windows properly or when getting a hard drive ready for an OS or when loading an OS from a CD-ROM drive that isn't recognized by the BIOS. For this reason, we take a look at common DOS commands and their uses here.

Command Syntax

To enter some commands, type the command and press ENTER. For example, to clear the screen, enter **CLS**. To view the OS version, type **VER**. Other commands require certain parameters. For example, when run by itself, the DIR command displays the contents of the *current* directory. By adding a parameter to the DIR command, you can display the contents of a different directory. The command that follows displays the contents of the GAMES directory:

```
DIR GAMES
```

The number of required parameters depends on the command itself. The COPY command, for instance, requires that you enter the command, the name of the file to copy, and the destination. The following command shown copies the RESUME document into the LETTERS directory, as long as the RESUME file and LETTERS directory are within your current location in the directory structure:

```
COPY RESUME LETTERS
```

Some commands have options that can be enabled by using switches. For example, when the DIR command is used, the /p switch can be used to pause the listing after every full screen, and the /w switch can be used to display the listing in wide format.

These commands are all case-insensitive, meaning that they can be entered in lowercase, uppercase, or a combination of the two. You must be careful to enter the appropriate spaces to differentiate between elements of the command. The only case in which the presence of a space doesn't matter is when you're entering a switch. For example, the DIR command can be entered to use the /p switch with a space or without:

```
DIR/p
DIR /p
```

When you enter a command improperly, you will receive a syntax error or an "Invalid switch" error. You can get help on the purpose, syntax, and available switches for any command by entering the command, followed by /?. For example, Figure 8-10 displays help for the DIR command.

Internal and External Commands

DOS commands are all either internal or external. *Internal commands* are included in the COMMAND.COM file. This means that if you can access a DOS prompt, you are able to use these commands. CLS, DIR, COPY, and DELETE are all

FIGURE 8-10

The Help screen for the DIR command.

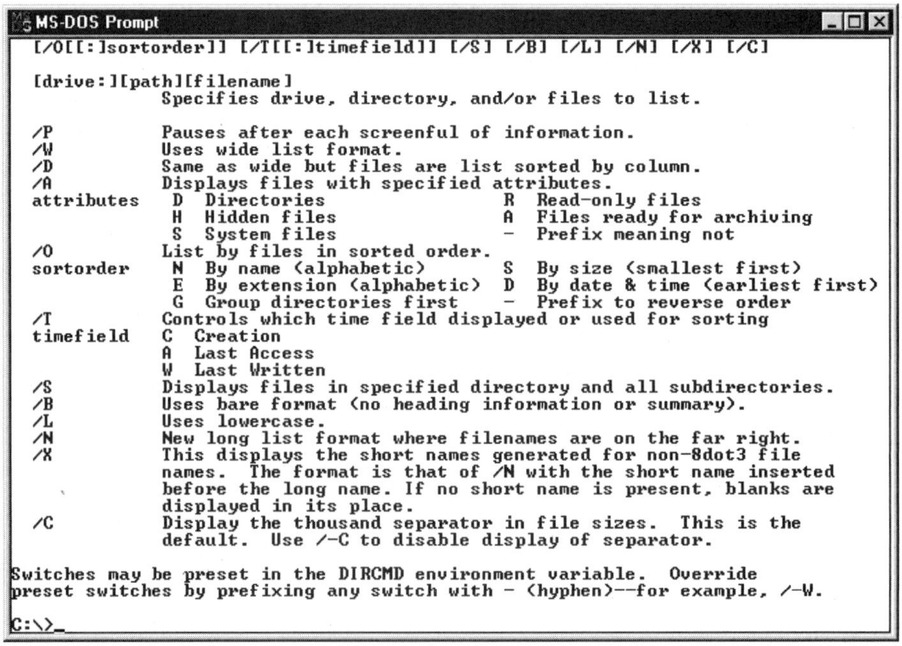

```
MS-DOS Prompt
  [/O[[:]sortorder]] [/T[[:]timefield]] [/S] [/B] [/L] [/N] [/X] [/C]

  [drive:][path][filename]
              Specifies drive, directory, and/or files to list.

  /P          Pauses after each screenful of information.
  /W          Uses wide list format.
  /D          Same as wide but files are list sorted by column.
  /A          Displays files with specified attributes.
  attributes   D  Directories                R  Read-only files
               H  Hidden files               A  Files ready for archiving
               S  System files               -  Prefix meaning not
  /O          List by files in sorted order.
  sortorder    N  By name (alphabetic)       S  By size (smallest first)
               E  By extension (alphabetic)  D  By date & time (earliest first)
               G  Group directories first    -  Prefix to reverse order
  /T          Controls which time field displayed or used for sorting
  timefield   C  Creation
              A  Last Access
              W  Last Written
  /S          Displays files in specified directory and all subdirectories.
  /B          Uses bare format (no heading information or summary).
  /L          Uses lowercase.
  /N          New long list format where filenames are on the far right.
  /X          This displays the short names generated for non-8dot3 file
              names.  The format is that of /N with the short name inserted
              before the long name. If no short name is present, blanks are
              displayed in its place.
  /C          Display the thousand separator in file sizes.  This is the
              default.  Use /-C to disable display of separator.

Switches may be preset in the DIRCMD environment variable.  Override
preset switches by prefixing any switch with - (hyphen)--for example, /-W.

C:\>_
```

internal commands. *External commands* are not part of COMMAND.COM and are contained in separate files. For example, to execute the XCOPY command, you must have the file XCOPY.EXE.

ATTRIB The ATTRIB command, which uses the file ATTRIB.EXE, can be used to view or modify a file's attributes. File attributes include hidden (h), archive (a), system (s), and read-only (r). These attributes affect your ability to modify or view the files. Attributes are explained in more detail later in the chapter.

To view a file's attributes, enter the ATTRIB command, followed by the filename. To add or remove a file's attribute, enter **ATTRIB**, a + or a – sign (add or remove, respectively), the letter representing the appropriate attribute (*h, a, s,* or *r*), then the filename. In the following command, the read-only and hidden attributes are applied to a file called RECIPE:

```
ATTRIB +H +R RECIPE
```

MEM The MEM command can be used to display memory allocation information. To view the used and available amounts of conventional, expanded, and extended memory, simply enter **MEM** at the command prompt.

You can use the /c (classify) switch to display memory use by application. That is, the switch will generate a report that lists each active application or driver and how much memory it is using. The /d (debug) switch is the most detailed and displays a block-by-block report of memory usage.

SCANDISK Recall from Chapter 2 that the Scandisk utility can be used to correct a disk's FAT errors and mark bad clusters. The DOS version of Scandisk is a file called SCANDISK.EXE. To start the Scandisk utility, enter **SCANDISK** at the command prompt.

DEFRAG The Disk Defragmenter, also discussed in Chapter 2, can be used to rearrange a disk's contents so that files occupy contiguous clusters. Like Scandisk, Disk Defragmenter comes in a version for DOS. Its file is called DEFRAG.EXE, and it is run by entering **DEFRAG** at the command prompt.

EDIT DOS includes a text editor that allows you to create batch files or small documents. The editor is available in a file called EDIT.COM. When you enter the

EDIT command, the text editor will open, allowing you to create, open, save, print, or search text files. This is a menu-driven application that is accessed using the keyboard in DOS mode or using the mouse in a DOS shell.

XCOPY   XCOPY is similar to the COPY command but allows you to copy entire directories and their files and subdirectories. The XCOPY command requires the presence of the XCOPY.EXE file. To use the XCOPY command, enter **XCOPY**, followed by the directory you want to copy, then the destination. There are several options for the XCOPY command, including /s, which copies all directories and subdirectories within the current directory, and /y, which overwrites existing files without prompting you for confirmation.

FORMAT   Recall that disks must be formatted before data can be stored on them. The DOS format command uses the FORMAT.COM file and is executed by entering **FORMAT**, followed by the appropriate drive letter. The FORMAT command is discussed in more detail later in this chapter, in the section entitled "Disk Management."

FDISK   Before a disk can be formatted, it must first be partitioned. The DOS tool for partitioning hard drives is the FDISK.EXE file. The FDISK command is discussed in more detail later in this chapter, in the section entitled "Disk Management."

MSCDEX   The Microsoft CD-ROM Extension (MSCDEX) driver enables DOS to use the CD-ROM drive. Although the driver can be loaded any time by entering the command **MSCDEX**, it is typically referenced in the AUTOEXEC.BAT file so that it is loaded automatically at startup. The MSCDEX driver file is called MSCDEX.EXE.

SETVER   The SETVER command, supplied by the SETVER.EXE file, allows you to manually set the DOS version that is reported to a particular application. That is, older applications might not be able to recognize newer versions of DOS. In this case, you can use the SETVER command to report that the version of DOS is older than it is. To use the command, enter **SETVER**, followed by the application, followed by the version number. For example, to inform the application Game that the DOS version is 6.22, use this command:

```
SETVER GAME.EXE 6.22
```

CERTIFICATION OBJECTIVE 8.03

File and Folder Management

Recall that one function of an OS is to manage files and folders. The Windows OSs also allow you to perform file and folder management, such as creating, renaming, moving, and deleting. In order to properly manage the files and folders on your system, you must be familiar with the folder structure, navigation techniques, and management procedures.

Creating Folders

A folder is simply a "container" that holds files and other folders. By organizing items into folders, it is easier for you and the OS to find the files you need. As an analogy, think of a dresser that holds your clothing. By placing different types of items into different drawers, you can find them more easily than you could if the items were simply piled on the floor. When you need a pair of socks, you open the sock drawer, and you can ignore other items that are in the shirts and belts drawers.

The same idea can be applied to OSs. If you place all your pictures, for example, in a different folder than your documents, you will be able to more quickly retrieve the pictures. However, just like a dresser, the ability of the OS to maintain an organized structure depends on your ability to keep items in the proper places. This means consistently saving files to the proper folders and not moving files into places where they don't belong.

To create a folder in Windows, you must first open the drive or folder in which you want to create the new folder. Once the folder is created, give it a name that will help you easily identify its contents. Folders can be created using either Windows Explorer or My Computer. Exercise 8-3 lists the steps required to create a folder in Windows Explorer (both the Explorer and My Computer are explained in more detail later in the chapter).

EXERCISE 8-3

Creating a Folder in Windows Explorer

1. Click Start, point to Programs, and click Windows Explorer. A window similar to the one in Figure 8-11 will open. The folder structure is displayed on the left, and the selected drive or folder contents are displayed on the right.

2. Click the drive or folder in which you want to create the new folder.

3. Select File in the menu bar, point to New, then select Folder.

4. A new folder icon will appear within the selected drive or folder. Enter a name using the keyboard, then press the ENTER key.

FIGURE 8-11

In Windows Explorer, the folder structure is displayed on the left and contents are displayed on the right.

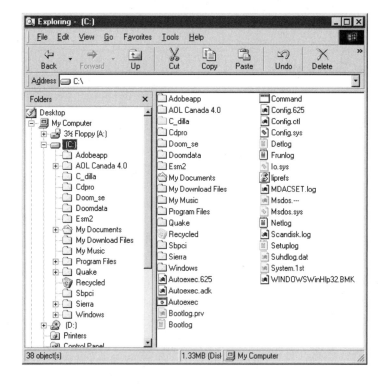

Navigating Through Windows

In Windows 9x and 2000, you can navigate through files and folders using either Windows Explorer or My Computer. Each provides the same management tools; the only difference between the two is their display methods. These two methods are provided simply to accommodate user preferences.

The term *navigation* refers to the ability to find files and ensure that they are saved in the proper locations. Your ability to save or move things to the proper places will determine your ability to find them later.

Windows Explorer

As described earlier, Windows Explorer displays the drive and folder structure in the left pane, and the selected folder's (or drive's) contents are displayed on the right. As shown in Figure 8-12, you can display the contents of a folder (in this case, the My

FIGURE 8-12

In Windows Explorer, the selected folder's contents are displayed in the right-hand pane.

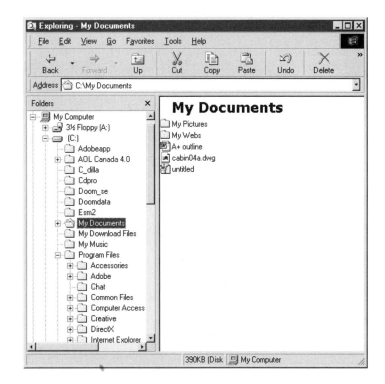

Documents folder) simply by clicking the folder's icon. As you can see, the My Documents folder contains two subfolders and three files.

To view the contents of a subfolder, click the + sign to the left of the main folder. The subfolders will be displayed in the folder structure on the left. In Figure 8-13, you can see the two subfolders under My Documents in the folder structure.

You can now view the contents of these subfolders by clicking them. For example, in Figure 8-14, the contents of the My Pictures subfolder is displayed.

My Computer

When you navigate using My Computer, a folder's contents are displayed in a window by themselves. To demonstrate My Computer navigation, we'll explore the same contents we explored in the Windows Explorer example—that is, the contents of C:\My Documents\My Pictures.

To start using My Computer, double-click the My Computer icon on the desktop. A window similar to the one shown in Figure 8-15 will appear. This window lists the system's drives as well as commonly used utilities such as the Control Panel.

FIGURE 8-13

You can view subfolders in the directory structure by clicking the parent folder's + icon.

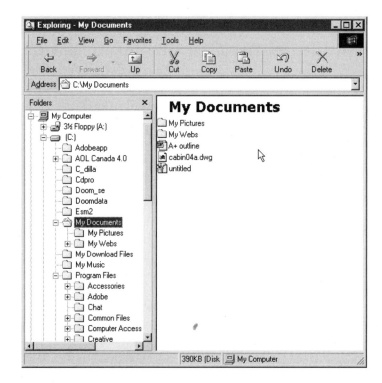

FIGURE 8-14

The contents of a subfolder are viewed using the same method used for parent folders.

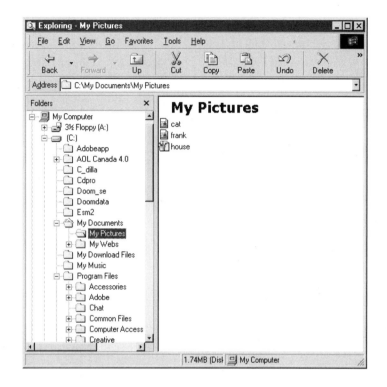

FIGURE 8-15

The My Computer Window displays the system's drives.

To view a drive's contents, double-click its icon. In this case, to access the My Documents folder, double-click the C: drive icon. The contents of this drive are displayed in Figure 8-16. Your computer might be configured to either open a new window to display these contents or replace the previous My Computer window with the new contents. Note that the folders shown here are the same ones that were listed in the Windows Explorer folder structure pane.

Using the double-click technique, you can open the My Documents folder. Within that window, double-click the My Pictures folder. The result is that the contents of the My Pictures folder will be displayed (see Figure 8-17). Note again that these are the same files that were displayed using Windows Explorer.

Note in Figure 8-17 that the path to this folder (C:\My Documents\My Pictures) is displayed in the Address line at the top of the window. To return to a previous window (folder), click the Back button. In this case, the contents of the My Documents folder will be redisplayed. If you click the Back button again, the contents of the C: drive will be redisplayed.

FIGURE 8-16

The contents of the C: drive.

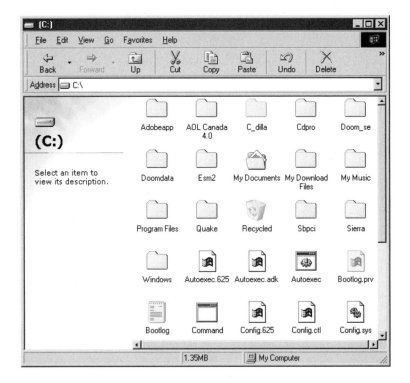

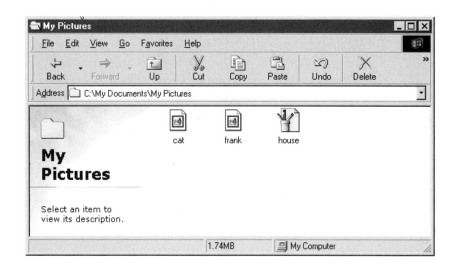

FIGURE 8-17

The contents of
the My Pictures
folder.

Management Tools

Whether you use Windows Explorer or My Computer, you can manage files and
folders using the same procedures. As you already know, when you double-click a
folder, it is opened. When you double-click a file, it is activated. If it is an executable
file, that program will be launched. If you double-click an application's file, the file
will be opened within the host application. For example, if you double-click a
Microsoft Word document icon, Microsoft Word will be launched and it will open
the selected document.

To delete a file, select it (by clicking it), then press the DEL key on the keyboard.
Because this is easy to do by accident, Windows will ask you to confirm the deletion.
You can also delete a file by right-clicking it, then selecting Delete from the shortcut
menu that appears. Files and folders that are deleted from the hard drive will be
placed in the Recycle Bin. They will stay there until they are either restored to their
original locations or removed permanently when you empty the Recycle Bin. If you
delete a hidden, read-only, or system file, Windows will ask you to confirm again.
Note that you cannot delete a file that is currently in use or that you do not have
proper permissions to access.

You can rename a file or folder by clicking its icon, then clicking its name. This is
two separate clicks, not a double-click. Next, type the new name, then either click in
a neutral area on the screen or press the ENTER key on the keyboard. You can also
rename a file (or folder) by selecting Rename from the file's shortcut menu. You
cannot rename a file that is currently in use. Furthermore, Windows will warn you if

you are about to give the file an improper name (naming conventions are described later in the chapter). Note that you cannot give a file a blank name (one with no characters) and you can't give a file the same name as another file in the same location.

Windows also lets you move and copy files from one location to another. To move a file, you must be able to see both the file itself and the destination folder or drive. Use your mouse to click and drag the file to the new location. Hold the CTRL key on the keyboard while you do this to copy the file. Again, as with other commands, you cannot move or copy a file that is in use.

on the **Job**

Because it is so easy to rename, delete, or move files and folders, Windows contains lots of safeguards, such as confirmation screens and an Undo feature on the desktop shortcut menu.

You can view the details of any file or folder by selecting Properties from its shortcut menu. As shown in Figure 8-18, a file's Properties window displays the type, full name, location, and size of the file. Also displayed are the date of creation, last modification, and last access. You can also use this window to view or apply file attributes. File attributes are discussed in more detail in the next section.

File Attributes

As mentioned earlier, a file or folder can have any or all the read-only, hidden, system, and archive attributes. These attributes can be viewed or altered using either a command prompt or the file's or folder's Properties dialog box. To apply an attribute in Windows, open the Properties dialog box, then place a check in the appropriate attribute's check box. You can apply more than one attribute to a file or folder. To remove an attribute, remove the check from the appropriate check box. Note that some attributes are applied automatically by the OS or other applications. In all cases, when an attribute is applied to a folder, it will not be applied to the files within that folder. That is, attributes must be applied to files independently of their folders.

The Read-Only Attribute

The Read-only attribute is used to ensure that the file or folder isn't modified, renamed, or deleted accidentally. In Windows, if you try to rename a read-only file, you will receive the message shown in Figure 8-19.

FIGURE 8-18

A file's Properties window.

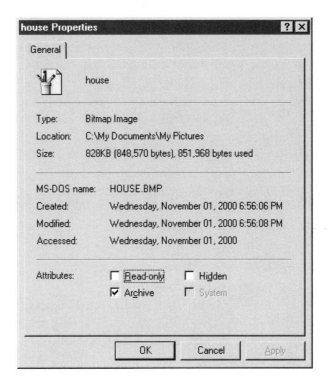

To carry out the renaming procedure, you must select Yes. Again, the purpose is to prevent accidental renaming. To cancel the renaming procedure, select No. A similar confirmation dialog box will appear if you try to delete a read-only file or folder.

When you open a read-only file such as document, you can view the file and make changes. However, to save the changes you have made, you must save the document as a new file. There will therefore be two files: The original file will be left intact, and a second file, which contains the modifications, will be created.

FIGURE 8-19

This confirmation dialog box appears when you try to rename a read-only file.

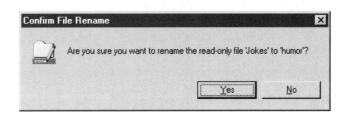

The Hidden Attribute

Under normal circumstances, hidden files and folders will not be displayed in Windows Explorer or My Computer and will not be listed by the Windows Find feature. The idea is that if a user can't see a file, the user can't accidentally change or delete it. However, by changing the Windows View options, as explained in Exercise 8-2, you can display all files and folders, even if they are marked as hidden. These files and folders will appear grayed out to indicate their status. It is recommended that you select either the "Do not show hidden files" or "Do not show hidden or system files" option so that hidden files truly remain hidden.

If a folder is hidden, the files in the folder cannot be viewed using My Computer or Windows Explorer, even if those files are not marked hidden. This is because if you cannot view a folder, you cannot open it to view the files inside. These files will be found by the Find command, however.

The Archive Attribute

The archive attribute can be used to select particular files or folders to back up. System backups are explained later in the chapter. However, to explain briefly here, many backup utilities include the option to back up only files marked with the archive attribute. By default, Windows applies the archive attribute to all files, but not to folders. You can, of course, manually add or remove the archive attribute.

The System Attribute

Windows does not allow you to apply or remove the system attribute from files or folders. Rather, files are given the system attribute automatically by the OS or the application, depending on their function. Most system files are also given the hidden attribute to keep users from accidentally modifying or deleting them. In DOS, you can apply or remove the system attribute, but in Windows, you can only view the presence or absence of the attribute. You can use the View command (described in Exercise 8-2) to view or hide files with the system attribute. Whenever you rename, delete, or move a system file, you will be required to confirm the action before it is carried out.

File-Naming Conventions

In Windows 9x and 2000, filenames (and folder names) can be up to 255 characters, including the full path name. A full path name includes the drive, folder, and subfolders in which a particular file is located. For example, suppose a file called JACKET is located in the WINTER subfolder, which is located in the CLOTHES folder on the C: drive. This file's full path name is C:\CLOTHES\WINTER\ JACKET. The file's name can include letters and numbers, spaces, and several other characters. Its name cannot include the following characters: \ / ? * : " < > |

Most files include a filename extension, which is separated from the remainder of the name by a period and is used to signify the file's type. For example, a file with the .SYS extension is a system file. The extension is very important because it indicates to Windows which application should be used to open a particular file. For example, when you double-click a file with the .XLS extension, Windows will launch the Microsoft Excel application to open the file. Table 8-1 contains some common extensions and their functions or associated applications.

Each extension is associated with a particular icon, which allows you to quickly determine the type of a particular file. This is especially handy if the Windows View settings have been configured to hide file extensions. Several common icons and their associated extensions are shown in Figure 8-20. Note that the last icon displayed here is used for files whose extensions do not have a Windows or application association.

If you rename or remove a file's extension when you rename the file itself, a warning message will appear, stating that if you change the extension, the file could become unusable. You must then confirm or cancel the operation because, without an extension, Windows might be unable to determine with which application a file is associated. Furthermore, some applications simply won't open a file without the proper extension. For example, suppose the file POEM.DOC was created in

TABLE 8-1	Extension	Function or Application
Common Extensions and Their Functions or Associated Applications	EXE	An executable file (a program)
	BAT	A batch file (a program)
	COM	A command file (a program)
	DOC	A document, typically associated with Microsoft Word or WordPad
	BMP	A bitmap (graphic)
	SYS	A system file
	CFG	A configuration file

FIGURE 8-20

Common
Windows icons
and their
extensions.

WordPad. If you change the file's name to POEM.ODE, WordPad will not open the file.

File and folder names in Windows 9x are case-sensitive when they are displayed, but no two items with the same name can exist in the same location, regardless of their use of uppercase or lowercase characters. That is, if you name a file POTATO, it will be displayed as POTATO. If you name a file Potato, it will be displayed as Potato (note the use of lowercase letters). However, although the names appear different, you cannot have a file called POTATO and a file called Potato in the same location. If you are using Windows 2000 on an NTFS volume, however, these two files are considered different because they use different upper- and lowercase letters.

Now that you are familiar with file characteristics in Windows, test your knowledge by answering the following Scenario & Solution questions.

SCENARIO & SOLUTION

What is the purpose of a file's extension?	To identify the file type or the application with which it is associated.
What is an .EXE file?	An executable file—in other words, a program or small application. When you double-click its icon, the application will be launched.
What is a hidden file?	A file that has the hidden attribute set and will not be displayed by default.
How can I view a system or hidden file?	Use the Windows View options to select Show All Files.

Backup and Restore

Windows 9x and Windows 2000 include a native backup utility, called simply Backup. This utility allows you to save large amounts of data on floppy disk or other storage media. One benefit of using the Backup utility is that it can compress data so that it takes up less storage space than is normal. Another benefit is that this utility allows you to save a single large file over more than one floppy disk. In most cases, you cannot split a file over two disks. The file must fit entirely on one floppy disk, or it cannot be saved at all. However, for files over 1.44MB (the capacity of most floppies), Backup will catalog and convert the file so that it can span two or more disks.

To access Backup in Windows 9x or 2000, click Start, then select Programs | Accessories | System Tools | Backup. Although the screens might differ, the procedure is similar for both OSs. Exercise 8-4 lists the steps necessary to back up select files to floppy disk in Windows 98. Note that the procedure differs only slightly in Windows 95 and 2000.

EXERCISE 8-4

Using the Windows 9x Backup Utility

1. When you launch the Backup utility, a welcome screen will appear. Elect to create a new backup job.

2. The Backup Wizard screen will appear. You can use this wizard to get step-by-step instructions. However, for this exercise, click Cancel to close the wizard. The Backup window is shown in Figure 8-21.

3. In the "What to back up" section, select the "All selected files" option (the alternative will back up only files that have been created or changed since the last backup).

4. Navigate through the file structure as you would in Windows Explorer to find the appropriate files. Click the check box for each file you want to back up.

5. In the "Where to back up" section, click the folder icon and select the floppy disk (A:).

FIGURE 8-21

The Windows 98 Backup utility.

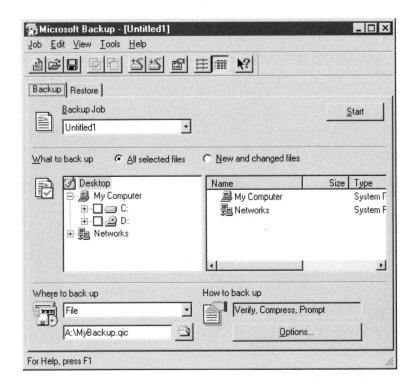

6. From the Job menu, select Save.

7. Enter a name for this backup job, then click Save.

8. Click the Backup utility's Start button.

To restore a backup job's files, open the Backup utility and select the Restore tab. Select the backup job to restore, then click Start.

Extract

The Windows 9x installation disks contain compressed cabinet (.CAB) files. These files are automatically extracted during the setup process. Windows 98 includes an extract tool, called EXTRACT.EXE, to allow you to manually extract .CAB files from the installation media. This is a handy tool when you want to install a single application, feature, or driver from the installation disk without rerunning the Windows setup.

The EXTRACT.EXE tool must be run from a command prompt. To use this tool, enter EXTRACT, followed by the name of the cabinet and the name of the file you want to extract. Follow this with the destination in which to place the specified file. For example, suppose the file DRIVER.DRV exists on the Win98_4 cabinet on the CD-ROM drive (D:). Use the following command to extract and place the driver in the WINDOWS folder:

```
EXTRACT D:\WIN98_4.CAB DRIVER.DLL C:\WINDOWS
```

Windows 2000 Compression and Encryption

Windows 2000 includes "native" file and folder compression and encryption. That means that files and folders can be compressed or encrypted without the use of a third-party utility. When you work with a compressed or encrypted file or folder, Windows 2000 must continually work in the background to uncompress or recompress or decrypt or re-encrypt it. These processes can make the computer seem to perform more slowly than normal.

Compression

Compressed files and folders are saved in a manner that allows them to take up less space than normal. Windows 2000 compression can be applied only to hard drives that use the NTFS file system (explained in detail at the end of the chapter). All files that are saved in or copied into a compressed folder will also be compressed. You can compress a folder in Windows 2000 by following the steps in Exercise 8-5.

EXERCISE 8-5

Compressing a Folder in Windows 2000

1. In My Computer or Windows Explorer, right-click the folder you want to compress.

2. Select Properties from the shortcut menu, then click Advanced. A window similar to the one shown in Figure 8-22 will be displayed.

FIGURE 8-22

The Windows
2000 Advanced
Properties
dialog box.

3. Enable the "Compress contents to save disk space" option, then click OK.

4. Click the OK button in the Properties dialog box.

5. A confirmation window will appear, prompting you to apply compression
   to the current folder only or the current folder and its subfolders and files.
   Select the appropriate option, then click OK.

Encryption   Windows 2000 native encryption can prevent users from accessing
files to which they have otherwise been given server-based permission to access.
Typically, Windows 2000 is configured to either permit or restrict access to files
based on a user's profile or group profile. Suppose, however, that a sensitive file has
been placed in an otherwise accessible folder. Encryption can be placed on that
single file to restrict access to it, without affecting access to the rest of the folder.

Encrypted files and folders are actually "encoded." Authorized users' computers
are given the "decoder" (decryption) key so that they can access the encrypted files
or folders. It is important to note here that compressed files and folders cannot be
encrypted. You can encrypt a file or folder by accessing its Advanced Properties

dialog box (as explained in Exercise 8-5). Enable the "Encrypt contents to secure data" option.

CERTIFICATION OBJECTIVE 8.04

Disk Management

The final OS function discussed in this chapter is disk management. OSs allow you to prepare disks for use by formatting and partitioning them. The Windows OSs also include utilities, such as Disk Defragmenter and Scandisk, discussed in Chapter 2. that allow you to maintain disks and prevent disk problems from occurring.

Disk Preparation

Before a new disk can be used to save data, it must first be partitioned and formatted. When you partition a disk, you simply divide the disk into several *volumes*. Each volume can have a different file system (explained in the following discussion). If you plan to install more than one OS on the computer, each should be loaded on its own partition. Each partition will be treated by Windows as a separate drive and will therefore get its own individual drive letter. If you don't want to divide the hard drive into several volumes, you must create a single partition that uses the entire drive.

When you format a drive, it is divided into usable areas, called *clusters*. Partitioning and formatting procedures are described in detail in Chapter 9. When you partition and format a disk, you must configure it to use a specific file system. The file system will determine the type of OS it can support and how much data the disk can hold. Some common file systems are described in the following sections.

FAT

The original file system was called FAT, short for *file allocation table*. The file system's name is a reference to the use of the FAT which behaves as a type of disk index. FAT is a 16-bit file system, meaning that it is capable of 16-bit addressing. File allocation tables that use the FAT file system can address up to 2GB of data. If you want to use FAT on a larger hard drive, you must create separate partitions of no more than 2GB each. FAT is a sort of "universal" file system, in that it can be used by DOS, Windows 9x, Windows NT, and Windows 2000.

exam
ⓦatch

Don't be confused by the term FAT. It actually has two meanings. First, it is used to describe a drive's "index" (its file allocation table). The first file system to use a FAT was called the FAT file system, to distinguish it from other file system types. The FAT file system was later renamed FAT16 to distinguish it from its successor, FAT32.

Due to its addressing and capacity limitations, FAT is not a particularly efficient file system. Here's why: The maximum number of addressable clusters in a FAT system is 65526, regardless of the drive's capacity. In a 500MB system with 65526 clusters, each cluster is roughly 8KB. However, in a 2GB system with 65526 clusters, each cluster will be 32KB.

Now consider this: When a file is saved, the entire cluster, even the leftover part of the cluster that the file is not using, becomes dedicated to that file. This leftover space is, in essence, wasted. This waste is called *slack*. The larger a drive's clusters, the greater the overall drive slack.

Suppose, for example, that a drive uses 32KB clusters. A 1KB file will reserve the entire cluster, resulting in 31KB of unusable "slack" space. However, if the clusters were 8KB, the same 1KB file would result in only 7KB of slack. Because of this characteristic as well as its capacity limitations, the FAT file system has been largely replaced by newer file systems.

FAT32

FAT32 is an improvement of the FAT16 file system because it supports up to 2 terabytes (TB) of drive capacity. Furthermore, its 32-bit addressing allows it to recognize a greater number of clusters (over 250 million), so its cluster sizes are typically much smaller (around 4KB), resulting in less drive slack.

on the
ⓙob

A terabyte is 1024 gigabytes. A gigabyte is 1024 megabytes. So, if you can imagine this, a terabyte is over a million megabytes!

The FAT32 file system can be used by Windows 95 OSR2 and later, as well as by Windows 98 and 2000. If you boot using one of these OSs, you will be able to view the contents of a FAT16 drive. However, if you boot using an older OS, you will not be able to view the FAT32 drive.

NTFS4

NTFS4, originally called *new technology file system (NTFS)*, was introduced with the Windows NT OS. Like FAT32, NTFS4 is a 32-bit file system. This means that it supports large capacities and small cluster sizes. NTFS4 also includes native file compression, so files and folders can be compressed individually, without the use of a third-party utility.

Furthermore, NTFS4 allows you to set access permissions on individual files and folders and supports a *spanned disk* (known as a *volume set* in Windows NT), a partition that is made up of space on more than one physical disk. This allows you to create partitions that exceed the size of a single hard drive and allows you to create a partition out of the extra space on multiple drives. NTFS volumes can be accessed by Windows 2000 but not Windows 9x.

exam
ⓦatch

Windows 9x can use and access FAT16 or FAT32 partitions. Windows NT can access FAT16 or NTFS4 partitions, and Windows 2000 can access FAT16, FAT32, NTFS4, and NTFS5 partitions.

NTFS5

NTFS5 is a new file system, released in Windows 2000. It has the same features as NTFS4 but includes several improvements, such as native encryption. NTFS5 also allows administrators to set server disk quotas for network users. NTFS5 can be used by Windows 2000 only.

exam
ⓦatch

It is important for you to know the differences between the four file systems discussed here, both in your career as a technician and in preparing for the A+ exam. The FAT file systems are typically used in the Windows 9x line, and the NTFS file systems are used in the NT line (including Windows 2000).

HPFS

HPFS stands for *high-performance file system*, and it is traditionally used in OS/2 systems. OS/2 stands for Operating System/2 and is IBM's native OS. HPFS cannot be used with Windows 9x or 2000. HPFS is able to support volumes up to 64GB and results in less slack space than FAT due to its use of much smaller storage units (single sectors rather than larger clusters).

HPFS uses a different disk structure than FAT file systems. FAT systems use a single file allocation table in the first cluster of the volume to keep an index of the volume's contents. HPFS volumes, however, are divided into 16 "bands." Each band includes its own index, meaning that the drive's read/write head travels less when accessing files, and file access is much faster. It also means that volumes become less fragmented. That is, fragmentation can occur within a single band, but it is unlikely to occur across the entire volume.

Drive Converter

Windows 98 includes a utility that allows you to convert existing FAT16 volumes to FAT32, without loss of information. This is an important utility, since, typically, the conversion of a file system type requires repartitioning and reformatting of the volume. When you partition and/or format a volume, all of that volume's data is lost.

To use the Windows 98 drive converter utility (CVT1.EXE), click Start, then select Programs | Accessories | System Tools | Drive Converter. An important note here is that although this utility will convert from FAT16 to FAT32 without data loss, the opposite is not true. That is, this is a one-way conversion utility. To revert back from FAT32 to FAT16, the volume must be partitioned and formatted.

Windows 2000 does not contain the Drive Converter utility. However, the Computer Management utility in Windows 2000, described previously in the chapter, provides a much more powerful file system conversion tool.

SCSI Versus IDE Drives

SCSI drives can be partitioned and formatted in the same manner as IDE hard drives. However, SCSI hard drives can require special care. In particular, if you mix SCSI and IDE drives in the same computer, you cannot boot from the SCSI hard drive. This has to do with the way that volumes are lettered. When there are mixed drives, the OS will give the first letters (starting with C:) to the IDE drives. SCSI drives are lettered last. However, Windows 9x will not boot properly unless it is located on the "first" drive. Drive lettering is described in more detail in Chapter 9.

Furthermore, some SCSI drives, such as CD-ROM and tape drives, require special drivers. If you are unable to view a SCSI drive in the Device Manager or My Computer windows, chances are that the computer hasn't recognized and loaded a driver for it. In this case, you must run the Setup or Install program that came with the drive.

In some cases, Windows might detect a SCSI drive and load an IDE driver for it. For example, many SCSI CD-ROM drives require the ASPI rather than the MSCDEX file to work properly. If you can see but not access a SCSI drive, ensure that the proper driver has been loaded.

Internal Versus External Drives

An *external drive* is one that is connected to the computer via a parallel port or SCSI chain. Common external disk types are Jaz and Zip drives. Like SCSI drives, external drives will be lettered *after* the IDE internal hard drives. You cannot boot from an external drive. However, if the external drive is a hard drive (in other words, not a backup device), it can be formatted and partitioned in the same manner as regular hard drives.

A large number of Windows utilities are discussed in this chapter. Use the following questions and answers to refresh your memory on the functions of these utilities.

CERTIFICATION SUMMARY

There are a great many components to the Windows OSs, including their system files, disk management tools, and configuration utilities. This chapter focused on the ones that are most important to the system and the ones you are most likely to have to deal with as a computer technician. However, even with all the differences between the Windows 9x and Windows 2000 platforms, they have a great many file and disk-related components in common.

For example, Windows 9x and Windows 2000 both rely on the system registry for most configuration and other system values. Both support Plug and Play, contain a registry editor, use virtual memory, and can be used to execute DOS prompt commands. The interface of the two platforms is also similar. They use a "desktop" concept that contains icons, a Start menu, a taskbar, and shortcut menus.

There are, however, a great number of differences between Windows 9x and 2000. Because Windows 9x is aimed at home users, it supports backward compatibility with older applications and therefore includes many legacy system files, such as SYSTEM.INI, WIN.INI, and memory management files (HIMEM.SYS and EMM386.EXE). Because Windows 2000 is intended for business networks, it supports more sophisticated file systems, networking components, security, compression, and configuration utilities.

TWO-MINUTE DRILL

Here are some of the key points from each certification objective in Chapter 8.

Operating System Functions and the Windows Family

❑ Some functions of an OS is to provide an interface between the user and the hardware, to manage an organized file and folder structure, and to provide procedures for preparing and managing disks.

❑ Windows 95 and 98 are part of the Windows 9x family, aimed at home users, and Windows 2000 is part of the Windows NT family, aimed at business networks.

❑ Windows 9x and 2000 have a similar-looking interface, which includes a desktop, My Computer, Windows Explorer, a Start button, and a taskbar.

❑ Windows 9x supports older applications and has more Plug and Play support for home computer devices; Windows 2000 has more sophisticated security, fault tolerance, and disk management utilities.

System Files and Utilities

❑ The majority of configuration information for the Windows 9x and 2000 OSs is located in the system registry.

❑ You can safely edit the registry using the Control Panel (in 9x and 2000) or the Computer Management utility (in 2000).

❑ You can directly edit the registry using the Registry Editor.

❑ Because Windows 9x supports older applications, it includes older system configuration files, such as SYSTEM.INI, WIN.INI, CONFIG.SYS, and AUTOEXEC.BAT.

❑ Windows 9x uses memory managers such as HIMEM.SYS and EMM386.EXE to maintain backward compatibility with older applications.

❑ Windows 9x includes the Device Manager, which allows you to view and modify hardware configurations.

❑ The Windows 98 Automatic Skip Driver detects and disables potentially problematic drivers.

- ❑ Windows 9x and 2000 both use virtual memory, which is space on the hard drive that is used temporarily as though it were RAM.

- ❑ Windows allows you run DOS commands, such as EDIT, DIR, MEM, and ATTRIB from a DOS command prompt.

File and Folder Management

- ❑ Windows allows you to view, create, rename, delete, move, or open files and folders using either My Computer or Windows Explorer.

- ❑ Windows 9x and 2000 include a Backup utility for storing and compressing files, and Windows 2000 includes native file encryption and compression.

Disk Management

- ❑ Before a disk can store data, it must be partitioned using DOS FDISK and formatting using the FORMAT command.

- ❑ Windows 9x supports the FAT16 and FAT32 file systems.

- ❑ Windows 2000 supports the FAT16, FAT32, NTFS4, and NTFS5 file systems.

SELF TEST

The following questions will help you measure your understanding of the material presented in this chapter. Read all of the choices carefully because there might be more than one correct answer. Choose all correct answers for each question.

Operating System Functions and the Windows Family

1. Which of the following procedures should you use to activate a shortcut menu in Windows?

    A. Click Start, then select Programs | Accessories | Short Cuts.

    B. Double-click the component for which you want to access the shortcut.

    C. Right-click the component for which you want to access the shortcut menu.

    D. Double-click My Computer, then select Menu | Shortcut.

2. When using a Windows OS, which feature can you use to view the system's active (running) applications?

    A. The taskbar

    B. Each running application's desktop icon will turn blue

    C. The Start menu

    D. The desktop's shortcut menu

3. Which of the following statements about Windows 9x and Windows 2000 is the most accurate?

    A. Windows 2000 can be networked, and Windows 9x cannot.

    B. Windows 9x is aimed at home users, and Windows 2000 is not.

    C. Windows 9x supports Plug and Play, and Windows 2000 does not.

    D. Windows 2000 is the successor to the Windows 9x line of operating systems.

System Files and Utilities

4. Which Windows OS(s) require(s) IO.SYS?

    A. Windows 9x

    B. Windows 98 only

    C. Windows 2000 only

    D. Windows 9x and 2000

5. When you started your Windows 9x computer, you received a message stating that the registry was corrupt. Which of the following files might be corrupt?

A. WIN.DAT

B. SYSTEM.INI

C. WIN.INI

D. USER.DAT

6. A user is nervous about losing data in the Windows 98 registry. Which utility should you advise the user to use?

A. REGEDIT

B. REGEDT32

C. SCANREG

D. MSCONFIG

7. Which of the following is required by both the Windows 9x and Windows 2000 OSs?

A. CONFIG.SYS

B. IO.SYS

C. BOOT.INI

D. The registry

8. What does Windows 2000 use the SYSTEM.INI file for?

A. To store required hardware settings for the system

B. To store application settings for legacy programs

C. To store hardware settings for older applications

D. Windows 2000 does not use SYSTEM.INI

9. What is the function of the NTLDR file?

A. To initialize and organize the Windows 2000 boot process

B. To initialize and organize the Windows 9x boot process

C. To allow users to select the OS in a multiboot configuration

D. To boot Windows 2000 from a SCSI drive

10. Which of the following can you use to *safely* make changes to the Windows 9x registry?

A. Computer Management utility

    B. Control Panel

    C. Registry Editor

    D. System Configuration utility

11. Which of the following most accurately describes the function of the HIMEM.SYS file?

    A. To initialize the Windows 9x boot process

    B. To enable access to extended memory

    C. To enable memory paging between extended and upper memory

    D. To store hardware configuration settings in Windows 9x

File and Folder Management

12. When using Windows, you double-click a file's icon on the desktop. Which of the following is most likely to happen?

    A. The file's Properties dialog box will open.

    B. You will be given an opportunity to rename the file.

    C. The file will open.

    D. Nothing will happen.

13. Which of the following file attributes are you unable to change in Windows?

    A. Archive

    B. Read-only

    C. System

    D. Hidden

14. A user has called you with a question about Windows. Several files that she knows should be hidden are showing up on the desktop. What do you tell the user?

    A. The hidden files will be listed but cannot be opened or modified.

    B. The hidden files can be truly hidden by selecting the appropriate option in the My Computer | View menu.

    C. The hidden files should be moved to the Recycle Bin.

    D. The user is incorrect because hidden files cannot be shown on the desktop.

15. Which of the following statements about a file's extension is *inaccurate?*

    A. The file's extension determines the type of icon used for that file.

    B. The file's extension indicates the file's type.

    C. You cannot change a file's extension.

    D. You can make a file unusable by changing its extension.

16. You have decided to compress several files on your Windows 9x computer. Which of the following procedures should you use?

    A. Use the Backup utility and select the option to compress the files.

    B. Right-click each file, select Properties, and enable the Compression option.

    C. Open the Disk Management utility and select the "Compress selected files" option.

    D. Use My Computer to move the appropriate files into the COMPRESSED folder.

Disk Management

17. An OS uses the NTFS5 file system. When you boot the computer with this OS, which other types of volumes will you be able to access?

    A. FAT16 only

    B. FAT16 and FAT32

    C. FAT16 and HPFS

    D. None

18. Which of the following statements about the FAT16 and FAT32 file systems is true?

    A. FAT16 supports volumes up to 16MB, and FAT32 supports volumes up to 32MB.

    B. FAT16 volumes typically have about half the amount of slack as FAT32 volumes.

    C. Some versions of Windows 9x cannot access FAT16.

    D. FAT16 can be used by more versions of Windows than FAT32.

19. Which of the following file systems support native file compression and encryption?

    A. FAT32, NTFS4, and NTFS5

    B. NTFS4 and NTFS5

    C. FAT32 and NTFS5

    D. NTFS5

20. Your computer contains two IDE hard drives and one SCSI hard drive. You have loaded Windows 9x on the SCSI hard drive, but the computer won't boot properly. Why?

    A. SCSI hard drives cannot be loaded with the Windows 9x OSs.

    B. The automatic lettering of the drives prevents the SCSI drive from booting the system.

    C. SCSI hard drives can be used to contain data only and cannot be used to boot the computer.

    D. The SCSI hard drive has probably not been given the proper SCSI ID.

LAB QUESTION

Throughout this chapter, you have been introduced to a great number of Windows 9x and 2000 utilities. As a technician and in preparation for the A+ exam, it is important for you to know which utilities are included with each OS and to understand their functions. Use Table 8-2 to fill in information about the function of each utility as well as how you can access the utility and which OSs include the utility.

TABLE 8-2   Lab Chart

Utility	Purpose	Access	Operating System(s)
Scanreg			
Registry Editor (REGEDIT.EXE)			
Registry Editor (REGEDT32.EXE)			
System Configuration Editor (SYSEDIT)			
System Configuration utility (MSCONFIG)			
Control Panel			
Device Manager			

TABLE 8-2   Lab Chart *(continued)*

Utility	Purpose	Access	Operating System(s)
Automatic Skip Driver			
Computer Management utility			
Backup			
EXTRACT.EXE			
Drive Converter (CVT1.EXE)			

SELF-TEST ANSWERS

Operating System Functions and the Windows Family

1. ☑ **C.** To access a Windows shortcut menu, right-click the component for which you want to access the shortcut menu. A menu with items pertaining to that component will appear.
    ☒ **A,** click Start, then select Programs | Accessories | Short Cuts, is incorrect. The only way to access a shortcut menu is to right-click the component. Furthermore, there is no Short Cuts option in the Accessories menu. **B,** double-click the component for which you want to access the shortcut menu, is also incorrect. When you double-click certain components, such as an empty area of the desktop or taskbar, there will be no result. Other components, such as folders or icons, will be opened or activated when you double-click them. **D,** double-click My Computer, then select Menu | Shortcut, is also incorrect. Again, the only way to access a shortcut menu is to right-click. Furthermore, there is no Menu or Shortcut option in the My Computer window.

2. ☑ **A.** You can use the taskbar to view the system's active applications. All applications, utilities, and folders that you open will appear in the taskbar until you close or end them. You can switch between open applications by clicking the appropriate application button on the taskbar.
    ☒ **B** is incorrect because it states that the icon of each running application will appear blue on the desktop. In fact, many applications do not have icons on the desktop. Icons on the desktop typically turn blue when they are selected, but will not turn blue to indicate the application is running. **C,** the Start menu, is incorrect because this provides access to programs, help, and utilities but does not list active applications. **D,** the desktop's shortcut menu, is incorrect because this displays configuration options for the desktop, not a list of running applications.

3. ☑ **B.** Windows 9x is aimed at home users, and Windows 2000 is not. Rather, Windows 2000 is designed for use by businesses, especially those with sophisticated networking needs. The required hardware, cost, and lack of backward compatibility makes Windows 2000 a poor choice for home use.
    ☒ **A** is incorrect because it states that Windows 2000 can be networked, and Windows 9x cannot. It is true that Windows 2000 is dedicated to networking and has more sophisticated network features, but Windows 9x can also be networked. Although networking is not the strength of Windows 9x, it can be set up in a peer-to-peer configuration and can even be configured to join a Windows 2000 network. **C,** Windows 9x supports Plug and Play, and Windows 2000 does not, is incorrect. Both OSs support Plug and Play. However, whereas Windows 9x supports home user-type devices, such as specialized video or sound cards, Windows 2000 supports business-type devices, such as NICs, printers, and card readers.

D is incorrect because it states that Windows 2000 is the successor to the Windows 9x line of OSs. In fact, these represent two different OS lines. Windows 2000 is the successor in the Windows NT line.

System Files and Utilities

4. ☑ **A.** Windows 9x requires IO.SYS. This file is responsible for initializing and organizing the OS's boot process, and it is required for the OS to load properly.
    ☒ **B,** Windows 98 only, is incorrect because IO.SYS is also required by Windows 95. Therefore, the most appropriate answer is Windows 9x. **C,** Windows 2000 only, is incorrect because Windows 2000 does not use IO.SYS. Instead, it uses NTLDR to initialize and organize the boot process. For this reason, **D,** Windows 9x and 2000, is also incorrect.

5. ☑ **D.** USER.DAT might be corrupt. This file, along with SYSTEM.DAT, makes up the Windows 9x registry. These files contain the bulk of the OS's operation and configuration settings. Windows 2000 also uses the same two files in its registry. (The files, of course, contain different settings in Windows 2000.)
    ☒ **A,** WIN.DAT, is incorrect because this is not a valid Windows system file. **B,** SYSTEM.INI, and **C,** WIN.INI, are incorrect because they are not part of the Windows registry. Windows 9x uses these files only for backward compatibility with older applications.

6. ☑ **C.** You should advise the user to use the SCANREG utility. Included in Windows 98, this utility will back up the registry's contents. If the registry becomes corrupt or otherwise unusable, the registry backup can be restored.
    ☒ **A,** REGEDIT, and **B,** REGEDT32, are incorrect because these utilities are used for directly editing the registry files. Editing the files can be dangerous and will not prevent the registry from losing data. Furthermore, REGEDT32 is available only in Windows 2000. **D,** MSCONFIG, is also incorrect. This is a Windows 98 utility that allows you to enable or disable the processing of legacy configuration files during startup. For example, using MSCONFIG, you can opt to skip the AUTOEXEC.BAT file or process only select lines of the SYSTEM.INI file.

7. ☑ **D.** The registry is required by both the Windows 9x and Windows 2000 OSs. Although the data contained in the registry is different for Windows 9x and Windows 2000, they both still require the registry's presence to function properly.
    ☒ **A,** CONFIG.SYS, is incorrect. Windows 9x includes this file so that older applications can access the hardware. However, it is not required in Windows 9x and is not even present in Windows 2000. **B,** IO.SYS, is incorrect because although this file is required to properly boot a Windows 9x system, it is not present in Windows 2000. **C,** BOOT.INI, is also incorrect.

This file is required by Windows 2000 only if the OS is not installed in the default WINNT directory or is part of a dual-boot configuration (a system with more than one operating system). BOOT.INI is not present in Windows 9x.

8. ☑ **D.** Windows 2000 does not use SYSTEM.INI. This file was required by older 16-bit OSs to store hardware settings. Windows 9x includes this file for backward compatibility, but it is not present in Windows 2000.
☒ **A,** to store required hardware settings for the system, is incorrect. Again, SYSTEM.INI is required in older OSs such as Windows 3.1 but not in Windows 2000. **B,** to store application settings for legacy programs, is incorrect. This is the function of the WIN.INI file, which is used in Windows 9x, not Windows 2000. **C,** to store hardware settings for older applications, is also incorrect. Although Windows 9x uses SYSTEM.INI for this purpose, Windows 2000 does not. Windows 2000 does not support backward compatibility with older applications, so it does not include the SYSTEM.INI file.

9. ☑ **A.** The function of NTLDR is to initialize and organize the Windows 2000 boot process. On startup, NTLDR is responsible for locating and initializing other startup files, including NTDETECT and the registry.
☒ **B,** to initialize and organize the Windows 9x boot process, is incorrect because this is the function of the IO.SYS file. NTLDR is not present in Windows 9x. **C,** to allow users to select the OS in a multiboot configuration, is incorrect because this is the function of the BOOT.INI file. **D,** to boot Windows 2000 from a SCSI drive, is incorrect because this is the function of the NTBOOTDD.SYS file, which, incidentally, is initialized by NTLDR.

10. ☑ **B.** You can use the Control Panel to safely make changes to the Windows 9x registry. The Control Panel provides you with applets to configure the keyboard, mouse, system colors, printers, and many other features. The Control Panel simply provides you with configuration options, none of which can damage the registry. When you make a change in the Control Panel, the registry is automatically updated with the new settings.
☒ **A,** Computer Management utility, is incorrect because this is available only in Windows 2000. **C,** Registry Editor, is incorrect because this utility allows you to edit the registry directly. It is therefore possible to delete important settings or to enter incorrect settings that could cause a fatal OS error. **D,** System Configuration utility, is incorrect because this utility, present only in Windows 9x, allows you to configure the settings of legacy configuration files such as CONFIG.SYS and WIN.INI.

11. ☑ **B.** The function of HIMEM.SYS is to enable access to extended memory. Many older applications were written when computers were limited to 1MB of RAM. The HIMEM.SYS

file allows these applications to use memory over 1MB (the extended memory area).
☒ **A,** to initialize the Windows 9x boot process, is incorrect because this is the function of the IO.SYS file. **C,** to enable memory paging between extended and upper memory, is incorrect because this is the function of the expanded memory manager, EMM386.EXE. **D,** to store hardware configuration settings in Windows 9x, is also incorrect. This is the function of SYSTEM.DAT and, to a lesser degree (for backward compatibility), SYSTEM.INI.

File and Folder Management

12. ☑ **C.** When you double-click a file's icon, the file will open. If this is an application file, such as a document or image, the host application will be launched and the file opened within it. If it is an executable file, the program will run.
☒ **A,** the file's Properties dialog box will open, is incorrect. To open the Properties dialog box, you can right-click the icon, then select Properties. **B,** you will be given an opportunity to rename the file, is also incorrect. To rename a file, click the file's icon once, then click the file's name. This process involves two separate clicks, not a double-click. **D,** nothing will happen, is incorrect. Any icon that is double-clicked will open, whether it is a file icon, folder, or navigation icon, such as My Computer or Network Neighborhood.

13. ☑ **C.** You cannot change the system attribute in Windows. This attribute is assigned automatically by the file's host application or by Windows itself. Although it is possible to view this attribute, you cannot change it.
☒ **A,** archive, **B,** read-only, and **D,** hidden, are all incorrect. You can apply or remove any of these attributes by right-clicking the file's icon, then selecting Properties. You can place a check beside each attribute you want to apply, or remove the check from attributes you want to remove.

14. ☑ **B.** The hidden files can be truly hidden by selecting the appropriate option in the My Computer | View menu. It is possible to view all files, even hidden ones, by selecting View in the My Computer window. The "Show all files" option will display hidden files as grayed-out icons. Use either the "Do not show hidden files" or "Do not show hidden or system files" option to keep hidden files from being displayed.
☒ **A** is incorrect because it states that the hidden files will be listed but cannot be opened or modified. If you can see a hidden file, you can manage it just as you would any other file. This means you can open, modify, move, rename, or delete it. You will, however, receive a confirmation message when renaming or deleting it to prevent accidental actions. **C,** the hidden files should be moved to the recycle bin, is incorrect. This action is the same as deleting the files. **D,** the

user is incorrect because hidden files cannot be shown on the desktop, is incorrect. Again, even hidden files can be displayed by choosing the appropriate Windows View option.

15. ☑ **C.** The statement that you cannot change a file's extension is inaccurate. You can remove or change the extension along with the rest of the file's name. However, when you change the extension, Windows will issue a warning that this can render the file unusable. By changing a file's extension, you essentially remove the file's association with its host application.
☒ **A,** the file's extension determines the type of icon used for that file, is incorrect because this statement is *true.* Windows automatically associates most extensions with a particular icon type. For example, the .DOC extension is indicated by a Word or WordPad icon, and the .TXT extension is indicated by a Notepad icon. **B,** the file's extension indicates the file's type, is also incorrect because this statement is true. Files will be given an extension according to their role in the system or by the host application. For example, executable files are indicated by the .EXE extension, and bitmaps are indicated by the .BMP extension. **D,** you can make a file unusable by changing its extension, is also incorrect because it is true. As explained, when you change a file's extension, you remove its association with the host application. When you later double-click the file, Windows will either open the wrong application or simply report an error, depending on the new extension.

16. ☑ **A.** To compress files in Windows 9x, use the Backup utility and select the option to compress the files. Short of using a third-party compression utility, this is the only way to compress files in Windows 9x.
☒ **B,** right-click each file, select Properties, and enable the Compression option, is incorrect because although this procedure can be used in Windows 2000, it is not supported in Windows 9x. **C,** which suggests using the Disk Management utility, is incorrect because this utility exists only in Windows 2000. **D,** use My Computer to move the appropriate files into the COMPRESSED folder, is also incorrect. There is no native COMPRESSED folder in Windows 9x. Although you can create a folder with this name, moving files into it will not compress them.

Disk Management

17. ☑ **B.** You will also be able to access FAT16 and FAT32 volumes. The NTFS5 file system can be used only by Windows 2000. Windows 2000 retains backward compatibility with older file systems and is able to access FAT16, FAT32, and NTFS4 volumes.
☒ **A,** FAT16 only, is incorrect. If the OS uses NTFS5, it must be Windows 2000. Again, Windows 2000 can access FAT16, FAT32, and NTFS4 volumes. **C,** FAT16 and HPFS, is also

incorrect. HPFS was developed for OS/2 and is not accessible to Windows 9x or Windows 2000. **D,** none, is incorrect because Windows 2000 is not limited to using only NTFS5.

18. ☑ **D.** FAT16 can be used by more versions of Windows than FAT32. FAT16 can be used by Windows 9x, Windows NT, and Windows 2000. FAT32, however, can be used only on later releases of Windows 95 (OSR2 or later), Windows 98, and Windows 2000.
☒ **A** is incorrect because it suggests that FAT16 and FAT32 support 16MB and 32MB of volume capacity, respectively. The numbers 16 and 32 actually indicate the bit addressing of the file system. Using 16-bit addressing, FAT16 can support up to 2GB of volume space. The FAT32 file system uses 32-bit addressing and can support volumes up to 2TB. **B** is incorrect because it suggests that FAT16 volumes have less slack than FAT32 volumes. In fact, FAT32 volumes have far less slack than FAT16 volumes. FAT16 is limited to 65,526 clusters, which, in a 2GB volume, means clusters are 32KB each. FAT32 volumes use much smaller clusters, meaning that less cluster space is left over when a file is saved, so there is less overall volume slack (leftover, unused space). **C** is incorrect because it states that some versions of Windows 9x cannot access FAT16. Although early versions of Windows 95 cannot access FAT32 volumes, all can access FAT16.

19. ☑ **D.** NTFS5 supports native file compression and encryption. This means that you can compress or encrypt files and folders simply by enabling those options in the file's or folder's Properties dialog box.
☒ **A,** FAT32, NTFS4, and NTFS5, is incorrect because FAT32 supports neither compression nor encryption, and NTFS4 supports native compression only. For this reason, **B,** NTFS4 and NTFS5, and **C,** FAT32 and NTFS5, are incorrect.

20. ☑ **B.** The automatic lettering of the drives prevents the SCSI drive from booting the system. In a system with IDE and SCSI drives, the IDE drives are lettered first, followed by the SCSI drives. For example, if each drive contains only one partition, the two IDE drives will be designated C: and D:, and the SCSI drive will be designated E:. However, Windows 9x must exist on the primary drive (C:) in order to boot properly.
☒ **A** is incorrect because it suggests that SCSI hard drives cannot be used to install the Windows 9x OS. If the system does not contain IDE drives, the SCSI drive can be used to store the OS and boot the system. For this reason, **C** is also incorrect, because it suggests that SCSI drives cannot be used to boot the system. Again, SCSI drives are able to hold and boot from an OS but are given lower priority than IDE drives. SCSI drives are unable to boot the system only if an IDE drive is present in the system. **D** is incorrect because it suggests that the problem lies with the SCSI drive's SCSI ID. Regardless of the SCSI drive's configuration in the SCSI chain, it will be unable to boot the computer as long as an IDE drive is present.

LAB ANSWER

TABLE 8-3   Lab Answer

Utility	Purpose	Access	Operating System(s)
Scanreg	To back up and restore the Windows registry files	Runs automatically, can be accessed by entering SCANREG on the Windows Run line	Windows 98
Registry Editor (REGEDIT.EXE)	To directly edit the registry files	Enter **REGEDIT** on the Windows Run line	Windows 95, Windows 98, and Windows 2000
Registry Editor (REGEDT32.EXE)	To directly edit the registry files	Enter **REGEDT32** on the Windows Run line	Windows 2000
System Configuration Editor (SYSEDIT)	Allows you to directly edit legacy configuration files (e.g., WIN.INI, SYSTEM.INI, AUTOEXEC.BAT, CONFIG.SYS)	Enter **SYSEDIT** on the Windows Run line	Windows 95 and Windows 98
System Configuration utility (MSCONFIG)	Allows you to safely modify legacy configuration files (WIN.INI, SYSTEM.INI, AUTOEXEC.BAT, CONFIG.SYS)	Enter **MSCONFIG** on the Windows Run line	Windows 98
Control Panel	Allows you to safely modify hardware, application, or desktop settings	Start | Settings | Control Panel *or* double-click My Computer	Windows 95, Windows 98, and Windows 2000
Device Manager	Allows you to view and modify hardware configurations and load device drivers	Right-click My Computer and select Properties	Windows 95, Windows 98, and Windows 2000

TABLE 8-3   Lab Answer *(continued)*

Utility	Purpose	Access	Operating System(s)
Automatic Skip Driver	Detects and disables potentially problem-causing device drivers	Runs automatically; to view results, enter **ASD** on the Windows Run line *or* select Start | Programs | Accessories | System Tools | System Information	Windows 98
Computer Management utility	Allows you to configure and manage hardware configurations, disks, printers, and security settings	Start | Programs | Administrative Tools | Computer Management	Windows 2000
Backup	Allows you to create backup copies of all or selected files; also enables you to compress backed-up files	Start | Programs | Accessories | System Tools | Backup	Windows 95, Windows 98, and Windows 2000
EXTRACT.EXE	Allows you to manually extract applications or drivers from the .CAB installation files	Enter **EXTRACT** at a DOS command prompt	Windows 98
Drive Converter (CVT1.EXE)	Allows you to convert a volume from FAT16 to FAT32 without loss of existing data	Start | Programs | Accessories | System Tools | Drive Converter	Windows 98

9

Installation, Configuration, and Upgrade

The focus of this chapter is the proper setup and configuration of Windows 9x and Windows 2000. Whether you are installing from scratch, upgrading, or configuring the system, you must follow certain guidelines and procedures. First, we discuss basic preparation and installation procedures, followed by upgrade paths and procedures. Alternative methods of booting Windows are also described. Finally, the chapter wraps up with a discussion about installing non-Plug and Play drivers and third-party applications. Note that although there are four versions of Windows 2000 (Professional, Server, Advanced Server, and Datacenter Server), the A+ exam (and this chapter) focuses on Windows 2000 Professional.

CERTIFICATION OBJECTIVE 9.01

Installing Windows

The installation of an operating system is a large undertaking. Many things can go wrong with a Windows installation, so the more familiar you are with the normal process, the easier it will be for you to determine the cause of installation problems. Because the Windows 9x and Windows 2000 installation procedures are quite different, they are discussed individually in the following subsections.

Before starting any OS installation, you must ensure that your computer meets the minimum hardware requirements. The minimum (min) and recommended (rec) requirements for Windows 95, 98, and 2000 are listed in Table 9-1. Additional required hardware includes a 1.44-inch high-density floppy disk drive and keyboard. Recommended hardware includes a CD-ROM drive and a mouse.

Windows 9x

The Windows 9x installation is almost completely automated; typically, little input is required on your part. However, you must carry out a number of

TABLE 9-1 Minimum and Recommended Hardware Requirements for Windows 95, 98, and 2000

	Windows 95		Windows 98		Windows 2000	
	Minimum	Recommended	Minimum	Recommended	Minimum	Recommended
Processor	386DX	486DX 66	486DX 66	Pentium	Pentium 133	
RAM	4MB	16MB	16MB	24MB	32MB	64MB
Hard disk space	55MB	120MB	175MB (FAT32)	255MB (FAT32)	650MB	1GB
Video	VGA	SVGA with 2MB VRAM	VGA	14- or 24-bit SVGA	VGA	16- or 24-bit SVGA

important preparation procedures, and you should be familiar with the installation options and how they will affect the outcome of the installation. It is important to note here that although the Windows 95 and Windows 98 installation procedures are very similar, the exercises contained within this section are specific to Windows 98. You might notice some slight screen differences if you use these procedures to install Windows 95.

Startup

The first challenge when installing an OS from scratch is that computers cannot boot without an OS of some kind. How, then, can you get the computer started to install an OS if an OS doesn't already exist in the computer?

The answer is that you use the boot disk that came with the installation CD. The Windows 9x boot disk contains drivers that will start the system and allow the computer to read from the CD. To use the boot disk, insert the appropriate floppy disk and start the computer.

If you do not have the proper OS's boot disk, your task is a bit more difficult. In these cases, you must create your own startup disk. The procedure for creating a startup disk is explained later in the chapter. In short, however, a startup disk contains just enough of an OS's components to allow you to access a DOS command prompt and access the CD-ROM drive. From there, you can initiate the Windows 9x Setup program.

Partitioning

Once the computer has booted properly and before you can install an OS, you must prepare the hard drive to store data. If the hard drive has already been prepared, you don't need to perform the procedures described in this section or in the "Format Drive" section later in the chapter.

The first step in preparing the hard drive is creating partitions. Recall that a partition is a division of the hard drive into one or several volumes. Most hard drives come from the manufacturer unpartitioned. To partition the drive, enter **FDISK** at the command prompt, then press ENTER. FDISK.EXE is included on the Windows 9x boot disk.

If the hard drive is 2GB or less, FDISK will automatically partition the drive using FAT16. If the drive is larger than 2GB, you will be given the option to use FAT16 or FAT32. Recall that you can create more than one partition on a hard drive. Windows 9x must be installed on the first primary partition. Follow the steps in Exercise 9-1 to create a primary partition and an extended partition with one logical drive. This exercise assumes that you are using the Windows 98 boot disk and that the hard drive is larger than 2GB.

EXERCISE 9-1

Using FDISK to Create Hard Drive Partitions

1. Enter **FDISK** at the command prompt. The FDISK utility will start, and you will first be asked if you want to enable large disk support. If you select Yes,

the drive will be partitioned using the FAT32 file system. If you select No, the FAT16 file system will be used.

2. Enter **Y** and press the ENTER key to use FAT32. The FDISK screen shown in Figure 9-1 will appear.

3. Press 1, then press ENTER to create a partition. The screen shown in Figure 9-2 will appear.

4. Select 1, then press ENTER to create the first primary partition. You will see "Verifying drive integrity."

5. You will be asked if you want to allocate all drive space to this partition. Press N, then press ENTER. You will again see "Verifying drive integrity."

6. Enter the size of the first partition in megabytes or percentage of total drive space, then press ENTER.

FIGURE 9-1   The primary FDISK screen.

```
                    Microsoft Windows 98
                   Fixed Disk Setup Program
            (C)Copyright Microsoft Corp. 1983 - 1998

                        FDISK Options

Current fixed disk drive: 1

Choose one of the following:

1. Create DOS partition or Logical DOS Drive
2. Set active partition
3. Delete partition or Logical DOS Drive
4. Display partition information


Enter choice: [1]




Press Esc to exit FDISK
```

The Create Partition screen.

```
                    Create DOS Partition or Logical DOS Drive
Current fixed disk drive: 1

Choose one of the following:

1. Create Primary DOS Partition
2. Create Extended DOS Partition
3. Create Logical DOS Drive(s) in the Extended DOS Partition


Enter choice: [1]




Press Esc to return to FDISK Options
```

7. Press ESC to return to the main FDISK menu.

8. Press 2, then press ENTER to set this partition active (bootable).Enter the number of the partition you want to make active. Enter 1 (C: is always 1).

9. Repeat Steps 3 to 7 to create the extended partition, ensuring that you select the Extended Partition option in Step 4, and use all remaining drive space.

10. At this point, you will be asked to enter logical drive size in Mbytes or percentage. Enter a size or percentage (up to 100%) for each additional drive you wish to create. Each time a logical drive is created fdisk will check its integrity. Press ESC *twice* to exit FDISK, then restart the computer.

When using FDISK, you can create a total of four partitions. At least one partition must be primary. All other partitions that you want to make bootable must also be primary partitions. However, if you want to create more than four volumes, you must use at least one extended partition. Extended partitions differ from primary partitions in that they are not assigned a drive letter. Rather, you use extended partitions to create logical drives. These logical drives are assigned drive letters. The number of logical drives you create on an extended partition is limited only by the number of available letters of the alphabet.

exam
ⓦatch

Primary partitions are bootable, and logical drives are not. However, you may create only four primary partitions. Although you may create up to four primary partitions, if you want more drive letters, you must create an extended partition with logical drives.

For example, if you create four primary partitions, you will have a C:, a D:, an E:, and an F: drive. However, suppose that you create three primary partitions and one extended partition. The primary partitions will receive the letters C:, D:, and E:. You can then use the extended partition to create up to 21 logical drives (lettered from F: to Z:).

Logical drives cannot contain the OS because they are not bootable. Furthermore, the system's first partition must be a primary partition. All other partitions, including those on secondary or slave drives, can be either primary or extended.

Primary partitions and logical drives also differ in the way that they are assigned letters. The system assigns drive letters starting with the primary hard drive's primary partitions, then the primary partitions on other drives (such as a slave). Next, the logical drives will be lettered, starting with the primary hard drive. For example, suppose a system has two hard drives with the following volumes:

Primary Hard Drive	Secondary Hard Drive
Primary partition	Primary partition
Logical drive	Logical drive
Logical drive	

The system will automatically letter these volumes as follows:

Primary Hard Drive	Secondary Hard Drive
C:	D:
E:	G:
F:	

Format Drive

Once the hard disk is partitioned, it is assigned a drive letter for each volume. However, these volumes cannot store data until they are formatted. (Fdisk requires that the computer be restarted before formatting can take place.) To format a partition, enter the FORMAT command, followed by the drive letter. For example, to format the C: drive, use the following command:

```
FORMAT C:
```

You will receive a message stating that all data on the specified volume will be lost; you'll receive this message even if the drive currently contains no data. Confirm the FORMAT command by entering **Y**, then pressing ENTER. A percentage counter will appear, indicating the progress of the formatting process. When the volume has been completely formatted, a message will appear asking you to enter a name for the volume. Enter a name, or simply press ENTER to leave the volume unnamed.

Running the Setup Utility

Once the hard drive is partitioned and formatted, you can proceed with the Windows 9x installation. You can start the Setup utility by entering **SETUP** at the command prompt. If you are using a homemade boot disk, you might need to access the CD-ROM drive first, then enter the SETUP command.

Pre-File Copy Phase   The first phase of the Windows 9x Setup is called the *pre-file copy phase*. In this phase, the installation utility checks the integrity of the hard drive by running ScanDisk. Next, the utility automatically selects the installation location and gives you an opportunity to change it.

You are then asked to select an installation type. The Typical option loads drivers and applications that most people tend to use. The Portable option is used for portable systems, and the Compact option loads minimal drivers and applications. The Custom option allows you to hand-pick which drivers and/or applications are installed. Finally, you will be prompted to create a Startup disk. Enter a blank floppy disk, and follow the on-screen instructions. You can also use the methods described later in the chapter to create a Startup disk after the OS is installed.

File Copy Phase   The *file copy phase* typically takes the longest but requires the least input from you. During this phase, the required files (depending on the selected installation option) are copied from the installation CD into the proper locations on the hard drive.

Detection Phase   When the file copy phase is complete, Windows will begin detecting Plug and Play hardware in the system and loading the appropriate device drivers in the *detection phase*. You will most likely be required to restart the computer so that the drivers can be initialized.

Configuring System Settings   *Configuring system settings* is the final phase of the Windows 9x installation. You will be asked to verify the Date/Time setting and select the proper time zone. Next, you will be prompted to install a printer (if one exists). Windows 9x will then continue to load, and the installation will be complete.

Throughout the entire installation process, Windows 9x keeps a log of installation processes. This log is contained in the SETUPLOG.TXT file. If any part of the installation has failed, you can restart the Setup utility. Choose Safe Recovery, and Windows will use the SETUPLOG.TXT file to determine where the interruption occurred, skip the failed step, then proceed with the rest of the installation process.

Windows 9x also keeps a log of the hardware detection phase during installation. A log called DETCRASH.LOG is generated and can be used by the Setup utility to determine and avoid failure points during the hardware detection phase of a safe recovery. A text (readable) version of the DETCRASH.LOG file is also produced so that users can view a listing of which hardware was or was not successfully detected. This file is called DETLOG.TXT.

Windows 2000

The Windows 2000 installation process differs significantly from that of Windows 9x. To begin with, although you can use the Windows 9x methods for partitioning and formatting the hard drive, the Windows 2000 Setup program itself contains a partition and format utility. The order of events is also different for the Windows 2000 installation.

Whether you are performing a clean installation or an upgrade, Windows 2000 has some pretty steep hardware requirements and compatibility specifications. Check the installation package or the Microsoft Web site (www.microsoft.com/windows2000) to ensure that your computer meets these requirements and specifications.

Startup

If the computer's BIOS supports booting from the CD-ROM drive, you can boot directly from the Windows 2000 installation CD. When this is the case, insert the CD and start the computer. The installation utility (WINNT.EXE) will begin automatically.

If your computer cannot boot from the CD-ROM drive, you must use the Windows 2000 boot disks (of which there are four). Place the first boot disk in the floppy drive, then start the computer. You will be prompted to insert the remaining disks as they are required.

Once you have started the computer using the Windows 2000 installation CD or boot disks, a welcome screen will be displayed. You will prompted to select one of three setup options. The options are to install Windows 2000, repair a failed installation, or exit the Setup utility. Choose to install Windows 2000.

Partitioning and Formatting

You can install Windows 2000 on a disk that has already been partitioned using FDISK. However, if you are installing Windows 2000 on an unpartitioned hard disk, you will automatically be prompted by the Setup program to create partitions. Therefore, unlike Windows 9x, partitioning and formatting can be done during the Windows 2000 installation rather than before.

This partitioning and formatting utility is recommended over FDISK for Windows 2000 because it, but not FDISK, supports the creation of NTFS partitions. Note that Windows 2000 also includes a partition utility called Disk Management that can be used after the OS is installed. This is completely different from the utility used during setup, so it is discussed separately in the "From the Classroom" sidebar. Follow the instructions in Exercise 9-2 to partition and format the hard drive during the Windows 2000 installation.

exam
ⓦatch

The Windows 2000 setup partitioning utility is very different from the FDISK utility. FDISK can create a total of four partitions. Furthermore, it can create only FAT16 or FAT32 partitions (the two types cannot be mixed). The Windows 2000 partitioning utility can create FAT16, FAT32, or NTFS partitions and is not limited in the number of partitions it can create.

EXERCISE 9-2

Partitioning and Formatting the Hard Drive During the Windows 2000 Installation

1. To create a new partition, press C.

2. Enter the size of the partition, and press ENTER.

3. You will be prompted to install Windows 2000 on this partition. Press ENTER to accept. Note that at this point you could also elect to continue creating partitions. However, Microsoft recommends creating only the boot partition at this step. The remaining partitions should be created using the Disk Management utility after the OS has been installed.

4. Select the file system for this partition. You can select either FAT or NTFS (recommended). The partition will be formatted with the selected file system. Note that if you select FAT on a drive that is less than 2GB, FAT16 will be used. If you select FAT for a drive larger than 2GB, FAT32 will be used.

The Setup utility will automatically copy required installation files to the new partition, then reboot the computer. When the computer starts up again, the Windows 2000 Setup Wizard will begin automatically.

The Setup Utility

At this point, the Setup utility will detect basic hardware components such as the mouse and keyboard. You will also be prompted to enter regional settings such as language and to enter personal and company information. Next, you will asked to supply the Windows 2000 product key and enter a computer name and administrator password.

FROM THE CLASSROOM

Windows 2000 Disk Management

Partitioning and formatting a disk is pretty serious business; if you use DOS or Windows tools to partition or format a volume that already contains data, that data will be lost. Furthermore, if you partition a volume incorrectly before loading the OS, the only way to change the partition is to remove the OS, repartition the volume, then reload the OS.

Although these rules apply to all Windows OSs, Windows 2000 has included a partitioning utility that can make partitioning much easier. This utility is Disk Management and can only be used once Windows 2000 is properly installed. This means that you will have to partition at least one volume—the

partition the OS is installed on—using basic methods.

The Disk Management utility isn't limited to creating primary and extended partitions the way FDISK is. Rather, Disk Management simply lets you create as many partitions as you want, using whichever file system you deem appropriate. You can create, remove, or modify partitions without having to reboot the system (this process is often called "on-the-fly" partitioning). The only partition you cannot modify or remove is the boot partition, which contains the OS itself.

—Amy Thomson, A+
Certified Technician,
MOUS Master

Because Windows 2000 is essentially a network OS, you will be asked to enter network settings, such as sharing options, protocols, services, and a workgroup or domain name. When the appropriate information has been gathered, the Windows 2000 Setup utility will begin copying the required files to the hard drive (depending on the options you selected and the information supplied). The computer will restart, and Windows 2000 will start for the first time.

Now that you are familiar with the setup procedures for Windows 9x and Windows 2000, test your knowledge by answering the following Scenario & Solution questions.

SCENARIO & SOLUTION

	Windows 9x	Windows 2000
How can I start the computer prior to installing the OS?	Use the Setup disk.	Use the Setup disks or boot from the installation CD.
How do I create partitions before installation?	Use FDISK.	Use the Windows 2000 installation's partition utility.
How do I start the Setup utility?	Enter the command SETUP.	The Setup utility starts automatically when you boot from the setup disks or installation CD.

CERTIFICATION OBJECTIVE 9.02

Upgrading Windows

In some cases, you might want to upgrade the Windows OS rather than performing a clean installation. When you upgrade the OS, you replace the old one with a new version. The main advantages to performing an upgrade rather than purchasing a full new version are the lower cost of the installation disk and the fact that you can keep most of the existing applications and settings. That is, when you upgrade from one Windows OS to another, all your network settings, applications, and nonsystem files are migrated into the new OS.

However, it is typically recommended that you perform a clean installation whenever possible. This eliminates the migration of problems from the old OS to the new. It also ensures that the new OS uses known compatible drivers rather than old ones that might not function properly, even though they worked with the old OS.

Before you perform an upgrade, it's a good idea to back up your computer in case the upgrade fails and you are left without an OS. You must also ensure that your computer has a sufficient OS to upgrade to the new OS. These are called *upgrade paths*. In short, you can upgrade to Windows 98 from Windows 95. You can also upgrade to Windows 2000 Professional from Windows 95, Windows 98, and Windows NT 4 Workstation.

Upgrading from Windows 95 to Windows 98

You can run the Windows 98 Setup utility directly from Windows 95. When you perform the upgrade, Windows 98 will overwrite the Windows 95 system files while leaving applications, nonsystem files, and settings intact. Follow the steps in Exercise 9-3 to begin the upgrade from Windows 95 to 98.

EXERCISE 9-3

Upgrading from Windows 95 to Windows 98

1. Start Windows 95 as you normally do, and close any running applications and utilities.

2. Insert the Windows 98 installation CD. In most cases, the Setup utility will start automatically. If it doesn't, access the CD using My Computer or Windows Explorer, and double-click the Setup icon.

3. The Setup utility will detect the existence of Windows 95 and ask if you want to perform an upgrade. Select Yes.

4. Follow the on-screen instructions to complete the upgrade, ensuring that you select Yes when prompted to save the system files. This will allow you to uninstall Windows 98 and revert to Windows 95 if problems occur. When Windows 98 is removed, the Windows 95 system files will be restored.

The remainder of the installation will proceed as described earlier in the chapter, with the exception of a few steps. To begin with, you will not be asked to select an installation type (compact, typical, and the like). Windows 98 will simply migrate existing features when possible or upgrade existing features that cannot be migrated. During the Windows 98 upgrade, the hardware detection and configuration steps will also be skipped. Again, Windows 98 will simply use the existing hardware configurations.

Upgrading from Windows 9x to Windows 2000

The upgrade process for Windows 9x to Windows 2000 is relatively simple. From within Windows 9x, launch the Windows 2000 Setup utility. Because you are currently using a 32-bit OS, the 32-bit Setup utility will be used (WINNT32.EXE).

The Setup utility will detect the Windows 9x OS and ask if you want to upgrade. Choose Yes.

The setup will proceed as normal, except that all existing compatible applications, OS settings, and network configurations (such as username, password, and IP address) will be migrated into Windows 2000. Some files that will not be upgraded include the Windows 9x System Tools and virtual device drivers. These files will be replaced with Windows 2000 versions.

on the **Job**

It is recommended that you back up the system before upgrading Windows 9x to Windows 2000. Windows 2000 does not have an uninstall feature, so the only way to revert to Windows 9x is to delete Windows 2000 and reinstall Windows 9x.

Upgrading from Windows NT 4 to Windows 2000

Like Windows 9x, Windows NT 4 provides an easy upgrade to Windows 2000. From the Windows NT 4 OS, launch the 32-bit Windows 2000 Setup utility (WINNT32.EXE). Choose to perform an upgrade and follow the on-screen instructions.

Like Windows 9x, some Windows NT 4 utilities will be replaced rather than migrated. However, all existing compatible applications and utilities, as well as network and other configuration settings, will be migrated.

Dual-Booting Windows

A dual-boot configuration includes two working OSs on a single computer. At startup, a boot menu will be presented; the user selects which OS to use from this menu. To create a dual-boot system, the two OSs must be installed separately. When users install applications or configure OS settings in one OS, the other OS will remain unaffected. In other words, if you want to access a particular application from both OSs, you must install the application twice—once from within each OS.

It is recommended that you install each OS in a dual-boot configuration on a separate partition. The OS that you boot with will determine whether you can access files on the other partitions in the system. For example, suppose a computer has Windows 9x installed on a FAT32 partition and Windows 2000 installed on an NTFS5 partition. If you boot from Windows 9x, you will be unable to access files on the NTFS partition, since Windows 9x cannot recognize this file system. However, since Windows 2000 is backward compatible with FAT32, you will be able to access the FAT32 partition if you boot from Windows 2000.

Recall that Windows 9x must be installed on the first primary partition. Windows 2000, on the other hand, can occupy any partition. Therefore, if you plan to create a dual-boot configuration in the future, don't install Windows 2000 on the first partition. Although the location of each OS is important, the *order* of installation is usually irrelevant. That is, it makes no difference which OS you install first when creating a dual-boot configuration. The exception is that if you are dual-booting with Windows 95 and Windows 2000, it is recommended that you install Windows 95 first.

Creating a dual-boot configuration is similar to performing an upgrade, except that you select a *different* location in which to install the second OS. Follow the steps in Exercise 9-4 to create a dual-boot configuration with Windows 9x and Windows 2000. Note that this basic procedure (not including network configuration) can also be used to dual-boot Windows NT 4 and Windows 2000.

EXERCISE 9-4

Creating a Dual-Boot Configuration with Windows 9x and Windows 2000

1. Install Windows 9x using the procedures discussed earlier in the chapter, ensuring that there are at least two partitions on the hard drive.

2. Insert the Windows 2000 installation CD. The Setup utility will run automatically. If not, activate it using the Windows 9x My Computer or Windows Explorer.

3. You will be asked to choose between upgrading or installing a new copy of Windows 2000. Choose to install a new copy.

4. The Windows 2000 installation will proceed, and the computer will be restarted.

5. When the computer restarts, you will be prompted to select the Windows 2000 installation location. Select a different partition than the one Windows 9x is using. This is not necessary, but it is recommended.

6. Follow the on-screen directions to complete the Windows 2000 setup. Windows 2000 will automatically detect the presence of Windows 9x and will automatically generate and configure the dual-boot menu (BOOT.INI), which will appear at startup.

By default, the system will display a boot menu for 30 seconds at startup. If no OS is selected, the system will automatically boot into Windows 2000. You can change these options by altering the Windows 2000 Startup and Recovery options. To access these options, right-click My Computer and select Properties. Click the Advanced tab, then click the Startup and Recovery button.

Test your familiarity with the concepts presented in this section by answering the following Scenario & Solution questions.

CERTIFICATION OBJECTIVE 9.03

Booting Windows

Under normal conditions, Windows will boot in normal mode, loading all its required device drivers and utilities. However, in some cases, when problems are encountered, you can use alternate boot methods to determine or troubleshoot the problem. These boot methods, as well how to manually boot or repair an OS that will not load, are discussed in the following sections.

Windows 9x

Windows 9x retains backward compatibility with older hardware and applications, so its boot files are different from those of Windows 2000. Furthermore, Windows 9x

SCENARIO & SOLUTION	
When should I perform an OS upgrade?	When you want to keep existing applications, configurations, and nonsystem files.
How do I perform an upgrade?	Load the original OS normally, and run the new OS installation utility. Select the upgrade option.
How do I create a dual-boot configuration?	Install the first OS using basic methods and start the computer normally. Run the Setup utility for the second OS and choose to perform a new installation rather than an upgrade.

includes a DOS mode that allows you to boot the computer without loading Windows. The normal boot sequence, boot modes, and boot troubleshooting procedures for Windows 9x are described in the following subsections.

Boot Sequence and Required Files

When you first turn on the computer, the BIOS performs a POST, then searches the drives for the *master boot record (MBR)*. This is known as the *BIOS bootstrap phase*. The BIOS then hands control to the OS loader, located in the MBR. The MBR also contains data about the partitions on the drive as well as which partition has been marked as active. The OS loader uses this information to find and initialize IO.SYS on the boot partition.

The boot process then enters what is called *real-mode boot*, indicating that real-mode files required to boot the system will be processed. See the "From the Classroom" sidebar that follows for more information about real mode and protected mode. First, IO.SYS locates and reads MSDOS.SYS, which contains boot parameters, such as how long to display the "Starting Windows 9x" message or which OSs exist if there is a non-Windows 2000 dual-boot configuration. The LOGO.SYS file (the Windows splash screen) is then displayed. Next, IO.SYS searches for the SYSTEM.DAT and USER.DAT files and checks the integrity of their data, then loads SYSTEM.DAT.

Next, the boot process enters the *real-mode configuration stage*, during which real-mode (legacy) configuration files will be processed, if they exist. CONFIG.SYS is processed first, followed by AUTOEXEC.BAT. Note that these files are not required by Windows 9x to boot properly. Values in the CONFIG.SYS file will override values in SYSTEM.DAT. IO.SYS will then load HIMEM.SYS, if it has not already been referenced in the CONFIG.SYS file.

The next boot stage is called *protected-mode boot* because it includes the initialization of protected-mode (32-bit) system files. First, WIN.COM is executed, and IO.SYS hands it control of the boot process. WIN.COM then locates and loads the virtual memory manager (VMM386.VXD). VMM386.VXD is responsible for loading 32-bit device drivers into memory. VMM386.VXD also switches the processor from real mode to protected mode. Next, WIN.COM reads SYSTEM.INI and its values are implemented. Note that values in the SYSTEM.INI file will be overridden by corresponding parameters in the registry.

Finally, the Windows 9x screen is loaded. The kernel (KRNL32.DLL) contains the actual screen components, and GDI.EXE and USER.EXE enable the graphical interface. Entries in the WIN.INI file are read, and the Windows shell (EXPLORER.EXE) is loaded.

exam
ⓦatch

It is essential that you be familiar with the phases and files of the Windows 9x boot process as well as how they differ from those of Windows 2000.

Boot Modes

The boot process described previously is known as *normal mode*. That is, it is how Windows 9x will boot when things are running normally. However, in some cases, you might want to alter the boot process so that some or most of the normal steps

FROM THE CLASSROOM

Real Versus Protected Mode

What are real and protected modes? The term *real mode* refers to older systems and applications—or rather, their behavior. Real mode indicates an inability to access extended and virtual memory. Real-mode systems also do not support multitasking, and applications that run in real mode typically run by trying to directly access the hardware. Another feature of real mode is that it is possible for an application to take over memory space that is already in use by a utility or driver. This is why the division of memory into conventional and upper, as described in Chapter 8, is so important.

Protected-mode systems, such as the Intel 286 and newer chips, support multitasking and access to extended and virtual memory. While most real-mode applications are 16-bit, protected-mode applications are usually 32-bit. The term *protected mode* refers to the fact that each application's memory space is protected from use by other applications.

DOS cannot run in protected mode, even if it is installed on a computer whose processor can run in protected mode. Windows 95 and higher can run in protected mode, and Windows 9x retains the ability to run real-mode applications. In general, Windows 9x legacy files and drivers work in real mode, and native 32-bit Windows 9x files and drivers work in protected mode.

—Amy Thomson, A+ Certified Technician, MOUS Master

are skipped. For example, if Windows 9x will not load properly, you can use an alternate boot method to at least get to a command prompt so that you can determine and troubleshoot the cause of the problem.

There are several boot modes for Windows 9x. To select an alternate boot mode, press F8 at startup, when you see the message "Starting Windows." On some Windows 98 systems, you might be required to press CTRL rather than F8. The two most commonly used alternate boot modes, safe mode and MS-DOS mode, are described in the subsections that follow.

Safe Mode   If Windows 9x contains a bad device driver or a corrupt legacy configuration file, the OS might not be able to load at all. By booting in Safe mode, you can instruct the OS to skip these files on startup. This might allow Windows 9x to load so that you can troubleshoot the problem. For example, suppose the device driver for a NIC is corrupted and is preventing the OS from loading. When you start the computer in Safe mode, the NIC device driver is skipped altogether. That is, the driver is not processed, so the error does not occur.

When the OS boots in Safe mode, the real-mode configuration phase is skipped. That is, legacy configuration files such as AUTOEXEC.BAT and CONFIG.SYS are not processed. Furthermore, the only device drivers to be loaded are the standard mouse, keyboard, and VGA display drivers. Again, you will not have the full functionality of Windows 9x when you boot in Safe mode, but enough of the OS will load to allow you to troubleshoot the problem.

When the OS boots in Safe mode, the text "Safe Mode" will appear in each corner of the monitor to indicate the status. While in Safe mode, you will be unable to access the Network Neighborhood or any mapped network drives.

MS-DOS Mode   In some ways, MS-DOS mode is the opposite of Safe mode. In Safe mode, only the protected-mode configuration files are processed. In MS-DOS mode, only the DOS-based real-mode configuration files, such as AUTOEXEC.BAT and CONFIG.SYS, are processed. You can run Windows 9x in real mode, either by selecting Command Prompt Only from the Startup menu or by selecting Start | Shutdown | Restart in MS-DOS mode.

There are several reasons for starting the computer in real (DOS) mode. For example, some DOS applications, such as games, will not run properly from within a Windows 9x DOS shell. These applications require full control of the hardware, so they cannot be run from Windows. You might also need to start the computer in real mode if the Windows 9x OS is too badly corrupted to start in Safe mode. The DOS mode might allow you to delete problematic utilities or drivers from the hard drive or to reinstall Windows 9x.

There are several other Windows 9x boot modes. These are listed in Table 9-2.

Creating a Startup Disk

In some cases, the Windows 9x OS will be too badly damaged to even present the Startup menu. In these cases, you must have an alternate method for booting the computer. A startup disk is one of the most useful tools you can have in troubleshooting serious OS problems. As described previously, a startup, or boot, disk contains just enough of an OS to provide you with a DOS command prompt.

TABLE 9-2   Windows 9x Boot Modes

Boot Mode	Description
Normal mode	The OS will load normally, using all drivers and registry values.
Logged mode	The OS will load normally and will log boot activities in a text file called BOOTLOG.TXT.
Safe mode	The OS will load with minimal drivers (mouse, keyboard, and standard VGA).
Safe mode with network support	Same as Safe mode but with network drivers and configurations to allow network access.
Step-by-step confirmation	The OS will load normally but will allow you to selectively process or skip individual AUTOEXEC.BAT and CONFIG.SYS lines.
Command prompt only	Begins the boot process normally but stops before the protected-mode boot phase.
Safe mode command prompt only	Loads in MS-DOS mode without the real-mode configuration files. The only files loaded are IO.SYS, MSDOS.SYS, and COMMAND.COM .
Previous version of MS-DOS	Loads an earlier version of DOS than the one that is included with Windows 9x. Can be used only if a previous version of DOS exists on the system.

There are several methods for creating a startup disk for a Windows 9x system. You can create the disk manually or use the Windows 9x startup disk utility. These methods are described in the following subsections.

Creating a Startup Disk Manually   The most important feature of a startup disk is that it is configured to be bootable. To make a floppy disk bootable, you can format it using the system switch, as shown in the following command:

```
FORMAT A: /S
```

Startup disks must contain the core DOS files: IO.SYS, MSDOS.SYS, and COMMAND.COM. As long as these files are loaded, the computer will boot and you will be able to carry out internal DOS commands. Transfer these files, as well as any configuration or external command files that you might need, to the system disk. Common startup disk files include FORMAT.COM, FDISK.EXE, MSCDEX.EXE, SCANDISK.EXE, CONFIG.SYS, and AUTOEXEC.BAT.

on the
job

The MSDOS.SYS file used on a startup disk is different from the MSDOS.SYS file used in the Windows 9x boot process. The startup disk must contain the DOS version, which is responsible for translating commands between COMMAND.COM and IO.SYS. The Windows 9x version of MSDOS.SYS is used only in startup and contains boot parameters, such as how long to display the "Starting Windows" message or which OS to use by default in a dual-boot configuration.

You can also use the SYS command to create a system disk. You can use this command only if the disk is already formatted. When you use the SYS command, the disk is made bootable, and the IO.SYS, MSDOS.SYS, and COMMAND.COM files are copied onto it. You will still be required to manually copy any driver, configuration, or external command files that you want to use.

Finally, you can create a bootable disk using the Windows 9x format utility. Right-click the floppy drive icon in either My Computer or Windows Explorer, then select Format. A window similar to the one shown in Figure 9-3 will open.

If the disk is already formatted, select the "Copy system files only" option. The disk will be marked as bootable, and IO.SYS, MSDOS.SYS, and COMMAND.COM will

FIGURE 9-3 The Windows 9x Format utility window

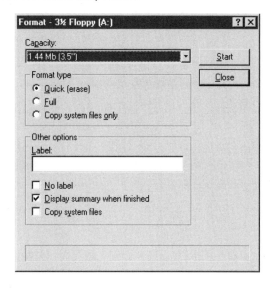

be copied to it. If the disk is not formatted, select the appropriate Format type, then enable the "Copy system files" option. The result will be the same, but the disk will be formatted first. As before, you will need to manually copy external command and driver files onto the disk.

on the job

When creating a startup disk, it's also a good idea to back up SYSTEM.DAT and USER.DAT. However, as long as you are running Windows 9x, these files are in use, so they cannot be copied. You can copy the registry files to the startup disk only if you are using the computer in real mode.

Creating a Windows Startup Disk You can create a Windows 9x startup disk during the OS installation. Simply follow the on-screen procedures when you are prompted to create the disk. Alternatively, you can create a Windows 9x startup disk at any time, once the OS is loaded. To create a startup disk in Windows 9x, follow the steps in Exercise 9-5.

EXERCISE 9-5

Creating a Windows 9x Startup Disk

1. Insert a blank, formatted floppy disk into the floppy drive.

2. Access the Control Panel by choosing Start | Settings | Control Panel or My Computer | Control Panel.

3. Double-click the Add/Remove Programs icon.

4. Click the Startup Disk Tab, then click the Create Disk button. You might be required to insert the Windows 9x installation CD at this time. A progress meter will be displayed.

5. When the process is finished, click OK or Cancel to exit the Add/Remove Programs window.

The startup disk will contain IO.SYS, MSDOS.SYS, and COMMAND.COM. It will also allow you to use external commands such as SCANDISK, FDISK, FORMAT, EDIT, and EXTRACT. Note that you will not see a separate file for each of these external commands, because they are compiled and contained in the EBD.CAB file. If you created the boot disk using Windows 98, the disk will also contain drivers for standard IDE and SCSI CD-ROM drives as well as the AUTOEXEC.BAT and CONFIG.SYS files.

Windows 2000

Windows 2000 cannot operate in real mode, so its boot process is quite different from that of Windows 9x. Furthermore, Windows 2000 provides more powerful troubleshooting and diagnostic boot modes.

Boot Sequence and Required Files

When a Windows 2000 computer is started, the BIOS bootstrap phase is conducted, just as it is in Windows 9x. Following this phase, the MBR locates the bootstrap loader, NTLDR. NTLDR is responsible for initiating and organizing the boot process, much like IO.SYS in Windows 9x. First, it switches the processor into 32-bit protected mode, then locates and reads the BOOT.INI file. BOOT.INI is responsible for providing the boot menu in a Windows 2000 dual-boot configuration.

Once Windows 2000 has been selected or if there are no other OSs in the computer, the message "Starting Windows" will appear on the screen. At this time, NTLDR runs NTDETECT.COM, which detects existing hardware configurations. This is known as the *hardware detection phase*. The information gathered during this phase is placed in the registry via NTLDR. As this process is being conducted, an on-screen bar indicator is displayed to indicate its progress.

When the hardware detection phase is over, the *kernel load phase* begins. This change is evident to the user because the display mode changes from text to graphics. During this phase, NTLDR locates the Windows 2000 kernel (NTOSKRNL.EXE) and loads it into memory. NTLDR then locates the hardware device drivers referenced in the registry. These files are not yet initialized; rather, they are simply located and prepared for initialization by the kernel. The last function of NTLDR is to initialize the kernel and hand it control of the rest of the boot process. The kernel will then initialize the device drivers and load the graphical interface.

Before continuing in the chapter, test your knowledge of the boot processes for Windows 9x and Windows 2000 by answering the following Scenario & Solution questions.

Boot Modes

Like Windows 9x, you can choose alternate boot modes during the Windows 2000 startup. To do so, press F8 when the boot menu is displayed. You'll see the Windows 2000 Advanced Options menu, from which you can select the appropriate boot mode. There are several choices, including Safe mode, Safe mode with networking, last known good configuration, and Debugging mode. A complete list of Windows 2000 boot modes is displayed in Table 9-3. The most commonly used (other than Normal) are Safe mode, Safe mode with command prompt, and last known good configuration.

SCENARIO & SOLUTION	
What is the function of IO.SYS?	To control the real-mode boot and real-mode configuration phases in Windows 9x.
What is the function of NTLDR?	To control the Windows 2000 boot process until the kernel is loaded.
Which Windows OSs load real-mode configuration files at startup?	Windows 95 and Windows 98.

| TABLE 9-3 | Windows 2000 Boot Modes |

Boot Mode	Description
Boot normally	The OS will boot using all drivers and registry values.
Safe mode	The OS will be loaded using Plug and Play drivers as well as standard mouse, keyboard, and VGA drivers only.
Safe mode with networking	Similar to Safe mode, with the inclusion of network settings and NIC drivers.
Safe mode with command prompt	Similar to Safe mode, except that the command-line interface (CMD.EXE) rather than the graphical interface is loaded.
Enable boot logging	Loads the OS normally but also generates a boot log file called NTBTLOG.TXT.
Enable VGA mode	Loads the OS normally, with the exception that a standard VGA driver is loaded.
Last known good configuration	Loads the OS using the registry settings that were generated the last time Windows loaded successfully.
Debugging mode	Allows the computer to be accessed by another computer via the serial port for debugging.

Safe Mode   The Windows 2000 Safe mode is very similar to the Windows 9x Safe mode. That is, the OS will load with minimal drivers and files. Standard drivers will be loaded for the mouse, keyboard, CD, and VGA video drivers. However, unlike Windows 9x, Windows 2000 Safe mode will load Plug and Play drivers. The idea behind this is to isolate problems related to third-party applications and drivers.

Safe Mode with Command Prompt   Because Windows 2000 cannot run in real mode, no MS-DOS mode is available. However, you can elect to load the OS in Safe mode with command prompt. The difference between this mode and regular Safe mode is that a command prompt, rather than the Windows graphical interface, will be displayed. This allows you to use command-line troubleshooting techniques to resolve graphical interface-related problems.

Creating a Startup Disk

The Windows 2000 setup disks also serve as startup disks that you can use to boot the computer when Windows 2000 will not load properly. Four startup disks are required to boot a Windows 2000 machine, and you can create them by entering the following command at the Windows Run line:

```
\BOOTDISK\MAKEBOOT A:
```

Note that the MAKEBOOT command must be executed from the installation CD unless it has been manually copied to the hard disk. When you boot the computer using the Windows 2000 startup (setup) disks, you will be prompted to either install Windows 2000 or repair a failed installation. Press R to select repair. You will then be provided with the option to repair the OS using either the recovery console or the emergency repair process.

The recovery console allows you to access the system's hard drives using basic DOS-like commands to repair the problem. These commands will allow you to move, copy, delete, and expand files. Other commands allow you to format drives, replace the registry from backup, and repair the boot sector or MBR. The emergency repair process is an automated utility that requires the use of an emergency repair disk (ERD). Procedures for creating and using the ERD are described in the following sections.

Creating an Emergency Repair Disk

An emergency repair differs from the recovery console process in that it is an automated process. To perform an emergency repair, start the computer using the Windows 2000 setup disks, elect to repair a failed installation, then choose the emergency repair process. You will then be prompted to select manual repair or fast repair. Fast repair will automatically perform all repair options; manual repair will allow you to select which repair functions to perform.

The repair process includes checking the existence and integrity of boot files, such as NTLDR and BOOT.INI and system files such as NTOSKRNL.EXE. If any of these files are missing or corrupt, they will be replaced by files on the installation CD. The repair utility will also check the integrity of the boot sector and rebuild it if necessary.

To create an ERD, access the Windows 2000 Backup utility and select Emergency Repair Disk from the Welcome tab. It is important to note here that the ERD will contain information about the computer's *current* configuration. If you use an ERD that was created with an older configuration, the repair utility might not function correctly. For this reason, you should create a new ERD each time you change the configuration of the system.

on the
Oob

If you look in the Help system for Windows 98 Backup, you will find instructions for creating ERDs. However, if you follow the instructions, you will see that the option to create these disks doesn't exist. Microsoft has since released technical documents stating that Windows 98 Backup (created by Seagate Software, Inc.) does not support the creation of ERDs. You can, however, create Windows 98 ERDs with the full third-party version of Seagate's Backup utility.

CERTIFICATION OBJECTIVE 9.04

Installing and Configuring Device Drivers and Applications

Depending on the options you select during the Windows installation, several or all of the native Windows utilities and applications will be installed. Furthermore, because Windows supports Plug and Play, a number of device drivers can be installed automatically. However, in many cases, you might want to install native Windows applications or Plug and Play drivers after the OS has been installed. The following subsections describe the procedures you should use, as well as the procedures for installing third-party (non-native) applications and device drivers.

Loading/Adding Device Drivers

In most cases, when you install or attach a new device, Windows will detect it automatically at startup. If the device is Plug and Play, a driver will automatically be installed, and if it is not Plug and Play, you will be prompted to supply the third-party driver. In other cases, Windows will not detect the device, and you will have to prompt Windows to load the driver. These procedures, as well as the procedure for using Device Manager to reinstall an existing driver, are discussed in the following subsections.

Loading Drivers on Startup

Every time Windows 9x starts, it compares the existing hardware in the system to the hardware values stored in the registry. In Windows 2000, information about the existing hardware is gathered and placed in the registry. All devices that have been previously configured in the system will be allocated system resources, and their device drivers will be initialized.

If Windows detects a new device (one that has not previously been configured), you will receive a message stating that Windows found a new device and is installing a driver for it. Windows then checks its driver library for the appropriate Plug and Play driver. If the appropriate driver exists, it will be initialized and loaded in the registry. You will then be able to use the new device. However, if an appropriate driver does not exist in the Windows driver library, you will be prompted to supply the proper third-party driver. Insert the manufacturer's driver disk and select the appropriate drive when prompted. Windows will locate and load the driver.

The Add Hardware Wizard

Anytime you install or attach a hardware device that Windows does not recognize at startup, you must prompt Windows to load the driver or you must load it manually. Many devices come with a manufacturer's setup disk. When you attach the device and restart the computer, run the Setup utility. In most cases, the driver will be installed without the use of the Add Hardware Wizard.

However, some manufacturers' driver disks do not have a Setup program, and sometimes Windows simply doesn't recognize a Plug and Play device at startup. In these cases, you will need to use the Add Hardware Wizard. To do this, access the Add New Hardware utility in the Windows 9x Control Panel or the Add/Remove Hardware utility in the Windows 2000 Control Panel. Follow the instructions in Exercise 9-6 to use the wizard to install a Plug and Play driver in Windows 98.

EXERCISE 9-6

Using the Add New Hardware Utility in Windows 98 to Install Plug and Play Drivers

1. Double-click the Add New Hardware icon in the Control Panel. The window shown in Figure 9-4 will be displayed.

2. Click Next. Windows will inform you that it will search for all new Plug and Play devices in the system.

FIGURE 9-4   The Windows 98 Add New Hardware Wizard.

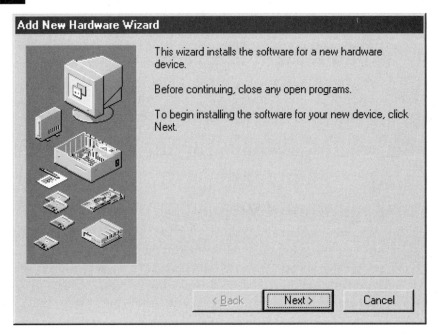

3. Click Next to begin the Plug and Play hardware search. If the device is found, Windows will automatically install the driver for it, and you can skip the remaining steps.

4. If the device is not detected, Windows will report that it can search for all new non-Plug and Play devices. For this exercise, select No. A window similar to the one shown in Figure 9-5 will be displayed.

5. Select the device type from the list, then click Next.

FIGURE 9-5   The Add New Hardware device list.

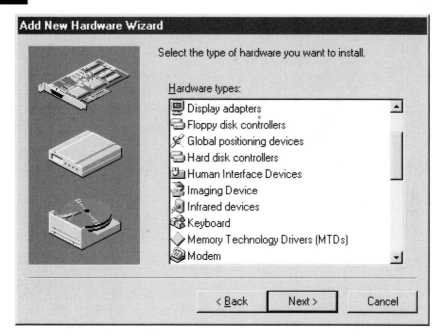

6. A list of supported manufacturers and models of the selected device type will be displayed (see Figure 9-6). The contents of this window will depend on the device type you selected in Step 5. Select the appropriate manufacturer and model, then click Next.

7. Click Finish. Windows will load the appropriate driver for the device. You might be prompted to insert the Windows installation disk at this point.

FIGURE 9-6   The Add New Hardware manufacturer and model selection window.

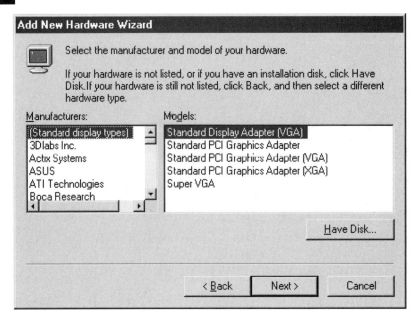

It is only in rare circumstances that you will have to use the Add Hardware Wizard to install drivers for Plug and Play devices. This wizard is more commonly used to install device drivers for third-party (non-Plug and Play) devices that did not come with their own Setup utility. It should be noted that some Plug-and-Play devices may be newer than the OS; therefore, the OS won't yet have the necessary drivers. Follow the steps in Exercise 9-7 to install a third-party driver in Windows 98.

EXERCISE 9-7

Using the Add New Hardware Utility in Windows 98 to Install Third-Party Drivers

1. Double-click the Add New Hardware icon in the Windows 98 Control Panel.

2. Click Next, then click Next again. Windows will search for Plug and Play devices that have not been configured yet.

FIGURE 9-7 Use this dialog box to indicate the location of the third party device driver.

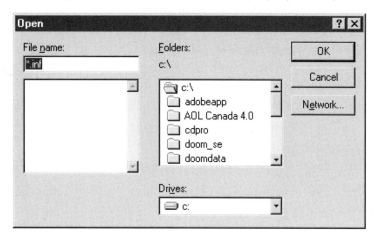

3. You will be asked to choose between letting Windows search for the device or selecting it yourself. For this exercise, choose to select it yourself.

4. Select the proper device type from the Hardware list, and click Next.

5. Click the Have Disk button.

6. Insert the third-party driver disk in the computer, and click the Browse button. A window similar to the one shown in Figure 9-7 will be displayed.

7. Select the drive and path location of the driver, then click OK.

8. Click OK again. The driver will be located and loaded by Windows.

Reinstalling and Replacing Drivers

If a device's driver becomes corrupted, you will need to reinstall it. In some cases, you might want to replace a working driver with another driver. For example, the manufacturer of a device could release an updated driver that is better than the one you are currently using, or you might decide to replace a generic Windows driver with a more sophisticated third-party driver.

To replace or reinstall an existing device driver, use the Windows Device Manager. In Windows 9x and 2000, right-click My Computer, select Properties, click the Hardware tab, then click the Device Manager button.

View the appropriate device's Properties and elect to update the driver. The Update Driver Wizard will launch. Follow the on-screen instructions to replace a bad driver with a good one or to update the driver with one from another location. You might need to restart the computer for the changes to take effect.

Installing and Launching Applications

The main objective in installing an OS is to be able to run applications such as word processors, games, or multimedia applications. In this section, three types of applications are discussed: first, native Windows applications and utilities, then non-native Windows applications, and finally, non-native non-Windows (DOS) applications.

Installing Native Windows Applications

A native Windows application is a program or utility that is included on the Windows installation disk. You can install all or most of these applications by selecting them when you install the OS. However, depending on the installation options you selected, you might later find yourself in need of a Windows application that hasn't yet been installed.

To install a Windows application, double-click the Add/Remove Programs icon in the Windows Control Panel and select the Windows Setup tab. In Windows 2000, click the Add/Remove Windows Components button. A window similar to Figure 9-8 will open. You can use this dialog box to add or remove any native Windows application or utility.

Select the appropriate category, and click Details. All applications and utilities within that category will be listed. Add a check mark beside all applications you want to add, and remove the check mark from all applications you want to remove. Windows will make the appropriate changes. You might be required to insert the Windows installation disk at this time.

Installing Non-native Windows Applications

The majority of applications you use will be designed to run in Windows but will not be part of the Windows OS itself. In these cases, you will need the third-party software manufacturer's installation disk(s). Most applications require more than simply

| FIGURE 9-8 | The Windows Setup dialog box. |

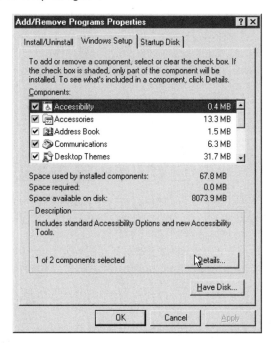

copying files to the hard drive. This is because many application installation disks do not contain the actual application files. Rather, the application files must be compiled, created, or uncompressed during the application's Setup process. Furthermore, many applications must register themselves in the Windows registry. This cannot be done by manually copying files from the installation disk to the computer. You can usually tell if an application has registered itself in the registry, because you will prompted to restart the computer before the application will run properly.

In most cases, you can install an application by running the Setup or Install program that is included on the installation disk. If the installation disk is an autorunning CD, the Setup program will be launched as soon as you insert the CD. Otherwise, access the Setup program by double-clicking its icon in My Computer or Windows Explorer. Application Setup programs differ from one manufacturer to another. Simply follow the on-screen instructions.

You can also install an application using the Add/Remove Programs utility. In the Install/Uninstall tab, click Install. You will be prompted to select the location and setup file for the application. The installation will proceed in the same manner as it would if you had run it from My Computer or Windows Explorer.

Non-native, Non-Windows Applications

Recall that Windows 9x retains the ability to run older DOS applications in real mode. Both Windows 9x and 2000 can run some DOS applications like any other third-party Windows application. That is, they will be run within a DOS shell inside Windows. Special procedures relating to the two types are described here.

DOS Shell Applications   You can alter the appearance and behavior of applications that run in a Windows DOS shell. By modifying the application's Program Information File (PIF), you can configure whether the application runs in a regular window or in full-screen mode. You can also select the font and resolution of text and specify memory access limits for the application. To modify a DOS application's PIF, locate the application's executable file icon in My Computer or Windows Explorer. Right-click the icon and select Properties (see Figure 9-9).

exam
ⓦatch   *An application's executable file is the file responsible for starting (launching) the application and initializing or using the application's supporting files.*

FIGURE 9-9   The DOS application's Properties window allows you to modify its PIF.

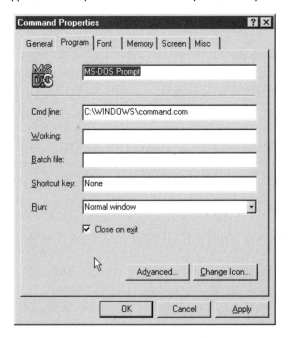

DOS Mode Applications   Some DOS applications cannot be run in a DOS shell and must instead be installed and run in DOS mode. To install the application, use the DIR command to determine the name of the Setup program, then enter the appropriate command to start the installation. For example, if the application's Setup program is SETUP.EXE, enter the command **SETUP** at the command prompt. Note again that Windows 2000 cannot run DOS applications in real mode.

To launch the application, start the computer in MS-DOS mode and enter the command to start the application's executable file. For example, if an application's executable file is GAME.EXE, enter the command **GAME** at the command prompt.

PIF files are used with DOS shell applications only. You cannot use Windows to alter the behavior or appearance of a real-mode DOS application. The behavior and appearance of real-mode DOS applications are configured using CONFIG.SYS.

The Windows Printing Subsystem

One feature of the Windows OSs is that they can control application-generated print jobs. That is, when you print from a third-party application, the print job is handed over to the OS so that the application can continue working on other things. This is an improvement over earlier systems in which each application was in control of its print jobs and could not continue working until the print job was complete. Furthermore, each application had to be configured with the appropriate printer settings.

In Windows, the printing subsystem provides a link between all applications and the printer. Printers are installed and configured in Windows, and every print job is intercepted by the OS and sent to the printer using the defined Windows print settings. Each installed printer will appear in a Printers list in most applications. Simply select the appropriate printer from within the application.

You can view all the installed printers in the system by double-clicking Printers in My Computer or the Windows Explorer or by selecting Start | Settings | Printers. Any printers that are currently unavailable will appear grayed out. This might occur when the printer is turned off, unplugged, or unavailable (if it is a network printer).

Installing and Configuring Printers

Windows includes extensive Plug and Play support for printers. As with other Plug and Play devices, most printers are automatically detected and configured by Windows at startup. However, in the event that you attach a non-Plug and Play printer, you will have to install and configure it manually. To install a printer, follow the instructions in Exercise 9-8. Note that this procedure is specific to Windows 98. The procedure to install a printer in Windows 95 and 2000 is similar but might use different screens.

Installing a Windows Printer

1. Double-click the Printers icon in My Computer or Windows Explorer, or select Start | Settings | Printers. The Printers windows will open (see Figure 9-10).

2. Double-click the Add Printer icon. Click Next to start the Add Printer Wizard.

3. You will be prompted to choose whether this is a local or network printer. Select Local, and click Next (network printers are discussed in the next section).

FIGURE 9-10   The Windows 98 Printers window.

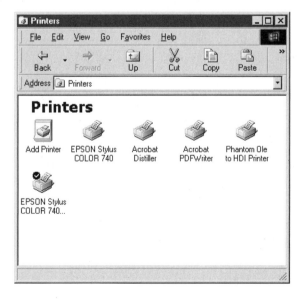

4. Select the manufacturer and model of the printer you want to install, then click Next. At this point, if you do not see your printer listed, click Have Disk and supply the manufacturer's third-party device driver.

5. Select the port to which the printer is physically attached, and click Next.

6. Enter a name for the printer, and choose whether or not this printer will be the default system printer.

7. Click Next.

8. Select whether to print a test page or not, then click Finish. Windows will load the printer's driver or ask you to supply a third-party driver.

on the **Job**

The default printer is the one to which all print jobs will be sent unless you specify otherwise in the application from which you are printing.

When the printer is successfully installed, the Printers window will be displayed with an icon representing all printers in the system (including the new one). The default printer might be indicated by a check mark. To configure a printer as the default, right-click its icon, then select Set as Default.

You can configure a printer's settings by accessing its properties. Right-click the appropriate printer's icon and select Properties. A window similar to Figure 9-11 will open. Note that this window could vary, depending on the printer model.

Depending on the manufacturer's design, you might be able to use this window to set the resolution, paper type, color use, and density of the printer. Many printers also include test and cleaning modes in this window.

An important printer configuration is its spool settings. If spooling is enabled, applications will write print jobs to the hard disk, where they will be picked up and handled by the OS. Again, this allows the applications to resume work on other things more quickly. To configure the printer's spool settings, select the Details tab in the printer's Properties window. The Details window allows you to configure the printer's port and timeout settings. Click the Spool Settings button. The windows shown in Figure 9-12 will be displayed.

Enable spooling by selecting "Spool print jobs so program finishes printer faster." The alternative to spooling is to select the "Print directly to the printer" option. If spooling is enabled, you will be able to select whether the printer begins printing after the first page is spooled or after the last page is spooled.

FIGURE 9-11 The Printer Properties window.

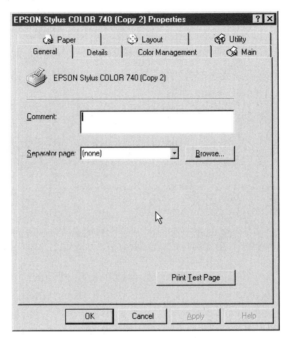

You will also be able to select the spool data format. Enhanced Metafile Format (EMF) is the default Windows graphic-rendering language. When you use EMF spooling, the printing application builds an EMF file representing the print job. Windows sends this file to the printer. The RAW option configures Windows to translate each print job into printer-specific code. RAW printouts look the same as EMF printouts. However, not all printers can print EMF print jobs. When this is the case, you should use the RAW option, although these print jobs will take longer because they must first be translated by the OS into a format the printer can understand.

Network Printing

If Windows is on a network, you can use the OS to access network printers. Recall from Chapter 7 that printers on a network might be true network printers or might simply be local printers that are shared on the network. In either case, their installation and access methods are the same.

FIGURE 9-12   The Windows 98 Spool Settings dialog box.

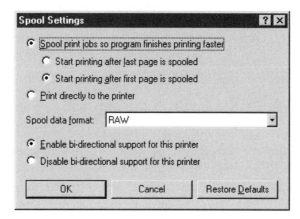

The procedure for installing a network printer is similar to the procedure outlined in Exercise 9-8. If you use that procedure, you will start the Add Printer Wizard by double-clicking Add Printer in the Printers window. However, you can also launch the Add Printer Wizard by using Network Neighborhood to find the printer on the network. Right-click the printer's icon, and select Install.

Within the Add Printer Wizard, you must select Network Printer instead of Local Printer, and you must navigate through the network to locate the proper printer. In some cases, the drivers from that printer or its server will be transferred to your computer. In other cases, you might need to install a third-party driver.

CERTIFICATION SUMMARY

As a computer technician, you will likely be required to set up Windows systems and configure them for use. The Windows installation programs are almost entirely automated, so it is a relatively simple matter to install or upgrade the OS. However, you might need to do some preparation work to partition and format the disks. Furthermore, you must be aware of the procedures for upgrading and dual-booting Windows because these are common OS configurations.

Once Windows is installed, it will be automatically loaded every time you start the computer. You must be familiar with these boot processes so that you can pinpoint and troubleshoot boot problems. For example, if a Windows 9x system is missing the WIN.COM file, you know that the protected-mode boot phase cannot be carried out. If the Windows 2000 BOOT.INI file is corrupted, dual-booting cannot be enabled.

When there is a problem with the boot process, you might be able to start the computer using an alternate boot mode. Safe mode, for example, will boot Windows with minimal drivers in the hopes that the faulty driver will be bypassed so that it cannot halt the boot process. If Windows is too badly damaged to boot in an alternate mode, you can start the computer and try to repair the problem by booting with a boot or startup disk. These disks can be made during the OS installation or within the OS itself.

Equally important to the proper function of Windows is the configuration of device drivers, applications, and printers. Because Windows supports Plug and Play, many devices will be automatically detected and configured at startup. However, you will need to use the Add Hardware utility or a third-party Setup program to install non-Plug and Play drivers. The same is true for third-party Windows utilities. These must be installed using either the manufacturer's Setup program or the Add/Remove Programs utility.

TWO-MINUTE DRILL

Here are some of the key points from each certification objective in Chapter 9.

Installing Windows

❑ When performing a clean install of Windows 9x, you must boot the computer using the Windows boot disks.

❑ Use the FDISK and FORMAT commands to prepare hard disks for Windows 9x installation.

❑ The Windows 2000 installation disk includes its own partitioning and formatting utility, and the CD itself can be used to boot the computer.

❑ Once the hard disk is prepared, install Windows by accessing its Setup program.

Upgrading Windows

❑ When you upgrade from one version of Windows to another, nonsystem files, applications, and configurations are migrated from the old OS to the new.

❑ You can revert from Windows 98 to 95 following an upgrade, but you cannot revert back to Windows 9x or NT after a Windows 2000 upgrade.

❑ To upgrade Windows, start the computer normally, insert the new OS's installation CD, and run the Setup program, ensuring that you select the Upgrade option.

❑ To create a Windows dual boot, start the computer normally and run the Setup program, ensuring that you install the new OS in a different location, or select the New Installation option (rather than the Upgrade option).

Booting Windows

❑ The Windows 9x boot process includes the BIOS bootstrap, real-mode boot, real-mode configuration, and protected-mode boot phases.

❑ Windows Safe mode loads minimal drivers to bypass potential problems and allow you to troubleshoot the OS.

❏ You can create a startup disk by accessing the Windows 9x Add/Remove Programs utility or by entering the Windows 2000 command \BOOTDISK\MAKEBOOT A:.

Installing Device Drivers and Applications

❏ Most Plug and Play devices are detected by Windows at startup and are automatically configured.

❏ Use the Add New Hardware (Windows 9x) or Add/Remove Hardware (Windows 2000) utilities to install third-party device drivers.

❏ Install third-party applications by running their Setup programs or by using the Windows Add/Remove Programs utility.

❏ Install and configure Windows printers using the Printers utility in the Control Panel.

SELF TEST

The following questions will help you measure your understanding of the material presented in this chapter. Read all of the choices carefully because there might be more than one correct answer. Choose all correct answers for each question.

Installing Windows

1. You are planning to partition a hard drive using FDISK. Which of the following can you do?

    A. Create two primary partitions and one extended partition with 14 logical drives.

    B. Create as many partitions as will fit on the drive.

    C. Create NTFS or FAT16 partitions.

    D. Create one FAT16 and one FAT32 partition.

2. A computer has two hard drives installed, each of which has been partitioned using FDISK. The primary hard drive has two primary partitions and one extended partition with two logical drives. The secondary hard drive has one primary partition and two extended partitions, each with one logical drive. Which drive letters will be assigned to the partitions on the secondary hard drive?

    A. D:, F:, H:

    B. E:, H:, I:

    C. G:, H:, I:

    D. This cannot be determined without knowing the order in which the partitions were created.

3. Which file does Windows 9x use to determine nonhardware-related failure points when performing a safe recovery installation?

    A. SETUPLOG.TXT

    B. RECOVER.LOG

    C. DETCRASH.LOG

    D. DETLOG.TXT

4. Which Setup utility does Windows 2000 use when you boot from the Windows 2000 installation CD?

   A. SETUP.EXE

   B. SETUP32.EXE

   C. WINNT.EXE

   D. WINNT32.EXE

5. You are planning to install Windows 2000 on an unpartitioned hard disk, and you have only the Windows 2000 setup disks and the installation CD-ROM. In which order will you perform the necessary installation procedures?

   A. Partition the disk, format the disk, restart the computer, run the Setup utility

   B. Partition the disk, restart the computer, format the disk, run the Setup utility

   C. Run the Setup utility, partition the disk, format the disk, restart the computer

   D. Partition the disk, restart the computer, run the Setup utility, format the disk

Upgrading Windows

6. A customer who currently uses Windows 95 has asked for your advice. He wants better security and networking abilities but is concerned about losing his existing documents and having to reinstall the system's applications. What is your advice?

   A. Back up the applications and files, remove Windows 95 and perform a clean install of Windows 2000, then restore the applications and files.

   B. Create a Windows 95 and Windows 2000 dual-boot configuration.

   C. Upgrade Windows 95 to Windows 98, then create a Windows 98 and Windows 2000 dual-boot configuration.

   D. Upgrade Windows 95 to Windows 2000.

7. You are planning to upgrade Windows 95 to Windows 98, but you are concerned that you might need to revert to Windows 95 if problems occur. Which step must you perform to revert from Windows 98 to Windows 95?

   A. Make sure that you elect to save the system files when prompted during the installation.

   B. Start the computer using the Windows 95 setup disk and choose Revert.

   C. Access the Windows 98 Startup menu and choose Previous Version of Windows.

   D. You cannot revert from Windows 98 to Windows 95.

8. A computer has recently been upgraded from Windows 98 to Windows 2000 but is experiencing problems. Which of the following must you do to remove Windows 2000 and use Windows 98?

   A. Uninstall Windows 2000, ensuring that you select the Restore Previous Operating System option.

   B. Delete Windows 2000 and reinstall Windows 98.

   C. Run the Windows 98 Setup utility and choose to install the OS in the WINNT folder.

   D. Access the Windows 2000 Startup menu and choose Previous Version of Windows.

9. A computer has a Windows 98 and Windows 2000 dual-boot configuration. Which file must you modify if you want to change the options in the system's boot menu?

   A. NTLDR

   B. MSDOS.SYS

   C. IO.SYS

   D. BOOT.INI

10. A computer has a Windows 2000 and Windows 95 dual-boot configuration. Windows 95 was installed first on a FAT32 volume, then Windows 2000 was installed on an NTFS volume. Which of the following is true?

   A. If you boot the computer using Windows 95, you will not be able to access the NTFS volume.

   B. When Windows 2000 was installed, it converted the Windows 95 volume to NTFS.

   C. The computer will not boot properly in this configuration.

   D. You can run Windows 95 from within Windows 2000, but not vice versa.

Booting Windows

11. What is the function of the IO.SYS file in the Windows 9x boot process?

   A. To store dual-boot configuration settings

   B. To initialize and conduct the real-mode boot and configuration stages

   C. To conduct the protected-mode boot stage

   D. To switch the processor into protected mode

12. Which of the following is true of the Windows 9x VMM386.VXD file?

    A.   It is responsible for initiating the protected-mode boot stage.

    B.   It contains Windows 9x 32-bit device drivers.

    C.   It reads the values in the SYSTEM.INI file during the boot process.

    D.   It is included in Windows 98 but not Windows 95.

13. Which of the following occurs when you start a Windows computer in Safe mode?

    A.   The boot process ends with the real-mode configuration stage.

    B.   The computer will provide a command-line interface rather than a graphical interface.

    C.   The Network Neighborhood will be unavailable.

    D.   The Device Manager will be unavailable.

14. Which of the following is not a proper method for creating a boot disk in Windows 9x?

    A.   Use the Backup utility.

    B.   Use the Format utility.

    C.   Use the Startup Disk tab in the Add/Remove Programs utility.

    D.   Use the SYS command in a DOS shell.

15. Which file is responsible for conducting the Windows 2000 boot process before the kernel is loaded?

    A.   IO.SYS

    B.   NTLDR

    C.   BOOT.INI

    D.   NTOSKRNL.EXE

Installing Device Drivers and Applications

16. Which of the following can you use to replace an existing device driver in Windows?

A. The Install/Uninstall tab of the Add/Remove Programs utility

B. The Windows Setup tab of the Add/Remove Programs utility

C. The Device Manager

D. The Hardware Configuration Manager

17. Which of the following is a function of a Program Information File (PIF)?

A. To configure the appearance of applications that run in DOS mode

B. To configure shared files for 32-bit Windows applications

C. To store information about the creation and modification dates of a nonsystem file

D. To configure the memory usage of applications that run in a DOS shell

18. Which of the following is true of the Windows printers?

A. The printer that you plan to use as the default must be installed first.

B. By default, the Printers window in the Control Panel displays only the default printer.

C. Applications can print only to whichever printer is set as the default.

D. The default printer will be used by Windows applications unless a different printer is specified within the application.

19. Which of the following will occur when you enable printer spooling in Windows?

A. Print jobs will be stored on the hard drive by the originating application.

B. The application, rather than Windows, will send the print job to the printer.

C. Windows will poll all printers and send the print job to the first available printer.

D. Print jobs will be processed in the order of the originating application's priority.

20. You have just installed a new printer, but it seems to take a long time for print jobs to start printing once they are sent. Which of the following could help speed up printing?

A. Disable printer spooling

B. Set this printer as the default

C. Set the data format to EMF

D. Reinstall the printer's device driver

LAB QUESTION

Throughout this chapter, a number of differences between Windows 9x and Windows 2000 have been discussed. As a technician, it is very important for you to be familiar with which files, processes, and utilities are associated with which OS. For each of the following items, indicate whether it is specific to Windows 9x or Windows 2000 or used by both.

____ Supports printer spooling

____ Has an Add Printer Wizard

____ Uses FDISK for partitioning

____ The installation file is SETUP.EXE

____ Requires a minimum of 32MB of RAM

____ Can partition the hard disk during OS installation

____ Allows you to create startup disks

____ Allows you to select Typical or Compact installation

____ Can automatically detect and configure Plug and Play devices

____ Can be booted in real mode

____ Can use FAT16 or FAT32 volumes

____ Can be used in a dual-boot configuration

____ Uses four startup disks

____ Can be uninstalled

____ Can be booted in Safe mode

____ Has an Add/Remove Programs utility

____ Uses PIFs to configure DOS applications

____ Allows you to access network printers

____ Uses IO.SYS

____ Loads real-mode configuration files

____ Uses a Windows kernel

____ Allows you to create an ERD

____ Has a Device Manager

SELF-TEST ANSWERS

Installing Windows

1. ☑ **A.** When using FDISK, you can create two primary partitions and one extended partition with 14 logical drives. The maximum number of partitions you can create with FDISK is four, and the number of logical drives you create on an extended partition is limited only by the remaining number of letters in the alphabet. In total, you can create four partitions, and if one is an extended partition, you can create up to 21 logical drives.

   ☒ **B,** create as many partitions as will fit on the drive, is incorrect. Although this is true for partitions in Windows 2000, FDISK is limited to four partitions only. **C,** create NTFS or FAT16 partitions, is incorrect because FDISK can create FAT16 and FAT32 partitions only. **D,** create one FAT16 and one FAT32 partition, is incorrect because FDISK does not allow you to mix file system types on a single drive.

2. ☑ **B.** The partitions on the secondary drive will be given the letters E:, H:, and I:. The system always letters the primary partitions first, starting with the primary drive. Next, the system letters the logical drives, starting with the primary drive. Therefore, the primary drive's primary partitions are given C: and D:. The secondary drive's primary partition is given E:. Next, the primary drive's logical drives are lettered F: and G:. Finally, the secondary drive's logical drives are lettered H: and I:.

   ☒ **A,** D:, F:, and H:, is incorrect because this would be the result of assigning letters equally back and forth from one drive to the next, regardless of partition type. **C,** G:, H:, and I:, is incorrect because this indicates that all partitions on the primary drive are lettered first, followed by the secondary drive. **D** is incorrect because it suggests partitions are lettered according to the order in which they were created. The lettering scheme for primary partitions and logical drives always follows the order described. When you create a new partition, it will be lettered according to this scheme, regardless of current drive-letter assignments.

3. ☑ **A.** Windows 9x uses SETUPLOG.TXT to determine nonhardware-related failure points when performing a safe recovery installation. Thre SETUPLOG.TXT file is generated at the start of the installation process and documents the success or failure of each step. If the installation process fails, you can choose to reinstall the OS. If you choose the safe recovery method, Windows 9x will use the values in SETUPLOG.TXT to determine where the installation failed, then skip that step in an attempt to complete the installation.

☒ **B,** RECOVER.LOG, is incorrect because this file is not generated or used by the Windows 9x installation process. **C,** DETCRASH.LOG, is incorrect because this file is generated during the hardware detection phase of the installation, and is used by the OS to determine which, if any, hardware devices failed to be detected. This file relates specifically to the system's hardware. **D,** DETLOG.TXT, is incorrect because this is the text version of the DETCRASH.LOG file. It is not used by Windows; rather, it is generated by Windows to allow you to view the information contained in DETCRASH.LOG.

4. ☑ **C.** Windows 2000 uses WINNT.EXE when you boot from a CD. By default and unless otherwise instructed, the processor runs in real mode. When you boot from the CD, the processor remains in real mode. Therefore, the real-mode installation utility, WINNT.EXE, is used.

☒ **A,** SETUP.EXE, is incorrect because this is the Setup utility used in Windows 9x, not Windows 2000. **B,** SETUP32.EXE, is incorrect because this is not a valid Windows Setup file. **D,** WINNT32.EXE, is incorrect because this Setup utility is used only if the computer is already running in protected mode. For example, if you run the Windows 2000 installation from within Windows 9x, WINNT32.EXE will be used.

5. ☑ **C.** To install Windows 2000 on an unpartitioned hard disk, run the Setup utility, partition the disk, format the disk, then restart the computer. The Windows 2000 Setup utility will start automatically when you boot the computer using either the Setup disks or the installation CD. You will then be prompted to create and format hard disk partitions. When the disk has been prepared, the computer will be restarted and the Setup process will continue.

☒ **A** and **D** are incorrect because they suggest partitioning the disk first. However, in the Windows 2000 installation, disk partitioning and formatting are part of the Setup and can only be conducted once the Setup utility has been started. **B,** partition the disk, restart the computer, format the disk, run the Setup utility, is incorrect. This procedure is used when installing Windows 9x on an unpartitioned hard disk. That is, you must first partition the disk using FDISK, then restart the computer for the changes to take effect. When the computer restarts, format the partitions, then start the Setup utility.

Upgrading Windows

6. ☑ **D.** Your advice should be to upgrade Windows 95 to Windows 2000. The customer's desire for better security and networking abilities indicates a need for Windows 2000. When you upgrade from one Windows OS to another, applications, nonsystem files, and other settings are migrated into the new OS.

☒ **A** is incorrect because it suggests backing up the applications and other files, replacing Windows 95 with Windows 2000, then restoring the applications and files. Although this procedure might satisfy the need to keep nonsystem files, it will not work for the applications. Most Windows applications must register themselves in the Windows registry. Simply restoring these applications from backup will not ensure their proper function. Furthermore, many applications place files in more than one folder, and it can be almost impossible to determine which files belong to which applications. **B**, create a Windows 95 and Windows 2000 dual-boot configuration, is incorrect. If the user boots in Windows 2000, he will be able to access the files and applications on the Windows 95 volume. However, these applications might not run correctly, because they will not be registered in the Windows 2000 registry. Furthermore, if the user boots to Windows 95, he cannot take advantage of the Windows 2000 OS features. **C** is incorrect because it suggests creating a dual-boot configuration after upgrading Windows 95 to Windows 98. Again, a dual boot is not the best configuration for this user's needs.

7. ☑ **A.** Make sure that you elect to save the system files when prompted during the installation. The Windows 95 installation files will be saved on the hard drive. When you uninstall Windows 98, the Windows 95 system files will be restored. If you do not opt to save the system files, you will be left without an OS when you uninstall Windows 98.

   ☒ **B**, start the computer using the Windows 95 setup disk and choose Revert, is incorrect. There is no Revert option on the Windows setup disks. **C**, access the Windows 98 Startup menu and choose Previous Version of Windows, is also incorrect. There is a startup option that allows you to use a previous version of DOS, but there is no option to use a previous version of Windows. **D** is incorrect because it suggests you cannot return to Windows 95 after upgrading to Windows 98. This is true only for Windows 2000, which does not have an Uninstall feature.

8. ☑ **B.** Delete Windows 2000 and reinstall Windows 98. Windows 2000 does not have an Uninstall feature and does not allow you to save and revert to an older OS the way Windows 9x does.

   ☒ **A**, uninstall Windows 2000, ensuring that you select the Restore Previous Operating System option, is incorrect. Again, Windows 2000 cannot be uninstalled or reverted to a previous OS. **C** is incorrect because it suggests installing Windows 98 over Windows 2000. Windows 2000 will not replace itself with an older version of Windows. **D** is incorrect because it suggests selecting the previous version of Windows in the Startup menu. This is not a Windows 2000 Startup menu option. Furthermore, when Windows 98 is upgraded to Windows 2000, none of the Windows 98 OS is saved by Windows 2000.

9. ☑ **D.** To change the boot menu in a computer with a Windows 2000 dual-boot configuration, you must modify the BOOT.INI file. This file is automatically generated by Windows 2000 and contains settings such as the default OS and countdown time until an OS is selected automatically.

   ☒ **A,** NTLDR, is incorrect because this file is the boot loader and is responsible for organizing and conducting the boot process. However, it does not contain the boot menu parameters. **B,** MSDOS.SYS, is incorrect because this file contains the boot menu in systems that use Windows 9x but not Windows 2000. **C,** IO.SYS, is incorrect because this is the boot loader for Windows 9x. That is, it organizes and conducts the early boot stages of Windows 9x.

10. ☑ **A.** If you boot the computer using Windows 95, you will not be able to access the NTFS volume. Windows cannot recognize NTFS volumes. However, if you boot into Windows 2000, you will be able to see the FAT32 volume because Windows 2000 can recognize FAT16, FAT32, NTFS4, and NTFS5 volumes.

   ☒ **B** is incorrect because it suggests that Windows 2000 converted the Windows 95 volume to NTFS. Windows 2000 does not convert volumes unless specifically instructed to do so. If the computer's volumes were converted to NTFS by the Windows 2000 installation, you couldn't create a Windows 9x dual boot, since Windows 9x cannot recognize NTFS volumes. **C,** the computer will not boot properly in this configuration, is incorrect. Although you cannot guarantee that no problems will exist, the configuration described here is perfectly legitimate. That is, the configuration itself will not be the cause of boot-related problems. **D,** you can run Windows 95 from within Windows 2000, but not vice versa, is incorrect. You cannot run a Windows OS from within another. You can run one *or* the other.

Booting Windows

11. ☑ **B.** The function of IO.SYS is to initialize and conduct the real-mode boot and configuration stages of the Windows 9x boot process. IO.SYS is responsible for locating MSDOS.SYS, SYSTEM.DAT, and other real-mode boot files. Next, IO.SYS locates and processes real-mode configuration files, such as CONFIG.SYS and AUTOEXEC.BAT. IO.SYS then locates WIN.COM and gives it control of the rest of the boot process. This marks the beginning of the protected-mode boot stage.

   ☒ **A,** to store dual-boot configuration settings, is incorrect because this is the function of the Windows 9x MSDOS.SYS file. **C,** to conduct the protected-mode boot stage, is incorrect because this the function of several protected-mode boot files such as WIN.COM and VMM386.VXD. **D,** to switch the processor into protected mode, is incorrect because this function is performed by VMM386.VXD.

12. ☑ **B.** The Windows 9x VMM386.VXD file contains Windows 9x 32-bit device drivers. These drivers are read and loaded into memory during the boot process, and they include devices such as the mouse, the keyboard, and the display adapter.

☒ **A,** it is responsible for initiating the protected-mode boot stage, is incorrect. The protected-mode boot stage begins when IO.SYS locates and runs WIN.COM. From there, WIN.COM is in control of the boot process. **C,** it reads the values in the SYSTEM.INI file during the boot process, is incorrect because this is done by WIN.COM. **D,** it is included in Windows 98 but not Windows 95, is incorrect because both OSs use VMM386.VXD.

13. ☑ **C.** When you start a Windows computer in Safe mode, the Network Neighborhood will be unavailable. Safe mode loads standard mouse, keyboard, and VGA display adapters only. This means the NIC will not be configured, and the computer will not have network access.

☒ **A,** the boot process ends with the real-mode configuration stage, and **B,** the computer will provide a command-line interface rather than a graphical interface, are both incorrect. These describe events that occur when you select the command prompt only or Safe mode command prompt only startup options. In the case of the latter, the boot process will end before the real-mode configuration stage. **D,** the Device Manager will be unavailable, is incorrect. While in Safe mode, you can still access the Device Manager, and if you are troubleshooting a driver problem, this will most likely be the utility you use to resolve the issue.

14. ☑ **A.** You cannot use the Backup utility to create a boot disk in Windows 9x. A boot disk must contain system files, which the Backup will allow you to create. However, boot disks must also be configured to be bootable. The Backup utility will not perform this function.

☒ **B,** use the Format utility, is incorrect. By using the Windows 9x Format utility, you can choose to format a disk *and* make it a system disk, or you can choose to configure it as a system disk without formatting it. **C,** use the Startup Disk tab in the Add/Remove Programs utility, is also incorrect. When you click Create Disk in the Startup Disk tab, the floppy disk will be made bootable, and several system files, external commands, and utilities will be copied onto the disk. **D,** use the SYS command in a DOS shell, is also incorrect. When you use this command, the disk is marked as bootable, and IO.SYS, MSDOS.SYS, and COMMAND.COM are transferred to it.

15. ☑ **B.** The NTLDR file is responsible for conducting the Windows 2000 boot process before the kernel is loaded. NTLDR locates and initializes startup files throughout the boot process. Once the kernel is loaded, it takes over control from NTLDR.

☒ **A,** IO.SYS, is incorrect because this file is used in the Windows 9x boot process but is not used in Windows 2000. **C,** BOOT.INI, is incorrect because this file contains boot menu settings. It is located and initialized by NTLDR. BOOT.INI is not responsible for locating or initializing other startup files. **D,** NTOSDRNL.EXE, is incorrect because this is the file name of the Windows 2000 kernel itself.

Installing Device Drivers and Applications

16. ☑ **C.** You can use the Device Manager to replace an existing device driver in Windows. View the device's properties, and in the Driver tab, select Update Driver.

☒ **A** and **B** are both incorrect because they suggest using tabs in the Add/Remove Programs utility. This utility is used to install applications or Windows utilities, not device drivers. **D,** the Hardware Configuration Manager, is incorrect because this is not a real Windows utility.

17. ☑ **D.** One function of a PIF is to configure the memory usage of applications that run in a DOS shell. By modifying a DOS application's PIF, you can also modify its window size, text font, and text resolution.

☒ **A,** to configure the appearance of applications that run in DOS mode, is incorrect. A PIF is used specifically for configuring the appearance and behavior of DOS applications that are run within Windows, not in DOS (real) mode. **B,** to configure shared files for 32-bit Windows applications, is incorrect. PIFs are associated with non-Windows applications only. **C,** to store information about the creation and modification dates of a nonsystem file, is incorrect. PIFs are used only with non-Windows executable files.

18. ☑ **D.** The default printer will be used by Windows applications unless a different printer is specified within the application. By setting a printer as the default, you are instructing Windows applications to use that printer unless you specify otherwise.

☒ **A,** the printer that you plan to use as the default must be installed first, is incorrect. You can set any printer as the default by right-clicking it and selecting Set as Default. **B,** by default, the Printers window in the Control Panel displays only the default printer, is incorrect. The Printers window displays all printers in the system. **C,** applications can print only to whichever printer is set as the default, is incorrect. Applications can print to any printer in the system, as long as the printer is selected within the application.

19. ☑ **A.** When you enable printer spooling in Windows, print jobs will be passed on to the Windows spooler by the originating application. From there, they will be saved to the hard drive. The application can then resume other functions. Windows will then retrieve the print job from the hard drive, process the job, and send it to the printer.

☒ **B,** the application, rather than Windows, will send the print job to the printer, is incorrect. In fact, this is the opposite of print spooling. When you elect to have applications send print jobs directly to the printer, you disable printer spooling. **C,** Windows will poll all printers and send the print job to the first available printer, is incorrect. Windows will send print jobs to the printer specified within the originating application. There is no option to configure Windows to send print jobs to the first available printer. **D,** print jobs will be processed in the order of the originating application's priority, is incorrect. Print jobs are processed in the order in which they are received by Windows. Applications cannot be given printing priorities.

20. ☑ **C.** Set the data format the EMF. EMF is the default rendering language of Windows. If the data format is set to RAW, Windows must first translate the print job into the printer's native code. This can take longer than sending EMF print jobs, so the print process might appear slow.

☒ **A,** disable printer spooling, is incorrect. If you disable spooling, the application itself, rather than Windows, will control the print job. The print job won't arrive at the printer any faster, and you will lose the ability to work in the application until the print job is finished. **B,** set this printer as the default, is incorrect. The default printer is the one that applications will print to unless otherwise specified. This prevents you from having to select the printer every time you print. The default printer is not given any time priority, so the speed of a print job is unrelated to the printer's status as default. **D,** reinstall the printer's device driver, is incorrect. If the device driver is missing or corrupted, the printer won't work slowly; it will probably not work at all.

LAB ANSWER

For the following items, "9x" indicates the function or feature is specific to Windows 95 and Windows 98; "2000" indicates it is specific to Windows 2000; and "B" indicates it is common to Windows 95, 98, and 2000.

B	Supports printer spooling
B	Has an Add Printer Wizard
9x	Uses FDISK for partitioning
9x	The installation file is SETUP.EXE
2000	Requires a minimum of 32MB of RAM
2000	Can partition the hard disk during OS installation
B	Allows you to create startup disks
9x	Allows you to select Typical or Compact installation
B	Can automatically detect and configure Plug and Play devices
9x	Can be booted in real mode
B	Can use FAT16 or FAT32 volumes
B	Can be used in a dual-boot configuration

2000	Uses four startup disks
9x	Can be uninstalled
B	Can be booted in Safe mode
B	Has an Add/Remove Programs utility
9x	Uses PIFs to configure DOS applications
B	Allows you to access network printers
9x	Uses IO.SYS
9x	Loads real-mode configuration files
B	Uses a Windows kernel
2000	Allows you to create an ERD
B	Has a Device Manager

10

Diagnosing and Troubleshooting

Y ou should now be familiar with the major functions of the Windows operating systems and the procedures they use to boot, run, and maintain computers. However, these procedures can fail, and it is important for you to know how to return the system to a normal functioning state in the event of a failure. A familiarity with the concepts presented in previous chapters is the best tool you can have in diagnosing and resolving OS errors. This chapter will help you use what you already know about Windows to locate and resolve some common OS problems.

Windows OS problems can be related to either boot processes or runtime processes. This chapter presents boot and runtime errors separately, focusing on the most common errors associated with each. As you work through this chapter, note that a majority of the information presented here relates specifically to Windows 9x. Windows 2000 does not support potentially problematic legacy files, and it has been specifically designed to fail less and to automatically recover from many types of errors. For these reasons, Windows 2000 typically requires less troubleshooting than Windows 9x.

CERTIFICATION OBJECTIVE 10.01

Boot Problems

Recall from previous chapters that the Windows 9x and 2000 boot processes are highly coordinated. Each boot file has a specific job, and in most cases, if a required file is missing, in the wrong place, or corrupt, the boot process will not continue. Fortunately, most boot problems can be reliably and easily diagnosed from the behavior of the computer or the error messages you receive. That is, because the Windows boot sequences are so predictable, it is usually quite simple to determine and troubleshoot the problem, as long as you are familiar with the normal boot process. Some common boot problems, along with typical resolution procedures, are discussed here.

Don't forget about the troubleshooting concepts and utilities that were discussed in Chapters 8 and 9. Keep in mind that you can use one of several boot modes in diagnosing and resolving boot errors. Furthermore, you can use utilities such as Automatic Skip Driver, Device Manager, System Configuration Utility, or the System Configuration Editor to resolve boot-related Windows 9x problems.

No Operating System Found

An "Invalid Partition" or "Bad or Missing Command Interpreter" message can occur immediately after the BIOS begins its search for a master boot record, from where it will launch an OS. This error indicates that the BIOS could not find a boot loader file (IO.SYS in Windows 9x and NTLDR in Windows 2000) to give control of the OS boot process. Note that this error might be worded differently, depending on the BIOS itself.

This error can occur if the boot loader file itself is missing or corrupted. In Windows 9x, boot from a startup floppy disk and SYS the boot drive. A good copy of the IO.SYS file on the boot disk will be placed on the boot drive. In Windows 2000, use the startup disks to boot the computer and select to perform a repair. Use the emergency repair process to replace the NTLDR file on the boot drive.

A missing or corrupted NTLDR file in Windows 2000 could also be indicated by the message "BOOT: Couldn't find NTLDR."

This error can also occur if the BIOS cannot find a valid MBR. First, run an antivirus application to be sure you don't have a boot sector virus. If this doesn't work, it may be possible to replace a Windows 9x MBR. To do so, boot from the startup disk and execute the following command:

```
FDISK /MBR
```

This command should update the MBR on the boot drive with a good copy if you have included a backup of MBR on the startup disk. Be aware that using this command can produce unexpected results and cause unrecoverable damage, however FDISK/MBR will not work if you have used the manufacturer's tools to partition the hard drive.

As a last resort, use the drive manufacturer's program to write zeros to the drive. You will find this on their web site.

If the problem persists, it could be due to a hardware problem. That is, the BIOS might not be able to communicate with the boot drive itself. If this is the case, use the hardware troubleshooting procedures discussed in Chapter 3.

CONFIG.SYS Errors

Problems with the CONFIG.SYS file are typically displayed as "Error in CONFIG. SYS Line *xx*" or "There is an unrecognized command in CONFIG.SYS on line *xx*." These messages indicate that the specified (*xx*) line in the CONFIG.SYS file contains an invalid command or parameter or that it references a file that doesn't exist. This error is specific to Windows 9x; Windows 2000 does not use the CONFIG.SYS file.

This is a nonfatal error, meaning that Windows 9x will boot properly, with the exception of the referenced command. When Windows has finished loading, use the System Configuration Editor (SYSEDIT) or Notepad to open and view the CONFIG.SYS file. Count the lines of text to find the line referenced in the error message. If the line contains spelling or syntax errors, make the appropriate changes, save the CONFIG.SYS file, then restart the computer.

If this doesn't solve the problem, look at the command variable itself (usually a filename). Check to ensure that the referenced file exists and is located in the specified path. If the problem persists, enter **REM** at the beginning of the specified line. This instructs the computer to skip over that line, thus avoiding the error message.

AUTOEXEC.BAT Errors

Recall that the AUTOEXEC.BAT file can be used to automatically launch applications or carry out other DOS commands during the Windows 9x startup process. The lines in the AUTOEXEC.BAT file must use the same syntax as commands that you would manually enter at a command prompt. If the AUTOEXEC.BAT file contains an invalid or incorrectly spelled command, an "Invalid Command" message will appear on the screen, just as it would if you manually entered a bad command. If the AUTOEXEC.BAT file references an invalid drive letter, you will receive a "Current drive is no longer valid" error.

These errors are nonfatal, meaning that the OS will continue to load in an otherwise normal manner. When Windows has finished loading, use the System Configuration Editor or Notepad to open the AUTOEXEC.BAT file. Ensure that the existing commands are all valid and spelled correctly. If the problem persists, configure the system to skip over suspect lines by placing the text **REM** at the beginning of the line.

HIMEM.SYS Not Loaded

The "HIMEM.SYS not loaded" error occurs only in Windows 9x startup. Windows 9x requires the presence of the HIMEM.SYS file in the Windows folder to boot properly. If this file is missing, corrupted, or in the wrong location, Windows will not start properly. However, at this point, the computer can run in real (DOS) mode and you will be presented with a DOS command prompt. Follow the steps in Exercise 10-1 to resolve the HIMEM.SYS file problem.

EXERCISE 10-1

Resolving HIMEM.SYS Boot Errors

1. Type the following commands to check the WINDOWS folder for the presence of the HIMEM.SYS file:

```
CD WINDOWS
DIR
```

If HIMEM.SYS is present, proceed to Step 2. If the file is not present, skip to Step 3.

2. The contents of the WINDOWS folder will be listed. If HIMEM.SYS is present, you should assume that it is corrupted (otherwise, the error wouldn't have occurred). To delete the HIMEM.SYS file, enter the following command:

```
DEL HIMEM.SYS
```

3. Insert a floppy disk that contains the HIMEM.SYS file and enter the following commands to copy the file from the disk into the hard drive's WINDOWS folder:

```
A:
COPY HIMEM.SYS C:\WINDOWS
```

4. Restart the computer.

exam
ⓦatch
Although Windows 9x doesn't require the SYSTEM.INI, CONFIG.SYS, and AUTOEXEC.BAT files, it does require HIMEM.SYS. Errors related to this file are fatal, meaning that Windows will not load.

Failure to Start GUI

In some cases, Windows 9x or 2000 could simply fail to load the graphical user interface. This problem might occur due to a missing or corrupted display driver. To determine if this is the cause, restart the computer and boot in Safe mode. A standard VGA driver will be loaded, bypassing potentially problematic third-party, 32-bit video drivers. If the system will boot in Safe mode, use the Device Manager to locate and/or reinstall the nonfunctioning video adapter. If the display driver is not the problem, turn your attention to other potentially corrupt drivers. Devices with corrupt drivers will be indicated in the Device Manager by a warning icon.

Another, more serious cause of a failure to load the GUI is a missing or corrupted GUI file. That is, during startup, Windows could simply be unable to load a file responsible for producing the interface, such as GDI.EXE or the Windows kernel. If you are using Windows 2000, restart the computer with the boot disks and try to repair the problem using the emergency repair process.

If the problem persists or if you are using Windows 9x, reinstall the operating system. To do this, boot from the Windows startup disk(s) and install the OS in the same location as the nonworking OS. Setup will overwrite the Windows system files while leaving other files and applications intact. Note that you will lose all OS-related configurations such as screen colors and Windows network settings.

Safe Mode

As discussed in Chapter 9, both Windows 9x and Windows 2000 can run in Safe mode. This is an excellent diagnostic tool, and you can use it by selecting Safe Mode from the Windows Startup menu (Windows 9x) or advanced startup options (Windows 2000). However, if Windows detects a potentially fatal driver error on startup, it might boot in Safe mode automatically. This action is typically accompanied by a message indicating the source of the problem. Use the Device Manager to find nonfunctioning hardware and to replace bad drivers. If you are using Windows 9x and suspect a problem with a 16-bit driver, use the System Configuration utility to bypass suspect 16-bit drivers, then restart the computer.

Windows Protection Errors

Windows protection errors occur during startup, before the GUI is loaded, when a 32-bit virtual driver fails to load. The failed driver will typically be indicated along with the error message. Restart the computer in Safe mode. If the OS loads properly, use the Device Manager to reinstall corrupted or missing drivers. If you are using Windows 9x and cannot determine which driver is at fault, restart the computer using step-by-step confirmation. This choice will allow you to select which drivers to process and will allow you to view the success or failure of each. Once you have determined the source, replace the driver.

If the OS will not load in Safe mode, there could be an error with the standard VGA driver or another Safe mode device driver. You will need to replace the driver by copying it from the installation disk into the WINDOWS\SYSTEM folder. If you are using Windows 9x, you can do this using the EXTRACT command from the boot disk. If you are using Windows 2000, boot from the startup disks and select the Repair option.

A Device Referenced in SYSTEM.INI or Registry Could Not Be Found

During Windows 9x startup, you could receive a message stating "A device referenced in SYSTEM.INI or registry could not be found" or "The Windows registry or System.ini file refers to this device file, but the device file no longer exists." These messages indicate that a file or device is listed in the SYSTEM.INI file or registry but Windows could not find it. For example, the SYSTEM.INI file could refer to a driver called DRIVER.DRV. If Windows cannot find DRIVER.DRV, one of these messages will be generated. The most common cause of this problem is that an application or device has been removed from the system, but references to it have been left in either the SYSTEM.INI file or the registry.

These errors are typically nonfatal, meaning that the computer will continue to boot after the error. When the error occurs, note the referenced file or device. If this file is required for a device or application in Windows 9x, use SYSEDIT or Notepad to open SYSTEM.INI. Determine where the referenced file should be located. Next, check for the presence of that file in the proper location. If it doesn't exist, reinstall or copy it. If it does exist, it might be corrupted and will have to be replaced. When you are finished, restart the computer.

If the problem persists or if the referenced file is not needed, open the SYSTEM.INI file and place a semicolon (;) in front of the line referencing the problem file. This symbol instructs Windows to skip over that line during startup. If the problem still persists or if you are using Windows 2000, you might need to look at registry entries. Before you open the registry and remove or change entries, make a backup copy of the registry that you can restore if more serious problems occur. Use the Registry Editor to search for and remove the referenced entries.

on the
job

One of the most common causes of this referencing error is deleting an application rather than uninstalling it. When you uninstall an application, its files are removed from the computer, its references are removed from the registry and SYSTEM.INI files, and its listing in the Programs menu is removed. If you simply delete an application's files, these references remain in the system. You should always remove applications using the manufacturer's uninstall utility or the Windows Uninstall utility, located in the Add/Remove Programs dialog box.

Corrupted Swap File

Recall that Windows 9x and 2000 can use space on the hard drive to store temporary data that will not fit in regular RAM. This space is the swap file, and it can become corrupted just like any other file on the hard drive. When there is a swap file problem, you will typically be notified by a "Swapfile Corrupt" error message. However, swap file problems can also manifest themselves as other problems, such as a system that frequently "hangs," or locks up.

Fortunately, corrupt swap file problems are easy to resolve. If Windows is configured to use a swap file but one doesn't exist, Windows will automatically generate it at startup. To force Windows 2000 to generate a new swap file, simply reboot the system. In Windows 9x, boot the computer using a boot disk (so that Windows doesn't load), locate the existing swap file, and delete it. This file is called WIN386.SWP in Windows 9x. To adjust the swap file, double-click on the System Control panel and select the Performance tab, then Virtual Memory. Once the file is deleted, restart the computer. Note that corrupted files sometimes indicate a failing hard drive. Run Scandisk to locate and eliminate other disk-related problems.

Your knowledge of the information presented in the preceding subsections should allow you to provide solutions to the following Scenario & Solution questions.

SCENARIO & SOLUTION

What does the "No Operating System Found" error message indicate?	The boot loader file cannot be accessed. Try replacing it (IO.SYS in Windows 9x and NTLDR in Windows 2000). This problem could also be caused by a bad MBR or bad hard drive connection.
The HIMEM.SYS file is missing. What should I do?	Boot from a startup disk and copy a good version of the HIMEM.SYS file from the floppy disk to the C:\Windows folder.
The swap file is corrupted. What should I do?	In Windows 9x, delete the file (WIN386.SWP). When you restart the computer, Windows will automatically rebuild the swap file. In Windows 2000, restart the computer.
A legacy configuration file contains an error. What should I do?	Windows should continue to load normally. Use SYSEDIT to view the file. Ensure that the device or command is valid and that its parameters are correct. If the device is no longer needed, remove the line that is causing the error.

exam
ⓦatch

It might seem like a trick, but it really is this simple: All you have to do to resolve a swap file error in Windows 9x is delete the existing swap file and restart the computer. Don't dismiss "Delete the swap file" as the correct answer on the exam simply because it sounds too easy.

In Windows 2000, it's not necessary to delete the swap file, as rebooting will generate a new one.

CERTIFICATION OBJECTIVE 10.02

Runtime Problems

Unlike boot problems, runtime problems can be quite difficult to diagnose. The problem could be inherent in the OS, the result of a recently conducted runtime operation, or the result of a user error. Some runtime problems are quite common, so they are easy to troubleshoot. However, the causes of most runtime problems will not be immediately apparent, and you will need to do some detective work to determine the cause. This section begins with basic troubleshooting guidelines and steps you can use to determine a problem's source. The section follows up with ways to resolve common problems once you have found their sources. Note that these procedures do not apply to Windows boot problems.

Diagnosing Problems

In some cases, the cause of a runtime error could be apparent from the error message displayed by Windows. In other cases, the error message might simply state that there has been an error, without indicating the potential source. A problem could even take the form of a nonfunctioning or locked-up component that is not accompanied by an error message. Whenever you must resolve a problem for which the cause is unfamiliar, you must do everything you can to narrow it down before troubleshooting. This will be easier to do if you establish some basic fact- finding and troubleshooting guidelines and stick to them.

The following subsections provide basic guidelines for you to following in determining the cause of common Windows problems. The procedures for troubleshooting printer problems are quite different from troubleshooting system problems, so they are presented individually later in the chapter.

Gathering Information

The first step in determining the cause of a Windows runtime error involves gathering as much information as you can about the problem. Ask the customer what happened to indicate an error. For example, did an application lock up, or is the system refusing to launch a utility? Ask the customer about the presence and content of error messages. This could be an excellent clue to the cause of the problem. For example, if the user can't save to the floppy drive and Windows produced a "Device is not ready" error, you will have pinpointed the source of the problem. Unfortunately, other messages, such as "Illegal operation," are more vague.

If possible, ask the user to reproduce the problem. That is, have him or her perform the procedure that brought on the problem. This will allow you to see error messages that the user might not have noticed or remembered; it will also allow you to watch the sequence of events that caused the problem. As the user reproduces the error, pay attention to the techniques he or she uses, because these could be the cause of the error. Is the user trying to save a file to the Recycle Bin? Or is he or she perhaps impatient and overloading the OS by clicking and double-clicking items too quickly?

It is also important to determine whether there have been recent changes to the system. For example, an application that worked normally until a virus scan utility was installed is most likely being affected by the virus scan utility.

General Troubleshooting Procedures

Sometimes the information you gather from the customer is sufficient to pinpoint the cause of an error. However, this is not always the case. If the error persists or if you have not yet determined its cause, restart the computer. It is not uncommon for applications to exit improperly, thus tying up resources that other applications are trying to access. By restarting the computer, you will clear the system's RAM and possibly put an end to the problem.

Once the computer has restarted, try again to reproduce the problem. This might help you determine if the problem occurs at random or with regularity. For example, does the screen go blank at random, or does it happen every time a particular application is started? If the problem persists, reboot the computer in Safe mode. If the problem does not occur in Safe mode, you can start looking at 16-bit configuration files as the cause.

Next, determine the components that are involved in the problem. That is, try to determine whether the problem is limited to a single utility or perhaps to a specific function within all applications. For example, if a utility won't start, try to start another utility. If one application won't import images from the scanner, try to access the scanner from another application. If a program won't save to the floppy drive, try to save from another application, or use the original application to save to a different drive.

If the problem seems to stem from a particular device, check its configuration in the Device Manager and ensure that the driver is not corrupted. (Refer to Chapter 3 for more hardware-related troubleshooting procedures.) If the problem seems to occur within a single application, uninstall it, then reinstall the application. If the problem persists, check with the application's manufacturer for bug fixes or patches, because the problem could be caused by an error within the application itself.

If the problem is more widespread or if the OS will not run at all, try reinstalling the OS itself.

Windows Troubleshooting Utilities

Windows includes several troubleshooting utilities that can help you quickly and easily pinpoint the causes of some problems. Some of the utilities described here can even help you resolve problems. Again, refer to Chapter 8 for information on other Windows utilities that can help you diagnose and resolve runtime errors.

Dr. Watson   Windows 9x and Windows 2000 include a utility called Dr. Watson, which can help you pinpoint the causes of errors in running applications. When an error occurs or when the program is initiated by the user, Dr. Watson takes a "snapshot" of the system's current configuration (see Figure 10-1). This information includes all currently running applications and tasks as well as currently loaded device and user drivers. Also included is a Diagnosis tab, where Dr. Watson will indicate error information such as which program experienced the error, which program caused the error, and which memory address was the site of the error.

FIGURE 10-1

The Windows 98
Dr. Watson utility.

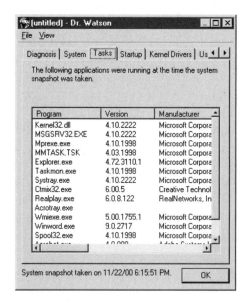

The Dr. Watson snapshot can be saved as a log file so that you can refer to it at a later time. Dr. Watson does not run automatically when you start Windows, so when an error occurs, you must initiate the utility right away to get an accurate record of the system's configuration. Note that some applications start the Dr. Watson utility automatically when you run them. Once Dr. Watson is running, it will continue to monitor application performance and can automatically inform you when an error occurs. Follow the steps in Exercise 10-2 to start Dr. Watson, take a system snapshot, and log the details in Windows 98.

EXERCISE 10-2

Using Dr. Watson to Log System Details

1. Select Start | Programs | Accessories | System Tools | System Information.

2. In the Tools menu, select Dr. Watson. An icon will appear in the taskbar to indicate that the Dr. Watson utility is running.

3. Double-click the Dr. Watson icon in the taskbar. The utility will create a snapshot of the system's current configuration and running applications and

FIGURE 10-2

The Windows 98
Dr. Watson
Diagnosis screen.

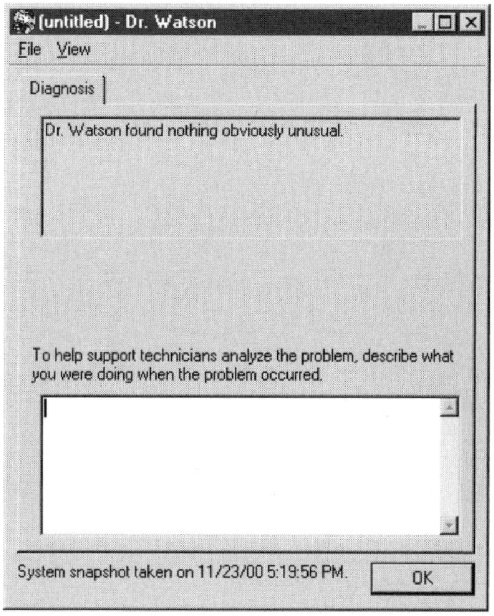

will open a window similar to the one shown in Figure 10-2. Note that in this case, no problems were detected.

4. Click the View menu and select Advanced View. The tabs displayed in Figure 10-3 will become available. You can click each of these tabs to view system details.

5. In the File menu, select Save As.

6. Select the path C:\Windows\Drwatson and enter a name for the snapshot.

7. Click Save. You can later open this snapshot by selecting Open Log File from the File menu.

To start Dr. Watson in Windows 2000, select Start | Administrative Tools | Computer Management | Tools | Dr. Watson. The alternative to starting Dr. Watson manually is to place the utility in the Windows Startup folder so that it launches automatically every time you start Windows.

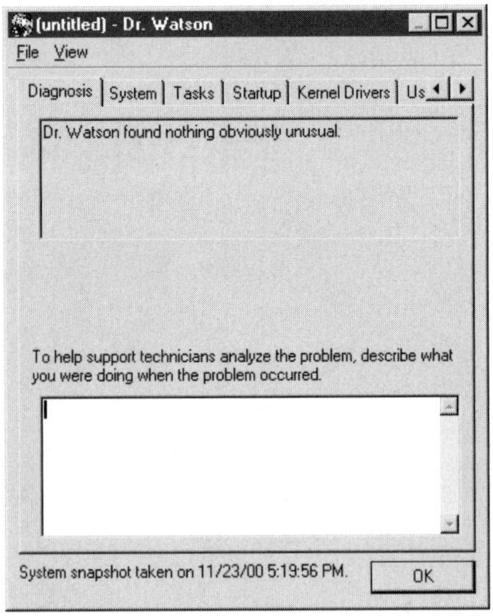

FIGURE 10-3

Windows 98
Dr. Watson
Advanced view.

Event Viewer   Windows 2000 includes a utility called the Event Log service. This service starts automatically when Windows 2000 loads and keeps three separate activity logs: a system log, an application log, and a security log. The system log records system-related events such as driver loading and display changes. The application log records application-specific activities such as loading, saving, and file access. The security log is available only to system administrators and records events such as log-on attempts and failures and network resource access attempts.

Each logged event is accompanied by the date and time as well as the event type (error, warning, information, success or failure notations). In the event of a problem, you can use the Windows 2000 Event Viewer to read these logs and see the events and tasks leading up to the problem. To open the Event Viewer, select Start | Programs | Administrative Tools | Event Viewer.

As well as reading the event logs, you can use the Event Viewer to set the log size, save logs, clear current entries in the logs, and select what happens when the log becomes full. In most cases, older events are replaced in the logs by newer events as they occur. However, you can configure the log service to display an error message when the log is full. This allows you to save the log before old items are overwritten with new items.

Common Runtime Problems

Every OS problem can be resolved. Whether it involves replacing a missing file or reinstalling the entire OS, you can get the system up and running again. The more familiar you are with the normal function and processes of the OS, the easier it will be to determine the source of a problem and repair it. You must also be familiar with the procedures described so far in this chapter and the troubleshooting techniques and tools described in this and previous chapters. However, you can save some time in troubleshooting Windows OS problems by familiarizing yourself with some of the most common problems and their resolutions.

General Protection Faults

A *general protection fault (GPF)* occurs when an application attempts a procedure that could compromise another application or the OS itself. GPFs can occur in Windows 9x and Windows 2000 when an application attempts to access a corrupted driver. More often, GPFs occur when an application attempts to directly access the system's hardware or to use memory space that is already being used by another application. These behaviors are typically limited to older 16-bit (real-mode) applications, unless the application has internal flaws.

When the computer experiences a GPF, a blue screen will appear, with white text outlining the nature of the problem. Unfortunately, GPF messages are typically cryptic and offer you no help in pinpointing the cause of the problem. Furthermore, GPF errors are often fatal on a systemwide scale. Under ideal conditions, a GPF error should result in the termination of the offending program only. However, in most cases, GPFs cause fatal OS errors, requiring you to restart the computer. The causes of GPFs can be obscure, and if the error never occurs again, you will probably never know what caused it in the first place.

You should, however, try to restart the offending application. If the GPF occurs again, reinstall the application. Note that the GPF can be localized within a particular application. For example, it might occur only when you try to access a particular printer from a particular program. If reinstalling does not resolve the problem, check with the manufacturer for a patch.

Illegal Operation

Illegal operations are caused in Windows 9x and 2000 when an application asks the OS to perform a function that cannot be carried out. This could be due to an error (bug) in the application's code, or it might occur when the application tries to access a corrupted system file. When an illegal operation occurs, a dialog box will appear with an error message, such as "This program has performed an illegal operation and will be shut down." You can click the Details button to view messages about the cause of the error. Like GPF messages, illegal operation details can be cryptic. For example, one illegal operation associated with Microsoft Internet Explorer is "Exception: access violation (0xc0000005), Address: <address>."

The only other option in the Illegal Operation dialog box is Close. When you click this button, the offending application will be shut down. In most cases, the OS and other applications will continue to function normally. Try to reproduce the error. Some illegal operations result from a very specific set of circumstances and will not be repeated. However, if the error persists, restart the computer. If you continue receiving illegal operation errors, try to resolve the problem by reinstalling the application.

In most cases, illegal operations are application specific, so you might have to check with the manufacturer of the application to solve the problem via a patch or an upgrade. Additionally, the Microsoft Web site contains an extensive list of known illegal operation causes in a variety of applications. When an illegal operation occurs, note its details, then search for its cause and resolution in Microsoft's Knowledge Base at http://search.support.microsoft.com/kb/c.asp.

exam
ⓦatch

Don't confuse GPFs with illegal operations. The main difference between the two is that GPFs occur when an application tries to perform a function that can disrupt or damage another application or device, such as taking over its memory space or trying to access the hardware directly. Illegal operations occur when an application tries to perform an operation that simply cannot be carried out, due to a corrupted file or an incorrect path. Both error types are often caused by bad code within the application itself.

Invalid Working Directory

When you first launch an application in Windows 9x or 2000, you might receive an "Invalid Working Directory" error. The application's working directory is typically the location in which the application itself is located. The application can use the working directory to create and save temporary files, create default backups, and look for other application files it might need to call during normal operation. The "Invalid Working Directory" error indicates that the working directory does not exist. This problem occurs most often if the working directory is located on a network to which the computer currently has no access. However, this error can also occur if you accidentally move or delete the application's working directory.

If the working directory has been accidentally moved or deleted, simply recreate it or place it in the proper location. If the working directory requires a network connection, wait until the computer can access the network, or change the working directory to a location on the local computer. To view and change an application's working directory in Windows 98, perform the steps listed in Exercise 10-3. Note that not all applications use a working directory.

Changing an Application's Working Directory

1. Right-click the Start button and select Open, or open the C:\Windows\Start Menu folder.

2. Navigate through the Programs folder until you have located the proper application shortcut.

3. Right-click the shortcut's icon and select Properties.

4. Select the Shortcut tab. A dialog box similar to the one shown in Figure 10-4 will appear. Note that in this example, the WinZip application has been selected.

5. View and modify the entry in the "Start in:" field. This is the application's working directory.

6. Click OK when you are finished. Note that Windows will not allow you to enter a working directory that doesn't exist.

FIGURE 10-4

An application's working directory is displayed in the "Start in:" field.

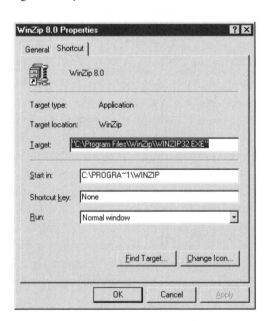

System Lockup

System lockups are one of the most common application/OS errors. They are characterized by an application or an entire system that appears "frozen" or "hung up." In some cases, you might not even be able to move the mouse pointer. System lockups can be caused by a variety of things, including a poorly written application or an application's attempt to access a corrupted or temporarily unavailable file or resource.

If a single application hangs, you can usually close it using the Windows Task Manager. Follow the steps in Exercise 10-4 to close an unresponsive application in Windows 98.

EXERCISE 10-4

Using the Windows 98 Task Manager to close an unresponsive application

1. Press CTRL+ALT+DEL on the keyboard. A dialog box similar to the one shown in Figure 10-5 will appear. Note that in this case, the hung application (Microsoft Word) is identified by the message "Not responding".

2. Select the application you want to close, and click End Task. The dialog box shown in Figure 10-6 will appear.

FIGURE 10-5

The Windows 98 Task Manager allows you to close unresponsive applications.

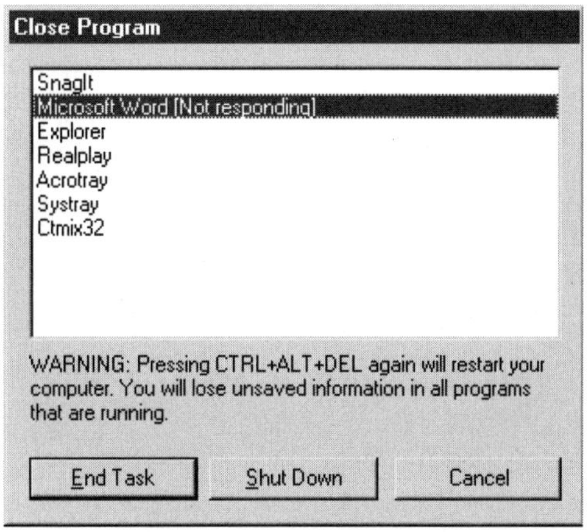

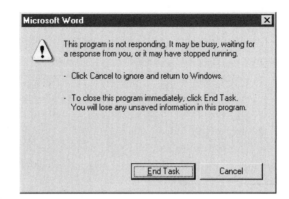

FIGURE 10-6

This dialog box informs you that the selected application is not responding.

3. Click End Task. The Task Manager and the offending application will close and the computer should return to a normal state.

In some cases, a hung application will continue to affect the entire system after you close it. That is, you could notice increased performance degradation. This situation typically occurs if the hung application's resources were not returned to the system once the application was shut down. The Windows 2000 Task Manager includes a more sophisticated tool for ending not only applications, but any other processes that might have been spawned by the unresponsive application (see Figure 10-7).

If the entire system is locked up, you need to restart the computer. You can do this by selecting Shut Down in the Windows Task Manager. If this doesn't work, or if you cannot open the Task Manager window, restart the computer manually, using the power or restart button.

When the computer has restarted, open the offending application and try to reproduce the error. In many cases, an application lockup stems from a very specific state and order of events, and you might not be able to reproduce it. If the application continues to hang, reinstall the application. Again, some applications simply lock up because they contain bugs. For example, Microsoft Word 2000 invariably locks up when you close a large document and elect to save the file when prompted. In cases like these, check with the manufacturer for an application patch.

FIGURE 10-7

FIGURE 10-7

The Windows
2000 Task
Manager allows
you to end
applications
and individual
processes.

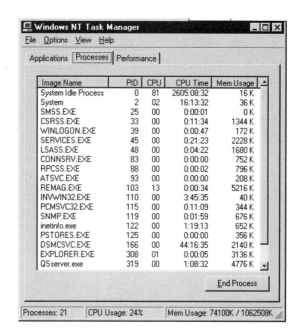

Option Will Not Function

Whenever a computer device doesn't function, examine its configuration in the OS before troubleshooting the hardware itself. First, retry the device, because it might have been busy when you first tried to access it. Next, close and restart the host application and try to access the device again. Try to access the device from another application. These steps can help you pinpoint whether the problem is caused by the device or the application.

If the application is at fault, restart the computer. If the problem persists, check the application's settings for accessing the device. For example, if you are trying to access a scanner, ensure that the imaging application is configured to access the proper device and that it is using valid scan settings for that device.

If the problem is not limited to a single application, check the device's configuration in Windows. Use the Device Manager to determine if there is a resource or driver problem. If the Device Manager indicates an error, you might need to reinstall the device driver.

If the Device Manager doesn't indicate a driver problem, or if reinstalling the driver doesn't resolve the problem, restart the computer. If the device still doesn't work, use the Device Manager to remove the device's configuration from the system. That is, select the device and click Remove. Restart the computer, then reinstall and reconfigure the device. If you are using Windows 2000, restart the computer using the Last Known Good Configuration option in the Windows 2000 Advance Options menu. The OS will load with a previous configuration in which the device might have worked.

Applications Don't Install

In some cases, an application installation will halt before the installation is complete. You might receive an error message, or the installation could simply stop. The first thing you should do is check the application's minimum computer and OS requirements. For example, if there is not enough memory or if the OS is too old, you will be unable to install or run the application. If the minimum requirements are met, restart the computer. This will free any resources or memory space that the installation utility requires.

Next, ensure that all other applications are shut down, because they could interfere with the installation process. You should also check for and shut down applications and utilities that are running in the background. These applications are often referred to as *terminate and stay resident (TSR)* applications because they continue to work even if they do not have an open and active window. TSRs include Windows and third-party monitoring utilities or virus scan programs. You can check for and close any running TSRs using the Windows Task Manager.

If the application still won't install, double-check the manufacturer's recommended installation instructions. Next, check the installation disk itself by using it to install the application on another computer. If the installation works, you can be confident that the problem is caused by the original computer, not the application itself. Finally, check with the manufacturer for known installation problems and obtain a patch or upgrade if necessary.

Application Will Not Start or Load

If an application will not start, you must determine whether the application has worked before or has just been installed. If the application has just been installed, it is likely that the problem lies within the application itself. If the application has worked before, you might need to look at other applications in the system or at the OS itself as the cause of the problem. In either case, watch the screen for error messages; these could provide you with important clues, such as insufficient resources, invalid working directory, missing .EXE file, or expired trial period.

The Application Has Worked Before   If the application has worked before, you should first restart the computer. Doing so will release the system's resources and free memory space that the application might need in order to load properly.

If the application still won't start, ensure that all required hardware or network resources are available. Next, determine whether the computer's configuration has been changed recently. If, for example, this problem started only after you installed a new device or another application, you can assume the problem and that installation are related. In this case, check the configuration of the other application or device, and focus your attention on troubleshooting it, not the original application, as the cause of the problem.

exam
ⓦatch   *One of the most common solutions for an application load failure is to reboot the computer.*

If the computer's configuration has not changed, reinstall the application. This will cause any corrupted application files to be replaced by working files from the installation media. If the application still won't start properly, check with the manufacturer for known causes of this problem, and obtain a patch or application upgrade if necessary.

The Application Has Just Been Installed   If you have just installed an application and can't get it to start, chances are that the problem lies within the application itself. You should first restart the computer. Many applications must make registry updates to function properly, and restarting the computer will force the OS to initialize those registry settings.

Next, ensure that the computer and the OS meet the minimum requirements for the application. If so, try reinstalling the application, and use the manufacturer's documentation for instructions on specific configuration or installation settings. If the application still won't run, treat this as you would a failed installation, as described above.

ⓦatch

Applications that won't start or install can be caused by other existing problems in the system, such as a file that has suddenly become corrupted or hardware that is configured incorrectly.

Cannot Log On to Network

Computer networks are complex entities, and a failure to log on properly can be caused by a variety of things. First, however, note any error messages that are displayed. If you are using an incorrect password, for example, try retyping it, and ensure that the Caps Lock feature is not enabled on the keyboard. If you have forgotten your password or if the password is otherwise not working, you will need the system administrator to reset it for you.

You might also be unable to log on to a network if the computer has been configured to use network resources that are already in use by another computer. Check the network configuration settings to ensure that the IP address or network ID (if used) is unique. Also ensure that the computer name is unique and that the proper workgroup or domain name is configured, if required.

If you are still unable to log on to the network, there is a more serious problem, such as an absent network connection or bad Windows network configuration. Refer to Chapters 7 and 11 for more information on troubleshooting network problems.

Use your knowledge of the concepts presented in this section to answer the following Scenario & Solution questions.

SCENARIO & SOLUTION

What causes GPFs?	GPFs occur when an application tries to perform an activity that would compromise the data or integrity of another application, such as trying to take over its memory space.
How do illegal operations affect the system?	They are typically limited to a single application. However, they could cause the gradual degradation of the system after the offending program has been closed.
What should I do if an application keeps causing errors, even after I have reinstalled it?	There could be a problem (bug) in the application itself. Check with the manufacturer for known errors and patches.

Windows-Specific Printing Problems

Recall that Windows has a printing subsystem in which all printers are configured, accessed, and monitored by the OS rather than by individual applications. This section focuses on troubleshooting printer problems related to this printing subsystem. (Connection and device-related printer problems are discussed in Chapters 3 and 6.)

Print Spool Is Stalled

When printer spooling is enabled in Windows, applications send print jobs to a spooler, which in turn saves the print jobs to the hard disk. This method allows the application to return to other functions more quickly and allows Windows to hold print jobs in a queue until the printer is available. However, the print spool can become stalled so that a print job, and all print jobs submitted after it, will not print.

Unfortunately, spool errors are not indicated by error messages. Rather, you will probably become aware of a spool problem only if a print job gets sent but is not printed. If the print job is large or contains a lot of high-resolution graphics, simply wait. It could take a long time for the print job to spool. However, if the job is not printed after an excessive amount of time, you should begin troubleshooting. The first thing you should do is access the Printer Properties window. You can do this by double-clicking the printer's icon in the Control Panel. A window similar to the one in Figure 10-8 will appear.

Each pending print job will be listed here, and its status will be indicated in the Status column. If the spool is stalled, right-click the print job marked "Spooling," and select Cancel Printing from the shortcut menu. The print job's status will be

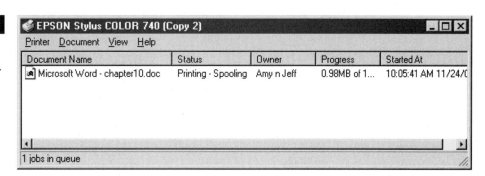

FIGURE 10-8

A Typical Windows Printer Properties window.

listed as "Deleting" and the job will be removed from the queue. This should allow other print jobs to continue normally.

Once you have cleared a print job from a stalled spool, try to print it again. If the spool continues to stall, restart the computer and the printer. If the problem continues, defragment the hard drive and ensure that there is at least 10MB of free hard drive space for spooled files.

If the problem continues, change the spool setting from EMF to RAW. (Refer to Chapter 9 for details about changing the spool settings.) You might also need to disable the spooling option. This action will instruct applications to print directly to the printer, thus bypassing the print spool altogether.

Incorrect or Incompatible Driver

The drivers for system printers are configured and managed by Windows. If a printer is configured to use the wrong driver, it will not print. Check the Device Manager for configuration problems. If the driver is corrupted or missing, reinstall it. Third-party manufacturer drivers are recommended over generic Windows drivers for Plug and Play printers. If the problem persists, remove the printer from the Device Manager and restart the computer. If the printer is Plug and Play, Windows will reload a driver for it. If the printer is not Plug and Play, you will be prompted to supply the manufacturer's driver.

Incorrect Port

Printers must be configured with the proper port settings as well as driver and spool settings. If a printer is configured to use the wrong port, open the Details tab in the printer's Properties window (see Figure 10-9).

Ensure that the port listed in the "Print to the following port:" field is the port to which the printer is actually attached. If it's not, use the drop-down list to select the proper port. If you are printing to a network printer, click the Capture Printer Port button. In the dialog box that appears, you will be able to create an association between a computer port and the actual network printer (see Figure 10-10).

FIGURE 10-9

The Windows 98 printer Properties window displays the port settings.

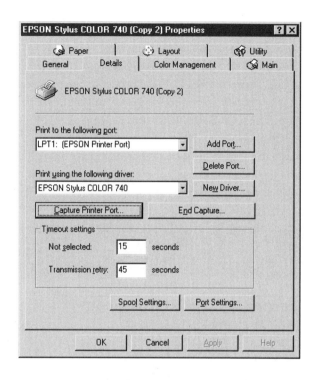

FIGURE 10-10

The Capture Printer Port dialog box allows you to associate a port with a

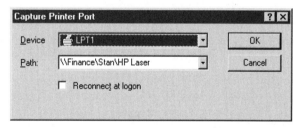

Viruses and Virus Types

A great number of computer problems can be caused by computer viruses. Effects of a virus could be minor or severe (fatal), and they might be predictable or sporadic. Unfortunately, diagnosing and removing viruses can be difficult, and with the increased information exchange brought on by access to the Internet, viruses are becoming more and more prevalent.

Computer viruses are not caused by corrupted files or internal OS or application flaws. Rather, they are intentionally created programs, the purpose of which is to cause some effect in the computer and replicate themselves to be passed on to other computers. The effect that a virus has on a computer is called its *payload*. A virus payload could be nondestructive to the computer, meaning that it could merely display a particular message, run a video clip, or change the display colors. However, if a payload is destructive, it can delete files, close running applications, or destroy a drive's master boot record.

FROM THE CLASSROOM

Viruses: Open Up and Say "ARRGGHHH!"

Computer viruses are no fun to deal with and can often be very frustrating. Although some viruses are simply destructive, others are quite creative and, if they didn't result in computer damage and lost files and time, would probably be considered awfully clever. Take, for example, the I Love You virus. This virus is transmitted via a Visual Basic e-mail attachment with the subject line "I Love You." When the attachment is opened, the I Love You virus destroys multimedia files, such as JPG and MP3 files, then sends itself to every user in your e-mail address book. Pretty clever.

Virus creators have also come up with a number of interesting activation methods. Some viruses are activated when their host application is activated; others are time sensitive. For example, the Michelangelo virus of 1992

was automatically activated when an invaded computer's date rolled to March 6, Michelangelo's birthday. Other viruses are activated when you use a particular key combination or access a particular feature.

Some viruses require you to play games. For example, one virus turns your mouse pointer into a graphic of a block of cheese. Out of nowhere comes a pack of mice, which follow the cheese wherever you move it. If you click the mouse, the cheese turns into a mousetrap and "squishes" any mice it touches. Once all the mice have been caught with the mousetrap, the computer returns to normal. The Oreo virus displays a message stating "I want a cookie." The user cannot use the computer until he or she enters the word *Oreo*. The message is repeated 15 minutes later, then

FROM THE CLASSROOM

repeated 10 minutes later, then 8 minutes later, and so on until it stops altogether.

Here's an example of one of the most clever viruses. It's called the Good Times virus and is reported to have devastating effects on a computer's system files. Recently, a "watchdog" group issued this warning via e-mail: "If you receive an e-mail message with the subject line "Good Times," *do not* read the message but delete it immediately." Being helpful by nature, people circulated this e-mail all over the world until—guess what? It was found that the Good Times virus didn't even exist. The punch line is that this virus hoax caused a tremendous amount of worry, preparation, increased Internet traffic, and wasted time, and the originator didn't have to do an ounce of coding.

—Amy Thomson, A+ Certified Technician, MOUS Master

Virus Types

Many types of computer infestations are actually not viruses at all. A true virus is a piece of code that attaches itself to an executable file and is not activated until the executable file is launched. A *worm*, on the other hand, is a program in itself and does not need to attach itself to a legitimate application in order to run. Viruses are typically more common than worms.

Viruses can be categorized by where they hide themselves. The most common virus type is the *file virus*. File viruses hide themselves in executable files. When the executable file is run, the virus is activated.

Another virus type is a *macro virus*. These viruses attach themselves to portions of applications and disguise themselves as macros. A *macro* is simply an automated process within an application, such as reading and automatically updating a date field or searching for and formatting specified text.

Another type of virus is a *boot sector virus*. This type of virus hides itself in the MBR and is activated during startup when the MBR is located and initialized.

Sources and Spreading of Viruses

When a virus is introduced into a computer system, it typically replicates (copies) itself into memory. From there, it can copy itself into other files in the system.

This is an intentional behavior, configured by the programmer who created the virus. These copies of the virus can then be spread via floppy disks, downloading files from the Internet, or executing e-mail attachments that launch a host program, such as a word processor.

You can minimize the spread of viruses by using antivirus programs that scan all new files introduced into the computer system. You should scan all files on floppies that have been used in other computers, all e-mail messages with attachments, and all files that you download from the Internet.

on the **Job**

You can help prevent infection of your computer by a boot sector virus by not leaving floppy disks in the computer at startup. When you receive the "Invalid System Disk" error, restart the computer using the restart or power key rather than pressing the SPACEBAR, as prompted. This practice ensures that the computer's memory is wiped clean of any boot sector viruses that might have copied themselves into RAM.

Detecting and Removing Viruses

Unfortunately, even if you take all the precautions we've mentioned, you are not immune to computer viruses. New viruses are created all the time and could be too new for your antivirus utility to detect. When the computer starts behaving sporadically or begins to unexpectedly crash, close, or launch applications or lose files, you should suspect a virus and begin troubleshooting the problem immediately. If you have an antivirus utility, run it and instruct it to perform a virus scan and removal. A variety of antivirus utilities are available from third parties, such as GriSoft, Symantec, and McAffee. Windows 2000 includes a native antivirus utility called AVBoot.

In most cases, antivirus utilities work by recognizing and removing specific viruses. They are typically useless against viruses that have been created since the release of the utility itself. For this reason, most third-party virus utility manufacturers keep an up-to-date list of new virus signatures and offer upgrades via the Internet. It is therefore important that you update your antivirus utility's capabilities often. In fact, you should configure your antivirus utility to automatically check for viruses at regular intervals, as well as automatically retrieve updates from the Internet.

If an antivirus utility has failed to detect and remove a virus and you suspect the virus is limited to the boot sector, use the FDISK/MBR command. This command will replace the infected MBR with a (hopefully) good copy from a floppy disk.

If you are unable to remove a virus before it has caused fatal damage, you will probably have to reinstall the OS from scratch. It is important in these cases to repartition and reformat the hard drive because viruses could still exist on the drive (especially in the boot sector).

Use the following Scenario & Solution questions to test your knowledge of the virus concepts discussed in the previous sections.

CERTIFICATION SUMMARY

Because the OS conducts so much activity, a great number of things can go wrong. The more familiar you are with an OS's normal processes, the more easily you will be able to troubleshoot problems when they occur. For example, if you know the steps of the boot process, you will be able to identify which file is at fault when you receive a specific error, such as "HIMEM.SYS not loaded" or a "Swapfile Corrupt" error.

When diagnosing runtime errors, keep in mind that a number of diagnostic utilities and boot modes are available to you. There might be no way to prevent system lockups, GPFs, and illegal operations, but you can certainly help resolve them by pinpointing and reinstalling suspect applications or improving the system's resources.

Some OS errors occur due to computer viruses. You can help protect a computer against viruses by using antivirus utilities to scan all incoming files. Viruses can cause unpredictable behavior, so they might be difficult to pinpoint. However, as long as you are aware of their potential and know the proper recovery steps, you can limit the amount of damage viruses do or stop their spread.

SCENARIO & SOLUTION

Where do viruses come from?	They are created by programmers. They are spread via the Internet, sharing disks, and e-mail.
What is the function of a virus?	To replicate itself and deliver its payload. The payload is simply the effect the virus has on the computer, such as deleting files or displaying messages.
How can I prevent viruses from attacking my system?	Keep an antivirus utility running in the background. Do not start the computer with floppies in the drive unless necessary. Scan all incoming files.
How can I eradicate a virus from my system?	Run an antivirus utility. If the virus is not detected and removed, get the latest utility update from the manufacturer.

TWO-MINUTE DRILL

Here are some of the key points from each certification objective in Chapter 10.

Boot Problems

❑ The "No operating system found" error indicates that the BIOS could not find and initialize the boot loader file (IO.SYS in Windows 9x and NTLDR in Windows 2000).

❑ Windows 9x CONFIG.SYS or AUTOEXEC.BAT startup errors can be resolved by booting in Safe mode and removing or modifying the problematic file entry.

❑ If the HIMEM.SYS file is missing or corrupted, Windows 9x will not start and the file will have to be replaced from the installation or boot disk.

❑ Faulty display driver, kernel, or graphical user interface files could cause a failure to load the GUI during startup.

❑ Windows protection errors occur in Windows when a 32-bit driver is corrupted or missing.

❑ Missing application files that are referenced in the registry or SYSTEM.INI files will result in nonfatal errors during startup.

❑ If the Windows 2000 swap file is corrupted, restart the computer. If the Windows 9x swap file is corrupted, start the computer using a boot disk and delete WIN386.SWP.

Runtime Problems

❑ When diagnosing a runtime error, gather as much information as you can about the nature of the problem, error messages, and recent changes to the computer.

❑ You can use the Dr. Watson utility to take a snapshot of the system's current configuration in either Windows 9x or Windows 2000.

❑ Windows 2000 uses an Event Log service that keeps a record of all system activities.

❑ GPFs occur when an application tries to perform an activity that might compromise another running application.

❑ If an application produces an illegal operation error or locks up, try restarting the computer and reinstalling the application. If those actions fail, check with the manufacturer for a resolution or patch.

❑ Use a printer's Properties window to troubleshoot stalled print spools or incorrectly set printer ports.

❑ Viruses are programs that are designed to have an unwanted effect on a computer and to replicate themselves so that they can be spread from one computer to another.

❑ Use an antivirus utility to detect and remove viruses, and update the utility often so that it recognizes new viruses.

SELF TEST

The following questions will help you measure your understanding of the material presented in this chapter. Read all of the choices carefully because there might be more than one correct answer. Choose all correct answers for each question.

Boot Problems

1. Which of the following could be the cause of a "No operating system found" error?

   A. A registry file is missing.

   B. The boot loader file cannot be accessed.

   C. The kernel file is corrupted.

   D. The BOOT.INI file could not be found.

2. A computer is experiencing boot problems because the IO.SYS file is corrupted. Which of the following procedures could help you resolve the problem?

   A. Start the computer in Safe mode and replace IO.SYS from the boot or installation disk.

   B. Start the computer using the boot disks and elect to use the emergency repair process.

   C. Start the computer using the boot disk and enter the command SYS C:.

   D. Start the computer using the boot disk and enter the command FDISK/MBR.

3. During a Windows 9x startup process, you notice the message "Invalid Command." Which file is responsible for the occurrence of this error?

   A. CONFIG.SYS

   B. AUTOEXEC.BAT

   C. SYSTEM.INI

   D. IO.SYS

4. Which of the following problems might you be able to resolve by using the System Configuration editor?

   A. The computer generates an "Error in CONFIG.SYS line 42" message.

   B. The swap file is corrupted.

   C. The computer generates a "HIMEM.SYS not loaded" message.

   D. The BOOT.INI file is missing.

5. When starting a computer, you received an error stating "HIMEM.SYS not loaded." Which of the following is true?

   A. The error is nonfatal and the OS will load.

   B. You should restart the computer in Safe mode.

   C. This is not a Windows 2000 computer.

   D. The error is caused by a faulty CONFIG.SYS file.

6. Why should you restart the computer in Safe mode if the system fails to load the GUI?

   A. Because Safe mode will detect and replace corrupted or missing drivers.

   B. Because Safe mode allows you to edit legacy configuration files.

   C. Because Safe mode loads a standard video driver.

   D. You shouldn't restart the computer in Safe mode.

7. A computer displays a Windows protection error message. Which of the following could be the cause of the error?

   A. Failure to load a virtual device driver

   B. A device resource conflict

   C. A corrupted 16-bit driver

   D. Bad internal code within the running application

8. A computer is generating an error that states that a device referenced in SYSTEM.INI could not be found. Which of the following is true?

   A. This error occurs when an application is started.

   B. This error can be resolved using the Dr. Watson utility.

   C. If the device is a video driver, the GUI will not load.

   D. This is a nonfatal error.

9. During startup, a Windows 9x computer displays the error, "A device referenced in SYSTEM.INI could not be found." Which of the following can you do to prevent this error from occurring during the next startup?

   A. Enter **REM** at the beginning of the corresponding SYSTEM.INI line to instruct Windows to skip the line.

   B. Enter a semicolon (;) at the beginning of the corresponding SYSTEM.INI line to instruct Windows to skip the line.

C. Enter **REM** at the beginning of the CONFIG.SYS line that references the SYSTEM.INI file to instruct Windows to skip the file.

D. Enter a semicolon (;) at the beginning of the CONFIG.SYS line that references the SYSTEM.INI file to instruct Windows to skip the file.

10. Your Windows 98 computer is reporting that the swap file is corrupted. What should you do to resolve the problem?

A. Delete the WIN386.SWP file.

B. Replace the PAGEFILE.SYS file from the startup or installation disk.

C. Ensure that the WIN98.SWP is properly referenced in the SYSTEM.INI file.

D. Defragment the hard drive.

Runtime Problems

11. Which of the following is a function of the Windows Dr. Watson utility?

A. To find and reload missing or corrupt device drivers

B. To keep a continuous log of all system events

C. To allow you to access and modify registry files

D. To record the system's current configuration

12. Which of the following items keeps a running log of runtime activities in Windows 2000?

A. The Event Log service

B. The Event Viewer

C. Dr. Watson

D. The Enable Boot Logging boot mode

13. Which of the following error is typically associated with an application that tries to use another application's memory space?

A. Illegal operation

B. Invalid working directory

C. General protection fault

D. Program not responding

14. A computer has generated an Illegal Operation dialog box. Which of the following is true?

    A. This is typically not a systemwide fatal error.

    B. The error resulted from the application trying to directly access the hardware.

    C. You must restart the computer.

    D. The application will be shut down automatically.

15. You are using an application and it hangs. Which of the following should you do *first*?

    A. Restart the application.

    B. Restart the computer.

    C. Click the Details button.

    D. Press CTRL+ALT+DEL on the keyboard.

16. You are installing an application, and the installation process hangs just before finishing. Which of the following is *least* likely to be the cause of the problem?

    A. The system doesn't meet the minimum requirements.

    B. There is bad internal code in the application.

    C. TSRs are running on the system.

    D. The installation utility has tried to use an occupied memory location.

17. When you select a program from the Start menu, nothing happens. After you repeat attempts to start the program, it continues to do nothing. Which of the following should you do first?

    A. Reinstall the application.

    B. Restart the computer.

    C. Check the Device Manager for device configuration errors.

    D. Install the application in another computer.

18. The Windows print spool is stalled, and documents aren't being sent to the printer. Which of the following actions is *least* likely to resolve this issue and allow you to print?

    A. Disable Windows print spooling.

    B. Restart the computer.

    C. Defragment the hard disk.

    D. Replace the printer's driver.

19. You suspected that your computer had a virus, so you ran an antivirus utility. However, the utility reported that no viruses were found. What should you do next?

    A. Reinstall the affected application(s).

    B. Delete the affected file(s).

    C. Download an update for your antivirus utility.

    D. Assume that there is no virus.

20. Which command should you use if you suspect your Windows 9x computer has a boot sector virus?

    A. CLEAR /VIRUS

    B. FDISK /MBR

    C. VIRUS /REMOVE

    D. MBR /CLEAR

LAB QUESTION

Familiarity with common Windows errors is key in your role as a computer technician. So that you can effectively troubleshoot problems, it is important for you to understand why errors occur and where the problems lie. For example, you shouldn't expect to see an "Error in CONFIG.SYS line *xx*" error message when you start an application, and you shouldn't expect to see an "Invalid working directory" error message during Windows startup.

This exercise tests your knowledge of Windows startup and runtime processes and the errors that can occur along the way. Place the following problems in the order in which they can occur, beginning with the Windows startup. For example, errors relating to IO.SYS must occur before errors relating to the registry, since IO.SYS is processed before the registry during startup. Note that some errors, such as GPFs or those caused by viruses, can occur at practically any time, so they are not listed here.

____ Windows protection error

____ Invalid working directory

____ Error in CONFIG.SYS line *xx*

____ HIMEM.SYS not loaded

____ No operating system found

____ Invalid command

____ Print spool is stalled

____ A device referenced in SYSTEM.INI could not be found

SELF-TEST ANSWERS

Boot Problems

1. ☑ **B.** The "No operating system found" error could occur when the boot loader file cannot be accessed. At startup, the BIOS performs a POST, loads drivers, then searches for a bootable drive. When one is located, it finds the boot loader file (IO.SYS in Windows 9x and NTLDR in Windows 2000) and gives it control of the boot process. If, for any reason, the BIOS cannot find the boot loader file, you could receive this message. This might be due to a hardware communication problem, a corrupted MBR, or corruption of the boot loader file itself.

☒ **A,** a registry file is missing, and **C,** the kernel file is corrupted, are incorrect. This error message is displayed during the beginning of the boot process, long before the kernel or registry files are located and loaded. **D,** the BOOT.INI file could not be found, is also incorrect. The BOOT.INI file is used by Windows 2000 to configure dual-boot settings. BOOT.INI is located and loaded by NTLDR (the boot loader). The "No operating system found" error occurs because the boot loader itself cannot be located. At this point, the system has not even tried to locate a BOOT.INI file.

2. ☑ **C.** Start the computer using the boot disk and enter the command SYS C:. This command replaces the IO.SYS file on the hard drive with a good copy from the boot disk.

☒ **A,** start the computer in Safe mode and replace IO.SYS from the boot or installation disk, is incorrect. If the IO.SYS file is corrupted, the computer cannot even begin to load the OS, so you will not even reach the point where you can elect to boot in Safe mode. **B,** start the computer using the boot disk and elect to use the emergency repair process, is incorrect. The emergency repair process exists for Windows 2000 only. Windows 2000 does not use the IO.SYS file, so it cannot produce IO.SYS-related errors. **D,** start the computer using the boot disk and enter the command FDISK/MBR, is also incorrect. Although this command could help resolve boot errors caused by a bad MBR, it will not replace or repair a corrupted IO.SYS file.

3. ☑ **B.** The AUTOEXEC.BAT file is responsible for the error. The AUTOEXEC.BAT file can be used to automatically execute DOS commands during the Windows 9x startup. If the file contains a syntax error or a bad command, the "Invalid command" error will occur, just as it would if you entered the command manually.

☒ **A,** CONFIG.SYS, is incorrect because errors in this file typically result in an "Error in CONFIG.SYS line *xx*" message. Furthermore, the CONFIG.SYS file contains parameters and settings, not actual DOS commands. **C,** SYSTEM.INI, is incorrect because errors in this file typically result in the following error message: "A device referenced in SYSTEM.INI could not be found." Furthermore, like CONFIG.SYS, SYSTEM.INI contains parameters and settings, not commands. **D**, IO.SYS, is incorrect because this file does not contain DOS commands. IO.SYS file errors are typically quite serious and tend to result in "No operating system found" errors.

4. ☑ **A.** The computer generates an "Error in CONFIG.SYS line 42" message. This message indicates a problem within the CONFIG.SYS file. You can use the System Configuration editor to open the CONFIG.SYS file and view, correct, or remove line 42.

☒ **B**, the swap file is corrupted, is incorrect because the System Configuration editor allows you to access legacy configuration files only. These files are AUTOEXEC.BAT, CONFIG.SYS, SYSTEM.INI, WIN.INI, and PROTOCOL.INI. For this reason, **C** and **D** are also incorrect because they suggest using the System Configuration Editor to resolve problems relating to the HIMEM.SYS and BOOT.INI files, respectively.

5. ☑ **C.** This is not a Windows 2000 computer. Windows 2000 does not use the HIMEM.SYS file, so this message cannot be generated on a Windows 2000 computer.

☒ **A**, the error is nonfatal and the OS will load, is incorrect. This message indicates a Windows 9x computer, and although Windows 9x can boot without other legacy configuration files, such as SYSTEM.INI and CONFIG.SYS, the HIMEM.SYS file is required. **B**, you should restart the computer in Safe mode, is incorrect. Booting in Safe mode will not bypass the HIMEM.SYS file, as it does with other legacy configuration files. If you boot in Safe mode, the HIMEM.SYS error will still occur and Windows will not load. **D**, the error is caused by a faulty CONFIG.SYS file, is incorrect. Although the CONFIG.SYS file can be used to load HIMEM.SYS, it is not required. If the CONFIG.SYS file does not reference HIMEM.SYS or does not load it properly, the IO.SYS file will search for it and load it.

6. ☑ **C.** You should restart the computer in Safe mode if the system fails to load the GUI because Safe mode loads a standard video driver. This allows you to determine if a third-party display driver or other device driver is causing the problem.

☒ **A**, because Safe mode will detect and replace corrupt or missing drivers, is incorrect because Safe mode is not a diagnostic tool. Safe mode is a boot method in which only standard video, mouse, and keyboard drivers are loaded. **B**, because Safe mode allows you to edit legacy configuration files, is incorrect because the System Configuration editor, not Safe mode, allows you to access these files. Furthermore, the GUI is loaded after the configuration files in the startup process. Problems with these files would have occurred before the system attempted to load the GUI. **D** is incorrect because it suggests that Safe mode cannot help you resolve this problem. However, as discussed, booting in Safe mode can actually be a helpful troubleshooting procedure in this case.

7. ☑ **A.** The Windows protection error could be caused by a failure to load a virtual device driver. During Windows startup, all 32-bit virtual device drivers are loaded. If one is corrupted or missing, the protection error will occur. When it does, reload the driver from the installation disk.
☒ **B,** a device resource conflict, is incorrect. This could result in one or two nonfunctioning devices, but not the Windows protection error (which occurs at startup). **C,** a corrupted 16-bit driver, is incorrect. These drivers are loaded by CONFIG.SYS or SYSTEM.INI and are not required by Windows. These errors are nonfatal and will not generate a Windows protection error. **D,** bad internal code within the running application, is incorrect. Although bad application code can be responsible for a number of runtime errors, it cannot cause startup errors such as the Windows protection error.

8. ☑ **D.** "A device referenced in SYSTEM.INI could not be found" is a nonfatal error. That is, once this error message is displayed, Windows will continue to boot normally. The SYSTEM.INI file contains legacy configurations to be used by older 16-bit applications. This file is not required by Windows to boot properly.
☒ **A,** this error occurs when an application is started, is incorrect because this error can be generated during startup only, when the SYSTEM.INI file is processed (if it exists). **B,** this error can be resolved using the Dr. Watson utility, is incorrect because that utility can be used only after Windows has loaded. SYSTEM.INI errors occur during startup, before the Dr. Watson utility can be used. **C,** if the device is a video driver, the GUI will not load, is incorrect. Devices in the SYSTEM.INI file are overridden by devices in the registry. If a 16-bit video driver fails to load from SYSTEM.INI, Windows 9x will simply ignore it and load a standard virtual device driver for the video adapter.

9. ☑ **B.** Enter a semicolon (;) at the beginning of the corresponding SYSTEM.INI line to instruct Windows to skip the line. Although this step will not resolve the underlying device problem, it will prevent the error from occurring the next time the computer is started.
☒ **A** is incorrect because it suggests entering **REM** at the beginning of the line to tell Windows to skip it. Although this technique can be is used in CONFIG.SYS and AUTOEXEC.BAT, a semicolon must be used in SYSTEM.INI and WIN.INI. **C** and **D** are incorrect because they suggest configuring the CONFIG.SYS file so that the line referencing the SYSTEM.INI file is skipped. However, SYSTEM.INI, if it exists, is read automatically during the Windows 9x startup. It is not referenced in the CONFIG.SYS file.

10. ☑ **A.** You can resolve a corrupted swap file in Windows 98 by deleting the WIN386.SWP file. When Windows is restarted, it will look for the presence of the WIN386.SWP swap file. If it doesn't exist, Windows will regenerate one.

☒　**B,** replace the PAGEFILE.SYS file from the startup or installation disk, is incorrect because this is the name of the swap file in Windows 2000, not Windows 98. **C,** ensure that WIN98.SWP is properly referenced in the SYSTEM.INI file, is incorrect because WIN98.SWP is not a valid Windows 98 file. **D,** defragment the hard drive, is incorrect because although this might speed up access to the swap file, it will not correct or restore a corrupted swap file.

Runtime Problems

11.　☑　**D.** A function of the Windows Dr. Watson utility is to record the system's current configuration. When enabled, Dr. Watson will take a snapshot of current configuration settings as well as all running applications. You can then use this information to pinpoint the cause of a runtime error.

　☒　**A,** to find and reload missing or corrupted device drivers, is incorrect. Although this is a function of the Windows 2000 emergency repair process, Dr. Watson is limited to information gathering. **B,** to keep a continuous log of all system events, is incorrect because this is a function of the Windows 2000 Event Log service. Although it is true that Dr. Watson snapshots can be saved as a log, this utility does not keep a running log of all activities. Rather, it gathers system information only when instructed by the user or when an application error occurs. **C,** to allow you to access and modify registry files, is incorrect because this is the function of the registry editor. Dr. Watson cannot be used to access the registry.

12.　☑　**A.** The Event Log service keeps a running log of runtime activities in Windows 2000. This service is started automatically and keeps logs of application, system, and security activities. You can later view these logs to view the events leading up to a runtime problem.

　☒　**B,** the Event Viewer, is incorrect because this is used to view the entries generated by the Event Log service. The Event Viewer does not itself log events. **C,** Dr. Watson, is incorrect because this utility can take a snapshot of the system's current configuration but does not maintain a running log. **D,** the Enable Boot Logging boot mode, is incorrect because this will generate a log of boot activities only. It will not log runtime activities.

13.　☑　**C.** The GPF is typically associated with an application that tries to use another application's memory space. GPFs can also occur whenever an application tries to access a resource that is currently in use or to control the hardware directly. Fortunately, GPFs are usually caused by 16 bit applications, so they occur less now than they did when all applications were 16 bit.

　☒　**A,** illegal operation, is incorrect because this error usually occurs when an application makes a request that the OS cannot carry out—for example, if an application tries to access a corrupted file or a device that does not exist. **B,** invalid working directory, is incorrect because this error is generated at application startup if the application's working directory no longer exists or has been moved. **D**, program not responding, is incorrect because this error is generated when you use the Task Manager to close an unresponsive (locked up) application.

14. ☑ **A.** This is typically not a systemwide fatal error. Illegal operations usually affect only the application that caused the problem in the first place. Click the Close button in the Illegal Operation dialog box to close the application. The OS as well as other open applications should continue to work normally.

☒ **B**, the error resulted from the application trying to directly access the hardware, is incorrect because this type of activity results in a GPF, not an illegal operation error. **C**, you must restart the computer, is incorrect because in most cases, once you close the offending application, the computer will continue to work normally. **D**, the application will be shut down automatically, is incorrect because the application won't be shut down until you click the Close button in the Illegal Operation dialog box.

15. ☑ **D.** When an application hangs, you should first press CTRL+ALT+DEL on the keyboard. This will open the Windows Task Manager, and you can close the application from there.

☒ **A**, restart the application, is incorrect because you should close the application before trying to start another instance of it. In some cases, you will not be able to open another instance of a hung application. **B**, restart the computer, is incorrect. Although this action might eventually be required, you should first try to shut down the hung application. The computer might continue to operate normally, once the offending application is closed. Furthermore, restarting the computer could cause problems such as corrupted or temporary files, and you will lose any unsaved work you have created in other applications. **C**, click the Details button, is incorrect because applications do not generate Details button when they hang. The Details button is a feature of an Illegal Operation dialog box.

16. ☑ **D.** The least likely cause of this problem is that the installation utility has tried to use an occupied memory location. This type of behavior will result in a GPF and is indicated by a blue screen, not a single hung application.

☒ **A**, the system doesn't meet the minimum requirements, is incorrect because this might be the cause of the problem. For example, if the computer doesn't have enough memory or a fast enough processor, the installation could fail. **B**, bad internal code in the application, is incorrect because the application itself could contain a bug or flaw that is preventing it from loading correctly. **C**, TSRs are running on the system, is also incorrect. Any running programs or TSRs could interfere with a Setup utility's ability to access system resources and therefore cause the installation to fail.

17. ☑   **B.** The first thing you should do is restart the computer. Some applications don't release their resources when they are closed. This could be preventing other applications from starting properly. When you restart the computer, you free the computer's resources and memory. If this application has just been installed, restarting the computer might allow registry entries for that application to be initialized.

☒   **A,** reinstall the application, is incorrect because although you could end up performing this step, you shouldn't reinstall until you have verified that the problem is not due to a temporary state of the system. **C,** check the Device Manager for configuration errors, is also incorrect. Applications can be affected by faulty device configurations, but you should examine this possibility after restarting the computer. Restarting the computer takes only a few moments and tends to eradicate a large number of application errors. Reconfiguring a device, on the other hand, can take longer and there is no clear way of telling whether the device is responsible for the failure of the application to start. Furthermore, in most cases, a device reconfiguration requires you to restart the computer anyway. **D,** install the application in another computer, is also incorrect. You could end up performing this step to determine if the application or installation medium itself is at fault. However, this typically takes longer and is less likely to resolve the problem than a system restart.

18. ☑   **D.** Replacing the printer's driver is least likely to resolve this issue. The driver itself is used to allow Windows to communicate with the printer. This is unrelated to the system's use of print spooling, which configures applications to send print jobs to the hard drive rather than to the printer directly.

☒   **A,** disable Windows print spooling, is incorrect. When you disable print spooling, you configure the system so that applications send print jobs directly to the printer. Print jobs will therefore bypass the spool service altogether. **B,** restart the computer, is incorrect because this is a common resolution to a stalled printer. The spool service can hang, just as other applications can. By restarting the computer, you also restart the spool service. **C,** defragment the hard disk, is incorrect. The print spooler places print jobs on the hard disk. By defragmenting the hard disk, you make it easier for the Windows printing subsystem to write and retrieve this print job information. This can result in faster print service and fewer stalls.

19. ☑   **C.** You should download an update for your antivirus utility. Because new viruses are being released all the time, antivirus software manufacturers typically provide regular updates so that your utility can recognize and remove new viruses. Most manufacturers make these updates available on the Internet.

☒   **A,** reinstall the affected application(s), and **B,** delete the affected file(s), are incorrect. Viruses are usually designed to remain hidden, so it will be nearly impossible for you to tell which applications and files have been affected. With the virus still in your computer, you could inadvertently help it spread. **D,** assume that there is no virus, is incorrect because antivirus utilities can deal only with viruses that they have been programmed to recognize. They cannot detect viruses that did not exist at the time the utility was released. Therefore, unless you receive regular antivirus utility updates, there is a good chance that the utility will miss a new virus.

20. ☑ **B.** You should use the FDISK /MBR command. Restart the computer using the startup disk(s). At the command prompt, enter **FDISK /MBR** to replace the MBR on the hard drive with uninfected data from the floppy disk.
☒ **A,** CLEAR /VIRUS, **C,** VIRUS /REMOVE, and **D,** MBR /CLEAR, are all incorrect because they are not valid commands.

LAB ANSWER

5   Windows protection error

7   Invalid working directory

2   Error in CONFIG.SYS line *xx*

4   HIMEM.SYS not loaded

1   No operating system found

3   Invalid command

8   Print spool is stalled

6   A device referenced in SYSTEM.INI could not be found

1. **No operating system found.** The first system file accessed during startup is IO.SYS or NTLDR. If there are problems accessing this file, the "No operating system found" error could appear.

2. **Error in CONFIG.SYS line *xx*.** IO.SYS then loads MSDOS.SYS and enters the real-mode configuration phase. First, it loads the settings in the CONFIG.SYS file.

3. **Invalid command.** Next, IO.SYS runs the AUTOEXEC.BAT file. If this file contains a bad command, the invalid command error will occur.

4. **HIMEM.SYS not loaded.** If HIMEM.SYS is not referenced in CONFIG.SYS or if it is not referenced correctly, IO.SYS will load it. If HIMEM.SYS is missing or corrupted, the HIMEM.SYS not loaded error could occur.

5. **Windows protection error.** The boot process then enters the protected-mode configuration phase. WIN.COM finds and initializes VMM386.VXD, which in turn loads the system's 32-bit virtual device drivers. If a required driver is missing or corrupted, a Windows protection error will occur.

6. **A device referenced in SYSTEM.INI could not be found.** WIN.COM then reads values in the SYSTEM.INI file. If this file refers to a file or device that does not exist or is in the wrong location, this message will be displayed.

7. **Invalid working directory.** If an application's working directory has been moved or deleted, this error could occur when you launch the application.

8. **Print spool is stalled.** This problem can occur when you try to print from within a running application. This error message means that the print spooler is not writing print jobs to the hard drive properly or is not retrieving them properly to send to the printer.

11

Networks

I n Chapter 7, you were introduced to networking concepts and the hardware configurations required to set up a physical network. The focus of this chapter is the concepts and procedures required to access an existing physical network using Windows OSs. This chapter discusses how to enable resource sharing and introduces some commonly used access protocols. The chapter ends with a discussion of concepts related to the largest network in the world: the Internet.

CERTIFICATION OBJECTIVE 11.01

Networking with Windows

As discussed in Chapter 8, Windows 9x and Windows 2000 are both able to join computer networks and access network information and resources. Windows 2000 is designed to support server-based networks, where network access is controlled (permitted or denied) by a single controlling computer, called a *server*. This design is also referred to as *user-level security*. That is, users log on when the OS starts up, and they are given or denied access to network resources based on their identities. Windows 9x is designed for use in peer-to-peer networks, where all computers can access the network and each computer is configured to manage its own resources. This is called *share-level security*. In this type of security, users can view all shared resources, but they could be asked for a password when they try to access a specific resource.

exam
⚠atch
In share-level security, restrictions are placed on individual resources via access passwords. In user-level security, restrictions are placed on users via profiles.

Note that these are simply the *common* implementations of Windows 9x and 2000. A Windows 9x computer can be configured to join a Windows 2000 server-based network, and a Windows 2000 computer can join a peer-to-peer network. Server-based networks can be quite complex, and most organizations with server-based networks employ systems administrators. A *systems administrator* is a specialist whose job it is to maintain and update network settings, privileges, and connectivity. These concepts are complex enough to warrant their own CompTIA certification exam—the Network + certification. For this reason, the A+ exam (and this chapter) focuses mainly on peer-to-peer networks.

Before introducing Windows networking concepts, it is important to note that a Windows computer cannot access a network simply by connecting to it. First, a network card must be properly installed and configured. Next, the OS must be configured for network access. (Refer to Chapter 7 for instructions on installing the network card and configuring the Windows network settings.)

Activating Network Neighborhood

Network Neighborhood isn't always automatically installed with the operating system. If you don't find it on your desktop:

1. Click Start | Settings | Control Panel, then double-click Network to open the Network dialog box.

2. Click Add.

3. Click Client and then click Add.

4. Follow the instructions on the screen to set up Network Neighborhood.

Enabling Network Sharing

The purpose behind connecting computers together in a network is to allow them to access each other's resources. Using Windows, you can configure which resources other users can and cannot access. However, before you can share your computer's resources, you must enable network sharing in the Network Properties. Follow the steps in Exercise 11-1 to enable sharing in Windows 98.

EXERCISE 11-1

Enabling Resource Sharing in Windows 98

1. Right-click the Network Neighborhood icon on the desktop, and select Properties. A dialog box similar to the one shown in Figure 11-1 will appear.

2. Click the File and Print Sharing button. The dialog box shown in Figure 11-2 will open.

3. Enable access to your files and/or printer(s) using the available check boxes.

FIGURE 11-1

The Windows 98
Network
Properties
dialog box.

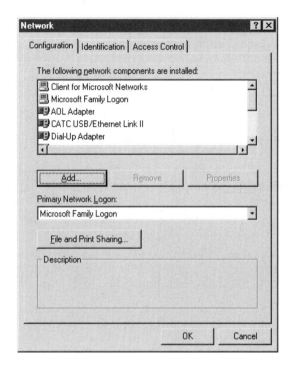

4. Click OK to return to the Properties dialog box.

5. Click OK. You will be prompted to restart your computer.

FIGURE 11-2

Use this dialog
box to enable or
disable access to
your computer's
resources.

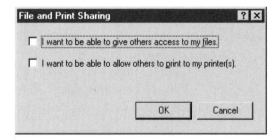

Sharing Disk Drives

One important shared resource on a network is the computer's disk drives. If a hard drive is configured as "shared," other users can access its data as though the hard drive resided in their own computers. You can also share floppy drives and CD-ROM drives. This is particularly useful if you want to install applications on several computers at once, using a single installation disk. To share a drive in Windows 98, follow the procedure in Exercise 11-2.

EXERCISE 11-2

Sharing a Drive in Windows 98

1. Open My Computer, and right-click the drive you want to share.

2. Select Sharing from the shortcut menu. The window shown in Figure 11-3 will open. Note that the default setting is Not Shared. If the Sharing option is not available, enable file sharing using the steps you followed in Exercise 11-1.

FIGURE 11-3

A hard drive's Sharing window.

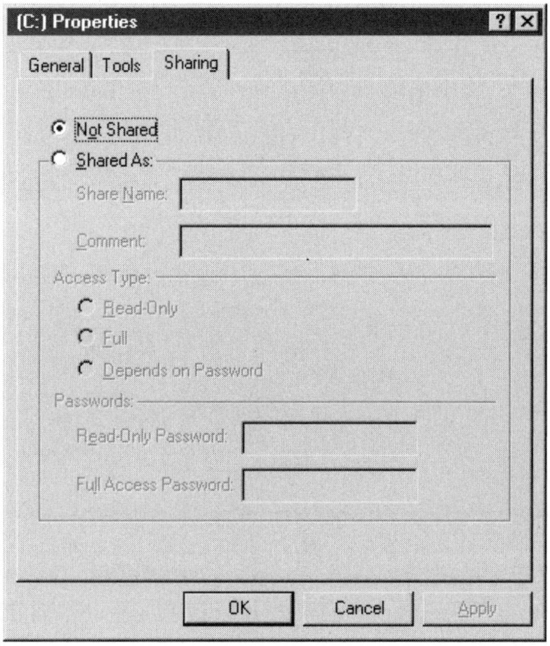

3. Select the "Shared As:" option. The remaining options in the dialog box will become available.

4. Enter a name for the drive in the Share Name field. The drive's letter or label will be entered by default, but you can enter a more descriptive name if you like.

5. Select the access type:

   A. The Read-Only option allows others to view and copy files on the shared drive but does not allow them to modify, move, or delete files.

   B. The Full option gives others full access to view, move, modify, and delete files.

   C. The Depends on Password option allows you to provide read-only or full access, depending on the password that others use. For example, you could want all employees in your department to have full access, whereas others outside the department will have read-only access.

6. If you want to limit access to the drive, enter a password in the appropriate Read-Only and/or Full Access Password fields. You can then control access to the drive by divulging the password only to users to whom you want to grant access. If you selected the Depends on Password option in Step 5, you can enter passwords in both fields. Read-only or full access will then be granted to users based on the passwords they supply.

7. Click OK. You will be asked to confirm any passwords you entered, to ensure that they weren't mistyped. The drive's icon in My Computer will change to indicate that the drive is shared (see Figure 11-4).

[C:]

FIGURE 11-4

This icon is used to indicate that the drive is shared.

To access a shared drive, users must find it using Windows Network Neighborhood. Double-click the Network Neighborhood icon on the desktop. All computers in your computer's workgroup or domain will be listed (see Figure 11-5). To view computers in other workgroups or domains, double-click the Entire Network icon.

FIGURE 11-5

The Network
Neighborhood
window.

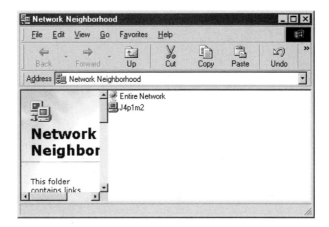

When you double-click a computer's icon in the Network Neighborhood window, its shared resources are listed. Note in Figure 11-6 that the selected computer has two shared drives and a shared printer.

To access data on a shared drive, double-click the drive's folder icon. If a password has been placed on the drive, you will be prompted to enter it. To enable faster access to shared drives, users can create *mapped drives*. A mapped drive appears in the user's My Computer window as though it existed on the local system. This option provides a faster method of accessing system drives than navigating through Network Neighborhood. Follow the steps in Exercise 11-3 to map a network drive in Windows 98.

FIGURE 11-6

The selected
computer has
two shared drives
and a shared
printer.

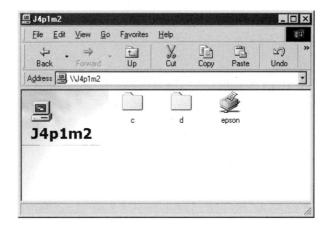

EXERCISE 11-3

Mapping a Network Drive

1. Navigate through Network Neighborhood until you locate the network drive you want to map.

2. Right-click the drive's icon, and select Map Network Drive. A dialog box similar to the one shown in Figure 11-7 will open. Note that the path to the network drive has been entered automatically.

3. The next available drive letter in your system will be selected by default. However, you can use a different drive letter by selecting it from the Drive drop-down list.

4. Enable the "Reconnect at logon" option if you want Windows to automatically map this drive every time you log on.

5. Click OK. You can now access the shared drive by accessing drive E: (or whichever drive letter you assigned) in My Computer.

FIGURE 11-7

The Map
Network Drive
window.

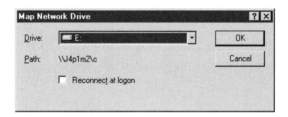

Sharing Print and File Services

When you share a drive, all its folders and files become accessible to other users on the network. If you prefer to share selected folders only, set the drive to "Not Shared." Next, enable sharing on the appropriate folders only, using the steps presented in Exercise 11-2. Each shared folder will appear as a separate icon in Network Neighborhood. Note that when you share a folder, all its files become accessible on the network. You cannot enable or disable sharing for individual files.

One of the most commonly shared resources is a printer. You can share printers the same way that you share drives or folders. The difference is that users can access drives and folders simply by opening them. Shared printers, however, can only be used once they are properly configured within the remote user's computer. The simplest way to configure access to a network printer is to locate the printer in Network Neighborhood. Right-click the printer's icon, and select Install. Carry out the installation as you would for a local printer (refer to Chapter 9 for printer installation procedures).

on the
Job

When accessing a network printer, you can pause or cancel your own print jobs but not the print jobs of other users. If the printer is attached to a print server, the print server can be used to pause or cancel all print jobs in the queue.

Now that you are familiar with procedures for sharing resources in Windows, you should be able to answer the following Scenario & Solution questions.

SCENARIO & SOLUTION

How can I share my hard disk on the network?	Enable File Sharing in the network Properties. Right-click the drive in My Computer, select Sharing, then set the appropriate share options.
How can I view a shared drive on the network?	Double-click Network Neighborhood, locate the appropriate computer, then navigate through the shared drive as you would in My Computer.
Is there a faster way to access a shared resource than using Network Neighborhood?	Yes, you can map the resource so that it appears as a local drive in My Computer. Navigate through Network Neighborhood until you find the resource. Right-click and select Map Network Drive. Assign a drive letter.

Protocols

A *protocol* is a set of rules and procedures that computers use to communicate with one another on a network. You have already been introduced to several access protocols, such as TCP/IP, IPX/SPX, and NetBEUI. You will be expected to answer questions about these protocols on both the Core and OS A+ exams, so make sure that you are familiar with the concepts presented in Chapter 7.

To recap, TCP/IP is the most common network protocol and is used to access the Internet. It requires configuration of a unique TCP/IP address and allows routing across networks. IPX/SPX is also routable, but it is designed specifically for use with Novell systems and cannot be used to access the Internet. NetBEUI is the simplest of the three protocols. It requires no ID configuration but is not routable.

IP Addresses

Recall from Chapter 7 that IP addresses can be assigned manually to computers using the TCP/IP network protocol. Every time a new computer is added to a network, it must be assigned an IP address and subnet mask. If the network is connected to another network, each computer must also be configured with a gateway address and, if they are present, the addresses of WINS and DNS servers (WINS and DNS are discussed in more detail later in this chapter). Furthermore, every time a computer moves between subnetworks (as in a portable computer), it must be configured with these new addresses. Because these configurations can be time consuming, many networks use automatic IP addressing. This concept as well as some supporting utilities are described in this chapter.

DHCP

A *Dynamic Host Configuration Protocol (DHCP)* server is used to dynamically assign IP addresses to computers as they join the network. The DHCP server is configured to use a specified range of IP addresses. When a computer joins the network, it first asks the DHCP server for an IP address. The DHCP server gives the computer an IP address and subnet mask as well as the addresses of the gateway, DNS server, and WINS server, if they exist. The setup and configuration of a DHCP server are beyond the scope of the A+ exam, but you should know how to configure computers to use DHCP services. Follow the steps in Exercise 11-4 to configure a Windows 98 computer as a DHCP client.

Configuring a Windows 98 Computer to Use DHCP

1. Right-click the Network Neighborhood icon, and select Properties.

2. Select the TCP/IP protocol from the list of installed components, and click Properties.

3. Select the Obtain an IP Address Automatically option.

4. Click OK to return to the Network Properties dialog box.

5. Click OK, and restart the computer when prompted.

WINIPCFG.EXE

Windows 9x includes an IP Configuration utility, which allows you to view the computer's current IP configuration. To run the IP Configuration utility, enter **WINIPCFG** on the Windows Run line. A dialog box similar to the one shown in Figure 11-8 will open.

If there is more than one network adapter in the system, select the appropriate one from the drop-down list. Its details will be listed. The adapter's Media Access Control (MAC) address is listed first. This is a hard-coded ID placed on the adapter by the manufacturer, and the adapter uses it to identify itself to the DHCP server at startup. You cannot change an adapter's MAC address. The computer's current

FIGURE 11-8

The Windows 9x
IP Configuration
utility.

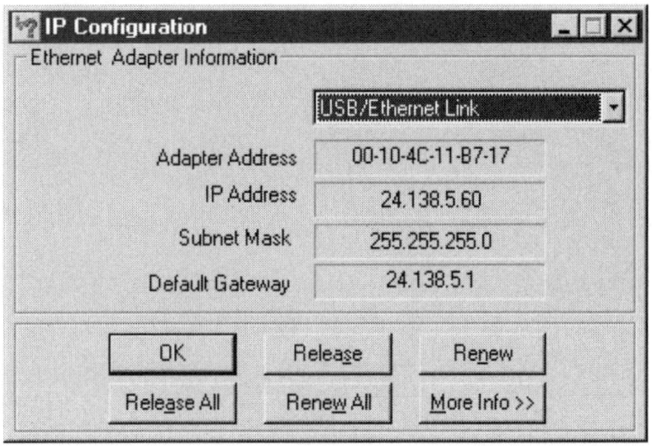

IP address, subnet mask, and default gateway are also listed. You can view more
details by clicking the More Info button (see Figure 11-9). Note that the DHCP,
DNS, and WINS servers are displayed.

If you want to obtain a new IP address from the DHCP server, click the Release
button. This action forces the adapter to stop using its currently assigned IP address.
Next, click Renew. The adapter will ask the DHCP server for a new IP address.

IPCONFIG.EXE

IPCONFIG.EXE is a command-line version of the IP Configuration utility and is
used in Windows 9x and Windows 2000. To use IPCONFIG.EXE, enter **IPCONFIG**
at a command prompt. The IP address, subnet mask, and default gateway of each
network adapter in the system will be listed (see Figure 11-10). To release an IP address,
enter the command **IPCONFIG /RELEASE**. To renew an IP address, enter
IPCONFIG /RENEW.

FIGURE 11-9

The IP
Configuration
utility's detailed
view.

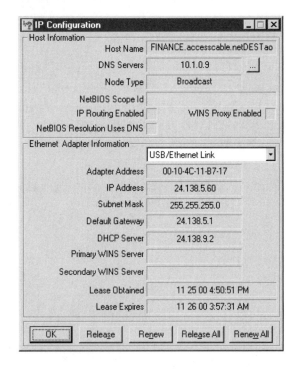

FIGURE 11-10

The IPCONFIG
utility screen.

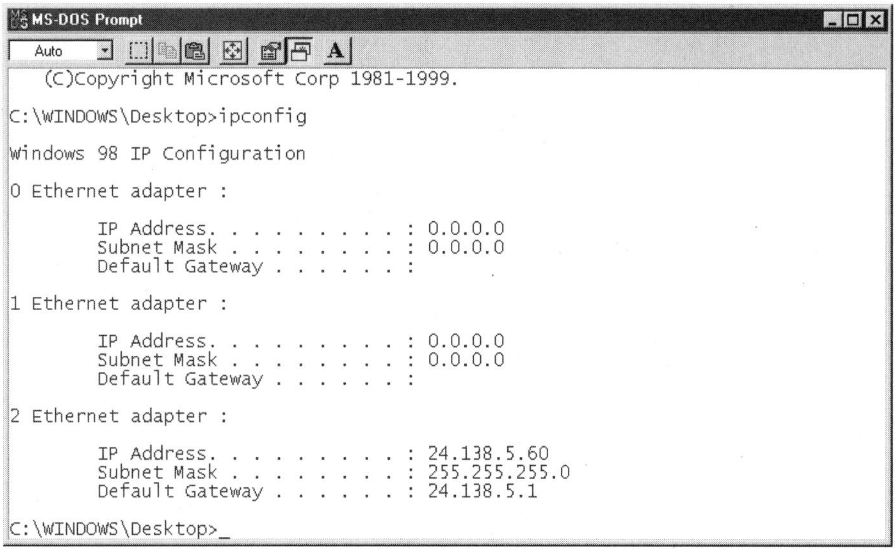

```
MS-DOS Prompt                                                    _ □ ✕
Auto    ▼  [] ▣▣ ▣ ▣▣ A
      (C)Copyright Microsoft Corp 1981-1999.

C:\WINDOWS\Desktop>ipconfig

Windows 98 IP Configuration

0 Ethernet adapter :

        IP Address. . . . . . . . . : 0.0.0.0
        Subnet Mask . . . . . . . . : 0.0.0.0
        Default Gateway . . . . . . :

1 Ethernet adapter :

        IP Address. . . . . . . . . : 0.0.0.0
        Subnet Mask . . . . . . . . : 0.0.0.0
        Default Gateway . . . . . . :

2 Ethernet adapter :

        IP Address. . . . . . . . . : 24.138.5.60
        Subnet Mask . . . . . . . . : 255.255.255.0
        Default Gateway . . . . . . : 24.138.5.1

C:\WINDOWS\Desktop>_
```

CERTIFICATION OBJECTIVE 11.02

Internet Concepts

The largest network in the world is the Internet. All computers that provide a service for or access the Internet are considered part of the Internet itself. The Internet contains a huge network of connected servers. Each server is responsible for some service, such as supplying Web pages, transferring e-mail, or simply relaying messages to the next server. The servers are connected using phone lines, cable lines, and fiber optic cabling.

There are many ways to access the Internet, including a single-computer dial-up connection to an Internet service provider (ISP), an entire network that accesses the Internet through a single server, a computer that has dial-up access to a network with Internet access, or simply two computers that exchange documents using servers already in place on the Internet. The list goes on and on. Because there are so many access methods, and due to the sheer volume of data transfer, a number of concepts, protocols, and procedures are associated with the Internet that are not used on simple internal networks.

Internet Service Providers

An ISP is a company that provides Internet access to home or business users. ISPs have traditionally been phone companies, but now the role of ISP is moving toward cable companies and third-party firms that simply lease phone or cable time. When you connect to the Internet from home or the office, you first connect to your ISP's server. All your data transfers are relayed to and from the appropriate Internet server via the ISP.

Dial-Up Access

Even with the advent of fast DSL and cable Internet access, dial-up access remains the most popular Internet access method. Dial-up access requires the use of a phone line and a modem that actually dials up and establishes a connection with the ISP's Internet server. Before you can connect to the ISP's server, however, you must configure Windows to use a dial-up connection. Here, you will configure the modem with the appropriate phone number and communication settings. Follow the steps in Exercise 11-5 to create a dial-up connection to your ISP using Windows 98.

EXERCISE 11-5

Creating a Dial-Up Connection

1. Double-click the Dial-up Networking icon in My Computer.

2. Double-click the Make New Connection icon. The Make New Connection Wizard will open.

3. Enter a name for the connection. Ensure that the name is descriptive because you can create dial-up connections to more than one server.

4. In the Select a Device drop-down list, select the modem you want to use for this connection. (Some computers have more than one modem installed.)

5. Click Next.

6. Enter the area code and phone number of the ISP's Internet server.

7. Click Finish. You can now establish a connection to your ISP. Note that you will be asked to enter a username and password. These must be obtained by the ISP.

on the

Job *If you are accessing the Internet using a cable modem, you do not need to configure dial-up access. Rather, an internal NIC is installed and communicates with the external cable modem using regular network protocols. The modem itself has a direct connection to the ISP.*

Internet Names and Addresses

The access protocol of the Internet is TCP/IP. That is, all computers on the Internet are identified by an IP address and can identify other computers by their IP addresses. However, when accessing a computer on the Internet, users tend to use domain names instead of IP addresses. This section describes these methods of computer identification on the Internet as well as their supporting services.

Domain Names

A *domain name* is a "common" name for a computer or group of computers on the Internet. By combining computers into domains, organizations can allow access to a group of computers without requiring users to enter individual addresses for each computer.

For example, Microsoft makes information available on the Internet through its *microsoft* domain. This domain contains more than one computer, each with a different IP address. When you access the microsoft domain on the Internet, you are able to access all the servers in the microsoft domain without addressing each one separately.

Domain Name Service

The function of Domain Name Service, or DNS, is to translate domain names into IP addresses, and vice versa. Recall that all computers are identified on the Internet by their IP addresses. However, remembering these addresses can be very difficult for users, so DNS allows users to identify computers on the Internet by their domain names instead. That is, it is much easier to remember *www.syngress.com* than it is to remember *205.181.158.215*. Note that when accessing Internet sites, you can use either the domain name or the IP address.

exam

Watch *You might also see DNS described as Domain Name System. Domain Name System and Domain Name Service are the same thing.*

FROM THE CLASSROOM

The Domain Name Game

When you visit a Web site by entering *www.website.com*, you are actually entering that site's domain name. The first part of the name (*www*) indicates the type of site. For example, WWW indicates a World Wide Web site; OWA stands for Outlook Web Access. The last part of the domain name (*.com*) is used as a Web site identifier. COM, the most common extension, is typically used for commercial businesses. Some common extensions and their uses are as follows:

AU	Australian
CA	Canadian
COM	Commercial business
EDU	An educational organization
GOV	Government agency
MIL	Military
ORG	Nonprofit organization
US	American

In addition, several new identifiers, such as .aero (aviation), .biz (business), info (Afilias.Ltd.) and .net (Verisign Global), have been added.

Domain names must be unique and must be registered with an Internet Corporation for Assigned Names and Numbers (ICANN)–accredited registrar. Domain names are no longer directly registered with the Internet Network Information Center (InterNIC). That is, you cannot configure a server to use a domain name that you selected out of the blue.

Fortunately, most large companies have domain names that are very similar or identical to the company name. For example, the Microsoft Internet domain name is *www.microsoft.com*, and the 3Com domain name is *www.3com.com*. This makes it easy for users to locate a company's Web site by "guessing" the name. Unfortunately, this is not always the case. For example, the Web site *www.scsi.com* is actually owned by Summit Computer Systems Inc. and has nothing to do with SCSI as in Small Computer Systems Interface technology, as you might expect.

—Amy Thomson, A+ Certified Technician, MOUS Master

Windows Internet Naming Service

WINS, which stands for Windows Internet Naming Service, has a function similar to that of a DNS server but is used to resolve IP addresses to computer (NetBIOS) names rather than host names.

exam
ⓦatch

DNS and WINS servers are both used to translate IP addresses. DNS translates into domain names, and WINS translates into computer (NetBIOS) names.

Uniform Resource Locator

A Uniform Resource Locator (URL) is the full address of an Internet location. A URL indicates the data transfer protocol and either a domain name or an IP address. For example, the URL *http://www.syngress.com* indicates an HTTP (Web) site that has the domain name *www.syngress.com*. The URL *ftp://128.102.34.2* indicates an FTP download site that uses the IP address *128.102.34.2*. FTP and HTTP are discussed in more detail later in the chapter.

Packet InterNetwork Groper

PING stands for Packet InterNetwork Groper. The PING utility allows you to determine the IP address of a particular Internet domain. You can run PING from a command prompt or the Windows Run line. Enter the command using the following syntax:

```
PING www.domainname.com
```

Here, *www.domainname.com* is the domain name, the IP address of which you want to find. An output similar to that shown in Figure 11-11 will be generated.

Note that the IP address is indicated (205.181.158.215). The PING utility works by sending a data packet to the specified location, then waiting for a reply. Using the reply data, the PING utility will then report the amount of data loss (if any) and the amount of time it took for packets to be transferred. An interesting history of PING is located at http://ftp.arl.mil/~mike/ping.html.

FIGURE 11-11

A PING command output.

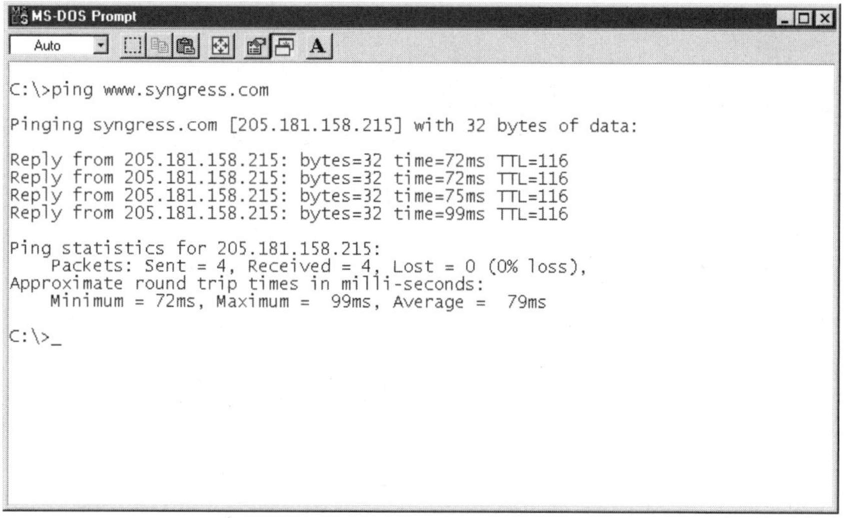

```
MS-DOS Prompt                                                   _ □ ×
Auto ▼  □ ▧▨▧ ▧ ☟▧ A

C:\>ping www.syngress.com

Pinging syngress.com [205.181.158.215] with 32 bytes of data:

Reply from 205.181.158.215: bytes=32 time=72ms TTL=116
Reply from 205.181.158.215: bytes=32 time=72ms TTL=116
Reply from 205.181.158.215: bytes=32 time=75ms TTL=116
Reply from 205.181.158.215: bytes=32 time=99ms TTL=116

Ping statistics for 205.181.158.215:
    Packets: Sent = 4, Received = 4, Lost = 0 (0% loss),
Approximate round trip times in milli-seconds:
    Minimum = 72ms, Maximum =  99ms, Average =  79ms

C:\>_
```

Although PING is an acronym, it is often used as a verb and is then represented in lowercase. For example "I pinged the address" or "Give that site a ping."

TRACERT.EXE

Because the Internet contains so many servers worldwide, data that you receive could take a different route each time between the Internet server and your computer. For example, suppose you are accessing data from a server in Europe. The data could be relayed to your computer through servers in England, New York, Iowa, and Colorado. The next time you access that server, the data may be relayed through servers in Minnesota, Wisconsin, Illinois, and Kansas.

Windows includes a utility that allows you to trace the current route to that server. The utility, Trace Route, can be executed from a command prompt, as long as your computer currently has Internet access. You can also use Trace Route within an internal network. To use the Trace Route utility, enter the following command:

```
TRACERT www.website.com
```

where *www.website.com* is the domain name of the server you want to trace. Figure 11-12 shows the results of a route trace to *www.syngress.com*. Note that the domain name and IP address of each server in the route are displayed. Note also

FIGURE 11-12	

The results of a TRACERT command.

```
MS-DOS Prompt                                                          _ □ ✕
Auto        ▼  □ 🖺 🖺  ⊠ 🖺🖺 A
C:\>tracert www.syngress.com

Tracing route to syngress.com [205.181.158.215]
over a maximum of 30 hops:

  1    24 ms    24 ms    28 ms  gw-5.accesscable.net [24.138.5.1]
  2    25 ms    29 ms    29 ms  CDR7-2.accesscable.net [24.138.7.2]
  3    28 ms    29 ms    30 ms  CDR7-149.accesscable.net [24.138.7.149]
  4    32 ms    29 ms    30 ms  205.150.223.33
  5    52 ms    47 ms    45 ms  202.at-6-0-0.XR2.MTL1.ALTER.NET [152.63.131.206]

  6    78 ms    59 ms    60 ms  293.ATM3-0.TR1.TOR2.ALTER.NET [152.63.128.174]
  7    71 ms    71 ms    71 ms  137.at-5-1-0.TR1.NYC9.ALTER.NET [152.63.7.77]
  8    73 ms    79 ms    77 ms  187.ATM6-0.XR1.BOS1.ALTER.NET [152.63.20.185]
  9    76 ms    78 ms    78 ms  191.ATM8-0-0.GW2.BOS1.ALTER.NET [146.188.176.241
]
 10    76 ms    80 ms    76 ms  shorenet-gw.customer.ALTER.NET [157.130.3.142]
 11    80 ms    76 ms    79 ms  lynn2-cr2-f0-0-10.wharf.shore.net [207.244.95.68
]
 12    79 ms    78 ms    78 ms  infoboard.f0-0.shore.net [204.167.97.74]
 13    80 ms    78 ms    81 ms  syngress.com [205.181.158.215]

Trace complete.

C:\>_
```

that this particular route went through servers in Toronto (TOR), New York (NYC9), and Boston (BOS1).

The TCP/IP suite is complex and is associated with many services and utilities. Before continuing in the chapter, test your understanding of these concepts by answering the following Scenario & Solution questions.

E-Mail

One of the most common activities on the Internet is the transmission of e-mail (electronic mail). E-mail is a messaging service in which users can create letters and send them to other users via the Internet. To send or receive e-mail, your computer must be using an e-mail application, must have access to the Internet, and must be connected to a server that provides e-mail services.

Most e-mail applications use the Simple Mail Transfer Protocol (SMTP) for sending mail and the Post Office Protocol 3 (POP3) for receiving mail. Both protocols are part of the TCP/IP suite. Each user must have an e-mail address, which is typically in the form of *name@domain*, where *name* is a username and *domain* is the domain name of the e-mail server. An example of an e-mail address is *joeb@hotmail.com*.

In most e-mail applications, you can send e-mail by electing to create a new message, entering the recipient's e-mail address, entering the message, then selecting Send. Furthermore, most e-mail applications poll the e-mail server on startup and automatically display all new (received) e-mail messages.

SCENARIO & SOLUTION

What is the function of a DNS server?	To translate IP addresses into domain names, which are much easier for users to remember than numbers.
What is the function of a DHCP server?	To dynamically assign IP addresses to computers as they join a network.
What is the function of a WINS server?	To translate IP addresses into computer names.
How can I determine the IP address associated with an Internet domain name?	Use the PING or TRACERT command.

The World Wide Web

Another commonly used Internet service is the World Wide Web. The "Web" comprises text and graphical Web pages that users can browse. Typically, Web pages contain links to other Web pages so that users can move from one site to another without having to enter new addresses each time.

exam

ⓦ**atch**

The World Wide Web is often confused with the Internet itself. However, the Internet is a huge worldwide network that supports many different services, including e-mail, FTP sites, bulletin boards, newsgroups, and HTTP sites. The World Wide Web refers to HTTP services on the Internet.

Web pages come from Web servers that organizations set up to make information available. When you access a Web page, either by requesting its URL or by clicking a link to that page, the hosting server sends that page to your computer. You can then view the page as though you were using the Web server itself. Every time you receive data from the Internet, whether by e-mail, FTP, or the Web, you are *downloading* that information. Every time you send data, such as sending an e-mail or posting a message, you are *uploading* data.

Installing and Configuring Browsers

To access Web pages on the Internet, you must be using a Web browser. A *Web browser* is simply an application that allows you to access and read Web pages on the Internet. Common Web browsers include Netscape Navigator (see Figure 11-13) and Internet Explorer (see Figure 11-14). Note in the figures that although these two browsers might look different, they contain similar navigation buttons, such as Back, Stop, Search, and Print. Both have a line in which you can enter a URL, and the two display the same Location or Address line for the selected Web page (*www.comptia.org*).

Most ISPs will give you a free copy of a Web browser installation disk when you subscribe to their Internet service. You can also get a Web browser application by buying it or even downloading it from the Internet. Obviously, the latter method works only if you already have a Web browser with which to download the new Web browser application. Furthermore, Windows comes with Internet Explorer built in, so as long as Windows is properly installed, you will have access to a Web browser.

Web browsers are installed like any other application, but they require quite a bit of configuration. You might be prompted by a wizard to configure the browser at

FIGURE 11-13 The Netscape Navigator Web browser.

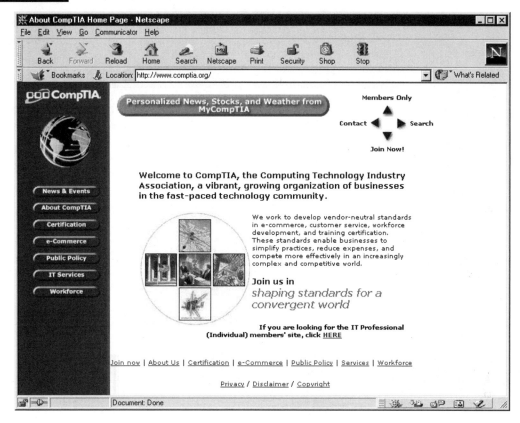

installation time, or you might need to configure it manually once the installation is complete. You will need to supply the browser with information such as the default page to open at startup, your Internet access setup (such as server names), and e-mail information (most Web browsers include a native e-mail service). You might need to obtain some settings from your ISP or systems administrator, such as the name of the mail server and the manual proxy settings, if required.

HyperText Markup Language

HyperText Markup Language (HTML) is the language of Web pages. The HTML language is used to create Web page code, which is converted by your browser into the Web pages that you see when you browse the Internet. HTML supports text,

FIGURE 11-14 The Internet Explorer Web browser.

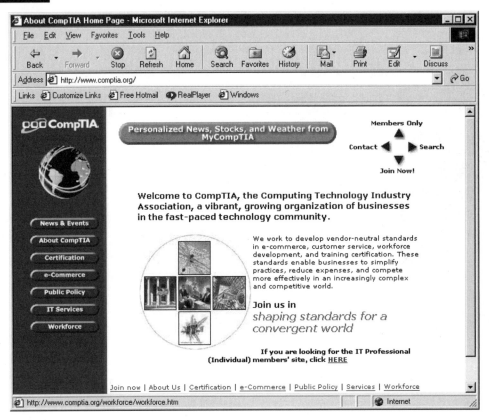

hyperlinks, graphics, and streaming media, such as video clips or sound files that play when you view the Web page. Figure 11-15 shows a Web page on the left and its underlying HTML code on the right.

HTML has evolved into HTML 4, XHTML, and XML, among others. To find more on these new versions, go to http://www.xhtml.org/. HTML pages can be created using graphics applications that can translate pages into HTML format. You can also create HTML pages using Notepad or another text editor to manually enter the HTML code. Follow the steps in Exercise 11-6 to create and view a small HTML Web page.

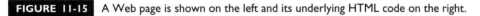

FIGURE 11-15 A Web page is shown on the left and its underlying HTML code on the right.

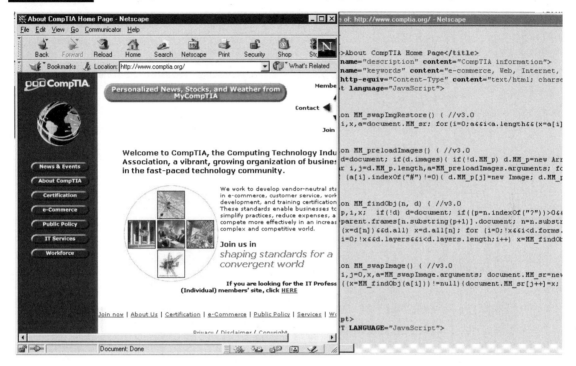

EXERCISE 11-6

Creating an HTML Web Page

1. Start Notepad by selecting Start | Programs | Accessories | Notepad.

2. Enter the following lines:

```
<html>
<h1>Welcome to my Web Page!!</h1>
<p>My name is (enter your name) and I am preparing to become an A+ Certified
Technician.
<p><font color=blue>The A+ certification is available through
CompTIA.</p></font>
```

```
<p><font color=green>You can visit their website by clicking <a
href="http://www.comptia.org">here</a>.</font>
<p><font color=red>I have been preparing for the exam using the A+
Certification Study Guide,
created by <a href="http://www.syngress.com">Syngress</a>.
```

3. Save the file on the desktop, and give it the filename testpage.htm.

4. Close Notepad.

5. Double-click the testpage icon on the desktop. Your default browser will open and the Web page you created will be displayed (see Figure 11-16). Note that you can visit the CompTIA and Syngress Web sites by clicking the hyperlinks you created.

The HTML page, as displayed in a browser.

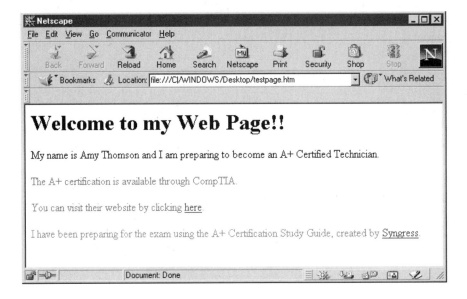

HyperText Transfer Protocol

HyperText Transfer Protocol (HTTP) is the protocol used for downloading HTML Web pages. HTTP is part of the TCP/IP suite and is responsible for locating and downloading pages in response to user requests. That is, when you request a Web page by entering a URL or clicking a hyperlink, the HTTP protocol works in the background to locate and retrieve that page.

File Transfer Protocol

FTP stands for File Transfer Protocol and is a much faster transfer protocol than HTTP. However, it does not support the transfer and display of graphical pages or the use of hyperlinks. FTP sites are therefore typically used for downloadable archives only. FTP sites typically contain a directory structure of downloadable files, as shown in Figure 11-17. Note that the URL of an FTP site starts with *ftp://* rather than *http://*. Because most browsers assume HTTP, you will have to manually specify FTP.

FIGURE 11-17

FTP sites contain directory structures of downloadable files.

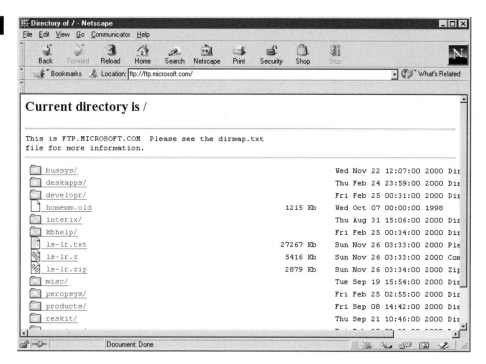

Make sure that you understand the differences between HTTP and FTP. HTTP allows you to download and view HTML-based Web pages, while FTP allows you to download files only, much as you would by accessing a shared drive on a network. FTP offers faster file downloading than HTTP.

Now that you are familiar with some common Internet protocols, test your knowledge by answering the following Scenario & Solution questions.

SCENARIO & SOLUTION	
What is HTTP used for?	For downloading and viewing HTML Web pages.
What is FTP used for?	Downloading non-HTML files.
What are the major differences between HTTP and FTP?	HTTP supports graphics, hyperlinks, and streaming media. FTP supports the simple transfer (copying) of files from one computer to another but is much faster than HTTP.

CERTIFICATION SUMMARY

In this chapter, you were introduced to a number of concepts and procedures associated with sharing and accessing network resources, including those on the Internet. To share a resource on an internal Windows network, you must first enable resource sharing in the Network Properties, then you can selectively share disk drives, individual folders, and/or printers. You can access data on an internal network using Network Neighborhood or by mapping a drive to the appropriate drive or folder.

Most users can only access the Internet via a connection to an ISP. To take advantage of Internet services such as e-mail or the World Wide Web, you must also have an appropriate e-mail or Web browser application installed. Most Web pages are created using HTML, XHTML, and XML, and are transferred using HTTP. FTP is used for simple file transfers such as downloading (copying) a file from an Internet server to your computer.

All computers on the Internet are identified by an IP address. Because these addresses can be difficult for users to remember, a number of supporting utilities and protocols have been developed to simplify access to Internet resources. For example, a DNS server can be used to translate IP addresses to domain names, which are much easier for users to remember than strings of numbers. The PING and TRACERT utilities can then be used to determine which IP address is associated with a particular domain name. The PING utility can also be used to measure packet loss, and the TRACERT utility can be used to show you which servers are being used to relay data between your computer and a destination Internet server.

TWO-MINUTE DRILL

Here are some of the key points from each certification objective in Chapter 11.

Networking with Windows

❑ Share-level security allows users to specify which of their computers' resources will be made accessible on the network, and user-level security allows or denies resource access according to each user's profile and permission settings.

❑ To share resources on a network, you must first enable sharing in the Network Properties dialog box.

❑ To share a resource, right-click it and select Sharing, then set the appropriate share type and passwords.

❑ To access a shared resource, use Windows Network Neighborhood.

❑ You can map a local drive to a network resource by right-clicking the resource in Network Neighborhood and selecting Map Network Drive.

❑ The function of a DHCP server is to automatically assign IP addresses to computers as they join the network.

❑ The IP configuration utilities (WINIPCFG and IPCONFIG) can be used to request a new IP address from a DHCP server.

Internet Concepts

❑ The Internet is a huge network that connects computers all over the world.

❑ Most home and business users access the Internet through an Internet service provider.

❑ A DNS server is used to translate IP addresses into more easily remembered domain names.

❑ A URL contains the transfer method (HTTP or FTP) and the domain name or IP address of the server to which you want to connect.

❑ You can use the PING utility to determine packet transfer speed and data loss from a particular Internet server, as well as its IP address.

❑ To use Internet e-mail, you must have an installed e-mail application and access to an Internet mail server.

❑ The World Wide Web is an Internet service that uses HTTP to transfer HTML (Web) pages from a Web server to your computer.

❑ FTP cannot be used to view Web pages, but it offers fast transfer rates for downloadable files.

SELF TEST

The following questions will help you measure your understanding of the material presented in this chapter. Read all of the choices carefully because there might be more than one correct answer. Choose all correct answers for each question.

Symptoms and Problems

1. To share your CD-ROM drive on the network, you right-clicked the CD drive in My Computer, but there was no "Sharing" option available. Why?

   A. You cannot share CD-ROM drives.

   B. File sharing has not been enabled in the Network Properties.

   C. This machine has no resources to share.

   D. The CD-ROM drive has already been configured as "Shared."

2. Which statement is true regarding shared resources in Windows?

   A. All files and folders on a drive are made available to other users when you share the drive.

   B. You can configure sharing options on individual files and folders.

   C. To share a folder, you must first share the drive, then configure the folder as "Shared."

   D. To access a shared folder, users must map a network drive to it.

3. You are planning to share a folder on the network. However, you would like to give some users full access while limiting others to read-only access. Which of the following can you do in Windows 9x to accomplish this goal?

   A. Map a network drive to each user who should have full access.

   B. Select each username from the list of users, and apply full or read-only access to each one.

   C. Use the Depends on Password option.

   D. You cannot apply more than one access type to a single shared folder.

4. Your computer is part of a Windows network, and you are planning to share your printer. Which of the following lists the appropriate order of the steps you should follow?

   A. Right-click the printer and select Share.

   B. Enable printer sharing in the Network Properties dialog box, access the printer's sharing dialog box, and select the "Shared as" option.

C. Access the printer's sharing dialog box, select the "Shared as" option, and enable printer sharing in the Network Properties dialog box.

D. Enable printer sharing in the Network Properties dialog box.

5. What is the purpose of mapping a network drive?

A. To receive automatic updates whenever data changes on the shared drive

B. To inform users of a shared drive's name

C. To access to a shared drive without having to navigate through Network Neighborhood

D. To specify which users can access a shared drive

6. Which type of server is used to automatically assign IP addresses to computers when they join the network?

A. DHCP

B. WINS

C. DNS

D. IP addresses cannot be automatically assigned

7. Which of the following cannot be provided to computers by a DHCP server?

A. Subnet mask

B. URL

C. Gateway address

D. WINS server address

8. Your Windows 2000 computer is part of a network that uses dynamic IP address assignment. Which utility can you use to request a new IP address?

A. WINIPCFG

B. IPCONFIG

C. PING

D. TRACERT

Basic Troubleshooting Procedures

9. You are configuring a computer for dial-up access. Which of the following will you need to supply?

A. The URL of the default Web page

    B. The address of the proxy server

    C. A username

    D. The name of the e-mail server

10. *www.website.com* is an example of which of the following?

    A. A URL

    B. An e-mail address

    C. An HTML filename

    D. A domain name

11. Which of the following services is used to translate domain names into IP addresses, and vice versa?

    A. HTTP

    B. DHCP

    C. WINS

    D. DNS

12. Which of the following most accurately describes the function of a WINS server?

    A. To assign IP addresses to computers on a network

    B. To supply and transfer HTML pages

    C. To translate IP addresses into computer names

    D. To establish and maintain a dial-up connection

13. You are accessing data on the Internet, and it seems to be taking a very long time for requested Web pages to load. A coworker has suggested that your computer is just being slow. Another coworker states that there is a bad connection between your computer and the Internet server. Which Windows utility can you use to rule out or pinpoint your Internet connection as the source of the problem?

    A. IPCONFIG

    B. WINIPCFG

    C. PING

    D. TRACERT

14. Which of the following is true of the URL *ftp://ftp.blitz.ca*?

    A. The site is served by the Blitz company.

    B. It is most likely a Canadian Web site.

    C. The site will not support streaming media.

    D. The URL is using an invalid syntax.

15. Which of the following is a function of the Windows TRACERT utility?

    A. To display the servers used to relay data between your computer and a specified Internet server

    B. To establish a connection between your computer and your ISP

    C. To request a new IP address from a DHCP server

    D. To measure packet loss between your computer and a specified Internet server

16. Which of the following must you have in order to send and receive e-mail on the Internet?

    A. A Web browser

    B. A connection to a mail server

    C. A dial-up connection

    D. All of the above

17. Complete the sentence: The World Wide Web …

    A. Uses the HTTP protocol.

    B. Uses the FTP protocol.

    C. Is the largest network in the world.

    D. Allows users to send e-mail and view Web pages.

18. What is HTML?

    A. A protocol used for transferring Web pages

    B. A service that resolves IP addresses to domain names

    C. A service that supplies computers with IP addresses

    D. A language used to create Web pages

19. Which of the following statements about HTTP is true?

    A. Most Web browsers use HTTP by default.

    B. HTTP is faster than FTP.

C. HTTP and FTP are used to transfer HTML Web pages.

D. HTTP is unable to support streaming media.

20. Which of the following would you expect to see on an FTP site?

A. A Web page with hyperlinks and graphics

B. A directory structure of downloadable files

C. A directory structure of Web sites

D. A directory structure of the servers used to relay data between your computer and the specified Internet server

LAB QUESTION

TCP/IP is the protocol of the Internet and the most popular protocol on internal networks. TCP/IP is the basis for an entire suite of information exchange protocols, services, and utilities. Match each of the following items on the left with the proper description of its function on the right.

1.	HTML	___ Reports packet transfer time and loss
2.	DNS	___ Translates IP addresses into computer names
3.	FTP	___ Transfers Web pages
4.	IPCONFIG	___ Language used to create Web pages
5.	WINS	___ Reports all servers used between your computer and a specified Internet server
6.	PING	___ Dynamically assigns IP addresses to computers
7.	DHCP	___ Requests a new IP address
8.	TRACERT	___ Resolves IP addresses to domain names
9.	HTTP	___ Provides fast transfer of non-Web downloadable files

SELF-TEST ANSWERS

Symptoms and Problems

1. ☑ **B.** File sharing has not been enabled in the Network Properties. Before you can share any resource in Windows, you must first access the Network Properties dialog box and enable file and/or printer sharing.

☒ **A,** you cannot share CD-ROM drives, is incorrect because you can share any type of drive on a Windows network, including a hard drive, a CD-ROM drive, a floppy drive, or a tape drive. **C,** this machine has no resources to share, is incorrect. If a printer or drive or folder exists on the computer, it can be shared. **D,** the CD-ROM drive has already been configured as "Shared," is incorrect because even devices that are already being shared will allow you to select the "Sharing" option when you right-click it. By doing so, you can view and/or modify the Sharing options.

2. ☑ **A.** All files and folders on a drive are made available to other users when you share the drive. That is, when you share a disk drive, all its contents are configured as "Shared." To share individual folders, configure the drive as "Not shared," then share each individual folder that you want to make available to other users.

☒ **B,** you can configure sharing options on individual files and folders, is incorrect because you can share individual folders but not files. **C,** to share a folder, you must first share the drive, then configure the folder as "Shared," is incorrect because when you share a drive, its folders and files are also shared. **D,** to access a shared folder, users must map a network drive to it, is incorrect. Users *can* access shared folders by mapping a network drive to it, but they don't have to. They can also access shared folders using Windows Network Neighborhood.

3. ☑ **C.** Use the Depends on Password option. In the folder's Sharing dialog box, select Depends on Password. Enter a password for full access and a different password for read-only access. Give the full-access password to users who should have full access, and give the read-only password to users who should have read-only access.

☒ **A,** map a network drive to each user who should have full access, is incorrect. You can map a network drive to a resource that is already shared, not to configure the resource for sharing with others. **B,** select each username from the list of users, and apply full or read-only access to each one, is incorrect. There is no option in the Sharing dialog box to apply different access options to individual network users. **D** is incorrect because it suggests that you can only apply either full or read-only access but not both. As described, you can accomplish both using the Depends on Password option.

4. ☑ **B.** Enable printer sharing in the Network Properties dialog box, access the printer's sharing dialog box, and select the "Shared as" option. Before you can share a printer, sharing must be enabled in Network Properties. Next, right-click the printer you want to share and select the Sharing option. The printer's Sharing dialog box will open. Select the "Share as" option.

   ☒ **A,** right-click the printer and select Share, is incorrect because there is no Share option in the printer's shortcut menu. Rather, you must select Sharing and select the appropriate options in the Sharing dialog box. **C** is incorrect because although it lists the appropriate steps, they appear in the wrong order. Printer sharing must be enabled in Network Properties before you can configure individual printers as shared. **D,** enable printer sharing in the Network Properties dialog box, is incorrect because this alone is not sufficient to share a printer. Once printer sharing is enabled, you must individually configure specific printers as shared.

5. ☑ **C.** The purpose of mapping a network drive is to access to a shared drive without having to navigate through Network Neighborhood. When you map a drive, that drive appears in My Computer, just as local drives do. You can then use My Computer rather than the Network Neighborhood to access the drive.

   ☒ **A,** to receive automatic updates whenever data changes on the shared drive, is incorrect. There is no Windows utility that will update users whenever you change data on a shared drive. **B,** to inform users of a shared drive's name, is incorrect because there is no such utility in Windows. It is therefore important that you give the drive a descriptive name when you share it. **D,** to specify which users can access a shared drive, is incorrect. Although you can create mixed access types to a shared drive, you cannot apply access to individual users.

6. ☑ **A.** A DHCP server can be used to automatically assign IP addresses to computers when they join the network. Rather than manually entering IP addresses on all computers, they can be configured to obtain an IP address from the DHCP server. When the computer joins the network, the DHCP will assign it a dynamic IP address.

   ☒ **B,** WINS, is incorrect because this type of server is responsible for translating IP addresses into computer names, and vice versa. **C,** DNS, is incorrect because this type of server translates IP addresses into domain names, and vice versa. **D** is incorrect because it suggests that IP addresses cannot be automatically assigned.

7. ☑ **B.** A URL cannot be provided to computers by a DHCP server. The function of a DHCP server is to provide computers with IP addresses. A URL is an address used on the Internet to identify the transfer method and domain name or IP address of an Internet server.

   ☒ **A,** subnet mask, **C,** default gateway, and **D,** WINS server address, are all incorrect. All computers are assigned a subnet mask by the DHCP server and are supplied with addresses of the gateway and WINS Server, if they exist.

8. ☑ **B.** You can use IPCONFIG to request a new IP address. Windows 2000 and Windows 9x allow you to run the IP Configuration utility from a DOS prompt, and by using the /release and /renew switches, you can request a new IP address from the DHCP server.

   ☒ **A,** WINIPCFG, is incorrect because this utility is available in Windows 9x only. **C,** PING, is incorrect because the purpose of this utility is to measure connectivity, view the IP address associated with a particular domain name, and measure packet speed and loss. **D,** TRACERT, is incorrect because this utility is used to report which servers are being used to relay data between your computer and another on the Internet.

Basic Troubleshooting Procedures

9. ☑ **C.** When configuring dial-up access, you need to supply a username. You also need to supply a password. The username must be obtained by the ISP to which you are trying to connect. Furthermore, you have to supply the phone number at which the ISP's server can be reached.

   ☒ **A,** the URL of the default Web page, **B,** the address of the proxy server, and **D,** the name of the e-mail server, are all incorrect because these are all settings that are entered when configuring a Web browser for Internet access. The dial-up access settings are required to make a dial-up connection to an ISP and are unrelated to the Web browser's settings.

10. ☑ **D.** *www.website.com* is an example of a domain name. The *www* indicates that this is a site on the World Wide Web. *website* is the name of the domain, and *com* indicates that this is a commercial site.

    ☒ **A,** a URL, is incorrect because a URL includes the transfer method (HTTP or FTP) and the domain name or IP address. *www.website.com* is not considered a URL because there is no HTTP or FTP reference. *http://www.website.com* is a URL. **B,** an e-mail address, is incorrect because e-mail addresses have the form *name@domain*. For example, *joe@hotmail.com* is an e-mail address. **C,** an HTML filename, is incorrect. HTML files are named in the same way that other files are named and have an HTM or HTML extension. For example, WEBPAGE.HTM is an HTML filename.

11. ☑ **D.** DNS is used to translate domain names into IP addresses, and vice versa. All computers on the Internet are identified by their IP addresses. However, these addresses can be difficult for users to remember, so DNS servers allow users to locate Internet locations using their easy-to-remember domain names. For example, *www.syngress.com* is much easier to remember than *205.181.158.215*.

☒   **A,** HTTP, is incorrect because this is the protocol responsible for transferring HTML Web pages on the Internet. **B,** DHCP, is incorrect because it is a protocol used to dynamically assign IP addresses on a network. **C,** WINS, is incorrect because this service is used to translate between computer names and IP addresses.

12.   ☑   **C.** The function of a WINS server is to translate IP addresses into computer names. This is similar to the function of a DNS server, except that a WINS server is able to keep track of which computers have been assigned which IP addresses in a DHCP environment.
☒   **A,** to assign IP addresses to computers on a network, is incorrect because this is the function of a DHCP server. The WINS server keeps track of which computers have been assigned which IP addresses, but it cannot assign addresses itself. **B,** to supply and transfer HTML pages, is incorrect. HTML pages are supplied by Web servers on the Internet and are transferred using HTTP. **D,** to establish and maintain a dial-up connection, is incorrect because this is the function of your computer's analog modem.

13.   ☑   **C.** You can use the PING utility. This will report the transmission times between your computer and the Internet server and will report the amount of packet loss (if any). If the transmission times are low and there is no packet loss, you should assume that the speed problem is originating within your own computer. If transmission times are high and there is significant packet loss, you can assume that your Internet connection is slow because data packets are taking a long time to travel from the server to your computer.
☒   **A,** IPCONFIG, and **B,** WINIPCFG, are incorrect because these utilities are used to view your computer's current IP address and the IP addresses of the gateway, WINS server, and DNS server (if they exist). **D,** TRACERT, is incorrect because this utility reports the servers that are being used to relay data between your computer and a specified Internet server, but it does not report on the fitness of the connection or the amount of packet loss.

14.   ☑   **C.** The site will not support streaming media. The URL *ftp://ftp.blitz.ca* indicates an FTP site. FTP supports fast file transfers but cannot support HTML-based components such as graphics, links to other sites, or streaming media.
☒   **A,** the site is served by the Blitz company, is incorrect because there is no way of knowing the relationship between the domain name and the organization until you visit the site. Although this site could be provided by a company called Blitz, it is conceivable that anyone could use this domain name, as long as the name was approved and purchased from InterNIC. **B,** it is most likely a Canadian Web site, is incorrect. Although the *ca* extension indicates that it is Canadian, the *ftp* identifies this as an FTP site, not a Web site. **D,** the URL is using an invalid syntax, is incorrect. URLs contain the data transfer method, followed by a colon and two forward slashes, followed by the domain name. The URL given here has a valid syntax.

15. ☑ **A.** The function of the Windows TRACERT utility is to display the servers used to relay data between your computer and a specified Internet server. Depending on where you are located, you will use a number of different servers to access a particular Internet server. These intermediary servers can be identified by the TRACERT utility.

  ☒ **B,** to establish a connection between your computer and your ISP, is incorrect. You can configure a dial-up connection between your computer and your ISP, then establish the connection by activating the appropriate dial-up icon. **C,** to request a new IP address from a DHCP server, is incorrect because this is the function of the WINIPCFG and IPCONFIG utilities. **D,** to measure packet loss between your computer and a specified Internet server, is incorrect because this is a function of the PING utility.

16. ☑ **B.** To send and receive e-mail on the Internet, you must have a connection to a mail server. For most users, mail servers are supplied by an ISP. You also need an e-mail application and a username to use e-mail.

  ☒ **A,** a Web browser, is incorrect because although many Web browsers include an e-mail application, you can purchase separate applications that provide e-mail only. **C,** a dial-up connection, is incorrect. Many users access the Internet using a cable or DSL connection, which does not require a dial-up connection. For these reasons, **D,** all of the above, is also incorrect.

17. ☑ **A.** The World Wide Web uses the HTTP protocol. The World Wide Web is an Internet service that uses HTTP to transfer HTML Web pages.

  ☒ **B,** uses the FTP protocol, is incorrect because the World Wide Web is composed of HTTP Web sites only. FTP sites use a different protocol and are not part of the World Wide Web. **C,** is the largest network in the world, is incorrect because the Internet is the largest network in the world. The World Wide Web is simply one of several services available on the Internet. **D** is incorrect because it suggests that the World Wide Web is used for both e-mail and Web page viewing. Again, the World Wide Web supports Web page access only. E-mail is simply another service that can be used on the Internet.

18. ☑ **D.** HTML is a language used to create Web pages. Web browsers can request and download HTML files from Web servers. The browser then translates the HTML code into the appropriate text and graphics that we view as Web pages.

  ☒ **A,** a protocol used for transferring Web pages, is incorrect. HTTP is used for transferring Web pages, and HTML might the format of the Web pages themselves. **B,** a service that resolves IP addresses to domain names, is incorrect because this service can be provided by a DNS or WINS server. **C,** a service that supplies computers with IP addresses, is incorrect because this is the function of the DHCP protocol, not the HTML language.

19. ☑ **A.** Most Web browsers use HTTP by default. That is, if you enter a domain name, the browser assumes that you are trying to contact an HTTP Web site. If you are trying to access an FTP site, you must specifically enter *ftp://* in the URL.

    ☒ **B,** HTTP is faster than FTP, is incorrect. Because FTP does not support the display of graphics or streaming media, it can transfer files much faster than HTTP. **C** is incorrect because it suggests that both HTTP and FTP can transfer Web pages. HTTP, not FTP, can be used for Web page transfer. **D,** HTTP is unable to support streaming media, is incorrect. HTTP supports graphics, text formatting, streaming media, and hyperlinks.

20. ☑ **B.** You should expect to see a directory structure of downloadable files on an FTP site. FTP does not support the display of Web pages; instead, it is used for locating and downloading files, much as you would in Network Neighborhood on an internal Windows network.

    ☒ **A,** a Web page with hyperlinks and graphics, is incorrect because this is what you could expect to see on an HTTP (Web) site, not an FTP site. **C,** a directory structure of Web sites, is incorrect because FTP sites contain files and folders, not hyperlinks or lists of Web sites. **D,** a directory structure of the servers used to relay data between your computer and the specified Internet server, is incorrect. Although the Windows TRACERT utility can be used to list these servers, there is no utility or Internet FTP site for providing them as a directory structure.

LAB ANSWER

1.	HTML	6	Reports packet transfer time and loss
2.	DNS	5	Translates IP addresses into computer names
3.	FTP	9	Transfers Web pages
4.	IPCONFIG	1	Language used to create Web pages
5.	WINS	8	Reports all servers used between your computer and a specified Internet server
6.	PING	7	Dynamically assigns IP addresses to computers
7.	DHCP	4	Requests a new IP address
8.	TRACERT	2	Resolves IP addresses to domain names
9.	HTTP	3	Provides fast transfer of non-Web downloadable files

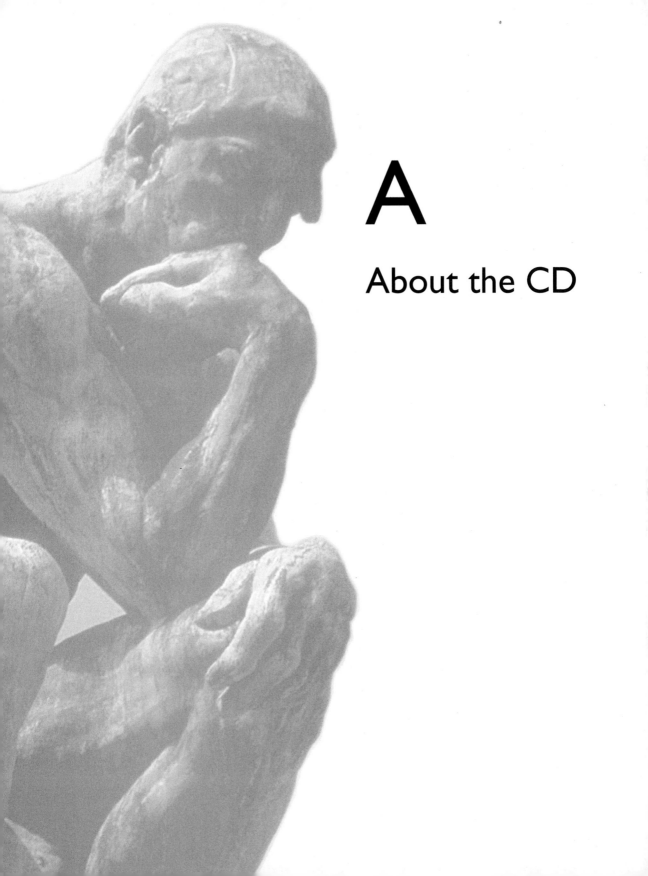

A

About the CD

The CD-ROM included with this book comes complete with MasterExam, MasterSim, CertCam movie clips, the electronic version of the book, and Session #1 of LearnKey's online training. The software is easy to install on any Windows 98/NT/2000 computer and must be installed to access the MasterExam and MasterSim features. You may, however, browse the electronic book and CertCams directly from the CD without installation. To register for LearnKey's online training and a second bonus MasterExam, simply click the Online Training link on the Main Page and follow the directions to the free online registration.

System Requirements

Software requires Windows 95 or higher, Internet Explorer 5.0 or above, and 20 MB of hard disk space for full installation. The electronic book requires Adobe Acrobat Reader. To access the Online Training from LearnKey you must have RealPlayer Basic 8 or Real1 Plugin, which will be automatically installed when you launch the online training. Please see the ReadMe file on the CD-ROM for more information on system requirements and setup instructions.

LearnKey Online Training

The **LearnKey Online Training** link will allow you to access online training from Osborne.Onlineexpert.com. The first session of this course is provided at no charge. Additional sessions for this course and other courses may be purchased directly from www.LearnKey.com or by calling (800) 865-0165.

The first time that you run the Training, you will required to register with the online product. Follow the instructions for a first time user. Please make sure to use a valid e-mail address.

Prior to running the Online Training you will need to add the Real plugin and the RealCBT plugin to your system. This will automatically be facilitated to your system when you run the training the first time.

Installing and Running MasterExam and MasterSim

If your computer CD-ROM drive is configured to auto run, the CD-ROM will automatically start up upon inserting the disk. From the opening screen you may install MasterExam or MasterSim by pressing the *MasterExam* or *MasterSim* buttons. This will begin the installation process and create a program group named "LearnKey." To run MasterExam or MasterSim use START | PROGRAMS | LEARNKEY. If the auto run feature did not launch your CD, browse to the CD and Click on the RunInstall icon.

MasterExam

MasterExam provides you with a simulation of the actual exam. The number of questions, the type of questions, and the time allowed are intended to be an accurate representation of the exam environment. You have the option to take an open book exam, including hints, references, and answers, a closed book exam, or the timed MasterExam simulation.

When you launch the MasterExam simulation, a digital clock will appear in the top center of your screen. The clock will continue to count down to zero unless you choose to end the exam before the time expires.

MasterSim

The MasterSim is a set of interactive labs that will provide you with a wide variety of tasks to allow the user to experience the software environment even if the software is not installed. Once you have installed the MasterSim you may access it quickly through this CD launch page or you may also access it through Start | Programs | Learnkey.

Electronic Book

The entire contents of the Study Guide are provided in PDF. Adobe's Acrobat Reader has been included on the CD.

CertCam

CertCam AVI clips provide detailed examples of key certification objectives. These clips walk you step-by-step through various system configurations. You can access the clips directly from the CertCam table of contents by pressing the CertCam link on the Main Page.

TheCertCam AVI files are stored on the CD. If the CD is removed, the CertCam clips will not play.

Help

A help file is provided through the help button on the main page in the lower left hand corner. Individual help features are also available through MasterExam, MasterSim, and LearnKey's Online Training.

Removing Installation(s)

MasterExam and MasterSim are installed to your hard drive. For *best* results for removal of programs use the Start | Programs | Learnkey | Uninstall options to remove MasterExam or MasterSim.

If you desire to remove the Real Player use the Add/Remove Programs icon from your Control Panel. You may also remove the LearnKey training program from this location.

Technical Support

For questions regarding the technical content of the electronic book, MasterExam, or CertCams, please visit www.osborne.com or email customer.service@mcgraw-hill .com. For customers outside the 50 United States, email: international_ cs@mcgraw-hill.com.

LearnKey Technical Support

For technical problems with the software (installation, operation, removing installations), and for questions regarding LearnKey Online Training and MasterSim content, please visit www.learnkey.com or email techsupport@learnkey.com.

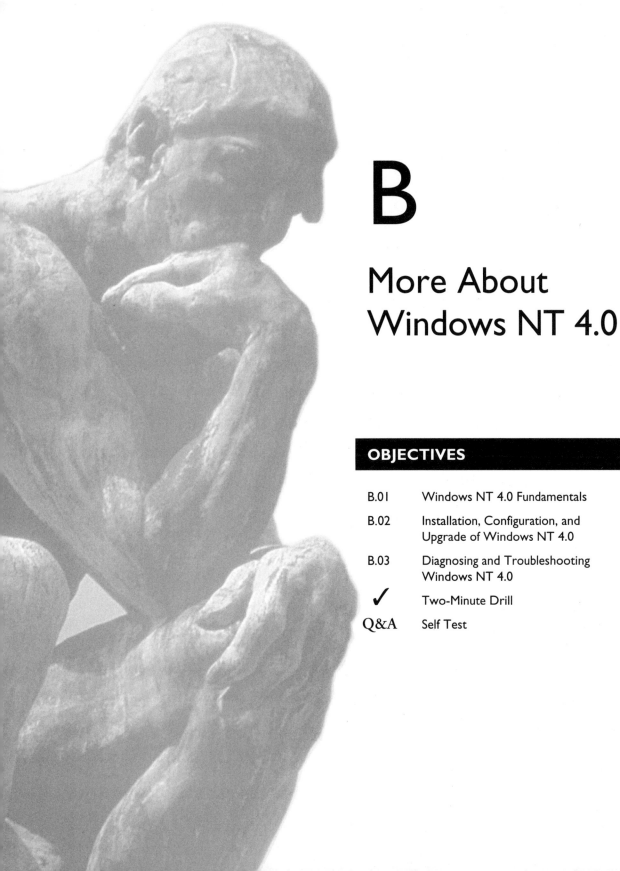

B

More About Windows NT 4.0

A fter receiving valuable feedback from readers, it was discovered that there was more Windows NT 4.0 coverage on the A+ exam than anticipated. As a result, this appendix has been created to assist you in your studies. Most of the Windows NT 4.0 questions you will see on the A+ exam focus on system files and troubleshooting procedures. Fortunately, this information is almost identical to that for Windows 2000. Windows NT 4.0 and Windows 2000 are both part of the NT platform. In fact, before its release, Windows 2000 was known as Windows NT 5.0.

You may also receive some questions about Windows NT 4.0 desktop navigation. Windows NT 4.0 and Windows 9x have an almost identical interface, so as long as you are familiar with the navigation procedures for Windows 9x (Chapter 8), you will be able to apply them to Windows NT 4.0. For example, to change the screen saver, you access the Display icon in the Control Panel. This is true whether you are using the Windows NT 4.0 or Windows 9x Control Panel.

CERTIFICATION OBJECTIVE B.01

Windows NT 4.0 Fundamentals

The Windows NT 4.0 desktop itself is identical to Windows 95 in color schemes, fonts, and taskbar, as well as the appearance of the Start menu and shortcut menus. Furthermore, like Windows 9x, Windows NT 4.0 provides My Computer and Windows Explorer for navigating files and folders and provides the Control Panel and Device Manager for configuring hardware and other system settings. (The Computer Management console does not exist in Windows NT 4.0.) Again, refer to Chapter 8 for information on using the Windows 9x/NT Control Panel and Device Manager.

However, like Windows 2000, Windows NT 4.0 is a network operating system. It is available in Workstation and Server editions to provide secure access to network resources using user-based security. Unlike Windows 9x and 2000, Windows NT 4.0 provides no support for Plug and Play. There is also no support in NT4.0 for USB where 9x and 2000 do support it.

System Files and Utilities

Like Windows 9x and 2000, Windows NT 4.0 relies on the Windows registry for most of its operating instructions and configuration parameters. The Windows NT 4.0 registry is more similar to that of Windows 2000 than 9x, being comprised of one file for each registry key, rather than the 9x USER.DAT and SYSTEM.DAT files. The following subsections describe other system files and utilities found in Windows NT 4.0.

BOOT.INI

The BOOT.INI file is used by Windows NT 4.0 only if the computer contains more than one OS (a dual-boot configuration). The BOOT.INI file is responsible for displaying the OS choices at startup. It also contains the location of each OS so that the computer knows where to look for the selected one. Once an OS has been selected by the user and found by the NTLDR file, the function of BOOT.INI is complete.

NTLDR

The NTLDR file is used by Windows NT 4.0 to coordinate the system's startup procedure. It is responsible for locating and initializing other required startup files, much like the NTLDR file in Windows 2000 or the IO.SYS file in Windows 9x.

NTDETECT.COM

The NTDETECT.COM file is used in the Windows NT 4.0 startup process to gather information about the hardware that currently exists in the system. This information is reported back to NTLDR and is written into the Windows registry.

Registry Editors

Windows NT 4.0 contains the same registry editors as Windows 2000: REGEDIT.EXE and REGEDT32. The two editors differ in that REGEDT32 displays each subtree in a separate window and REGEDIT does not. REGEDT32 also allows you to enter longer key values and set security restrictions on individual keys, subkeys, or values. However, REGEDT32 does not have REGEDIT's ability to set bookmarks and has a less powerful search feature.

SCANREG

Windows NT 4.0 contains the same SCANREG utility found in Windows 9x. This is a registry backup utility that runs in the background and backs up the registry each time the computer is started successfully.

Like Windows 2000, Windows NT 4.0 provides limited support for legacy applications through its use of the AUTOEXEC.NT and CONFIG.NT files.

Compression and Encryption

Windows NT 4.0 can make use of either the FAT16 or NTFS 4 file systems. If NTFS is used, Windows NT 4.0 will support native drive, file and folder compression. To compress an individual file or folder in Windows NT 4.0, access the file or folder's properties, enable the Compress option on the General tab, and click OK. Windows NT 4.0 does not, however, support the native file and folder encryption found in Windows 2000.

CERTIFICATION OBJECTIVE B.02

Installation, Configuration, and Upgrade of Windows NT 4.0

Because Windows NT 4.0 and Windows 2000 are built on the same platform, the procedures for installing and configuring them are quite similar. The same is true for the boot sequence and boot modes.

Installing Windows NT 4.0

To install Windows NT 4.0, you must first boot the computer using the three installation floppy disks or the installation CD-ROM (if your computer's BIOS supports booting from CD). The installation utility (WINNT.EXE) will begin automatically. A welcome screen will appear, prompting you to either install Windows or repair a failed installation.

The setup utility will begin the installation by confirming the existing hardware and prompting you to create or configure partitions on the existing hard drives. Note that the partitioning utility will allow you to convert an existing FAT16 drive to NTFS. However, this conversion is not reversible. Once the appropriate partitions have been created, you will be prompted to select a drive and folder for the Windows NT 4.0 installation.

At this point, you will be prompted to restart the computer. When the computer restarts, the installation wizard will begin automatically and will start to gather information about your computer. During this stage, you will be asked to select an installation type and enter personal, product key, and administrator account information, much like the Windows 2000 installation.

Because Windows NT 4.0 is a network operating system, you will be asked to enter network settings, such as sharing options, protocols, services, and a workgroup or domain name. When the appropriate information has been gathered, the Windows NT 4.0 setup utility will begin copying the required files to the hard drive. The computer will restart, and Windows NT 4.0 will start for the first time.

On systems with more than one operating system, Windows NT 4.0 must be installed as the last one because an installation of a Windows 9x OS will overwrite the bootstrap and make NT unbootable.

The Windows NT 4.0 Boot Process

Like most other processes, the Windows NT 4.0 boot process is very similar to that already described for Windows 2000. When the computer is first started, the BIOS bootstrap phase is conducted. The MBR then locates the bootstrap loader, NTLDR. The NTLDR file is responsible for initiating and organizing the boot process. First, it switches the processor from real mode into 32-bit (protected) mode, then it locates and reads the BOOT.INI file, if one exists (as in a dual-boot configuration).

Once Windows NT 4.0 has been selected from the boot menu (or if Windows NT 4.0 is the only existing operating system), the message "Starting Windows" will appear on the screen. At this time, NTLDR runs NTDETECT.COM whose function is to detect and report on the computer's existing hardware. NTLDR uses these hardware settings to generate the Windows registry. NTLDR then loads the Windows NT kernel, NTOSKRNL.EXE and provides it with the values stored in NTDETECT.COM. NTOSKRNL.EXE will then initialize required device drivers and load the graphical interface.

CERTIFICATION OBJECTIVE B.03

Diagnosing and Troubleshooting Windows NT 4.0

Because Windows NT 4.0 uses many of the same files as Windows 2000, it typically runs into similar problems and requires similar troubleshooting procedures, such as those described in Chapter 10. Like Windows 2000, Windows NT 4.0 includes the Dr. Watson and Event Viewer utilities to help you pinpoint the causes of runtime errors such as GPFs and Illegal Operations. Also, like Windows 2000, many Windows NT 4.0 boot problems can be resolved using the emergency repair process (Chapter 10).

Creating an Emergency Repair Disk

The Windows NT 4.0 emergency repair disk can be used to boot the computer when the Operating System fails to load properly and is used to initiate an emergency repair process similar to that of Windows 2000. You may create an emergency repair disk when prompted during the Windows NT 4.0 installation, or you may create one manually after installation.

To manually create an emergency repair disk, format a blank floppy disk within Windows NT. Run the RDISK.EXE utility from the Run line. The files required to initiate and run the emergency repair process will be copied to the floppy disk. You should use the RDISK utility to update the emergency repair disk each time you make a configuration change in Windows NT 4.0.

You may also wish to create a recovery disk, which will allow you to boot Windows NT 4.0 without using the emergency repair process. This disk can be used when only the startup files are at fault for a failed startup. Format a floppy disk within Windows NT 4.0. Next, copy the NTLDR, NTDETECT.COM, BOOT.INI, OSLOADER.EXE, NTBOOTDD.SYS (when booting from a SCSI disk), and HAL.DLL files to the floppy disk.

CERTIFICATION SUMMARY

Windows NT 4.0 looks very similar to Windows 95, but is functionally more similar to Windows 2000. Use the same navigation techniques in Windows NT 4.0 as you would use in Windows 9x to access programs, files, the Control Panel, and the Device Manager. Because Windows NT 4.0 is architecturally similar to Windows 2000, they share many of the same system files and have the same boot sequence. The Windows NT 4.0 installation is also very similar to that of Windows 2000.

When troubleshooting Windows NT 4.0, use the same procedures you would use in Windows 2000. The Dr. Watson and Event Viewer utilities are available to help you pinpoint problems. As with any operating system, the better your knowledge of the boot system and required files, the more easily and efficiently you will be able to pinpoint and resolve problems.

TWO-MINUTE DRILL

Here are some of the key points from each objective in Appendix B.

Windows NT 4.0 Fundamentals

❑ The Windows NT 4.0 interface is almost identical to that of Windows 95.

❑ Windows NT 4.0 provides the Control Panel for configuration, the Device Manager for installing and troubleshooting hardware, and provides My Computer and the Windows Explorer for navigating files and folders.

❑ Windows NT 4.0 has many of the system files found in Windows 2000, such as BOOT.INI, NTLDR and NTDETECT.COM.

Installation, Configuration, and Upgrade of Windows NT 4.0

❑ Like Windows 2000, you may install Windows NT 4.0 from the three installation floppy disks or the installation CD.

❑ During the installation, you will be prompted to select a file system, enter personal and administrator information, and enter network settings such as protocols, services and domain names.

Diagnosing and Troubleshooting Windows NT 4.0

❑ Windows NT 4.0 typically experiences problems similar to those experienced in Windows 2000.

❑ Use the RDISK.EXE utility in Windows NT 4.0 to create or update an emergency repair disk.

SELF TEST

The following questions will help you measure your understanding of the material presented in this appendix. Read all of the choices carefully because there might be more than one correct answer. Choose all correct answers for each question.

Windows NT 4.0 Fundamentals

1. The Windows NT 4.0 desktop:

   A. Most closely resembles the Windows 9x desktop

   B. Most closely resembles the Windows 2000 desktop

   C. Does not resemble either the Windows 9x or 2000 desktop

   D. Does not support click-and-drag

2. To view your NT 4.0 system's hardware configuration, use

   A. The Control Panel

   B. The Hardware Manager

   C. The Device Manager

   D. The Computer Management Console

3. Which of the following can you use to create a new folder in Windows NT 4.0? (Choose two.)

   A. Control Panel

   B. Folder Manager

   C. Windows Explorer

   D. Desktop Manager

   E. My Computer

4. Which Operating Systems support Plug and Play?

   A. Windows 9x only

   B. Windows 9x and NT 4.0 only

   C. Windows 9x and Windows 2000 only

   D. Windows NT 4.0 and Windows 2000 only

5. Which of the following statements is true?

   A. The Windows NT 4.0 registry is comprised of the SYSTEM.DAT and USER.DAT files.

   B. The files that make up the Windows NT 4.0 registry have the same file names as the files that make up the Windows 2000 registry.

   C. The Windows NT 4.0 registry is contained in the WINNT4.DAT file.

   D. Windows NT 4.0 does not have a system registry.

6. Which of the following are required files in Windows NT 4.0? (Choose two.)

    A. IO.SYS

    B. NTDETECT.COM

    C. NT.DAT

    D. USER.DAT

    E. NTLDR

7. What is the function of the Windows NT 4.0 SCANREG utility?

    A. To scan the registry for viruses

    B. To create a backup copy of the registry

    C. To allow you to manually edit the registry

    D. The SCANREG utility does not exist in Windows NT 4.0.

8. Which of the following statements is true?

    A. Any operating system that can use the NTFS 4 file system can make use of native file and folder encryption.

    B. Windows 2000 supports native file and folder compression and encryption.

    C. Windows NT 4.0 and Windows 2000 support native file and folder compression and encryption.

    D. Windows NT 4.0 supports native file and folder encryption.

Installation, Configuration, and Upgrade of Windows NT 4.0

9. Which file is launched when you perform a clean install of Windows NT 4.0?

    A. SETUP.BAT

    B. WINNT32.EXE

    C. WINNT.EXE

    D. INSTALL.EXE

10. What is the function of the Windows NT 4.0 NTDETECT.COM file?

    A. To initiate and organize the Windows NT 4.0 startup process

    B. To detect the presence of more than one operating system at startup

    C. To detect and remove known viruses from the system at startup

    D. To detect and report the existing system hardware at startup

Diagnosing and Troubleshooting Windows NT 4.0

11. Which utility can you use to create a Windows NT 4.0 emergency repair disk?

    A. REPAIR.EXE

    B. ERDNT4.EXE

    C. The Device Manager

    D. RDISK.EXE

SELF TEST ANSWERS

Windows NT 4.0 Fundamentals

1. ☑ **A.** The Windows NT 4.0 desktop most loosely resembles the Windows 9x desktop. In fact, it uses identical color schemes and fonts and contains the same Recycle Bin, My Computer, and Network Neighborhood icons.

   ☒ **B** is incorrect because it states that the Windows NT 4.0 desktop resembles the Windows 2000 desktop. The two desktops are actually quite different in that they use different colors, fonts, start menus, and contain different system icons. **C** is incorrect because it states that the Windows NT 4.0 desktop does not resemble either the Windows 9x or 2000 desktops. However, as described above, Windows NT 4.0 is visually almost identical to Windows 9x. **D** is incorrect because Windows NT 4.0, like Windows 9x, supports a variety of mouse actions, including click, double-click, right-click, and click-and-drag.

2. ☑ **C.** To view your NT 4.0 system's hardware configuration, use the Device Manager. Like Windows 9x, this applet allows you to view, remove, create, or edit hardware configurations, and can help you pinpoint hardware problems.

   ☒ **A** is incorrect because the Control Panel allows you to configure Windows, but not your system's hardware. **B** is incorrect because the Hardware Manager is not a valid Windows applet. **D** is incorrect because the Computer Management Console exists in Windows 2000 only.

3. ☑ **C, E.** You can use either Windows Explorer or My Computer to create a new folder in Windows NT 4.0. These are the same file and folder management utilities found in Windows 9x.

   ☒ **A** is incorrect because the Control Panel allows you to configure Windows, but not to manage files and folders. **B**, Folder Manager, and **D**, Desktop Manager, are incorrect because these are not a valid Windows utilities.

4. ☑ **C.** Plug and Play is supported by Windows 9x and Windows 2000 only. That is, Windows NT 4.0 includes no support for Plug and Play devices.

   ☒ **A** is incorrect because although they differ in the devices they support, Windows 9x and Windows 2000 both support Plug and Play. **B** and **D** are incorrect because there is no support for Plug and Play in Windows NT 4.0.

5. ☑ **B.** The files that make up the Windows NT 4.0 registry have the same file names as the files that make up the Windows 2000 registry. That is, the registry is comprised of a file for each registry key.

☒   **A** is incorrect because the SYSTEM.DAT and USER.DAT files make up the Windows 9x registry, not the Windows NT 4.0 or Windows 2000 registry. **C** is incorrect because WINNT4.DAT is not a valid Windows NT 4.0 system file name. **D** is incorrect because it states that Windows NT 4.0 does not have a system registry.

6.   ☑   **B, E.** NTDETECT.COM and NTLDR are both required in Windows NT 4.0. NTLDR is responsible for initiating and organizing the boot process and NTDETECT.COM is responsible for detecting and reporting information about the existing hardware during startup.
☒   **A** and **D** are incorrect because IO.SYS and USER.DAT are required in Windows 9x, but do not exist in Windows NT 4.0. **C** is incorrect because NT.DAT is not a valid NT 4.0 system file name.

7.   ☑   **B.** The function of the Windows NT 4.0 SCANREG utility is to create a backup copy of the registry. This is done automatically each time the Windows NT 4.0 OS is properly loaded. At the next OS startup, if the registry files are corrupt, the backup copies will be used instead.
☒   **A** is incorrect because SCANREG is not an anti-virus tool. **C** is incorrect because in Windows NT 4.0, registry editing utilities are REGEDIT.EXE an REGEDT32.EXE. **D** is incorrect because the SCANREG utility is present and is run automatically in Windows NT 4.0.

8.   ☑   **B.** Windows 2000 supports native file and folder compression and encryption. This is only supported on NTFS partitions.
☒   **A, C,** and **D** are incorrect because although Windows NT 4.0 supports native file compression on NTFS drives, it does not support native file and folder encryption.

Installation, Configuration, and Upgrade of Windows NT 4.0

9.   ☑   **C.** WINNT.EXE is launched when you perform a clean install of Windows NT 4.0. This file is the 16-bit installation file.
☑   **A** and **D** are incorrect because SETUP.BAT and INSTALL.EXE are not valid Windows NT 4.0 installation file names. **B** is incorrect because WINNT32.EXE is the 32-bit installation file, used when you are upgrading from an existing 32-bit system.

10.   ☑   **D.** The function of NTDETECT.COM is to detect and report the existing system hardware at startup. This information is used by NTLDR to build the Windows NT 4.0 registry.
☒   **A** is incorrect because the file responsible for initiating and organizing the Windows NT 4.0 startup process is NTLDR. **B** is incorrect because the BOOT.INI file is responsible for storing the OS choices, but there is no file in Windows NT 4.0 that will search for and detect the presence of more than one OS at startup. **C** is incorrect because NTDETECT.COM is responsible for detecting hardware configurations, not viruses.

Diagnosing and Troubleshooting Windows NT 4.0

11. ☑   **D.** You can use the RDISK.EXE utility to create a Windows NT 4.0 emergency repair disk. RDISK.EXE will copy all files required to run the emergency repair process onto a floppy disk. You can then use this disk to repair Windows NT 4.0 if it fails to load properly.
☒   **A** and **B** are incorrect because REPAIR.EXE and ERDNT4.EXE are not valid Windows NT 4.0 utilities. **C** is incorrect because although the Device Manager may allow you to pinpoint and troubleshoot hardware problems, it will not allow you to create an emergency repair disk.

Glossary

Access Methods   Also known as *network access*, these are the methods by which a device communicates on a network. Network access provides a standard that all devices that wish to communicate on a network must abide by in order to eliminate communication conflicts.

Active Matrix Display   Active matrix displays are based on Thin Film Transistor technology. Instead of having two rows of transistors, active matrix displays have a transistor at every pixel, which enables much quicker display changes than passive matrix displays and produces display quality comparable to a CRT.

ANSI.SYS   ANSI.SYS is a DOS system file that is loaded by CONFIG.SYS if required. This file loads an extended character set for use by DOS and DOS applications that includes basic drawing and color capabilities. Normally used for drawing and filling different boxes for menu systems, it is seldom in use today. By default, it carries no attributes, and is not required for OS startup.

ARCHIVE Attribute   The ARCHIVE attribute is set automatically when a file is created or modified, and is automatically removed by back-up software when the file is backed up.

ATTRIB.EXE   ATTRIB.EXE is a command line utility that can be used to change the attributes of a file or group of files.

AUTOEXEC.BAT   A user-editable system file, AUTOEXEC.BAT contains commands to modify the PC environment (PATH, COMSPEC, other SET commands), and to execute applications. It can be used to create a menu system, prompt for user input, or *call* other batch files to maintain a modular structure. By default, it carries no attributes, and is not required for OS startup.

Basic Input Output System   See BIOS.

Bi-Directional Print Mode   Most common in some of the newer and more advanced printers, bi-directional print mode means that the printer is able to talk back to the computer, enabling, for example, the printer to send the user exact error messages that are displayed on the workstation. It also helps the spooler to avoid print spooler stalls.

BIOS   Most commonly known as BIOS, Basic Input Output System is a standard set of instructions or programs that handle boot operations. When an application needs to perform an I/O operation on a computer, the operating system makes the request to the system BIOS, which in turn translates the request into the appropriate instruction set used by the hardware device.

Brownout   Momentary lapses in power supply. Brownouts can cause problems with computer components that are not designed to withstand these events.

Bus   A bus is the actual pathway used to transmit electronic signals from one computer device to another.

Bus Topology   In a local area network, a bus topology has each device on the network connected to a central cable, or bus. Most common with coaxial cabling.

Cache Memory   Cache memory is used to store frequently used instructions and data so that they can be accessed quickly by the computer.

Carrier Sense Multiple Access/Collision Detection   See CSMA/CD.

Central Processing Unit   See CPU.

Chip Creep   A phenomenon whereby a computer chip becomes loose within its socket.

Cleaning Blade   This rubber blade inside a laser printer extends the length of the photosensitive drum. It removes excess toner after the print process has completed and deposits it into a reservoir for re-use.

CMOS   The Complementary Metal-Oxide Semiconductor (or CMOS) is an integrated circuit composed of a metal oxide that is located directly on the system board. The CMOS, which is similar to RAM in that data can be written to the chip, enables a computer to store essential operating parameters after the computer has been turned off, enabling a faster system boot.

Coaxial Cable   A high-bandwidth network cable that consists of a central wire surrounded by a screen of fine wires.

COMMAND.COM   COMMAND.COM is a DOS system file that is automatically executed in the ROOT directory at startup. This file contains the internal command set and error messages. By default, it carries no attributes, but is required for OS startup.

Complementary Metal-Oxide Semiconductor   See CMOS.

CONFIG.SYS   A user-editable system file that provides the ability to install device drivers. Windows 9x does not require any specific settings to be made in CONFIG.SYS.

Cooperative Multitasking   There are two different types of multitasking: cooperative and preemptive. Cooperative multitasking means that applications must voluntarily relinquish control of the CPU. When an application relinquishes control of the CPU, Windows then decides which application will execute next. The most common way for an application to relinquish control is by asking Windows if any messages are available.

CPU   The CPU (Central Processing Unit) is the operations center of a computer. Its job is to provide the devices attached to the computer with directives that retrieve, display, manipulate, and store information.

CSMA/CD   Most commonly found on Ethernet networks, carrier sense multiple access/collision detection (CSMA/CD) is a network communication protocol and operates in much the same way as humans communicate. With CSMA/CD, a device listens to the network for a pause in communication, and attempts to transmit data onto the network during the pause. The device then detects if any other devices have transmitted onto the network at the same time. If it detects that another device has transmitted data onto the network at the same time, the device then waits an unspecified random amount of time and retransmits its data.

Defragmentation   A process that reorganizes fragmented files back in a proper, contiguous fashion. This is done by moving several of them to an unused portion of the drive, erasing the previous locations in contiguous clusters, then rewriting the files back in proper sequence. Performed periodically, defragmentation is probably the single best operation a user can perform to maintain a high-performance system.

Device Driver   Device drivers are programs that translate necessary information between the operating system and the specific peripheral device for which they are configured, such as a printer.

Dial-Up Access   Dial-up access is defined as access provided to the Internet, a LAN, or even another computer by using a phone line and a modem.

Dial-Up Networking   Refers to the type of network in which a modem is used to connect two or more workstations.

DIMM   A Dual In-Line Memory Module (DIMM) is very similar to a SIMM; it's a small plug-in circuit board that contains the memory chips that you need to add certain increments of RAM to your computer. Because the memory chips run along both sides of the chip, DIMM chips can hold twice as much memory as SIMM chips.

DIP Switch   Dual in-line package (DIP) switches are very tiny boxes with switches embedded in them. Each switch sets a value of 0 or 1, depending on how they are set. These switches are used to provide user-accessible configuration settings for computers and peripheral devices.

Direct Memory Access   See DMA.

Dirty Current   Noise present on a power line is referred to as dirty current. This noise is caused by *electro-magnetic interference (EMI)* and can stray, or leak, from the current into nearby components. When EMI leaks from power current, it is called a magnetic field and can easily damage computer components.

DMA   Direct memory access (DMA) is a facility by which a peripheral can communicate directly with RAM, without intervention by the CPU.

DNS   Domain Name System (DNS) is the Internet-based system that resolves symbolic, called host names, names to IP addresses (which are a series of numbers) that the computer is able to understand.

Docking Station   Docking stations allow users to add "desktop-like" capabilities, such as a mouse, monitor, or keyboard, to their portable computer by plugging these components into a docking station and connecting their portable only to the docking station, rather than to each individual component.

Domain Name System   See DNS.

DOS Mode   DOS Mode, or DOS Compatibility Mode as it is commonly known, allows execution of some older MS-DOS applications that are not capable of running in Windows 95. Applications that require use of MS-DOS mode are usually blocked from operation within Windows 95. DOS itself stands for Disk Operating System.

Download   Downloading refers to the process of transferring a file or files from one computer to another. Unlike uploading, the transfer is always initiated by the computer that will be receiving the file(s).

Downtime   Downtime is the time wasted as a result of a malfunctioning computer or network.

DRAM   Dynamic Random Access Memory (DRAM) chips abandoned the idea of using the unwieldy transistors and switches in favor of using the smaller capacitors that could represent 0s and 1s as an electronic charge. This resulted in the ability to store more information on a single chip, but also meant that the chip needed a constant refresh and hence more power.

Dual In-Line Memory Module   See DIMM.

Dual In-Line Package Switch   See DIP Switch.

Dynamic RAM   See DRAM.

EBKAC Error   A common error that most technicians face, the EBKAC error stands for Error Between Keyboard and Chair. As that implies, EBKAC errors are not technical errors, but rather errors on the part of the end user. Common EBKAC errors include power cords being unplugged, no paper in printer, and power switches being turned off.

ECP   ECP (Extended Capability Port) is a parallel printer interface designed to speed up data transfer rates by bypassing the processor and writing the data directly to memory.

EDO RAM   Extended Data Output RAM (EDO RAM) is a type of DRAM chip designed for processor access speeds of approximately 10 to 15 percent above fast-page mode memory.

EISA   Extended Industry Standard Architecture (EISA) is an industry standard bus architecture that allows for peripherals to utilize the 32-bit data bus that is available with 386 and 486 processors.

Electrophotographic Printing Process   See EP Process.

EMM386.EXE   EMM386.EXE is a DOS system file that, along with HIMEM.SYS, controls memory management. It is not required for system startup in pre-Windows 95 machines. Basically, this is an expanded memory emulator that performs two major functions: It enables and controls EMS, if desired, and enables the use of upper memory as system memory.

EMS   Meaning Expanded Memory Specification, EMS is an expanded memory standard that allows programs that recognize it to work with more than 640K of RAM.

Enhanced Parallel Port   See EPP.

EP Process   The EP (Electrophotographic Printing) process is the six-step process that a laser printer goes through to put an image on a page. The process follows these six steps: Cleaning, Charging, Writing, Developing, Transferring, and Fusing.

EPP   EPP (Enhanced Parallel Port) is an expansion bus that offers an extended control code set. With EPP mode, data travels both from the computer to the printer and vice versa.

Error Between Keyboard and Chair   See EBKAC Error

Exit Roller   One of four different types of rollers found in printers, exit rollers aid in the transfer and control of the paper as it leaves the printer. Depending on the printer type, they direct the paper to a tray where it can be collated, sorted, or even stapled.

Expanded Memory Specification   See EMS.

Extended Capability Port   See ECP.

Extended Data Output RAM   See EDO RAM.

Extended Industry Standard Architecture   See EISA.

eXtended Memory Specification   See XMS.

FDISK   A DOS-based utility program used to partition a hard disk in preparation for installing an operating system.

Feed Roller   One of four different types of rollers found in printers. Also known as paper pickup roller, the feed roller, when activated, rotates against the top page in the paper tray and rolls it into the printer. The feed roller works together with a special rubber pad to prevent more than one sheet from being fed into the printer at a time.

Fiber Optic Cable   Extremely high-speed network cable that consists of glass fibers that carry light signals instead of electrical signals. Fiber optic cable is best used for transmission over long distances, and is much less susceptible to environmental difficulties, such as electronic and magnetic interference.

File Transfer Protocol   See FTP.

Flash Memory   A faster version of ROM that, while still basically developed as ROM, can be addressed and loaded *thousands* of times.

Fragmentation   Because DOS writes files to the hard disk by breaking the file into cluster-sized pieces and then storing each piece in the next available cluster, as files are deleted and then rewritten, they can be written in noncontiguous clusters scattered all over the disk. This is known as file fragmentation.

FTP   Much older than the HTTP protocol, the File Transfer Protocol(FTP) is the protocol used to download files from an FTP server to a client computer. FTP is much faster than HTTP.

Fully Qualified Path   A fully qualified path is the entire path of a file, starting from the root of the file system, to the file being referenced.

Fusing Rollers   One of four different types of rollers found in laser printers, fusing rollers comprise the final stage of the Electrophotographic Printing (EP) process, bonding the toner particles to the page to prevent smearing. The roller on the toner side of the page has a non-stick surface that is heated to a high temperature to permanently bond the toner to the paper.

Ghosted Image "Ghosting" is what occurs when a portion of an image previously printed to a page is printed again, only not as dark. One cause of this is if the erasure lamp of the laser printer sometimes fails to operate correctly, not completely erasing the previous image from the EP drum. Another cause of ghosting may be due to a malfunction in the cleaning blade such that it doesn't adequately scrape away the residual toner.

Handshaking The process by which two connecting modems agree on the method of communication to be used.

HIDDEN Attribute The Hidden attribute keeps a file from being displayed when a DIR command is issued.

HIMEM.SYS HIMEM.SYS is a DOS system file that, along with EMM386.EXE, controls memory management. It is not required for system startup in pre-Windows 95 machines.

HTML Derived from the Standard General Markup Language (SGML), the Hypertext Markup Language(HTML) is the markup language that dictates the layout and design of a Web page.

HTTP Hypertext Transfer Protocol (HTTP) is the TCP/IP-based protocol that is most commonly used for client/server communications on the World Wide Web.

Hub Hubs are common connection points for devices in a network. Hubs contain multiple ports and are commonly used to connect segments of a LAN.

Hypertext Markup Language See HTML.

Hypertext Transfer Protocol See HTTP.

Impact Printer Impact printers, like the name suggests, require the impact with an ink ribbon to print characters and images. An example of an impact printer is a daisy wheel.

Industry Standard Architecture See ISA.

Input Device   Input devices take data from a user, such as the click of a mouse or the typing on a keyboard, and convert that data into electrical signals used by your computer. Several devices that provide input are: keyboards, mice, trackballs, pointing devices, digitized tablets, and touch screens.

Internet Service Provider   See ISP.

Internetwork Packet Exchange/Sequenced Packet Exchange
See IPX/SPX

Interrupt Request Line   See IRQ.

IO.SYS   IO.SYS is a DOS system file that defines basic input/output routines for the processor. By default, it carries the hidden, system, and read-only attributes, and *is* required for OS startup

IPX/SPX   Internetwork Packet Exchange/Sequenced Packet Exchange (IPX/SPX) is a very fast and highly established network protocol most commonly used with Novell Netware

IRQ   Interrupt Request (IRQ) lines are the physical lines over which system components such as modems or printers communicate directly with the CPU when the device is ready to send or receive data.

ISA   Industry Standard Architecture (ISA) is an industry standard bus architecture that allows for peripherals to utilize the 16-bit data bus that is available with 286 and 386 processors.

ISP   An Internet Service Provider (ISP), as its name suggests, is a company that provides folks with access to the Internet, usually for a fee. On the other hand, a company that gives their employees Internet access through a private bank of modems is usually not considered an ISP.

Jumper   Jumpers, like DIP switches, are used to accomplish configuration manually. Jumpers are actually made of two separate components: a row of metal pins on the hardware itself and a small plastic cap that has a metal insert inside of it. The two parts together form a circuit that sets the configuration. This form of configuration device is only used to set one value for a feature at a time, as opposed to DIP switches, which can handle multiple configurations.

LAN   A local area network (LAN) is created whenever two or more computers in a limited geographic area (within about a two-mile radius) are linked by high-performance cables so that users can exchange information, share peripheral devices, or access a common server.

Local Area Network   See LAN.

Material Safety Data Sheets   See MSDS.

MEM.EXE   MEM.EXE is a simple command line utility that, using various command switches, can display various reports of memory usage.

MEMMAKER.EXE   A Microsoft utility that automatically determines the best possible configuration and load sequence for a given set of applications and drivers used. Before using MEMMAKER, the PC should be configured for normal operation (i.e. mouse driver, network operation, sound support, and so forth), including any items that are loaded from the AUTOEXEC.BAT and CONFIG.SYS files.

Memory Address   The memory address is used to receive commands from the processor that are destined for any device attached to a computer. Each device must have a unique memory address in order for it to function.

Memory Bank   A memory bank is the actual slot that memory goes into.

Memory Effect   When a Nickel Cadmium, or NiCad, battery is recharged before it is fully discharged, the battery loses the ability to fully recharge again, which is known as the memory effect.

MSD   MSD, Microsoft Diagnostics, is a DOS-based utility that provides a great deal of information about the system. It is most useful in determining what the system has installed in it, such as memory and hard drives.

MSD.EXE   A Microsoft System Diagnostics program, MSD.EXE roots out almost every conceivable item about your system that you'd ever want to know (and then some!) and displays it in a menu-driven format for you to browse

MSDOS.SYS MSDOS.SYS is a DOS system file that defines system file locations. By default, it carries the hidden, system, and read-only attributes, and is required for OS startup.

MSDS Material Safety Data Sheets (MSDS) are white pages that contain information on any substance that is deemed hazardous, most notably cleaning solvents. The purpose of MSDS is to inform employees about the dangers inherent in hazardous materials and the proper use of these items to prevent potential injuries from occurring.

Multi-Boot Configuration A system that has been configured to allow a user to select one of multiple installed operating systems at boot time.

Multimeter A multimeter is a device that measures current, resistance, or voltage, used to determine whether certain computer components are functioning correctly based on these electrical measurements.

NetBEUI The NetBios Extended User Interface (NetBEUI) is an extremely fast network transport protocol that is most commonly found on smaller networks.

NetBios Extended User Interface See NetBEUI.

Network Interface Card See NIC.

Network Topology The arrangement of cable links in a local area network. There are three principal network topologies: bus, ring, and star.

NIC A network interface card (NIC) is used to connect a PC to a network cable.

Noise Filter UPS's contain a special filter, called a *noise filter*, that reduces the amount of noise present in electrical current and eliminates magnetic fields caused by noise, thus providing some protection to the components that utilize the current or are nearby.

Non-Impact Printer Non-impact printers do not use an ink ribbon, and therefore do not require direct contact with the paper for printing. An example of a non-impact printer is a laser printer.

Normal Mode   Normal Mode is the mode in which Windows 95 is started by default, which provides full functionality of the Windows 95 Explorer.

Null Modem Cable   A null modem cable is a special cable that has the send and receive lines reversed on the connector. It enables you to connect two computers directly, without using a modem.

Operating System   See OS.

Operator Error   Operator error occurs when the customer inadvertently makes a configuration change.

OS   By definition, an Operating System (OS) is a set of computer instruction codes, usually *compiled* into executable files, whose purpose is to define input and output devices and connections, and provide instructions for the computer's central processor to operate on to retrieve and display data.

Output Device   Output devices take electronic signals *from* a computer and convert them into a format that the user can use. Examples of output devices include monitors and printers.

Overlays   Rather than put all available functions into a single huge executable file, most developers choose to modularize their applications by creating library files that include additional commands and functions. These additional executable enhancement files are usually referred to as overlays.

Page Description Language   See PDL.

Parallel Port   One of two types of communication ports found on a motherboard (the other is the serial port), the parallel port is used to connect a peripheral device (most commonly a printer for this type of port) to the computer. A parallel port allows transmission of data over eight conductors at one time. The processor socket is the actual socket used to attach the processor to the motherboard.

Parallel Processing   The Intel 586 (Pentium) chip combined two 486DX chips into one, called the *Dual Independent Bus Architecture*. This allowed each processor inside the chip to execute instructions simultaneously and independently from each other, which is called parallel processing.

Parity   Parity is an error-checking mechanism that enables the device to recognize single-bit errors.

Partition   A section of the storage area on a computer's hard disk. A hard disk must be partitioned before an operating system can be installed.

Passive Matrix Display   Most common on portable systems, the passive matrix display is made from a grid of horizontal and vertical wires. At the end of each wire is a transistor. In order to light a pixel at (X, Y), a signal is sent to the X and Y transistors. In turn, these transistors then send voltage down the wire, which turns on the LCD at the intersection of the two wires

PC Card   The PC Card (Personal Computer Memory Card International Association, or PCMCIA) bus was first created to expand the memory capabilities in small, hand-held computers. It is a type of bus used mostly with laptop computers that provides a convenient way to interchange PCMCIA-compatible devices, which are only slightly larger than credit cards.

PCI   The Peripheral Component Interconnect(PCI) was designed in response to the Pentium class processor's utilization of a 64-bit bus. PCI buses are designed to be processor-independent.

PCMCIA   See PC Card.

PDL   Laser printers use a Page Description Language(PDL) to send and receive print job instructions one page at a time, rather than one dot at a time, as with other types of printers.

Peripheral Component Interconnect   See PCI.

Personal Computer Memory Card International Association   See PC Card.

Photosensitive Drum   This light-sensitive drum is the core of the electrophotographic process inside the laser printer. This drum is affected by the cleaning, charging, writing, and transferring processes in the six-step laser printing process.

Plug and Play   Plug and Play offers automatic driver installation as soon as hardware or software is "plugged in," or installed. Microsoft first offered PnP support on the PC with Windows 95.

Pointing Stick   One of the three most common types of pointing devices found on portable systems, the pointing stick is a small pencil-eraser-size piece of rubber in the center of the keyboard. The on-screen pointer is controlled by simply pushing the pointing stick in the desired direction.

Point-To-Point Protocol   See PPP.

POLEDIT.EXE   The Windows 95 System Policy feature, POLEDIT.EXE, is used to build a Registry template that will later be used during logon to set common-denominator defaults for all network users, and add certain restrictions on a global basis if deemed necessary

POP   Post Office Protocol (POP) is a common protocol by which an Internet server lets you receive e-mail and download it from the server to your own machine.

POST   As its name suggests, a Power On Self Test (POST) is self test performed by the computer that occurs during boot time. It is used to diagnose system-related problems.

Post Office Protocol   See POP.

Power On Self Test   See POST.

Power Spike   When there is a power spike, there is a sudden, huge increase in power that lasts for a split second. Power spikes can literally fry computer components.

PPP   The Point-To-Point protocol, PPP is a serial communications protocol used to connect two computers over a phone line via a modem. SLIP is the alternate protocol that is acceptable to most browsers, though it's not as common as PPP.

Preemptive Multitasking   There are two different types of multitasking: cooperative and preemptive. Preemptive multitasking means that control is passed from one program to another automatically by the Windows process scheduler.

Primary Corona Wire   This highly negatively charged wire inside a laser printer is responsible for electrically erasing the photosensitive drum, preparing it to be written with a new image in the writing stage of the laser print process.

Processor Socket   The processor socket is the actual socket used to attach the processor to the motherboard.

Protocol   A set of communication standards between two computers on a network. Common protocols include TCP/IP, NetBEUI, and IPX/SPX.

READ ONLY Attribute   The READ ONLY attribute prevents a user or application from inadvertently deleting or changing a file.

Refresh   Refresh refers to the automatic process of constantly updating memory chips to ensure that their signals are correct. The refresh rate is the frequency by which chips are refreshed, usually about every 60 to 70 thousandths of a second.

Registration Roller   One of four different types of rollers found in laser printers, the registration roller synchronizes the paper movement with the writing process inside the EP cartridge. Registration rollers do not advance the paper until the EP cartridge is ready to process the next line of the image.

Registry   A complex database used by Windows NT and Windows 95 (and later) pertaining to both application settings and hardware configuration.

Rollers   Rollers are located inside a printer to aid in the movement of paper through the printer. There are four main types of rollers: feed, registration, fuser, and exit.

Safe Mode   Safe Mode is a special diagnostic mode of Windows 95 that starts the operating system without any network, CD-ROM, and printer drivers. This special mode allows you to change an incorrect setting, which will in most cases allow you to return an abnormally functioning system to its correct operation.

Serial Port   One of two types of communication ports found on a motherboard (the other is the parallel port), the serial port connects to a serial line that leads to a computer peripheral<@151>the type most common with modems and mice. The serial port transmits data sequentially, bit by bit over a single conductor.

SIMD   Single Instruction Multiple Data (SIMD) works by allowing a single instruction to operate on multiple pieces of data when an application is performing a repetitive loop.

SIMM   A Single In-Line Memory Module(SIMM) is a small plug-in circuit board that contains the memory chips that you need to add certain increments of RAM to your computer. The chips are positioned along one side of the board.

Simple Mail Transfer Protocol   See SMTP.

Single In-Line Memory Module   See SIMM.

Single Instruction Multiple Data   See SIMD.

Slack   Slack is the space left between the end of a file and the end of the cluster in which the file resides.

SLIP   The Serial Line Interface Protocol, SLIP is a protocol used to manage telecommunications between a client and a server over a phone line. PPP is the alternate protocol that is acceptable to most browsers, and is in fact the most common.

SMTP   Simple Mail Transfer Protocol (SMTP) is the underlying protocol for Internet-based e-mail.

Socket Services   Socket Services is a layer of BIOS-level software that isolates PC Card software from the computer hardware and detects the insertion or removal of PC Cards.

Solenoid   The solenoid is a resistive coil found in dot matrix and daisy wheel printers. When the solenoid is energized, the pin is forced away from the printhead and impacts the printer ribbon and ultimately the paper, thus impressing the image on the page.

SRAM   Unlike DRAM, Static RAM (SRAM) retains its value as long as power is supplied. It is not constantly refreshed. However, SRAM does require a periodic update and tends to use excessive amounts of power when it does so.

Star Topology   In a local area network, a star topology has each device on the network connected to a central processor, usually a hub. Most common with twisted pair cabling.

Static RAM   See SRAM.

Stylus   Shaped like a pen, a stylus is used to select menu options and the like on a monitor screen or to draw line art on a graphics tablet.

Sync Frequency   Monitors use a *sync frequency* to control the refresh rate, which is the rate at which the display device is repainted. If this setting is incorrect, you get symptoms such as: a "dead" monitor, lines running through the display, a flickering screen, and a reduced or enlarged image.

SYSTEM Attribute   The SYSTEM attribute is usually set by DOS or Windows, and cannot be modified using standard DOS or Windows commands, including the ATTRIB command or File Manager.

SYSTEM.INI   SYSTEM.INI is a Windows system file that configures Windows to address specific hardware devices and their associated settings. Errors in this file can and do cause Windows to fail to start, or crash unexpectedly.

TCP/IP   The most common protocol suite in use today, Transmission Control Protocol/Internet Protocol (TCP/IP) is the suite of protocols upon which the Internet is based. It refers to the communication standards for data transmission over the Internet, although TCP/IP can also be used on private networks without Internet connectivity.

Time Slicing   The process of the CPU dividing up time between applications for preemptive multitasking is called time slicing.

Token Passing   Token passing is a network communication protocol by which a token is passed from device to device around a virtual (and frequently physical) ring on a network. Whenever a device receives the token, it is then allowed to transmit onto the network.

Token Ring   A Local Area Network (LAN) specification that was developed by IBM in the 1980s for PC-based networks and classified by the (Institute of Electrical and Electronics Engineers) IEEE as 802.5. It specifies a star topology physically and a ring topology logically. It runs at either four Mbps or 16 Mbps, but all nodes on the ring must run at the same speed.

Toner   Toner is comprised of finely divided particles of plastic resin and organic compounds bonded to iron particles. It is naturally negatively charged, which aids in attracting it to the written areas of the photosensitive drum during the transfer step of the laser printing process.

Touch Pads   A touch pad is a stationary pointing device commonly used on laptop computers in replace of a mouse or trackball. They are pads that have either thin wires running through them, or specialized surfaces that can sense the pressure of your finger on them. You slide your finger across the touchpad to control the pointer or cursor on the screen.

Trackball   Most commonly, trackballs are used in older portable computers in replace of a mouse. Trackballs are built the same way as an opto-mechanical mouse, except upside-down with the ball on top.

Transfer Corona   This roller inside a laser printer contains a positively charged wire designed to pull the toner off of the photosensitive drum and place it on the page.

Transistor   A transistor is the most fundamental component of electronic circuits. A CPU chip, for example, contains thousands to millions of transistors, which are used to process information in the form of electronic signals. The more transistors a CPU has, the faster it can process data.

Transmission Control Protocol/Internet Protocol   See TCP/IP.

Twisted Pair   By far the most common type of network cable, twisted pair consists of two insulated wires wrapped around each other to help avoid interference from other wires.

Uninterruptible Power Supply   See UPS.

Upload   Uploading is the process of transferring files from one computer to another. Unlike downloading, uploading is always initiated from the computer that is sending the files.

UPS   The uninterruptible power supply (UPS) is a device that was designed to protect your computer and its components from possible injury from the problems that are inherent with today's existing power supply structure.

VESA Local Bus   See VL-Bus.

Virtual Memory   Virtual memory is memory that the processor has been "tricked" into using as if it were actual physical memory.

Virus   Any program that is written with the intent of doing harm to a computer. Viruses have the ability to replicate themselves by attaching themselves to programs or documents. They range in activity from extreme data loss to an annoying message that pops up every few minutes.

VL-Bus   Originally created to address performance issues, the VESA Local Bus (VL-Bus) was meant to enable earlier bus designs to handle a maximum clock speed equivalent to that of processors.

WAN   A wide area network (WAN) is created whenever two or more computers are linked by long-distance communication lines that traverse distances greater than those supported by LANs (or, greater than about two miles).

Wide Area Network   See WAN.

WIN.INI   WIN.INI is a dynamic Windows system file that contains configuration information for Windows applications. Errors made in this file seldom have global implications to Window's operation, but can cripple specific applications or features. Printing is also controlled by settings in this file.

Windows Accelerator Card RAM   See WRAM

WINFILE.INI   In pre-Windows 95 systems, this is the configuration file that stores the names of the directories that File Manager displays when starting.

WRAM   The Windows Accelerator Card was introduced into the market out of a need to assist some environments with running Microsoft Windows. WRAM utilizes memory that resides on the card itself to perform the Windows-specific functions, and therefore speeds up the OS.

XMS   Meaning eXtended Memory Specification, XMS is a set of standards that allows applications to access extended memory.

Zoomed Video   See ZV.

ZV   Zoomed Video (ZV) is a direct data connection between a PC Card and host system that allows a PC Card to write video data directly to the video controller.

INDEX

16-bit SCSI systems, 75
32-bit SCSI systems, 75
802.3 (Ethernet), 276

A

"A: is not accessible" error message, 118–119
AC adapter, 27
AC (alternating current) voltage, 7
accelerated graphics ports (AGP), 125, 210
access
    dial-up, 13, 484
    network, 273–274
    shared drive, 476–477
active matrix displays, 29
Add Hardware Wizard, 395–399
Add Printer Wizard, 407
address/termination conflicts, 71–74, 76
address translation, 132–133
addresses, 31–32, 485–488. *See also* IP addresses
Advanced Technology (AT) motherboards, 205
advanced transfer cache (ATC), 195
AGP (accelerated graphics port), 125, 210
alcohol, 162, 163, 244
alternating current (AC) voltage, 7
AMD Athlon processor, 196
AMD Duron processor, 196
AMD K5 processor, 193
AMD K6 processor, 195
AMD processor, 192
American National Standards Institute (ANSI), 67
analog modems, 13

ANSI (American National Standards Institute), 67
antistatic spray, 173, 174
antistatic wristband, 4
antivirus utilities, 454–455
application file, 308
application log, 439
applications
    boot error and, 431–432
    installing and launching, 400–407
    runtime errors of, 439–448
    troubleshooting, 141, 435, 436–439
architecture, network, 266
archive attribute, 338
ASD (Automatic Skip Driver), 317–318
asynchronous serial communications, 44
AT (Advanced Technology) motherboards, 205
ATA (AT Attachment), 62
ATC (advanced transfer cache), 195
Athlon processor, AMD, 196
attenuation, 269
ATTRIB command, 327
ATX motherboard, 205–207
audio errors, 121, 122–124
AUTOEXEC.BAT, 313
AUTOEXEC.BAT (system file), 386, 428–429
Automatic Skip Driver (ASD), 317–318

B

Baby AT motherboard, 205
backup
    of CMOS settings, 213

of data in Windows, 341–342
    network, 283
    before upgrade, 379, 381
Backup utility, 393–394
backward compatibility, 320, 383–384
"Bad or Missing Command Interpreter" message, 427–428
bandwidth, 281–282
baseband networks, 282
Basic Input/Output System. *See* BIOS (Basic Input/Output System)
batteries
    CMOS, replacing, 91–92
    portable computers and, 93–94
    safety procedures for, 170, 175
    of UPS, 167–168
bi-directional cables, 38
bi-directional communication, 274–275
bi-directional mode, 213
binary numbers, 31–32
BIOS (Basic Input/Output System)
    boot process and, 18–19
    bootstrap phase, 384, 390–391
    CMOS settings for, 216
    described, 17–18
    operating system not found error, 427–428
    POST error codes, 114–115
    settings, 121, 133
    troubleshooting, 128
    upgrading, 92–93
    USB keyboards and, 129
bit width, 202–203
blackout, 166–167
blue screen, 440
Bluetooth infrared standard, 36

549

INTERNATIONAL CONTACT INFORMATION

AUSTRALIA
McGraw-Hill Book Company Australia Pty. Ltd.
TEL +61-2-9417-9899
FAX +61-2-9417-5687
http://www.mcgraw-hill.com.au
books-it_sydney@mcgraw-hill.com

CANADA
McGraw-Hill Ryerson Ltd.
TEL +905-430-5000
FAX +905-430-5020
http://www.mcgrawhill.ca

GREECE, MIDDLE EAST,
NORTHERN AFRICA
McGraw-Hill Hellas
TEL +30-1-656-0990-3-4
FAX +30-1-654-5525

MEXICO (Also serving Latin America)
McGraw-Hill Interamericana Editores S.A. de C.V.
TEL +525-117-1583
FAX +525-117-1589
http://www.mcgraw-hill.com.mx
fernando_castellanos@mcgraw-hill.com

SINGAPORE (Serving Asia)
McGraw-Hill Book Company
TEL +65-863-1580
FAX +65-862-3354
http://www.mcgraw-hill.com.sg
mghasia@mcgraw-hill.com

SOUTH AFRICA
McGraw-Hill South Africa
TEL +27-11-622-7512
FAX +27-11-622-9045
robyn_swanepoel@mcgraw-hill.com

UNITED KINGDOM & EUROPE
(Excluding Southern Europe)
McGraw-Hill Education Europe
TEL +44-1-628-502500
FAX +44-1-628-770224
http://www.mcgraw-hill.co.uk
computing_neurope@mcgraw-hill.com

ALL OTHER INQUIRIES Contact:
Osborne/McGraw-Hill
TEL +1-510-549-6600
FAX +1-510-883-7600
http://www.osborne.com
omg_international@mcgraw-hill.com

CORE HARDWARE/OPERATING SYSTEM EXAMS

TEST YOURSELF

A+ Certification

Third Edition

CORE HARDWARE/OPERATING SYSTEM EXAMS

TEST YOURSELF

A+ Certification

Third Edition

Syngress Media, Inc.

Osborne/McGraw-Hill

New York Chicago San Francisco Lisbon London Madrid Mexico City
Milan New Delhi San Juan Seoul Singapore Sydney Toronto

Osborne/**McGraw-Hill**
2600 Tenth Street
Berkeley, California 94710
U.S.A.

For information on translations or book distributors outside the U.S.A., or to arrange bulk purchase discounts for sales promotions, premiums, or fund-raisers, please contact Osborne/**McGraw-Hill** at the above address.

Test Yourself A+ Certification, Third Edition

567890 CUS CUS 01987654321

ISBN 0-07-212-637-X

KEY	SERIAL NUMBER
001	T3HA3QY45V
002	T6W2A1KNY7
003	TH6F4D3C2A
004	923UBC4DS8
005	BJ635FVXZP

Publisher
Brandon A. Nordin

**Vice President and
Associate Publisher**
Scott Rogers

Editorial Director
Gareth Hancock

Associate Acquisitions Editor
Timothy Green

Editorial Management
Syngress Media, Inc.

Project Editor
Maribeth A. Corona

Acquisitions Coordinator
Jessica Wilson

Series Editor
D. Lynn White

Technical Editor
Joli Ballew

Copy Editor
Julianna Smith

Computer Designer
Maureen Forys,
Happenstance Type-O-Rama

Illustrator
Jeff Wilson

Series Design
Maureen Forys,
Happenstance Type-O-Rama

Cover Design
Greg Scott

Cover Image
imagebank

This book was composed with QuarkXPress 4.11 on a Macintosh G4.

About Syngress Media

Syngress Media creates books and software for Information Technology professionals seeking skill enhancement and career advancement. Its products are designed to comply with vendor and industry standard course curricula, and are optimized for certification exam preparation. You can contact Syngress via the Web at www.syngress.com.

Author

Pawan K. Bhardwaj (MCSE, MCP+I, CCNA, A+) is a consultant, technical trainer, and a freelance author. He started his IT career in 1986 as a polytechnic instructor and since then has spent nearly 14 years in this industry working at various systems and network support levels.

He has been involved in designing and implementing Windows NT–based LAN and WAN solutions for several small- and medium-sized companies. These include manufacturing industries, one of India's largest newspaper groups, Hind Samachar, and a large e-commerce Web site in the United States, where he took an active part in Windows 2000 migration team.

Pawan also teaches MCSE classes. He is currently working towards attaining his MCT certification. He dedicates his work to his parents Sudarshan and Santosh. He can be reached at pawan_bhardwaj@hotmail.com.

Series Editor

D. Lynn White (MCPS, MCSE, MCT, MCP+Internet, CTT) is President of Independent Network Consultants, Inc. Lynn has more than 15 years in programming and networking experience. She has been a system manager in the mainframe environment, as well as a software developer for a process control company. She is a technical author, editor, trainer, and consultant in the field of networking and computer-related technologies. Lynn has been presenting mainframe, Microsoft official curriculum and other operating systems and networking courses in and outside the United States for more than 13 years. Lynn is the Series Editor for Syngress for both the Network + and A+ Series. Her latest certification has been to

v

receive her CTT (Certified Technical Trainer) by the Chauncey Group International. Lynn would like to extend thanks to her family and friends for always being there over the years.

Technical Editor

Joli Ballew (MCSE, MCT, A+) is a technology trainer, writer, and network consultant in the Dallas area. Some of her previous employment positions have included technical writing, educational content consulting, working as a PC technician, a network administrator, a high school algebra teacher, and an MCSE instructor at Eastfield Community College. While teaching in the public school system, she achieved many acclamations for student achievement.

Joli attended high school at the Performing Arts Magnet in Dallas where she studied music and the arts and was a member of the National Honor Society. She attended college at the University of Texas at Arlington and graduated with a Bachelor's degree in Mathematics and a minor in English. The following year, she earned her Texas Teaching Certificate from the State of Texas. After teaching math and algebra for 10 years, she decided to change careers and enter the world of computing. She earned all of her certifications in 14 months and entered the field of computer training and consulting soon thereafter. Joli spends her spare time golfing and surfing the net and spending time with her wonderful family and friends. Joli can be reached at Jballew@swynk.com

ACKNOWLEDGMENTS

We would like to thank the following people:

- All the incredibly hard-working folks at Osborne/McGraw-Hill: Brandon Nordin, Scott Rogers, Timothy Green, Gareth Hancock, and Jessica Wilson.
- Maureen Forys for her help in fine-tuning the project.
- Bob Glennon of ComputerCrafters, Hingham, MA, www.compucrafters.com, for use of their equipment.

CONTENTS

This book's primary objective is to help you prepare for and pass the required A+ exam so you can begin to reap the career benefits of certification. We believe that the only way to do this is to help you increase your knowledge and build your skills. After completing this book, you should feel confident that you have thoroughly reviewed all of the objectives that CompTIA has established for the exam.

In This Book

This book is organized around the actual structure of the A+ exam administered at Sylvan Prometric and VUE Testing Centers. CompTIA has let us know all the topics we need to cover for the exam. We've followed their list carefully, so you can be assured you're not missing anything.

In Every Chapter

We've created a set of chapter components that call your attention to important items, reinforce important points, and provide helpful exam-taking hints. Take a look at what you'll find in every chapter.

Test Yourself Objectives

Every chapter begins with a list of Test Yourself Objectives—what you need to know in order to pass the section on the exam dealing with the chapter topic. Each objective in this list will be discussed in the chapter and can be easily identified by the clear headings that give the name and corresponding number of the objective, so you'll always know an objective when you see it! Objectives are drilled down to the most important details—essentially what you need to know about the objectives and what to expect from the exam in relation to them. Should you find you need further review on any particular objective, you will find that the objective headings correspond to the chapters of Osborne/McGraw-Hill's *A+ Certification Study Guide, Third Edition*.

Exam Watch Notes

Exam Watch notes call attention to information about, and potential pitfalls in, the exam. These helpful hints are written by authors who have taken the exams and received their certification; who better to tell you what to worry about? They know what you're about to go through!

Practice Questions and Answers

In each chapter you will find detailed practice questions for the exam, followed by a Quick Answer Key where you can quickly check your answers. The In-Depth Answers section contains full explanations of both the correct and incorrect choices.

The Practice Exams

If you have had your fill of explanations, review questions, and answers, the time has come to test your knowledge. Turn toward the end of this book to the Test Yourself Practice Exams where you'll find simulation exams. Lock yourself in your office or clear the kitchen table, set a timer, and jump in.

A + Certification

This book is designed to help you pass the A+ Certification exam. At the time this book was written, the exam objectives for the exam were posted on the CompTIA Web site, www.comptia.org. We wrote this book to give you a complete and incisive review of all the important topics that are targeted for the exam. The information contained here will provide you with the required foundation of knowledge that will not only allow you to succeed in passing the A+ certification exam, but will also make you a better A+ Certified Technician.

HOW TO TAKE AN A+ CERTIFICATION EXAM

This Introduction covers the importance of your A+ certification as well as prepares you for taking the actual examinations. It gives you a few pointers on methods of preparing for the exam, including how to study, register, what to expect, and what to do on exam day.

IMPORTANCE OF A+ CERTIFICATION

The Computing Technology Industry Association (CompTIA) created the A+ certification to provide technicians with an industry-recognized and valued credential. Due to its acceptance as an industry-wide credential, it offers technicians an edge in a highly competitive computer job market. Additionally, it lets others know your achievement level and that you have the ability to do the job right. Prospective employers may use the A+ certification as a condition of employment or as a means of a bonus or job promotion.

Earning A+ certification means that you have the knowledge and the technical skills necessary to be a successful computer service technician. Computer experts in the industry establish the standards of certification. Although the test covers a broad range of computer software and hardware, it is not vendor-specific. In fact, more than 45 organizations contributed and budgeted the resources to develop the A+ examinations.

To become A+ certified you must pass two examinations: the Core exam and an OS Technologies exam. The Core exam measures essential competencies for a break/fix microcomputer hardware service technician with six months of experience. The exam covers basic knowledge of desktop and portable systems, basic networking concepts, and printers. Also included on the exam is safety and common preventive maintenance procedures.

The newest revision of the A+ certification (January 2001) includes the OS Technologies exam, which covers basic knowledge of Windows 95, Windows 98, and Windows 2000 Operating Systems for installing, upgrading, troubleshooting, and repairing microcomputer systems.

Computerized Testing

As with Microsoft, Novell, Lotus, and various other companies, the most practical way to administer tests on a global level is through Sylvan Prometric or VUE testing centers, who provide proctored testing services for Microsoft, Oracle, Novell, Lotus, and the A+ computer technician certification. In addition to administering the tests, Sylvan Prometric and VUE also score the exam and provide statistical feedback on each section of the exam to the companies and organizations that use their services.

Typically, several hundred questions are developed for a new exam. The questions are reviewed for technical accuracy by subject matter experts and are then presented in the form of a beta test. The beta test consists of many more questions than the actual test and provides for statistical feedback to CompTIA to check the performance of each question.

Based on the performance of the beta examination, questions are discarded based on how good or bad the examinees performed on them. If a question is answered correctly by most of the test-takers, it is discarded as too easy. The same goes for questions that are too difficult. After analyzing the data from the beta test, CompTIA has a good idea of which questions to include in the question pool to be used on the actual exam.

TEST STRUCTURE

Currently the A+ exam consists of a *form* type test (also called *linear* or *conventional*). This type of test draws from a question pool of some set value and randomly selects questions to generate the exam you will take. We will discuss the various question types in greater detail later in this Introduction.

Some certifications are using *adaptive* type tests. This interactive test weights all of the questions based on their level of difficulty. For example, the questions in the form might be divided into levels one through five, with level one questions being the easiest and level five being the hardest. Every time you answer a question correctly you are asked a question of a higher level of difficulty, and vice versa when you answer incorrectly. After answering about 15–20 questions in this manner, the scoring algorithm is able to determine whether or not you would pass or fail the exam if all the questions were answered. The scoring method is pass or fail.

The exam questions for the A+ exams are all equally weighted. This means that they all count the same when the test is scored. An interesting and useful characteristic of the form test is that questions may be marked and returned to later. This helps you manage your time while taking the test so that you don't spend too much time on any one question. Remember, unanswered questions are counted against you. Assuming you have time left when you finish the questions, you can return to the marked questions for further evaluation.

The form test also marks the questions that are incomplete with a letter "I" once you've finished all the questions. You'll see the whole list of questions after you finish the last question. The screen allows you to go back and finish incomplete items, finish unmarked items, and go to particular question numbers that you may want to look at again.

Question Types

The computerized test questions you will see on the examination can be presented in a number of ways. The A+ exams are comprised entirely of one-answer multiple choice questions.

True/False

We are all familiar with True/False type questions, but due to the inherent 50 percent chance of guessing the right answer, you will not see any of these on the A+ exam. Sample questions on CompTIA's Web site and on the beta exam did not include any True/False type questions.

Multiple Choice

A+ exam questions are of the multiple choice variety. Below each question is a list of four or five possible answers. Use the available radio buttons to select one item from the given choices.

Graphical Questions

Some questions incorporate a graphical element to the question in the form of an exhibit either to aid the examinee in a visual representation of the problem or to present the question itself. These questions are easy to identify because they refer to the exhibit in the question and there is also an "Exhibit" button on the bottom of the question window. An example of a graphical question might be to identify a component on a drawing of a motherboard.

Test questions known as hotspots actually incorporate graphics as part of the answer. These types of questions ask the examinee to click a location or graphical element to answer the question. As a variation of the above exhibit example, instead of selecting A, B, C, or D as your answer, you would simply click the portion of the motherboard drawing where the component exists.

Free Response Questions

Another type of question that can be presented on the form test requires a *free response* or type-in answer. This is basically a fill-in-the-blank type question where a list of possible choices is not given. You will not see this type of question on the A+ exams.

Study Strategies

There are appropriate ways to study for the different types of questions you will see on an A+ certification exam. The amount of study time needed to pass the exam will vary with the candidate's level of experience as a computer technician. Someone with several years experience might only need a quick review of materials and terms when preparing for the exam.

For others, several hours may be needed to identify weaknesses in knowledge and skill level and working on those areas to bring them up to par. If you know that you are weak in an area, work on it until you feel comfortable talking about it. You don't want to be surprised with a question knowing it was your weak area.

Knowledge-Based Questions

Knowledge-based questions require that you memorize facts. The questions may not cover knowledge material that you use on a daily basis, but they do cover material that CompTIA thinks a computer technician should be able to answer. Here are some keys to memorizing facts:

- **Repetition** The more times you expose your brain to a fact, the more it "sinks in" and increases your ability to remember it.

- **Association** Connecting facts within a logical framework makes them easier to remember.

- **Motor Association** It is easier to remember something if you write it down or perform another physical act, like clicking on the practice test answer.

Performance-Based Questions

Although the majority of the questions on the A+ exam are knowledge-based, some questions may be performance-based scenario questions. In other words, the performance-based questions on the exam actually measure the candidate's ability to apply one's knowledge in a given scenario.

The first step in preparing for these scenario type questions is to absorb as many facts relating to the exam content areas as you can. Of course, actual hands-on experience will greatly help you in this area. For example, knowing how to install a video adapter is greatly enhanced by having actually done the procedure at least once. Some of the questions will place you in a scenario and ask for the best solution to the problem at hand. It is in these scenarios that having a good knowledge level and some experience will help you.

The second step is to familiarize yourself with the format of the questions you are likely to see on the exam. The questions in this study guide are a good step in that direction. The more you're familiar with the types of questions that can be asked, the better prepared you will be on the day of the test.

The Exam Makeup

To receive the A+ certification, you must pass both the Core Hardware and the OS Technologies exams. For up-to-date information about the number of questions on each exam and the passing scores, check the CompTIA site at www.comptia.org, or call the CompTIA Certification Area: (630) 269-1818 extension 359.

The Core Hardware Exam

The Core Hardware exam is comprised of six domains (categories). CompTIA lists the percentages as the following:

Installation, configuration, upgrading	30%
Diagnosing and troubleshooting	30%
Preventive maintenance	5%
Motherboard, processors, memory	15%
Printers	10%
Basic networking	10%

The Operating System Technologies Exam

CompTIA's breakdown of the OS Technologies exam is as follows:

OS Fundamentals	30%
Installation, configuration, and upgrading	15%
Diagnosing and troubleshooting	40%
Networks	15%

SIGNING UP

After all the hard work preparing for the exam, signing up is a very easy process. Sylvan operators in each country can schedule tests at any authorized Sylvan Prometric Test center. To talk to a Sylvan registrar, call 1-800-77 MICRO (1-800-776-4276). There are a few things to keep in mind when you call:

1. If you call Sylvan during a busy period, you might be in for a bit of a wait. Their busiest days tend to be Mondays, so avoid scheduling a test on Monday if at all possible.

2. Make sure that you have your social security number handy. Sylvan needs this number as a unique identifier for their records.

3. Payment can be made by credit card, which is usually the easiest payment method. If your employer is a member of CompTIA you may be able to get a discount, or even obtain a voucher from your employer that will pay for the exam. Check with your employer before you dish out the money. The fee for one exam is $78.00 for members and $128 for non-members.

4. You may take one or both of the exams on the same day. However, if you only take one exam, you only have 90 calendar days to complete the second exam. If more than 90 days elapse between tests, you must retake the first exam.

TAKING THE TEST

The best method of preparing for the exam is to create a study schedule and stick to it. Although teachers have told you time and time again not to cram for tests, there just may be some information that doesn't quite stick in your memory. It's this type of information that you want to look at right before you take the exam so that it remains fresh in your mind. Most testing centers provide you with a writing utensil and some scratch paper that you can utilize after the exam starts. You can brush up on good study techniques from any quality study book from the library, but some things to keep in mind when preparing and taking the test are:

1. Get a good night's sleep. Don't stay up all night cramming for this one. If you don't know the material by the time you go to sleep, your head won't be clear enough to remember it in the morning.

2. The test center needs two forms of identification, one of which must have your picture on it (i.e., a driver's license.) Social security cards and credit cards are also acceptable forms of identification.

3. Arrive at the test center a few minutes early. There's no reason to feel rushed right before taking an exam.

4. Don't spend too much time on one question. If you think you're spending too much time on it, just mark it and go back to it later if you have time. Unanswered questions are counted wrong whether you knew the answer to them or not.

5. If you don't know the answer to a question, think about it logically. Look at the answers and eliminate the ones that you know can't possibly be the answer. This may leave with you with only two possible answers. Give it your best guess if you have to, but most of the answers to the questions can be resolved by process of elimination.

6. Books, calculators, laptop computers, or any other reference materials are not allowed inside the testing center. The tests are computer based and do not require pens, pencils, or paper, although as mentioned above, some test centers provide scratch paper to aid you while taking the exam.

AFTER THE TEST

As soon as you complete the test, your results will show up in the form of a bar graph on the screen. As long as your score is greater than the required score, you pass! Also a hard copy of the report is printed and embossed by the testing center to indicate that it's an official report. Don't lose this copy; it's the only hard copy of the report that is made. The results are sent electronically to CompTIA.

The printed report will also indicate how well you did in each section. You will be able to see the percentage of questions you got right in each section, but you will not be able to tell which questions you got wrong.

After you pass the Core exam and the OS Technologies exam, an A+ certificate will be mailed to you within a few weeks. You'll also receive a lapel pin and a credit card–sized credential that shows your new status: A+ Certified Technician. You're also authorized to use the A+ logo on your business cards as long as you stay within the guidelines specified by CompTIA. If you don't pass the exam, don't fret. Take a look at the areas where you didn't do so well and work on those areas for the next time you register.

Once you pass the exam and earn the title of A+ Certified Technician, your value and status in the IT industry increases. A+ certification carries along an important proof of skills and knowledge level that is valued by customers, employers, and professionals in the computer industry.

Part I

A+ Core Hardware

CORE HARDWARE/OPERATING SYSTEM EXAMS

Identifying, Adding, and Removing System Components

A ll components of the computer system, whether internal or external, are connected to the system board or the motherboard. The motherboard houses the processor that receives user inputs through input devices, such as the keyboard, and makes computations and produces the results using output devices, such as a monitor or a printer. The power supply unit produces various DC voltages required for the operation of the system board and internal components. The system uses random access memory (RAM) for temporary storage, cache memory for storing instructions that the processor requires, and read-only memory (ROM) to store the basic input/output system (BIOS).

Floppy disks, hard disks, and CD-ROMs are common storage devices. Most personal computers use Enhanced IDE (Integrated Device Electronics) hard disk controllers, whereas some others use Small Computer System Interface (SCSI) controllers. All devices in the computer use some system resources, such as interrupt request (IRQ) and input/output (I/O) addresses, and no two devices can share a single resource. Hard disks and floppy drives are connected to the motherboard using ribbon cables. External devices use special cables and are connected either to on-board controllers or to adapters mounted on the motherboard.

TEST YOURSELF OBJECTIVE 1.01

System Modules

The computer system contains several devices such as the motherboard, processors, memory and storage devices, and a variety of input/output devices such as the keyboard, mouse, monitor, and printer. These are some of the common system modules that might require replacement in the event that any of them becomes faulty. Pentium II and higher processors use Single Edge Contact (SEC) sockets or connectors, whereas older processors use Pin Grid Array (PGA) connectors. Computers use several types of memory such as cache memory, read-only memory (ROM), and random access memory (RAM), the latter being the most commonly referred to as "memory." Portable computers use proprietary hardware. EIDE controllers are limited to four devices in a computer.

- All components, including external peripherals, are connected to each other via the system board.

- The computer's processor uses RAM as a temporary storage space for its processes and uses the system BIOS to communicate with other devices in the system.

■ Data is stored permanently on storage devices, such as hard, floppy, and CD-ROM disks, each of which offers a different capacity and portability.

■ Portable systems are proprietary (non-standardized) and use components that desktop systems do not, such as LCD displays.

You must be familiar with different types of processors, their names, shapes, clock speeds, and the types of sockets on the motherboard where these processors can be mounted. Although it is very unlikely that you will be asked about very old processors such as 8088 or 80286, basic familiarity with these processors must not be ignored. Questions addressing differences between memory types such as RAM, ROM, and cache must be studied carefully before answering. Another potential exam question might involve identifying differences between SIMMs and DIMMs. Similarly, capacities and sizes of floppy drives and types of hard disk controllers must be studied in detail. You must also be aware of the variety of color display and resolution capabilities of video monitors .

QUESTIONS

1.01: System Modules

1. The clock speed of the motherboard in your PC is 100MHz. The socket for the processor looks like the socket for an adapter card. Which of the following types of processors can be used in the PC? Select all correct answers.

   A. 80486DX2 66MHz

   B. Pentium II 350MHz

   C. Pentium II 400MHz

   D. Pentium 150MHz

2. You open up your PC to install a second hard drive with a capacity of 6.4GB. You find by looking at the motherboard that there are only two connectors for hard drives, as shown in the following illustration. Each of these connectors has a

ribbon cable with two black connectors. You disconnect the ribbon cables from the motherboard.

Which of the following is the type of hard drive that you are going to install?

A. EIDE

B. IDE

C. SCSI

D. ESDI

3. **Current Situation:** You decided to purchase the monitor separately for your new PC that has a 15-pin connector for the monitor. The PC will primarily be used to connect to the Internet and do some word processing. You will also be working with graphics programs. The PC vendor told you that the PC has a SVGA video adapter. Here is what you have to do:

Required Result: Purchase a color monitor that must be able to give 1280×1024 resolution and be able to display 256 colors simultaneously.

Optional Desired Results:

1. The monitor must be capable of displaying 32-bit true color.

2. The cost of the monitor must be kept as low as possible.

Proposed Solution: Purchase a SVGA monitor that is not very expensive and attach it to the 15-pin connector on the PC.

What results does the proposed solution produce?

A. The proposed solution produces the required result and both of the optional results.

B. The proposed solution produces the required result but none of the optional results.

C. The proposed solution produces the required result and only one of the optional results.

D. The proposed solution does not produce the required result.

4. If the CMOS battery becomes weak, which of the following settings of the computer will not be affected?

A. System time

B. CPU clock

C. Keyboard settings

D. System boot sequence

TEST YOURSELF OBJECTIVE 1.02

Adding and Removing Field Replaceable Modules

The most important aspect of replacing or removing any system component is that you follow standard procedures and ensure safety. When removing an adapter, you must remove any connected external devices first, unscrew the adapter, and then "rock" it lengthwise to make it free from the expansion slot on the motherboard. When removing internal components such as a floppy drive or a hard disk drive, you must remove the power cable first and then remove the ribbon cable. You may then remove the mounting screws and pull the drive out of the cage. When connecting hard disks and floppy disks, the red stripe on the ribbon cable must be aligned to pin 1 on the connector on the disk. The power connectors on the motherboard must be connected last of all, ensuring that the black wires on P8 and P9 connectors face each other.

■ Always turn the computer off and follow ESD procedures before installing or removing a computer component.

■ If you must rock a component to remove or install it, always rock it lengthwise (from end to end), never back and forth (from side to side).

■ The red stripe on a drive ribbon must be aligned with pin 1 on the port.

■ When installing the P8 and P9 power connectors, place the two black wires together.

exam
Watch

There are certain defined procedures for adding, replacing, and removing filed replacement units in a computer. The most common mistakes made by technicians are also the most common questions that you should expect in the exam. For example, you might be asked to select the correct method for removing an adapter. When making connections, you must not forget that the red stripe on any ribbon cable identifies its pin 1 and that it must be aligned to pin 1 on the disk drive connector. It is also important to note that the primary hard disk is always connected to the end connector on the ribbon cable. Similarly, the power supply connectors P8 and P9 must be connected with their black wires facing each other.

QUESTIONS

1.02: Adding and Removing Field Replaceable Modules

5. **Current Situation:** The power supply of your computer was blown last week and you have purchased a new compatible supply. Here is what you have to accomplish:

   Required Result: Mount the power supply in the computer and make power connections to the motherboard, floppy disk drive, and the hard disk drives.

Desired Optional Results:

1. The power supply must be tested before mounting in the computer case.

2. The motherboard must be tested before connecting power to disk drives to ensure that there is no critical fault.

Proposed Solution: Mount the new power supply unit in the computer case and tighten all screws. Connect the two motherboard supply connectors, ensuring that the black wires face each other. When this is done, connect the power connectors to the hard disks and the floppy drive. Close the computer case and switch on the power supply.

What results does the proposed solution produce?

- A. The proposed solution produces the required result and both of the optional results.

- B. The proposed solution produces the required result but none of the optional results.

- C. The proposed solution produces the required result and only one of the optional results.

- D. The proposed solution does not produce the required result.

6. Which of the statements correctly describes the actions you must perform while taking out a Pentium II processor?

- A. Release the lever of the socket and pull out the processor carefully.

- B. Push the retaining clips on each side, and the processor will become free in the slot.

- C. Push the retaining clips outwards on each side and pull the processor safely out of the socket.

- D. Release the lever of the socket and use the chip puller to take out the processor.

7. If you were asked to install an ATAPI CD-ROM drive on a PC, which of the following actions would make it a primary slave drive?

- A. Use the central connector of the primary hard drive cable and set the configuration jumper to slave.

- B. Use the central connector of the primary hard drive cable and leave the default configuration jumper setting.

C. Use the end connector of the primary hard drive cable and set the configuration jumper to slave.

D. None of above. The CD-ROM drive cannot be connected to the hard drive controller.

8. One of your friends has sought your advice on how to replace the keyboard of his laptop computer. Which of the following would be your best suggestion to him?

A. Get a compatible keyboard from the market.

B. Get any laptop keyboard since all laptops use similar keyboards.

C. Get a replacement keyboard from the manufacturer.

D. Send the laptop to the manufacturer to replace the keyboard.

TEST YOURSELF OBJECTIVE 1.03

IRQs, DMAs, and I/O Addresses

Each device connected to the computer requires system resources to function. These resources are interrupt request (IRQ), input/output (I/O) addresses, and Direct Memory Access (DMA). These resources are allocated to each device, and the processor loads this information in the RAM on system startup. Devices use IRQs to interrupt the processor. The processor uses the I/O addresses to communicate with the devices. The DMA is used by devices to directly communicate with each other without interrupting the processor. The IRQs and I/O addresses for standard critical system components such as the system timer, hard disk controllers, floppy drive controller, and the keyboard are reserved and cannot be allocated to other devices. It is very important that no two devices use the same IRQ or I/O address.

■ The processor uses I/O addresses to locate and communicate with devices, and devices use IRQs (interrupt requests) to get the attention of the processor.

■ The range of maskable IRQs is 0 to 15 with IRQ 0 having the highest priority.

■ Some devices use DMA (Direct Memory Access) channels to read from or write to RAM directly.

■ No two devices can share an IRQ or I/O address.

e x a m

ⓦ a t c h

Be aware of the functions of IRQs and I/O addresses. An important distinction between the two is that the IRQs are used by the devices, whereas the I/O addresses are used by the processor. Remember each IRQ and its default assignment to critical and non-critical devices or ports. You might get a question in which the default assignments of IRQs are reversed. For example, the question might say that IRQ 3 is used by COM1 and IRQ 4 is used by COM2, or IRQ 5 is used by LPT1 and IRQ 7 by LPT2, both of which are reversed and incorrect. IRQs in the range of 0 to 15 are known as maskable with IRQ 0 having the highest priority. It is very unlikely that you will be asked to identify I/O addresses, but you must memorize these addresses for the most common ports such as COM ports and LPT ports.

QUESTIONS

1.03: IRQs, DMAs, and I/O Addresses

Questions 9–11   The Pentium PC you are using is running Windows 98 operating system. It has two hard disk controllers, a PS/2 mouse, a printer connected to the LPT2 port, and a modem connected to the COM2 port.

The current IRQ assignments to various devices are given in the following table:

IRQ	Device
IRQ 3	Modem
IRQ 5	Printer
IRQ 12	PS/2 Mouse
IRQ 13	Math Co-processor
IRQ 14	Primary Hard Disk Controller
IRQ 15	Secondary Hard Disk Controller

Based on these assumptions, answer the following three questions, selecting the best answer for each.

9. You have just purchased a sound card that requires setting the jumpers for configuring the IRQ setting. Which of the following IRQs are available on your PC for the sound card?

   A. IRQ 3 and IRQ 5

   B. IRQ 4 and IRQ 10

   C. IRQ 10 and IRQ 13

   D. IRQ 12 and IRQ 15

10. Replace the PS/2 mouse with a serial mouse, connecting it to COM2, and move the modem to COM1 port.

    Which of the following IRQs will now be available?

    A. IRQ 3 and IRQ 4

    B. IRQ 4 and IRQ 12

    C. Only IRQ 12

    D. Only IRQ 4

11. With the configuration changes given in question 10, and assuming that you have assigned IRQ 10 to the sound card, how will you assign an IRQ to a Plug and Play network adapter?

    A. Replace the serial mouse with the PS/2 mouse and assign IRQ 3 to the Plug and Play network adapter.

    B. Use the free IRQ 7.

    C. Change the sound card IRQ from 10 to 7 and assign IRQ 10 to the Plug and Play network adapter.

    D. Do nothing.

12. Which of the following statements correctly describes the function of Direct Memory Access?

    A. It is used by the processor to communicate directly with devices.

    B. It is used by devices to communicate directly with one another.

    C. It is used by devices to interrupt the processor.

    D. It is used by the processor to directly access the RAM.

TEST YOURSELF OBJECTIVE 1.04

Peripheral Ports, Cabling, and Connectors

Serial and parallel ports are used to connect a variety of external devices such as modems, printers, and mice. Some of the ports are integrated into the motherboard, whereas others use adapters. Common examples of adapters are the video adapter and the network interface card (NIC). These ports use connectors that have standard names, pin configurations, and male or female types. Cables used by these peripherals are also known by names such as the RS-232 serial cable and the Centronics parallel printer cable.

The DB type connectors always have an odd number of pins that identify the type of connector. DB-9 connectors are used for EGA and CGA monitors and serial devices, whereas VGA and higher resolution video adapters have DB-15 connectors. Networks adapters have either RJ-45 connectors for twisted pair cables or BNC connectors for coaxial cables. Min-DIN (or mini-DIN-6) connectors are used for PS/2 keyboards and mouse connections. USB ports have different connectors for the slow USB and fast USB ports. IEEE 394 connectors are a bit smaller than DB-15 connectors but have round edges to ensure proper orientation.

- Common electronic cables include straight pair, twisted pair, and coaxial.

- Most cables are physically configured to fit only one way in a port or device.

- Common connectors include DB-9, DB-25, RJ-11, RJ-45, BNC, and Mini-DIN-6.

- Serial devices transmit one bit at a time, whereas parallel devices transmit more than one bit at a time.

exam
watch

It is important for you to be able to identify the types of cables, connectors, and ports available in a computer for connecting internal or external devices. You must be able to differentiate between a serial and a parallel port on the back side of the computer, and between RJ-11 and RJ-45 connectors. The DB type connectors usually tell you the number of pins in the connector. The RJ-11 connector has only two cables and is used to connect modems. For network connections, the most common connector used is either the RJ-45 connector or the BNC connector. The RJ-45 connector has eight twisted pair cables, where as the BNC connector has only one coaxial cable.

QUESTIONS

1.04: Peripheral Ports, Cabling, and Connectors

13. Your friend has purchased a new parallel printer that he wishes to attach to his PC. Unfortunately, he lost the cable that was to be used for connecting the PC to the printer. He has asked you to buy a new cable for him. Which of the following types of connectors would you look for on the cable that would be suitable for this purpose?

    A. DB-25 male connectors on both ends

    B. DB-25 male on one end and Centronics 36-pin male on the other

    C. Centronics 36-pin connectors: female on one end and male on the other

    D. DB-25 female on one end and Centronics 26-pin female on the other

14. Fiber-optic cables are immune to which of the following type of interference?

    A. Electrical

    B. Magnetic

    C. Electromagnetic

    D. All of above

15. Which of the following types of cables cannot be connected in reverse direction? Select all correct answers.

    A. A cable connecting the network adapter to the wall jack

    B. A cable connecting the modem to the telephone jack

    C. A cable connecting the monitor to the computer

    D. A cable connecting the cable modem to the wall socket

    E. A cable connecting the printer to the computer

A QUICK ANSWER KEY

Objective 1.01

1. **B** and **C**
2. **A**
3. **A**
4. **B**

Objective 1.02

5. **B**
6. **C**
7. **A**
8. **D**

Objective 1.03

9. **B**
10. **C**
11. **D**
12. **B**

Objective 1.04

13. **B**
14. **D**
15. **C** and **E**

IN-DEPTH ANSWERS

1.01: System Modules

1. ☑ **B** and **C.** Since the socket for the processor on the motherboard looks like the socket for an adapter card, it is the Single Edge Contact (SEC) processor socket. Only Pentium II and higher processors use the SEC socket and can be mounted in these sockets on the motherboard. Pentium II processors work on motherboard speeds of either 66MHz or 100MHz.

   ☒ **A** is incorrect because these processors use Pin Grid Array (PGA) sockets that are horizontal and square in shape. Moreover, a 80486DX2 66MHz processor cannot be used with a 100MHz motherboard. The 80486 family of processors is supported on motherboards with a maximum clock speed of 33MHz. **D** is incorrect because these processors also use PGA connectors on the motherboard. Furthermore, the Pentium 150MHz supports a maximum clock speed of 60MHz on the motherboard.

2. ☑ **A.** EIDE stands for Enhanced Integrated Device Electronics. EIDE is an advanced version of Integrated Device Electronics (IDE) that allows you to have up to four hard drives in a PC. There are typically two connectors on the motherboard known as primary and secondary controllers. Each of the controllers can have two EIDE hard drives installed as master and slave drives. This gives you the ability to have a maximum of four hard drives in the PC.

   ☒ **B** is incorrect because IDE has a limit of only two hard drives. **C** is incorrect because the SCSI controller has only one cable with multiple connectors, usually more than two. With a SCSI interface, all the devices are connected in a chain with a SCSI terminator attached to the last device. **D** is incorrect because the ESDI (Enhanced Small Device Interface) hard drive controller also has a limit of two hard drives per computer.

3. ☑ **A.** The proposed solution produces the required result and both of the optional results. The SVGA monitor can display 1280×1024 resolution and can display 256 colors simultaneously. This produces the required result. The

SVGA monitor can also display 32-bit true colors. This produces the first optional result. The second optional result is produced because it is suggested to purchase the monitor that is comparatively less expensive. Since the PC has a SVGA video adapter, you can attach only a SVGA monitor with the PC.

☒   **B, C,** and **D** are incorrect because the proposed solution produces the required result and both of the optional results. Keeping in mind the capabilities of EGA and VGA monitors, the type of video adapter, and the required result, the best choice is the SVGA monitor, choosing a comparatively less expensive make.

4.   ☑   **B.** The CPU clock is built into the microprocessor and has no relation to the CMOS battery. The CPU clock sets the processing speed of the processor. The CMOS battery is used to supply power to the CMOS chip so that it can retain certain computer configurations when the power is turned off.

☒   **A, C,** and **D** are incorrect because the system time, keyboard settings, and system boot sequence are all stored in the CMOS chip. If the CMOS battery becomes weak or is not able to supply power to the CMOS chip, these settings will be lost each time the computer power is turned off. You will have to configure the CMOS settings every time you start up the computer.

1.02: Adding and Removing Field Replaceable Modules

5.   ☑   **B.** The proposed solution produces the required result but none of the optional results. The required result is produced because the power supply is mounted and all connections are made as suggested in the proposed solution. Considering that the power supply was the only problem in the system, the system should work after the replacement is complete. The first optional result is not produced because there is no suggestion in the proposed solution as to how the power supply unit should be tested. Although a new power supply should be working, it is always better to check the DC output using a multimeter. The second optional result is not produced because all the power connectors for disk drives are being connected without first testing the motherboard. It is a common practice to test the motherboard alone by connecting the power supply. This is typically done by listening for a beep generated by the system during the power-on self-test (POST). This ensures that there is no critical fault in the motherboard.

☒ **A, C,** and **D** are incorrect because the proposed solution produces only the required result and none of the optional results.

6. ☑ **C.** Push the retaining clips outwards on each side and pull the processor safely out of the socket. Pentium II processors use vertical Single Edge Contact (SEC) sockets. The correct method to take out a Pentium II processor is to first locate the retaining clips on each side of the processor and push them outside simultaneously. The processor can then be pulled out of the socket safely. If there is a locking tab to secure the processor in its place, it must be removed before pushing out the retaining clips.

☒ **A** is incorrect because the SEC connectors do not have any lever that makes the processor free in the socket. A lever typically exists in Zero Insertion Force (ZIF) connectors. **B** is incorrect because the processor does not become free in the slot but has to be pulled out after removing the retaining clips. **D** is incorrect because there is no lever in a SEC connector and the Pentium II processor does not come in the shape of a chip. Hence a chip puller cannot be used to take out the processor.

7. ☑ **A.** Use the central connector of the primary hard drive cable and set the configuration jumper to slave. In order to make the CD-ROM drive a slave drive on the primary hard drive controller, you must connect it to the central connector of the ribbon cable and set its configuration jumper to slave position.

☒ **B** is incorrect because the configuration jumper on the CD-ROM drive must be set to the slave position. **C** is incorrect because the end connector of the hard drive cable is connected to the hard disk that is set to act as a master drive. **D** is incorrect because the ATAPI CD-ROM drive is always attached to the hard drive controller.

8. ☑ **D.** Send the laptop to the manufacturer to replace the keyboard. Most of the laptop components are integrated with the motherboard, and it is not an easy process to replace them. The best option to replace the keyboard is to send it to the manufacturer.

☒ **A** and **B** are both incorrect because usually laptop keyboards are proprietary and you might not be able to find a replacement in the market. **C** incorrect because it is not advisable to attempt replacing a laptop keyboard yourself.

1.03: IRQs, DMAs, and I/O Addresses

9. ☑ **B.** IRQ 4 and IRQ 10 are available for the sound card. IRQ 4 is used by serial port COM1 and is free. The IRQ 10 is also not used by any component and is available for assigning to the sound card.

   ☒ **A** is incorrect because both IRQ 3 and IRQ 5 are not free. IRQ 3 is being used by COM2 port where a modem is connected, and IRQ 5 is used by the printer connected to LPT2. **C** is incorrect because although IRQ 10 is free, IRQ 13 is in use by the math co-processor, since the PC is using a Pentium processor. All processors above 80486DX2 have a math co-processor that uses IRQ 13. **D** is incorrect because neither IRQ 12 nor IRQ 15 is free. The PS/2 mouse is using IRQ 12 and the secondary hard disk controller is using IRQ 15.

10. ☑ **C.** Only IRQ 12. The changes made to the ports make available IRQ 12 that was previously used by the PS/2 mouse. The modem is moved from COM2 port to COM1 port, and the new serial mouse is connected to COM2; therefore, both IRQ 3 and IRQ 4 are being utilized.

    ☒ **A** is incorrect because IRQ 3 is now in use by the serial mouse connected to COM2, and IRQ 4 is in use by the modem that is now connected to COM1. **B** is incorrect because only IRQ 12 is now available because of the removal of the PS/2 mouse. **D** is incorrect because IRQ 4 is not free; it is in use by the modem connected to serial port COM1.

11. ☑ **D.** Do nothing. You need not assign an IRQ manually to a Plug and Play network adapter. Operating systems such as Windows 98 support Plug and Play. When Plug and Play devices are installed in computers, the computers detect the new devices and automatically configure the resource settings.

    ☒ **A, B,** and **C** are incorrect because you need not assign IRQ settings manually to Plug and Play devices when the operating system supports these devices.

12. ☑ **B.** Two or more devices use the DMA channels to communicate with one another. DMA channels allow devices to write to the RAM without having to ask the processor for any action. Any device that requires this data can read it directly from the RAM.

    ☒ **A** is incorrect because the processor uses I/O addresses to communicate with different devices. **C** is incorrect because interrupting the processor is handled by interrupt requests (IRQs). **D** is incorrect because the processor does not need DMA to read data from or write data to RAM.

1.04: Peripheral Ports, Cabling, and Connectors

13. ☑ **B.** The standard printer cable has a DB-25 male connector on one end and a Centronics 36-pin male on the other. The DB-25 male connector is attached to the LPT1 port on the back panel of the computer. The Centronics 36-pin male connector is attached to the printer.

☒ **A** is incorrect because one end of the cable should have a Centronics 36-pin connector. **C** is incorrect because one end of the cable should have a DB-25 male connector. **D** is incorrect because both the DB-25 and the Centronics connectors should be male and not female. Pins protruding inside the D type case identify the male connector.

14. ☑ **D.** All of above. The fiber-optic cable is made of glass. The data travels in these cables by means of light signals that are immune to electrical, magnetic, and electromagnetic interferences. These interferences do not produce any signal deterioration or attenuation. Data can be transmitted larger distances using fiber-optic cables than using shielded or unshielded copper wires.

☒ **A, B,** and **C** are incorrect because electrical, magnetic, and electromagnetic interferences have no affect on fiber-optic cables.

15. ☑ **C** and **E.** A cable connecting the monitor to the computer and a cable connecting the printer to the computer. The cable that connects the monitor to the computer is a unidirectional cable. A unidirectional cable can be connected in only one direction. Usually you will find that the monitor cable has only one end that should be attached to the video connector on the PC. Similarly, the printer cable has a DB-25 male connector on one side that connects to the computer and a Centronics 36-pin connector on the other end that connects to the printer. The direction of this cable also cannot be changed.

☒ **A** is incorrect because the twisted pair network cable has RJ-45 connectors on both ends and can be connected in reverse direction. **B** is incorrect because this cable is also reversible. **D** is incorrect because the cable modem uses a coaxial cable that has similar connectors on both ends and can be reversed.

CORE HARDWARE/OPERATING SYSTEM EXAMS

2

Installation, Configuration, and System Optimization

There are certain standard procedures for adding and removing hard disk drives, CD-ROM drives, and other components in the computer such as memory, video adapters, and modems. Following these procedures will ensure that the components function in the desired way after the changes have been made. Most desktops have IDE or EIDE and ATA hard disks that are connected to the computer motherboard using ribbon cables. Desktops can use SCSI interfaces to support faster SCSI devices, the number of which is limited by the type of SCSI standard used in the system. Newer computers and the latest operating systems support USB and IEEE 1394 devices that are Plug and Play and support hot swapping.

One of the common upgrades in a computer system is the addition of RAM to enhance performance. The computer BIOS is usually upgraded to support newer features offered by operating systems or to address some limitations. Portable computers are commonly used at home and in the office. The docking stations allow you to attach the portable computer to almost any external device that a standard desktop system uses. Portable computers use Type I, Type II, and Type III PC Cards that support memory, I/O devices, and hard disks respectively.

TEST YOURSELF OBJECTIVE 2.01

Installing and Configuring IDE/EIDE Devices

Most personal and desktop computers use Enhanced Integrated Device Electronics (EIDE) or AT Attachment hard disk controllers that allow up to four hard disks or a combination of hard disks and CD-ROMs in the system. The ATA drives have faster data transfer speeds compared to EIDE drives. The ATA and EIDE drives are configured in master and slave fashion when two drives are connected to primary or secondary controllers. The red stripe on the disk ribbon cable identifies pin 1 on the controller and the hard disk. Master and slave drives are connected to the end and middle connectors of the ribbon cable with proper jumper settings on the drives. The primary master drive usually holds the operating system.

■ Most computers support the installation of up to four hard drives, CD drives, or a combination of hard drives and CD drives.

- Master drives must be configured with the proper jumper setting and are installed at the end of the drive's ribbon cable.

- To install a slave drive, set the jumper to the "slave" position, and attach the drive to the middle ribbon cable connector.

- An additional master and slave configuration can be added by using the system's secondary drive controller.

You must be well conversant with the procedures for configuring master and slave hard disks in a system. If you have four hard disks that are to be connected to the EIDE controllers, the drives are named as primary master, secondary master, primary slave, and secondary slave. The drive letters are also assigned to these drives in this fashion. The most important aspect of master and slave configuration is that the slave drive cannot work if the master drive is not present, and a secondary drive cannot work in the absence of a primary drive. If you have only one drive in the computer, it must be a primary master. You must set the configuration jumpers to the master or slave position before they are physically installed. Polarity of the ribbon cable is shown by the red stripe that indicates pin 1 on both the drive connector and the connector on the motherboard.

QUESTIONS

2.01: Installing and Configuring IDE/EIDE Devices

Questions 1–3   Your PC has three hard disk drives, two with 6.4GB and the third with 10.6GB capacity. The system also has a CD-ROM drive. All these drives are connected to the motherboard as shown in the following illustration.

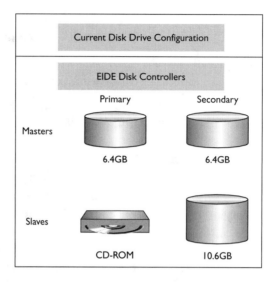

The computer also has a PS/2 mouse port, two serial ports, and a parallel port that is connected to a color printer. An external modem is connected to one of the serial ports. The system uses a Pentium II 533MHz processor and is running Windows 98 operating system.

Based on the given scenario answer the following three questions, selecting the best answer for each.

1. If the drive letters were assigned automatically by the operating system, which of the following letters would be assigned to the hard disk with 10.6GB capacity and the CD-ROM drive, respectively?

   A. D and E

   B. F and E

   C. D and F

   D. C and E

2. If you decide to remove the drive connected to the primary slave connector, which of the following drives will be assigned the drive letters D and E respectively when the computer is restarted?

   A. 6.4GB and 10.6GB

   B. CD-ROM and 10.6GB

C. 6.4GB and CD-ROM

D. No change

3. Taking into account the hard disks and other devices connected to the computer, if one of the slave hard disks were removed, which of the following additional devices cannot be connected to this system without adding any supporting adapters?

A. 9.1GB SCSI disk

B. Sound card

C. ATAPI CD-ROM

D. Serial mouse

4. **Current Situation:** You were working with your supervisor on a PC, adding a second hard disk. He had removed all the cables from the floppy disk and the hard disks to make space to mount the new hard disk, but he had to leave before the job could be completed. He asked you to connect the remaining cables. Considering that the new drive has been mounted and power connectors inserted to both the old and new hard disks, here is what is left for you to do to complete the job:

Required Result: Attach the ribbon cables to the floppy drive and the hard disk drives with proper connectors and correct orientation.

Optional Desired Results:

1. Attach the second hard drive so that it becomes a slave to the existing hard drive.

2. The second hard drive should be attached to a separate ribbon cable.

Proposed Solution: Attach the floppy drive ribbon cable by aligning the red stripe to pin 1 of the connector on the floppy drive. Attach the two hard drives using separate ribbon cables for each of the hard drives, ensuring that the red stripe on the cables are attached to pin 1 on the hard drive connector. Set the configuration jumper settings on the second hard drive so that it becomes slave to the first hard drive.

What results does the proposed solution produce?

A. The proposed solution produces the required result and both of the optional results.

B. The proposed solution produces the required result but none of the optional results.

C. The proposed solution produces the required result and only one of the optional results.

D. The proposed solution does not produce the required result.

TEST YOURSELF OBJECTIVE 2.02

Installing and Configuring SCSI Devices

Small Computer System Interface (SCSI) controllers can be used to connect a variety of devices such as hard disks, CD-ROMs, tape drives, scanners, and printers. The computer can have either an on-board SCSI controller or a SCSI adapter to support SCSI devices. SCSI hard disks are faster than EIDE or ATA hard drives, and depending on the SCSI system you are using, you can have 7, 15, or 31 SCSI devices attached to the SCSI chain. Each SCSI adapter must be assigned an IRQ and I/O address, and each SCSI device connected to the SCSI chain must be assigned a unique SCSI ID. The SCSI chain must be terminated for proper functioning of the SCSI devices.

- A SCSI system is controlled by a SCSI controller card, also called a SCSI host adapter.

- SCSI-1, SCSI-2, and SCSI-3 systems support different speeds, bus widths, and maximum cable lengths.

- Each device in a SCSI chain must be assigned a unique SCSI ID.

- Each end of the SCSI chain must be properly terminated.

You must be conversant with different types of SCSI standards, their bus widths, limitations of cable length, and the maximum number of devices supported by the SCSI system. This data is important from the exam point of view, and the questions might confuse you by mixing up different standards and figures. You may also expect questions dealing with installation of SCSI hard disks, SCSI termination, and SCSI ID conflicts. Remember that the SCSI devices are connected in a daisy chain fashion, rather than in master and slave or primary and secondary configuration. The SCSI adapter always gets the highest priority, which is typically ID 7 or ID 15. Another important point is that the system resources such as IRQs and I/O addresses are required only by the SCSI adapter and not by each SCSI device.

QUESTIONS

2.02: Installing and Configuring SCSI Devices

5. Which of the following statements is correct regarding the difference between Enhanced IDE and SCSI devices?

A. EIDE controllers are much faster than SCSI devices because they have to handle a maximum of four devices.

B. The number of EIDE devices is limited to four, whereas there can be up to 31 SCSI devices in a system.

C. EIDE devices are connected in a daisy chain fashion, whereas the SCSI devices have to be configured as master and slave.

D. EIDE devices require a separate IRQ and I/O address for each device, and SCSI devices require only an ID.

6. You want to add hard disks to your computer to increase the storage capacity. The computer has a SCSI-1 controller card. If there are two SCSI hard disks and a SCSI scanner attached to the system, how many SCSI IDs are free to allow you to add new hard disks?

    A. Two

    B. Four

    C. Eight

    D. Ten

7. Your computer has two SCSI adapters, one of which is connected to three SCSI hard drives, and the other is meant for external SCSI devices such as a scanner and printer. Which of the following will be the most likely problem if the terminator is missing in the external SCSI chain?

    A. The last device connected to the SCSI chain will not work.

    B. The SCSI hard disks will not work.

    C. None of the SCSI devices in the system will work.

    D. None of the external SCSI devices will work.

8. Which of the following types of SCSI cables is known as an A cable?

    A. A cable that has 50 pins and is used to connect only the external SCSI devices

    B. A cable that has 68 pins and can be used for connecting 16-bit SCSI devices

    C. A cable that has 50 pins and supports only 8-bit SCSI devices

    D. A SCSI cable that has 50-pin or 68-pin connectors, used for 16-bit SCSI devices

Installing and Configuring Peripheral Devices

Peripheral devices include video adapters and monitors, internal or external modems, network interface cards (NIC), Universal Serial Bus (USB) devices, IEEE 1394 devices, and a host of other devices. Depending on whether the adapter or device is Plug and Play and whether the operating system is in use, there may be certain configuration procedures to complete the installation of these devices. Video adapters and monitors offer a variety of color display and resolution capabilities, and you must configure these settings in the operating system. When you install a modem you must configure the dial-up properties in the operating system to make it functional. Although most of the USB and IEEE 1394 devices are Plug and Play and the operating systems that support these standards can automatically detect and configure these devices, there may be certain situations when you might have to upgrade or reinstall the device drivers.

- Video cards and modems require additional configuration, such as their display settings and dial-up properties, to work properly.

- USB systems require the use of USB hubs to attach more than one or two devices.

- IEEE 1394 (Firewire) systems are similar to USB, but support faster devices such as DVD and video cameras.

- Most portables can make use of desktop components through the use of port replicators or docking stations.

exam
Watch

You may expect questions on installation of video adapters, modems, NICs, USB, and IEEE 1394 devices. You must understand some compatibility issues related to video adapters and monitors, installation of modems and configuring dial-up properties in the operating system, and the number of maximum devices supported by USB and IEEE 1394 standards. Note that USB ports can be extended to support a maximum of 127 devices by using USB hubs, whereas IEEE 1394 devices are connected in a daisy chain fashion and support a maximum of 63 devices. Most of the newer computers have two USB ports, and a hub can be connected to either of them. Furthermore, the USB hubs can be cascaded to support additional devices.

QUESTIONS

2.03: Installing and Configuring Peripheral Devices

9. You have purchased a new Pentium 533MHz PC that the vendor claimed to be USB compliant. When you open up the packaging, you find that there are only two USB ports on the back of the PC. If you want to connect four USB devices to the PC, which of the following would be the most appropriate action to increase the USB ports?

    A. Install a USB hub.

    B. Install one more USB adapter.

    C. Use an extension cable.

    D. Nothing; the PC supports only two USB devices.

10. Select the statement that incorrectly describes the features of IEEE 1394 compliant devices.

    A. They support fast transmission rates.

    B. The devices are connected in daisy chain fashion.

    C. IEEE 1394 devices support Plug and Play and hot swapping.

    D. Up to 127 devices can be connected in the IEEE 1394 chain.

    E. IEEE 1394 adapters can be installed if not already present.

11. **Current Situation:** The computer that you are using at home has two hard disk controllers, a serial mouse connected to the COM1 port, and a printer connected to the LPT1 port. The sound card in your system is configured to use the resources that are typically reserved for a PS/2 mouse. You have purchased an internal ISA modem card and need to connect it to your PC and configure its settings so that you can connect to the Internet. Considering that you are using Windows 98 operating system that supports Plug and Play, here is what you have to accomplish.

Required Result: Install the modem card inside the computer and configure the dial-up properties in Windows 98. The modem must be in working condition when the task is complete.

Optional Desired Results:

1. Windows 98 should be able to automatically detect the modem and install its driver when the computer is started after installation.

2. The system resources assigned to the modem should not be in conflict with any resources used by other devices.

Proposed Solution: Open the computer case and find a free expansion slot. Install the modem card in the selected slot and close the computer cover. When the computer restarts, Windows 98 will detect the modem and load its device drivers. When this is done, configure the Dial-up Networking properties and set the telephone number of the Internet Service Provider and other settings as required. Refer to the following illustration showing the dial-up properties dialog box.

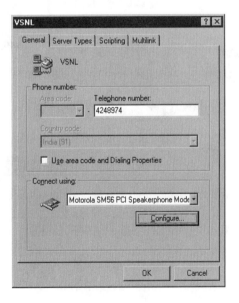

Type in the telephone number of the Internet Service Provider. Click the Configure button to set modem properties.

What results does the proposed solution produce?

A. The proposed solution produces the required result and both of the optional results.

B. The proposed solution produces the required result but none of the optional results.

C. The proposed solution produces the required result and only one of the optional results.

D. The proposed solution does not produce the required result.

12. Which of the following operating systems do not support IEEE 1394 compatible devices? Select all correct answers.

A. Windows for Workgroups 3.11

B. Windows 95

C. Windows 98

D. Windows 2000 Professional

TEST YOURSELF OBJECTIVE 2.04

Upgrading and System Optimization

Upgrading the RAM in a computer is the most common upgrade that improves performance of the system. In addition, an external cache, known as a level 2 or L2 cache, can be installed to enhance system performance. Most motherboards allow processor and BIOS upgrades. Hard disk drives become fragmented by continuous usage, and the Disk Defragmenter utility helps restore disk access performance. The Scandisk utility helps restore proper information about the data stored in hard disks by updating information about lost or cross-linked clusters in the File Allocation Table (FAT). When upgrading a portable computer, the PC Card and the type of slot in the portable computer must be compatible.

■ A computer system's speed can be increased by defragmenting the hard drive, installing RAM, installing additional processors, and by installing external cache memory.

■ Scandisk allows you to update the information in the File Allocation Table (FAT) regarding lost and cross-linked clusters on the hard disk.

■ The computer's BIOS can be upgraded (flashed or replaced) to recognize new types of devices.

■ Portable computers can use Type I, Type II, or Type III PC cards to access additional RAM, I/O devices, or additional storage, respectively.

e x a m
ⓦatch

Memory upgrades are common solutions to resolve the performance of computers, and BIOS upgrades are done so that the computer can recognize newer devices. Hard disk performance can be enhanced using Disk Defragmenter and Scandisk utilities, but it is very important that you understand the difference between defragmentation and scan disk utilities, as well as their respective limitations. Defragmentation helps in redistributing data on contiguous clusters of the hard disk, thus improving hard disk access performance, whereas Scandisk merely scans the hard disk and updates the File Allocation Table (FAT) regarding cross-linked or lost clusters on the hard disk. Remember that none of these utilities can fix any problems related to master boot record (MBR).

QUESTIONS

2.04: Upgrading and System Optimization

13. You have deleted a large number of files from your hard disk, and now you feel that the disk performance has degraded. The hard disk seems to be very slow in responding when you have to open a file or save your work in a file. Which of the following options would you use to resolve this problem?

   A. Run Scandisk to pinpoint the performance problem.

   B. Run the FDISK command.

   C. Run the Disk Defragmenter.

   D. Reformat the hard disk.

14. One of your friends advised you to run Scandisk regularly on your computer.
    He did not tell you exactly why he was suggesting this. By looking at the
    Windows 98 Scandisk dialog box shown in the following illustration, can you
    tell which of the following will not be accomplished by running Scandisk?
    Select all correct answers.

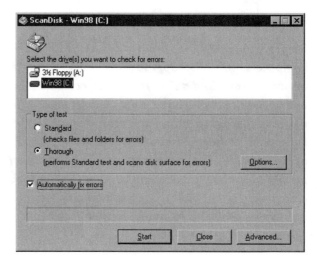

A. Fixing the master boot record of the hard disk

B. Restoration of corrupt files

C. Fixing bad sectors on the hard disk

D. Resolution of problems related to lost clusters

15. Which of the following is the easiest and most common upgrade to your
    computer that will provide the best performance enhancement?

A. Install Level 2 cache.

B. Install a large capacity hard disk.

C. Install more read-only memory.

D. Install more random access memory.

16. You are using an old desktop computer that is running Windows 95 operating system and ISA adapters for video and sound. You wish to upgrade the operating system to Windows 98 because of its advanced features. The desktop has a Pentium 166MHz processor with 512KB cache memory. Considering that you wish to have full Plug and Play functionality in your system after the upgrade, which of the following must you have to ensure support for Plug and Play? Select all correct answers.

   A. The operating system

   B. The system BIOS

   C. The cache memory

   D. The adapters

   E. The CMOS battery

QUICK ANSWER KEY

Objective 2.01

1. B
2. A
3. A
4. C

Objective 2.02

5. B
6. B
7. D
8. C

Objective 2.03

9. A
10. D
11. D
12. A and B

Objective 2.04

13. C
14. A and C
15. D
16. A, B, and D

IN-DEPTH ANSWERS

2.01: Installing and Configuring IDE/EIDE Devices

1. ☑ **B.** F and E. When the drives are assigned drive letters automatically, the letters C, D, E, and F are assigned to primary master, secondary master, primary slave, and secondary slave, respectively. The 10.6GB hard disk is connected as secondary slave and thus is assigned letter F, and the CD-ROM is connected as primary slave and thus gets letter E.

    ☒ **A** is incorrect because the letter D is assigned to the secondary master hard disk that has 6.4GB capacity. **C** is incorrect because of the same reason. **D** is incorrect because the letter C is reserved for the primary master drive that has 6.4GB capacity.

2. ☑ **A.** 6.4GB and 10.6GB. When any drive is removed from the system, the operating system reassigns the drive letters to the remaining drives, provided the primary master drive is not removed. In this scenario, the CD-ROM drive was connected to the primary slave connector and was assigned the drive letter E. The change in drive letters affects only the secondary slave drive that is a 10.6GB hard disk. This hard disk will now be assigned letter E. The 6.4GB hard disk was earlier using drive letter D and that remains unchanged. Thus the 6.4GB and 10.6GB drives are assigned drive letters D and E respectively.

    ☒ **B** and **C** are incorrect because the CD-ROM drive has been removed and cannot have a drive letter assigned to it. **D** is incorrect because the drive letters have been changed. The drive letters would have remained unchanged in the case that the removed drive was the secondary slave 10.6GB hard disk. Removal of the last drive does not affect the drive letter assignment.

3. ☑ **A.** 9.1GB SCSI disk. The only device that cannot be connected to this system is the SCSI disk that requires a SCSI controller. Since the question states that no supporting adapter should be used, you cannot add a SCSI hard

disk without adding an adapter. The hard disk controllers present are EIDE that can use only IDE or EIDE hard disks.

☒ **B** is incorrect because a sound card can be installed in this system. **C** is incorrect because the CD-ROM can be connected to the EIDE hard disk controller as a slave drive in place of the drive that was removed. **D** is incorrect because the serial mouse can be connected to the second free serial port COM2.

4. ☑ **C.** The proposed solution produces the required result and only one of the optional results. The proposed solution produces the required result because the ribbon cables have been properly attached to the hard drives, ensuring that the red stripe is aligned to pin 1 on the male connectors on each of the hard drives. Similarly, the floppy drive is also connected properly. The first of the optional results is not produced because the hard drive is being connected to the second ribbon cable. This essentially means that the hard drive will become a secondary drive. In order to configure the second hard drive as slave to the first hard drive, you must connect it to the same ribbon cable using the central connector. It is suggested that you set the configuration jumper on the second hard drive to make it a slave drive. This setting will not work because the second hard drive is connected to the secondary controller at the far end connector of the cable. You must connect the drive to the same cable and set the jumpers to make it a slave drive. Otherwise, if the drive has to be connected to the secondary controller, the default jumper setting, which is typically set to master, should not be changed.

☒ **A, B,** and **D** are incorrect because the proposed solution produces only the required result and one of the optional results. The second optional result is produced because you are using a separate cable for the second hard drive.

2.02: Installing and Configuring SCSI Devices

5. ☑ **B.** The Enhanced IDE controller allows you to have a maximum of four hard disk drives in a system. This limitation is overcome by the SCSI controller that allows you to have up to 31 devices, depending on the type of controller

used. The latest Ultra-3 SCSI standard that is still under development supports up to 32 devices.

☒   **A** is incorrect because EIDE is not faster, but rather is slower than most of the SCSI versions. **C** is incorrect because the SCSI devices are connected in daisy chain fashion, whereas the EIDE devices have to be configured as master and slave. **D** is incorrect because it is the SCSI controller that requires the IRQ and I/O address. These resources are typically automatically assigned by the system BIOS.

6.   ☑   **B.** Four. Since the computer has a SCSI-1 controller, it will support a maximum of only eight devices. There are already three devices attached, leaving you with the option of a maximum of four additional hard disk drives. Remember that the SCSI adapter also needs an ID; typically ID 7 or ID 15 is reserved for the SCSI adapter because these IDs get the highest priority.

☒   **A** is incorrect because there are four free SCSI IDs that allow you to add four more SCSI hard disks. **C** is incorrect because SCSI-1 can have a maximum of eight devices, and three devices are already connected using three SCSI IDs. **D** is incorrect because SCSI-1 is limited to eight devices.

7.   ☑   **D.** If a SCSI chain is missing the terminator, none of the SCSI devices in the chain will be able to work. The SCSI chain must be terminated in order to have a fully functional set of SCSI devices connected to a particular SCSI adapter. The SCSI terminator is usually connected to the last device in the chain on the specified free SCSI connector.

☒   **A** is incorrect because not only the last device, but none of the SCSI devices connected to the chain will be able to work. **B** is incorrect because there are other SCSI devices in the computer connected to another SCSI adapter. **C** is incorrect because the SCSI hard disks are connected to a separate SCSI adapter.

8.   ☑   **C.** A cable that has 50 pins and supports only 8-bit SCSI devices. The A cable is either a ribbon cable used to connect internal SCSI devices, or an external cable having a Centronics 50-pin connector for connecting external SCSI devices such as SCSI printers and scanners. The A cables support only 8-bit SCSI devices.

☒   **A** is incorrect because the A cables can be used to connect both external and internal SCSI devices. **B** is incorrect because this type of SCSI cable is known as a P cable. P cables support 16-bit SCSI systems and have 68 pins. Like A cables, P cables are used to connect both external and internal SCSI devices. The internal P cable is a 68-pin ribbon cable. **D** is incorrect because the A cable has only 50 pins and cannot be used to connect 16-bit devices.

2.03: Installing and Configuring Peripheral Devices

9.   ☑   **A.** Install a USB hub. USB hubs are used to increase the number of ports so that additional USB devices can be attached to the computer. A USB hub allows you to attach up to seven additional USB devices to the system. Although USB devices are very fast, care must be taken because the performance of the system decreases with each additional device. A maximum of 127 USB devices can be attached to a single USB root port.

☒   **B** is incorrect because an external hub is a better solution that also provides additional free ports so that you may add or remove USB devices as required. **C** is incorrect because using an extension cable cannot increase USB ports. Such a cable does not exist. You must use a USB hub. **D** is incorrect because USB supports up to 127 devices.

10.   ☑   **D.** Up to 127 devices can be connected in the IEEE 394 chain. This is the only incorrect statement in the given options. The IEEE 1394 standard supports a maximum of 63 devices in the chain. Remember that the 127 figure is associated with the maximum number of USB devices that can be attached to a USB port. You must be careful in exams regarding mixed up figures.

☒   **A, B, C,** and **E** are all incorrect answers because these correctly describe the features of IEEE 1394 standards. IEEE 1394 devices support fast transmission rates and are connected in a daisy chain fashion. If a computer does not have an IEEE 1394 adapter, it can be installed on one of the available expansion slots in the computer. All IEEE 1394 compatible devices support Plug and Play and hot swapping.

11. ☑ **D.** The proposed solution does not produce the required result because it does not correctly address the issues associated with installing the modem. Looking carefully at the question statement, you will notice that the modem card is an ISA (Industry Standard Architecture) standard card. This type of card is usually not Plug and Play and must be configured manually. The manual configuration includes setting jumpers on the card to use a particular IRQ and I/O address. This has not been done in the proposed solution. Both the operating system and the device to be installed must support the Plug and Play feature. Even with Windows 98 operating system, the modem card will not be detected and you must install the device driver manually using the files provided by the manufacturer. If you implement the suggested solution, the modem will not work and hence, the required result will not be produced.

☒ **A, B,** and **C** are incorrect because the proposed solution produces neither the required result nor any of the optional results. The first optional result is not produced because although Windows 98 supports Plug and Play, the modem card is not a Plug and Play device. Windows 98 will not detect the new hardware and will not install a device driver for it. The second optional result is not produced because there is no suggestion as to how the jumpers should be set on the modem card. It is difficult to say whether there is a resource conflict or not because the proposed solution does not deal with this issue. In order to have a working configuration, you must first set the jumpers on the modem card to assign it an IRQ 3 that is reserved for COM2 serial port. This must be done manually before physically installing the card inside the computer. Start the computer and manually install the device driver for Windows 98 by running the appropriate setup file provided by the manufacturer and selecting COM2 as the modem port. Configure the dial-up properties of the modem and set the telephone number of the Internet Service Provider.

12. ☑ **A** and **B.** Windows for Workgroups 3.11 and Windows 95 are older operating systems that do not support IEEE 1394 compatible devices. If you wish to attach IEEE 1394 compatible devices to your computer, you must be running a Windows 98 or later operating system. Windows 2000 Professional also supports IEEE 1394.

☒ **C** and **D** are incorrect because these operating systems are fairly new and have built-in support for IEEE 1394 devices.

2.04: Upgrading and System Optimization

13. ☑ **C.** Run the Disk Defragmenter. The data on the hard disk is usually stored in noncontiguous clusters. When you delete a large number of files from the hard disk, a number of clusters become free, resulting in fragmentation of the hard disk. Fragmentation causes further performance problems when reading or writing to the hard disk because the system has to read or write from a large number of noncontiguous clusters. Running Disk Defragmenter will resolve the problem by rewriting data on contiguous clusters of the hard disk. Although defragmentation might not resolve the disk performance problems completely, placing the disk data on contiguous clusters, as far as possible, certainly helps in improving disk access.

☒ **A** is incorrect because Scandisk will only update the File Allocation Table (FAT) on lost or cross-linked clusters and will not resolve the fragmentation problem suspected to be the cause of slow disk response. Scandisk will not indicate what exactly is causing the hard disk to work slowly. **B** is incorrect because this command is used to create and delete disk partitions and has nothing to do with hard disk performance. **D** is incorrect because this will result in a loss of data.

14. ☑ **A** and **C.** Fixing the master boot record of the hard disk and fixing bad sectors on the hard disk. These two problems cannot be resolved by using Scandisk. By updating information in the File Allocation Table (FAT), the Scandisk is used to fix problems with corrupted files due to lost or cross-linked clusters. Since it is a software utility, it cannot fix the bad sectors on the hard disk.

☒ **B** is incorrect because this is the basic function of Scandisk. It attempts to move the data residing on the bad sectors to good sectors, and update the file entries in the FAT appropriately. **D** is also an incorrect answer because Scandisk can locate the lost and cross-linked clusters in the hard disk and restore the files if required.

15. ☑ **D.** Installing additional random access memory (RAM) significantly enhances the performance of the computer. RAM upgrades are one of the easiest and most common upgrades of the computer to improve performance.

The installation of RAM is easy because you do not have to detach any cables or reconfigure the system. All you have to do is remove the computer case and insert the RAM modules in the appropriate slots.

☒   **A** is incorrect because this is not a common upgrade to enhance system performance. **B** is incorrect because this will not enhance system performance. Furthermore, upgrading a hard disk is a complex process because the hard disk might contain the operating system and critical data files. **C** is incorrect because the read-only memory (ROM) cannot be upgraded.

16.   ☑   **A, B,** and **D.** The operating system, the BIOS, and the adapters must be present to support Plug and Play functionality in the system. In the absence of any of these, the Plug and Play features will not work. If the Pentium 166MHz computer does not have a Plug and Play supporting BIOS, you may upgrade the BIOS to a newer version that supports this functionality. The BIOS in most newer computers supports Plug and Play.

☒   **C** is incorrect because it has no involvement in Plug and Play functions of the computer. **E** is incorrect because the battery is required only to supply continuous power to CMOS memory.

CORE HARDWARE/OPERATING SYSTEM EXAMS

3

Diagnosing and Troubleshooting Problems

TEST YOURSELF OBJECTIVES

3.01   Symptoms and Problems

3.02   Basic Troubleshooting Procedures

Computer problems are countless; however, there are a few basic problems that appear in almost all computers, as well as some standard methods to resolve them. Problems associated with motherboards, processors, and memory are known as fatal in that they usually do not allow the system to boot successfully. These problems are indicated by a variety of beeps or errors displayed on the monitor. Although humidity and Electrostatic Discharges (ESDs) are the major causes of computer faults, components such as the keyboard and mouse are mainly subject to wear and tear and the hazards of a dirty environment.

There are some standard procedures to diagnose problems in computer systems. Gathering first-hand information from the customer is the first thing you should do when a problem is reported. After the facts have been collected, carefully analyze them to find the cause of the problem. Hardware problems arise from faulty adapters and the devices connected to them, as well as from connectors and cables. Corrupt device driver files and incorrect configurations are also causes of hardware problems.

TEST YOURSELF OBJECTIVE 3.01

Symptoms and Problems

Computer problems associated with the motherboard, processor, and memory can be fatal in that they will not allow the boot process to complete successfully. This is indicated either by error codes or beeps. Even when the boot process is successful, other components such as the video adapter, mouse, keyboard, sound card, and modem can develop faults caused by mishandling, wear and tear, or improper configuration. Most of the problems can be fixed by replacement of faulty components, reconfiguring their settings, or by reloading corrupted device driver files. Whatever the cause of the problem, it is important that proper diagnosis be done before deciding on replacing a component.

- POST error codes, such as 1**, 2**, and 3**, can indicate system board, memory, or keyboard failures, respectively.

- Most system board, processor, and memory errors are fatal, meaning that the computer cannot properly boot up.

- The most common mouse problem is irregular movement, which is resolved by cleaning the internal rollers in the mouse.

- A hard drive that begins to develop corrupted data should be replaced before all of the information is lost.

■ When troubleshooting a video or audio problem, start with the most accessible component, and check to ensure it is getting power and is properly connected to the computer.

■ When resolving modem errors, make sure the modem is properly attached and configured, and that there is a connection to the phone jack and a good dial tone.

■ Motherboard errors can be the most difficult to pinpoint, and because of the cost and effort of replacement, they should be the last device you suspect when a subsystem, or the entire computer, fails.

■ Never open the power supply or try to replace the fan; rather, replace the entire power supply when the fan stops working.

exam
Watch

It is important that you be well acquainted with the computer boot process and the components that are involved in the process. There are several visual and audible error codes that occur if the boot process does not complete successfully. Based on the error code displayed on the monitor or the number of beeps, you might be asked to identify a possible cause of the problem. The exam will test your ability to diagnose a problem successfully given a set of problem symptoms and will expect you to be able to apply your knowledge to find an appropriate resolution.

QUESTIONS

3.01: Symptoms and Problems

1. Which of the following errors is not a possible cause of problems associated with the boot process?

    A. Errors with the system board

    B. Errors with the processor

    C. A faulty monitor

    D. Problems with on-board memory

2. In which of the following conditions would you assume that the computer has passed the power-on self-test and that the problem is not a fatal one?

    A. When you see error 201

    B. When you hear one long beep

    C. When you hear one long and one short beep

    D. When you do not hear any beeps

3. Which of the following statements correctly describes the order of tests done on the components during the POST?

    A. Processor, keyboard, memory

    B. Processor, memory, keyboard

    C. Memory, processor, keyboard

    D. Memory, keyboard, processor

4. A customer calls you and tells you that his computer reboots itself when he is working on it. He also tells you that sometimes it just switches off and does not reboot. What is the likely cause of the problem?

    A. A loose power connection

    B. Bad CMOS battery

    C. Hard disk failure

    D. A stuck key on the keyboard

5. One of your friends told you that he loaded a small application from three floppy drives. The setup program prompted him to restart the computer. When he pressed the ENTER key to restart the computer, the system could not boot and was giving the following error:

    ```
    Non-system disk or disk error.

    Replace disk and press any key to continue.
    ```

    Which of the following could be the possible cause of the problem?

    A. The application corrupted the operating system on the hard disk.

    B. He left the last disk in the floppy disk drive.

C. He should not have restarted the computer after installation.

D. The floppy disks corrupted the floppy drive.

6. The mouse pointer in a computer is stuck on a particular place and is not moving with the physical movement of the mouse. This is a new serial mouse and you are sure that there is no resource conflict. You have checked all connections and found no problems. You tried to solve the problem by restarting the computer several times, but on many of these occasions the pointer does not appear at all. You have also opened the mouse and found that the ball and the rubber rollers look neat and clean, as shown in the following illustration.

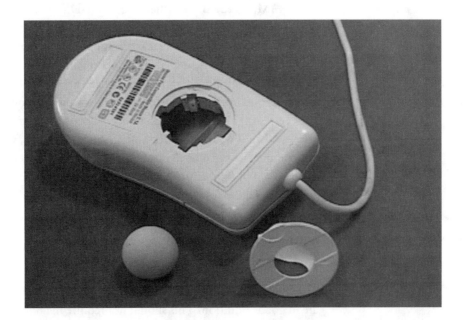

What else could possibly be the cause of the problem?

A. The mouse driver needs to be replaced.

B. The mouse needs reassignment of IRQ.

C. Serial mice are no longer supported.

D. The mouse port is defective.

7. You have an 80486 DX2 computer that was running very slowly. You added two new SIMM modules to this computer to increase its performance. When you started the computer after the upgrade, the BIOS gave you a "Memory size mismatch" error. What should you do to resolve the problem?

   A. Change the size of the memory in the BIOS.

   B. The new SIMM modules may be faulty; replace them.

   C. Insert the SIMM modules in reverse order.

   D. Invert the SIMM orientation in the sockets.

8. **Current Situation:** A computer is built on a Pentium 200MHz processor with 32MB of RAM, a 512KB L2 cache, a 4.3GB EIDE hard disk drive, a 32X CD-ROM drive, a PS/2 mouse, and a standard 101-key keyboard. The computer is running Windows 95 and several applications. The system was purchased two years ago, and since then several computer games have been installed on this system. In recent months, you have noticed a few problems with this computer. The computer gives errors when opening some older files. You have also noticed that the speed of the computer has reduced significantly compared to its speed when it was purchased. Since about a week ago, you have noticed that the computer is not able to open files that are shown in Windows Explorer. When you attempt to open such a file, an error message is displayed that the file is corrupt. Here is what you have to do.

   Required Result: Resolve the performance problem of the computer.

   Optional Desired Results:

   1. Find a permanent solution to the corrupted data problem.

   2. The solution should be able to preserve some of the critical data files that are in good condition. This should not require making a backup copy on floppies.

   3. The expense of the solution should be moderate.

   Proposed Solution: To resolve the performance problem, add more RAM to the system. This can be a single 32MB memory module. Since a large number of files are shown as corrupt, it is likely that the hard disk has developed a large number of bad sectors. To resolve this problem, install a new hard disk and reinstall the operating system on it. Reconfigure the operating system to restore all settings previously used by the system.

What results does the proposed solution produce?

A. The proposed solution produces the required result and all of the optional results.

B. The proposed solution produces the required result and only one of the optional results.

C. The proposed solution produces the required result and only two of the optional results.

D. The proposed solution does not produce the required result.

TEST YOURSELF OBJECTIVE 3.02

Basic Troubleshooting Procedures

Computer problems can be caused by a number of things going wrong. If you are familiar with the workings of different parts of the computer, it becomes an easy job to determine the cause of the problem. Whereas most hardware problems can be resolved by identifying and replacing the faulty component, software problems are a little more difficult to resolve and may require the use of diagnostic tools provided by the operating system. Corrupted application files and device driver files can be reinstalled from original source disks to resolve software problems.

- When faced with a computer problem, gather information from the customer, such as what the problem is, what happened before the problem occurred, and what, if anything, has changed recently in the computer.

- Determine whether the problem is hardware- or software-related by accessing suspect devices with more than one type of application, and vice versa.

- To resolve software problems, check the software's configuration and its minimum requirements, and then try to reinstall it.

- To resolve a hardware problem, first identify and test the components that belong to the affected subsystem.

■ Always check to ensure that a failed device has power and is connected to the computer.

■ Verify a suspect component's status by trying to use it in another computer, or by replacing it with a known working component.

■ Check the configuration of a failed device to ensure it does not have a resource conflict with another device.

exam

ⓦatch

The key to resolving hardware failures is to check whether the computer works with a known working component. Remember that there are different methods of diagnosing software problems depending on whether they occur in a fresh installation or in an existing application. In the case of fresh installations, make sure that proper resources exist for running the application and that the minimum required configuration has been performed. The A+ exam will focus on testing your ability to perform a diagnosis of a problem and on how you would proceed if there were no information on the cause of the problem.

QUESTIONS

3.02: Basic Troubleshooting Procedures

9. Which of the following actions would you take first when you start a computer and find there is no display on the monitor even though its power indicator is on?

A. Change the video adapter.

B. Try connecting a compatible working monitor.

C. Change the video driver.

D. Replace the power cord of the monitor.

10. You have installed a new hard disk in the customer's computer and installed Windows 98 Second Edition on it. Prior to this the customer was using Windows 3.11 operating system. When you arrive back at your office you get a call from him saying that every time he starts his computer, Scandisk starts

running. He said that the system runs fine otherwise and he likes the new features. What could be the cause of the problem?

A. Windows 98 is not installed properly.

B. There are bad sectors on his hard disk.

C. Windows 98 is not shut down properly.

D. There is a virus on the hard disk.

11. If a customer complains to you about problems in the sound system of his computer without giving any particular symptoms of the problem, which of the following would you check first?

A. The configuration of the sound card driver

B. The jumper settings on the sound card

C. The speakers and connecting cables

D. The volume and tone control settings

Questions 12–16   You have been asked to attend to a computer problem at a customer's site. The customer reported that when he starts his computer he hears a series of beeps but nothing is visible on the monitor. He could not provide any other information on phone.

The customer told you that the computer has a Pentium 166MHz processor and 64MB of RAM. He uses Windows 95 operating system. He has also connected a modem for accessing the Internet and a printer that he seldom uses. Besides this, he told you that the mouse has a D-shaped connector.

The following five questions describe the series of events at the customer's site. Answer these questions selecting the best answer for each.

12. You asked the customer if he counted the number of beeps, but he said he did not remember. Based on the symptoms given by the customer, what should be your first action?

A. Observe the problem symptoms yourself.

B. Replace the video adapter.

C. Replace the monitor.

D. Ensure that the video adapter is seated properly.

13. You open up the computer case and find that the video adapter has come out of the expansion slot. After you fix it and restart the computer, the monitor starts displaying video output. However, the system cannot boot and the following error is displayed:

    ```
    Boot from ATAPI CD-ROM: Failure…

    DISK BOOT FAILURE, INSERT SYSTEM DISK AND PRESS ENTER..
    ```

    You observe that when the POST is complete, the lights on the CD-ROM and floppy drive light up once. Which of the following will you rule out as a possible cause of this problem?

    A. Disconnected hard disk drive

    B. Corrupted operating system files

    C. Misconfigured hard disk drive

    D. Insufficient RAM

14. You fixed the problem given in question 13 by fixing the hard disk ribbon cable that had become disconnected. When you restart the system, Windows 95 loads but you cannot find the mouse pointer on the screen. You move the mouse on the mouse pad but the pointer does not appear. What should you do to resolve this problem?

    A. Clean the mouse ball and its internal rollers.

    B. Restart the computer.

    C. Reinstall the mouse driver.

    D. Make sure that the mouse is connected.

15. You find that the mouse was connected properly to the COM1 port, but the cable from the motherboard to the connector on the computer chassis was disconnected. You fix the problem by reconnecting the cable, and the mouse starts working. The customer now wants to test the system himself and ensure that his modem works and that he can connect to the Internet. He dials up his Internet Service Provider, the modem produces the usual sounds, but when the

post-dial terminal screen appears, it displays garbled characters as shown in the following illustration.

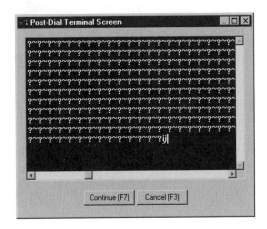

Which of the following could cause this problem?

A. Improper dial-up configuration

B. Incorrect modem driver

C. Static on the phone line

D. Bad COM2 port

16. After you have made sure that the computer is working fine in every respect, the customer thanks you for your efforts. What would you advise the customer before you leave?

A. That his bill will be high because the repairs have taken a long time

B. That he should try to observe fault symptoms before calling customer service

C. That he should get such repairs done by another company

D. That he should not mess up his system again

QUICK ANSWER KEY

Objective 3.01	
1.	C
2.	B
3.	B
4.	A
5.	B
6.	A
7.	A
8.	C

Objective 3.02	
9.	B
10.	C
11.	C
12.	A
13.	D
14.	D
15.	C
16.	B

IN-DEPTH ANSWERS

3.01: Symptoms and Problems

1. ☑ **C.** A faulty monitor will not be a possible cause of problems associated with the boot process. Similarly, a defective video adapter or a video adapter with an incorrect driver will not cause any problems with the boot process. In any of these cases the computer will boot properly, but you will not be able to view the display.

   ☒ **A**, **B,** and **D** are all incorrect. Any errors with the system board, processor, or memory are known as fatal errors that do not allow the boot process to complete.

2. ☑ **B.** In most PCs, one long beep during the power-on self-test indicates that the computer has successfully passed the POST and that there is no fatal problem with the system. The problem is thus caused by some other component.

   ☒ **A** is incorrect because errors starting with digit 2 are associated with memory. Memory errors are fatal errors that will not allow the computer to boot properly. **C** is incorrect because this indicates a problem with the system board in most common PCs. **D** is incorrect because this indicates that the system board is not responding at all. The system board is either not getting power or has developed some fault.

3. ☑ **B.** Processor, memory, keyboard. The computer checks all components during the POST routine, such as the processor, memory, BIOS ROMs, DMA controllers, Interrupt controller, video adapters, keyboard, floppy drive, and hard drive controllers. The order of testing components is not similar with all BIOS manufacturers, but the key components in question are always tested in the given order. The processor is tested before memory, and memory is tested before testing the keyboard.

   ☒ **A** is incorrect because the keyboard is an external component that is tested when the memory tests have been completed. **C** and **D** are incorrect because these suggest that memory is tested first. In every computer system, the processor is always first to be tested during the POST, irrespective of the manufacturer. Although it is not listed in any of the given answer options, remember that the motherboard itself is the first thing to be tested by the BIOS.

4.   ☑   **A.** The most likely cause of the problem is a loose power connection. Loose power connections are caused by a loose power cord or loose power connections on the system board. Any of these can cause the system to reboot and just turn off. Change the power cord and the problem will be resolved.

☒   **B** is incorrect because the CMOS battery does not cause the system to reboot or turn off by itself. **C** is incorrect because the problem is associated with the power source and not with the hard disk or floppy disk. **D** is incorrect because this will not cause the system to reboot.

5.   ☑   **B.** The "non-system disk or disk error" is typically caused by a nonbootable floppy disk in the floppy disk drive. Since your friend pressed the ENTER key immediately after seeing the restart prompt on the screen, the possible cause of the problem is that the floppy disk, which was not bootable, was left in the disk drive. The computer searched for the operating system in the floppy disk, and when it did not find the operating system there, it gave the "non-system disk or disk error" message.

☒   **A** is incorrect because had this been the problem, the system would have reported the "missing operating system" error. **C** is incorrect because several applications require a restart to complete installation. This is not the cause of the current problem. **D** is incorrect because the disk drive cannot be "corrupted." You must be on the lookout for incorrect statements in the answer options. This statement does not make any sense.

6.   ☑   **A.** The mouse driver needs to be replaced. All devices come with device driver files. The cause of the problem could be that you replaced the mouse but did not install the new mouse driver. The old driver might not be compatible with the new mouse. Loading a new mouse driver will resolve the problem.

☒   **B** is incorrect because the older mouse was working well with the same serial port, and there does not seem to be any problem with IRQ assignment. Remember that it is the serial port that needs an IRQ and I/O address assignment, and not the device connected to the serial port. **C** is incorrect because serial mice are still supported on nearly all computer systems. **D** is incorrect because it is very unlikely that a working port would become defective just by replacing a device. However, serial ports are very sensitive and become faulty quickly if proper safety procedures are not followed.

7. ☑ **A.** Change the size of the memory in the BIOS. Several older computer BIOS programs do not automatically detect changes in the size of the RAM when memory is upgraded. Therefore you must enter the BIOS setup during computer startup and manually enter the size of the memory. Most newer BIOS programs automatically detect changes in the size of the physical memory (RAM).

☒ **B** is incorrect because if this were the problem, the error would not have appeared at all. The computer BIOS would not have detected the change in memory size if the SIMMs were faulty. **C** is incorrect because this will not make any difference. **D** is incorrect because you cannot reverse the orientation of the SIMM modules.

8. ☑ **C.** The proposed solution produces the required result and only two of the optional results. The required result is produced because added RAM will improve system performance. The first optional result is produced because replacing the hard disk will be a permanent solution to the bad sectors in the older hard disk. The third optional result is produced because the expense of an additional 32MB of RAM and a new hard disk will not be very high. The second optional result is not produced because the proposed solution does not suggest how the older files will be preserved. To accomplish this, the new and old hard disks can be connected in a master and slave fashion. When the operating system is installed on the new hard disk and it is fully configured, the critical data files that are in good condition should be copied to the new hard disk. When this is done the old hard disk can be removed from the system.

☒ **A, B,** and **C** are incorrect because the proposed solution produces the required result and only two of the optional results.

3.02: Basic Troubleshooting Procedures

9. ☑ **B.** The first action you should take in this situation is to try connecting a compatible working monitor. This would rule out the possibility of the monitor being faulty. Remember that whenever you start troubleshooting or diagnosing a problem, you must start by first trying things that do not require

any configuration changes. Since the power indicator on the monitor is on, it is possible that either the monitor is faulty or there is some problem with the video adapter.

☒ **A** is incorrect because this should not be your first action for the given problem. You must not change any component unless you are certain that it is faulty. **C** is incorrect because it is unlikely that the video driver has been corrupted. Moreover, like changing the video adapter, this should not be your first action to resolve the stated problem. **D** is incorrect because we know the monitor is getting power since its power indicator is on.

10. ☑ **C.** Windows 98 is not shut down properly. The reason Scandisk starts running every time the computer is started is that the customer is probably not shutting down the system using the shutdown option in the start menu. This causes the operating system to suspect that the hard disk is corrupted, and Scandisk starts scanning the hard disk for possible errors.

☒ **A** is incorrect because the customer said that Windows 98 runs fine. **B** is incorrect because it is very unlikely that a new hard disk has bad sectors. **D** is incorrect because viruses usually do not cause Scandisk to run on startup.

11. ☑ **C.** The speakers and connecting cables. The first thing you must check in the given situation is that the speakers are connected properly to the computer and that they are getting power. When you are sure that there is no problem caused by connections and speaker power, you may check other things such as volume control, configuration of the sound card driver, and hardware configuration such as jumper settings on the sound card.

☒ **A** is incorrect because even if the sound card driver is configured correctly, the sound system will not work if the speakers are not properly connected or if there is no power. These two things must be checked first. **B** is incorrect because the jumper settings are not the first things to check unless this is a fresh installation. **D** is incorrect because you must first make sure that the speakers are connected and powered on before checking the controls. These controls should be checked if the system is working but the desired level and quality of sound is not being achieved.

12. ☑ **A.** The first thing you must do after arriving at the customer's site is to observe the problem symptoms yourself. Since the number of beeps plays an

important part in problem diagnostics, you must listen carefully to the beeps produced by the POST. Although this may not tell you the cause of the problem, it is often a good start in diagnostics.

☒   **B** is incorrect because you must make sure that the video adapter is faulty before replacing it. The beeps during the POST routine are caused not only by a faulty video adapter but also by other problems. **C** is incorrect because a monitor problem does not produce beeps during the system startup. **D** is incorrect because although this may be the cause of the problem, you cannot make this decision until you first carefully check the system startup.

13.   ☑   **D.** Insufficient RAM is not a possible cause of the problem because the system has 64MB of RAM which is sufficient for running Windows 95 operating system. The error indicates that the system is not able to boot from the CD-ROM drive, the floppy drive, or the hard disk.

☒   **A, B,** and **C** are incorrect because any of these could be a possible reason for the error displayed. A disconnected hard disk, corrupted operating system files, or misconfigured hard disk drives could cause the BIOS to fail in loading the operating system. When the BIOS does not find the operating system from any of the bootable devices, it will display the given message.

14.   ☑   **D.** Make sure that the mouse is connected. The mouse pointer is missing because Windows 95 did not detect the mouse during startup. The mouse is probably disconnected from the computer. You should first check the mouse connection. If it is disconnected, shut down the computer, connect the mouse, and restart.

☒   **A** is incorrect because the stated problem is not related to a dirty mouse ball or rollers. **B** is incorrect because the mouse will again fail to appear on restarting the computer if it is not connected properly. **C** is incorrect because if the mouse driver were corrupted, the mouse pointer would have appeared. An incorrect driver usually causes the mouse pointer to move sporadically across the screen. In certain cases the mouse pointer may not move at all.

15.   ☑   **C.** The garbled characters on the post-dial terminal screen indicate that there is static on the phone line.

☒   **A** is incorrect because if this were the problem the modem would not have dialed a correct number, or it may not have dialed at all. **B** is incorrect because an incorrect modem driver will not activate the modem. **D** is incorrect because the modem is sending and receiving signals on this port, indicating that the COM2 port is working well.

16. ☑ **B.** That he should try to observe fault symptoms before calling customer service. It is a good idea to advise customers to observe fault symptoms when a computer develops problems. Getting first-hand information contributes to a speedier resolution of the problem either by allowing the customer to obtain a solution to the problem on the phone or by saving the time required to collect facts in order to diagnose the cause of the problem when you arrive at the customer's site for repairs.

☒ **A, C,** and **D** are all incorrect because these are bad customer service ethics.

CORE HARDWARE/OPERATING SYSTEM EXAMS

4

Power Protection and Safety Procedures

TEST YOURSELF OBJECTIVES

4.01   Preventive Maintenance Products
        and Procedures

4.02   Power Protection and Safety
        Procedures

Regular cleaning of computer parts not only extends the computer's life but also is helpful in preventing common problems that may arise from the dust buildup on internal and external components. Dust can cause electrostatic charge and heat to build up on internal components that ultimately results in premature failure of the affected component. External components such as the keyboard, mouse, and monitor attract dust on exposed surfaces. Cleaning computer parts is an essential part of preventive maintenance, and the method used for cleaning depends on the type of part being cleaned. You must know the correct cleaning procedures for both internal and external components.

Following proper safety procedures is very important in preventive maintenance, and you must be very careful in handling chemicals and high voltage equipment like monitors and power supplies. Power causes the majority of problems in computers. Sudden increases and decreases in power voltages must be prevented using surge suppressors and uninterrupted power supplies (UPS). Electrostatic Discharge (ESD) can be prevented using ESD wrist straps, and any spare components must be stored in antistatic bags. It is also important to properly dispose of used chemicals and hazardous materials, such as empty toner cartridges and batteries.

TEST YOURSELF OBJECTIVE 4.01

Preventive Maintenance Products and Procedures

Dust buildup on computer parts, such as the power supply fan, causes the components inside the computer to heat up, which is harmful and often results in failure of one or more internal components. External parts such as the keyboard and mouse are prone to collect dust and dirt and must be cleaned regularly. While you are cleaning internal parts, it is essential that you look for any loose contacts and fix them properly. Distilled water and isopropyl alcohol are common cleaning liquids used for keyboards, mouse rollers, and monitor screens. Dirty contacts can be cleaned using white erasers. A vacuum cleaner is used to blow off dust from internal parts that are not easily accessible.

■ Cleaning the computer and replacing worn-out components before they stop working can help you prevent problems.

■ Use mild soapy water to clean the mouse ball and plastic casings.

■ Clean a sticky keyboard with distilled water.

- Use isopropyl alcohol to clean mouse rollers and floppy drives.

- Use regular glass cleaner to remove smudges and fingerprints from the glass screen on a CRT monitor.

- Check all connections to ensure there is no corrosion or other buildup.

- Use a plain white eraser or isopropyl alcohol to clean contacts.

- Use compressed air or a vacuum to remove dust from the fan and the inside of the computer.

Different parts of the system require different methods of cleaning. Most of the visible dust inside the computer can be blown off using compressed air. Some parts can be cleaned using soapy water, whereas others require the use of isopropyl alcohol, and still others can be damaged by liquids. An example is the LCD display of a portable computer that should not be cleaned using a glass cleaner or soapy water. Similarly, water cannot be used to clean dirty or corroded contacts and expansion slots. The exam might have questions that will test your knowledge of the proper type of cleaning method for a given component. Be aware that hard disks cannot be cleaned and floppy drives should be cleaned only when necessary using cleaning diskettes.

QUESTIONS

4.01: Preventive Maintenance Products and Procedures

1. Which of the following computer parts can you clean using soapy water and a damp cotton cloth? Select all correct answers.

    A. Mouse ball

    B. LCD display

    C. Keyboard

    D. Gold contacts on adapters

    E. CRT display of the monitor

2. You have a computer that runs Windows 98 operating system. You use this computer at home for your personal accounting, Internet access, and email. The computer performance has degraded a little, and you want to download a disk maintenance utility from the Internet and try it on your computer. Which of the following is the most important thing that you must do to protect your critical data before you decide to run the disk maintenance utility on your hard disk?

   A. Back up the data.

   B. Rearrange the data in folders.

   C. Empty the Recycle Bin.

   D. Set file permissions.

3. You opened your computer case to change a jumper on the sound card, and you noticed that some of the metal parts have developed a residue. You tried to remove the residue but were not successful. Which of the following methods should you use to remove this residue?

   A. Use a rubber knife.

   B. Use a flat bit screwdriver.

   C. Use isopropyl alcohol.

   D. Use soapy water and a damp cloth.

4. **Current Situation:** The computer you purchased last year has never been opened, and you suspect that it is very dirty inside. You turn around the computer and notice that a lot of dust has accumulated on the power supply fans. Here is what you have to do:

   Required Result: Clean the computer parts from inside and check that there are no loose components.

   Optional Desired Results:

   1. The motherboard, adapter cards, and the free expansion slots should be clean after the cleaning process is complete.

   2. Dust should not be removed from components in such a manner that it settles on other components.

   3. The monitor and computer case should also be cleaned to a shine.

Proposed Solution: Switch off the computer and open its case. Use a vacuum cleaner to collect dust from the motherboard, adapter cards, and free expansion slots. Take a dry cloth and wipe off the dust that settles on external parts such as the computer case and the monitor. Before you close the computer case, check that the adapters, power cables, and ribbon cables are connected properly and there are no loose connections. These rough guidelines are shown in the following illustration.

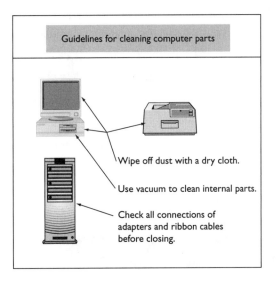

What results does the proposed solution produce?

A. The proposed solution produces the required result and all the optional results.

B. The proposed solution produces the required result and only one of the optional results.

C. The proposed solution produces the required result and only two the optional results.

D. The proposed solution does not produce the required result.

5. Which of the following methods can be used for maintaining hard disk drives? Select all correct answers.

A. Clean with hard disk cleaning diskettes.

    B.   Defragment hard disks regularly.

    C.   Run a low-level format.

    D.   Use Scandisk for corrupted files.

    E.   Use virus scan software.

6.   You work on your home computer, store some files on floppies, and take them to your office. Since you use the floppy drive very frequently, you want to perform a thorough check to ensure that it keeps working well, even though the drive has never created any problem so far. Which of the following procedures is the best way to protect the floppy drive?

    A.   Use compressed air and blow out dust from inside the floppy drive.

    B.   Use a head cleaner disk cassette to clean the read-write heads of the floppy drive.

    C.   Use a cotton swab, rinse it in isopropyl alcohol, and clean the read-write heads.

    D.   Do not clean the drive, since it is working fine.

TEST YOURSELF OBJECTIVE 4.02

Power Protection and Safety Procedures

Electrostatic Discharge and power protection are two topics that need to be understood to safeguard against possible computer failures. You must also follow safety procedures to prevent personal injuries and damage to components when working with computer parts. A UPS provides backup power in case of a power failure and protects the computer from power surges and spikes. It also helps prevent Electromagnetic Interference (EMI) in the power supply caused by nearby high voltage equipment. Keep spare components inside antistatic bags or on antistatic mats, and store them in low humidity places. High voltage components such as the monitor and power supplies should be handled carefully and must not be repaired in the field.

◼ Use a UPS to provide backup power in the event of a brownout or blackout.

◼ Suppressors can be used to absorb excess voltage.

- Noise filters "condition" the electrical supply by removing EMI.

- Monitors and power supplies are considered to be high voltage equipment and should never be opened.

- Many computer components, such as batteries, contain harmful substances and must be disposed of properly.

- Clean the computer often and use ESD straps and mats to reduce the possibility of ESD damage.

- Always store computer components in ESD bags, and place them in cool, dry places.

exam
watch

You must understand the differences between various power problems, such as power surges, power spikes, and Electromagnetic Interference (EMI), and how these can be prevented using appropriate equipment. There may be questions in the A+ exam asking you to select appropriate protection equipment based on the given power problem. You must also be aware of proper methods of storage and disposal of used parts, such as toner cartridges, batteries, and chemicals.

QUESTIONS

4.02: Power Protection and Safety Procedures

7. If you are working on adapter cards without wearing antistatic wrist straps or using any other static prevention method, how much electrostatic voltage is sufficient to damage the chips on the card?

   A. 30 volts

   B. 1,000 volts

   C. 3,000 volts

   D. 20,000 volts

8. Which of the following is an acceptable level of humidity in a room that houses computers and associated peripherals, such as scanners and printers?

   A. 20 percent to 50 percent

   B. 30 percent to 60 percent

   C. 50 percent to 80 percent

   D. 50 percent to 95 percent

9. The customer support engineer has just left your office after servicing your computer and laser printer. You notice that he has left behind a used chemical bottle that looks hazardous. You cannot contact the engineer and do not find any Workplace Hazardous Materials Information System (WHMIS) labels or warnings on the bottle or its packaging. Which of the following is your best option to dispose of the chemical? Select all correct answers.

   A. Throw the bottle in the garbage.

   B. Search for WHMIS disposal methods on the Internet.

   C. Contact the manufacturer.

   D. Put the bottle in the recycle can.

   E. Call 1-800-DISPMSDS.

10. One of your friends has purchased a new 1 KVA UPS system that will be able to supply power to two computers, a scanner, and a laser printer. The older 500 VA UPS is now free, and he wants to keep it just in case the new one fails. He has asked for your advice on how to store the UPS so that the battery is not damaged if it is not used for another six months. Which of the following is correct advice?

    A. Discharge the battery.

    B. Take out the battery and keep it in a cool, dry place.

    C. Keep the UPS connected to power so that it remains charged.

    D. Refer to the manufacturer's documentation.

11. You have a computer that is located near a high voltage transformer. Which of the following should you be concerned about if you want to protect yourself from injuries, and the computer from damage, caused by this transformer? Select all that apply.

    A. Electromagnetic Interference

    B. Electrostatic Discharge

    C. Humming sound

    D. Electric shock

    E. Magnetic interference

12. The following table presents some problems related to power supplies and the equipment suggested to prevent them.

Problem	Equipment to Prevent
Electromagnetic Interference	Noise filter
Sudden rise in AC voltage	Surge suppressor
Sudden dip in AC voltage	UPS
Backup power	CVT

    Identify the equipment that has been inappropriately suggested for the given problem?

    A. Noise filter

    B. Surge suppressor

    C. UPS

    D. CVT

    Questions 13–16   A customer has called you for preventive maintenance. His equipment includes an 80486 DX2 computer running Windows 95 Second Edition, which is connected to a laser printer. The computer uses an EIDE hard disk, a serial mouse connected to COM1 port, and an internal modem.

    Although the customer has not told you about any specific problems, you could judge from his tone of voice on the phone that he is not very happy with his computer.

Your visit to the customer's site reveals several correlated things. These are explained in the following questions. Answer these questions, selecting the best answer for each.

13. The first thing you notice when you start the computer is that after loading the operating system, the computer runs very slowly when you try to open files. You check Windows Explorer and find that the space on the hard disks is nearly 50 percent free. You check the Recycle Bin and find about 150 files there. You try to open several files, but the system performance does not change, and you do not get any errors indicating that any of the files are corrupted. Which of the following utilities will you use to resolve the file access problem?

    A. Scandisk

    B. Norton AntiVirus™

    C. Disk Defragmenter

    D. CHKDSK

14. After you have defragmented the hard disk drive, you notice that the power supply fan is not working. There is a lot of dust on it. You clean the fan using a vacuum cleaner, but the fan still does not move. What should you do with the power supply?

    A. Replace the power supply unit.

    B. Replace the faulty fan with a new fan.

    C. Open the power supply and check the voltage on fan connections.

    D. Disconnect the fan because the room is air-conditioned.

15. The customer has a lot of empty toner cartridges stored in one corner of the room. He wants to know what he should do with these cartridges, since they are now useless to him. What should be your advice?

    A. Throw them in the garbage.

    B. Buy toner powder and refill them himself.

    C. Sell them to a refilling company.

    D. Any of the above.

16. The customer wishes to know what type of fire extinguisher he should install in his computer room. Which of the following types of fire extinguishers would you suggest, considering that the customer is interested in a multipurpose product that would extinguish not only an electrical fire, but would also be suitable to extinguish a paper or wood fire?

    A. Class A

    B. Class B

    C. Class C

    D. Class ABC

QUICK ANSWER KEY

Objective 4.01	
1.	**A, C,** and **E**
2.	**A**
3.	**A**
4.	**B**
5.	**B, D,** and **E**
6.	**D**

Objective 4.02	
7.	**A**
8.	**C**
9.	**B** and **C**
10.	**D**
11.	**A** and **D**
12.	**D**
13.	**C**
14.	**A**
15.	**C**
16.	**D**

IN-DEPTH ANSWERS

4.01: Preventive Maintenance Products and Procedures

1. ☑ **A, C,** and **E.** The mouse ball, keyboard, and CRT display of the monitor can be cleaned using soapy water or a damp cotton cloth. Care must be taken that when these parts are reassembled, water is not dripping from them and they are absolutely dry. These parts can also be cleaned with isopropyl alcohol if any stain marks cannot be removed using water. The CRT of the monitors can also be cleaned using liquid glass cleaners.

    ☒ **B** is incorrect because you should not clean the LCD display of a portable computer with soapy water *and* a damp cloth. You can use only the damp cloth for this purpose. You should also not use isopropyl alcohol or liquid glass cleaners on the LCD display. **D** is incorrect because these contacts usually get corroded, and water is not sufficient to clean them. Instead, use a pencil eraser or a cotton swab dipped in isopropyl alcohol to clean the gold contacts.

2. ☑ **A.** The most important thing you must do before trying a new utility on your system is secure the existing data by taking a backup. Although chances are rare that any commercially available utility will damage your hard disk, it is always better to take the precaution of protecting your data. The question states that you want to download a utility and run it on your hard disk. The first thing you actually should do is read the documentation of the utility that should be available on the Web site. (This should have been your answer, if it were one of the options.) Then if you decide to download the utility and try it on your hard disk, you must make a backup of your data first.

    ☒ **B** is incorrect because this does not protect your data. **C** is incorrect because this action does not make any difference. **D** is incorrect because it is not possible in Windows 98 to set file level permissions.

3. ☑ **A.** A rubber knife is the best tool to remove hardened residue from metal components. Rubber knives are strong enough to do this job and do not conduct electricity, thereby preventing electrical shock.

    ☒ **B** is incorrect because you should not use a metallic tool to clean residue on metallic parts. **C** is incorrect because isopropyl alcohol is not suitable for cleaning residue. **D** is incorrect because you cannot remove the residue on metallic parts with soapy water and a damp cloth.

4. ☑ **B.** The proposed solution produces the required result and only one of the optional results. The required result is produced because you have used a vacuum cleaner to collect dust from the internal components, and you have ensured there are no loose connections. The first optional result is produced because you have cleaned the motherboard, adapter cards, and free expansion slots. The second optional result is not produced because using a vacuum cleaner will cause the dust removed from the motherboard, adapter cards, and expansion slots to settle on other parts of the computer. The blown off dust might settle on the keyboard, mouse pad, monitor, and printer. A better method would have been to disconnect the computer and take it away from the other external components for cleaning or cover the other parts with a sheet of cloth before using the vacuum cleaner. The third optional result is not produced because using a dry piece of cloth to clean the computer case and monitor will not produce shine on these parts. You should use a mild detergent and a damp cloth to clean these parts to shine.

    ☒ **A, C,** and **D** are incorrect because the proposed solution produces the required result and only one of the optional results. The two other optional results were not produced.

5. ☑ **B, D,** and **E.** Defragment hard disks regularly, use Scandisk for corrupted files, and use virus scan software. Fragmentation causes hard disks to lose read and write performance. Defragmentation helps by rearranging data in contiguous clusters on the hard disk, thus improving disk access. Scandisk is used to fix problems related to corrupted files. Virus scanners are helpful in saving the hard disk from fatal virus programs that might cause loss of system or data files.

    ☒ **A** is incorrect because hard disk cleaning diskettes do not exist. Only floppy drives can be cleaned using head cleaning disks. **C** is incorrect because this will result in loss of all the data on the hard disk. You will have to reload the operating system every time you perform a low-level format.

6. ☑ **D.** If the floppy drive is working well and has not shown any problems, you should not clean it. Cleaning drives reduces the life of read-write heads and must be avoided if you do not have any problem reading or writing to floppy disks. When you actually need to clean the floppy drive heads, you should use a head cleaning diskette.

☒ **A** is incorrect because you must not use compressed air to clean floppy drives. **B** is incorrect because you need not clean a floppy drive when it is working fine. **C** is incorrect because this requires you to dismantle the disk drive, open the disk covers, and expose the read-write heads. This method should never be used for cleaning floppy drives. You must first decide whether the drive needs cleaning or not. If required, the only correct method is to use a head cleaner diskette. Note that this question requires careful reading to determine whether or not to clean the drive.

4.02: Power Protection and Safety Procedures

7. ☑ **A.** It takes a static charge of only about 30 volts to destroy a computer component. This is known as *hidden* ESD, an amount of Electrostatic Discharge that can neither be felt nor be seen, but is still present in and around the working area. Whenever you work on computer components such as the motherboard, adapters, and memory chips, you should be careful about static discharge from your body. As a matter or practice, you should wear antistatic wrist straps while working on these parts.

☒ **B** is incorrect because it requires only about 30 volts of charge to damage semiconductor chips. Most static discharges are nearly 1,000 volts, which is highly damaging for computer components. **C** is incorrect because this much static discharge can cause heavy damage to static sensitive devices. **D** is incorrect because this charge is so high that it can produce an electric spark.

8. ☑ **C.** The acceptable level of relative humidity in a room that houses computers and associated equipment, such as scanners and printers, is between 50 and 80 percent. A humidity level below 50 percent is considered extremely dry, and a level of more than 80 percent is extremely humid. Both of these conditions cause ESD buildup in the room and are not suitable for the normal functioning of computers.

☒   **A** is incorrect because 20 percent humidity indicates extremely dry conditions that cause ESD buildup. **B** is incorrect because although computers can work well if the humidity remains between these limits, these are not the suggested limits of acceptable humidity. **D** is incorrect because 95 percent humidity indicates an extremely humid room that is not suitable for the normal functioning of computers.

9.   ☑   **B** and **C.** The two options you have in the given situation are to search the Internet for information on how to handle and dispose of the hazardous chemical, and to contact the manufacturer for these details. If the information on the bottle includes a contact number for the manufacturer, it would be better to contact them first. The manufacturer of a chemical is the best source of information concerning handling and disposal of the chemical. If you are not able to contact the manufacturer, search the Internet for information on WHMIS hazardous materials handling and disposal.

☒   **A** is incorrect because hazardous chemicals should not be thrown in the garbage. They are harmful to the environment and can cause injuries to anyone coming into contact with them. **D** is incorrect because you should not put a bottle containing a hazardous chemical in a recycle can. **E** is incorrect because this number does not exist.

10.   ☑   **D.** The best advice to your friend would be to ask him to check the manufacturer's documentation on how to store the UPS for long periods. Although it is a good idea to keep the UPS online so that the battery remains charged, it might not be suitable for every customer. The best course of action would be to consult the manufacturer's documentation that came with the UPS.

☒   **A** is incorrect because if the battery is discharged before disconnecting the UPS, it might not be able to work in the event the UPS is required urgently at a later date. **B** is incorrect because this action will result in discharge of the battery after some time. **C** is incorrect because in certain situations it may not be possible to do so.

11.   ☑   **A** and **D.** A high voltage transformer near a computer or your work area can cause Electromagnetic Interference (EMI) in your computer, and can give you an electric shock should there be any exposed wires. High voltage equipment should be kept away from computers and any place where you usually work.

☒ **B** is incorrect because the high voltage transformer will not be a source of Electrostatic Discharge. **C** is incorrect because although high voltage equipment produces a humming sound caused by the transformers, it is not the major concern in terms of personal safety or the safety of computers. **E** is incorrect because high voltage equipment will not create an electromagnetic field and will not generate magnetic fields.

12. ☑ **D.** The incorrect equipment in the table is the CVT (Constant Voltage Transformer). The CVT does not provide backup power when the power fails. It is used only to maintain a constant AC voltage output when the AC voltage varies.

☒ **A** is incorrect because a noise filter can be used to prevent Electromagnetic Interference (EMI) or noise in power lines. **B** is incorrect because a surge suppressor is capable of containing sudden increases and decreases in input AC voltage. **C** is incorrect because a UPS is capable of handling several power problems such as surges, spikes, and EMI, as well as providing backup power in case of a power failure.

13. ☑ **C.** Disk Defragmenter. If you read the question carefully, you will see the cause of the slow hard disk access. The hard disks are nearly 50 percent empty, but the Recycle Bin has a large number of files in it, indicating that the customer is deleting files frequently. Therefore, the likely cause of the problem is that the hard disk is fragmented. Running Disk Defragmenter will help improve disk access performance.

☒ **A** is incorrect because Scandisk will only check for corrupt files and lost links in the File Allocation Table (FAT), and the question states that there are no corrupted files. **B** is incorrect because there is no mention of any kind of virus. The problem is related only to slow performance of the hard disks when files are opened. **D** is incorrect because CHKDSK will check the hard disks for errors but will not defragment them to improve performance.

14. ☑ **A.** Replace the power supply unit. When you have any problems with the power supply unit of a computer, especially at a customer's site, the best course of action is to replace the unit itself. The power supply unit has high voltages inside the case, and it must not be opened to repair the fan or any other component.

☒ **B** is incorrect because the power supply unit should be replaced. You must not attempt to replace the fan. **C** is incorrect because the power supply case must not be opened, especially at a customer's site. **D** is incorrect because even if the room is air conditioned, the fan in the power supply is required to supply cool air from outside the computer to the internal components to prevent them from heating up.

15. ☑ **C.** The best way to deal with empty toner cartridges is to sell them to a company that can refill them. Toner cartridges are sold in large quantities, and there are several companies that buy old cartridges, refill them, and sell them again. Even if you do not buy the refilled toner cartridges, getting them refilled is an option that prevents waste.

☒ **A** is incorrect because toner cartridges can be refilled and reused. It is important, however, that this job be done either after proper training or by experienced people. **B** is incorrect because refilling toner cartridges requires specialized training, so not everyone should attempt it. Toner powder can spill on clothes, the printer, and all over the floor if not handled carefully. **D** is incorrect because the toner cartridges should be sold to a company that refills them.

16. ☑ **D.** A class ABC fire extinguisher is useful for all types of fires, such as paper and wood (class A), flammable liquids (Class B), and electrical fires caused by short circuits (class C). The Class ABC fire extinguisher contains dry chemical powder that not only extinguishes the fire but also helps to reduce temperatures.

☒ **A** is incorrect because this type of fire extinguisher is not suitable for electrical fires. **B** is incorrect because a class B fire extinguisher is suitable for flammable liquids but not for electrical fires. **C** is incorrect because class C fire extinguishers are not suitable to put out fires caused by paper and wood. If the customer wants a multipurpose product, he should install a class ABC fire extinguisher.

5

Motherboard, Processors, and Memory

TEST YOURSELF OBJECTIVES

The Intel Pentium family of processors was introduced at a speed of 60MHz, and it has now surpassed the speed of 1.4GHz as of the writing of this book. In addition to Intel, AMD and Cyrix are also popular brands of processors. Non-Intel processors offer almost the same speeds and are less expensive, but they have other limitations, such as lesser cache memory than Intel processors. Use of a particular type of processor requires that the motherboard support the selected processor in terms of the mounting socket or slot, bus speeds, and power supply requirements. AT and Baby AT are older types of motherboards, and a majority of newer motherboards are ATX, which have integrated I/O ports.

Random access memory (RAM) is primarily classified into Static RAM (SRAM) and Dynamic RAM (DRAM). SRAM is fast and very expensive compared to DRAM and is used only as system cache, whereas DRAM is used as the main memory of the computer. The computer saves its BIOS configuration in CMOS chips. The CMOS settings can be changed to suit a particular system and working environment.

TEST YOURSELF OBJECTIVE 5.01

Popular CPU Chips

Intel Pentium processors are mounted on the motherboard using sockets, and most of them require ±3.3vDC power supply. All Pentium processors are capable of parallel processing. Pentiums come in speeds ranging from 60MHz to 200MHz, and they have a 64-bit data bus and a 32-bit address bus that enables them to use up to 4GB of random access memory (RAM). The speed of Pentium II ranges from 233MHz to 333MHz, and they are mounted using Slot 1 or a Single Edge Contact (SEC) connector. These processors also have a 64-bit data bus, a 32-bit address bus, and they can handle up to 64GB of RAM. Pentium Pro processors were meant for servers with speeds ranging from 150MHz to 200MHz, with a wider address bus of 36 bits. Pentium III processors start from 450MHz and include MMX and Single Instruction Multiple Data (SIMD) technology. Pentium Pro, Pentium II, and Pentium III have an on-board L2 cache.

- Processors in the Pentium family include the Pentium, Pentium Pro, Pentium with MMX, Pentium II, and Pentium III.

- Pentium II and Pentium III processors connect to the motherboard using Slot 1; other Pentium processors use sockets.

- The L1 cache is located within the processor, whereas the L2 cache is either integrated with the processor (on-board), enabling it to run at the speed of the processor, or installed separately on the motherboard.

- Pentium Pro, Pentium II, and Pentium III processors include an on-board L2 cache.

Since a majority of desktops use Intel processors, you should concentrate on the variants of Intel processors, mounting methods on the motherboard, the voltages they use, the width of their address bus and data bus, the amount of L1 and L2 cache they include, and the amount of memory they can handle. All Pentium and Pentium II processors work on 3.3vDC with the exception of Pentium 150MHz, which uses 3.1vDC. Pentium III processors work on 2.0vDC, and they come in two forms that can be mounted using either SEC or a 370-pin PGA ZIF socket. Do not confuse external cache with on-board cache, and remember the maximum amount of cache and RAM that each of these processors can support.

QUESTIONS

5.01: Popular CPU Chips

1. One of your friends has a computer with a Pentium 200MHz processor and a motherboard with a bus speed of 100MHz. There is an additional Single Edge Contact (SEC) slot to support Pentium II and Pentium III processors. Your friend wants to upgrade the processor to a Pentium III processor with a speed over 600MHz. This will enable him to benefit from faster cache memory and a larger amount of RAM compared to the existing processor. Your friend has selected a Pentium III E processor. Which of the following is an additional performance benefit of this processor compared to other Pentium III processors?

   A. It can use either a PGA socket or Slot 1.

   B. It has a 64-bit wide data bus.

   C. It has a 36-bit wide address bus.

   D. It has a 256KB Advanced Transfer Cache.

2. The following illustration represents the System Properties dialog box of a computer running Windows 98.

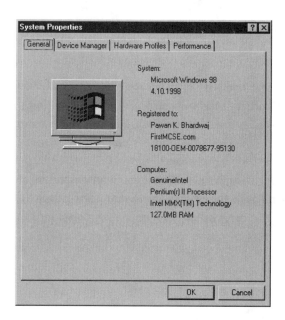

Which of the following is a correct statement regarding the type of processor used in the computer?

A. This is an Intel Pentium MMX processor.

B. This is an Intel Pentium II processor with a 127.0MB L2 cache.

C. This is an Intel Pentium II processor with MMX technology.

D. This is an Intel Pentium II clone with MMX technology.

3. The following table shows some popular Pentium chips and their corresponding data bus, address bus, and internal bus widths.

Processor Type and Speed	Data Bus	Address Bus	Internal Bus
Pentium 166MHz	64-bit	32-bit	64-bit
Pentium Pro 180MHz	64-bit	32-bit	32-bit
Pentium MMX 233MHz	64-bit	32-bit	32-bit
Pentium III 450MHz	64-bit	36-bit	32-bit

Which of the following processors has incorrect specifications in this table?

A. Pentium 166MHz

B. Pentium Pro 180MHz

C. Pentium MMX 233MHz

D. Pentium III 450MHz

4. **Current Situation:** You have a computer that is currently using a Pentium 100MHz processor and 2 modules of 16MB EDO RAM. You wish to upgrade this computer by replacing the processor and increasing its RAM. You also intend to upgrade the operating system from Windows 95 to Windows 98. Here is what you have to accomplish.

    Required Result: Upgrade the computer using a higher speed Intel Pentium processor.

    Optional Desired Results:

    1. The new processor should not require a different type of processor socket on the motherboard.

    2. The new processor should have at least 32KB of L1 cache for better performance.

    3. The new memory modules should be sufficient to run Windows 98.

    Proposed Solution: Purchase a new Pentium 200MHz processor and install it on the motherboard, replacing the old processor. Add two more modules of 16MB EDO RAM to increase the total RAM to 64MB.

    What results does the proposed solution produce?

    A. The proposed solution produces the required result and all of the optional results.

    B. The proposed solution produces the required result and only one of the optional results.

    C. The proposed solution produces the required result and only two of the optional results.

    D. The proposed solution produces only the required result.

TEST YOURSELF OBJECTIVE 5.02

Random Access Memory

Random access memory (RAM) provides temporary storage space for the operating system and the applications. Static RAM (SRAM) is expensive and is mainly used for system cache, whereas Dynamic RAM (DRAM) is less expensive, has a higher capacity, and is used for main memory. Most common DRAM variants include EDO RAM, SDRAM, and RDRAM. SDRAM runs at motherboard bus speeds from 100MHz to 133MHz and is twice as fast as the EDO RAM. The type of DRAM used in the computer depends on the type supported by the motherboard. Another type of RAM is Video RAM (VRAM), used only on video adapters for enhanced video performance. Some RAM chips use parity for error checking.

- SRAM is very fast, very expensive, and is used for L2 cache in most systems.

- DRAM is slower than SRAM but is less expensive and has a higher capacity. It is used as main memory in the computer.

- You must install SIMMs, DIMMs, and RIMMs in full memory banks so that their total bit width matches the width of the processor's data bus.

- Some memory modules use an error-checking method called odd or even parity.

exam
Watch

Adding or replacing RAM is the most common type of computer upgrade. RAM is widely classified into two types: SRAM and DRAM. Remember that SRAM is used only for system memory or cache memory. When installing RAM in a computer, you must be aware of the type of RAM supported by the motherboard. The number of SIMM or DIMM modules used should satisfy the requirements for creating a full memory bank after considering the width of the data bus on the motherboard and the bit width of the RAM being used. Remember that SIMM packaging is used for EDO RAM, and DIMM packaging is used by SDRAM. In addition, VRAM cannot be used as main memory in a computer. It is meant for video adapters only.

QUESTIONS

5.02: Random Access Memory

5. Random access memory comes in mainly two forms: Static RAM (SRAM) and Dynamic RAM (DRAM). Which of the following statements is incorrect regarding these two types of memory?

    A. SRAM is commonly used in computers for cache memory.

    B. SRAM is faster than DRAM because of its faster access time.

    C. Both SRAM and DRAM are used as main memory in the computer.

    D. EDO RAM, SDRAM, and VRAM are types of DRAM.

6. The computer you are using was purchased in 1997. It has a Pentium 133MHz processor with 16MB of RAM. You want to upgrade the RAM in this computer to 32MB, and the computer dealer has asked you to specify the type of RAM used in the computer. You know only that the RAM is Dynamic RAM. Which of the following can you rule out as a possible type of RAM?

    A. EDO RAM

    B. RDRAM

    C. DRAM

    D. Parity RAM

7. You want to add more memory to your computer, but the computer dealer says that the type of memory used in your computer is not easily available these days. Which of the following memory modules is possibly used and supported by your computer?

    A. 30-pin SIMM

    B. 72-pin SIMM

    C. 168-pin DIMM

    D. 184-pin RIMM

8. Which of the following statements is correct concerning the parity used by memory in a computer?

    A. Odd parity is used to ensure that the number of 1s in the data stream is not odd.

    B. Even parity is used to ensure that the number of 0s in the data stream is always even.

    C. Parity is used for error checking, and even and odd parity add 0 and 1 respectively to the number of 1s in the data stream.

    D. Parity is used for error checking, and odd parity adds 1 to the number of 1s in the data stream if the number of 1s is even.

TEST YOURSELF OBJECTIVE 5.03

Motherboards

Computer motherboards come in a variety of forms, sizes, and layouts, and they support different types of bus architectures, processors, and memory types. It is not possible to install just any type of processor, or any type of memory, on a motherboard. Two common forms of motherboard are AT and ATX. ISA, EISA, VESA, and PCI are some of the commonly used I/O bus architectures that provide bus widths ranging from 8-bit to 32-bit and have corresponding expansion slots for additional adapters on the motherboard. PCI supports a 32-bit bus width and is the most commonly used I/O bus architecture. Newer motherboards support AGP ports for video graphics performance, USB ports for faster Plug and Play, and hot-swappable serial devices.

- The most common type of motherboard in current computers is the ATX form, which includes 3.3vDC support, Mini-DIN-5 keyboard connectors, and a single P8/P9 power connector.

- The most common type of bus architectures are ISA, PCI, and AGP.

- VESA, PCI, and AGP bus architectures are considered "local" because they connect more directly with the processor.

- When using a drive interface, such as IDE or SCSI, use a bus architecture that supports the interface's bit width, and use a local bus architecture for faster devices.

It is quite possible that no two motherboards in the market match each other's features, but for the purpose of the A+ exam you must concentrate on some standard features such as support for processors, power supply, and I/O bus architecture. All new motherboards have support for ±3.3vDC power supply required by Pentium processors. Remember that a majority of new motherboards support both ISA and PCI I/O buses and have support for new IEEE 394, AGP, and USB buses.

QUESTIONS

5.03: Motherboards

9. A computer has a Baby AT motherboard, a 486DX2 processor running at 66MHz, with two serial ports and a parallel port. The motherboard has two power connectors and a DIN-5 keyboard connector. Which of the following additional features are you not likely to find on this motherboard?

   A. Support for a keyboard with a DIN-5 connector

   B. ±3.3vDC power supply

   C. Support for ISA I/O bus

   D. Support for 3.5-inch floppy disk drive

10. The computer you are using has only a 32-bit Extended Industry Standard Architecture (EISA) I/O bus standard. Which of the following types of adapters cannot be used in this computer?

   A. 8-bit ISA

   B. 16-bit ISA

   C. 32-bit PCI

   D. 32-bit EISA

11. **Current Situation:** One of your friends has an older computer that uses a Baby AT motherboard. This computer is built using an 80486DX2 processor, 2 modules of 16MB EDO RAM, and one EIDE hard disk controller. The power supply being used in the computer has a ±3.3vDC output. He wants to upgrade this computer. Here is what he has asked you to do.

    Required Result: Upgrade the computer to a faster, Pentium class processor, and replace the keyboard with a new 104-key keyboard.

    Optional Desired Results:

    1. The cost of the new processor should not be very high.

    2. The new processor should support the MMX technology.

    Proposed Solution: Check the socket type on the processor and see if it can support installation of a Pentium processor. Replace the 80486DX2 processor with a Pentium 166MHz processor. Replace the keyboard with a new one that has a compatible mini-DIN-5 connector.

    What results does the proposed solution produce?

    A. The proposed solution produces the required result and both of the optional results.

    B. The proposed solution produces the required result and only one of the optional results.

    C. The proposed solution produces the required result but none of the optional results.

    D. The proposed solution does not produce the required result.

12. You have just purchased a new Pentium III 600MHz computer that has 128MB of SDRAM. You call up your friend and tell him about the purchase. He asks you what type of motherboard it has and what I/O bus it supports. If the computer uses the most common motherboard, a part of which looks like the illustration shown on the next page, which of the following do you think is the correct answer?

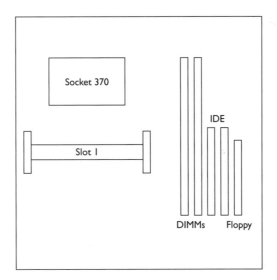

A. ATX motherboard with EISA bus

B. Baby AT motherboard with PCI bus only

C. ATX motherboard with PCI and ISA bus

D. Baby AT motherboard with ISA bus only

TEST YOURSELF OBJECTIVE 5.04

Complementary Metal-Oxide Semiconductor (CMOS) Settings

CMOS settings are used to customize the way the computer recognizes and uses components. These settings affect the way the computer starts up; how it accesses and loads the operating system; how the processor accesses and uses memory; and, if the BIOS supports Plug and Play (PnP), how PnP devices are detected and resources allocated to them. You can configure the boot sequence and set passwords for protecting BIOS settings. Common CMOS settings include setting system date and time and enabling or disabling I/O ports, PnP support, and configuration of floppy drives and hard drives.

■ The CMOS settings program allows you to alter the behavior and configuration of many of the system's components.

■ Parallel ports may be set to unidirectional, bi-directional, ECP, or EPP mode.

■ You can use the CMOS settings to disable or enable the I/O ports, floppy drive, hard drive, or Plug and Play support.

■ The CMOS settings program allows you to set the time and date, user passwords, and boot sequence.

exam
Watch

Some of the important CMOS settings in a computer are the boot sequence, date and time, and enabling or disabling I/O ports. Be aware of the different options available in different CMOS configuration screens. You might find an answer option that does not exist in the CMOS settings or a question that will attempt to confuse you by mixing up the CMOS setting options. It is important to note that the RAM cannot be configured in CMOS settings, but is always calculated during the system startup.

QUESTIONS

5.04: Complementary Metal-Oxide Semiconductor (CMOS) Settings

Questions 13–17 A computer has an ATX motherboard with a Pentium II 450MHz processor. It has two SDRAM DIMMs, each with a 64MB capacity and integrated two serial ports and a parallel port.

The computer has two integrated EIDE hard disk controllers designated as primary and secondary. The primary master disk is the main C drive of the computer having a 6.4GB capacity. An ATAPI CD-ROM is connected as a primary slave drive. The computer also has a 1.44MB floppy disk drive. The computer has a 104-key keyboard and a PS/2 mouse. A color inkjet printer is connected to the parallel port.

When you press the DEL key immediately after switching on the computer, the computer enters the CMOS setup utility.

You need to work on this computer to add a second hard disk. The user working on this computer has some other correlated problems described in the following questions. Answer these questions selecting the best answer for each.

13. The user wants you to change some of the power management features of the computer. Which of the following options should you perform first before configuring the power management settings of the computer?

    A. Set the Frequency/Voltage Control.

    B. Check the PC Health Status.

    C. Note the current settings.

    D. Load Optimized Defaults.

14. The user has called you about adding a second hard drive in his computer. He got this hard disk from his friend who upgraded his Pentium 150MHz computer with a new larger capacity hard disk. You are not able to get any information about the number of heads, sectors, or tracks, except that the hard disk has a 1.2GB capacity. The label on the hard disk is not readable. Considering that you have to enter the hard disk type in the CMOS settings manually, which of the following settings should you select?

    A. Auto detect

    B. Auto head detect

    C. Auto Sector/track detect

    D. User type

15. The current boot sequence of the computer is A:, C:. The user does not use the floppy drive very frequently, but he wants to keep the drive for emergency situations. On the other hand, he does not want the system to seek the floppy drive on startup. What will happen if you change the boot sequence from A:, C: to C:, A:?

    A. The BIOS will first search the C: drive for the operating system and then the A: drive.

    B. The BIOS will always load the operating system from the C: drive.

C. The BIOS will never seek the A: drive for loading the operating system.

D. The BIOS will attempt three times to load the operating system from the C: drive and then seek the A: drive.

16. You have installed the additional hard disk. The user wants you to check the printing quality of the inkjet printer. When you send a page from the word processing program for printing, you notice that the printer software gives an indication of the ink in the print cartridge. In which of the following modes is the parallel port of the computer working? Select all correct answers.

A. ECP mode

B. EPP mode

C. Transfer mode

D. Bi-directional mode

17. When you have finished your job, the user tells you that he stores his important files in this computer. He wants you to set passwords in the system so that no one is able to boot the system without his knowledge. Which of the following methods is most secure for this requirement?

A. Log-on password in Windows 98

B. Supervisor password in the CMOS setup

C. User password in the CMOS setup

D. None of the above

QUICK ANSWER KEY

Objective 5.01

1. D
2. C
3. B
4. C

Objective 5.02

5. C
6. B
7. A
8. D

Objective 5.03

9. B
10. C
11. D
12. C

Objective 5.04

13. C
14. A
15. A
16. A and D
17. C

IN-DEPTH ANSWERS

5.01: Popular CPU Chips

1. ☑ **D.** The major difference between Pentium III E and other variants of Pentium III processors is that this processor has an on-board 256KB Advanced Transfer Cache (ATC) that improves the performance by nearly 25 percent.

    ☒ **A** is incorrect because there are several variants of Pentium III processors that can be mounted using either the PGA socket or Slot 1 (SEC). This is not an advantage so far as the performance of the processor is concerned. **B** and **C** are incorrect because all Pentium III processors have a 64-bit wide data bus and a 36-bit wide address bus. These processors support up to 64GB of RAM because of the wide address bus.

2. ☑ **C.** This is an Intel Pentium II processor with MMX technology. The System Information dialog box in Windows 98 shows the type of processor being used in the computer. In the given diagram, the information displayed about the processor indicates that it is a genuine Intel Pentium II processor. Intel MMX technology indicates that the processor has built-in extensions to support multimedia. All Intel Pentium processors released after the Pentium MMX support the MMX technology. The speed of the processor is not indicated in this dialog box.

    ☒ **A** is incorrect because the first Intel processor with MMX technology was named Intel Pentium MMX. All later processors, including the Pentium II shown in the dialog box, include MMX capabilities. Intel Pentium II and Intel Pentium MMX are two different types of processors. **B** is incorrect because 127.0MB is the amount of RAM in the system and is not indicative of the L2 cache on the processor. **D** is incorrect because the processor is a genuine Intel processor and not a *clone* of Intel Pentium II.

3. ☑ **B.** Pentium Pro 180MHz. The Pentium Pro processors have a 36-bit address bus. These processors were designed specially to address the processing needs of servers. Because of the wider address bus compared to its predecessors,

the Pentium Pro processors can support up to 64GB of RAM. In addition, these processors can support up to 1MB of L2 cache.

☒ **A** is incorrect because the specifications given in the table for this processor are correct. **C** is incorrect because the Pentium MMX processors have a 64-bit data bus, a 32-bit address bus, and a 32-bit internal bus, as correctly given in the table. **D** is incorrect because the data given in the table is correct: these processors have a 64-bit address bus, 36-bit data bus, and a 32-bit internal bus.

4. ☑ **C.** The proposed solution produces the required result and only two of the optional results. The required result is produced because you can replace the currently installed Pentium 100MHz processor with a higher speed Pentium 200MHz processor, since both processors use PGA socket 7. This also produces the first optional result. The second optional result is not produced because the new Pentium 200MHz processor has only 16KB of L1 cache memory. The third optional result is produced because adding two more modules of 16MB EDO RAM will produce a total RAM of 64MB. This much RAM is sufficient to run Windows 98 operating system.

☒ **A, B,** and **D** are incorrect because the proposed solution produces the required result and only two of the optional results. The second optional result that the L1 cache should be 32KB is not produced.

5.02: Random Access Memory

5. ☑ **C.** This statement is incorrect because only DRAM is used as main memory in the computer. Main memory refers to the random access memory (RAM), and several variants of DRAM are used as main memory or RAM in computers. SRAM, on the other hand, is faster but very expensive and is used only as system cache memory.

☒ **A** is an incorrect answer because this statement is true. SRAM is used as system cache. **B** is incorrect because the statement is true. SRAM has a faster access time of approximately 10 ns. **D** is incorrect because it is true that the given types of RAM are all types of DRAM.

6. ☑ **B.** RDRAM stands for Rambus Dynamic RAM, a type of RAM introduced in 1999. Since the computer you are using is three years old, it cannot be using RDRAM, as it was not available at that time.

☒ **A** is incorrect because the computer might have EDO RAM. **C** is incorrect because DRAM is a general acronym for all kinds of dynamic RAM. **D** is incorrect because the dynamic RAM used by the computer might be using parity for error checking.

7. ☑ **A.** The 30-pin SIMM was used in older computers and has almost vanished from the marketplace. If your computer uses this type of SIMM, it is quite possible that the computer memory cannot be upgraded due to unavailability of these SIMMs.

☒ **B** is incorrect because, although these modules are not widely used, they are not very old and are still available. **C** is incorrect because the SDRAM DIMM which uses a 168-pin connector is the most common type of RAM currently available. **D** is incorrect because this type of memory is not very old and is widely available these days.

8. ☑ **D.** Parity is used by RAM for error checking, and odd parity checks the number of 1s in the data stream and adds 1 if the number of 1s is even. When even parity is used, the number of 1s in the data stream is counted, and 1 is added if the number is odd. This is a question with very confusing options. You must be careful while answering this type of question.

☒ **A** is incorrect because parity is used for error *checking*, rather than to *ensure* that the number of 1s in the data stream remains odd or even. In odd parity, the number of 1s in the data stream should remain 1, and if it is not, 1 is added as a parity bit. **B** is incorrect because only 1s are counted for calculating parity and not 0s. **C** is incorrect because the parity bit is either 1 or 0, and it is incorrect to say that both even and odd parity add 0 and 1 respectively to the data stream.

5.03: Motherboards

9. ☑ **B.** ±3.3vDC power supply. The Baby AT motherboard is an older type of motherboard that does not support the ±3.3vDC power supply. This supply is typically used by the newer Pentium class of processors that did not exist when the Baby AT motherboards were in use. These motherboards support only ±5vDC and ±12vDC.

⊠ **A** is incorrect because the Baby AT motherboards typically support 84-key keyboards with a round DIN-5 connector. **C** is incorrect because the ISA I/O bus is supported by Baby AT motherboards. **D** is incorrect because Baby AT motherboards support 3.5-inch floppy drives as well as 5.25-inch floppy drives.

10. ☑ **C.** 32-bit PCI. A computer that has only a 32-bit EISA I/O bus standard supports only 8-bit ISA, 16-bit ISA, and 32-bit EISA adapters. 32-bit PCI adapters need a 32-bit PCI I/O bus architecture on the motherboard and use smaller white-colored PCI slots. A PCI card cannot be inserted into an ISA or EISA expansion slot.

⊠ **A, B,** and **D** are incorrect answers because the 32-bit EISA I/O bus does support 8-bit ISA, 16-bit ISA, and 32-bit EISA adapters. The EISA expansion slots can be used to install any of the three types of adapters.

11. ☑ **D.** The proposed solution does not produce the required result because the Pentium processor selected has a speed of 166MHz that needs a ±3.3vDC power supply. Although the power supply unit has a ±3.3vDC output, the Baby AT motherboard does not support it. Typical Baby AT motherboards support only ±5vDC and ±12vDC power supplies. Supposing that the Pentium 166MHz processor were supported on this motherboard, let us see whether the optional results are produced or not. The first optional result is produced because the Pentium 166MHz processor is not very expensive (provided it is still available in the market!). The second optional result is not produced because the Pentium 166MHz processor does not support MMX technology.

⊠ **A, B,** and **C** are incorrect because the proposed solution does not produce the required result. You must either change the motherboard to an ATX type or install a Pentium processor with a maximum of 66MHz speed that does not require the motherboard to support the ±3.3vDC power supply. This is also true if the Baby AT motherboard has a socket 4 for the processor.

12. ☑ **C.** ATX motherboard with PCI and ISA bus. Read the question carefully: it says, '*if the computer uses the most common motherboard.*' Since there are several types of motherboards available on the market, you must concentrate on standard and common computer components. Commonly used motherboards today use the ATX layout and have both ISA and PCI I/O buses.

☒ **A** is incorrect because the EISA I/O bus is very rare to find in newer computers. **B** is incorrect because the Baby AT motherboard is not very common. Even if the computer uses a baby AT motherboard (because some manufacturers do use it), it should have support for the ISA I/O bus. **D** is incorrect because all newer motherboards have the PCI I/O bus.

5.04: Complementary Metal-Oxide Semiconductor (CMOS) Settings

13. ☑ **C.** Whenever you need to alter CMOS settings, make it a point to note the current settings. Although you have the option of exiting the CMOS settings without saving the changes, taking note of the current settings gives you an option of rolling back to previous working settings, even when you have saved the new configuration, if the system refuses to work after the changes take effect. This is a good practice that saves you from embarrassment in case the CMOS settings get misconfigured by accident.

☒ **A** is incorrect because it is not necessary to change this setting for configuring power management of the computer. Even if you were to alter frequency or voltage settings, this should not be your first action when starting to work on CMOS settings. **B** is incorrect because this setting is checked when you suspect that something is wrong with the normal working of the computer, and it does not help in configuring power management features. **D** is incorrect because this refers to loading optimized default values in case the CMOS settings are misconfigured such that manual reconfiguration is time consuming or cannot be done. Rather than being the *first* action that you should perform when you need to configure CMOS settings, this action is taken usually as a last resort.

14. ☑ **A.** If you are not sure about the type of hard disk, you should select 'Auto detect' or 'Auto' in the CMOS settings. This enables the BIOS to detect the number of heads, sectors, and tracks automatically. All of the BIOS software manufacturers have this auto detect functionality for hard disks.

☒ **B** and **C** are incorrect because neither the 'Auto head detect' nor the 'Auto Sector/track detect' option exists in any BIOS software. These functions are performed by the hard disk auto detect feature and are not available individually. **D** is incorrect because if you are not sure about the number of heads and sectors in the hard disk, you will not be able to configure it correctly. The User type setting was required in older computers.

15. ☑ **A.** The BIOS will first search the C: drive for the operating system and then the A: drive. You must be careful about simple questions in the A+ exam that might try to confuse you with the answer options, and this is one such question. The boot sequence just tells the BIOS the preferred order of drives for seeking and loading the operating system. If the boot sequence of the computer is changed from A:, C: to C:, A: this means that the BIOS will seek the C: drive first for locating the operating system, and if it does not find it there, it will search the floppy drive A:.

 ☒ **B** is incorrect because the BIOS will always *first* attempt to load the operating system from the C: drive. **C** is incorrect because the BIOS will first attempt to load the operating system from the C: drive and then seek the floppy drive if it is not able to find the operating system on the C: drive. **D** is incorrect because the BIOS will make only one attempt to load the operating system from the C: drive before looking for it from the A: drive.

16. ☑ **A** and **D.** ECP mode and bi-directional mode. The ECP (Enhanced Capability Port) and bi-directional modes of the parallel ports in a computer allow data to travel in both directions: from computer to printer and from printer to computer. Since the printer is sending the status of ink in the cartridge, data is traveling from the printer to the computer in addition to the print data that is flowing from the computer to the printer.

 ☒ **B** is incorrect because the EPP (Enhanced Parallel Port) mode is used for devices other than printers and scanners. **C** is incorrect because the transfer mode is a unidirectional mode in which data travels only from computer to the printer through the parallel port.

17. ☑ **C.** The User password in the CMOS settings ensures that no one except the intended user of the computer who knows the correct password is able to boot the computer. When a user enters an incorrect password, the boot sequence does not complete, and the system does not load the operating system.

☒ **A** is incorrect because this password does not stop the system from booting. The Windows 98 password works only after the system has loaded the operating system. This password is not secure and will not meet the requirements of the user. **B** is incorrect because this password is meant to secure the CMOS settings only. Any user who does not know the Supervisor password cannot alter the CMOS settings. This password does not prevent any unintended user from booting the system. **D** is incorrect because one correct answer does exist in the given options.

CORE HARDWARE/OPERATING SYSTEM EXAMS

6

Printers

The various types of computer printers differ in their printing mechanisms, cost, and print quality. Dot matrix printers use a matrix of pins and ink ribbon to form a character on the paper. They are the least expensive and offer the lowest print quality. Inkjet, deskjet, and bubblejet printers are non-impact printers that use ink cartridges, produce better print quality than dot matrix printers, and can print in color. Laser printers, on the other hand, are very fast—they can print a full page at a time. Laser printers use toner cartridges instead of ink, give the best print quality in color or black and white, and are the most expensive.

Whatever type of printer is being used, it is important that proper preventive maintenance procedures be followed to avoid problems. Regular cleaning of printers and replacement of ribbons, ink cartridges, and toner cartridges not only maintains printing quality at its best but also prevents several printing problems. The most common printer problems are caused by dust, humidity, and poor paper quality. Laser printers are difficult to service and, in order to resolve a particular problem, you must know the function of each part involved in the printing process.

TEST YOURSELF OBJECTIVE 6.01

Basic Printer Concepts

Printers are mainly classified into three categories: dot matrix, inkjet, and laser. Dot matrix and inkjet printers are called impact printers and print one line at a time, whereas laser printers are non-impact, print the whole page at a time, and are thus called page printers. Laser printers are the most expensive printers and employ a complex printing technology using high negative voltages for charging drums and fusing purposes. They use toner for printing as opposed to the ink used by dot matrix and inkjet printers. Printers are either connected to a computer, or they can be directly connected to the network as a network node and shared by multiple users.

- Dot matrix printers are called impact printers because they create images by striking an array of pins against the page.

- Inkjet printers use a small pump to spray ink on the page, and bubblejet printers use heat to place bubbles of ink on the page.

- Laser printers use a drum to transfer toner to the page.

- Dot matrix and inkjet printers are line printers, and laser printers are page printers.

- The six steps in the laser print process are charging, writing, developing, transferring, fusing, and cleaning.

- Printers can be attached locally to a computer using a parallel or USB connection.

- True network printers contain a NIC and are stand-alone network devices.

- Regular local printers can be shared on the network as long as the print server is turned on and has network access.

exam
ⓦatch

You must be able to differentiate among the types of commonly used printers and how they function. Laser printers employ the most complex printing mechanisms, and it is important for you to understand the steps involved in their print process, that is, charging, writing, developing, image transfer, fusing, and drum cleaning. In addition, it is important that you be aware of the parts that accomplish these jobs. Once you are familiar with the laser printing process, it will be easy for you to answer questions in the A+ exam.

QUESTIONS

6.01: Basic Printer Concepts

1. Which of the following is used for making an impact on paper in dot matrix printers and also enables them to create multiple carbon copies?

    A. Rotating daisy wheel

    B. Ink cartridge

    C. Toner powder

    D. Solenoid activated pins

2. One of your friends is seeking your advice on the types of printers available in the market and how each type of printer would meet his requirements. Which of the following would you suggest as a non-impact printer that is capable of printing acceptable color prints and is not very expensive? Select all correct answers.

    A. Dot matrix printer

    B. Laser printer

    C. Inkjet printer

    D. Bubblejet printer

3. Which of the following printers does not use friction feed rollers for movement of paper?

    A. Laser printer

    B. Inkjet printer

    C. Deskjet printer

    D. Dot matrix printer

4. When you install a printer locally, connecting it to the LPT1 port of your computer, what should be the maximum length of cable?

    A. 6 feet

    B. 8 feet

    C. 10 feet

    D. 25 feet

5. **Current Situation:** You have purchased a Pentium III 750MHz computer that has 128MB of SDRAM and Windows 98 preinstalled. You will use this printer for advertisements you design for your clients. You also want to print your invoices for clients in triplicate. You want to buy a printer for this computer. Here is what you have to accomplish.

    Required Result: Select a printer that can print high-resolution graphic designs for the advertisements that you will be preparing with your design applications.

    Optional Desired Results:

    1. The printer should be the able to print full pages at a time instead of printing line-by-line.

    2. The printer should be able to print carbon copies of invoices.

    Proposed Solution: Buy a laser printer because it is the fastest printer available in the market. Install the printer on your Windows 98 computer after connecting it to the parallel port.

What results does the proposed solution produce?

A. The proposed solution produces the required result and both of the optional results.

B. The proposed solution produces the required result and only one of the optional results.

C. The proposed solution produces the required result but none of the optional results.

D. The proposed solution does not produce the required result.

6. In laser printers, the image is transferred from the charged drum to paper using a transfer corona wire. What happens immediately after this process?

A. Cleaning of the drum

B. Recharging of the drum with a high negative voltage

C. Fusing the toner on the paper

D. Writing the image on the photosensitive drum

7. The following statements describe some of the steps involved in the laser printing process. Identify the statement that is incorrect.

A. In the charging phase, the high voltage power supply charges the photosensitive drum with a high negative voltage.

B. In the writing phase, the toner is attracted to the charged drum at the places that do not have a high negative charge.

C. In the transferring phase, the transfer corona wire applies a small positive charge to the paper that attracts the toner from the drum.

D. In the cleaning phase, the drum is cleaned using a cleaning blade to remove excess toner.

8. Which of the following statements correctly describes the difference between the primary corona wire and the transfer corona wire in a laser printer?

A. The primary corona wire charges the paper with a positive charge, whereas the transfer corona wire transfers high negative voltage to the drum.

B. The primary corona wire is used to charge the drum with a high positive voltage, whereas the transfer corona wire transfers a negative charge onto the paper.

C. The primary corona wire is used to charge the drum with a high negative voltage, whereas the transfer corona wire transfers a positive charge onto the paper.

D. Primary and transfer corona wire are mutually exclusive, and a laser printer can have either of them but not both.

9. You have installed a parallel printer, with your computer running Windows 98 operating system. The office has five more Windows 98 computers, and your boss wants the printer to be available for use by all computer users. A coaxial cable connects all the computers, and NetBEUI is used as the network protocol. See the following illustration for details of this setup.

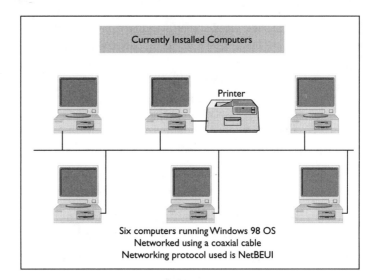

You are already sharing folders, and File and Printer Sharing is enabled on the computers. Which of the following is the best way to allow all users access to the printer?

A. Share the printer from Printer Properties.

B. Install print sharing software on all computers.

C. Use a 6-way printer switch.

D. Nothing; the printer will be automatically shared since File and Printer Sharing is enabled.

TEST YOURSELF OBJECTIVE 6.02

Care, Service, and Troubleshooting

Preventive maintenance is a must for proper printer functioning. Dot matrix printers are more prone than other printers to problems caused by dust because of their paper feed mechanisms, the type of paper they use, and their open printing parts. Problems in print quality are related to the ribbons in dot matrix printers, ink cartridges in inkjet printers, and toner cartridges in laser printers. These ribbons or cartridges must be replaced for better print output. Improper communication between the computer and the printer also causes several problems, such as garbled print output or no print output at all.

- Tractor feeds use sprocketed wheels to pull a continuous roll of paper through the printer, whereas friction feeds use rubber or plastic rollers to pull single pages through.

- Paper jams can be caused by pages sticking together because of static, worn out feed mechanisms, particle build-up, or using the wrong paper weight.

- Blank pages are usually resolved by replacing the printer ribbon, ink cartridge, toner cartridge, or drum.

- If a printer produces a repeated blotch, clean the printer, or, in the case of a laser printer, replace the drum.

- Ghosted images are caused by failure of the laser printer's cleaning step, and can usually be resolved by replacing the drum.

- If the printer produces garbled text, or if it cannot be found by the computer, the computer is not communicating properly with the printer.

- The most important preventive maintenance procedure you can carry out on a printer is regular cleaning.

exam
Watch

It is very important that you understand the causes of common printer problems, so you must be familiar with the printing process of each type of printer. Although cleaning the printer resolves most paper feed problems in all types of printers, you must be aware that paper feed problems are often caused by poor paper quality. In laser printers, replacing the drum or toner cartridge resolves several problems related to print quality, such as ghosted images and poor resolution.

QUESTIONS

6.02: Care, Service, and Troubleshooting

10. Which of the following preventive maintenance procedures will help you keep your dot matrix printer working well without any expenditure?

    A. Regular replacement of the ribbon cartridge

    B. Regular cleaning of the print head pins

    C. Regular cleaning of printer parts

    D. Regular use of refilled ribbon cartridges

11. A previous customer of yours has recently purchased an inkjet printer. He uses his printer only for printing some letters and envelopes. You cleaned the printer only last week. He calls and tells you that the printer has suddenly started having frequent paper jam problems. Which of the following should be your suggestion to the customer to resolve the problem?

    A. Order a new paper tray.

    B. Try a different type of paper.

    C. Stop printing envelopes.

    D. Replace the paper rollers.

12. **Current Situation:** The laser printer in your office was purchased two years ago. The manufacturer has given you training in preventive maintenance and basic troubleshooting for this printer. In recent weeks this printer has started having several problems. Here is what you have to accomplish.

    Required Result: Keep the printer free of dust and toner particles to maintain its printing quality and enhance its life.

    Optional Desired Results:

    1. The preventive maintenance procedure you adopt should take care of paper jam problems.

    2. The preventive maintenance should not cost the company any extra expenditure.

Proposed Solution: Depending on the usage of the laser printer, set a schedule for regular cleaning. While cleaning the printer, make sure that the paper path is free of dust and that toner particles are not spilled on the internal parts of the printer. When the printer display indicates that the toner is low, immediately change the toner cartridge. Change the drum every four months to maintain printing quality.

What results does the proposed solution produce?

A. The proposed solution produces the required result and both of the optional results.

B. The proposed solution produces the required result and only one of the optional results.

C. The proposed solution produces the required result but none of the optional results.

D. The proposed solution does not produce the required result.

13. A laser printer is producing print outputs with a few blotches of toner spilled on one corner of the paper. The printer was cleaned only last week, and you are sure that there is no toner residue inside the printer. Which of the following components of the printer needs replacement?

A. Drum

B. Toner cartridge

C. Cleaning blade

D. Fuser assembly

14. A laser printer is producing print output that contains the image of previous printing. Which of the following processes do you think is causing the problem?

A. Fusing

B. Writing

C. Cleaning

D. Developing

Questions 15–17   One of your friends has purchased a secondhand laser printer to replace his old bubblejet printer. He needs your help to install this printer with his computer. He has a Pentium II 450MHz computer running Windows 95. He uses his computer for word processing applications and some graphics designs.

The printer he purchased is a black and white printer manufactured over two years ago. He also bought the parallel cable with the printer and the device driver disks that contain printer drivers for Windows 98, Windows NT, Mac OS, and SCO UNIX.

When you arrive at your friend's house, you find that he has already connected the printer to his computer and is trying to print from a word processing program. The following questions describe the various problems you are faced with during your stay at your friend's house. Answer these questions selecting the best answer for each question.

15. Your friend is trying to print a page from his word processing program, but the first page does not print. The lights of the printer panel flicker a couple of times, but nothing happens after that. You try to print a test page, but the printer again shows the same symptoms, and nothing is printed. You check all connections and find that they are okay. What should you do next to further diagnose the cause of the problem?

   A. Replace the printer cable.

   B. Check the IRQ assignment of the parallel port.

   C. Check the BIOS to see if the parallel port is disabled.

   D. Check to see if the correct printer driver is installed.

16. After installing the correct printer driver, you try to print a page from the word processing program, but the paper comes out blank. The printer display on the front panel is not showing any error message. Which of the following would you rule out as the likely cause of the problem?

   A. High voltage power supply

   B. Toner cartridge

   C. Primary corona wire

   D. Transfer corona wire

17. Once the printer is operational and you are able to print a test page, your friend is happy because all the problems have been taken care of. However, when your friend picks up the printed page from the printer, the toner smears off the page and sticks to his hand. Which of the following parts of the printer should you tell him to replace?

    A. Fusing assembly

    B. Drum

    C. Transfer corona wire

    D. High voltage power supply

QUICK ANSWER KEY

Objective 6.01		Objective 6.02	
1.	D	10.	C
2.	C and D	11.	B
3.	D	12.	C
4.	C	13.	A
5.	B	14.	C
6.	C	15.	D
7.	B	16.	B
8.	C	17.	A
9.	A		

IN-DEPTH ANSWERS

6.01: Basic Printer Concepts

1. ☑ **D.** Solenoid activated pins. Dot matrix printers use metal pins that are activated by a solenoid upon getting signals from the printer main board, also called the motherboard or logic board. The print head contains the solenoid as well as the pins, which strike the paper through a ribbon. The impact is strong enough to create impressions on multiple carbon copies. For this reason, dot matrix printers are best suited for accounting applications, such as printing invoices, checks, and account statements.

   ☒ **A** is incorrect because the daisy wheel is not used in dot matrix printers. A daisy wheel is a circular shaped plastic part that prints complete characters, unlike the dot matrix printer, which uses a matrix of pins to create the shape of the characters. Daisy wheels are used in electronic typewriters and can produce quality text printing. **B** is incorrect because ink cartridges are used in inkjet and bubblejet printers. **C** is incorrect because toner cartridges contain the black powder known as toner which is used in laser printers.

2. ☑ **C and D.** Both the inkjet printer and the bubblejet printer are non-impact printers, are able to produce color prints with an acceptable resolution, and are not very expensive compared to laser printers.

   ☒ **A** is incorrect because this printer falls in the impact printer category and is not able to produce good quality color resolution. **B** is incorrect because although these printers are non-impact printers and give the best resolution, they are very expensive. The requirement is that the color resolution be acceptable, and this requirement is satisfied by inkjet and bubblejet printers.

3. ☑ **D.** The dot matrix printer does not use friction feed rollers for moving the paper inside the printer from the paper tray, or to move it out after printing. These printers use the continuous form feed or the tractor feed mechanism for moving the paper in and out of the printer. This method uses two wheels, one on the left and another on the right side of the printer. The wheels have spokes

or stubs that fit into the corresponding holes in the continuous roll of paper, and the paper moves when the wheels rotate. The paper is usually perforated to mark the end of the page and can be torn off when a page completes printing.

☒ **A, B,** and **C** are incorrect answers because the laser printer, inkjet printer, and deskjet printer all use friction feed rollers for pulling the paper inside the printer from the paper tray and to move it out when the printing is complete.

4. ☑ **C.** 10 feet. The LPT1 port is a parallel port on the computer. The maximum length of the parallel cable connecting the computer's LPT1 port and the printer should not exceed 10 feet. The longer the cable, the more it becomes susceptible to interference that causes printing problems.

☒ **A** and **B** are incorrect because the maximum length of parallel cable is 10 feet. A shorter cable is a better choice, if available. **D** is incorrect because 25 feet is the limit for serial printer cables. The parallel cable must be kept within the length of 10 feet.

5. ☑ **B.** The proposed solution produces the required result and only one of the optional results. The required result is produced because a laser printer is capable of giving you the best resolution print output among all types of printers. Depending on the make and model of the laser printer, these printers are capable of producing high-quality prints for your graphics designs. The first optional result is produced because laser printers print one full page at a time instead of printing line-by-line. The second optional result is not produced because it is not possible to print carbon copies with a laser printer. A dot matrix printer is best suited for printing invoices with carbon copies.

☒ **A, C,** and **D** are incorrect because the proposed solution produces the required result and only one of the optional results. The requirement of printing copies of invoices in triplicate is not produced.

6. ☑ **C.** Fusing the toner on the paper. Immediately after the image is transferred to paper using toner, the paper moves to the fusing assembly in the laser printer. The fusing assembly has heated rollers that melt the toner, which until now is held on the paper with only electrical charge, and permanently sets the toner on the paper.

☒ **A** is incorrect because this is typically the last process in laser printing. When the fusing process finishes, completing the printing process, the drum is cleaned with the help of a cleaning blade to remove excess toner. **B** is incorrect because this is the first process when the laser printer starts printing. **D** is incorrect because the image is *written* to the drum before the developing phase.

7. ☑ **B.** In the writing phase, the toner is attracted to the charged drum at the places that do not have a high negative charge. This step is known as the developing phase and not the writing phase, as described here. In the writing phase, the laser beam moves along the drum and creates an image that will finally appear on the paper. The moving laser beam removes the high negative charge from selective places on the drum, depending on the signals received from the computer.

   ☒ **A** is incorrect because the statement is true. The high voltage power supply charges the drum to nearly −5000vDC. **C** is incorrect because this step is correctly described. During the transfer phase, the image is transferred to the paper, which is positively charged by transfer corona wire in order to attract toner from the drum. **D** is an incorrect answer because the statement correctly describes the cleaning step. A cleaning blade removes the excess toner from the drum so that it can be charged again for a new image.

8. ☑ **C.** The primary corona wire is used to charge the drum with a high negative voltage, whereas the transfer corona wire transfers a positive charge onto the paper. The difference between primary corona wire and the transfer corona wire is that the former applies a high negative charge of nearly −5000vDC to the drum, and the latter applies a small positive charge to the paper. Whereas the negative charge is used to develop an image on the drum with the help of a laser beam, the positive charge on the paper attracts the toner from the drum. The key to remembering the difference is that the transfer corona wire is used to actually *transfer* the image from the drum to the paper.

   ☒ **A** is incorrect because the functions of the wires have been interchanged in the statement. The primary corona wire charges the drum with a high negative voltage, whereas the transfer corona wire charges the paper with small positive voltage. **B** is incorrect because the charges described in the statement have been interchanged. The primary corona wire transfers the high negative charge, and the transfer corona wire administers the positive charge. **D** is incorrect because these wires are not mutually exclusive. The two corona wires have specific functions in the laser printing process, and all laser printers have both primary and transfer corona wires.

9. ☑ **A.** Share the printer from Printer Properties. All non-network printers can be shared on the network from the Properties dialog box of Windows 98 as well as other operating systems. If you are using Windows 98, click the Start menu and then click Printers, which opens the Printers window. Right-click the installed printer, and select Properties. This opens the Properties sheet of the printer. If File and Printer Sharing is enabled on the computer, a Sharing tab appears in this dialog box. Click this tab, and click Share This Printer to enable printer sharing.

☒ **B** is incorrect because you need not install any additional software to enable the computers to use the shared printer. **C** is incorrect because there is no need to install another piece of hardware when the printer can already be shared on Windows 98 operating system. **D** is incorrect because even if File and Printer Sharing is enabled, you have to share the printer from its Properties page.

6.02: Care, Service, and Troubleshooting

10. ☑ **C.** Regular cleaning of printer parts. Dot matrix printers are known for repeated problems caused by dirty parts. These printers attract more dust than any other type of printer because of their open print mechanisms, such as the tractor feed and the print heads. It is common practice for users to remove the printer cover and keep it aside when printing. This exposes the printing parts which continuously attract dust, and this dirt collects inside the printer as a result. Furthermore, the special paper used by dot matrix printers creates and leaves behind a lot of paper particles inside the printer. It is very important to perform regular cleaning of dot matrix printers.

☒ **A** is incorrect because although it is a good practice to replace ribbon cartridges before they become worn out or run out of ink, this requires spending money. The question asks for the preventive maintenance method that does not require expenditure. **B** is incorrect because general cleaning of the dot matrix printer is more important than cleaning the print head pins. **D** is incorrect because this is against preventive maintenance practices. As far as possible, new ribbons should be used instead of refilled ribbons in order to maintain high print quality.

11. ☑ **B.** Try a different type of paper. Most paper jam problems are caused by quality of paper. A possible cause of the paper jam problem in this case is that the customer is using poor quality paper. Changing the paper with another type will help to resolve the problem.

    ☒ **A** is incorrect because the problem does not seem to be caused by the paper tray. **C** is incorrect and unwise advice, and it will certainly not solve the problem. Your job is to resolve the problem and not restrict the customer from using a particular feature of the printer. **D** is incorrect because the paper rollers are not likely causing the problem. The printer has recently been purchased and is not heavily used. The chance of the rollers already being worn out is very unlikely.

12. ☑ **C.** The proposed solution produces the required result but none of the optional results. The required result is produced because the solution suggests that the printer be regularly cleaned. Dust and toner particles inside the printer cause several problems which will be taken care of by regular cleaning. The first optional result is not produced because the solution does not present a way to prevent paper jam problems. Apart from clearing the paper path from dust particles, you must also use good quality paper. Humidity on paper also causes paper jam problems, so wet or damp paper should not be used. The second optional result is not produced because it is suggested that the drum be changed every four months. There is no need to change the drum until it starts creating problems. This suggestion will cause extra expenditure that is not warranted.

    ☒ **A, B,** and **D** are incorrect because the proposed solution produces the required result but does not produce any of the optional results.

13. ☑ **A.** If there is a small nick on the drum, the toner will collect there and then get transferred to the paper. Even the cleaning blades do not clean this excessive toner on the damaged part of the drum. Replacing the drum will resolve the problem.

    ☒ **B** is incorrect because the toner cartridge is not causing the problem, but rather the drum that transfers toner onto the paper. **C** is incorrect because if the cleaning blade is not functioning properly, the print output appears like ghosted images. **D** is incorrect because if the fuser assembly does not work, the toner does not stick to the paper but comes off if you rub your hand on the printed paper.

14. ☑ **C.** It is evident from the problem symptoms that the drum is not being cleaned properly before it is recharged with a new print image. The drum must be free of any previous image that was charged on it with toner before it gets another image. The leftover toner on the drum from previous images is causing these prints to get mixed up with future prints.

    ☒ **A** is incorrect because the fusing process is responsible for melting the toner onto the paper once the image has been transferred to paper in the form of toner. **B** is incorrect because this process involves creating a fresh image on the drum. If the leftover toner on the drum from a previous image has not been completely cleaned, the new image will contain an impression of the previous image. **D** is incorrect because during the developing process, the toner is applied to the drum in areas that have been *touched* by the laser beam.

15. ☑ **D.** Check to see if the correct printer driver is installed. The most likely cause of the problem is that the printer is using the incorrect printer driver. There is a strong possibility of an incorrect printer driver because the user was earlier using a bubblejet printer and most likely did not install a new printer driver or may have installed an incorrect printer driver for the new printer.

    ☒ **A** is incorrect because if the printer cable were faulty, there would have been no printer activity at all. **B** is incorrect because the user was printing on a bubblejet printer connected to the same port. **C** is incorrect because the parallel port was in use with the bubblejet printer.

16. ☑ **B.** Toner cartridge. The blank page could be caused by failure of any of the given components. However, most laser printers would give a toner empty or toner low error message when the amount of toner in the cartridge reaches a low level. Although there are several low-end laser printers that do not warn about low toner, printers that have a display usually are high-end laser printers that show an error message when a problem is detected in the printer.

    ☒ **A, C,** and **D** are incorrect answers because any of these parts could be the cause of the blank page output. If the high voltage power has failed, the primary corona wire will not be able to charge the photosensitive drum. If the primary corona wire has failed, the drum will not get charged. If the transfer corona wire has failed, the toner will not get transferred to the paper from the drum.

17. ☑ **A.** Fusing assembly. The problem symptoms indicate that the toner is not being fused or melted properly onto the paper before the paper comes out of the printer. This causes the toner particles to come off the paper when you touch it. Fuser rollers are heated up, and when the paper passes through these rollers, the toner should melt and permanently stick to the paper.

☒ **B** is incorrect because the function of the drum is to create and transfer the image to the paper. The fusing assembly does the final toner conditioning. **C** is incorrect because if the transfer corona wire were defective or broken, there would be no image on the paper at all. **D** is incorrect because the creation of the image and its successful transfer to paper indicate that there is no problem with the high voltage power supply. The image is created on the drum by charging it with a high voltage of nearly –5000vDC.

7

Basic Networking

Networks enable computer users to share files and printers. The different network topologies are Bus, Star, and Ring. The Star topology is the most commonly used in networks today. Networks can be built using thin and thick coaxial cables, shielded and unshielded twisted pair cables, and fiber-optic cables. Each of the cable types is associated with different network topology and has limitations such as network speed and maximum cable length. Each computer that participates in a network has a network interface card (NIC) that needs to be configured with its driver, and a suitable networking protocol such as NetBEUI, TCP/IP, IPX/SPX, or a combination of these.

NetBEUI is the simplest network protocol. It requires the least configuration and is suitable for small networks. TCP/IP is the most complex network protocol, and it is routable and has cross-platform support. When setting up a network, the choice of network topology, network cable, and networking protocol must be planned in advance. The hub in Star networks is the single point of failure that can bring down the entire network. Bus networks require a terminator at the end of the coaxial cable, and such a network cannot function without this terminator. Large networks employ server mirroring and clustering for reducing down times and ensuring the safety of data. Network speed can be enhanced using 100 Mbps hubs and switches.

TEST YOURSELF OBJECTIVE 7.01

Networking Concepts

A Star network topology using a hub and twisted-pair cabling is the most widely used among the networking topologies Bus, Ring, and Star. It runs at 10 or 100 Mbps speeds and is easy to build, upgrade, and maintain. NetBEUI, IPX/SPX, and TCP/IP are main networking protocols. Larger networks use the TCP/IP protocol, also used on the Internet. CAT5 is the type of twisted-pair cable that is commonly used with RJ-45 connectors. Ethernet networks support up to 100 Mbps speeds using CSMA/CD technology, whereas Token Ring networks use Token passing and are typically limited to a 16 Mbps speed. Fiber-optic cabling provides the fastest network speeds but is very expensive.

- Computers are connected to a hub in a Star topology, to a main backbone in a Bus topology, and to each other in a Ring topology.

- The TCP/IP protocol is the most commonly used, is more difficult to configure, and is the protocol of the Internet.

▨ The NetBEUI protocol is simple to implement but is not routable.

▨ The most commonly used twisted-pair cable is CAT5, which can transmit up to 100 Mbps.

▨ Twisted pair cable may be shielded (STP) or unshielded (UTP), and uses an RJ-45 connector.

▨ Coaxial cable is more shielded than shielded twisted pair (STP), contains a single copper wire, and uses a BNC connector.

▨ Fiber-optic cable transmits light signals, and although it can transmit longer distances and at faster speeds, it is not commonly used because of its expense.

▨ In CSMA/CD access, each computer is free to transmit as long as no other computer is also transmitting.

▨ Ethernet networks, such as 10BaseT or 100BaseFX, use CSMA/CD and can transmit data at either 10 or 100 Mbps.

▨ Token-passing networks support speeds of 4 or 16 Mbps, and computers can communicate only if they have the network's empty token.

e x a m
ⓦa t c h

Since networking is a vast subject, you have to concentrate only on very basic concepts, terminology, cable types, network speeds supported, and advantages and limitations of the three major network topologies: Bus, Star, and Token Ring. You might be asked about the network speeds or the maximum lengths of cable supported by different types of networks. Based on requirements of data speed, cost factors, and number of computers that need to be joined, you might be asked to select an appropriate type of network cabling and a suitable protocol to build a network.

QUESTIONS

7.01: Networking Concepts

1. Which of the following network topologies is widely used as a backbone, uses coaxial cable, and requires termination at both ends?

    A. Star

    B. Bus

C. Ring

D. None of above

2. Which of the following statements is incorrect concerning the Ethernet Star network in which all the computers are connected to a central hub using twisted pair cables?

   A. If one of the connected computers goes down, the rest of the network continues to work.

   B. These networks can be expanded without bringing down the network.

   C. The network continues to work even if the hub fails.

   D. Two or more Ethernet networks can be joined in a Bus fashion.

3. One of your friends has sought your advice on Ring networks. The following options describe the features of a Ring network. Identify the feature that has been incorrectly listed here.

   A. Difficult to set up and upgrade

   B. Very high signal loss

   C. More prone to failures

   D. Most expensive

4. **Current Situation:** One of your friends has taken a new job in a small company. This company has eight computers. The first task he has been assigned is to connect the computers to make a workgroup. He has sought your help in setting up the network. Here is what you have to do.

   Required Result: Implement a network topology that is easy to build, maintain, and troubleshoot. Even if one or more computers break down, the rest of the network should continue to work in the network environment.

   Optional Desired Results:

   1. It should be easy to add more computers to the network without bringing down the whole network.

   2. When the network is active, the signals should flow in such a way that data travels only from the sending computer to the receiving computer.

Proposed Solution: Purchase a 12-port active hub and twisted-pair cable. Place the hub on one side of the computer room and connect all the computers to the hub using RJ-45 connectors as shown in the following illustration.

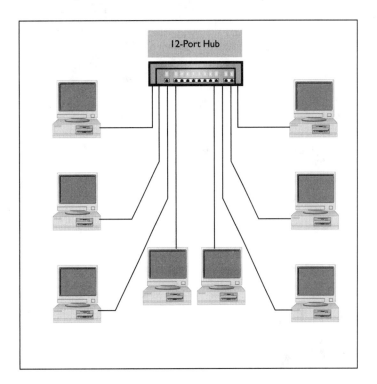

What results does the proposed solution produce?

A. The proposed solution produces the required result and both of the optional results.

B. The proposed solution produces the required result and only one of the optional results.

C. The proposed solution produces the required result but none of the optional results.

D. The proposed solution does not produce the required result.

5. You have been asked to select a suitable networking protocol to implement an Ethernet network in a company that has two departments. The network will have two separate network segments for each of its departments, but selected users in one department should be able to connect to computers in the other department. The selected protocol should be easy to configure and should work well if the network grows to 150 computers. There are no plans to connect the network to the Internet, and the company is using Windows 98 operating system on all the computers. Which of the following network protocols will meet all these requirements?

A. NetBEUI

B. TCP/IP

C. IPX/SPX

D. Microsoft DLC

6. The following table specifies the properties of some of the commonly used twisted-pair cables standards.

Cable Type	Speed	Common Usage
CAT2	10 Mbps	Token Ring networks
CAT3	16 Mbps	Ethernet networks
CAT4	20 Mbps	Token Ring networks
CAT5	100 Mbps	Ethernet networks

Which of the listed cable types has incorrect data?

A. CAT2

B. CAT3

C. CAT4

D. CAT5

7. A customer is telling you that he is using a 10BaseT Ethernet network in his office. He wants to know why this network is known as a CSMA/CD based network. Which of the following statements would you use to describe how signals are transmitted in these networks, and what is the first action a device takes before transmitting a packet in a CSMA/CD network?

A. Attempts to possess an empty token

   B. Sends a signal to all computers to stop transmitting

   C. Listens to the network medium for silence

   D. Waits for a random interval of time so that the medium becomes free

8. One of your friends has purchased a second computer for his small home office. Both of the computers have network adapters with RJ-45 connectors. He wants to connect the two computers so that he can copy files from one computer to the other and share the printer that is connected to the existing computer. The older computer has a serial mouse connected to COM1 port and a modem connected to COM2 port. He does not want to purchase a hub right now but knows that the two computers can be joined with only a twisted-pair cable. Which of the following cables can be used in this situation?

   A. Parallel

   B. Serial

   C. Straight

   D. Cross-over

TEST YOURSELF OBJECTIVE 7.02

Network Setup and Troubleshooting

The basic element of networking in a computer is the network interface card (NIC), which may have one or more types of connectors, such as an RJ-45 for 10BaseT, BNC for Bus, or a DB-15 for Token Ring. The network adapter driver is installed in the operating system with a suitable networking protocol such as TCP/IP so that the computer can communicate with other computers. Network problems can be as small as a broken cable or as complex as network traffic congestion. In large networks, network problems can be difficult to diagnose and resolve.

   ▨ A computer's NIC (for example, Ethernet or Token Ring) must support the type of network it is joining.

   ▨ The NIC must be configured for use by the computer and also to communicate on the network.

■ Network communications can occur only as fast as the slowest element involved, such as the NIC, hub, or cable.

■ Some network servers use mirroring or clustering to prevent or reduce data loss in the event of a server failure.

■ Network slowdowns can be caused by interference, heavy traffic, or insufficient equipment.

e x a m
ⓦa t c h
In 10BaseT networks, hubs transmit the data received on one of their ports to all other ports, and this creates undesired network traffic, resulting in congestion. Apart from physical connectivity, the causes of network problems include the use of inappropriate networking protocol, an incorrectly configured adapter or protocol, and duplicate computer names. If the computer you use supports only a 10 Mbps speed, it will run at only 10 Mbps, even if the network is Fast Ethernet which can run at a speed of 1 Gb per second.

QUESTIONS

7.02: Network Setup and Troubleshooting

9. You have purchased a second computer for your home office. The new and the existing computers are both fitted with network adapters. You want to connect the two computers to build a small network. Since the network adapters in both computers have RJ-45 connectors, you are sure that you can use UTP cable. So you join the two network adapters using a cross-over cable. Which of the following actions must you perform after installing the cable so that you can test the network?

A. Install the networking protocol.

B. Configure the Dial-up Networking.

C. Check that the two adapters are communicating.

D. Install the drivers for the network adapters.

10. Which of the following should be unique when you use TCP/IP as your network protocol? Select all correct answers.

    A. Computer name

    B. The IP address

    C. Subnet mask

    D. The default gateway address

11. The following table specifies several network types and the data speed, cable type, and maximum cable length used in each network.

Network	Speed	Cable Type	Maximum Length
10BaseT	10 Mbps	Twisted-pair	100 Meters
10Base2	16 Mbps	Thinnet	185 Meters
10Base5	10 Mbps	Thicknet	500 Meters
100BaseTX	100 Mbps	Twisted-pair	100 Meters

    Which of the following network types has an incorrect specification in the table?

    A. 10BaseT

    B. 10Base2

    C. 10Base5

    D. 100BaseTX

12. A user on the network is complaining that he cannot print to a shared printer from his Windows 98 computer. You are asked to attend to the problem, and you know that all other users can print to the printer. If you suspect that the network might be a problem, which of the following is the best way to start your diagnosis?

    A. Check the printer sharing on the computer connected to the printer.

    B. Check the configuration of the network adapter.

    C. Check the Network Neighborhood in the user's computer.

    D. Check the configuration of the NetBEUI protocol.

13. Which of the following methods is most commonly used for saving critical data on servers so that it is available in emergency situations?

    A. Server clustering

    B. Floppy disks

    C. Tape backups

    D. CD-ROM

Questions 14–16 You have joined a small company as a help desk technician. The main business of the company is to produce graphics designs for major advertising agencies. The company has three departments, namely, accounts, marketing, and production. There are four computers in the accounts department, 6 computers in marketing, and 12 computers in the production department.

The technician whom you have replaced built the computer network using 10 Mbps hubs and CAT3 cabling. All computers have network adapters with RJ-45 connectors to connect the computers to the hub, and BNC connectors for coaxial cabling.

All computers in the network are using Windows 98 operating system with NetBEUI as the networking protocol. There is no server in the office, and the three computers that have HP LaserJet 5000 printers are being used as print servers.

The company has just secured a large order, and management has decided to purchase 15 new computers so that the order can be expedited. The following questions present some problems with this network. Answer these questions, selecting the best answer for each question.

14. The IT manager has received complaints from several users that the network runs very slow when all users are working on their computers. You are afraid that the problem will become more severe when 15 new computers are added to this network. Which of the following do you think will help increase the network speed without having to change any software configuration?

    A. Change the network adapters from half duplex to full duplex.

    B. Upgrade Windows 98 to Windows NT Workstation.

    C. Replace the CAT3 cable with a CAT5 cable.

    D. Split the network into two or more segments.

15. In order to cope with the increase in business, the company has decided to open another office in a neighboring state. The two offices will be connected by routers using a leased line. Although you will not be involved in setting up the links, your boss has asked you what basic software changes will have to be carried out so that all computers in the local network will be able to access all computers in the neighboring state. Which of the following should be your answer?

    A. The networking protocol will have to be changed from NetBEUI to TCP/IP.

    B. The network adapters will need new drivers to access the remote network.

    C. The operating system has to be changed from Windows 98 to Windows NT.

    D. All computers will need two protocols: one for the local network and another for the remote network.

16. The manager now wants to upgrade the network speed from 10 Mbps to 100 Mbps. He has ordered a 100 Mbps Fast Ethernet hub for this purpose. When you find out about this purchase order, which of the following should be your first concern? Select all correct answers.

    A. The UTP cable

    B. The network adapters

    C. The networking protocol

    D. The operating system

A

QUICK ANSWER KEY

Objective 7.01		Objective 7.02	
1.	B	9.	D
2.	C	10.	A and B
3.	B	11.	B
4.	B	12.	C
5.	C	13.	C
6.	A	14.	D
7.	C	15.	A
8.	D	16.	A and B

IN-DEPTH ANSWERS

7.01: Networking Concepts

1. ☑ **B.** The Bus topology is widely used as a network backbone. This network topology uses coaxial cable and requires that both ends of the cable be terminated.

   ☒ **A** is incorrect because the Star topology is not used as a network backbone. The Star network neither uses coaxial cable nor requires terminators at the ends. The Star network typically uses twisted-pair cables or fiber-optic cables. **C** is incorrect because the Ring topology is not used as a backbone. **D** is incorrect because a correct answer is within the given options.

2. ☑ **C.** The network continues to work even if the hub fails. This statement is incorrect because the Ethernet Star network depends on the hub to operate normally. All the computers communicate with one another through the hub, and a faulty hub can bring down the entire network.

   ☒ **A** is incorrect because the statement is true. Failure of one or more computers in a Star network does not cause the network to fail. **B** is incorrect because it is possible to expand the network by connecting more computers or other network devices to the network by free ports on the hub. **D** is incorrect because the statement is true. When two or more hubs are cascaded (one hub joined to another using the uplink port), the physical structure becomes a Bus network.

3. ☑ **B.** Very high signal loss. This feature is incorrectly listed in the given options. Ring networks are known for lower signal loss because each computer that participates in the network amplifies the signal before retransmitting it.

   ☒ **A, C,** and **D** are incorrect because the given features are correct. Ring networks are difficult to set up compared to Star and Bus networks, they are more prone to failures, and they are very expensive because of the special equipment they require.

4. ☑ **B.** The proposed solution produces the required result and only one of the optional results. The required result is produced because Star networks are easy to build, maintain, and upgrade. These networks typically use a central device known as a hub that received signals, amplifies them, and retransmits them on the network. Since each computer is connected to the hub independently, the network continues to function even if one or more computers are shut down or break down because of a problem. The first optional result is produced because the Star topology with its central hub makes it easy to add new computers to the network. You simply have to connect a computer to a free port of the hub, and this does not affect existing computers. The second optional result is not produced because the data received on one port of the hub is usually transmitted to all other computers on the network instead of being transmitted to only the intended receiving computer. For this requirement, a switch is a better option than a hub since it allows the data to travel only from the sending computer to the receiving computer.

☒ **A, C,** and **D** are incorrect since the proposed solution produced the required result and only one of the optional results. The second optional result was not produced.

5. ☑ **C.** The IPX/SPX compatible protocol in Windows 98 meets all the requirements in the question. This is because this protocol is not very difficult to configure, and it is routable. A routable protocol is required when the network is divided into two or more segments, as indicated in the question. Although IPX/SPX is commonly used in Novell networks, even Windows networks can use this protocol in small- to medium-sized networks. The only limitation in using this protocol is that you cannot connect to the Internet; however, this was not a requirement stipulated by the company.

☒ **A** is incorrect because although this protocol is the easiest to configure, it is suited for very small workgroups and is not routable. This protocol cannot be used when the network has more than one segment. **B** is incorrect because among the given options, this protocol is the most difficult one to configure. Moreover, this protocol is not required since the company does not want to connect to the Internet. **D** is incorrect because this protocol is also not a routable protocol and is used mainly by network printers and to connect to an IBM mainframe computer.

6. ☑ **A.** The CAT2 cable specifications given in the table incorrectly list the data transfer speed as 10 Mbps. Remember that the CAT2 cable is limited to a

4 Mbps speed. This cable was typically used in Token Ring networks that had a maximum speed of 4 Mbps, and it is no longer used.

☒ **B, C,** and **D** are incorrect because the given data regarding speed and common usage is correctly specified in the table. The CAT3 cable supports a speed of 16 Mbps and is commonly used in 10BaseT Ethernet networks. CAT4 supports up to 20 Mbps and is commonly used in Token Ring networks. CAT5 is the most common cable type and supports up to 100 Mbps speeds. CAT5 is used in both Ethernet and Fast Ethernet networks.

7. ☑ **C.** Listens to the network medium for silence. CSMA/CD stands for Carrier Sense Multiple Access/Collision Detect. In such networks, the computer that wants to transmit a signal first listens to the network medium to see if there is *silence,* which means no other computer is transmitting data. The computer starts transmitting data only if the network medium is silent.

☒ **A** is incorrect because tokens are used in Token Ring networks and not in CSMA/CD networks. **B** is incorrect because the computer only listens for silence on the network medium. The signal sent to all computers to stop transmission is known as a *jamming signal.* This signal is sent when the computer detects that a collision has occurred on the network medium. Collision refers to two computers transmitting at the same time because they were not able to sense silence due to the large distance between them. **D** is incorrect because this action is taken when a collision is detected on the network medium, and a jamming signal has been sent to all computers. All computers wait for a random interval of time before transmitting a signal again.

8. ☑ **D.** Cross-over. The twisted-pair cable (commonly known as UTP cable) comes in only two types, straight and cross-over, both with RJ-45 connectors. The cross-over cable is used to connect two computers without using a hub. It is also used to connect two hubs when expanding the network. Remember that the straight cable cannot be used for a *straight* connection between two computers.

☒ **A** is incorrect because the parallel cable cannot be used for connecting the two computers in this case because one of the computers has a printer attached to its parallel port. **B** is incorrect because both of the serial ports on the older computer are occupied, one by the serial mouse and the other by the modem. **C** is incorrect because a straight cable is typically used for connecting computers to a hub.

7.02: Network Setup and Troubleshooting

9. ☑ **D.** The first thing you have to do to configure your network is install device drivers (or simply drivers) for your network adapters in both computers. Even if these drivers are already installed, you should check that they are in place.

☒ **A** is incorrect because if the drivers are not present for the network adapters, the network will not work. Network protocols *bind* to existing network adapters during installation. **B** is incorrect because the Dial-up Networking need not be configured for local networking. It is typically configured when you want to connect to the Internet or some other remote network that you can access using your modem. Dial-up Networking does not need a physical network adapter. **C** is incorrect because unless the network adapters and the operating system are configured for networking, the functionality of the network adapters cannot be checked.

10. ☑ **A** and **B.** No two computers in a network can have the same computer name or IP address. These properties are unique for each computer. Although they can be assigned to a computer during installation of the operating system, you can change or modify the IP address at a later date. If a duplicate computer name or a duplicate IP address exists on a network, only one of the computers will be able to access the network.

☒ **C** is incorrect because the subnet mask is common for all computers in a network segment. **D** is incorrect because this address is common to all computers in a network segment. The default gateway address is used by a computer in a network segment to access computers in another network segment.

11. ☑ **B.** The specifications for 10Base2 networks are incorrectly listed in the table. The data speed supported by these networks is 10 Mbps instead of 16 Mbps as stated in the table.

☒ **A, C,** and **D** are all incorrect answers because the specifications listed are all correct. 10BaseT networks have a 10 Mbps speed, use twisted-pair cables, and have a maximum cable length of 100 meters. 10Base5 networks have a 10 Mbps speed, use thicknet (thick coaxial) cables, and have a maximum cable length of 500 meters. 100BaseTX networks have a 100 Mbps speed, use twisted-pair cables, and have a maximum cable length of 100 meters.

12. ☑ **C.** The best way to start your diagnosis of a network-related problem in Windows 98 is to check the Network Neighborhood. This icon is located on the desktop and gives a first-hand view of the computers and workgroups in the network. If you do not find any computers in Network Neighborhood or get a message saying Unable to Browse Network, you should check that the network cables are properly attached to the network adapter. Most network adapters indicate whether the adapter is connected to the hub or not.

☒ **A** is incorrect because other users are able to print from their computers. **B** is incorrect because this is not the first thing you should check when an option exists on the desktop to check the computers on the network. **D** is incorrect because the only thing you can check with the NetBEUI protocol is whether it is installed or not. There is nothing else in the configuration of this protocol that you can check.

13. ☑ **C.** Tape backups are the most commonly used method for saving data so that it is available in case there is an emergency, such as a server breakdown. Data saved on tapes can be restored when the server problem is fixed and the server is brought online again.

☒ **A** is incorrect because clustering is implemented to provide fault tolerance and load balancing. It only stores a copy of the data and is not the most commonly used method to save critical data for emergencies. **B** is incorrect because floppy disks have a limited storage capacity and are not suitable for large amounts of server data. **D** is incorrect because CD-ROMs are read-only disks. Instead, CD-W (CD-writeable) could be used for storing data, but this again is not the most commonly used storage medium.

14. ☑ **D.** When the network is experiencing slow speeds, it is often best to divide the network into two or more segments according to functional requirements. For example, the computers in the accounts department can be separated from those in marketing or production, or both. This helps keep the departmental traffic local to the network segment. Unless required, the local network traffic does not travel to other segments.

☒ **A** is incorrect because this will have no effect on the network speed, since the hubs usually do not support full duplex communications. **B** is incorrect because this will have no affect on the network speed. **C** is incorrect because this will not help increase the network speed. The network is a 10 Mbps network, and both CAT3 and CAT5 cables support this speed.

15. ☑ **A.** The networking protocol will have to be changed from NetBEUI to TCP/IP. When two networks are joined by routers, it becomes a routed network. Since NetBEUI is not a routable protocol, it cannot be used in a routed network. You must change the networking protocol from NetBEUI to TCP/IP for accessing the remote network. In case you are planning to install dedicated servers at both of the locations such that the computers will use these servers to access remote networks, and if the servers support NetBEUI and TCP/IP, then reconfiguration of all computers will not be required.

☒ **B** is incorrect because the device drivers for network adapters need not be changed. **C** is incorrect because the computers can access the remote network using the existing Windows 98 operating system. **D** is incorrect because a single protocol can be used to access both local and remote networks. You need not add a networking protocol when you add remote networks.

16. ☑ **A** and **B.** The UTP cable and the network adapters should be your first concern. The network cable being used is CAT3, which supports only up to a 16 Mbps speed. This must be replaced with a CAT5 cable to support a 100 Mbps network. The installed network adapters support only 10 Mbps data speeds. Although these network adapters will work with the 100 Mbps Fast Ethernet hub, they will be able to communicate with only a 10 Mbps speed. You must change the network adapters to either 10/100 Mbps or 100 Mbps adapters.

☒ **C** is incorrect because the installed network protocol will work well with the 100 Mbps network. Network protocols are typically independent of network speeds. **D** is incorrect because the operating system has nothing to do with the speed of the network.

CORE HARDWARE/OPERATING SYSTEM EXAMS

Part II

A+ Operating Systems Technologies

CHAPTERS

CORE HARDWARE/OPERATING SYSTEM EXAMS

8

Operating System Fundamentals

The operating system is the platform that computer users rely on for interacting with the hardware. Desktop operating systems such as Windows 95 and Windows 98, and network operating systems such as Windows NT and Windows 2000, offer different levels of features and capabilities. Each of these operating systems offers various tools and utilities to manage and organize the system, devices, and data. System and device management is accomplished using the Control Panel in Windows 9x, and by using the Computer Management Console in Windows 2000.

Data in the form of files is organized by using Windows Explorer, which is present in all these operating systems. The hard disks are partitioned and formatted using FAT16, FAT32, and NTFS file systems. Each of these file systems has its advantages and limitations. Whereas Windows 9x systems can have only FAT16 and FAT32 file systems, the Windows 2000 operating system supports FAT16, FAT32, and NTFS file systems.

TEST YOURSELF OBJECTIVE 8.01

Operating System Functions and the Windows Family

The basic function of an operating system is to provide an interface between users and the computer, and to manage system devices. It is not possible to use a computer without an operating system. Windows 9x and Windows 2000 operating systems, targeted at personal and business applications respectively, offer different levels of features for managing files, disks, and devices. The newer operating systems, such as Windows 2000, support the strongest security features for protection of critical data.

■ The function of an operating system is to provide an interface between the user and the hardware, to manage an organized file and folder structure, and to provide procedures for preparing and managing disks.

■ Windows 95 and Windows 98 are part of the Windows 9x family and are aimed at home users, whereas Windows 2000 is part of the Windows NT family, aimed at business networks.

■ Windows 9x and Windows 2000 have a similar interface, which includes a desktop, My Computer, Windows Explorer, the Start button, and the taskbar.

■ Windows 9x supports older applications and has more Plug and Play support for home computer devices, whereas Windows 2000 has more sophisticated security, fault tolerance, and disk management utilities.

e x a m
⒲ a t c h

The focus of this section is on your understanding of operating systems, the features offered by Windows 95, Windows 98, and Windows 2000 operating systems, and the advantages of Windows 2000 versus Windows 9x. Although it is not expected that you have an in-depth understanding of how the operating system works, you must at least understand the benefits and limitations of each of these operating systems, and, if given a particular scenario, you must know which operating system is best suited to fulfill the given requirements. For example, a home user who needs only multimedia capabilities should use Windows 98, compared to a network user who requires strong security and should use Windows 2000.

QUESTIONS

8.01: Operating System Functions and the Windows Family

1. Which of the following is not a function of an operating system?

    A. Providing a user interface

    B. Disk management

    C. Interpreting commands and run files

    D. Managing the basic input output system

2. A friend has sought your advice on the basic differences between Windows 98 and Windows 2000 operating systems. Which of the following statements incorrectly describes the feature similarities of these two operating systems? Select all correct answers.

    A. Both Windows 2000 and Windows 98 support Plug and Play.

    B. Both Windows 2000 and Windows 98 have strong support for multimedia applications.

    C. Both Windows 2000 and Windows 98 support preemptive multitasking for running multiple applications.

D. Both Windows 2000 and Windows 98 support multiprocessing.

E. Both Windows 2000 and Windows 98 have a similar user interface.

3. **Current Situation:** You have just purchased a new Pentium III 750MHz computer with a 20GB hard disk drive and a dual processor motherboard. Currently there is only one processor installed on this system. The vendor has asked you to specify which operating system you would like to install on this computer. Here is what you would like to incorporate into your suggestions to him.

Required Result: The operating system must have the option to set passwords and user profiles. Besides this, you should be able to connect to the Internet, and the most common multimedia functions should be supported.

Optional Desired Results:

1. The operating system should be capable of protecting files and folders by setting permissions on them.

2. The operating system should be capable of using a second processor when you want to upgrade the computer.

Proposed Solution: Ask the vendor to make two partitions on the hard disk and install Windows 98 operating system. This will enable you to protect your files and folders by storing them in the second partition and setting the hidden attribute on them. The user profiles can be set from the User Profiles tab of Passwords Properties, as shown in the following illustration.

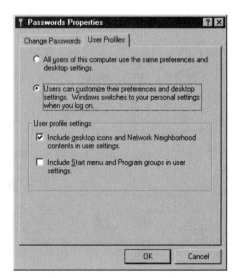

What results does the proposed solution produce?

A. The proposed solution produces the required result and both of the optional results.

B. The proposed solution produces the required result but none of the optional results.

C. The proposed solution produces the required result and only one of the optional results.

D. The proposed solution does not produce the required result.

4. A Windows 98 computer has an internal adapter that is not being recognized by the operating system. The device is shown as an Unknown Device in the Device Manager. Which of the following files or utilities is not involved in preventing the operating system from loading its device driver?

A. Registry

B. Automatic skip driver

C. Application configuration

D. Device driver

TEST YOURSELF OBJECTIVE 8.02

System Files and Utilities

System files refer to those files that must be available for any operating system to successfully load itself and the installed devices, and to run application programs. These files are typically located in the Windows folder on the root drive in Windows 9x. They include Registry files and device drivers. The Registry is the database of system configuration, and it exists in both Windows 9x and Windows 2000, although each of them has a different structure. Changes to the Registry database is made every time we change system settings, or install or uninstall applications or device drivers.

▪ The bulk of the Windows 9x and Windows 2000 operating systems is the system Registry. Whereas System.dat and User.dat files form the Registry in

Windows 9x, Windows 2000 Registry files are System, Security, Software, and Security Account Manager (SAM).

■ You can safely edit a subset of the Registry using the Control Panel (Windows 9x and Windows 2000) or the Computer Management Console (Windows 2000).

■ You can directly edit the Registry using the Registry Editor.

■ Because Windows 9x supports older applications, it includes older system configuration files, such as SYSTEM.INI, WIN.INI, CONFIG.SYS, and AUTOEXEC.BAT.

■ Windows 9x uses memory managers such as HIMEM.SYS and EMM386.EXE to maintain backward compatibility with older applications.

■ Windows 9x includes the Device Manager, which allows you to view and modify hardware configurations.

■ The Windows 98 automatic skip driver detects and disables potentially problematic drivers.

■ Windows 9x uses WIN386.SWP, and Windows 2000 uses PAGEFILE.SYS, as virtual memory. This additional storage space is used as virtual memory when there is insufficient physical memory (RAM) in the system to handle execution of programs.

■ Windows allows you to run DOS commands, such as edit, dir, mem, edit, and attrib from a DOS command prompt.

exam
ⓦatch
It is always better to use the Control Panel in Windows 9x and the Computer Management Console in Windows 2000 to configure your system, as opposed to using the Registry Editor program. When you go to take the A+ exam, you must be familiar with some of the commonly used DOS commands, such as COPY, XCOPY, ATTRIB, and FORMAT. You might be asked to spell the correct syntax of a DOS command. Besides this, you should be familiar with different applets in the Control Panel for configuring the system, and which applet you should use for a given configuration requirement. Be aware that the Dial-up Networking applet is located in My Computer and not in Control Panel.

QUESTIONS

8.02: System Files and Utilities

5. You have installed a new application in Windows 98 and accepted all default settings during the installation. If C: is the root drive of the computer, where will you find the folder for this application?

    A. C:\Program Files

    B. C:\Windows

    C. C:\Windows\Program Files

    D. C:\Windows\Application Data

6. You have a Windows 2000 Professional computer with a 10.6GB hard disk. The computer technician who set up this computer told you that the hard disk has been divided into two partitions, namely, C: and D:. The C: drive is the system partition, and the D: drive is the boot partition. Which of the following gives the correct meaning of system and boot partitions?

    A. The system partition is used for storing system files, and the boot partition is used to store boot files.

    B. The system partition is used to store files to boot the system, and the boot partition is used to store the system files.

    C. The boot partition is used to store the files used during system startup, and the system partition is used to store Windows setup files.

    D. The system and boot partitions have the same meaning.

7. You are using Windows 98 operating system on your computer. Which of the following should you prefer to use for making changes to system settings that affect how the computer will behave during normal operation?

   A. Use the Control Panel.

   B. Make changes to the BOOT.INI file.

   C. Use the Registry Editor program.

   D. Use the RUNAS command.

8. Which of the following options would you use to create a bootable floppy disk in a system running Windows 98?

   A. Format a floppy disk using the FORMAT A: /Q command.

   B. Use the Startup Disk tab in Add/Remove Programs in the Control Panel.

   C. Use the Startup Disk option in System Tools under the Accessories menu.

   D. Use the Maintenance Wizard in the Accessories menu.

TEST YOURSELF OBJECTIVE 8.03

File and Folder Management

Files and folders are organized from Windows Explorer, which is present in both Windows 9x and Windows 2000. You can set the file attributes, make new folders, delete files and folders, and copy and move them as and when required. The files that are sparingly used and are large in size can be compressed to save disk space. Windows 2000 allows you to set file level permissions and encrypt the files for better security.

■ Windows allows you to view, create, rename, delete, move, or open files and folders using either My Computer or Windows Explorer.

■ Most common file operations can be accomplished in Windows Explorer by right-clicking the selected file and selecting an appropriate function, such as cut, copy, rename, or delete.

■ Windows 9*x* and Windows 2000 include a backup utility for storing and compressing files, and Windows 2000 includes native file encryption and compression.

■ Several Internet functions are integrated in Windows 98 and Windows 2000, and it is even possible to visit Web sites from within Windows Explorer.

Some of the points that need to be stressed here concern the backup utility and file compression during the backup process. The backup utilities in Windows 9x and Windows 2000 look similar and have several common features. It is possible with both operating systems to back up files from a network location. Become familiar with the Backup Wizard and the various options it offers, such as selection of files for backup, the importance of the archive bit, and scheduling the backup job to run after office hours. Make sure you understand the difference between local and networked backups. The second point is compression. When you run a backup job, files are compressed by default.

QUESTIONS

8.03: File and Folder Management

9. Assuming that your Windows 98 computer is currently connected to the Internet, which of the following Internet tasks cannot be accomplished using Windows Explorer? Select all correct answers.

A. Visiting your home page

B. Configuring the home page settings

C. Viewing the disk contents as a Web page

D. Visiting a saved favorite Web site

E. Configuring the Internet connection

10. The MYFILES folder in the C: drive of your Windows 98 computer has some important files that you do not want disclosed to anyone. The files have been arranged in subfolders named MYACC, MYBANK, and MYCREDIT within the MYFILES folder, as shown in the following illustration.

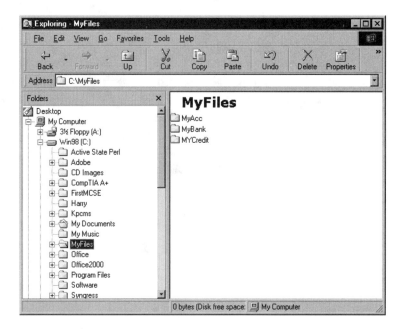

Which of the following commands would you use to set these files up so they are hidden, but even when they are visible, no one can modify them without changing the settings?

A. ATTRIB C:\MYFILES H R

B. ATTRIB C:\MYFILES +H +R

C. ATTRIB C:\MYFILES +H +R /S

D. ATTRIB C:\MYFILES*.* +H +R /S

11. You are using Windows 2000 Professional on your home computer. Because of space limitations, you have compressed some files using the built-in compression utility. Your computer is connected to the Internet, and you want to secure some of the folders by encrypting them. When you attempt encryption on one

of the folders, you find that the files in the folder get decompressed. Which of the following describes the correct reason for this?

A. The folder was not compressed properly.

B. Encryption and compression cannot be used on the same disk drive.

C. Encryption and compression cannot be used on the same folder.

D. You should encrypt the folder before compressing it.

12. You have some personal account files in your computer that you want to make as safe as possible. Assuming that the system is running Windows 98 operating system, which of the following attributes are you unable to set on these files using Windows Explorer?

A. Read Only

B. Hidden

C. Archive

D. System

TEST YOURSELF OBJECTIVE 8.04

Disk Management

A new disk must be partitioned and formatted before it can be used to store data. The options for using a file system depend on the operating system you are using. Windows *9x* operating systems support FAT16 and FAT32 file systems. Windows 2000 has native support for NTFS5 (New Technology File System 5), and also supports FAT16, FAT32, and NTFS4 for backward compatibility. NTFS5 has better disk management features, such as compression, encryption, auditing, and file level security.

■ Before a disk can store data, it must be partitioned using DOS FDISK and formatted using the FORMAT command.

■ Windows *9x* supports the FAT16 and FAT32 file systems. FAT16 disks can be converted to FAT32 for better disk space utilization and efficiency.

■ Windows 2000 supports the FAT16, FAT32, NTFS4, and NTFS5 file systems.

■ NTFS5 can be used only with Windows 2000 operating system.

exam
ⓌatchΦ

You must choose an appropriate file system when you format a hard disk. It is important that you understand the benefits and limitations of a particular file system. The exam might test your ability to select an appropriate file system, based on a complex scenario describing the requirements. Remember that once you format a disk using NTFS5, or convert a disk from FAT16 to FAT32, or from FAT32 to NTFS5, you cannot reconvert to an older file system. You must repartition the hard disk and reformat it. In simpler words, you cannot convert your hard disk to an older file system without losing your data.

QUESTIONS

8.04: Disk Management

13. Which of the following file systems provides file level security, data compression, data encryption, and auditing file access?

    A. FAT16

    B. FAT32

    C. NTFS4

    D. NTFS5

Questions 14–16   You are using a computer that you purchased two years ago. The computer has one IDE hard disk with Windows 98 operating system on it. Over the last two years, this computer has been heavily used for your personal accounts and for accessing the Internet.

You recently attended a crash course on maintaining Windows 98 computers, and you now want to perform some disk maintenance. This will primarily be aimed at enhancing disk performance.

Once this is done, you want to add another hard disk in your system and make this computer a dual boot system by installing Windows 2000 Professional on the second hard disk. Based on these assumptions, answer the following three questions, selecting the best answer for each.

14. **Current Situation:** Your hard disk has become very slow after two years of continuous use. You are running Windows 98 operating system on your computer. Here is what you have to accomplish.

Required Result: Clean up the hard disk in order to speed up the execution of frequently used programs.

Optional Desired Results:

1. You should be able to schedule your disk maintenance tasks during a time when your system is free.

2. The disk maintenance should also defragment your hard disk.

3. You should be able to check and mark bad sectors on the hard disk.

Proposed Solution: Click Start | Programs | Accessories | System Tools and select Maintenance Wizard from the drop-down menu. This opens the Maintenance Wizard dialog box. Click Custom radio button, and click Next. Select Custom Settings from the next dialog box, which opens the screen shown in the following illustration. Configure your settings, and click OK.

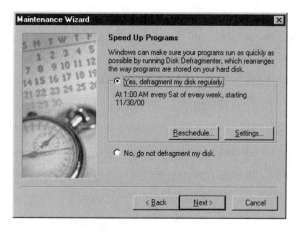

What results does the proposed solution produce?

A. The proposed solution produces the required result and all of the optional results.

B. The proposed solution produces the required result but none of the optional results.

    C. The proposed solution produces the required result and only two of the optional results.

    D. The proposed solution does not produce the required result.

15. The hard disk has reached an optimized stage and runs efficiently. You are now using disk management utilities regularly to keep your hard disk running well. Recently you learned that the NTFS5 file system is much more efficient in managing disks than FAT. What should you do to convert the hard disk to NTFS5?

    A. Use the Drive Converter utility from the command line, and specify NTFS as the file system.

    B. Run the CONVERT.EXE command at the MS-DOS prompt.

    C. Download the latest Drive Converter from the Microsoft Web site that supports conversion from FAT to NTFS5.

    D. None of above.

16. You have added another hard disk in your system and want to install Windows 2000 Professional to make the computer dual boot between Windows 98 and Windows 2000. Which of the following file systems should you use on the second disk if you want to access files on the Windows 2000 partition while running Windows 98?

    A. HPFS

    B. FAT

    C. NTFS4

    D. NTFS5

A QUICK ANSWER KEY

Objective 8.01

1.	D
2.	C and D
3.	B
4.	C

Objective 8.02

5.	A
6.	B
7.	A
8.	B

Objective 8.03

9.	B and E
10.	D
11.	C
12.	D

Objective 8.04

13.	D
14.	A
15.	D
16.	B

IN-DEPTH ANSWERS

8.01: Operating System Functions and the Windows Family

1. ☑ **D.** Managing the basic input output system is not a function of the operating system. The basic input output system of a computer is handled by the computer BIOS. The operating system utilizes the information provided by the BIOS to communicate with the input output devices.

   ☒ **A, B,** and **C** are incorrect because all of these functions are handled by the operating system. The operating system provides a user interface that enables the user to enter commands or run program files, and see the results. Disk management is also a function of the operating system that includes tasks such as partitioning and formatting the disk and carrying out routine disk maintenance. Files are run and user commands are interpreted by the operating system, and the results are shown to the user.

2. ☑ **C** and **D.** Both Windows 2000 and Windows 98 support preemptive multitasking for running multiple applications, and both Windows 2000 and Windows 98 support multiprocessing. These two statements are incorrect because Windows 98 supports cooperative multitasking, and Windows 2000 supports preemptive multitasking. Multiprocessing, the ability to support more than one microprocessor in a computer, is supported only in Windows 2000 Professional, which supports up to two microprocessors, or Windows 2000 Server, which supports up to four microprocessors. Windows 98 does not support more than one processor.

   ☒ **A, B,** and **E** are incorrect because the stated features are supported in both Windows 2000 and Windows 98. Both operating systems support Plug and Play, have strong support for multimedia applications, and have a similar interface.

3. ☑ **B.** The proposed solution produces the required result but none of the optional results. The required result is produced because the Windows 98 operating system allows you to set passwords and user profiles so that all users of the computer can have individual settings. Windows 98 also has full

multimedia capabilities, and it can be configured to connect to the Internet using Internet Explorer, which is built in. The first optional result is not produced because Windows 98 does not give you the option of setting permissions on individual files and folders. Any user who has access to a Windows 98 computer can access all the data on the computer. The second optional result is not produced because Windows 98 cannot make use of more than one processor.

☒ **A, C,** and **D** are incorrect because the proposed solution produces the required result but none of the optional results. The two optional results would be produced if Windows 2000 operating system were installed. Windows 2000 offers all the features of Windows 98 operating system, and, in addition, it supports two processors and enables you to set file level permissions on NTFS partitions.

4. ☑ **C.** The application configuration of Windows 98 is not involved in marking the internal adapter as Unknown Device. The application configuration, as the name suggests, is involved in configuring the applications during installation and during the time they are run.

☒ **A** is incorrect because the Registry is involved in preventing the operating system from loading the device drivers successfully. The device configuration is stored in the Registry. **B** is incorrect because this utility in Windows 98 operating system is used to prevent corrupted or incompatible device drivers from loading during the system startup. **D** is incorrect because it is essentially the fact that the device driver is either corrupt or incompatible with Windows 98 that prevents it to load.

8.02: System Files and Utilities

5. ☑ **A.** C:\Program Files. The default setting for all Windows 9x compatible applications is to install them in the Program Files folder on the root drive. Since C: is the root drive of the computer running Windows 98, the files will be placed in C:\Program Files. Remember that these are only the default settings, and you can modify these settings during installation if you wish to install any application in a different folder.

☒ **B** is incorrect because the C:\Windows folder contains system files in Windows 98. **C** is incorrect because this folder does not exist. **D** is incorrect because this folder contains settings for Microsoft applications, such as MS Office and Internet Explorer.

6. ☑ **B.** Microsoft terminology defines the partition used to boot the system as the system partition, and the partition used to install the Windows system files as the boot partition. The system and boot partitions can be on the same partition of the hard disk, on different partitions of the same hard disk, or on different hard disks.

   ☒ **A** is incorrect because the inverse is true. **C** is incorrect because the Windows setup files are stored in the boot partition. **D** is incorrect because, as specified above, the system partition is used to start up the system, and the boot partition refers to the partition that contains the Windows directory (WINNT in Windows 2000).

7. ☑ **A.** The easiest and safest way to make changes to the operating system and its utilities is to use the Control Panel. The Control Panel contains applets for configuring various operating system functions, such as adding and removing programs, adding and removing hardware devices, and setting up Windows components and other utilities, such as setting passwords and configuring modems and networking. As far as possible, you should use the Control Panel to configure your system.

   ☒ **B** is incorrect because the BOOT.INI file does not exist in a system that has only Windows 98 operating system. Furthermore, modifying this file modifies only the boot order of the Windows 2000 or dual boot system, and the location of the operating system to load. **C** is incorrect because the use of Registry Editor is recommended only for those settings that are not possible using the Control Panel and other interactive utilities. Incorrect changes in the Registry can create a lot of problems and even render the OS unable to boot. **D** is incorrect because this command is typically used by system or network administrators in a networked environment when they log on the computer with a less privileged user name and password, but wish to run a program that requires higher privileges.

8. ☑ **B.** A startup disk in Windows 98 can be created from the Startup Disk tab under Add/Remove Programs applet. This utility not only formats the new floppy disk, as desired in the question, but also copies system files to the disk, thus making it bootable.

☒   **A** is incorrect because the /Q switch is used for a quick format of the floppy disk. This does not make the disk bootable. To make a bootable disk from the command prompt, the FORMAT A:/S command should be used. **C** is incorrect because there is no option in System Tools to create a startup disk. **D** is incorrect because the Maintenance Wizard also does not have an option to create a startup disk.

8.03: File and Folder Management

9.   ☑   **B** and **E.** Configuring the home page settings and configuring the Internet connection are the two *configurations* that cannot be accomplished using Windows Explorer. These settings have to be made from the Control Panel or by using Dial-up Networking.

☒   **A** is incorrect because you can click on the Go menu and select Home Page to visit your home page when you are connected to the Internet. **C** is incorrect because Windows 98 Explorer allows you to display the disk contents as a Web page. This option is in the View menu. **D** is also incorrect because once you are connected to the Internet, you can click on the Favorites menu and click the Web page to which you wish to connect.

10.   ☑   **D.** ATTRIB C:\MYFILES*.* +H +R /S. This is the only correct command among the given answer options. The "*.*" is the wildcard that specifies all the files. The "+H" sets the hidden attribute on the files, "+R" sets the read only attribute, and "/S" tells the operating system to select all the subfolders under the MYFILES folder.

☒   **A** is an invalid command because you must specify the "+" sign with H and R to set the attribute. The "+" sign sets the attribute, and the "–" sign removes it. **B** and **C** are incorrect answers because neither of these commands has the correct syntax.

11.   ☑   **C.** Encryption and compression cannot be used on the same folder. Windows 2000 encryption and compression are mutually exclusive. If you wish to compress a folder, you cannot encrypt it, and vice versa. When you encrypt a compressed folder, its contents are first decompressed, and then encrypted.

☒   **A** is incorrect because when you compress a folder in Windows 2000, it either gets compressed properly or does not compress at all. If a problem is encountered during compression, Windows 2000 does not process the compression. **B** is incorrect because you can use compression and encryption on the same disk drive, as long as the folders are different. **D** is incorrect because this will not work. When you attempt to compress an encrypted folder, the folder will be decrypted.

12. ☑ **D.** The System attribute is set by the operating system. Users cannot set or remove the System attribute, which is typically meant to secure the files used by the operating system.

☒ **A, B,** and **C** are incorrect answers because you can set or remove the Read Only, Hidden, and Archive attributes on any files. For the safety of your personal files, the Read Only and Hidden file attributes should be set. By default, Windows does not show the System and Hidden files, which secures these files from accidental deletion.

8.04: Disk Management

13. ☑ **D.** The only file system that provides all these features is NTFS5. NTFS5 file system is supported in Windows 2000 operating systems. It offers features such as file level security, data compression, encryption, and the ability to audit file access.

☒ **A** is incorrect because this file system does not offer any of the required features for file protection. **B** is incorrect for the same reason. **C** is incorrect because although it offers file level security, data compression, and auditing, it does not offer file encryption. NTFS4 is used in Windows NT operating systems.

14. ☑ **A.** The proposed solution produces the required result and all of the optional results. The required result is produced because the Maintenance Wizard in System Tools can be used to perform several common disk management functions, such as cleaning up unnecessary temporary files created by programs or downloaded from the Internet, and rearranging program files, which helps speed up the execution of programs. The optional results are produced because the Custom Settings in the Maintenance Wizard allow you to schedule when the Maintenance Wizard will run. It also allows you to defragment the hard disk regularly at specified time and intervals.

☒ **B, C,** and **D** are incorrect because the proposed solution produces the required result and all three of the optional results. The Maintenance Wizard in System Tools is an ideal utility to use for performing and scheduling common disk maintenance functions.

15. ☑ **D.** None of above. The NTFS5 file system is supported only in Windows 2000 operating system. It is not possible to convert a hard disk in Windows 98 from FAT16 or FAT32 to NTFS simply by running a disk utility. Your system must be running Windows 2000 operating system to use NTFS file system.

☒ **A** is incorrect because this utility converts disks only from FAT16 to FAT32. **B** is incorrect because this command is supported only in Windows NT and Windows 2000 to convert FAT32 disk partitions to NTFS4 or NTFS5. **C** is incorrect because there is no such utility on the Microsoft Web site. You must remember that Windows 98 does not support NTFS4 or NTFS5 file systems. You can, however, access the NTFS4 and NTFS5 partitions on other network computers from your Windows 98 computer.

16. ☑ **B.** The FAT file system on the second disk will allow you to access files on the Windows 2000 disk while running Windows 98. Windows 98 can read only from FAT16 and FAT32 file systems and is not able to access NTFS disks locally. However, you can access shared NTFS4 and NTFS5 disks on other network computers.

☒ **A** is incorrect because the HPFS (high-performance file system) is not supported in Windows 2000, and you will not be able to format the second disk using HPFS. **C** is incorrect because Windows 2000 does not format hard disks with NTFS4. **D** is incorrect because you cannot access an NTFS5 disk locally while running Windows 98 operating system. As described earlier, you can access shared NTFS drives on the network.

CORE HARDWARE/OPERATING SYSTEM EXAMS

9

Installation, Configuration, and Upgrading

TEST YOURSELF OBJECTIVES

9.01 Installing Windows

9.02 Upgrading Windows

9.03 Booting Windows

9.04 Installing Device Drivers and
Applications

The first thing to do before installing any operating system (OS) is ensure you have the minimum hardware required to install and run it. You should check the Hardware Compatibility List to make sure that your hardware is supported by the OS you want to install. If necessary, you should obtain updated device drivers to ensure that the installed devices will work. Windows 9x and Windows 2000 have different boot sequences.

Whereas Windows 95 can be upgraded to Windows 98, both of these operating systems can be upgraded to Windows 2000, or you can make a dual boot system. In the latter case, you need to install Windows 2000 on a separate directory if you are installing on the same partition or a separate partition. When you want to make a dual boot system, the common applications you need to run should be installed from within each operating system. Each operating system requires dedicated device drivers, and the Device Manager makes it easy to install, replace, or update drivers. Windows Setup under the Add/Remove Programs in Control Panel is used to add or remove built-in Windows utilities.

TEST YOURSELF OBJECTIVE 9.01

Installing Windows

Setup boot disks make it easy to install an operating system on new computers. Windows 9x boot disks have all the necessary files, such as FDISK and FORMAT, to partition and format the hard disk before you start the installation. In Windows 2000, the hard disk partitioning and formatting can be done during the installation process, and it is recommended that initially you create only the boot partition. In Windows 9x, the SETUP.EXE command is used to start the installation, whereas in Windows 2000, the installation and upgrading files are WINNT.EXE and WINNT32.EXE, respectively, and are located in the \I386 folder. Windows 2000 operating system comes with four startup disks.

- When performing a clean install of Windows 9x, you must boot the computer using Windows boot disks.

- Use the FDISK and FORMAT commands to prepare hard disks for Windows 9x installation.

- The Windows 2000 installation disk includes its own partitioning and formatting utility, and the CD itself can be used to boot the computer.

- Once the hard disk is prepared, install Windows by accessing its Setup program.

e x a m
ⓦa t c h

One of the most important things you should be aware of for installing any operating system is that your hardware must meet the minimum requirements of, and all parts must be compatible with, the new operating system. For installing Windows 9x, you must prepare the hard disk by creating partitions using FDISK, and formatting the partitions using the FORMAT command. In Windows 2000, you have the option of creating the partitions during the installation. Windows 2000 also has a Disk Management utility that makes is easy to manage your hard disk partitions after installation, and you can select either FAT or NTFS file systems, a feature that is not available with Windows 9x.

QUESTIONS

9.01: Installing Windows

1. Your computer has the following configuration:

   Processor: Pentium 100MHz

   RAM: 64MB

   Video adapter: SVGA

   Free hard disk space: 2.5GB

   Current operating system: Windows 98

   Which of the following will prevent you from installing Windows 2000 Professional on this computer?

   A. Processor

   B. RAM

   C. Video adapter

   D. Hard disk space

2. You have just purchased a copy of Windows 98 operating system. You are currently running Windows 3.1 on your computer. Which of the following is the first thing you should do before you start installing the new operating system?

   A. Create fresh partitions on the hard disk so that you have two or more partitions.

   B. Reformat the hard disk to a FAT32 file system.

   C. Check the minimum hardware requirements and the Hardware Compatibility List.

   D. Make sure that your games will run with the new operating system.

3. **Current Situation:** You have assembled a computer at home. This computer has a 13.6GB hard disk. You want to install Windows 98 operating system on this computer. Here is what you have to accomplish.

   Required Result: Prepare the hard disk completely for installation of Windows 98 operating system.

   Optional Desired Results:

   1. It is desired that the hard disk should have two partitions: one for Windows 98 system files, and the other for your data files.

   2. The two partitions should be formatted using FAT32 file system for better disk access and faster performance.

   Proposed Solution: Boot the new computer using the Windows 98 setup disk. Run the FDISK program from the floppy disk, which displays the initial screen as shown in the following illustration.

```
                    Microsoft Windows 98
                 Fixed Disk Setup Program
            (C)Copyright Microsoft Corp. 1983 - 1998

                         FDISK Options

Current fixed disk drive: 1

Choose one of the following:

 1. Create DOS partition or Logical DOS Drive
 2. Set active partition
 3. Delete partition or Logical DOS Drive
 4. Display partition information


Enter choice: [1]




Press Esc to exit FDISK
```

Select 1 and press ENTER to view the second screen where you can create the primary and extended partitions. Create one primary partition and set it active by selecting 2 from the illustration shown on the previous page.

What results does the proposed solution produce?

A. The proposed solution produces the required result and both of the optional results.

B. The proposed solution produces the required result and only one of the optional results.

C. The proposed solution produces the required result but none of the optional results.

D. The proposed solution does not produce the required result.

4. You have purchased a new Pentium III 800MHz computer and a copy of Windows 2000 Professional. You want to create two or more partitions on the hard disk. Which of the following do you think is the recommended method for creating the hard disk partitions?

A. Use the FDISK utility to create all partitions before you start the installation.

B. Use Disk Management to create the primary and extended partitions.

C. Create the primary partition using Disk Management before installation, and create the other extended partitions using FDISK.

D. Create the primary partition during installation, and the other partitions using Disk Management after installation.

TEST YOURSELF OBJECTIVE 9.02

Upgrading Windows

When you upgrade your Windows 95 system to Windows 98, most of your existing programs are migrated to the new operating system. When you upgrade Windows 9*x* systems to Windows 2000, remember that you cannot restore the previous Windows 9*x* operating system. It is also important to note that Windows 3.1 cannot be directly upgraded to Windows 2000, and you must first upgrade to Windows 9*x*, or better still, perform a clean install. In case you want to install Windows 2000 to make your system dual boot, you must install it on a separate directory or on a separate disk partition. Windows 2000 supports FAT16, FAT32, and NTFS5 file systems, and in dual boot systems, you can access the Windows 9*x* partitions from within Windows 2000 only if the Windows 2000 partition is FAT.

- When you upgrade from one version of Windows to another, non-system files, applications, and configurations are migrated from the old OS to the new.

- You can revert from Windows 98 to Windows 95 following an upgrade, but you cannot revert back to Windows 9*x* or Windows NT after a Windows 2000 upgrade.

- To upgrade Windows, start the computer normally, insert the new operating system installation CD, and run the Setup program, ensuring you select the Upgrade option.

- To create a Windows dual boot, start the computer normally and run the Setup program, ensuring you install the new OS in a different location, or select the New Installation option, rather than the Upgrade option.

exam
ⓦatch

Hardware compatibility and software portability are two major issues that should be addressed before upgrading the current operating system. It is important to back up your data files to avoid accidental loss of critical files. Remember that you can upgrade from Windows 9x to Windows 2000, or make your system dual boot between Windows 9x and Windows 2000, but you must install the applications again on the Windows 2000 partition. In case you want to access the Windows 2000 partition from within Windows 9x, you must not use NTFS on the Windows 2000 partition.

QUESTIONS

9.02: Upgrading Windows

5. You want to upgrade your Windows 98 computer to Windows 2000 Professional. Compatibility of the current applications is not a major issue for you, but you want to make sure that the critical data files are available after the upgrade.

Which of the following should be your first concern before you start the upgrade installation?

A. Consider making a dual boot system.

B. Back up your data files.

C. Learn about uninstalling Windows 2000.

D. Compress the existing data.

6. You are unable to upgrade to Windows 2000 Professional from which of the following operating systems? Select all correct answers.

A. Windows 95 OSR2

B. Windows NT Server 3.51

C. Windows 98

D. Windows for Workgroups 3.11

E. Windows NT 4.0 Workstation

F. Windows NT 4.0 Server with Service Pack 4

7. Which of the following statements is correct regarding the existing formatted partitions and the default action of the Setup program when you are running a Windows 2000 Professional upgrade on a Windows 98 system. Select all that apply.

A. If the system will dual boot with Windows 98, and the partition is less than 2GB, Setup converts it to FAT32.

B. If the system will dual boot with Windows 98, but the partition is greater than 2GB, Setup converts it to NTFS.

C. If the system will not dual boot with Windows 98, and the partition is less than 2GB, Setup converts it to FAT.

D. Whatever the size or formatting of the partition, by default Setup will keep it intact.

8. **Current Situation:** The computer used by Ted has the following configuration: hard disk C: is 10.6GB, hosts the Windows 98 operating system, and is formatted in its native file system. This partition contains the word processing, Internet, accounts software, and email programs. The capacity of the second

hard disk D: is 4.3GB, and it contains other important data files. You want to make this computer a dual boot system with Windows 98 and Windows 2000 Professional. Here is what you have to accomplish.

Required Result: The computer should be able to dual boot between Windows 98 and Windows 2000 Professional, and the two operating systems should be installed on separate disks.

Optional Desired Results:

1. All the programs should be able to run from both Windows 2000 and Windows 98.

2. The data files on the Windows 2000 disk should be available when running Windows 98 after the install.

Proposed Solution: Start the Windows 98 computer. Insert the Windows 2000 Setup CD-ROM in the CD-ROM drive. After a few seconds, the following dialog box will appear.

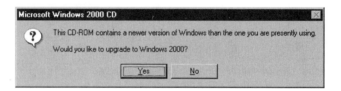

Click the No button, which will allow you to install Windows 2000 Professional, rather than upgrading Windows 98 to Windows 2000. When prompted, select the target as drive D: to ensure that the new operating system is installed on a separate drive. Format the D: drive using FAT32 file system.

What results does the proposed solution produced?

A. The proposed solution produces the required result and both of the optional results.

B. The proposed solution produces the required result but none of the optional results.

C. The proposed solution produces the required result and only one of the optional results.

D. The proposed solution does not produce the required result.

TEST YOURSELF OBJECTIVE 9.03

Booting Windows

Windows 9*x* uses the IO.SYS file to initiate the boot sequence after the power-on self-test (POST). In Windows 2000, this function is handled by NTLDR, in which the BOOT.INI is read in order to locate the operating system files and to display the choice of operating systems in dual-boot systems. In Windows 9x, the Add/Remove Programs has a Startup Disk tab to make a bootable disk. In Windows 2000, the four startup disks can be created by running the MAKEBOOT command. In case of startup problems, the emergency repair disk in Windows 2000 is used along with the Setup CD-ROM to fix startup problems by analyzing the startup environment and replacing any corrupted or missing files.

- The Windows 9*x* boot process includes the BIOS bootstrap, real-mode boot, real-mode configuration, and protected-mode boot phases.

- Windows Safe Mode loads a minimal set of device drivers to bypass potential problems and allow you to troubleshoot the OS.

- You can create a startup disk by accessing the Windows 9*x* Add/Remove Programs utility.

- To create a Windows 2000 boot disk set, run the MAKEBOOT.EXE command from the \BOOTDISK folder of the Setup CD-ROM.

exam
Watch

Both Windows 9x and Windows 2000 have distinct bootstrap routines which should not be mixed up. In Windows 9x, the IO.SYS initiates the boot process after the POST, whereas the same function is handled by NTLDR in Windows 2000 until the NTOSKRNL takes over. It is important for you to remember the correct sequence of the boot process and the function of each file involved. The exam might ask you to spell out the correct sequence, or it might attempt to confuse you by mixing up Windows 9x and Windows 2000 boot sequences. One last word: the emergency repair disk (ERD) in Windows 2000 is not bootable!

QUESTIONS

9.03: Booting Windows

9. You borrowed Windows 2000 Professional from your system administrator who asked you to install it on a new computer. Unfortunately, the administrator has lost the original set of startup disks and has requested you to prepare a set of disks for him. Which of the following commands can you use to create the Windows 2000 startup disks on a computer running Windows 98? Assume that the floppy disk drive is lettered A: and the CD-ROM drive is lettered F: on the Windows 98 computer. The Windows 2000 Setup files are located in the \I386 folder.

   A. F:\I386\WINNT32.EXE /OX

   B. F:\I386\WINNT32.EXE A:

   C. F:\BOOTDISK\MAKEBOOT.EXE A:

   D. None of above; you cannot create Windows 2000 startup disks on a Windows 98 computer.

10. Which of the following statements correctly describes the boot sequence of a Windows 2000 computer?

   A. NTLDR loads the operating system. NTOSKRNL loads the graphics mode and runs the NTDETECT to detect the hardware.

   B. NTLDR loads the operating system, NTDETECT is run to detect the hardware, and NTOSKRNL loads the graphics mode.

   C. NTLDR runs the POST and loads the operating system, NTDETECT is run to detect the hardware, and NTOSKRNL loads the graphics mode.

   D. NTLDR loads the operating system, NTDETECT loads the graphics mode, and NTOSKRNL detects the hardware and loads the device drivers.

Questions 11–13   You have a Pentium III 750MHz computer that has 128MB of SDRAM. The computer has a 10.6GB hard disk with 2 partitions, the second partition still being unused. The computer is currently running Windows 98 operating system. You have just purchased a copy of Windows 2000 Professional and want to make your computer a dual boot system.

You called a technician expert in Windows 2000 operating systems and asked him to install Windows 2000 Professional in the free partition of the hard disk. He did this. After the installation, he reinstalled several applications and had to restart the system several times.

Based on these assumptions answer the following three questions, selecting the best answer for each question.

11. You started your computer after the technician left, but instead of giving you an option for selecting the operating system, the system immediately started loading Windows 2000 Professional. Thinking that you might not have noticed the option screen, you restarted the system, but it again jumped to starting Windows 2000. Which of the following options can you use to view the operating system options to load during startup?

   A. Start the System applet in Windows 2000 Control Panel, and increase the wait time to 20 in the Startup/Shutdown tab.

   B. Windows 98 is possibly deleted from the system, and you must call the technician again to have it reinstalled.

   C. Boot the system using Windows 98 boot disk, and modify the BOOT.INI file to correct the timing of the OS option screen.

   D. Windows 98 should have been installed after installing Windows 2000 Professional, and it must be reinstalled now.

12. You downloaded a new updated driver for your sound card from the manufacturer's Web site. When you installed it on your Windows 2000 computer and restarted, the computer did not start up. Which of the following boot options should you use so that the system boots up normally and does not load the updated driver?

   A. Boot normally

   B. Step-by-step confirmation

    C. Last Known Good Configuration

    D. Enable Boot Logging

13. To better prepare yourself for emergency situations, you want to ensure that you are equipped with the tools you might need to restore the system in case of a failure. You decide to make an emergency repair disk (ERD). Which of the following can be accomplished with ERD?

    A. Starting Windows 2000 Professional

    B. Restoring system files

    C. Repartitioning the hard disk

    D. Restoring data files

TEST YOURSELF OBJECTIVE 9.04

Installing Device Drivers and Applications

Windows 9x and Windows 2000 make it easy to add or remove new applications, new hardware, and Windows components through interactive dialog boxes. Most of the applications come with their own Setup programs, and you need not install them from the Add/Remove Programs utility. All Windows components are not installed by default, and you can use the Windows Setup tab to install additional components as and when required. The Device Manager is used to add or remove devices, replace corrupted drivers, and install updated drivers.

- Most Plug and Play devices are detected by Windows at startup and are automatically configured.

- Use the Add New Hardware (Windows 9x) or Add/Remove Hardware (Windows 2000) utilities to install third party device drivers.

- Install third party applications by running their Setup programs or by using the Windows Add/Remove Programs utility.

- Install and configure Windows printers using the Printers utility in the Control Panel.

Plug and Play hardware is usually detected automatically by Windows 9x and Windows 2000, but it is necessary that the BIOS of your computer also be Plug and Play compliant. If the Device Manager shows a device as Unknown Device, you should update its driver with a compatible new driver. The Add/Remove Programs utility in Control Panel can be used to install any third party applications or to add or remove Windows components. Certain applications and Windows components modify the system Registry and make it mandatory for you to restart the system.

QUESTIONS

9.04: Installing Device Drivers and Applications

14. You have installed a new Plug and Play PCI network adapter in your Windows 98 computer and restarted. Surprisingly, the operating system did not detect the network adapter automatically. Which of the following is true?

    A. The operating system does not support Plug and Play.

    B. PCI adapters are not Plug and Play.

    C. The system BIOS does not support Plug and Play.

    D. Plug and Play software is not installed.

15. You have just upgraded your Windows 98 computer to Windows 2000. When you try to connect to the Internet, the modem does not respond. You open Device Manager and find that the modem is listed as an Unknown Device. What should you do with the modem?

    A. Replace the modem.

    B. Install Windows 2000 Service Pack 1.

    C. Install an updated driver for the modem.

    D. Reconfigure the Dial-up Networking.

16. **Current Situation:** You have installed a printer with your computer and have been assigned the job of printing page proofs for documents that are usually stored on your hard disk. The hard disk is constantly full of documents, and there is very little space left. Most of the documents span several pages, and the printing of the page proofs must finish by the end of each day. You want to configure the printer settings so that you can finish the printing job on time. Here is what you have to accomplish.

    Required Result: The printer should be able to handle large documents.

    Optional Desired Results:

    1. The printing should start as soon as you send the document to the printer.

    2. The printing process should be fast and take the minimum possible time.

    Proposed Solution: Open the Properties window of the printer. Click the Spool Settings button, and configure the various settings as shown in the following illustration.

    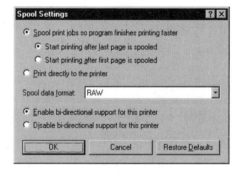

    What results does the proposed solution produce?

    A. The proposed solution produces the required result and both of the optional results.

    B. The proposed solution produces the required result and only one of the optional results.

    C. The proposed solution produces the required result but none of the optional results.

    D. The proposed solution does not produce the required result.

A QUICK ANSWER KEY

Objective 9.01

1. **A**
2. **C**
3. **D**
4. **D**

Objective 9.02

5. **B**
6. **B** and **F**
7. **D**
8. **C**

Objective 9.03

9. **C**
10. **B**
11. **A**
12. **C**
13. **B**

Objective 9.04

14. **C**
15. **C**
16. **D**

IN-DEPTH ANSWERS

9.01: Installing Windows

1. ☑ **A.** Windows 2000 requires at least a Pentium 133MHz processor. Remember that the minimum requirements for installing Windows 2000 Professional are a Pentium 133MHz processor, 32MB of RAM, a VGA video adapter, and 800MB of free hard disk space. In this case, you must upgrade the processor to 133MHz or higher.

   ☒ **B** is incorrect because the amount of RAM in the computer meets the minimum memory requirements for a successful installation. You should, however, increase the RAM to at least 64MB to get better performance. **C** is incorrect because Windows 2000 can be installed with a VGA adapter. An SVGA adapter is recommended for better video performance and color display. **D** is incorrect because the current disk has 2.5GB (2,500MB) of free hard disk space, which is sufficient to install the new Windows 2000 Professional operating system.

2. ☑ **C.** The first thing you should do before installing Windows 98, or any other operating system, on your computer is see if the existing hardware meets the minimum hardware requirements, and make sure that it is on the Hardware Compatibility List. This will ensure that you will not face any hardware related problems during the installation process.

   ☒ **A** is incorrect because this can be done after you determine if your hardware meets the minimum hardware requirements of the new operating system. **B** is incorrect because this is certainly not the first step to perform when you are preparing to install a new operating system. **D** is incorrect because the only thing you should be concerned about before installing Windows 98 is that your computer has the minimum requirements. The games and other entertainment software are a secondary issue.

3. ☑ **D.** The proposed solution does not produce the required result. The required result is not produced because the hard disk is not *completely* ready for

installing Windows 98 operating system, as required in the question. After you have created the partitions, you must format them before you can start installing the operating system. Assuming that you had formatted the disk partitions, the first and second optional results would also be produced.

☒   **A, B,** and **C** are incorrect because the proposed solution does not produce the required result, since the hard disk is not completely ready to install the Windows 98 operating system.

4.   ☑   **D.** Create the primary partition during installation, and the other partitions using Disk Management after installation. Windows 2000 gives you an option of creating one or all partitions during the installation process, but it is recommended that you create only the first partition during the installation, which is necessary to complete the installation process, and when the installation is complete, use the Disk Management Console to create and format other partitions. Disk Management allows you to create as many partitions as you wish, whereas the FDISK utility limits the number of primary partitions to four (or three primary and one extended partition). Besides this, Disk Management can format the partitions using NTFS file system, and offer conversion to Dynamic disks, some features that are not available when you use FDISK.

☒   **A** is incorrect because Microsoft does not recommend this due to limitations of the FDISK utility. **B** is incorrect because the Disk Management console becomes available only after you have installed Windows 2000 operating system. **C** is incorrect for the same reason. Disk Management cannot be used before the installation of Windows 2000 is complete.

9.02: Upgrading Windows

5.   ☑   **B.** Since the data files are critical for you, you must back up these files before you run the upgrade install. Although the upgrade install does not harm any data files, it is always better to back up important files before upgrading the existing operating system in case of accidental data loss.

☒   **A** is incorrect because the safety of data files is critical, and this should be your first concern. **C** is incorrect because Windows 2000 Setup does not include an uninstall option. **D** is incorrect because data compression does not ensure the safety of critical data. It only saves hard disk space.

6. ☑ **B** and **F.** Windows NT Server 3.51 and Windows NT 4.0 Server with Service Pack 4. Remember that you can upgrade to Windows 2000 Professional only from a workstation or desktop operating system and not from a server operating system. You can upgrade to Windows 2000 Professional from Windows for Workgroups 3.11, Windows 95 OSR2, Windows 98, Windows NT 3.51 Workstation, and Windows NT 4.0 Workstation. Options **B** and **F** are incorrect because they list server operating systems. Direct upgrade is supported only from Windows 9x and Windows NT, so you must first upgrade Windows for Workgroups 3.11 to Windows 9x or Windows NT Workstation before you can upgrade to Windows 2000 Professional.

   ☒ **A, C, D,** and **E** are all incorrect answers because all these operating systems can be upgraded to Windows 2000 Professional. When you insert the Windows 2000 Professional Setup CD-ROM, the Autorun program in the CD-ROM detects the previous operating system and prompts you to select whether you wish to perform a clean install or an upgrade install.

7. ☑ **D.** Whatever the size or formatting of the partition, by default Setup will keep it intact. The Setup program does not change the file system on any partition when you are dual booting with Windows 98. Instead you are given an option to make your selection.

   ☒ **A** is incorrect because the Setup will not convert any partition less than 2GB to the FAT32 file system. **B** is incorrect because the partition will not be automatically converted to NTFS. **C** is incorrect because this action is also not performed automatically.

8. ☑ **C.** The proposed solution produces the required result and only one of the optional results. If Windows 2000 is to dual boot with Windows 98, it has to be installed on a drive that is different from Windows 98. The proposed solution satisfies this requirement, since Windows 2000 is installed on drive D:, a separate hard disk. The first optional result is not produced because the applications installed on Windows 98 will not be able to run from Windows 2000. You need to install the applications while running Windows 2000 Professional. This, again, is subject to compatibility issues, and only those applications that are compatible with Windows 2000 operating system will run. The second optional result is produced because the file system on drive D: has been kept as FAT32, which allows you to access the data files while working on Windows 98.

☒ **A, B,** and **D** are incorrect because the proposed solution produces the required result and only one of the optional results. To produce the first optional result you would have to install the applications from within Windows 2000 Professional.

9.03: Booting Windows

9. ☑ **C.** The startup disks for Windows 2000 Professional can be created by running the MAKEBOOT.EXE command, located in the \BOOTDISK folder on the Setup CD-ROM. Be careful, because the question tries to confuse you by stating that the Windows 2000 Setup files are in the \I386 folder. The MAKEBOOT.EXE command can be run on any computer running MS-DOS or Windows operating systems. It is important to note that the Setup disks for Windows 2000 Professional and Windows 2000 Server are different.

☒ **A** is an incorrect command because this command is used in Window NT and is no longer valid in Windows 2000. **B** is incorrect for two reasons. First, the WINNT32.EXE command is used for upgrading a previous Windows 2000 operating system to Windows 2000 Professional, and secondly, you cannot specify A: as the destination drive. **D** is incorrect because the MAKEBOOT.EXE command can be used on any computer running MS-DOS or Windows operating systems.

10. ☑ **B.** NTLDR loads the operating system, NTDETECT is run to detect the hardware, and NTOSKRNL loads the graphics mode. When a Windows 2000 computer is started, the POST is run and NTLDR locates and loads the operating system as specified in the BOOT.INI file. NTLDR then loads the NTDETECT file that detects the installed hardware. After this, NTLDR locates and loads NTOSKRNL, which runs the graphics mode. Finally, the boot process is handed over by NTLDR to NTOSKRNL, which then loads the device drivers and initializes them as specified in the Registry. In other words, the sequence is NTLDR, NTDETECT, and NTOSKRNL.

☒ **A** is incorrect because NTOSKRNL is loaded after the NTDETECT file. **C** is incorrect because NTLDR does not run the POST. The POST is run by the BIOS, and the BIOS locates and runs the NTLDR file, which starts the actual Windows 2000 boot process. **D** is incorrect because neither does NTDETECT load the graphics mode, nor does NTOSKRNL detect installed hardware.

11. ☑ **A.** Start the System applet in Windows 2000 Control Panel, and increase the wait time to 20 in the Startup/Shutdown tab. In Windows 98 and Windows 2000 dual boot systems, the boot loader gives you the option of selecting an operating system to load. This option screen is displayed for 30 seconds by default, unless this timing is modified. A possible reason that you are not able to see the option screen is that this wait time has been set to zero seconds. This is quite likely because the technician had to restart the system several times and probably did not want to wait every time while the options screen was displayed. You can modify this wait time in the Startup/Shutdown tab of the System applet in Control Panel after starting the system in Windows 2000 Professional.

☒ **B** is incorrect because there is no indication in the question that Windows 2000 Professional was installed as an upgrade. If the system were upgraded, the question should have stated so. **C** is incorrect because the BOOT.INI is a system file, and its attributes are Read Only by default. Unless you change these attributes, you cannot modify this file. When a better option exists to correct the problem, you should not alter any files manually. **D** is incorrect because when you wish to boot Windows 2000 with any other operating system, it must be the last operating system to be installed.

12. ☑ **C.** When you select the Last Known Good Configuration, the Windows 2000 computer reverts to the saved configuration that was previously used to boot the system successfully. Any changes made to the system files and the Registry after that will be lost. This startup option is best used when you have loaded a device driver that prevents the system from booting normally after restart. It is important to note that the Last Known Good Configuration will be different for different users, so in order to restore the previous system state, you must log on with the same username that was previously used to load the correct driver.

☒ **A** and **B** are incorrect answers because these options do not exist in Windows 2000 as startup modes. These are Windows 98 startup options. **D** is incorrect because this mode enables you to collect boot information in a log file that you can analyze later to resolve the problem.

13. ☑ **B.** The emergency repair disk in Windows 2000 will be able to restore only the system files in the event the computer fails to boot because of a corrupted system file. The ERD copies only the files from the \Winnt\Repair

folder to the floppy disk. When you restore the system files using the ERD, it prompts you to insert the original Windows 2000 Setup CD-ROM. It is worth noting that you should create the ERD every time you make changes to your system configuration. When you create the ERD, the process makes a copy of the system Registry files in the \Winnt\Repair\RegBack folder.

☒ **A** is incorrect because the ERD is not bootable and cannot be used to start Windows 2000 Professional. **C** is incorrect because the ERD cannot make partitions on the hard disk. **D** is incorrect because the ERD does not have a copy of any data files. To fully prepare for emergency situations, you should regularly back up your system and data files on tape drives.

9.04: Installing Device Drivers and Applications

14. ☑ **C.** The only possible reason for the operating system not being able to detect the new Plug and Play network adapter is that the system BIOS does not support Plug and Play. Several older computer BIOSs did not support Plug and Play. In order to have full Plug and Play functionality in a computer, it is recommended that you ensure that the system BIOS, the operating system, and the devices are all Plug and Play compatible.

☒ **A** is incorrect because Windows 98 supports Plug and Play functionality. **B** is incorrect because all PCI adapters are Plug and Play. **D** is incorrect because you need not install Plug and Play software separately on a Windows 98 system. Plug and Play support is built in to the operating system itself.

15. ☑ **C.** Install an updated driver for the modem. The modem is listed in the Device Manager as Unknown Device because Windows 2000 did not recognize it during installation. You should get an updated Windows 2000 compatible driver for the modem and install it.

☒ **A** is incorrect because you should first try to get and install an updated driver for the modem. **B** is incorrect because unless you are sure that the problem can be addressed by Service Pack 1, you should not install it. The manufacturer of the modem is the right source of an updated driver for the modem. **D** is incorrect because the Dial-up Networking is dependent on the modem, and if the modem is not working, this reconfiguration will not resolve the problem.

16. ☑ **D.** The proposed solution does not produce the required result because given the situation, the printer attached to your computer will not be able to handle large documents. With the spooler enabled, the printer will essentially use the hard disk space to store the spooled documents. The question states that the hard disk is almost full, and there is hardly any space. To produce the required result, you must free up space in your hard disk. Assuming that this is done and the hard disk has sufficient space to spool large documents, the first optional result still is not produced because the spooler settings are configured to start printing *after* the last page is spooled, which delays the printing process. You must check the Start Printing After First Page is Spooled button in order to start the printing immediately after the document is sent to the printer. The second optional result is also not produced because the RAW format selected results in delayed printing. If the printer supports EMF (Enhanced Metafile Format) printing, it should be selected. When you select the RAW format, the operating system has to translate every document into the printer's language, which delays the printing process.

☒ **A, B**, and **C** are incorrect because the proposed solution is able to produce neither the required result nor either of the two optional results.

CORE HARDWARE/OPERATING SYSTEM EXAMS

10

Diagnosing and Troubleshooting

M ost of the problems in Windows 9x and Windows 2000 computers are related to starting up the operating system. Both Windows 9x and Windows 2000 offer a variety of startup options, such as Safe Mode in Windows 9x and Last Known Good Configuration in Windows 2000. The startup problems usually arise when the system is unable to locate the files that are necessary to initiate the boot process, or there is a missing, corrupt, or incompatible device driver. The Device Manager in Windows 9x and the Computer Management Console in Windows 2000 are very helpful in fixing problems with devices.

Apart from problems in Windows paging files, application bugs cause the majority of runtime problems. Runtime problems are more difficult to diagnose, and you should observe the errors displayed. In any case, you should gather as much information as you can and follow the correct diagnostics procedure to resolve the problem. Problems in Windows printers are usually caused by incorrect drivers or incorrectly installed printers. The settings in the Printer Properties page should be checked.

TEST YOURSELF OBJECTIVE 10.01

Boot Problems

Most of the boot problems in Windows 9x and Windows 2000 can be resolved using one of the various boot options. The Safe Mode can be used when there is a problem in loading a device driver in a Windows 9x system. The emergency repair disk in Windows 2000 is used with the Setup CD-ROM to fix problems in the startup environment. Often possible, the settings in the Control Panel should be preferred for making changes to the system configuration, rather than reinstallation of the operating system, which should be done only as a last resort.

- The No Operating System found error indicates that the BIOS could not find and initialize the boot loader file (IO.SYS in Windows 9x and NTLDR in Windows 2000).

- Windows 9x CONFIG.SYS or AUTOEXEC.BAT startup errors can be resolved by booting in Safe Mode and removing or modifying the problematic file entry.

- If the HIMEM.SYS file is missing or corrupt, Windows 9x will not start, and the file will have to be replaced from the installation or boot disk.

- Faulty display driver, kernel, or graphical user interface files may cause a failure to load the GUI during startup.

- Windows Protection Errors occur in Windows when a 32-bit driver is corrupt or missing.

- Missing application files that are referenced in the Registry or SYSTEM.INI files will result in non-fatal errors during startup.

- If the Windows Swapfile is corrupt, simply delete it, and then restart Windows.

You should be familiar with the boot process in both Windows 9x and Windows 2000, and with the importance of critical files, such as IO.SYS, MSDOS.SYS, and HIMEM.SYS in Windows 9x, and NTLDR, BOOT.INI, NTDETECT.COM, and NTOSKRNL.EXE in Windows 2000. You should also be able to differentiate among various boot options in Windows 9x and Windows 2000 operating systems, and know which particular startup option to choose for a given problem. Do not confuse the emergency repair disk in Windows 2000 with the boot disk, because the ERD cannot be used for booting a Windows 2000 system. When a problem scenario is given, you should choose to modify the Registry or reinstall the operating system as a last resort—that is, only if there is no other option to fix the startup problem.

QUESTIONS

10.01: Boot Problems

1. You have installed a new adapter in your computer, which is running Windows 98. After the installation, you modified the CONFIG.SYS file manually. When you start the computer, the following error message is displayed:

```
Error in CONFIG.SYS line 5.
```

Which of the following would you rule out as a possible cause of the error?

A. The adapter is faulty.

B. You have not installed the adapter driver.

C. The file referenced in CONFIG.SYS does not exist in the specified location.

D. There is a syntax error in CONFIG.SYS line 5.

2. One of your friends upgraded his Windows 98 computer to Windows 2000 a few days ago. He has called you to inform you that his computer does not start. You visit him and find that the problem is caused by a corrupted startup file. How will you fix a startup problem in his Windows 2000 computer?

A. Boot the system with a Windows 2000 boot disk, and run the SYS command.

B. Boot the system using the emergency repair disk, and replace the corrupt files from the CD-ROM.

C. Boot the system using boot disks, start the installation, and when prompted, choose the Repair option.

D. Boot the system using the emergency repair disk, and run the SYS command.

3. A computer that was running Windows 98 is exhibiting some boot problems. You want to diagnose the problem that is preventing the system from booting normally. Which of the following utilities are you unable to use for your diagnosis?

A. Device Manager

B. Automatic skip driver

C. System Configuration utility

D. System Configuration Editor

E. None of the above

4. One of your colleagues has told you that he was working on the Registry files of his Windows 98 computer, and now his computer does not boot. The applications installed on his computer are the same as on your computer, so you copy the Registry from your computer onto a floppy disk, and then copy it

onto your friend's computer. What will happen when your friend's computer is started?

    A. The computer will boot normally because both computers have the same applications.

    B. The computer will not boot because Windows 98 Registry is computer specific.

    C. The computer will boot normally, but the applications will need reconfiguration.

    D. The computer will boot only in Safe Mode, and some of the applications will work.

5. In which of the following situations will the Windows 98 Safe Mode not be helpful in resolving startup problems?

    A. When you have a display driver problem

    B. When the Safe Mode with Networking does not work

    C. When the Step-by-Step Confirmation Mode is not helpful

    D. When the Safe Mode with Command Prompt does not work

6. **Current Situation:** You have a computer that was purchased two years ago with a preinstalled version of Windows 98. This computer has ISA adapters for an internal modem and sound. Since the computer has PCI slots, you have decided to replace the older ISA cards with new PCI cards for sound and the modem. After consulting some magazines, you go to a computer store and buy two new adapters, one for the sound card and the other for the internal modem. Here is what you have to accomplish.

    Required Result: Remove the older sound and modem cards, and replace them with new PCI cards. There should be no problems after the installation is complete.

    Optional Desired Results:

    1. The operating system should not produce any errors after the installation.

    2. You should take precautions and use proper methods while performing the removal and installation of cards.

Proposed Solution: Make sure that you have Windows 98 compatible driver files for the two adapters. Open the Registry Editor as shown in the following illustration, and search for and delete all references to these cards and their drivers.

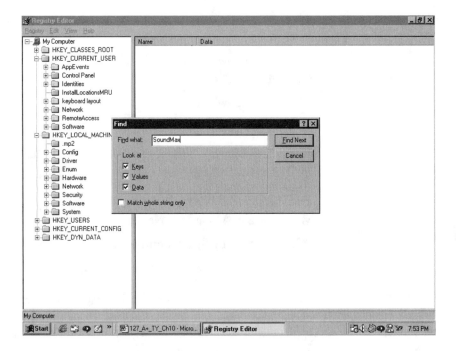

Open the cover of the computer and remove the cards. Insert new cards in two free PCI slots. When you restart the computer, the cards will be detected by the operating system. Follow the prompts to install suitable drivers for the new cards.

What results does the proposed solution produce?

A. The proposed solution produces the required result and both of the optional results.

B. The proposed solution produces the required result and only one of the optional results.

C. The proposed solution produces the required result but none of the optional results.

D. The proposed solution does not produce the required result.

7. A computer running Windows 2000 Professional operating system is running very slow. This computer has a Pentium II 450MHz processor and 32MB of RAM. You have noticed that there is a lot of activity on the hard disk. This hard disk was defragmented only two days ago, and when you run Scandisk, it does not report any problems. You suspect that the Windows swapfile might be causing the problem. What should you do to resolve the problem?

   A. Delete the WIN386.SWP file and restart the computer.

   B. Increase the size of PAGEFILE.SYS.

   C. Create another Paging file on the hard disk.

   D. Increase the RAM in the computer.

TEST YOURSELF OBJECTIVE 10.02

Runtime Problems

Runtime problems are different from startup problems. They appear in a running system because of corrupt or missing files and application bugs. When there are no clear symptoms to help locate the cause of the problem, there are certain established procedures for performing a diagnosis. Dr. Watson, available in both Windows 9x and Windows 2000, can take a snapshot of the system activities when a problem occurs. The Event Viewer in Windows 2000 can be used to track problem areas. The anti-virus utility you are using should be updated with new virus signatures on a regular basis. Use the Printer Properties page to diagnose common printer problems and to change ports, spooler settings, and update or replace printer drivers.

- When diagnosing a runtime error, gather as much information as you can about the nature of the problem, error messages, and recent changes to the computer.

- You can use the Dr. Watson utility to take a snapshot of the system's current configuration in either Windows 9x or Windows 2000.

- Windows 2000 uses an Event Log service that keeps a record of all system activities.

- General Protection Faults (GPFs) occur when an application tries to perform an activity that may compromise another running application.

- If an application produces an Illegal Operation error or locks up, try restarting the computer, reinstalling the application, and then checking with the manufacturer for a resolution or patch.

- Use the Printer Properties window to troubleshoot stalled print spools or incorrectly set printer ports.

- Viruses are programs that are designed to have an undesired effect on a computer and to replicate themselves so that they can spread from one computer to another.

- Use an anti-virus utility to detect and remove viruses, and update the utility often so that it recognizes new viruses.

exam
ⓦatch

The A+ exam might try to confuse you regarding runtime error messages, such as Illegal Operation, General Protection Fault, and Invalid Working Directory, and you should understand when and why these errors are produced. If a problem has occurred in a running application or a device, make sure to check any recent changes in configuration. As well, there are different kinds of viruses that infect the system in different manners and work in different ways. Be aware that Event Logs are available only in Windows 2000 and do not exist in Windows 9x operating system.

QUESTIONS

10.02: Runtime Problems

8. You installed new accounting software in your Windows 98 computer, but it does not work according to your expectations. You do not want to keep the application in your system but would rather remove it and free up system resources. Which of the following options should you consider first for removing the application?

   A. Use the Add/Remove Programs utility in Control Panel.

   B. Delete the folder created by the application.

C. Use the uninstall utility that came with the application.

D. Use an uninstall utility from a third-party vendor which will also clean the Registry.

9. Whenever you launch a game program in your Windows 98 computer, it starts, but after some time the system locks up. This causes problems with other applications that are running. You click several times to exit from the game program, but your mouse does not seem to work in the game window. What should you do to exit from the faulty game program?

A. Press CTRL-ALT-DEL and click Shut Down.

B. Press CTRL-ALT-DEL, select the game program in the dialog box, and click End Task.

C. Press CTRL-ALT-DEL and click End Task.

D. Press CTRL-ALT-DEL twice.

10. You are using a Windows 2000 Professional workstation in your office. You suspect that someone is trying to log on your computer in your absence. Your network administrator has suggested that you turn on auditing on your system. Which of the following logs would you check in the Event Viewer console to track unauthorized access to your computer once the auditing has been configured?

A. System Logs

B. Security Logs

C. Data Access Logs

D. Application Logs

11. An application in Windows 98 is trying to execute a function that cannot be carried out because of a bug in one of the files associated with the application. Which of the following errors is this action likely to produce on the screen?

A. Illegal Operation

B. General Protection Fault

C. Invalid Working Directory

D. The system will lock up.

12. You are sharing the printer attached to your Windows 98 computer with four of your office colleagues in a peer network. Your computer is heavily loaded with several applications, and a large number of data files have stacked up in your hard disk. Recently your colleagues have started complaining that sometimes their print jobs are not printed at all. Your inquiries reveal that none of the users has received any printing errors so far. What should you do?

    A. Change the port in Printer Properties.

    B. Increase the space in your hard disk.

    C. Increase RAM in your computer.

    D. Increase the timeout settings in Printer Properties.

    Questions 13–16 Just after passing your A+ Core and DOS/Windows exams, you accepted a job as a field technician with a major computer vendor in town. After spending a few days in the office learning customer support procedures, you are now ready to work offsite.

    Incidentally, the first call you get is from one of your friends. He purchased his Pentium II 450MHz computer from your company a few months ago. The computer runs Windows 98 operating system. He also purchased a new printer and has attached it to his computer. He is calling with a complaint about some problems that appeared after he installed the printer.

    You arrive at the customer's site (your friend's house) and find the problems that are presented in the following four questions. Answer each of the questions, selecting the best answer for each.

13. After connecting the printer to his computer, you friend installed a printer driver on his Windows 98 computer. When he restarted the computer, it did not start up. Which of the following modes would you use to correct the startup problem in the system caused by the new printer driver?

    A. Boot the system using the Last Known Good Configuration. The changes made will not be saved.

    B. Boot the system using the Safe Mode, and use the Device Manager to remove the faulty printer driver.

C. Boot the system using the Safe Mode with Command Prompt, and replace the printer driver files.

D. Boot the system using the VGA mode so that the printer driver is not visible to the system.

14. When the boot problem is solved, you connect the Epson Stylus Color 460 printer to the parallel port. When you open the Printer Properties page, you find the printer settings shown in the following illustration.

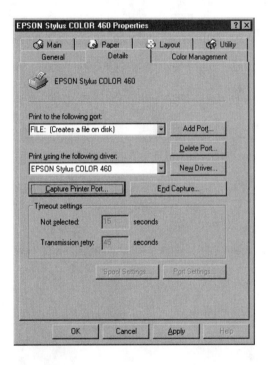

Which of the following correctly states why your friend will not be able to print to the printer?

A. The timeout settings have been disabled.

B. The spooler settings have not been enabled.

C. The printer driver is incorrect.

D. An incorrect printer port has been selected.

15. You correct the printer settings by selecting the LPT1 port. When this is done, your friend seeks your advice on protecting his computer from viruses. He tells you that he is worried about new viruses that might infect his hard disk. The anti-virus utility that he is using was purchased six months ago, and you know that it needs to be updated with new virus signature files. Which of the following should you suggest to him as the best source of getting updated files?

    A. The Microsoft Web site

    B. The manufacturer of the anti-virus software

    C. The Windows 98 Setup CD-ROM

    D. None of the above. Purchase a new copy of the anti-virus utility.

16. Your further diagnostics indicate that your friend's computer might have a boot sector virus. How would you remove it?

    A. Restart the computer with a clean boot disk, and run the FDISK /MBR command.

    B. Restart the computer and run the FDISK /MBR command.

    C. Restart the computer using an anti-virus disk, and run the anti-virus program.

    D. Restart the computer using a clean boot disk, and run McAfee.

QUICK ANSWER KEY

Objective 10.01		Objective 10.02	
1.	A	8.	C
2.	C	9.	B
3.	E	10.	B
4.	B	11.	A
5.	D	12.	B
6.	D	13.	B
7.	D	14.	D
		15.	B
		16.	A

IN-DEPTH ANSWERS

10.01: Boot Problems

1. ☑ **A.** The adapter is certainly not causing the reported error in the CONFIG.SYS file. Such errors are reported when the operating system is unable to process any code specified in a particular line of the CONFIG.SYS file. Usually this error is produced either when a file specified in the CONFIG.SYS line is not found, or when the specified path is incorrect.

   ☒ **B** is incorrect because it is possible that the CONFIG.SYS line 5 is referencing one of the driver files and is not able to find it. If you have modified the CONFIG.SYS file, which typically is done to load a specific driver file, and you have not installed the adapter driver, you will get this error. **C** is incorrect because this may also cause the given error. **D** is incorrect because if there is a syntax error in the CONFIG.SYS file, the operating system will not be able to process that line.

2. ☑ **C.** Boot the system using boot disks, start the installation, and when prompted, choose the Repair option. The corrupted files in Windows 2000 can be replaced by using the setup boot disks and selecting the Repair option. This option prompts you to insert the emergency repair disk The emergency repair process replaces the corrupted file with an undamaged copy from the original CD-ROM and makes the system bootable.

   ☒ **A** is incorrect because the SYS command does not work in Windows 2000. You should replace the corrupted startup file from the original CD-ROM by following the proper startup process explained above. **B** is incorrect because the emergency repair disk cannot be used to boot a Windows 2000 computer. You should remember that an emergency repair disk in Windows 2000 is not a bootable disk. **D** is incorrect because neither is the emergency repair disk bootable, nor can the SYS be used to restore startup files in Windows 2000.

3. ☑ **E.** None of the above. All of the listed utilities can be used to correct problems in the Windows 98 startup environment. This is a typical example of a confusing question that you might get on the A+ exam. All answer options are correct from the perspective that they can be used for a startup diagnosis, so you must select the best answer *after* carefully reading the question to be sure to choose the option that corresponds to the question asked, in this case, the utility that can *not* be used.

    ☒ **A** is incorrect because the Device Manager can be used to fix any problems with device drivers or resource conflicts. **B** is incorrect because this utility is used to locate a problem driver. Windows 98 includes this utility to skip the loading of the driver files for any device that prevents the operating system from loading normally. **C** is incorrect because you can use this utility to correct problems with the configuration of system devices, and to enable or disable components. **D** is incorrect because this utility is used to edit configuration files such as WIN.INI, SYSTEM.INI, CONFIG.SYS, and AOTUEXE.BAT.

4. ☑ **B.** The computer will not boot because Windows 98 Registry is computer specific. The Registry is unique to every Windows 9*x* computer. If you copy the Registry files from one computer to another, it is certain that the latter computer will not work. Although both computers have the same applications installed, there might be several other configuration differences between the two computers. As a general rule, you should remember that the Registry from one computer does not work on another.

    ☒ **A** is incorrect because the Registry contains not only application configuration information, but also configuration of the entire computer system, including hardware and software. **C** is incorrect because the computer will not be able to boot normally after copying the Registry. **D** is incorrect because it cannot be predicted whether the computer will boot in Safe Mode or whether any of the applications will work.

5. ☑ **D.** When the Safe Mode with Command Prompt does not work. The Safe Mode with Command Prompt starts the Windows 9*x* computer in real mode. If the real mode is not able to work, which is the most basic mode of starting Windows 9*x*, you will not be able to load the Safe Mode, because the Safe Mode works in protected mode and needs 32-bit device drivers.

☒ **A** is incorrect because the Safe Mode can be used to boot a Windows 9x computer if there is a display driver problem. If you have a problem with the display driver, boot Windows 9x in Safe Mode, and change the display driver. **B** is incorrect because if this mode does not work because of a network driver problem, you can use the Safe Mode and change the network settings or network drivers. **C** is incorrect because this mode allows you to load device drivers selectively. When you boot a Windows 9x computer in Safe Mode, Windows 9x loads using the most basic device drivers.

6. ☑ **D.** The proposed solution does not produce the required result because the procedure suggested is not the correct one for removing and adding adapters in Windows 9x or newer operating systems. You should first use the Add/Remove Hardware utility in the Control Panel to remove the two adapters. This will modify the Registry to reflect the changes. Turn off your computer. When this is done, you can open the computer and remove the cards physically. If you delete certain items in the Registry manually, the system will produce errors after restart. The Registry should not be modified manually unless there is no other way to solve a problem. This implies that you are not taking necessary precautions nor following proper procedures when removing the old cards, as desired in the second optional result.

☒ **A, B,** and **C** are incorrect because the proposed solution produces neither the required result nor any of the optional results.

7. ☑ **D.** Increase the RAM in the computer. The problem symptoms indicate that the excessive paging that is taking place on the hard disk is causing the system slowdown. The paging file in Windows 2000 is used by the operating system as virtual memory. Windows 2000 uses this file when the system is low on random access memory (RAM). If you increase the RAM in the computer, the problem will be resolved.

☒ **A** is incorrect because the WIN386.SWP file exists in Windows 9x and not in Windows 2000. The name of the Swapfile in Windows 2000 is PAGEFILE.SYS. **B** is incorrect because this will not help in resolving the problem. A better way to prevent paging is to increase the amount of RAM in the computer. **C** is incorrect because this is also not an appropriate solution. When you have two or more hard disks, creating a paging file on each disk does help, but increasing the RAM in the computer is a better way to resolve the problem.

10.02: Runtime Problems

8. ☑ **C.** The best method to uninstall an application is to use the uninstall utility that may have come with the application. If this utility exists, you should consider using it to remove the application. The built-in uninstall utility not only removes the application, but also removes any program short cuts, deletes folders created by the installation, and cleans up entries in the Registry that pertain to the application.

   ☒ **A** is incorrect because you should first check for a built-in uninstall utility within the application. **B** is incorrect because you should not delete the folder created by the application before you uninstall it properly. **D** is incorrect because you need not use a third-party utility to uninstall an application. Most newer applications come with an uninstall feature. Otherwise, you can use the Add/Remove Programs utility in the Control Panel. When you use a proper method to uninstall an application, the uninstall utility also cleans the Registry.

9. ☑ **B.** Press CTRL-ALT-DEL, select the game program in the dialog box, and click End Task. When you press CTRL-ALT-DEL together, the Close Program window opens. You can select the game program that is not responding and click the End Task button. You will notice that after a few moments another dialog box appears that prompts you to click the End Task button again. This happens because the system is not able to end the program normally.

   ☒ **A** is incorrect because if you shut down your system, you are likely to lose any unsaved data. Although you will be prompted again about whether or not you wish to shut down the system, this answer remains an incorrect option. **C** is incorrect because after you press CTRL-ALT-DEL, you should select the game program that is not responding. Pressing the End Task button will abruptly close whatever program is currently selected in the Close Program dialog box. **D** is incorrect because if you press this key combination twice, the system will abruptly shut down, and you might lose unsaved data without even getting a warning screen.

10. ☑ **B.** The Security Logs in Windows 2000 Event Viewer keep a record of unauthorized access to your system after the auditing has been configured. Remember that the Security Logs will not have any records unless auditing is properly configured. In order to track users trying to log on your system, you should audit log-on success and failure events.

☒ **A** is incorrect because System Logs keep a record of system activities, such as system boot time and whether each device driver has loaded successfully or not. **C** is incorrect because this kind of log does not exist in Windows 2000 or Windows 9*x* computers. There are only three types of logs in Windows 2000: System Logs, Security Logs, and Application Logs. In addition to these logs, Windows 2000 domain controllers have DNS (Domain Name System) logs. **D** is incorrect because this category contains the events written by applications.

11. ☑ **A.** An Illegal Operation error is produced when an application, or a particular function in the application, cannot be executed because of either a bug or an incorrect path specified somewhere in the application code. These errors can usually be removed either by reinstalling the application or by installing a patch that addresses the underlying bug.

☒ **B** is incorrect because this type of error is produced when an application attempts to carry out a function that is not permitted by the system. For example, if an application tries to capture memory space that is used either by another application or by the system itself, a General Protection Fault will occur. **C** is incorrect because this error is produced when an application is launched but the working directory is incorrectly specified in the short cut. **D** is incorrect because the symptoms stated in the question will not cause the system to lock up.

12. ☑ **B.** Increase the space in your hard disk. The symptoms of the problem indicate that the hard disk of the computer where the printer is defined does not have enough space to spool the print jobs. When a large number of print jobs are sent to the printer, the computer where the printer is installed holds the print jobs in the print spooler, that is, on the hard disk, until the print device is ready to accept the job. When this happens, however, if there is insufficient space on the hard disk, the print job cannot be spooled and therefore does not print, but no error message is displayed. You should delete any undesired files from your hard disk to free up space for the print spooler.

☒ **A** is incorrect because the printer port is not causing the problem. If you change the printer port, no one will be able to print to the printer. **C** is incorrect because the problem is not caused by low memory in your computer. **D** is incorrect because this will also not help resolve the problem. In most cases, the default timeout settings work fine.

13. ☑ **B.** When there is a problem starting up the Windows 98 system, you can boot the system using the Safe Mode and open Device Manager to remove any faulty device drivers. When Windows 9*x* systems boot using the Safe Mode, only very basic device drivers are loaded that are absolutely necessary to start the operating system. This mode is very useful in resolving problems that arise from faulty device drivers.

   ☒ **A** is an incorrect answer because this mode is available only in Windows 2000 operating system. You must be careful in the exam, because you might be given startup options that mix up Windows 9*x* and Windows 2000 operating systems. **C** is incorrect because replacing the driver files using the Command Prompt will not reflect the changes in Registry, and the problem will not be solved. **D** is incorrect because the VGA mode has nothing to do with hiding device drivers from the system. The VGA mode is used to fix display problems.

14. ☑ **D.** An incorrect printer port has been selected. The illustration shows that your friend has selected FILE as the printer port. With this setting, the printing jobs will be saved as print files in the hard disk of the computer, but will not actually be printed. Since the printer is connected to the parallel port, he should have selected LPT1 as the printer port.

   ☒ **A** and **B** are both incorrect answers because when you select to print to a file, you do not need timeout settings or print spooler settings, and these are disabled automatically. **C** is incorrect because a correct printer driver has been installed, according to the question.

15. ☑ **B.** The best source of updated files for any anti-virus utility is the manufacturer of the software. All manufacturers post new virus signature files on their Web sites, and usually these files are free to current customers. You should check the Web site of the manufacturer regularly to download the latest virus signature files.

   ☒ **A** is incorrect because Microsoft does not keep updates to any anti-virus programs on its Web site. **C** is incorrect because you will not find any anti-virus update files on the Windows 98 Setup CD-ROM. **D** is incorrect because it is not necessary to purchase a new copy of the anti-virus utility. Most anti-virus utilities only need to have updated virus signature files. All your friend needs to do is update the virus signature files that can be downloaded from the manufacturer's Web site.

16. ☑ **A.** Restart the computer with a clean boot disk, and run the FDISK /MBR command. Boot sector viruses in Windows 98 computers can be removed by starting the computer with a virus free boot disk and running the FDISK /MBR command. This command removes the virus from the master boot record.

☒ **B** is incorrect because when you boot the computer from the hard disk, the virus in the master boot record will become active. You must boot the system using a clean boot disk. **C** is incorrect because anti-virus disks are not usually bootable. Even if they were bootable, anti-virus programs do not remove viruses in the master boot record. **D** is incorrect because McAfee will not be able to clean the virus in the master boot record.

11

Networks

W indows 9*x* operating systems are mainly used in peer-to-peer networks where all computers share resources. Windows NT and Windows 2000 are network operating systems that offer centralized administration of users and network resources. Small and unsegmented peer networks can operate using the native NetBEUI protocol, whereas segmented Windows networks need a routable protocol, such as TCP/IP, which is also required for connecting the network to the Internet. Windows NT and Windows 2000 offer better control of users and network resources than Windows 9*x* operating systems, which offer only share-level or user-level access control.

The Internet is a collection of small and large networks worldwide that offers various services such as The World Wide Web, Internet email, news groups, and several other services. The Internet works on the TCP/IP protocol suite, which is the most complex network protocol, and which has several advantages over proprietary protocols. Internet Service Providers (ISPs) throughout the world provide connections to the Internet. The Domain Name System (DNS) is utilized to resolve host names to IP addresses. Internet Control Message Protocol (ICMP), TRACERT, and PING are some of the troubleshooting utilities in the TCP/IP protocol suite.

TEST YOURSELF OBJECTIVE 11.01

Networking with Windows

If you have physically installed a network adapter and loaded the appropriate driver files, you can enable sharing of local resources, such as files and printers, from the Network applet in the Control Panel. In Windows 9*x*, you can configure share-level access control by selecting different passwords for different types of access. Windows 2000 offers centralized administration by keeping security information on domain controllers. The DHCP server is used in large networks to automatically assign IP address configuration to client computers. The WINIPCFG utility in Windows 9*x* and the IPCONFIG utility in Windows 2000 enable you to view and change the IP address configuration of computers.

- Share-level security allows users to specify which of their computer's resources will be made accessible on the network, and user-level security allows or denies resource access according to each user's profile and permission settings.

■   To share resources on a network, you must first enable sharing in the Network Properties dialog box.

■   To share a resource on a Windows 9*x* computer, right-click on the resource and select Sharing, and then set the appropriate share type and passwords.

■   To access a shared resource, use the Windows Network Neighborhood.

■   You can map a local drive to a network resource by right-clicking the resource in Network Neighborhood and selecting Map Network Drive.

■   The function of a DHCP server is to automatically assign IP addresses to computers as they join the network.

■   The IP configuration utilities (WINIPCFG and IPCONFIG) can be used to request a new IP address from a DHCP server.

exam
ⓦatch
Become familiar with the configuration options available in the Network Properties page. You should be aware of what options should be configured and how they are to be configured for a given scenario. Even when networking is installed, you will not see the Sharing tab in the Properties page of a drive or folder unless you enable File Sharing. There are several ways to connect to a shared resource, such as the My Computer and Network Neighborhood icons on the desktop, Windows Explorer, and from a command prompt.

QUESTIONS

11.01: Networking with Windows

1. You are using two Windows 98 computers at home and want to network them so that you can share files and a common printer connected to one of the computers. You have purchased two network adapters, and you have just completed installing the network adapters and drivers on both computers and

connecting the two computers using a crossover UTP cable. Where should you start configuring the network?

A. From the My Computer icon on the desktop

B. From the Network applet in Control Panel

C. From the Device Manager in System Properties

D. From the Network Neighborhood icon on the desktop

2. You want to configure the TCP/IP protocol properties in your Windows 98 computer, and your network administrator has given you the address of the DHCP server. The following statements describe some of the properties of a DHCP server. Identify the incorrect statement.

A. The DHCP server assigns IP addresses and subnet masks automatically to DHCP clients.

B. The DHCP server can also assign the addresses of DNS and WINS servers.

C. The DHCP server often assigns the IP addresses for a predetermined time called a lease.

D. The DHCP server machine is either a Windows NT server or a Windows 2000 server.

3. You want to share some of your folders on a small Windows 98 peer network. Which of the following options do you have in order to control access to the shared drives and folders?

A. Read Only and Full Access

B. Full Access and Modify

C. Read Only and Take Ownership

D. Read Only and Full Control

4. You and your friend have just joined a small company and have been given two new Windows 98 computers. You are working jointly on a training project, and you want to share one of the folders related to the project with your colleague. When you open the Properties dialog box of the folder in Windows Explorer, you find that the Sharing tab does not exist. You check the Network Properties

in the Control Panel, but the Sharing tab does not exist there either, as shown in the following illustration.

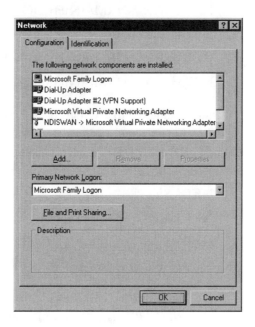

You check your friend's computer and find the same problem there. When you try to connect to the shared folders on other older computers, you do not have any problems. What could be the reason?

A. Networking software is not properly installed.

B. File and Print Sharing has not been enabled.

C. There is a problem with the network drivers.

D. An incorrect network protocol is being used.

5. The file HRPOLICY.DOC is located in the HRDOCS folder on the Windows 2000 computer named HRMAIN in the human resources department. The folder is shared as HRSHARE. Assuming that you have

appropriate permissions to work on this file, which of the following is the correct syntax for connecting to the shared folder?

A. NET USE X: \\HRMAIN\HRDOCS

B. NET USE X: \\HRMAIN\HRSHARE

C. NET USE X: \\HRMAIN\HRSHARE\HRDOCS

D. NET USE X: \\HRMAIN\HRSHARE\HRPOLICY.DOC

6. A printer connected to a Windows 98 computer named PRINTSRV is shared as HP4V1. You want to connect to this printer from the DOS prompt of your computer, named WKSTN21, and print some documents. Which of the following is the correct command to establish this connection?

A. NET USE LPT1: \\WKSTN21\HP4V1

B. NET PRINT: \\PRINTSRV\HP4V1

C. NET USE LPT1: \\PRINTSRV\HP4V1

D. NET USE LPT1: \\PRINTSRV\WKSTN21\HP4V1

7. **Current Situation:** You are the HR administrator of your company. You keep highly sensitive HR related files, which are currently not shared with anyone, on your Windows 98 computer. The company has made a new policy that allows all employees to read the newly implemented 401K plans, and some of the managers to make amendments to them. The filename of the plans is 401KPLAN.DOC, and it is stored in the HRPOLICY folder on your computer. You want to share this folder. Considering that share-level access control is set on your computer, here is what you have to accomplish.

Required Result: Share the HRPOLICY folder with other users on the Windows 98 peer-to-peer network.

Optional Desired Results:

1. All users should be able to read the files in the HRPOLICY folder, including 401KPLAN.DOC.

2. Only managers should be able to modify the files in the HRPOLICY folder.

Proposed Solution: Open Windows Explorer. Right-click the HRPOLICY folder, and then click Sharing. This opens the Sharing dialog box. Click the Shared As button and specify a Share Name for the folder. Under Access Type, click the Depends on Password button. Type two different passwords in the Read-Only Password and Full Access Password boxes, as shown in the following illustration. When this is done, advise all users of the Share Name and the Read-Only Password, and give the Share Name and Full Access Password to the managers.

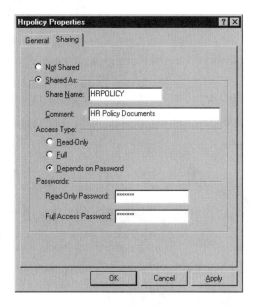

What results does the proposed solution produce?

A. The proposed solution produces the required result and both of the optional results.

B. The proposed solution produces the required result and only one of the optional results.

C. The proposed solution produces the required result but none of the optional results.

D. The proposed solution does not produce the required result.

Questions 8–10   You have been asked to report at a customer's site where your company installed a small Windows 98 peer-to-peer network last year. There seems to be some connectivity issues and sharing problems.

When you arrive at the customer's site, you find that they are using a bus network with a thin coaxial cable. After making sure that there are no issues related to cabling or termination, you start working on one of the computers.

You discover that the network, although very small, is using TCP/IP network protocol. The manager of the company tells you he uses TCP/IP because he is a bit technically minded and likes to experiment on his network.

You start your diagnosis. Some interesting problems start to surface, as described in the following questions. Answer these questions by selecting the best answer for each.

8.   Since all the computers have manually configured IP addresses, what is the quickest method to learn the IP configuration of computer A?

   A.   Check the statistics of computer A from the DHCP server.

   B.   Ping from computer B to computer A, and the IP address of computer A will be listed.

   C.   Run WINIPCFG from the command prompt of computer A.

   D.   Run WINIPCFG A: from the command prompt of computer B.

9.   There seems to be an interesting story about two of the computers. The manager of the company tells you that he configured the TCP/IP on both of these computers a few days ago. From that time onwards, only that computer which is turned on first works on the network. What could be the reason?

   A.   Both computers have the same IP address.

   B.   Both computers are configured with the same subnet mask.

   C.   The computers are using each other's IP address as a default gateway.

   D.   None of the above; this is a common problem in bus networks.

10.   After you have solved the problem of duplicate addresses, you are told that one of the computers is working as a print server. An HP LaserJet printer is

connected to this computer and is shared by all users. Sometimes it is difficult to manage print jobs when a print job gets stuck. The manager is asking for your suggestions as to how to get around this problem without having to resubmit all print jobs. What should be your answer?

A. Stop sharing the printer as soon as a job gets stuck, delete the job, and then share the printer again.

B. Open the Printer dialog box, click the Printer menu, and then click Purge Print Documents.

C. Open the Printer dialog box, click the Documents menu, and then click Pause Printing.

D. Open the Printer dialog box, select the stuck print job, and then click Cancel.

TEST YOURSELF OBJECTIVE 11.02

Internet Concepts

The Dial-up Networking icon in My Computer is the starting point for configuring your connection to the Internet. The ISP is your gateway to the Internet. The Dial-up Networking configuration should match the requirements of your ISP. The hierarchy of DNS servers on the Internet translates, or resolves, the host name in the URL to its IP address in order to take you to the intended Web site. HTTP is used to transfer Web pages written in HTML code from Web sites to your Web browser. Secure Web sites require you to enter your username and password to access the contents of their sites.

- The Internet is a huge network that connects computers all over the world.
- Most home and business users access the Internet through an ISP.
- A DNS server is typically used to translate domain names to IP addresses.
- A URL contains the transfer method (HTTP or FTP) and the domain name or IP address of the server to which you wish to connect.

■ You can use the PING utility to determine packet transfer speed and data loss from a particular Internet server, as well as its IP address.

■ To use Internet email, you must have an installed email application and access to an Internet mail server.

■ The World Wide Web is an Internet service that uses HTTP to transfer HTML pages (Web pages) from a Web server to your computer.

■ The FTP protocol cannot be used to view Web pages, but it offers fast transfer rates for downloadable files.

exam
ⓦatch

The A+ exam will focus on testing your knowledge of Internet fundamentals, and you must be able to differentiate between protocols, based on their functions and usage. The TCP/IP protocol suite has several constituent protocols, and you should be familiar with their basic functions. Make sure that you do not confuse protocols with utilities. For example, the TELNET and TRACERT utilities are parts of the TCP/IP protocol stack, but they are not protocols. You should also be familiar with the configuration options available with Dial-up Networking.

QUESTIONS

11.02: Internet Concepts

11. Which of the following protocols is used for downloading email from an email server on the Internet?

A. POP3

B. SMTP

C. TFTP

D. FTP

12. Which of the following would you use to configure additional settings for your Dial-up Networking connection to the ISP, such as automatic log-on authentication?

    A. TCP/IP settings

    B. Server Types

    C. Scripting

    D. Multilink

13. You are residing in a country in South Asia and have connected successfully to www.website.com, the servers for which are located in the United States. Which of the following utilities will you use to display detailed information of the route used by packets traveling from your computer to the said Web site?

    A. PING

    B. TRACERT

    C. NETSTAT

    D. ARP

14. **Current Situation:** You have just brought home a new Pentium III 800MHz computer already loaded with Windows 98 operating system. This is the first time you have purchased a computer for use at home. You want to configure the computer so that you can connect to the Internet and check your email. Here is what you want to accomplish.

    Required Result: Configure Dial-up Networking to connect to the Internet. The connection is to be made using an internal modem and a 1-800 number provided by the ISP.

    Optional Desired Results:

    1. The connection should be fast, and there should be no delays when the ISP server is contacted.

    2. The ISP requires a username and password, which should be supplied either manually when prompted or using a script.

Proposed Solution: Open the Dial-up Networking dialog box and double-click the Make New Connection icon. Configure the connection in the dialog boxes that follow, specifying a name for the connection and typing the phone number of the ISP. Select 115200 as the maximum speed for the connection. When this is done, right-click the new icon of the dial-up connection and select Properties. Configure the Server Types tab as shown in the following illustration.

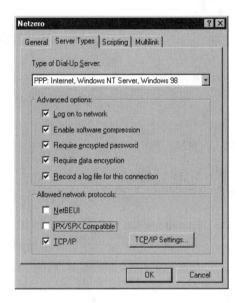

What results does the proposed solution produce?

A. The proposed solution produces the required result and both of the optional results.

B. The proposed solution produces the required result and only one of the optional results.

C. The proposed solution produces the required result but none of the optional results.

D. The proposed solution does not produce the required result.

15. You are all set to attend an interview with an ISP for a position as a technician. The interviewer is likely to ask you some questions to test your knowledge of Internet basics. What will you tell the interviewer if he asks you which of the following protocols is used to browse Web sites on the Internet?

    A. HTML

    B. ASP

    C. HTTP

    D. SNMP

16. A cable company is providing the Internet connection for your friend's home computer. You have learned from your friend that a coaxial cable is connected from a wall jack to the back of the computer. Which of the following options do you think your friend is using to make a dial-up connection to the Internet?

    A. He double-clicks the Dial-up Networking icon in My Computer.

    B. He double-clicks the Network Neighborhood icon on the desktop.

    C. He double-clicks the Shortcut to the Internet connection on the desktop.

    D. None; a cable modem does not require dial-up to connect to the Internet.

A

QUICK ANSWER KEY

Objective 11.01	
1.	B
2.	D
3.	A
4.	B
5.	B
6.	C
7.	A
8.	C
9.	A
10.	D

Objective 11.02	
11.	A
12.	C
13.	B
14.	D
15.	C
16.	D

IN-DEPTH ANSWERS

11.01: Networking with Windows

1. ☑ **B.** Networking on Windows 98 computers is configured from the Network applet in Control Panel. In the Network configuration dialog box, you can add or remove network protocols, enable file and print sharing, and add or remove network services. This is the centralized location to manage networking on Windows 9*x* computers.

   ☒ **A** is incorrect because although you can open the Control Panel and find the Network applet from the My Computer icon, this is not the best answer. **C** is incorrect because the Device Manager cannot be used to configure network properties. However, you can use it to add, remove, or update network drivers. **D** is incorrect because this icon is available only when networking is fully configured and File and Print Sharing is enabled. After the configuration is complete, you can right-click this icon to map or disconnect network drives and change network configurations.

2. ☑ **D.** This statement is not correct because the DHCP server machine need not be a Windows NT server or a Windows 2000 server. It can be any machine running a network operating system, such as UNIX. Windows computers can also get IP addresses from UNIX-based DHCP servers apart from Windows NT and Windows 2000 servers.

   ☒ **A, B**, and **C** are incorrect because these statements correctly describe the properties of DHCP servers. **A** is correct because this is the basic function of a DHCP server. **B** is correct because although these entries are optional, they are very useful in large networks for resolving host names and NetBIOS names to IP addresses. **C** is correct because the DHCP server uses leases (or durations) determined by the network administrator to make efficient use of available IP addresses.

3. ☑ **A.** The only two options for controlling access to shared resources on a Windows 98 computer in a peer network are Read Only and Full Access. These

access control security options can be configured in the Sharing Properties page of a particular drive or a folder. Select the Depends on Password option and specify two different passwords for each type of access.

☒ **B** is incorrect because there is no such access control option as Modify in Windows 98. **C** is incorrect because the Take Ownership permission exists on Windows NT and Windows 2000 computers. It is not available on Windows 98 computers. **D** is incorrect because although Full Control is equivalent to Full Access, this type of access is available only in Windows NT and Windows 2000 operating systems.

4. ☑ **B.** The reason that you cannot see the Sharing tab on the Properties dialog box of the folder is that File and Print Sharing is not enabled on both of the computers. Since the computers are new, it is possible that the technician who installed Windows 98 did not enable this feature. Unless File Sharing is enabled, you will not be able to share the folders on your computers. It is important to note that you need not select both the file and the printer sharing checkboxes if you want to share only files. To enable File Sharing only, open the Network Properties in Control Panel and click the File and Print Sharing tab. Click the "I want to be able to give others access to my files" check box and click OK. When the computer restarts after this, the Sharing tab will be added in Network Properties and in the folder properties in Windows Explorer.

☒ **A** is incorrect because there should be no problems with the installation of networking software since you can connect to shared folders on other computers. **C** is incorrect because if you can connect to other computers, there cannot be any problem with the network drivers. **D** is also incorrect because if you are able to connect to shared folders on other computers, there should be no problems with the installation of network software, network drivers, or the networking protocol. If you were trying to connect to another computer that uses a different network protocol, both computers would need to have at least one common protocol, but this is not the case here.

5. ☑ **B.** NET USE X: \\HRMAIN\HRSHARE. The correct syntax for connecting a drive, for example, drive X:, to a network share is NET USE X: \\COMPUTERNAME\SHARENAME. If the name of the computer is HRMAIN and the name of the share is HRSHARE, the command becomes NET USE X: \\HRMAIN\HRSHARE.

☒ **A** is incorrect because HRDOCS is the name of the folder. You have to use the share name of the folder and not its actual name. **C** is incorrect because only the share name of the folder is used. **D** is incorrect because this specifies the path of the file in the shared folder. You need to select only the correct command to connect to the shared folder.

6. ☑ **C.** NET USE LPT1: \\PRINTSRV\HP4V1. The correct command syntax to connect to a network printer is NET USE LPT1: \\COMPUTERNAME\ SHARENAME. Accordingly, if the computer sharing the printer is named PRINTSRV, and the name of the share is HP4V1, the correct command becomes NET USE LPT1: \\PRINTSRV\HP4V1. A printer port such as LPT1 should be specified while connecting the shared printer.

☒ **A** is incorrect because the printer is shared on the computer named PRINTSRV. The name of the computer from which the connection is being made does not appear in the command. **B** is incorrect because this command is used to view the print queue information on the printer. It does not establish the actual connection to the printer. **D** is incorrect because the name of the computer WKSTN21 has been incorrectly introduced into the command.

7. ☑ **A.** The proposed solution produces the required result and both of the optional results. The proposed solution produces the required result because you have correctly shared the HRPOLICY folder with all users so that they have access to the 401KPLAN.DOC file. The first optional result is produced because all users, by giving the specified Read-Only Password, will be able to read the files in the HRPOLICY folder. The second optional result is produced because only the managers have been given the Full Access Password. Other users will have only read-only access because they know only that password, and thus, those users will not be able to modify the 401KPLAN.DOC file stored in the shared HRPOLICY folder.

☒ **B, C,** and **D** are incorrect because the proposed solution produces the required result and both of the optional results. When the computer has share-level access, individual users, or groups of users, can be given different types of access to a shared folder, based on the passwords they specify when they access the shared folder.

8. ☑ **C.** Run WINIPCFG from the command prompt of computer A. WINIPCFG provides a quick view of the IP configuration of a computer. Whether the IP addresses are configured manually or are assigned automatically

by a DHCP server, the complete IP configuration can be viewed by running this command.

☒ **A** is incorrect because the DHCP server is not being used in the network. Even if a DHCP server were in use, you need not check the IP configuration of a computer from the DHCP server when you can do it on the local computer. **B** is incorrect because although PING can reveal the IP address of a computer, it cannot be used to view all TCP/IP parameters configured on a computer. **D** is incorrect because this is an invalid command. WINIPCFG cannot be used from remote computers.

9. ☑ **A.** Both computers have the same IP address. Remember that IP addresses are unique to each computer in a TCP/IP network. If two computers have the same IP address, only one of them will be able to use the network. In a small network, like the one in this situation, the computer that is turned on first will work. When you turn on the second computer with the same IP address, an IP address conflict will be detected, and TCP/IP will not initialize on the second computer.

☒ **B** is incorrect because the subnet mask is always the same in the network, whether it is a small network or a large network with several segments. **C** is incorrect because this is not the cause of the problem. Even if this were true, both the computers should have been capable of using the network. **D** is incorrect because this problem is not common in bus networks, nor in networks of any topology. It is certainly not a limitation or drawback of any network topology in particular.

10. ☑ **D.** Open the Printer dialog box, select the stuck print job, and then click Cancel. This is a simple question, and you should not let the answer options confuse you. The easiest way to prevent a stuck job from holding up other print jobs in the queue is to select it in the Printer window and click the Cancel button. This will not harm the other print jobs in the queue, and users can continue printing their documents.

☒ **A** is incorrect because even if you stop sharing the printer when a print job gets stuck, this will not clear the printer queue. **B** is incorrect because this will cancel all print jobs, and each user will have to resubmit their jobs, which is what the manager is trying to avoid. **C** is incorrect because this will produce no results. The printer might already have paused because of the bad print job stuck in the print queue.

11.02: Internet Concepts

11. ☑ **A.** The POP3 (Post Office Protocol version 3) is used to download email from the email servers on the Internet. POP3 is an enhanced version of the older POP protocol.

☒ **B** is incorrect because SMTP (Simple Mail Transfer Protocol) is used to send email, not to download email. **C** is incorrect because the TFTP (Trivial File Transfer Protocol) is a part of the TCP/IP protocol suite used to transfer files between two TCP/IP computers. **D** is incorrect because the FTP (File Transfer Protocol) is used to upload and download files to and from Internet FTP servers. FTP is also used for file transfers in private Intranets, and provides user authentication.

12. ☑ **C.** Scripting provides a method for writing a text file, known as script, that is passed on to the ISP when a connection has been established. This text file may contain additional options, such as providing a valid username and password, that are processed by remote servers on the Internet.

☒ **A** is incorrect because this button is located in the Server Types tab, and it allows you to select automatic or manual assignment of IP addresses. **B** is incorrect because these options are typically available and thus cannot be called *additional* options. **D** is incorrect because Multilink is used when you have more than one modem and phone line and you want to combine them for better connection bandwidth and faster speed.

13. ☑ **B.** TRACERT stands for Trace Route. This utility is a part of the TCP/IP protocol suite that is used to check the route taken by a network packet from the source computer to the destination host. The TRACERT command lists all the IP addresses of all the routers and hosts that the packet passes on its way to the destination. TRACERT is a useful troubleshooting utility and is widely used for diagnosing network problems.

☒ **A** is incorrect because the PING command tests only the connectivity between the source host and the destination. It does not trace the path taken from source to destination. The only result it displays is whether the connection exists or not. PING is also a TCP/IP troubleshooting utility. **C** is incorrect because NETSTAT gives detailed statistical information on the TCP/IP protocol and does not help in tracing the route. **D** is incorrect because the ARP (Address

Resolution Protocol) is used to translate or resolve IP addresses to MAC addresses, also known as the physical address or hardware address, of the machines.

14. ☑ **D.** The proposed solution does not produce the required result because although the connection has been configured correctly and your computer will be able to dial up the ISP server and make a connection, you will not be able to use the Internet. The reason is that neither are you using a script to supply a username and password, nor have you configured the modem properties to bring up a post-dial terminal window that prompts for these credentials. Unless you supply a username and password to the ISP server, the connection will not be completed. This also explains that the second optional result is not produced. The first optional result is not produced because you have checked all optional components. These options include logging on the network, encryption, compression, and logging activities. All these options result in delayed transmissions. You should select only those options that are necessary for a successful connection. The more options you use, the more delays you introduce. Merely selecting the highest speed for the modem does not ensure quick access to the Internet servers.

☒ **A, B,** and **C** are incorrect because the proposed solution does not produce the required result nor either of the optional results.

15. ☑ **C.** HTTP stands for Hypertext Transfer Protocol. This protocol is used to transfer pages from Web sites to your Internet Browser. You can remember this by the fact that the URL of a Web site starts with HTTP.

☒ **A** is incorrect because HTML (Hypertext Markup Language) is not a protocol, but rather a language used to build Web pages. **B** is incorrect because ASP (Active Server Pages) is also a language used to build Web pages. This language is proprietary to Microsoft and has certain advantages over HTML. **D** is incorrect because SNMP (Simple Network Management Protocol) is used to manage network services and is not involved in transferring information from Internet Web sites to Web browsers.

16. ☑ **D.** None; a cable modem does not require dial-up to connect to the Internet. When a cable company provides Internet connectivity, a cable modem is installed, and dial-up is no longer required. The cable companies typically provides a continuous connection to the Internet.

☒   **A** is incorrect because double-clicking Dial-up Networking brings up the configured Dial-up Connections window and does not actually dial any connection. **B** is incorrect because Network Neighborhood contains the list of shared resources available on a network. **C** is incorrect because no dialing is involved when Internet service is provided by a cable company. This statement describes the method for dialing the number of the ISP when you have a dial-up connection to the Internet.

CORE HARDWARE/OPERATING SYSTEM EXAMS

Part III

Practice Exams

EXAMS

A+ Core Hardware Practice Exam

A+ Operating Systems Technologies
Practice Exam

CORE HARDWARE/OPERATING SYSTEM EXAMS

A+ Core Hardware
Practice Exam

QUESTIONS

1. You have selected the NetBEUI protocol for connecting 12 computers in your office. When you configure the network properties in these computers, which of the following information must you supply in order to have a functional network?

   A. Computer name

   B. IP address

   C. Subnet mask

   D. None of the above

2. If you were to have only two IDE hard disks in a system that has two hard disk controllers, which of the following configurations would work? Select all correct answers.

   A. One hard disk as primary master and the other as secondary master

   B. One hard disk as primary master and the other as secondary slave

   C. One hard disk as secondary master and the other as primary slave

   D. One hard disk as primary master and the other as primary slave

3. You have purchased a new ATAPI CD-ROM drive that you want to install in your PC. The PC has only one hard disk controller. Which of the following statements correctly describes why the CD-ROM cannot be connected to the end connector of the ribbon cable?

   A. The ribbon cable is too short and cannot reach the CD-ROM drive.

   B. The CD-ROM has to act as a secondary hard disk because some bootable CD-ROMs can automatically upgrade the existing operating system.

   C. The hard disk needs to be the master drive, and the hard disk controller can treat the CD-ROM as a slave drive.

   D. All CD-ROMS are preconfigured as slave drives and must be connected to the middle connector of the ribbon cable.

4. Which of the following tools cannot be used for preventive maintenance of a personal computer that has two hard disks, a sound card, and a network adapter?

    A. Antistatic wrist strap

    B. Compressed air

    C. Pencil eraser

    D. Key ring knife

5. The switching mode power supply unit of your PC has an AC input range of 110 to 120 volts. Which of the following DC voltages is not available from this power supply?

    A. 3.0 volts

    B. −12 volts

    C. +5.0 volts

    D. −3.3 volts

6. Which of the following types of ESD damage is not visible immediately, but rather affects one or more components in such a way that the component may keep functioning normally?

    A. Catastrophic damage

    B. Degradation

    C. Intermittent

    D. None of the above

7. You are sharing your printer with ten other users in a small departmental workgroup running Windows 98. Since you are the supervisor of the team of users in your department, some users share your computer to store important data files containing large document drafts that you have to finalize. In recent weeks, these users have started complaining that printing on your printer has become extremely slow, and yet they find no problem when accessing files from your computer. What could be the reason for this problem?

    A. Slow network

    B. Decreasing hard disk space

C. Malfunctioning printer cable

D. Corrupt printer driver

8. If you were asked to remove a hard disk from a PC that has already been powered off, in what order would you remove the following parts? Refer to the illustration below for a view of the location of the three parts in question.

A. Screws, ribbon cable, power connector

B. Power connector, ribbon cable, screws

C. Ribbon cable, power connector, screws

D. The order is not important if the system power is off.

9. Which of the following are the benefits of non-Intel processors, compared to Intel Pentium processors with approximately equal speeds? Select all correct answers.

A. They are less expensive.

B. They have a large L1 cache.

C. They do not require an L2 cache.

D. They do not require heat sinks.

E. They can be installed in standard sockets.

10. Which of the following SCSI controllers has a maximum data transfer speed of 40 Mbps?

    A.   Fast SCSI-2 -10

    B.   Fast Wide SCSI-2 -20

    C.   Ultra-2 SCSI -40

    D.   Wide Ultra-2 SCSI -80

11. **Current Situation:** You are planning to install a SCSI adapter that will be used to replace your EIDE hard disk with four SCSI drives. Here is what you have to accomplish:

    Required Result: The SCSI adapter must be able to support a data transfer speed of at least 20 Mbps to and from the hard disks.

    Optional Desired Results:

    1.   The SCSI adapter must be able to support 12 hard disks in the SCSI chain.

    2.   The SCSI adapter should be assigned the highest priority.

    Proposed Solution: Choose a 16-bit SCSI adapter, such as the Fast Wide SCSI-2 or Wide Ultra SCSI-3, that supports 16 SCSI devices. Set the SCSI IDs of the hard disks as 2, 3, 4, and 5. Connect the SCSI hard disks to the SCSI chain and terminate the last device. Since this will be the only SCSI adapter in the computer, set its SCSI ID as 0. The proposed configuration is shown in the following illustration.

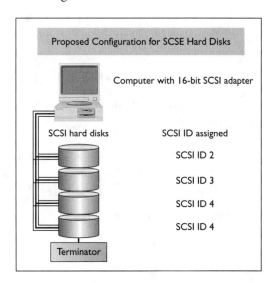

What results does the proposed solution produce?

A. The proposed solution produces the required result and both of the optional results.

B. The proposed solution produces the required result but none of the optional results.

C. The proposed solution produces the required result and only one of the optional results.

D. The proposed solution does not produce the required result.

12. Your computer dealer has advised you that the computer you are using has an ATX motherboard. Which of the following features are you unlikely to find on this motherboard? Select all correct answers.

A. Power management controlled by the BIOS

B. Integrated serial and parallel ports

C. Layout of components similar to the Baby AT

D. Support for Pentium class processors

E. DIN-5 connector for the keyboard

13. You have just received a new replacement power supply. After the power supply has been mounted inside the computer case, you want to connect it to the motherboard. Which of the following must you be careful to do when making this connection?

A. The red wires on the two connectors must be kept together.

B. The black wires on the two connectors must be kept together.

C. The black wires must be kept on the extreme ends.

D. The black wire on one connector should face the red wire on the other connector.

14. When your computer is switched on, the power supply fans start running, indicating that it is working properly, but nothing is displayed on the monitor. What should be your first step to identify the cause of the problem?

A. Listen to the number of beeps.

B. Use a different power outlet.

C. Try changing the memory modules.

D. Try changing the monitor.

15. After you connect a laser printer on a computer running Windows 98 operating system and install the printer driver, and before sharing the printer on the network, what should be your next step so that other users do not complain of printing problems?

A. Check that the network is working.

B. Print a self-test page.

C. Set permissions for other users.

D. Install a networking protocol.

16. Which of the following Intel processors is limited to 16KB of L1 cache but can access up to 512KB of external L2 cache memory?

A. Pentium III

B. Pentium II

C. Pentium Pro

D. Pentium

17. You have created a 60-page document in Microsoft Word 6.0 and formatted it using several fonts and character sizes. When you tried to send the document to the printer to obtain a hard copy, it did not print. You opened Microsoft Excel and found that a 2-page document was printing well. You also tested and found that you could print from Notepad. Which of the following would you suspect to be the likely cause of the problem?

A. The configuration of Microsoft Word 6.0

B. The large number of pages in the document

C. A corrupted printer driver

D. Incompatibility between Microsoft Word 6.0 and the printer

18. Which of the following configurations is imperative when attaching a third SCSI hard disk to a SCSI controller that already has two hard disks?

A. IRQ 15

B. I/O address

C. Terminator

D. SCSI ID

19. **Current Situation:** You are working in a publishing company that specializes in computer-aided designs. You are planning to upgrade the memory of your Pentium MMX computer that already has four modules with 256MB SDRAM each. Finances are not an issue, and you would like to double the RAM in your computer. Considering that there are only eight slots in the computer for RAM, here is what you have to do.

Required Result: Double the amount of memory in the computer.

Optional Desired Results:

1. The processor must be able to support the total amount of memory you plan to have in your computer.

2. The video performance of the computer should be enhanced by the addition of RAM.

Proposed Solution: Purchase four more modules of 256MB SDRAM and install them in the free memory slots of the computer.

What results does the proposed solution produce?

A. The proposed solution produces the required result and all of the optional results.

B. The proposed solution produces the required result and only one of the optional results.

C. The proposed solution produces the required result but none of the optional results.

D. The proposed solution produces only the required result.

20. Which of the following printers can be called a network printer and is installed as a separate node on the network? Select all correct answers.

A. Any printer that has a built-in network interface card

B. Any printer that is installed on a Windows 98 computer and shared with other users

C. Any printer installed on a Windows 2000 Server and shared on the network

D. A printer that supports networking protocols such as TCP/IP

21. A computer has gathered a lot of dust inside the case, and you want to clean it. Which of the following methods would you use if you do not want the dust to settle on other parts and accessories while cleaning?

    A. Dusting cloth

    B. Compressed air

    C. Vacuum

    D. Water

22. A company wants to connect its 100BaseTX networks which are in two buildings, 200 meters apart. The company wants the data transfer to be as fast as possible, and there should be no data loss caused by magnetic or electromagnetic interference. Which of the following cable types would you suggest?

    A. CAT-3

    B. CAT-4

    C. CAT-5

    D. Fiber optic

23. **Current Situation:** You need to install a sound card in a customer's computer. The computer has been in use for the last two years and has never been opened yet. When you open the computer, you see a lot of dust inside. Here is what you have to accomplish.

    Required Result: Clean the computer completely inside and install the sound card.

    Optional Desired Results:

    1. You must use proper tools for cleaning the computer parts.

    2. While installing the sound adapter, you must take ESD precautions.

    Proposed Solution: Open the computer case and use a cotton cloth duster to wipe the computer parts thoroughly so that they look clean. Take a cotton swab, dip it in isopropyl alcohol, and clean the expansion slot where you want to insert the sound card. Take the sound card out of its packing, put it on the table, and read the installation instructions. When you are ready, wear an antistatic wrist strap, and install the adapter in the spare expansion slot.

What results does the proposed solution produce?

A. The proposed solution produces the required result and both of the optional results.

B. The proposed solution produces the required result but none of the optional results.

C. The proposed solution produces the required result and only one of the optional results.

D. The proposed solution does not produce the required result.

24. The mouse connected to a serial port has not been working properly for the last several days. It does not move as intended and jumps rapidly from one spot to another on the monitor. Which of the following is a possible cause of the problem?

A. A crack in the serial cable

B. The IRQ or I/O address of the serial port

C. An incorrect mouse driver

D. Dirty mouse ball and rollers

25. In which of the listed situations is isopropyl alcohol more suitable for cleaning than using soapy water?

A. When isopropyl alcohol is freely available

B. When you need to observe ESD precautions

C. When soapy water is not capable of removing stains

D. When you are working on high voltage parts

26. You use your laptop computer at home and at your office. When you are working in your office, you find it difficult to work with the touch pad mouse, the LCD display, and the built-in keyboard continuously for eight hours. Which of the following options would allow you to use external components such as a color monitor or an external keyboard and mouse, considering that you also require network connectivity and sometimes use external hard disks, a scanner, and a printer?

A. Use the port replicator.

B. Use the extended port replicator.

C. Use a full docking station.

D. Any of the above.

27. You are at a customer's site to attend to a video problem. Your diagnostics have revealed that the monitor is faulty but there are no problems with the video adapter, connections, or the video configuration of the operating system. You want to disconnect the monitor and tell the customer to send it to your office for replacement. Which of the following is a correct method to accomplish this?

A. Disconnect the monitor, let it cool down, and pack it in the original packaging.

B. Disconnect the monitor, discharge it with a screwdriver, and pack it in the original packaging.

C. Disconnect the monitor, discharge it with a jumper wire, and pack it in the original packaging.

D. Disconnect the monitor, discharge it using a steel scale, and pack it in any empty box.

28. Your boss is planning to implement a network in the office based on a Token Ring standard, and he has asked you to suggest which topology would be the most suitable for building a network, supporting up to a 100 Mbps data speed, and providing fault tolerance. Which of the following should be your answer?

A. Token Ring

B. Token bus

C. FDDI

D. Token Star

29. Which of the following is a correct statement describing why the on-board L2 cache is faster than L2 cache memory on the motherboard?

A. On-board cache is another name for the L1 cache, and the L1 cache runs at the speed of the processor.

B. On-board cache works at the processor speed, whereas the external L2 cache runs at the speed of the motherboard.

C. On-board cache is usually smaller than the external L2 cache and hence, is more efficient.

D. On-board L2 cache runs at the cumulative speed of the processor and the motherboard, whereas the external cache runs at the speed of the processor only.

30. Out of the following IRQs, which will have the highest priority?

A. The IRQ used for the system timer

B. The IRQ used by the math co-processor

C. IRQ 15, when available

D. The IRQ used by the real time clock

31. Which of the following errors indicates that the ribbon cable on the floppy disk drive is not connected properly to the motherboard?

A. The light on the floppy disk drive glows continuously.

B. A:\ is not accessible.

C. Cannot read from the disk.

D. The disk in the destination drive is full.

32. When comparing paper feed mechanisms, which of the following statements incorrectly describes an advantage of inkjet printers versus dot matrix printers?

A. Inkjet printers use a friction feed mechanism, and you do not have to worry about the alignment of perforations.

B. Inkjet printers can print only on fixed-length paper.

C. You do not have to worry about separating the pages of the continuous paper after printing.

D. It is possible to print conveniently on envelopes and cards.

33. Which of the following components on the motherboard makes it possible to save CMOS BIOS settings in the computer when there is no power being supplied?

A. RAM

B. Battery

C. Cache

D. Hard disk

34. Considering that you are using Windows 98 operating system and an SVGA video adapter with high-resolution and high color display settings, which of the following is a possible reason for a flickering display on the monitor?

A. Display settings in Windows 98

B. Bad monitor cable

C. Incorrect video driver

D. Faulty monitor

35. If you were asked to install memory modules in a new Pentium III computer, and the motherboard has four sockets for installing Synchronous Dynamic RAM modules, what number of memory modules would you use to fill up the memory bank?

A. Two 16-bit DIMMs

B. One 64-bit DIMM

C. Two 16-bit RIMMs

D. Four 32-bit SIMMs

36. You have turned on your computer and can hear the power supply fan running. The system passes the POST, but you cannot hear the hard disk. What could be the cause of the problem?

A. A broken ribbon cable on the hard disk

B. Incorrect type of ribbon cable

C. Incorrect connection of the ribbon cable on the hard disk

D. Disconnected power connection on the hard disk

37. Which of the following statements about Token Ring networks is incorrect?

A. Token bus networks are based on the IEEE 802.5 standard.

B. All Token Ring networks require Multistation Access Units.

C. Token Ring networks have speeds between 4 Mbps and 16 Mbps.

D. Token Ring networks can use coaxial, twisted-pair, or fiber-optic cables.

38. Which of the following parts of a laser printer causes the paper to attract toner from the drum when the image is ready to be transferred?

    A. A positive charge on the paper

    B. The transfer corona wire

    C. The fusing rollers

    D. The cleaning blade

39. EGA monitors will connect to which of the following types of D connectors?

    A. DB-9 male

    B. DB-9 female

    C. DB-15 male

    D. DB-25 female

40. A customer has reported a certain problem in his computer. You arrive at his site, and he says he does not remember if any error codes were displayed on the screen. What should your first step be in resolving the problem?

    A. Try changing suspected components one by one.

    B. Try to reproduce the problem.

    C. Write down the details of the problem.

    D. Ask if the customer has made any changes recently.

41. The dot matrix printer you are using has been producing print outputs that show a white line across the width of the page on every line. Which of the following parts of the printer needs replacement?

    A. Ribbon cartridge

    B. Tractor feed

    C. Printer driver

    D. Print head

42. A bubblejet printer is producing print outputs that are not readable. The strange characters printed are not what the user intended to print, and he has asked for your help. Which of the following cannot be a cause of the problem?

    A. Incorrect printer driver

B. Dirty ink cartridge

C. Communication problem

D. Bad parallel port

43. Which of the following components is used in bus networks to prevent signals from bouncing back and forth in the cable?

A. Vampire tap

B. BNC T-connector

C. 50-Ohm coaxial cable

D. 50-Ohm terminator

44. **Current Situation:** The company where you work as a helpdesk technician has installed a Windows NT server. Nearly 50 desktop users, including those from the accounting and marketing departments, store their files on this server. Since this is the only server in the office and it is heavily loaded, management wants to install one more server. Here is what you have to do.

Required Result: Install the second server so that data is always available to users in case one of the servers fails.

Optional Desired Results:

1. The solution should also provide a mechanism to distribute the load between the two servers.

2. The data should be equally divided between the servers.

Proposed Solution: Install the second server as a mirror of the existing server.

What results does the proposed solution produce?

A. The proposed solution produces the required result and both of the optional results.

B. The proposed solution produces the required result and only one of the optional results.

C. The proposed solution produces the required result but none of the optional results.

D. The proposed solution does not produce the required result.

45. You have just added a second hard disk to your computer. When the cabling is complete and the power supply is connected, you put back the computer cover. Considering that you do not want to partition the hard disk, which of the following should be your first action immediately after switching on the computer?

    A. Check to see that the hard disk is recognized by the BIOS.

    B. Run FDISK program.

    C. Format the drive.

    D. Test the drive by copying some files onto it.

46. A customer has reported that his inkjet printer, connected to the LPT1 port of his Pentium II 333MHz computer, is giving a communication error when he tries to print. He said that the printer power is on, but there is no activity when he sends a print document. Which of the following would you suspect to be the cause of the problem?

    A. The printer driver

    B. The configuration of the word processor

    C. The printer cable and connection

    D. The inkjet cartridge

    E. The LPT port

47. Which of the following statements is correct when installing an EIDE hard disk as a primary slave drive?

    A. The drive must be connected to the end connector on the ribbon cable with the jumper set to slave position.

    B. The drive must be the first drive to be installed in the system and it must hold the operating system.

    C. The drive must be connected to the middle connector with the jumper set to the slave position.

    D. The primary slave drive cannot work unless a secondary master hard disk is present.

48. Antistatic wrist straps prevent the electrostatic discharge that can cause some computer components to fail. In which of the following cases should you not wear them when working on computers and printers?

    A. When you are using an antistatic mat

    B. When you are sure that you will not touch any static-sensitive device

    C. When you are working on high voltage equipment

    D. When you have used antistatic spray

49. A customer is telling you on the phone that none of the 12 computers in his 10BaseT Ethernet network is able to connect to the others. He could not give any other information beyond this. Which of the following could be causing the problem?

    A. Excessive network traffic

    B. Broken cable on one of the computers

    C. Faulty hub

    D. Missing terminator

50. The PC you are now using was upgraded some time ago. Several components in this PC were replaced during the upgrade, including the floppy disk drive, which used to be a 5.25-inch drive. The new drive can read only double-density, 3.5-inch floppy disks. If you were to replace this drive with a high-density drive, which of the following floppy disks would you be able to read from? Select all correct answers.

    A. 720KB

    B. 1.2MB

    C. 1.44MB

    D. 2.88MB

IN-DEPTH ANSWERS

1. ☑ **D.** None of the above. The NetBEUI protocol is the simplest of all protocols to configure. You have to install only the protocol; no other configuration is necessary. In Windows 98, open the Network dialog box from Control Panel, click Add, select Protocol, and select NetBEUI from the Microsoft list under the list of manufacturers.

    ☒ **A** is incorrect because the computer name is usually specified during the installation of the operating system. However, you may specify a different computer name during networking installation. **B** and **C** are incorrect because these addresses are required when installing the TCP/IP protocol.

2. ☑ **A** and **D. A** is correct because when the two hard disks are connected to the end connectors of the primary and secondary connectors, they will become primary master and secondary master, respectively. **D** is correct because when both the hard disks are connected to the ribbon cable of the primary hard disk controller, the one connected to the end connector will become the primary master drive, and the other connected to the middle connector will act as primary slave, provided the configuration jumper is set to the slave position.

    ☒ **B** is incorrect because the secondary slave drive cannot work without a secondary master drive. **C** is incorrect because one of the hard disks has to be the primary master. The other hard disk can be either primary slave or secondary master.

3. ☑ **C.** The hard disk needs to be the master drive, and the hard disk controller can treat the CD-ROM as a slave drive. The system that has only one hard disk controller must have the hard disk operating as primary master drive. The end connector on the ribbon cable will thus be reserved for the hard disk drive. The ATAPI CD-ROM can be connected to the middle connector, and the hard disk controller can treat the CD-ROM drive as a slave drive.

    ☒ **A** is incorrect because this is not the reason that the CD-ROM cannot be connected to the end connector. **B** is incorrect because the CD-ROM does not have to be a secondary master. Moreover, bootable CD-ROMs do not automatically upgrade the existing operating system. *Bootable* simply means that the system can use a CD-ROM to boot up when the boot sequence in BIOS is appropriately configured or when the BIOS cannot find an operating system on the hard disk. **D** is incorrect because all CD-ROMs are not preconfigured as slave drives.

4. ☑ **D.** A small knife attached to a key ring can be found with several PC technicians. This knife is an improper tool for any kind of maintenance job. A knife is sometimes needed to remove residue on metallic surfaces, but the only type of knife that should be used for this purpose is a rubber knife. A rubber knife is hard enough to remove this residue. A metallic knife must not be used in any case. Note that the question mentions two hard disks, a sound card, and an adapter. Although you must read each question carefully before deciding on an answer, beware of any details or statements such as this that are included just to draw your attention away from the main objective and waste your time.

☒ **A** is incorrect because this is a common safety device used when performing preventive maintenance and repairing computers. Antistatic wrist straps prevent electrostatic discharge from your body. **B** is incorrect because compressed air is used to blow dust off components inside the computer. **C** is incorrect because a pencil eraser is commonly used to clean dirty contacts.

5. ☑ **A.** 3.0 volts. The switching power supply unit of PCs typically gives DC voltages of 3.3, 5.0, and 12 volts. 3.0 volts is not a standard DC output from the power supply unit of the PC.

☒ **B, C,** and **D** are incorrect options because –12 volts, +5.0 volts, and –3.3 volts DC voltage output is available from the power supply unit. The three standard DC voltage outputs from the power supply unit are +3.3, +5.0, and +12 volts.

6. ☑ **B.** Degradation. When ESD damage is not visible immediately but has harmed one or more components, it is known as degradation. Although it does not damage any specific component immediately, it can cause intermittent problems. This is more harmful than catastrophic damage caused by ESD.

☒ **A** is incorrect because catastrophic ESD damage is visible immediately and damages the component. The affected component has to be replaced. Catastrophic ESD damage is less harmful than degradation because the effect of ESD can be known and the problem can be resolved by replacing the component that failed because of the ESD damage. **C** is incorrect because

ESD damage is classified broadly into only two categories: catastrophic and degradation. **D** is incorrect because we have a correct answer for the given symptoms. Note that the notorious options *none of the above*, *all of the above*, and *any of the above* will appear in several questions on the A+ exam.

7. ☑ **B.** Decreasing hard disk space. When a printer is shared on the network, print jobs from network computers are first stored on the hard disk of the computer where the printer is installed and shared. If this computer is low on hard disk space, as indicated in the question, the printing will become slow. To resolve this problem, make more free space on your hard disk so that print jobs can be expedited.

☒ **A** is incorrect because users are not finding any problems when accessing shared files on your computer. **C** is incorrect because a bad printer cable will not cause printing to slow down. **D** is incorrect because if the printer driver were corrupted, the problem would show up as incorrect print outputs, such as garbled prints, rather than slow printing.

8. ☑ **B.** Power connector, ribbon cable, screws. The correct order for removal of a hard disk is to first remove the power connector and then the ribbon cable. When the disk is free of cables, you can remove the screws. This order is important because the ribbon cable could be pulled accidentally if the screws were removed first, or the hard disk could be damaged while pulling the power connector or the ribbon cable.

☒ **A** is incorrect because you must remove the power connector first. This is done because a little force is required to pull the power connector, and it is best to pull it when the hard disk is held firmly in its cage by mounting screws. **C** is incorrect because the power connector must be removed before removing the ribbon cable. **D** is incorrect because the order of removal does matter, whether or not the system is powered off. You must make sure that the system power is turned off before removing the computer case.

9. ☑ **A** and **E.** They are less expensive and can be installed in standard sockets. Non-Intel processors come in speeds that closely match the speeds of Intel Pentium processors. However, they are comparatively less expensive than the corresponding Intel processors and can be installed in standard processor sockets.

☒ **B** is incorrect because most non-Intel processors have a smaller or equal size L1 cache when processors of equal speeds are compared. **C** is incorrect because the majority of processors use an L2 cache for enhanced performance. **D** is incorrect because all processors, regardless of their speed or manufacturer, require a heat sink for dissipation of the heat generated during the normal working of the computer.

10. ☑ **C.** The maximum data transfer speed of the Ultra-2 SCSI controller is 40 Mbps. The Ultra-2 SCSI is an 8-bit SCSI controller. The wide version of this SCSI controller is a 16-bit controller known as a Wide Ultra-2 SCSI that supports data transfer rates of up to 80 Mbps.

☒ **A** is incorrect because the Fast SCSI-2 is an 8-bit controller that supports up to only a 10 Mbps data transfer rate. **B** is incorrect because this SCSI controller is also limited to only a 20 Mbps data transfer rate. However, the Double Wide SCSI-2 version, which is a 32-bit system, does support 40 Mbps. **D** is incorrect because this SCSI controller is not limited to a 40 Mbps data transfer rate, but rather can support up to 80 Mbps.

11. ☑ **C.** The proposed solution produces the required result and only one of the optional results. The required result is produced because the suggested 16-bit SCSI adapters offer 20 Mbps data transfer speeds. The Fast Wide SCSI-2 adapter and the Wide Ultra SCSI-3 offer speeds of 20 Mbps and 40 Mbps, respectively. The first optional result is produced because both of these adapters support up to 16 SCSI devices in the chain. Configuring SCSI IDs of the hard disks, and terminating the last disk in the chain, ensures that the devices will work properly.

☒ **A, B,** and **D** are incorrect because the proposed solution produces the required result and only one of the optional results. The second optional result is not produced because the SCSI adapter must be assigned ID 7, the highest priority, as opposed to ID 0, as suggested in the proposed solution. The SCSI adapter is always given ID 7, regardless of the type of SCSI system and the number of devices it can support.

12. ☑ **C** and **E.** The ATX motherboard has a completely different component layout compared to the Baby AT motherboard. The keyboard connector is also a mini-DIN-5, rather than a DIN-5. Besides these dissimilar features, ATX motherboards have an additional ±3.3vDC power supply and a single power supply connector to the motherboard.

☒ **A, B,** and **D** are incorrect answers because these features *are* present on ATX motherboards. ATX motherboards have power management features that are typically controlled by the system BIOS, they have serial and parallel ports integrated into the motherboard, and they support Pentium class processors.

13. ☑ **B.** The black wires on the two connectors must be kept together. When connecting the P8 and P9 power connectors to the motherboard, the black wires on the two connectors must be kept together. This essentially means that these wires will be connected to the center of the connector on the motherboard. Any other orientation of the power connectors will not work.

☒ **A** is incorrect because it is physically not possible to do this. One of the connectors has a red wire (+5-vDC) and the other has an orange wire (power good signal) on the end. **C** is incorrect because the computer will not work with this orientation. **D** is incorrect because the black wires on both connectors should face each other.

14. ☑ **A.** When nothing is displayed on the monitor, the first thing you must do is listen to the number of beeps that the computer produces during the POST. These beeps are a clear indication of the type of problem the computer has encountered. For example, if there is only one long beep, it indicates that the POST has completed and there is some non-fatal error, such as a bad video adapter or a faulty monitor.

☒ **B** is incorrect because there is no problem with the AC power supply since the power supply fan is working. **C** is incorrect because this is not the first action you should take to resolve an unknown problem. **D** is also incorrect because you must first diagnose the problem properly before changing any parts.

15. ☑ **B.** Whether or not you share the printer with other users, you should print a self-test page immediately after the installation is done. This ensures that the printer has been installed correctly with the appropriate printer driver. When you are satisfied that the printer installation is done and you can print successfully from your computer, which will be evident from the test page, you can share the printer with other users. The self-test page option is available in the Properties dialog box of all printers.

☒ **A** is incorrect because this is not the first thing you should do after installing the printer. Network problems, if there is one, can be checked later if a user complains that he is not able to connect to the shared printer. **C** is incorrect because it is not possible to set permissions for individual users in Windows 98.

The printer is either shared by all users or not shared at all. **D** is incorrect because if you are sharing your computer with others on the network, you need not install a separate networking protocol for sharing the printer. Note that the answer options seem to distract your attention away from the actual question. You must concentrate on the *first* thing you should do after installing the printer.

16. ☑ **D.** Pentium processors with speeds ranging from 60MHz to 200MHz are limited to 16KB of internal L1 cache memory but can support up to 512KB of external L2 cache on the motherboard.

☒ **A** is incorrect because these processors have 32KB of built-in L1 cache memory. **B** is incorrect for the same reason. These processors also have 32KB of internal L1 cache. **C** is incorrect because although these processors have a built-in L1 cache of 16MB, the L2 cache is on board and not on the motherboard. The on-board L2 cache runs at the speed of the processor.

17. ☑ **A.** The configuration of Microsoft Word 6.0. The likely cause of the problem is that this application is not configured to use the connected printer, since the printer is printing documents sent from other applications. Check to ensure that the application is configured correctly and that the configuration matches the printer settings.

☒ **B** is incorrect because printers do not limit the number of pages that you can print, unless you request a specific number of pages for printing from the application. **C** is incorrect because if the printer driver were corrupted, you would not have been able to print from any other application. In this case, the printer is printing documents from Microsoft Excel and Notepad, which means that the printer driver files are not corrupted. **D** is incorrect because compatibility is not an issue between printers and applications. However, printers have different drivers for different operating systems.

18. ☑ **D.** From the given options, the only configuration required by the third SCSI hard disk when attaching it to the system will be the SCSI ID. All SCSI devices in the SCSI chain are identified by a unique SCSI ID, and no two SCSI devices can share the same SCSI ID.

☒ **A** and **B** are incorrect because SCSI devices require SCSI IDs as opposed to IRQ addresses. Similarly, the I/O address is assigned to the SCSI controller, not to individual SCSI devices. **C** is incorrect because the system is already using other SCSI devices, so a terminator must already be present in the SCSI bus.

19. ☑ **B.** The proposed solution produces the required result and only one of the optional results. The required result is produced because four more modules of SDRAM will increase the current amount of RAM to 2GB, which is double the existing RAM. Since the computer has eight slots for RAM and four slots are already in use by existing SDRAM modules, it is possible to add four more SDRAM modules of 256MB each. The first optional result is produced because the Pentium MMX computer supports up to 4GB of RAM. The second optional result is not produced because the addition of SDRAM modules will not enhance the video performance of the computer. You must use a video adapter that has a fairly high capacity of Video RAM (VRAM). VRAM is specifically used for enhanced video performance.

    ☒ **A, C,** and **D** are incorrect because the proposed solution produces the required result and only one of the optional results. The second optional result for enhancing video performance is not produced. To satisfy this requirement, you should use another video adapter with larger VRAM.

20. ☑ **A** and **D.** Any printer that has a built-in network interface card and that supports networking protocols such as TCP/IP. Although any printer can be considered as a network printer when it is shared on the network, the only printer that can become a node on the network is one that has a built-in network interface card. True network printers are those that are connected directly to the hub or switch as a node and can either be accessed directly using a networking protocol such as TCP/IP, or through a print server.

    ☒ **B** is incorrect because a printer cannot be called a network printer only because it is shared on the network. **C** is incorrect for similar reasons. A printer installed either on Windows 98 or Windows 2000 Server may or may not have a built-in network interface card that enables it to directly connect to the network.

21. ☑ **C.** The best way to remove dust is to use a vacuum cleaner to suck up the dust settled on the internal components of the computer. This is the preferred method because the vacuum cleaner will remove the dust without allowing it to settle on other parts. Vacuum cleaners come with a variety of nozzle sizes, and an appropriate nozzle to use would be one that can reach most of the areas inside the computer.

    ☒ **A** is incorrect because cleaning with a dust cloth will cause dust removed from one component to settle on other components. **B** is incorrect because when you blow dust off a component using compressed air, the dust will settle on other internal components of the computer, as well as on the external devices, such as the mouse, mouse pad, keyboard, and speakers. **D** is incorrect because dust inside the computer should never be removed using water or a damp cloth.

22. ☑ **D.** The fiber-optic cable is the best cable for connecting networks that are separated by large distances. Apart from providing high data speeds, this cable is also immune to magnetic and electromagnetic interference, because the data travels in the form of optical (light) signals. Moreover, this cable can be used in lengths up to 2,000 meters without any attenuation of signal.

☒ **A** and **B** are incorrect because these cables do not support the 100 Mbps data speeds required by the 100BaseTX networks. **C** is incorrect because although this cable can support up to 100 Mbps data speeds, it is not suitable because it is prone to magnetic and electromagnetic interference. CAT-5 also cannot be used in distances over 100 meters.

23. ☑ **D.** The proposed solution does not produce the required result because the computer cannot be cleaned completely using a cotton cloth duster. You must use either compressed air or a vacuum to clean the computer properly. Moreover, the expansion slots on the motherboard must not be cleaned using a cotton swab dipped in isopropyl alcohol. Instead, a vacuum cleaner should be used. The first and second optional results are not produced because you are not taking all ESD precautions, nor are you handling the sound card properly. When you are changing an adapter or installing a new one, you should take static precautions right from the beginning. The proposed solution suggests you wear the antistatic wrist strap only when inserting the adapter in the expansion slot. You should begin the process by placing an antistatic mat on the table where you can rest the spare adapters temporarily. The new adapter must not be taken out of the protective cover until you are ready to insert it in the expansion slot. If you need to read the installation instructions, you should do this before taking the adapter out of the protective cover, or better still, before you open the computer cover. If it is necessary to configure some settings manually on the card, you should do this while wearing the antistatic wrist strap.

☒ **A, B,** and **C** are incorrect because the proposed solution produces neither the required result nor either of the optional results.

24. ☑ **D.** Dirty mouse ball and rollers. The mouse usually moves on a mouse pad that is not covered and thus collects dust. This dust is picked up by the rubber ball on the bottom of the mouse and is transferred to internal rollers inside the roller compartment. This causes the mouse pointer to "jump" across the screen. Cleaning the rubber ball and rollers inside the roller compartment will solve the problem.

    ☒ **A** is incorrect because if the serial cable were cracked, the mouse would not work at all. **B** is incorrect because this does not cause the specified problem. However, a resource conflict can occur causing a total failure if more than one device is using the same resources. For example, if a modem and a mouse were using the same IRQ, only one of them would be able to work at a time. **C** is incorrect because if this were the case, the mouse would not have worked at all. Note that the question says, "The mouse has not been working *properly* for the last several days."

25. ☑ **C.** When soapy water is not capable of removing stains. This question is quite simple. You have to use common sense to answer it. When there are stains on computer parts, you can use isopropyl alcohol instead of soapy water to remove them. However, care should be taken not to use water on gold contacts, LCD displays, or power supplies.

    ☒ **A** is incorrect because this should not be the criterion for deciding what method to use for cleaning. Isopropyl alcohol should be used only when you cannot clean certain plastic parts using soapy water. **B** is incorrect because ESD precautions should be taken in addition to being cautious about the cleaning method used. Isopropyl alcohol does not protect computer equipment from ESD. **D** is incorrect because neither water nor isopropyl alcohol should be used on high voltage parts.

26. ☑ **C.** The full docking station provides access to most components and peripherals that a regular desktop system uses. When using a docking station, you simply have to plug your laptop computer into the docking station and restart it. The laptop disables the built-in components for which it finds an alternative attached to the docking station.

    ☒ **A** is incorrect because the port replicator has limited functionality and does not allow all of the external components mentioned in the question to be used externally. **B** is incorrect because the extended port replicator will also not be an appropriate alternative in the given situation. **D** is incorrect because only a docking station can facilitate connection to all the external devices mentioned in the question.

27. ☑ **B.** After you disconnect the monitor, you should discharge it using a screwdriver and then pack it in the original packing. Discharging it is necessary because the monitor can cause electric shock even after it is disconnected. The original packaging must be used because it is specially designed to protect the monitor from damage during transportation.

☒ **A** is incorrect because after you disconnect the monitor from power, it must be discharged before you pack it. **C** is incorrect because if you use a jumper wire for discharging the monitor, you might get an electric shock. The tool used for discharging must have an insulated handle. **D** is incorrect because neither should a steel scale be used for discharging the monitor because it can give you an electric shock, nor should the monitor be packed in an empty box. For discharging, use a tool that has an insulated handle, and use the original packaging to pack the monitor in order to protect it from transportation damages.

28. ☑ **C.** FDDI stands for Fiber-Distributed Data Interface. This network topology is based on Token Ring but uses fiber-optic cable that supports a 100 Mbps data transfer speed. The dual-ring FDDI network consists of two rings to provide fault tolerance. If one of the rings breaks down, the other ring takes over, and the network continues to function.

☒ **A** is incorrect because Token Ring networks support a maximum data transfer speed of 16 Mbps. **B** is incorrect because this network supports a maximum speed of 4 Mbps. Neither Token Ring nor token bus networks provide any kind of fault tolerance. **D** is incorrect because a Token Star network is actually a Token Ring network that uses a Multistation Access Unit (MAU). These networks may or may not support a 100 Mbps speed, depending on whether or not they use either a CAT5 cable or fiber-optic cable.

29. ☑ **B.** On-board cache works at the processor speed, whereas the external L2 cache runs at the speed of the motherboard. On-board simply means that it is housed in the processor casing and is able to run at the speed of the processor. The L2 cache on the motherboard is able to run only at the bus speed of the motherboard, typically attaining a maximum speed of 133MHz.

☒   **A** is incorrect because the L2 cache is not another name for the L1 cache. An L2 cache may be either an on-board cache (built inside the processor package) or an external cache (on the motherboard), whereas the L1 cache is on board. However, it is true that the L1 cache runs at the processor speed. **C** is incorrect because the on-board cache may or may not be smaller than the external cache, and this is not the reason that the on-board cache is faster than the external cache. **D** is incorrect because the on-board cache runs at the speed of the processor, not the cumulative speed of the processor and the motherboard.

30. ☑ **A.** The IRQ used for the system timer. The system timer is responsible for synchronizing the processor speed with various components. IRQ 0 is assigned to the system timer, and since it is a critical component of the computer, it is given the highest priority.

☒   **B** is incorrect because the highest priority is given to IRQ 0. **C** is incorrect because although IRQ 15 is the highest IRQ number available, it does not have the highest priority. **D** is incorrect because the real-time clock is responsible for maintaining only the actual date and time. The system timer with IRQ 0 is the most important function and hence, has the highest priority.

31. ☑ **A.** A continuously glowing light on the floppy disk drive indicates that the ribbon cable connecting the floppy disk drive is not connected properly or is connected in reverse orientation.

☒   **B** is incorrect because this error is displayed when there is no disk in the floppy disk drive and you are trying to read from or write to the drive. **C** is incorrect because this error is produced when the system is unable to read from the floppy disk because either the file or the floppy disk is corrupted. **D** is incorrect because this error indicates that you are trying to save a file on the floppy disk and there is not enough free space left.

32. ☑ **B.** It is incorrect to say that inkjet printers can print only on fixed-length paper. Inkjet printers allow you to print on a variety of paper sizes and even on envelopes and cards.

☒   **A** is an incorrect answer because it is true that inkjet printers use a paper tray from which friction feed rollers pull the paper into the printer. **C** is an incorrect answer because inkjet printers usually do not use continuous paper, but instead use a stack of paper already cut to size. **D** is incorrect because it is possible to print envelopes and cards using an inkjet printer. The dot matrix printer typically uses continuous paper with a tractor feed mechanism, which makes it difficult to print on envelopes and cards.

33. ☑ **B.** The BIOS settings in the CMOS chips are retained in the absence of power to the computer by a battery commonly known as a CMOS battery. This battery is charged when the computer is powered and supplies power to the CMOS chips when the computer is turned off.

☒ **A** is incorrect because the BIOS settings are not stored in RAM, but on CMOS chips. **C** is incorrect because the purpose of cache memory is to keep ready those instructions that the processor might be calling for. **D** is incorrect because again, the hard disk is not used for storing CMOS BIOS settings. Moreover, the question asks for *a component on the motherboard,* and the hard disk is not installed on the motherboard.

34. ☑ **D.** A faulty monitor is usually the cause of a flickering display. Since monitors cannot be repaired in the field, it is advisable to replace the faulty monitor in order to resolve the problem.

☒ **A** is incorrect because incorrect display settings usually cause problems such as a missing display, an improper display size, and overlapped images. **B** is incorrect because this will not cause a flickering display. **C** is incorrect because if the video driver were incorrect, the operating system would not have been able to utilize full video resolution and color depth.

35. ☑ **B.** The memory bank will be filled up using only one 64-bit DIMM. When installing RAM modules, you must remember that the memory bank does not refer to the number of slots on the motherboard, but the width of the address bus. Since the Pentium III motherboard supports a 64-bit address bus, you will need at least one 64-bit DIMM to fill up the memory bank.

☒ **A** is incorrect because a DIMM is not available in a 16-bit bus width. DIMMs have a 64-bit bus width. **C** is incorrect because you need at least four 16-bit RIMMs (16MB × 4 = 64MB) to fill up the memory bank. **D** is incorrect because the question clearly states that the motherboard has slots for Synchronous Dynamic RAM (SDRAM), and SDRAM typically comes in DIMMs. SIMM modules cannot be installed in DIMM slots.

36. ☑ **D.** Disconnected power connection on the hard disk. The hard disk produces sound only when the power is connected to it. If there is no power connection, the hard disk will not turn, and there will be no sound.

☒ **A** is incorrect because a broken ribbon cable will cause data access problems. **B** is incorrect because it is unlikely that the ribbon cable has been changed, since it is not mentioned in the question. **C** is also incorrect because this will cause hard disk access problems. In all the ribbon connection problems stated in options A, B, and C, the hard disk will still produce a turning sound when there is a power connection.

37. ☑ **B.** All Token Ring networks require Multistation Access Units. The Multistation Access Unit (MAU) is used only in Token Ring networks that have the star topology. This is also known as a Token Ring hub. Each computer is connected to the MAU in a star fashion, but the data travels in a ring fashion.

☒ **A, C,** and **D** are incorrect answers because all these statements are true. The Token Ring is based on the IEEE 802.5 standard. A variation is the token bus topology that is defined in IEEE 802.4 and uses coaxial cable instead of twisted-pair cable. Token Ring networks support either 4 Mbps or 16 Mbps data speeds, depending on the type of topology being used. Token Ring networks can use coaxial cable (token bus), twisted-pair cable (Token Ring), or fiber-optic cable (Fiber-Distributed Data Interface).

38. ☑ **A.** The positive charge on the paper attracts the negatively charged toner from the photosensitive drum. The transfer corona wire applies this positive charge on the paper after the image has been *developed* on the drum with toner powder. Since opposite charges attract each other, when the positively charged paper moves under the drum, it attracts the negatively charged toner.

☒ **B** is incorrect because it is responsible for applying the positive charge on the paper. This positive charge attracts the toner. **C** is incorrect because the fusing rollers are not responsible for transferring the toner from drum to paper. The paper moves to the fusing assembly for melting (or *fusing*) of the toner after the image has been transferred to the paper. **D** is incorrect because the cleaning blade is used to clean the drum after the image has been transferred to the paper and the printer is ready to receive a new page for printing.

39. ☑ **B.** DB-9 female. EGA (Enhanced Graphics Adapter) monitors have a DB-9 male connector. These monitors are connected to EGA video adapters that have a female DB-9 connector for attaching the monitor. There are only two rows of pins in DB-9 connectors—5 pins in the upper row and 4 pins in the lower row. The VGA and SVGA video adapters and monitors have DB-15

female connectors, and the pins are divided into 3 rows. Serial ports, CGA video adapters, and CGA monitors also have DB-9 connectors.

☒ **A** is incorrect because the EGA monitor has a DB-9 male connector, and a male connector cannot be attached to another male connector. **C** is incorrect because the DB-15 male connector is found on VGA and SVGA monitors. **D** is incorrect because this type of connector is used for LPT1 and LPT2 parallel ports. Serial ports on some computers also use DB-25 connectors.

40. ☑ **B.** If the customer is unable to provide sufficient information, the first step in successfully diagnosing a problem is to try to reproduce the problem. This will allow you to make your own observations. In such cases, the customer can help you reproduce the problem by outlining the steps he followed when the problem occurred.

☒ **A** is incorrect because you must not change any component unless you are absolutely sure that the component is faulty. **C** is incorrect because the customer does not remember any error codes, so you will not be able to get the details unless you reproduce the problem. **D** is incorrect because if this were the cause of the problem, the customer most likely would have informed you.

41. ☑ **D.** Print head. The defect symptoms indicate that one of the pins of the dot matrix printer is not being activated. This causes the print output to look like a continuous white line on paper. Replacing the print head will resolve the problem.

☒ **A** is incorrect because the problem is caused by a missing print head pin and not the ribbon cartridge. **B** is incorrect because tractor feed problems usually cause paper movement problems. **C** is incorrect because if the printer driver were incorrect or corrupted, either the print output would have been garbled or there would be no print output at all.

42. ☑ **B.** A dirty ink cartridge is certainly not the cause of the problem. Ink cartridges should be suspected when there are problems in the quality of the print output or if there is no printing at all, caused by an empty cartridge.

☒ **A, C,** and **D** are incorrect because any of these problems can cause garbled printing or unreadable characters. An incorrect printer driver, a communication problem between the computer and the printer, or a bad parallel port can all cause garbled print output.

43. ☑ **D.** A 50-Ohm terminator is used to terminate the ends of a coaxial cable in bus networks. The terminator prevents signals from bouncing back and forth on the wire. If the terminators are not present on the ends of the coaxial cable, the bus network cannot function.

    ☒ **A** is incorrect because the vampire tap is a connector that connects a computer to the coaxial cable. **B** is incorrect because the T-connector is used to connect a network adapter to the running coaxial cable. **C** is incorrect because the cable cannot be used to terminate itself.

44. ☑ **C.** The proposed solution produces the required result but none of the optional results. The required result is produced because a mirror server will provide access to data even if one of the servers fails. A mirror server keeps a copy of the data from the main server. The first optional result is not produced because the mirror server will not provide any load balancing. To achieve load balancing, you must build a cluster server. Cluster servers provide not only fault tolerance but also load balancing. When two servers in the cluster are working, they share the load, and when one of them breaks down, the other one takes over. The second optional result is not produced because mirror servers do not distribute data among themselves, but rather each server keeps a full copy of the data. Even if you install a cluster server, the data will not be distributed between the two servers.

    ☒ **A, B,** and **D** are incorrect because the proposed solution produces only the required result. The two optional results are not produced.

45. ☑ **A.** The first thing you must do immediately after installing a hard disk is check whether it is recognized by the computer BIOS or not. Every PC displays BIOS information upon startup that includes information on hard disks, floppy disks, keyboards, and so on. Although most of the newer BIOSs automatically recognize the hard disk types, it is best to check the BIOS display to make sure that the disk will work properly.

    ☒ **B** is incorrect because this utility is used to create or delete disk partitions. The question states that the hard disk will not have any partitions. Although it is not possible to use a hard disk without first partitioning it, the question is asking about your first action after switching on the computer. Partitioning has to be done *after* it is verified that the hard disk is being recognized by the BIOS. **C** is incorrect because you must first check that the hard disk is recognized by the system BIOS. Formatting can be done later. **D** is incorrect because the drive has to be formatted before it can be used for copying data.

46. ☑ **C.** The printer cable and connection. The communication error indicates that the computer is not able to communicate with the printer. This problem is caused by either a loose connection or a detached printer cable. Check to ensure that the printer is connected properly. If the connection is perfect, the cable might have become faulty. Replace the cable and try printing again.

☒ **A** is incorrect because an incorrect printer driver usually does not produce a communication error. **B** is incorrect because again, this will not produce a communication error. **D** is incorrect because insufficient ink in the cartridge is not a cause of the problem. **E** is incorrect because the printer had been working earlier.

47. ☑ **C.** The drive must be connected to the middle connector with the jumper set to the slave position. The hard disk is installed as a slave drive by connecting it to the middle connector on the ribbon cable. The configuration jumper on the drive must be set to the slave position. A primary slave hard disk requires that the primary master hard disk be present in the system.

☒ **A** is incorrect because the end connector on the ribbon connector is reserved for the master hard disk. If you connect a hard disk to the end connector with its configuration jumper in the slave position, it will not work. **B** is incorrect because the first hard disk in the system is always the primary master, which holds the operating system. **D** is incorrect because the primary slave drive requires a primary master drive, not a secondary master drive.

48. ☑ **C.** Antistatic wrist straps should not be used when you are working on high voltage devices. Computers, printers, and monitors contain high voltage parts, including power supplies. Antistatic wrist straps are designed to ease out excessive static voltage through your body. If you wear them while working on high voltage equipment, there is a chance that any leaking high voltage will pass through your body, giving you a severe electric shock.

☒ **A** is incorrect because even when you are using an antistatic mat, you must wear antistatic wrist straps as additional protection against static electricity, provided the device you are working on is not a high voltage device. **B** is incorrect because this is not the criterion for not using an antistatic wrist strap. **D** is incorrect because antistatic spray is not a substitute for an antistatic wrist strap, but additional protection against static discharge.

49. ☑ **C.** The problem is caused by a faulty hub. From the information given by the customer, it is clear that the network is a star network using UTP cables and a hub. If there is a faulty hub, the entire network is down because the computers communicate to one another through the hub.

☒ **A** is incorrect because there are only 12 computers in the network, and the network speed is 10 Mbps. Such a small numbers of computers cannot cause excessive network traffic. **B** is incorrect because a single broken cable on one of the computers cannot bring down the entire network. Since each computer is independently connected to the hub, only the computer that has a broken network cable would have a problem. **D** is incorrect because terminators are not used in 10BaseT networks. They are used only in bus networks that use coaxial cables.

50. ☑ **A** and **C.** The high-density floppy disk drive can read data from 720KB and 1.44MB floppy disks. Both types of floppy disks have 80 tracks on each side. The double-density and high-density floppy disks have 9 and 18 sectors per track, respectively.

☒ **B** is incorrect because the 3.5-inch floppy disk drives cannot read the 1.2MB floppy disks typically available with 5.25-inch floppy disk drives. It is not possible to insert a 5.25-inch disk in a 3.5-inch disk drive. **D** is incorrect because you need an extra high-density disk drive to read from 2.88MB floppy disks. Any of the higher density floppy disk drives can read data from and write data to a lower density floppy disk, but the opposite is not true. For example, the extra high-density floppy disk drive can read data from 1.44MB and 720KB floppy disks, in addition to the 2.88MB floppy disks.

A+

CORE HARDWARE/OPERATING SYSTEM EXAMS

A+ Operating Systems Technologies
Practice Exam

QUESTIONS

1. Which of the following methods cannot be used in Windows 98 to modify Registry entries? Select all correct answers.

   A. The Computer Management Console

   B. The Control Panel

   C. The REGEDT32.EXE command

   D. The REDEDIT.EXE command

2. You want to install Windows 2000 Professional on a Pentium 200MHz computer that is currently running Windows 98. This computer has two hard disk partitions named C: and D:. The computer does not have a CD-ROM, and you have mapped drive X: on your computer to the CD-ROM drive of another computer. Which of the following is a correct command to start the installation from the MS-DOS command prompt, considering that the destination drive will be C:?

   A. X:\I386\WINNT.EXE

   B. X:\I386\WINNT32.EXE C:

   C. X:\I386\SETUP.EXE

   D. X:\I386\WINNT32.EXE

3. When you open the TCP/IP Properties sheet of your network adapter, you find that it is configured to obtain an IP address automatically. You are using a Windows 98 computer, and a DHCP server in your office provides IP addresses to all desktops. Which of the following options would you use to check the IP address of your computer?

   A. Run the WINIPCFG utility.

   B. Run IPCONFIG/ALL at the command prompt.

   C. Click the Binding tab to find out the IP address.

   D. Restart the computer and check the BIOS.

4. **Current Situation:** You are working in a small company that has a peer network of 12 computers running Windows 98. Recently, users in this office have started raising concerns about the safety of data. You have been asked to attend to the users' concerns. You decide to use Windows 98 Backup utility to back up data on tape drives. You select a computer that is rarely used and install a tape drive on it. Here is what you have to accomplish.

    Required Result: Install Windows 98 Backup utility on the selected computer, and regularly back up the data as requested by users.

    Optional Desired Results:

    1. The backed up data should be protected using a password.

    2. The data should be compressed to minimize the space used on the tapes.

    3. The data backup should be done after office hours every day.

    Proposed Solution: Use Windows Explorer to map the network computer data folders that need data backup as network drives. Open the Windows Backup utility from Start | Programs | Accessories | System Tools. Select Networks, and select the network drives that need to be backed up. This is shown in the following illustration.

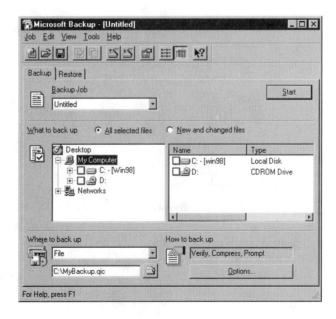

Next, click the Options button and select the Password tab. This opens the password dialog box. Click Protect this backup with a password check box. Specify a password, as shown in the following illustration. Click OK.

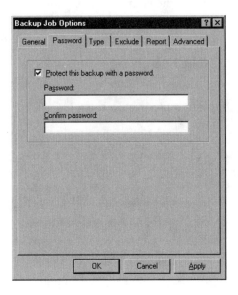

When this configuration is done, click Start in the main Backup window.

What results does the proposed solution produce?

A. The proposed solution produces the required result and all of the optional results.

B. The proposed solution produces the required result and only two of the optional results.

C. The proposed solution produces the required result but none of the optional results.

D. The proposed solution does not produce the required result.

5. You are using Windows 2000 operating system on your computer. The hard disk of the computer is almost full, even after you have compressed a large number of files. You currently have 20MB of free disk space. When you attempt to copy a 15MB compressed file on this hard disk, you get an error

message saying that the disk space is insufficient. Why does this message appear, when there is 20MB of free space on the disk?

A. The size of the uncompressed file must be counted.

B. You cannot copy compressed files to a compressed folder.

C. The file is corrupted after compression.

D. All of the above.

6. You have just arrived at a customer's site to resolve a problem in his Windows 98 computer. The complaint is that the system produces some unknown errors when the customer is working on certain applications. Unfortunately, the customer has not noted any of the error codes. What should be your first step when you start your diagnosis?

A. Start uninstalling the applications one by one.

B. Gather as much information as you can.

C. Ask the customer to reproduce all the error codes.

D. Search the Registry to locate the error codes.

7. You have decided to convert the hard disk of your Windows 98 computer to FAT32 using the Drive Converter utility. Which of the following benefits of this conversion is incorrectly described here?

A. Creates extra disk space

B. Runs programs faster

C. Can be converted back to FAT16

D. Efficient storage of disk data

8. Which of the following commands should you run to install Windows 98 operating system, assuming that you have already booted the system and the CD-ROM drivers have been loaded to access the Setup CD-ROM?

A. WINSETUP.EXE

B. SETUP.EXE

C. WINNT.EXE

D. WINSTALL.EXE

9. Which of the following statements about system files in Windows 9x and Windows 2000 operating systems is incorrect?

    A. System files can be located anywhere in the hard disk.

    B. System files are necessary to load and run the operating system.

    C. System files are required for loading Plug and Play device drivers and allocating system resources to them.

    D. System files are required to configure the system after installing the operating system.

10. Which of the following operating systems provides the easiest upgrade path to Windows 2000?

    A. Windows 3.1, because of its simple configuration

    B. Windows 95 and Windows 98, since they also use Registry

    C. Windows NT 4.0, because the Registry structure is similar

    D. Windows NT 3.51, because all device drivers are compatible

11. You have a computer that is configured to dual boot between Windows 98 and Windows 2000. You have installed a new Plug and Play modem while running Windows 98. The modem works fine in Windows 98, but when you start the computer in Windows 2000, the same modem does not respond. Which of the following is correct?

    A. The modem requires installation within Windows 2000 with the same driver.

    B. The modem requires installation within Windows 2000 with a Windows 2000 compatible driver.

    C. The modem can work with only one operating system.

    D. There is an IRQ conflict in the system.

12. Which of the following options can you use without any configuration to quickly track the processes running on a Windows 2000 Professional computer and the resources used by each process?

    A. Task Manager

   B. System Monitor

   C. Event Log

   D. Performance Console

13. **Current Situation:** You have just started a job as a helpdesk technician in a medium-sized company. The first day you are asked to format a box of ten floppy disks on a computer running Windows 98 operating system. Here is what you have to accomplish.

    Required Result: Format the ten 1.44MB floppy disks and label them as Disk 1, Disk 2, and so on.

    Optional Desired Results:

    1. The floppies should be bootable.

    2. The process should take as little time as possible.

    Proposed Solution: Open Windows Explorer and insert the first floppy disk in the floppy disk drive. Click the floppy disk drive icon, and you will be prompted to answer whether you wish to format the disk or not. Click the Yes button, which opens the Format dialog box. Make your selections, as shown in the following illustration. Type Disk 1 in the Label box and click the Start button. When the first disk is complete, take it out. Repeat the procedure for the rest of the floppy disks until the job is complete.

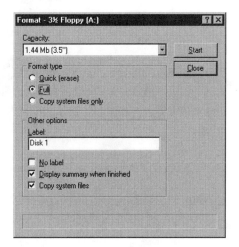

What results does the proposed solution produce?

A. The proposed solution produces the required result and both of the optional results.

B. The proposed solution produces the required result and only one of the optional results.

C. The proposed solution produces the required result but none of the optional results.

D. The proposed solution does not produce the required result.

14. Which of the following files in Windows 98 operating system is used to switch from real mode to 32-bit protected mode during the system startup?

A. VMM386.VXD

B. EMM386.EXE

C. IO.SYS

D. WIN.COM

15. What happens when Windows 98 is not able to locate a suitable driver for a new Plug and Play adapter?

A. You are prompted to locate and install a third-party driver yourself.

B. You are warned that the adapter will not work and should be removed.

C. Windows 98 installs a substitute driver.

D. None of the above.

16. You have four files named FOOT.EXE, FOOT.COM, FOOT.WPD, and FOOT.BAT in one of the folders of a Windows 98 computer. Which of the files will be executed when you type FOOT at the MS-DOS command prompt?

A. FOOT.EXE

B. FOOT.COM

C. FOOT.WPD

D. FOOT.BAT

17. The computer you are using at home was purchased two years ago with a preloaded version of Windows 98 and several other free applications. During these two years, you have installed many other applications and attached several devices to this computer. You are thinking of cleaning up the system by formatting the hard drive and reinstalling the operating system. In which of the following situations should you reinstall the operating system?

    A. When none of the applications and none of the devices respond

    B. When one of the applications does not respond

    C. When one of the devices does not work

    D. When the system locks up frequently on launching an application

18. You have two phone lines at home and have purchased an additional modem for your computer. After connecting the modem to a free serial port and configuring the dial-up numbers, you want to combine the two modems to dial the Remote Access Server in your office. Which of the following options in Dial-up Networking Properties will you use to define additional modems?

    A. From the Configure button in the General tab of Connection Properties

    B. From the Multilink tab of Connection Properties

    C. From the Options tab in Modem Properties

    D. From the Connection tab in Modem Properties

19. You installed a new network adapter in your computer running Windows 98 operating system. You installed the driver files from the floppy disk that came with the adapter. When you restarted the computer, it did not boot, but froze on the Windows 98 startup screen and wouldn't fully load. Which of the following can help you resolve the problem?

    A. Start the computer using Boot Normally Mode, and replace the driver with a Windows 98 generic driver for the adapter.

    B. Start the computer using the Safe Mode with Networking option, and replace the driver files.

    C. Start the computer in Safe Mode, and replace the driver using Device Manager.

    D. Start the computer in Step-by-step Confirmation Mode, and when prompted, replace the driver files.

20. You are working in a small company that has six computers configured in a peer network. The only color printer in the office is connected to your computer and is shared with other users. The users work on word processing programs and print several documents every day. The documents average ten printed pages. These users complain that when they come to collect their documents from the printer, they find the documents mixed up by other users. Which of the following will help you quickly address their grievances?

    A. Ask the users to stand by the printer.

    B. Allocate different time slots to each user.

    C. Use separator pages with the documents.

    D. Pause the printer after every print job.

21. The following symptoms are related to some problems in a Windows 98 computer. Which of them does not indicate a possible problem with the Windows Swapfile?

    A. Systems lock up frequently.

    B. System response is very slow.

    C. The printer does not respond.

    D. The system takes a long time to load applications.

22. Which of the following statements incorrectly describes the function of the BOOT.INI file in Windows 2000 operating system?

    A. It is responsible for presenting the user with a list of operating systems and the time duration for which the options menu will be displayed.

    B. It displays the Windows 2000 startup options when the user presses the F8 key in case there is a startup problem.

    C. It specifies the location of the boot files once the user selects an operating system to load.

    D. It specifies the default operating system in case the user does not select a particular operating system.

23. **Current Situation:** You have a Windows 98 computer on which several applications have been installed. This computer is exhibiting some application-related problems, and sometimes a particular application does not work at all. Here is what you have to accomplish.

    Required Result: Diagnose the system problems caused by applications.

    Optional Desired Results:

    1. You should be able to log detailed diagnostic reports.

    2. The diagnostics utility used should be capable of suggesting a solution to the problem.

    3. The diagnostic program should be capable of helping you in the event you have to contact Microsoft for technical support.

    Proposed Solution: Launch the applications that you suspect are causing the problems in your Windows 98 system. Launch Dr. Watson, the built-in diagnostics utility, from Programs | Accessories | System Tools | System Information. In the System Information window, click Tools and select Dr. Watson. An icon will appear on the right-hand side of the taskbar. Right-click the icon, and click Dr. Watson to open the utility screen. Click the View menu and select Advanced View. This displays advanced options, as shown in the following illustration.

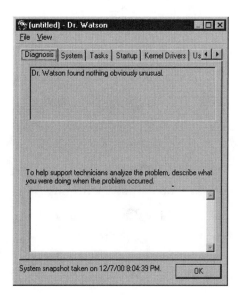

If there is a problem, it will appear in the upper part of the window. Enter your comments in the lower part of the Window. Click the File menu and click Save As. If required, the saved file can be sent to Microsoft Technical Support.

What results does the proposed solution produce?

A. The proposed solution produces the required result and all three of the optional results.

B. The proposed solution produces the required result but none of the optional results.

C. The proposed solution produces the required result and only two of the optional results.

D. The proposed solution does not produce the required result.

24. Which of the following statements correctly describes the reason Windows 2000 Professional is preferred over Windows 98 as a client operating system in a networked environment?

A. Windows 2000 has better Plug and Play and multimedia support.

B. Windows 2000 supports NTFS permissions and has better processing power.

C. Windows 2000 can serve as client to Windows 2000 Servers.

D. Windows 2000 is interactive and user friendly.

25. You have made some changes to a Windows 98 computer configuration. The new configuration does not work, and it has become evident that there is no other means of repairing the configuration than editing the Registry. What should be your first action before you start changing the Registry values to change the configuration?

A. Restart the computer.

B. Back up the existing Registry.

C. Export the Registry to some other computer.

D. Set the Registry file attributes to Read Only.

26. You install a SCSI hard disk in your computer that already has an IDE drive. When the adapter and disk drive have been installed, you start your computer and find that Windows 98 does not recognize the new drive. Which of the following is not essential to successfully configuring the SCSI hard disk?

    A. Setting the SCSI ID on the hard disk

    B. Installing the SCSI driver

    C. Assigning an IRQ to the SCSI drive

    D. Running the SCSI utility to partition the disk

27. A Windows 2000 computer is not starting up, and you feel that the problem is very complex. Which of the following would be your last option before making a decision to reinstall the operating system?

    A. Replace the existing Registry with a good copy from another computer.

    B. Use the Recovery Console to start the computer in DOS mode.

    C. Use the emergency repair disk.

    D. Try resolving the problem by removing hardware components one by one.

28. You were working on your Windows 98 computer and accidentally deleted some system files. Which of the following files do you think is the most critical for booting Windows 98 and, if missing, would produce a fatal error?

    A. SYSTEM.INI

    B. CONFIG.SYS

    C. HIMEM.SYS

    D. AUTOEXEC.BAT

29. Which of the following anti-virus utilities is included with Windows 2000 operating system?

    A. Norton

    B. Symantec

    C. AVBoot

    D. McAfee

30. A computer is showing the following error when it starts up:

    `NTLDR missing. Replace disk and press any key to continue.`

    What does this error indicate? Select all correct answers?

    A. The computer has Windows 95 operating system.

    B. The computer has Windows NT operating system.

    C. The computer is a dual boot system with Windows 98 and Windows 2000.

    D. The computer is running Windows 3.11.

31. A network adapter with appropriate driver is already installed on your Windows 98 computer. As well, networking is installed using the NetBEUI protocol. Which of the following states the correct sequence of actions necessary to connect to shared drives on other computers?

    A. Enable File Sharing in Network Properties, right-click Network Neighborhood, and select Map Network Drive.

    B. Enable File and Print Sharing in Network Properties, right-click Network Neighborhood, and select Map Network Drive.

    C. Enable File Sharing in Network Properties, click Tools in Windows Explorer, and select Map Network Drive.

    D. Right-click Network Neighborhood and select Map Network Drive.

32. There are some files on your Windows 98 home computer that contain important business data. You do not want these files to be visible to anyone else using your computer in your absence. Which of the following is the best way to hide these files when someone uses your computer?

    A. Set the File Properties as Hidden in Windows Explorer.

    B. Copy the files to floppy disks and hide them.

    C. Click View in Windows Explorer, and click As a Web Page.

    D. Set permissions so that only you have permission to view the files.

33. Assuming that your Internet connection is live, which of the following is an incorrect URL to connect to a Web site and will not make a connection?

    A. www.website.com

    B. http://website

    C. http://www.website.com

    D. www.web1.website.com

34. Which of the following methods can you not use to connect to a shared network drive when you are working on a computer running Windows 98 operating system?

    A. Right-click My Computer and click Map Network Drive.

    B. Right-click Network Neighborhood and click Map Network Drive.

    C. Type MAP DRIVE F: \\COMPUTERNAME\SHARENAME from the DOS prompt.

    D. Click Map Network Drive from the Tools menu in Windows Explorer.

35. You were trying to connect to http://www.syngress.com when your friend dropped in. He asked you what the popular term is for this Internet address. Which of the following should be you answer?

    A. UDP

    B. URL

    C. UNC

    D. FQDN

36. Which of the following is your best defense against data loss if there is a disaster? Select two answers.

    A. Back up your data regularly on tape drives and store the tapes offsite.

    B. Back up your data regularly on two servers.

    C. Keep the backup tapes locked inside the server room.

    D. Take a full system backup at least once a week.

37. You have a Windows 98 computer in your office and an Epson Stylus color printer connected to it. There are five more Windows 98 computers in the same office. All the computers have color monitors. Your boss has requested a computer dealer to connect all computers so that resources on these computers can be shared. What are the resources he is referring to? Select all correct answers.

    A. Disk drives

    B. Folders

    C. Files

    D. Monitors

    E. The printer connected to your computer

38. You do not want to upgrade your Windows 98 computer to Windows 2000 Professional, but you would like to know if your hardware and software are compatible so that you can do the upgrade at a later date. Which option of the WINNT32.EXE setup command will enable you to perform this compatibility check?

    A. /checkupgradeonly

    B. /syspart <drive_letter>

    C. /checkupgrade

    D. /copydir <folder_name>

39. One of the computers in your office is a Pentium 166MHz computer with a 512KB L2 cache, 64MB of RAM, and 560MB of free hard disk space. The computer is currently running Windows 98 operating system. Which of the following components will cause a problem if you were to make this computer dual boot with Windows 2000 Professional?

    A. Processor

    B. Cache memory

    C. Hard disk space

    D. RAM

40. You have a dual boot system running Windows 98 and Windows 2000 Professional. This system has two hard disks, and each operating system is

installed on a different disk. You have converted your Windows 2000 disk (drive D:) from FAT32 to NTFS5 using the Disk Management utility in Windows 2000, but now you are not able to see the Windows 2000 disk when running Windows 98. Which of the following options would you use to convert the file system back to FAT32 without losing any data?

A. Run the Reconvert utility in Disk Management.

B. Run CONVERT D: /FS:FAT32 from the command prompt.

C. Format the disk using the FAT file system.

D. None; FAT to NTFS conversion is a one-way process.

41. An internal modem is listed as an Unknown Device in the Device Manager in a Windows 98 computer. Which of the following problems could possibly be causing this?

A. An incorrect driver has been installed.

B. The driver files have not been installed.

C. There is a resource conflict with another device.

D. All of the above.

42. Which of the following types of servers on the Internet are configured to prompt you for a username and password before you are allowed to see the contents on the server? Select all correct answers.

A. An HTTP server

B. An FTP server

C. A WWW server

D. A secure Web site

43. You were working on a Windows 98 computer and accidentally deleted a file specified in SYSTEM.INI that is required by a legacy device. What will happen when the computer restarts?

A. Windows 98 will not boot successfully.

B. The boot process will fail during the GUI mode.

C. You will get an operating system error.

D. Nothing; Windows 98 will boot normally.

44. Most of your work on the Internet involves downloading files from several FTP and WWW Web sites. You are planning to set up an additional connection to the Internet. Which of the following options will suit your requirements?

    A. ISDN

    B. PSTN

    C. DSL

    D. POTS

45. A Windows 98 computer is not starting up, and you suspect that it is either the video adapter or the network adapter that might be causing the problem. Which of the following boot options is the best for starting Windows 98 on this computer?

    A. Boot normally

    B. Safe Mode

    C. Step-by-step Confirmation

    D. Debugging mode

46. One of your friends told you that when you type a URL in the address box of an Internet browser, the name is translated to its IP address. Which of the following services do you think is used to perform this translation?

    A. DHCP

    B. WINS

    C. DNS

    D. ISP

47. One of the Web sites that you tried to connect to has sent a warning message that Secure Socket Layer is not enabled on your computer. Which of the following tabs in Internet Options will you use to enable Secure Socket Layers?

    A. Security

    B. Content

    C. Advanced

    D. Programs

48. You have been given a new computer that will be connected to the office network. You will use this computer to design graphics advertisements for the your company's clients. Each of the design files takes nearly three days to complete, and you usually do not let anyone touch your design files before they are complete. If you were given a choice of Windows 98 or Windows 2000 operating systems for this computer, on which of the following factors would you base your decision? Select all correct answers.

   A. Ease of use

   B. File compression

   C. Security

   D. Processing power

   E. Networking features

49. You want to configure the TCP/IP network protocol on your Windows 2000 computer, which is part of one of the three segments of a network. It is essential that you be able to access shared resources on all computers in the network. Which of the statements given below is incorrect?

   A. The IP address is necessary and should not be in use by any other computer in any segment of the network.

   B. The subnet mask is optional and when specified, should be unique to the computer.

   C. The default gateway entry is essential because this is a multiple segment network.

   D. The DNS and WINS server entries are optional.

50. You were trying to install Windows 98 operating system on a computer, but the installation did not succeed. You suspect that some hardware component is preventing the installation from completing successfully. When you attempt to reinstall Windows 98, you select the Safe Recovery option to reduce installation time. Which of the following files does Windows 98 Setup use during the installation? Select all correct answers.

   A. DETCRASH.LOG

   B. DETSETUP.LOG

   C. SETUPLOG.TXT

   D. DETCRASH.TXT

IN-DEPTH ANSWERS

1. ☑ **A** and **C.** The Computer Management Console and the REGEDT32.EXE command exist only in Windows 2000 and are not available in Windows 98 operating system. The Registry can be modified indirectly by changing system settings through the Control Panel, or by direct editing.

   ☒ **B** is incorrect because modifying computer configuration using one or more of the options in Control Panel is an indirect and safe method to modify the Registry. **D** is incorrect because you can use this command in Windows 98 as well as in Windows 2000 to edit the Registry.

2. ☑ **D.** X:\I386\WINNT32.EXE. The Windows 2000 setup files for the Intel platform are located in the \I386 folder on the Setup CD-ROM. When installing from within a running Windows 98 operating system, you need to run the WINNT32.EXE file. If X is the letter for the network drive mapped to the CD-ROM, the correct command becomes X:\I386\WINNT32.EXE.

   ☒ **A** is incorrect because the WINNT.EXE setup command is used for clean installations. **B** is incorrect because you need not specify the destination drive with this command. The setup program will prompt you for the installation drive during installation. **C** is incorrect because SETUP.EXE is not a valid setup command in Windows 2000. This command is used to start installation of Windows 3.x and Windows 9x operating systems.

3. ☑ **A.** The WINIPCFG utility in Windows 98 is the best source to find out the IP address assigned to the computer by a DHCP server. This utility can also be used to force the release of an IP address or renew an existing IP address.

   ☒ **B** is incorrect because this utility is not available in Windows 9x computers. Windows NT and Windows 2000 computers have this utility. When used with the /ALL switch, the IPCONFIG utility displays detailed IP configuration for the computer. **C** is incorrect because the Bindings tab does not show the IP address of the computer. This tab lists the protocols to which a service is bound and allows you to set the binding order. **D** is incorrect because the BIOS will not report the IP address of the computer.

4. ☑ **B.** The proposed solution produces the required result and only two of the optional results. The required result is produced, because the required data will be backed up with the given configuration. The first optional result is produced because you have configured the backup options with a password to protect the data. The second optional result is produced because the Windows Backup program compresses the data during the backup process by default. The third optional result is not produced because you have not scheduled the data backup to start after office hours. When you click Start, the backup process starts running immediately.

   ☒ **A, C,** and **D** are incorrect because the proposed solution produces the required result and only two of the optional results. The third optional result is not produced.

5. ☑ **A.** The size of the uncompressed file must be counted. When you copy a compressed file to a folder in Windows 2000, the size of the uncompressed file is taken into account. The uncompressed size of the file you are trying to copy is more than 20MB, and this is why you are getting the error.

   ☒ **B** is incorrect because this is not true. Both compressed and uncompressed files can be copied to a compressed folder in Windows 2000. **C** is incorrect because Windows 2000 does not corrupt files when compressing them. **D** is incorrect because there is only one correct reason that you are not able to copy the compressed file. Although it is very unlikely that you will get difficult questions on Windows 2000 or Windows 9x file and folder management in the A+ exam, there are certain well-known features and limitations of these operating systems that you must be aware of.

6. ☑ **B.** Gather as much information as you can. When the cause of a problem is not known and the customer or computer user does not remember the error codes, you should try to gather as much information as you can. If you ask the customer a few questions, such as how the problem started, what particular application produced the errors, and what happened when the errors were displayed, you would have enough information to start your initial diagnosis.

   ☒ **A** is incorrect because unless you know the exact cause of the problem, you should not uninstall any applications. **C** is incorrect because the customer might not be able to produce *all* the errors again, as stated in the answer. You should, however, ask the customer if he can reproduce some of the errors, because if he can, then he essentially knows how the errors happened, and this will provide valuable information as to the sequence of events leading up to the errors. **D** is incorrect because the Registry contains configuration information and does not store any error codes generated by applications.

7. ☑ **C.** This is an incorrect statement regarding the benefits of the FAT32 file system in Windows 98. The drive, once converted to FAT32, cannot be converted back to the FAT16 file system without first repartitioning and reformatting it.

☒ **A, B,** and **D** are incorrect because all these features are benefits of the FAT32 file system. A hard disk using the FAT32 file system stores disk data more efficiently than FAT16, the conversion to FAT32 creates several megabytes of additional disk space, and FAT32 is capable of running programs faster.

8. ☑ **B.** SETUP.EXE. The simple command to start Windows 98 installation is SETUP.EXE, assuming that you are in the correct folder on the CD-ROM drive that has the installation files. If you are at the C: prompt, you must change to the appropriate folder on the CD-ROM drive so that the SETUP.EXE file can be located and run.

☒ **A** is incorrect because this file does not exist and thus is an incorrect command. **C** is incorrect because this file is used in Windows 2000 to start the installation from the DOS prompt. **D** is incorrect because this command does not exist for installation of Windows 98 operating system.

9. ☑ **A.** This statement is incorrect because the system files are usually located in the boot partition in Windows 98 and Windows 2000, typically in the WINDOWS and WINNT folders, respectively. The boot partition refers to the partition on the hard disk that contains these folders. If these files are moved from their original location, the operating system either will not load or will not run properly.

☒ **B, C,** and **D** are incorrect answers because these statements are true. The system files are necessary to load and run the operating system. They are required to load drivers for Plug and Play devices and allocate resources to them. When you install any application programs after the installation of the operating system, the system files are required to successfully complete the configuration of the application.

10.   ☑   **C.** Windows NT 4.0 because the Registry structure is similar. Windows NT 4.0 provides the easiest upgrade path to Windows 2000 because of the similar Registry structure and the fact that a majority of the configuration can be migrated to the new operating system.

☒   **A** is incorrect because you cannot upgrade from Windows 3.1 to Windows 2000. You must first upgrade Windows 3.1 to Windows 9*x* or Windows NT, and then to Windows 2000. In fact, this is the most complex upgrade path. Microsoft recommends that if you have a running Windows 3.1 system, you should perform a clean install instead of an upgrade. **B** is incorrect because the Registry structures of Windows 95 and Windows 98 are similar to each other, but they are entirely different from the Registry structure of Windows 2000. **D** is incorrect because the device drivers for Windows NT 3.51, Windows NT 4.0, and Windows 2000 are all different. Windows 95 and Windows 98 have the most compatible device drivers, but these again are not compatible with Windows NT and Windows 2000. Windows 2000 requires different device drivers to work with the operating system.

11.   ☑   **B.** You need to install the modem while running Windows 2000 operating system and using a Windows 2000 driver. Although both Windows 98 and Windows 2000 support Plug and Play and will detect the modem as soon as a particular operating system is started, in some cases, you might have to load the driver files from the disk supplied by the manufacturer.

☒   **A** is incorrect because the modem drivers might be different for Windows 98 and Windows 2000. **C** is incorrect because most modems are compatible with multiple operating systems and have corresponding device drivers. **D** is incorrect because if there were an IRQ conflict, the modem would not have worked with Windows 98 either.

12.   ☑   **A.** The Task manager in Windows 2000 displays a list of currently active processes on the computer. It also displays the different resources in use by individual processes. The Task Manager is brought up by pressing CTRL-ALT-DEL or by right-clicking the taskbar.

☒   **B** is incorrect because it is used to collect information on processes and will not display any results unless some basic configuration is performed. The configuration involves adding counters for different objects. **C** is incorrect because Event Logs also collect information on system, application, and security events after proper configuration. **D** is incorrect because the System Monitor discussed above is a part of the Performance Console. None of these options gives you the quick results required by the question.

13. ☑ **B.** The proposed solution produces the required result and only one of the optional results. The required result is produced because the procedure suggested for formatting the floppy disks and labeling them is correct. The first optional result is produced because when you click the Copy system files check box, the system files are copied to the floppy disk after formatting, and the disk becomes bootable. The second optional result is not produced because this is not the fastest method to create bootable floppy disks. A better option is to use the MS-DOS command prompt and use the FORMAT A: /S /V [:Label] command.

☒ **A, C,** and **D** are incorrect because the proposed solution produces the required result and only one of the optional results. The second optional result is not produced.

14. ☑ **A.** VMM386.VXD. During the Windows 98 startup process, the WIN.COM file locates and loads the virtual memory manager VMM386.EXE. This file loads device drivers into memory and also switches the processor from real mode to 32-bit protected mode. This mode is called the protected-mode boot because the system loads and initializes the critical system files and device drivers.

☒ **B** is incorrect because this file is used for expanded memory and does not switch the processor from real mode to protected mode. **C** is incorrect because the IO.SYS file is the file that initializes the loading of Windows 98 operating system. **D** is incorrect because the WIN.COM file is the first file used after the boot process has entered the protected mode. It loads the VMM386.VXD file.

15. ☑ **A.** When Windows 98 is not able to locate a suitable driver for any new adapter, it prompts you to locate and install a third-party driver yourself. If you have received a driver disk with the adapter, you may insert it and install the driver supplied by the manufacturer.

☒ **B** is incorrect because Windows 98 does not give any such warning to remove the adapter. **C** is incorrect because a substitute driver is not installed. **D** is incorrect because one correct answer option does exist.

16. ☑ **B.** FOOT.COM. When you do not specify an extension with a file at the MS-DOS command prompt, the operating system looks for the file with a COM extension. If found, that file is executed. If there is more than one file with the same name but with COM, EXE, and BAT extensions, the files will be executed in the order COM, EXE, and BAT.

    ☒ **A** is incorrect because this file is executed if the OS is unable to locate the FOOT.COM file. **C** is incorrect because this file cannot be executed using only the file name. If you are in Windows Explorer, you can execute the WPD file by double-clicking it. **D** is incorrect because this file is executed when there are no FOOT.COM or FOOT.EXE files.

17. ☑ **A.** When none of the applications and none of the devices attached to the computer respond, it becomes evident that there is a serious problem with the operating system. Since it is not feasible to diagnose each application or device problem separately, reinstalling the operating system is a good decision.

    ☒ **B** and **C** are incorrect answers because the decision to reinstall the operating system should not be based on failure of a single application or a single device. A better decision is to diagnose the problem or remove the faulty application or device. **D** is incorrect because in this case you should suspect low system memory, a faulty application, or limited space in the Windows Swapfile. This problem should not necessitate reinstallation of the operating system.

18. ☑ **B.** The Multilink tab in Connection Properties allows you to specify additional modems for use in conjunction with the existing modem. Multilink allows you to combine the bandwidth of two or more lines and get a better connection speed. You should configure the modem before you enable Mulitilink in Connection Properties.

    ☒ **A** is incorrect because the Configure button in the General tab is used for configuration of modem properties. **C** is incorrect because this tab is in the Modem Properties sheet and is used to configure dial-up options, such as bringing up the terminal screen before and after dialing. **D** is incorrect because this tab is used to configure port settings and start and stop bits for the modem communication.

19. ☑ **C.** Start the computer in Safe Mode, and replace the driver using Device Manager. When a Windows 98 computer refuses to boot normally after installing a driver or after updating an existing device driver, you can use Safe Mode to boot the computer. In this mode, Windows 98 loads only very basic drivers to run the system. You can then use the Device Manager to replace the bad driver files.

    ☒ **A** is incorrect because this is what you were doing when the system locked up. **B** is incorrect because the computer will load the driver for the network adapter, which is the driver causing the problem. **D** is incorrect because this mode gives you the option of selecting which drivers to load, but does not prompt you to replace any drivers, as stated in the answer.

20. ☑ **C.** Use separator pages with the documents. This option will help resolve the problem quickly and without much configuration. A separator page with each document will help the users identify their documents, and the chances of pages getting mixed up will be reduced. The Use Separator Page option is available in Printer Properties.

    ☒ **A** is incorrect because this is a waste of time. **B** is incorrect because this will prevent users from printing important or urgent documents even when the printer is free. **D** is not a practical option because you will always have to watch the printer window, which is very difficult and will not help resolve the problem.

21. ☑ **C.** If the printer attached to a Windows 9*x* computer does not respond, you should not suspect the Windows Swapfile. There are likely to be other reasons for this problem, such as connections, cables, printer drivers, or a faulty printer. The Swapfile is used when the system needs additional memory to process user requests or to run application programs.

    ☒ **A, B,** and **D** are incorrect answers because if the system locks up frequently, if its response is slow, or if it takes a long time to load applications, either the Swapfile has become corrupt or it has insufficient space to accommodate requests.

22. ☑ **B.** This is not a function of the BOOT.INI file in Windows 2000. The BOOT.INI file does not invoke the startup options menu if the user presses the F8 key when Windows 2000 begins to load.

☒   **A, C**, and **D** are incorrect answers because these statements correctly describe functions of the BOOT.INI file. The BOOT.INI file displays the operating systems menu, specifies for how long this menu is to be displayed, specifies a default operating system if the user does not make a selection, and tells NTLDR the location of boot files for each operating system.

23.   ☑   **A.** The proposed solution produces the required result and all three of the optional results. Dr. Watson is a built-in diagnostics utility that is very helpful in tracking sources of problems in applications and device drivers. The utility can take a snapshot of the current condition of the system, and the snapshot file can be saved as a log file. The log file can be viewed later to diagnose the problem. Often, Dr. Watson also suggests a solution to fix a problem. The snapshot taken by Dr. Watson is very detailed, and most of the time, you will be able to fix the problem caused by malfunctioning applications or devices. Microsoft recommends saving the snapshot file in case you have to contact Technical Support for assistance in resolving a problem. This indicates that the proposed solution produces the required result and all three of the optional results.

☒   **B, C,** and **D** are incorrect because the proposed solution produced the required result and all three of the optional results. Dr. Watson can be used to diagnose problems caused by applications, collect data, suggest a resolution to the problem, and save system snapshots as log files in the event that you need to contact Microsoft Technical Support.

24.   ☑   **B.** The correct reason out of the given options for preferring Windows 2000 Professional over Windows 98 as a client operating system in a networked environment is that it has better control over system resources because it supports NTFS and has better processing power. In Windows 2000 Professional, up to two microprocessors are supported, whereas in Windows 98, the limit is one.

☒   **A** is incorrect because although Windows 2000 Professional has better support for multimedia and Plug and Play devices than Windows 98, this is not the reason Windows 2000 Professional is a preferred client operating system. **C** is incorrect because Windows 98 and several other operating systems can also connect to Windows 2000 Servers as clients. **D** is incorrect because both Windows 98 and Windows 2000 operating systems are equally interactive and user friendly.

25. ☑ **B.** Before you start changing the computer configuration by editing the Registry, you should take a backup of the existing Registry. This is helpful if you accidentally make a change that further damages the system configuration. A backup copy of the Registry can be used to restore the original configuration.

    ☒ **A** is incorrect because this will make no difference. **C** is incorrect because this is possible only when you are in a network environment. Since it is not specified in the question whether the computer is a stand-alone or a network computer, this is not the best answer. **D** is incorrect because if you make the Registry Read Only, you will not be able to make any changes to it.

26. ☑ **C.** Assigning an IRQ to the SCSI drive. The IRQ is assigned to the SCSI adapter and not to any device attached to the SCSI chain. Usually when you install the SCSI driver, the program will assign an IRQ to the SCSI adapter.

    ☒ **A, B,** and **D** are incorrect answers because all these are essential to make the SCSI hard disk work. You must set the SCSI ID on the hard disk or at least check to make sure it is correct. You should install the SCSI driver and run the SCSI utility to partition the hard disk. The hard disk cannot be used until you partition it using the SCSI utility.

27. ☑ **B.** The Recovery Console in Windows 2000 offers advanced users a unique tool to repair the system startup and other problems. The Recovery Console either is installed on the hard disk or can be run using the Windows 2000 Setup CD-ROM. This console has advanced command-line features that enable you to fix complex problems in the system.

    ☒ **A** is incorrect because the Registry in Windows 2000 (and Windows 9x) is computer specific, so the Registry of one computer would not work in another. **C** is incorrect because the emergency repair disk is usually the first option used to fix startup problems, not the *last* option, as stated in the question. **D** is incorrect because it is not a good idea to remove standard computer hardware to resolve a startup problem.

28. ☑ **C.** The HIMEM.SYS file is critical for booting Windows 98 operating system, and if this file is missing from the \Windows folder, the system will produce the "HIMEM.SYS not loaded" error and fail to boot. As a result, you will be able to run the operating system only in real mode (MS-DOS mode).

    ☒ **A** is incorrect because this file is used for legacy devices and is not required by Windows 98. **B** is incorrect for the same reason. **D** is incorrect because this file is not critical for booting Windows 98. All configurations given in these files reside in the System Registry in Windows 9*x* systems. The values given in the Registry override the values specified in these files.

29. ☑ **C.** AVBoot. Windows 2000 Professional and Windows 2000 Server operating systems contain a copy of InoculateIT Anti-virus AVBoot anti-virus utility. This utility is located in the \VALUEADD\3RDPARTY\ CA_ANTIV folder on the Windows 2000 Setup CD-ROM. The AVBoot anti-virus utility is a command-line tool that can scan computer memory and all hard disks, and can even remove viruses in the master boot record. But you should remember that this utility should be updated regularly with the latest virus signature files from the original vendor. To make a bootable disk for Windows 2000 that automatically starts the AVBoot command-line tool, run the MAKEDISK.BAT file from the \VALUEADD\3RDPARTY\ CA_ANTIV folder.

☒ **A, B,** and **D** are incorrect because none of these utilities is included with Windows 2000 operating system. The only anti-virus utility that is bundled with the operating system is AVBoot.

30. ☑ **B** and **C.** The NTLDR (NT Loader) file is used by Windows NT and Windows 2000 operating systems. This file is used to locate and load the operating system from the hard disk. When the computer dual boots between Windows NT or Windows 2000 and another operating system, the NTLDR program displays a menu of operating system options listed in the BOOT.INI file. The presence of the NTLDR file indicates that the computer is running Windows NT or Windows 2000, or is dual booting between one of these two operating systems and another operating system, such as Windows 9*x*.

☒ **A** and **D** are incorrect answers because neither Windows 95 nor Windows 3.11 uses the NTLDR file.

31. ☑ **D.** Right-click Network Neighborhood and select Map Network Drive. The answer options try to confuse connecting to shares on other computers and sharing your files or printers. Note that you want only to connect to shared folders on *other* computers. This means you need to map a network drive on your computer. No other action is necessary.

☒ **A** is incorrect because enabling file and print sharing is not necessary. This is required when you want to share the resources on your computer. **B** is incorrect for the same reason. **C** is also incorrect because you need not enable file and print sharing to connect to shared resources on other computers. You can use either the My Computer or the Network Neighborhood icon on the desktop to map a network drive. Map Network Drive in the Tools menu in Windows Explorer can also be used to connect to a network share.

32. ☑ **A.** The easiest way to hide important files is to set their attributes as Hidden using the File Properties sheet. By default, Windows does not show System and Hidden files when someone opens Windows Explorer.

☒ **B** is incorrect because it is neither easy nor the best answer to copy the files to floppy disks. The floppy disks may not have the capacity to store your files, and it is not advisable to use this solution. **C** is incorrect because it will make things worse. Setting this option not only displays the files but also displays the attributes of a selected file on the left-hand side. **D** is incorrect because it is not possible to set file permissions on a Windows 98 computer.

33. ☑ **B.** http://website. This is an incorrect URL (Universal Resource Locator). The given address is missing the root domain type, such as .com, .net, or .org. A complete URL should specify the type of root domain. If you specify a domain name without a domain suffix, the connection will not be established.

☒ **A, C,** and **D** are valid URLs and can be used to connect to the Web site www.website.com. **A** is correct because it is not necessary to type http:// with the Web site address. **C** is correct because this specifies a complete URL. **D** is correct because it points to a second level domain named WEB1 in the website.com domain.

34. ☑ **C.** This command cannot be used to map a network drive because there is no such command as MAP DRIVE. The valid command to map a shared drive is

```
NET USE F: \\COMPUTERNAME\SHARENAME
```

☒ **A** is incorrect because you can use this method to connect to a shared drive on the network. **B** is an incorrect answer because this is also a correct method to map a shared network drive. **D** is incorrect because you can map a network drive using this method. In all three cases, you are prompted with a dialog box where you can specify a drive letter and the path of the shared network drive. You can also choose to reconnect the drive every time your computer restarts.

35. ☑ **B.** URL stands for Universal Resource Locator. The URL specifies how the domain names are formatted when accessing The World Wide Web (WWW). To access a Web site you must know the correct URL of the site.

☒ **A** is incorrect because UDP stands for User Datagram Protocol. UDP is a transport protocol in the TCP/IP suite of protocols and is mainly used for faster file transfers. **C** is incorrect because UNC stands for universal naming convention. A UNC path is required to connect to shared resources on the network. **D** is incorrect because a host name on the Internet is known as the FQDN (fully qualified domain name). The FQDN is a part of the URL.

36. ☑ **A** and **D**. The best defense against disasters is to regularly back up your data and store the tapes offsite, preferably out of town. In case you are performing incremental backups to save the cost of tapes, your schedule should include performing a full system backup at least once a week.

　　☒ **B** is incorrect because it is not a defense against disasters. This might save backup time, but it is not helpful because a disaster situation will most likely affect both servers. **C** is incorrect because this is not an adequate defense against disasters.

37. ☑ **A, B**, and **E**. Disk drives, folders, and the printer connected to your computer are the only resources that you can share. When networking is fully configured, you can share any of these resources with your colleagues in the office. You will be able to use files and folders on other computers, and other users will likewise be able to share these resources. These users will also be able to print to the printer connected to your computer when it is shared.

　　☒ **C** is incorrect because it is not possible to share individual files in Windows 98. However, you can share the folder where the file is located. When a user is connected to the shared folder, he will be able to access the files inside the folder. Although the popular term in Windows 9x is *File and Printer Sharing*, the files cannot be shared individually. **D** is incorrect because a monitor is not a network resource and cannot be shared on the network.

38. ☑ **A.** /checkupgradeonly. This switch performs a check on your current system and creates a compatibility report. When used with the /checkupgradeonly switch, the WINNT32.EXE setup command cannot be used to perform setup. It creates a detailed compatibility report that you can use to analyze the effects of upgrading the current operating system.

　　☒ **B** is incorrect because this switch is used to prepare additional hard disks for installation of Windows 2000. This option copies the Windows 2000 installation files to multiple hard disks and makes them active. These disks can then be installed on different computers and you can run the installation independently. **C** is incorrect because this is an invalid switch. **D** is incorrect because this switch is used to copy a specified folder within the Windows folder, which is not deleted after the setup is over.

39. ☑ **C.** Hard disk space. The minimum requirements for installation of Windows 2000 Professional include a 133MHz processor (166MHz recommended), 32MB of RAM (64MB recommended), and 650MB of hard disk space (2GB recommended). The hard disk in the computer in question has only 560MB of free space. This is insufficient for installing Windows 2000 Professional which requires a separate directory for installing system files.

    ☒ **A, B,** and **D** are incorrect answers because these components meet the minimum requirements for installation of Windows 2000 Professional operating system.

40. ☑ **D.** The conversion of a disk or a partition from FAT to NTFS is a one-way process and cannot be reversed without losing data. You need to delete the partition on drive D:, recreate a new partition, and format it using the FAT32 file system. But be aware that you will loose all your data, including the operating system, since Windows 2000 is installed on drive D:.

    ☒ **A** is incorrect because there is no such utility available in Windows 2000 Disk Management. **B** is incorrect because the CONVERT command allows only /FS:NTFS as a switch; /FS:FAT32 is invalid. **C** is incorrect because this will cause loss of all data on the disk, including the currently installed Windows 2000 operating system.

41. ☑ **D.** All of the above. An internal modem being listed as an Unknown Device in the Device Manager can be caused by any of the listed problems. An incorrect driver, a missing device driver, or a resource conflict will all cause the internal modem to be listed as an Unknown Device.

    ☒ **A, B,** and **C** are incorrect answers because none of them can be identified as the sole reason for the internal modem to be listed as an Unknown Device in the Device Manager. Even if a device driver has been installed, it might not be compatible with the operating system. Assuming that the device driver were compatible, it might have been corrupted. Supposing a compatible device driver were installed and that it has not been corrupted, there could still be a resource conflict with another device in the computer.

42. ☑ **B** and **D.** An FTP server and a secure Web site. FTP servers are configured to prompt the user to supply a username and password before being allowed access to the contents on the server or a particular directory on the server. FTP servers are mainly used to facilitate users in uploading and

downloading files to and from the Internet, respectively. Secure Web sites always prompt the user for a username and password to verify the authenticity of the user. Examples of such Web sites are online stores and other Web sites that deal with online financial transactions, such as the Web sites of banks, credit unions, and so on.

☒ **A** and **C** are incorrect answers because neither HTTP nor WWW servers on the Internet are configured to prompt the user to supply a username and password. A majority of Web sites on the Internet are either HTTP or WWW sites.

43. ☑ **D.** Nothing; Windows 98 will boot normally. The Windows 98 boot process does check the files specified in SYSTEM.INI during system startup, but any missing or corrupt files do not prevent the operating system from loading. In the given situation, the operating system will probably generate an error during the boot process, but will continue to load normally.

☒ **A** is incorrect because a missing file specified in SYSTEM.INI for a legacy device will not stop the OS from loading. **B** is incorrect for the same reason. **C** is incorrect because no error relating to the operating system will be reported.

44. ☑ **C.** DSL stands for digital subscriber line. This line provides downloads at the rate of 8.448 Mbps, whereas the uplink is limited to 2.7 Mbps. The DSL is an ideal choice when your work involves downloading files from Internet sites.

☒ **A** is incorrect because ISDN is required when you need higher bandwidth for both uplink and downlink. The ISDN (Integrated Services Digital Network) Basic Rate Interface (BRI) provides channels of 64 Kbps each, totaling up to 128 Kbps of speed. **B** is incorrect because the PSTN (Public Switched Telephone Network) provides a maximum speed of 56 Kbps. **D** is incorrect because the POTS (plain old telephone system) is another name for PSTN, which has a speed limitation of 56 Kbps.

45. ☑ **B.** The Safe Mode is the best mode to start a Windows 98 computer when you are not sure which component is preventing the system from booting successfully. Windows loads only basic and necessary drivers in this mode. You can then check the Device Manager to locate the actual component that is causing the problem.

☒ **A** is incorrect. This mode will not work because it will attempt to load the faulty components. **C** is incorrect because this mode is used if you are not able to find the problem in Safe Mode. You should try the Safe Mode first. **D** is incorrect because this mode does not exist in Windows 98, but is available only in Windows 2000.

46. ☑ **C.** The DNS (Domain Name System) is responsible for translating the domain name to its corresponding IP address. The name of the server is technically known as a fully qualified domain name (FQDN) or host name, and the process of locating the IP address of the domain is called name resolution. A hierarchy of DNS servers on the Internet accomplishes this name resolution process.

    ☒ **A** is incorrect because the purpose of the DHCP (Dynamic Host Configuration Protocol) is to assign IP address configurations to its clients. A DHCP server may assign the name of the DNS server to a DHCP client, but it does not resolve domain names to IP addresses. **B** is incorrect because the WINS service exists only in Windows networks and is used to resolve NetBIOS names, popularly known as computer names, to their respective IP addresses. WINS servers keep a database of IP addresses and corresponding computer names, and when queried by WINS clients, they supply the IP address of the specified computer name. **D** is incorrect because the ISP (Internet Service Provider) does not resolve host names to IP addresses on the Internet. An ISP does have one or more DNS servers for host name resolution.

47. ☑ **C.** The Advanced tab in Internet Options found in Internet Explorer 4.0 and above allows you to configure your Web browser by giving you several options. If you are getting a warning message from a particular Web site, you should check the Advanced tab in Internet Options. You will find that the Secure Socket Layer (SSL) under Security is not checked. Click SSL 2.0 and SSL 3.0 check boxes to solve the problem.

    ☒ **A** is incorrect because this tab is used to configure security zones, and security levels for a particular security zone. **B** is incorrect because this tab is used to configure ratings and install security certificates. **D** is incorrect because this tab is used to configure the programs that Windows starts automatically for a particular Internet service.

48. ☑ **C** and **D.** Security and processing power. These two features make Windows 2000 an ideal choice for the type of work you will be doing on the new computer. Since your work involves graphics designs, you need as much processing power as possible. Windows 2000 is a powerful operating system

that even supports dual processor computers. The graphics designs take significant time to complete, and protecting your files is your primary concern. Windows 2000 will allow you to secure your files using file level permissions, a feature that is not present in Windows 98.

☒ **A** is incorrect because both Windows 98 and Windows 2000 offer the same level of ease of use. **B** is incorrect because both Windows 98 and Windows 2000 offer file compression utilities. **E** is incorrect because Windows 98 and Windows 2000 are equally good choices as far as networking capabilities are concerned. Although Windows 2000 offers advanced networking features, this is not particularly relevant in terms of the current requirements.

49. ☑ **B.** This statement is incorrect because the subnet mask must be specified when configuring the IP address of a computer. The subnet mask address is not unique to the computer, but is common to all the computers in all segments of the network.

☒ **A** is incorrect because the statement is true. You should remember that the IP address and the subnet mask address are two essential entries, and that the IP address is unique to the computer. All computers in this network segment share the same subnet mask. **C** is incorrect because this statement is also true. When you have a multiple segment network, you should specify the address of the default gateway. This address is used to send network packets to other (or remote) network segments. **D** is a correct statement. These are optional entries and are required only if your network is very large and is dependent on DNS and WINS servers for translating host names and NetBIOS names to their respective IP addresses.

50. ☑ **A** and **C.** DETCRASH.LOG and SETUPLOG.TXT. These two files are using by Windows 98 installation when you choose to reinstall the operating system by selecting the Safe Recovery installation mode. These files are used to skip any files that have already been installed and to avoid loading any drivers for those devices that do not respond. This saves a lot of time during the reinstallation process by skipping the steps that previously failed.

☒ **B** is incorrect because there is no such file. **D** is incorrect because this file is the text version of the DETCRASH.LOG, which can be viewed by any user to determine the cause of installation failure. The Windows 98 Setup program does not use this file during the Safe Recovery installation process.

Glossary

Access Methods   Also known as *network access*, these are the methods by which a device communicates on a network. Network access provides a standard that all devices that wish to communicate on a network must abide by in order to eliminate communication conflicts.

Active Matrix Display   Active matrix displays are based on Thin Film Transistor technology. Instead of having two rows of transistors, active matrix displays have a transistor at every pixel, which enables much quicker display changes than passive matrix displays and produces display quality comparable to a CRT.

ANSI.SYS   ANSI.SYS is a DOS system file that is loaded by CONFIG.SYS if required. This file loads an extended character set for use by DOS and DOS applications that includes basic drawing and color capabilities. Normally used for drawing and filling different boxes for menu systems, it is seldom in use today. By default, it carries no attributes, and is not required for OS startup.

ARCHIVE Attribute   The ARCHIVE attribute is set automatically when a file is created or modified, and is automatically removed by back-up software when the file is backed up.

ATTRIB.EXE   ATTRIB.EXE is a command line utility that can be used to change the attributes of a file or group of files.

AUTOEXEC.BAT   A user-editable system file, AUTOEXEC.BAT contains commands to modify the PC environment (PATH, COMSPEC, other SET commands), and to execute applications. It can be used to create a menu system, prompt for user input, or *call* other batch files to maintain a modular structure. By default, it carries no attributes, and is not required for OS startup.

Basic Input/Output System   See BIOS.

Bi-Directional Print Mode   Most common in some of the newer and more advanced printers, bi-directional print mode means that the printer is able to talk back to the computer, enabling, for example, the printer to send the user exact error messages that are displayed on the workstation. It also helps the spooler to avoid print spooler stalls.

BIOS   Most commonly known as BIOS, basic input/output system is a standard set of instructions or programs that handle boot operations. When an application needs to perform an I/O operation on a computer, the operating system makes the request to the system BIOS, which in turn translates the request into the appropriate instruction set used by the hardware device.

Brownout   Momentary lapses in power supply. Brownouts can cause problems with computer components that are not designed to withstand these events.

Bus   A bus is the actual pathway used to transmit electronic signals from one computer device to another.

Bus Topology   In a local area network, a bus topology has each device on the network connected to a central cable, or bus. Most common with coaxial cabling.

Cache Memory   Cache memory is used to store frequently used instructions and data so that they can be accessed quickly by the computer.

Carrier Sense Multiple Access/Collision Detection   See CSMA/CD.

Central Processing Unit   See CPU.

Chip Creep   A phenomenon whereby a computer chip becomes loose within its socket.

Cleaning Blade   This rubber blade inside a laser printer extends the length of the photosensitive drum. It removes excess toner after the print process has completed and deposits it into a reservoir for re-use.

CMOS   The Complementary Metal-Oxide Semiconductor (or CMOS) is an integrated circuit composed of a metal oxide that is located directly on the system board. The CMOS, which is similar to RAM in that data can be written to the chip, enables a computer to store essential operating parameters after the computer has been turned off, enabling a faster system boot.

Coaxial Cable   A high-bandwidth network cable that consists of a central wire surrounded by a screen of fine wires.

COMMAND.COM   COMMAND.COM is a DOS system file that is automatically executed in the ROOT directory at startup. This file contains the internal command set and error messages. By default, it carries no attributes, but is required for OS startup.

Complementary Metal-Oxide Semiconductor   See CMOS.

CONFIG.SYS   A user-editable system file that provides the ability to install device drivers. Windows 9*x* does not require any specific settings to be made in CONFIG.SYS.

Cooperative Multitasking   There are two different types of multitasking: cooperative and preemptive. Cooperative multitasking means that applications must voluntarily relinquish control of the CPU. When an application relinquishes control of the CPU, Windows then decides which application will execute next. The most common way for an application to relinquish control is by asking Windows if any messages are available.

CPU   The CPU (central processing unit) is the operations center of a computer. Its job is to provide the devices attached to the computer with directives that retrieve, display, manipulate, and store information.

CSMA/CD   Most commonly found on Ethernet networks, carrier sense multiple access/collision detection (CSMA/CD) is a network communication protocol and operates in much the same way as humans communicate. With CSMA/CD, a device listens to the network for a pause in communication, and attempts to transmit data onto the network during the pause. The device then detects if any other devices have transmitted onto the network at the same time. If it detects that another device has transmitted data onto the network at the same time, the device then waits an unspecified random amount of time and retransmits its data.

Defragmentation   A process that reorganizes fragmented files back in a proper, contiguous fashion. This is done by moving several of them to an unused portion of the drive, erasing the previous locations in contiguous clusters, then rewriting the files back in proper sequence. Performed periodically, defragmentation is probably the single best operation a user can perform to maintain a high performance system.

Device Driver   Device drivers are programs that translate necessary information between the operating system and the specific peripheral device for which they are configured, such as a printer.

Dial-Up Access   Dial-up access is defined as access provided to the Internet, a LAN, or even another computer by using a phone line and a modem.

Dial-Up Networking   Refers to the type of network in which a modem is used to connect two or more workstations.

DIMM   A dual in-line memory module (DIMM) is very similar to a SIMM; it's a small plug-in circuit board that contains the memory chips that you need to add certain increments of RAM to your computer. Because the memory chips run along both sides of the chip, DIMM chips can hold twice as much memory as SIMM chips.

DIP Switch   Dual in-line package (DIP) switches are very tiny boxes with switches embedded in them. Each switch sets a value of 0 or 1, depending on how they are set. These switches are used to provide user-accessible configuration settings for computers and peripheral devices.

Direct Memory Access   See DMA.

Dirty Current   Noise present on a power line is referred to as dirty current. This noise is caused by electro-magnetic interference (EMI) and can stray, or leak, from the current into nearby components. When EMI leaks from power current, it is called a magnetic field and can easily damage computer components.

DMA   Direct Memory Access (DMA) is a facility by which a peripheral can communicate directly with RAM, without intervention by the CPU.

DNS   Domain Name System (DNS) is the Internet-based system that resolves symbolic names, called host names, to IP addresses (which are a series of numbers) that the computer is able to understand.

Docking Station   Docking stations allow users to add "desktop-like" capabilities, such as a mouse, monitor, or keyboard, to their portable computer by plugging these components into a docking station and connecting their portable only to the docking station, rather than to each individual component.

Domain Name System   See DNS.

DOS Mode   DOS Mode, or DOS Compatibility Mode as it is commonly known, allows execution of some older MS-DOS applications that are not capable of running in Windows 95. Applications that require use of MS-DOS mode are usually blocked from operation within Windows 95. DOS itself stands for Disk Operating System.

Download Downloading refers to the process of transferring a file or files from one computer to another. Unlike uploading, the transfer is always initiated by the computer that will be receiving the file(s).

Downtime Downtime is the time wasted as a result of a malfunctioning computer or network.

DRAM Dynamic random access memory (DRAM) chips abandoned the idea of using the unwieldy transistors and switches in favor of using the smaller capacitors that could represent 0s and 1s as an electronic charge. This resulted in the ability to store more information on a single chip, but also meant that the chip needed a constant refresh and hence more power.

Dual In-Line Memory Module See DIMM.

Dual In-Line Package Switch See DIP Switch.

Dynamic RAM See DRAM.

EBKAC Error A common error that most technicians face, the EBKAC error stands for Error Between Keyboard and Chair. As that implies, EBKAC errors are not technical errors, but rather errors on the part of the end user. Common EBKAC errors include power cords being unplugged, no paper in printer, and power switches being turned off.

ECP ECP (Extended Capability Port) is a parallel printer interface designed to speed up data transfer rates by bypassing the processor and writing the data directly to memory.

EDO RAM Extended Data Output RAM (EDO RAM) is a type of DRAM chip designed for processor access speeds of approximately 10 to 15 percent above fast-page mode memory.

EISA Extended Industry Standard Architecture (EISA) is an industry standard bus architecture that allows for peripherals to utilize the 32-bit data bus that is available with 386 and 486 processors.

Electrophotographic Printing Process See EP Process.

EMM386.EXE   EMM386.EXE is a DOS system file that, along with HIMEM.SYS, controls memory management. It is not required for system startup in pre-Windows 95 machines. Basically, this is an expanded memory emulator that performs two major functions. It enables and controls EMS, if desired, and enables the use of upper memory as system memory.

EMS   Meaning Expanded Memory Specification, EMS is an expanded memory standard that allows programs that recognize it to work with more than 640KB of RAM.

Enhanced Parallel Port   See EPP.

EP Process   The EP (Electrophotographic Printing) process is the six-step process that a laser printer goes through to put an image on a page. The process follows these six steps: Cleaning, Charging, Writing, Developing, Transferring, and Fusing.

EPP   EPP (Enhanced Parallel Port) is an expansion bus that offers an extended control code set. With EPP mode, data travels both from the computer to the printer and vice versa.

Error Between Keyboard and Chair   See EBKAC Error.

Exit Roller   One of four different types of rollers found in printers, exit rollers aid in the transfer and control of the paper as it leaves the printer. Depending on the printer type, they direct the paper to a tray where it can be collated, sorted, or even stapled.

Expanded Memory Specification   See EMS.

Extended Capability Port   See ECP.

Extended Data Output RAM   See EDO RAM.

Extended Industry Standard Architecture   See EISA.

eXtended Memory Specification   See XMS.

FDISK   A DOS-based utility program used to partition a hard disk in preparation for installing an operating system.

Feed Roller   One of four different types of rollers found in printers. Also known as paper pickup roller, the feed roller, when activated, rotates against the top page in the paper tray and rolls it into the printer. The feed roller works together with a special rubber pad to prevent more than one sheet from being fed into the printer at a time.

Fiber-Optic Cable   Extremely high-speed network cable that consists of glass fibers that carry light signals instead of electrical signals. Fiber-optic cable is best used for transmission over long distances, and is much less susceptible to environmental difficulties, such as electronic and magnetic interference.

File Transfer Protocol   See FTP.

Flash Memory   A faster version of ROM that, while still basically developed as ROM, can be addressed and loaded *thousands* of times.

Fragmentation   Because DOS writes files to the hard disk by breaking the file into cluster-sized pieces and then storing each piece in the next available cluster, as files are deleted and then rewritten, they can be written in noncontiguous clusters scattered all over the disk. This is known as file fragmentation.

FTP   Much older than the HTTP protocol, the File Transfer Protocol (FTP) is the protocol used to download files from an FTP server to a client computer. FTP is much faster than HTTP.

Fully Qualified Path   A fully qualified path is the entire path of a file, starting from the root of the file system, to the file being referenced.

Fusing Rollers   One of four different types of rollers found in laser printers, fusing rollers comprise the final stage of the Electrophotographic Printing (EP) process, bonding the toner particles to the page to prevent smearing. The roller on the toner side of the page has a non-stick surface that is heated to a high temperature to permanently bond the toner to the paper.

Ghosted Image   Ghosting is what occurs when a portion of an image previously printed to a page is printed again, only not as dark. One cause of this is if the erasure lamp of the laser printer sometimes fails to operate correctly, not completely erasing the previous image from the EP drum. Another cause of ghosting may be due to a malfunction in the cleaning blade such that it doesn't adequately scrape away the residual toner.

Handshaking   The process by which two connecting modems agree on the method of communication to be used.

HIDDEN Attribute   The Hidden attribute keeps a file from being displayed when a DIR command is issued.

HIMEM.SYS   HIMEM.SYS is a DOS system file that, along with EMM386.EXE, controls memory management. It is not required for system startup in pre-Windows 95 machines.

HTML   Derived from the Standard General Markup Language (SGML), the Hypertext Markup Language (HTML) is the markup language that dictates the layout and design of a Web page.

HTTP   Hypertext Transfer Protocol (HTTP) is the TCP/IP-based protocol that is most commonly used for client/server communications on the World Wide Web.

Hub   Hubs are common connection points for devices in a network. Hubs contain multiple ports and are commonly used to connect segments of a LAN.

Hypertext Markup Language   See HTML.

Hypertext Transfer Protocol   See HTTP.

Impact Printer   Impact printers, like the name suggests, require the impact with an ink ribbon to print characters and images. An example of an impact printer is a daisy wheel.

Industry Standard Architecture   See ISA.

Input Device   Input devices take data from a user, such as the click of a mouse or the typing on a keyboard, and convert that data into electrical signals used by your computer. Several devices that provide input are: keyboards, mice, trackballs, pointing devices, digitized tablets, and touch screens.

Internet Service Provider   See ISP.

Internetwork Packet Exchange/Sequenced Packet Exchange   See IPX/SPX.

Interrupt Request Line   See IRQ.

IO.SYS   IO.SYS is a DOS system file that defines basic input/output routines for the processor. By default, it carries the hidden, system, and read-only attributes, and *is* required for OS startup

IPX/SPX   Internetwork Packet Exchange/Sequenced Packet Exchange (IPX/SPX) is a very fast and highly established network protocol most commonly used with Novell Netware

IRQ   Interrupt Request (IRQ) lines are the physical lines over which system components such as modems or printers communicate directly with the CPU when the device is ready to send or receive data.

ISA   Industry Standard Architecture (ISA) is an industry standard bus architecture that allows for peripherals to utilize the 16-bit data bus that is available with 286 and 386 processors.

ISP   An Internet Service Provider (ISP), as its name suggests, is a company that provides folks with access to the Internet, usually for a fee. On the other hand, a company that gives their employees Internet access through a private bank of modems is usually not considered an ISP.

Jumper   Jumpers, like DIP switches, are used to accomplish configuration manually. Jumpers are actually made of two separate components: a row of metal pins on the hardware itself and a small plastic cap that has a metal insert inside of it. The two parts together form a circuit that sets the configuration. This form of configuration device is only used to set one value for a feature at a time, as opposed to DIP switches, which can handle multiple configurations.

LAN   A local area network (LAN) is created whenever two or more computers in a limited geographic area (within about a two-mile radius) are linked by high-performance cables so that users can exchange information, share peripheral devices, or access a common server.

Local Area Network   See LAN.

Material Safety Data Sheets   See MSDS.

MEM.EXE   MEM.EXE is a simple command line utility that, using various command switches, can display various reports of memory usage.

MEMMAKER.EXE   A Microsoft utility that automatically determines the best possible configuration and load sequence for a given set of applications and drivers used. Before using MEMMAKER, the PC should be configured for normal operation (i.e., mouse driver, network operation, sound support, and so forth), including any items that are loaded from the AUTOEXEC.BAT and CONFIG.SYS files.

Memory Address   The memory address is used to receive commands from the processor that are destined for any device attached to a computer. Each device must have a unique memory address in order for it to function.

Memory Bank   A memory bank is the actual slot that memory goes into.

Memory Effect   When a Nickel Cadmium, or NiCad, battery is recharged before it is fully discharged, the battery loses the ability to fully recharge again, which is known as the memory effect.

MSD.EXE   MSD, Microsoft Diagnostics, is a DOS-based utility that provides a great deal of information about the system. It is most useful in determining what the system has installed in it, such as memory and hard drives.

MSD.EXE   A Microsoft System Diagnostics program, MSD.EXE roots out almost every conceivable item about your system that you'd ever want to know (and then some!) and displays it in a menu-driven format for you to browse

MSDOS.SYS   MSDOS.SYS is a DOS system file that defines system file locations. By default, it carries the hidden, system, and read-only attributes, and is required for OS startup.

MSDS   Material Safety Data Sheets (MSDS) are white pages that contain information on any substance that is deemed hazardous, most notably cleaning solvents. The purpose of MSDS is to inform employees about the dangers inherent in hazardous materials and the proper use of these items to prevent potential injuries from occurring.

Multi-Boot Configuration   A system that has been configured to allow a user to select one of multiple installed operating systems at boot time.

Multimeter   A multimeter is a device that measures current, resistance, or voltage, used to determine whether certain computer components are functioning correctly based on these electrical measurements.

NetBEUI   The NetBios Extended User Interface (NetBEUI) is an extremely fast network transport protocol that is most commonly found on smaller networks.

NetBios Extended User Interface   See NetBEUI.

Network Interface Card   See NIC.

Network Topology   The arrangement of cable links in a local area network. There are three principal network topologies: bus, ring, and star.

NIC   A network interface card (NIC) is used to connect a PC to a network cable.

Noise Filter   UPS's contain a special filter, called a *noise filter*, that reduces the amount of noise present in electrical current and eliminates magnetic fields caused by noise, thus providing some protection to the components that utilize the current or are nearby.

Non-Impact Printer   Non-impact printers do not use an ink ribbon, and therefore do not require direct contact with the paper for printing. An example of a non-impact printer is a laser printer.

Normal Mode   Normal Mode is the mode in which Windows 95 is started by default, which provides full functionality of the Windows 95 Explorer.

Null Modem Cable   A null modem cable is a special cable that has the send and receive lines reversed on the connector. It enables you to connect two computers directly, without using a modem.

Operating System   See OS.

Operator Error   Operator error occurs when the customer inadvertently makes a configuration change.

OS   By definition, an Operating System (OS) is a set of computer instruction codes, usually *compiled* into executable files, whose purpose is to define input and output devices and connections, and provide instructions for the computer's central processor to operate on to retrieve and display data.

Output Device   Output devices take electronic signals *from* a computer and convert them into a format that the user can use. Examples of output devices include monitors and printers.

Overlays   Rather than put all available functions into a single huge executable file, most developers choose to modularize their applications by creating library files that include additional commands and functions. These additional executable enhancement files are usually referred to as overlays.

Page Description Language   See PDL.

Parallel Port   One of two types of communication ports found on a motherboard (the other is the serial port), the parallel port is used to connect a peripheral device (most commonly a printer for this type of port) to the computer. A parallel port allows transmission of data over eight conductors at one time. The processor socket is the actual socket used to attach the processor to the motherboard.

Parallel Processing   The Intel 586 (Pentium) chip combined two 486DX chips into one, called the *Dual Independent Bus Architecture.* This allowed each processor inside the chip to execute instructions simultaneously and independently from each other, which is called parallel processing.

Parity   Parity is an error-checking mechanism that enables the device to recognize single-bit errors.

Partition   A section of the storage area on a computer's hard disk. A hard disk must be partitioned before an operating system can be installed.

Passive Matrix Display   Most common on portable systems, the passive matrix display is made from a grid of horizontal and vertical wires. At the end of each wire is a transistor. In order to light a pixel at (X, Y), a signal is sent to the X and Y transistors. In turn, these transistors then send voltage down the wire, which turns on the LCD at the intersection of the two wires

PC Card   The PC Card (Personal Computer Memory Card International Association, or PCMCIA) bus was first created to expand the memory capabilities in small, hand-held computers. It is a type of bus used mostly with laptop computers that provides a convenient way to interchange PCMCIA-compatible devices, which are only slightly larger than credit cards.

PCI   The Peripheral Component Interconnect (PCI) was designed in response to the Pentium class processor's utilization of a 64-bit bus. PCI buses are designed to be processor-independent.

PCMCIA   See PC Card.

PDL   Laser printers use a Page Description Language(PDL) to send and receive print job instructions one page at a time, rather than one dot at a time, as with other types of printers.

Peripheral Component Interconnect   See PCI.

Personal Computer Memory Card International Association   See PC Card.

Photosensitive Drum   This light-sensitive drum is the core of the electrophotographic process inside the laser printer. This drum is affected by the cleaning, charging, writing, and transferring processes in the six-step laser printing process.

Plug and Play   Plug and Play offers automatic driver installation as soon as hardware or software is "plugged in," or installed. Microsoft first offered PnP support on the PC with Windows 95.

Pointing Stick   One of the three most common types of pointing devices found on portable systems, the pointing stick is a small pencil-eraser-size piece of rubber in the center of the keyboard. The on-screen pointer is controlled by simply pushing the pointing stick in the desired direction.

Point-To-Point Protocol   See PPP.

POLEDIT.EXE   The Windows 95 System Policy feature, POLEDIT.EXE, is used to build a Registry template that will later be used during logon to set common-denominator defaults for all network users, and add certain restrictions on a global basis if deemed necessary

POP   Post Office Protocol (POP) is a common protocol by which an Internet server lets you receive email and download it from the server to your own machine.

POST   As its name suggests, a power-on self-test (POST) is self test performed by the computer that occurs during boot time. It is used to diagnose system-related problems.

Post Office Protocol   See POP.

Power On Self Test   See POST.

Power Spike   When there is a power spike, there is a sudden, huge increase in power that lasts for a split second. Power spikes can literally fry computer components.

PPP   The Point-to-Point protocol (PPP) is a serial communications protocol used to connect two computers over a phone line via a modem. SLIP is the alternate protocol that is acceptable to most browsers, though it's not as common as PPP.

Preemptive Multitasking   There are two different types of multitasking: cooperative and preemptive. Preemptive multitasking means that control is passed from one program to another automatically by the Windows process scheduler.

Primary Corona Wire   This highly negatively charged wire inside a laser printer is responsible for electrically erasing the photosensitive drum, preparing it to be written with a new image in the writing stage of the laser print process.

Processor Socket   The processor socket is the actual socket used to attach the processor to the motherboard.

Protocol   A set of communication standards between two computers on a network. Common protocols include TCP/IP, NetBEUI, and IPX/SPX.

READ ONLY Attribute   The READ ONLY attribute prevents a user or application from inadvertently deleting or changing a file.

Refresh   Refresh refers to the automatic process of constantly updating memory chips to ensure that their signals are correct. The refresh rate is the frequency by which chips are refreshed, usually about every 60 to 70 thousandths of a second.

Registration Roller   One of four different types of rollers found in laser printers, the registration roller synchronizes the paper movement with the writing process inside the EP cartridge. Registration rollers do not advance the paper until the EP cartridge is ready to process the next line of the image.

Registry   A complex database used by Windows NT and Windows 95 (and later) pertaining to both application settings and hardware configuration.

Rollers   Rollers are located inside a printer to aid in the movement of paper through the printer. There are four main types of rollers: feed, registration, fuser, and exit.

Safe Mode   Safe Mode is a special diagnostic mode of Windows 95 that starts the operating system without any network, CD-ROM, and printer drivers. This special mode allows you to change an incorrect setting, which will in most cases allow you to return an abnormally functioning system to its correct operation.

Serial Port   One of two types of communication ports found on a motherboard (the other is the parallel port), the serial port connects to a serial line that leads to a computer peripheral<@151>the type most common with modems and mice. The serial port transmits data sequentially, bit by bit over a single conductor.

SIMD   Single Instruction Multiple Data (SIMD) works by allowing a single instruction to operate on multiple pieces of data when an application is performing a repetitive loop.

SIMM   A single in-line memory module (SIMM) is a small plug-in circuit board that contains the memory chips that you need to add certain increments of RAM to your computer. The chips are positioned along one side of the board.

Simple Mail Transfer Protocol   See SMTP.

Single In-Line Memory Module   See SIMM.

Single Instruction Multiple Data   See SIMD.

Slack   Slack is the space left between the end of a file and the end of the cluster in which the file resides.

SLIP   The Serial Line Interface Protocol (SLIP) is a protocol used to manage telecommunications between a client and a server over a phone line. PPP is the alternate protocol that is acceptable to most browsers, and is in fact the most common.

SMTP   Simple Mail Transfer Protocol (SMTP) is the underlying protocol for Internet-based email.

Socket Services   Socket Services is a layer of BIOS-level software that isolates PC Card software from the computer hardware and detects the insertion or removal of PC Cards.

Solenoid   The solenoid is a resistive coil found in dot matrix and daisy wheel printers. When the solenoid is energized, the pin is forced away from the printhead and impacts the printer ribbon and ultimately the paper, thus impressing the image on the page.

SRAM   Unlike DRAM, Static RAM (SRAM) retains its value as long as power is supplied. It is not constantly refreshed. However, SRAM does require a periodic update and tends to use excessive amounts of power when it does so.

Star Topology   In a local area network, a star topology has each device on the network connected to a central processor, usually a hub. Most common with twisted-pair cabling.

Static RAM   See SRAM.

Stylus   Shaped like a pen, a stylus is used to select menu options and the like on a monitor screen or to draw line art on a graphics tablet.

Sync Frequency   Monitors use a *sync frequency* to control the refresh rate, which is the rate at which the display device is repainted. If this setting is incorrect, you get symptoms such as: a "dead" monitor, lines running through the display, a flickering screen, and a reduced or enlarged image.

SYSTEM Attribute   The SYSTEM attribute is usually set by DOS or Windows, and cannot be modified using standard DOS or Windows commands, including the ATTRIB command or File Manager.

SYSTEM.INI   SYSTEM.INI is a Windows system file that configures Windows to address specific hardware devices and their associated settings. Errors in this file can and do cause Windows to fail to start, or crash unexpectedly.

TCP/IP   The most common protocol suite in use today, Transmission Control Protocol/Internet Protocol (TCP/IP) is the suite of protocols upon which the Internet is based. It refers to the communication standards for data transmission over the Internet, although TCP/IP can also be used on private networks without Internet connectivity.

Time Slicing   The process of the CPU dividing up time between applications for preemptive multitasking is called time slicing.

Token Passing   Token passing is a network communication protocol by which a token is passed from device to device around a virtual (and frequently physical) ring on a network. Whenever a device receives the token, it is then allowed to transmit onto the network.

Token Ring   A local area network (LAN) specification that was developed by IBM in the 1980s for PC-based networks and classified by the (Institute of Electrical and Electronics Engineers) IEEE as 802.5. It specifies a Star topology physically and a Ring topology logically. It runs at either four Mbps or 16 Mbps, but all nodes on the ring must run at the same speed.

Toner   Toner is comprised of finely divided particles of plastic resin and organic compounds bonded to iron particles. It is naturally negatively charged, which aids in attracting it to the written areas of the photosensitive drum during the transfer step of the laser printing process.

Touch Pad   A touch pad is a stationary pointing device commonly used on laptop computers in replace of a mouse or trackball. They are pads that have either thin wires running through them, or specialized surfaces that can sense the pressure of your finger on them. You slide your finger across the touchpad to control the pointer or cursor on the screen.

Trackball   Most commonly, trackballs are used in older portable computers in replace of a mouse. Trackballs are built the same way as an opto-mechanical mouse, except upside-down with the ball on top.

Transfer Corona   This roller inside a laser printer contains a positively charged wire designed to pull the toner off of the photosensitive drum and place it on the page.

Transistor   A transistor is the most fundamental component of electronic circuits. A CPU chip, for example, contains thousands to millions of transistors, which are used to process information in the form of electronic signals. The more transistors a CPU has, the faster it can process data.

Transmission Control Protocol/Internet Protocol   See TCP/IP.

Twisted Pair   By far the most common type of network cable, twisted pair consists of two insulated wires wrapped around each other to help avoid interference from other wires.

Uninterruptible Power Supply   See UPS.

Upload   Uploading is the process of transferring files from one computer to another. Unlike downloading, uploading is always initiated from the computer that is sending the files.

UPS   The uninterruptible power supply (UPS) is a device that was designed to protect your computer and its components from possible injury from the problems that are inherent with today's existing power supply structure.

VESA Local Bus   See VL-Bus.

Virtual Memory   Virtual memory is memory that the processor has been "tricked" into using as if it were actual physical memory.

Virus   Any program that is written with the intent of doing harm to a computer. Viruses have the ability to replicate themselves by attaching themselves to programs or documents. They range in activity from extreme data loss to an annoying message that pops up every few minutes.

VL-Bus   Originally created to address performance issues, the VESA Local Bus (VL-Bus) was meant to enable earlier bus designs to handle a maximum clock speed equivalent to that of processors.

WAN   A wide area network (WAN) is created whenever two or more computers are linked by long-distance communication lines that traverse distances greater than those supported by LANs (or greater than about two miles).

Wide Area Network   See WAN.

WIN.INI   WIN.INI is a dynamic Windows system file that contains configuration information for Windows applications. Errors made in this file seldom have global implications to Window's operation but can cripple specific applications or features. Printing is also controlled by settings in this file.

Windows Accelerator Card RAM   See WRAM.

WINFILE.INI   In pre-Windows 95 systems, this is the configuration file that stores the names of the directories that File Manager displays when starting.

WRAM   The Windows Accelerator Card was introduced into the market out of a need to assist some environments with running Microsoft Windows. WRAM utilizes memory that resides on the card itself to perform the Windows-specific functions, and therefore speeds up the OS.

XMS   Meaning eXtended Memory Specification, XMS is a set of standards that allows applications to access extended memory.

Zoomed Video   See ZV.

ZV   Zoomed Video (ZV) is a direct data connection between a PC Card and host system that allows a PC Card to write video data directly to the video controller.